Ohhh Yeahhh!

History of Hawaiian Wrestling

By Mike Rodgers

Edited by Frank Culbertson

Introduction

Mike Rodgers

In late 1971, I bought my first Ring Wrestling Magazine. I was eleven years old. In the pages were articles by Dave Cameron, Jeff Walton, and Joe Pottgeiser Jr, who would later all become acquaintances.

There were articles on Bull Ramos, Mad Dog Vachon, and Ivan Koloff, who I would later interview for my bulletin.

George Steele and Johnny Fargo (Greg Valentine) were listed in the ratings section. I would share the ring with them as a referee.

At the magazine's end were various correspondents' arena reports listing the results of a card they had witnessed. My favorite part of this magazine was entitled 'Pleasant, Peaceful Hawaii? Get a Load of This Action' by Carlos Gaivar. I read this piece over and over again. When I thought of starting this book, I thought I should share this piece of writing.

At 11 years old, I knew the wrestlers that had been in Oregon but was just learning the wrestlers on the National level. I had not heard of Sam Steamboat or King Curtis Iaukea until this.

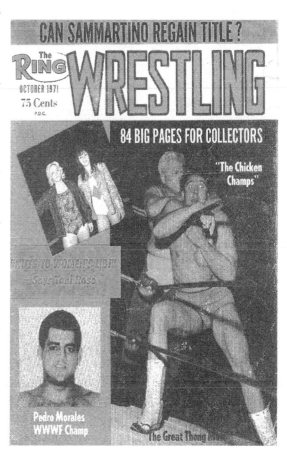

""The main event was a Sicilian Stretcher match between Sam Steamboat Mokuahi and Curtis "The Bull" Iaukea. The loser would be carried out on a stretcher and had to leave Hawaii.

Local hero Sammy was so impatient that he attacked Iaukea while he was still on his way to the ring. Fists and chairs were thrown, and when the Hawaiians finally got into the ring, Iaukeau's face was a gory mess.

With the match officially underway, it became more of a fight than a wrestling match. Iaukea's low blows enraged the fans, as Steamboat lay writhing on the canvas in pain.

Referee Beauregard tried pulling the crazed Bull off Sam, but became the target of his attack. While Iaukea was busy throwing the referee out of the ring, Steamboat had a chance to recover.

Iaukea stood on the apron of the ring gloating over the battered Beauregard, while Steamboat had recovered enough to sneak up behind him. Sam snuck one arm up between the Bulls legs and brought it straight up. The fans went crazy seeing justice served.

Steamboat wrapped it up by putting the abdominal stretch on Iaukea. The Bull was trying to concede, but the referee was right where he had left him, on his back outside of the ring. So Sam held and held and held. Wally Tsutsumi finally jumped in the ring and signaled the end of the match. It took 6 men to carry out the Bull.'""

The imagery brought out your imagination and made you want to learn more about these wrestlers and about the Hawaiian promotion.

When I was in college (pre-internet), I learned about interlibrary loans. I could request newspapers and books from other places. They would come on microfilm. Then, you could use a microfilm reader to see them. I discovered that the Honolulu Star-Advertiser could be borrowed from a college in Illinois.

I would get three months at a time and just be thrilled to read about these dream matches that took place in Hawaii. Matches like King Curtis VS Don Leo Jonathan, Pat Patterson and Ray Stevens VS Pampero Firpo and Nick Bockwinkel, Giant Baba VS Johnny Barend, King Curtis VS Dory Funk JR.

During this time, Hawaii was the perfect spot. They would have a good crew, and then wrestlers on their way to or from Japan or Australia would stop off for a few matches in Hawaii to bolster their cards.

I had a chance to interview Lord Blears, which you will read in this book. He told me time and time again that it was the local wrestlers who stayed that drew the money. The other one-off stars didn't really draw any money. Despite me wanting him to talk about these great, great cards he reiterated something that is important for fans to remember, it was all about the money.

I want to mention a wonderful coffee table book that Ed Francis put out in 2000. It is entitled 'Gentleman Ed Francis presents 50th State Big Time Wrestling.' It has glossy pages and is excellent. I think that you will find this book different, perhaps with more details on the week-by-week happenings.

A very well-respected wrestling historian and author asked me what story I wanted to tell with this book. I talked about these unbelievable cards. He mentioned the fans were just as big of a story. During a brief time, a 2nd promotion came to Hawaii with very big names, and the fans were able to support them as well. The Hawaii promotion knew their fans and what would attract them to the matches.

This person also mentioned that Hawaii was neutral in much of the politics of the wrestling world and was able to attract top talent from many territories.

It is easy to focus on these dream cards with unbelievable talent. I found Hawaii wrestling to be such a great story all the way to the beginning of the century. Al Karasick is a name that only a few will know, but he was a great promoter. I was amazed at the hustle he had to keep wrestling going through Pearl Harbor and World War 2.

Wrestling in Hawaii has a very long tradition. We want to shine a light on this often-forgotten territory.

Thank You!

In the other books I have written on the Pacific Northwest, I haven't needed too much help.

However, this book has taken a village to get to the finished product.

First of all, I have to thank Rock Rims. This was going to be his project and, no doubt, would have been fantastic. Rock Rims does research and background like no one else.

Then I have to thank Mark Hewitt. I have seen Mark's name on various wrestling historian conversations for years. Something told me to reach out to him for some help with the early years. Let me tell you that passing thought was probably the most important aspect of this book. He had already done the research, and it was there waiting for me. To top it off, he welcomed me to use it. So, just know the first part of this book is all Mark Hewitts with a few smart aleck remarks thrown in by me.

Next, I want to thank Ed Francis, Lord Blears, and Pampero Firpo. Many, many years ago, they did interviews with me. I was so fascinated by the Hawaiian territory, and their interviews were essential.

I have also taken excerpts from other interviews that have had info on Hawaii. I thank Beauregard, Bill Savage, Danno O'Shocker, Ricky Hunter, Billy Whitewolf, Don Leo Jonathan, Dutch Savage, Don Manoukian, Lou Thesz, and Rick Martel.

The next thank you goes to George Atkinson, who does the 50th State Big Time Wrestling website. www.50thstatebigtimewrestling.com. It is a truly remarkable site that has photos, recaps of matches, results, collectibles, history, and so much more. George was always available when I had questions.

Thank you to Mary Fries, Anita Barend, Renee Ane, and Sonny Francis, who were related to the wrestlers and helped show us their personal side.

Thank you to Doug Wulff, Steve Ogilvie, Jeff Walton, Kurt Beyer, Billy Anderson, Ed Moretti, Mickey Doyle, Matt Farmer, Dave Cameron, Jeff Sharkey, and Bruno Bekkar, who were able to pull back the curtain just a little bit to give a glimpse or add a story.

Photography is such a big bonus to this and every book. Some of the photographers that were so instrumental in bringing the names to life include Dr. Michael Lano, Viktor Berry, Dan Wesbrook, Paul Stratoti, Jim Brooks, and so many others. This would not be the book it is without your contributions.

One other person to mention and thank. Even though he is not directly involved, he is indirectly involved in everything wrestling. He should probably be mentioned in every historical wrestling book that is produced and that is J Michael Kenyon. Nearly every current wrestling historian throws up their hands and bows to the work that he has done. For that groundwork, we thank you, Sir!

I hope this book will give you the story of how special and unique Hawaiian wrestling was, not only in the 60s and 70s when we were able to see those dream cards but all the way back to the beginning.

Let's get started.....**OHHH YEAHHH!**

Hawaii's Journey to Statehood

In the mid-20th century, against the backdrop of the vast Pacific Ocean, a transformative chapter unfolded in the history of the Hawaiian Islands. The journey towards statehood, culminating in Hawaii becoming the 50th state of the United States on August 21, 1959, was a significant milestone that reshaped this tropical paradise's political, cultural, and economic landscape.

Hawaii's path to statehood was intertwined with its complex history of annexation. Annexed by the United States in 1898, Hawaii had long been a strategic outpost in the Pacific. The islands had played a crucial role in American military and economic interests, particularly in the aftermath of World War II.

The quest for statehood gained momentum in the post-war era. The returning veterans and the burgeoning tourism industry underscored the islands' integral role within the American fabric. The Organic Act of 1900 granted Hawaii territorial status. Over the ensuing decades, efforts were made to transition the islands from a territory to a fully-fledged state.

Hawaii's geopolitical significance was thrust into the spotlight during World War II when the attack on Pearl Harbor catapulted the United States into a global conflict. The war effort brought unprecedented attention to the islands and solidified their strategic importance. Subsequent military build-up and infrastructure development further intertwined Hawaii with the mainland.

Statehood discussions were not solely based on political and strategic considerations. Hawaii's unique cultural tapestry, blending native Hawaiian, Asian, and mainland influences, contributed to the islands' distinct identity. Advocates for statehood argued that Hawaii's multiculturalism could enrich the broader American experience.

The road to statehood faced hurdles, including debates over issues such as land ownership and Native Hawaiians' rights. However, a significant milestone came with Hawaii's residents' overwhelming approval of statehood in a 1959 referendum. A staggering 94% of voters supported the proposition.

The Star on the Flag:

On August 21, 1959, President Dwight D. Eisenhower signed the proclamation welcoming Hawaii into the Union as the 50th state. The iconic image of the 50th star was added to the American flag, symbolizing the culmination of Hawaii's long and intricate journey from annexation to full statehood.

Statehood brought about changes that resonated across every aspect of Hawaiian life. While it brought increased federal funding, economic opportunities, and political representation, it also prompted discussions about preserving Hawaiian culture in the face of mainland influences.

Hawaii's transformation into a state was a watershed moment, marking the end of a territorial era and the beginning of a new chapter in the islands' history. The unique blend of cultures, the resilience of the Hawaiian people, and the islands' strategic importance all played a role in shaping Hawaii into the 50th star of the American flag. As Hawaii joined the Union, it not only became an integral part of the United States but also retained its distinct identity, forever influencing the cultural mosaic of the nation.

Transportation to Hawaii, 1930-1941

In the exciting history of professional wrestling in Hawaii, the journey to the beautiful islands was more than just a simple trip—it was a challenging adventure. For the wrestlers who performed in Hawaii, the excitement of being in this tropical paradise was met with the difficulties of getting there. As you read through the pages of "Ohhh Yeahhhh," it's important to understand the travel details. Imagine a time before modern air travel was easy, when big ships sailed across the Pacific Ocean, and planes had propellers. The names you'll read about—like Al Karasick, Lord Blears, and Vic Christy—made their mark not only in the wrestling ring but also faced challenges on their way to the Hawaiian islands. So, step into the world of these wrestling pioneers, experience the ups and downs of their journeys across the Pacific, and appreciate the importance of their successes and struggles in a world where the ocean both connected and separated the realm of professional wrestling.

1930: The Maritime Gateway

In the early 1930s, reaching the idyllic shores of Hawaii required a maritime odyssey. Steamships like the Matson liners were the lifelines connecting the mainland United States to the distant archipelago. These vessels embarked on voyages from San Francisco to Honolulu, with stops in Los Angeles and occasionally Seattle. The journey was an expedition, taking several days and providing passengers with a leisurely passage across the Pacific.

1936: The Wings of Progress

The winds of change began to blow in 1936 when Pan American Airways initiated the first transpacific air service, the "China Clipper." This marked a significant shift in the paradigm of travel to Hawaii. The inaugural flight departed from San Francisco on November 22, 1935, and reached Honolulu on November 26, 1935. The advent of air travel not only slashed travel time but also heightened the allure of Hawaii as a premier tourist destination.

1941: Aerial Advancements and the Shadow of War

As aviation technology advanced, so did the accessibility of Hawaii. By the late 1930s, the Sikorsky S-42 flying boats were plying the route, offering a more refined and efficient means of transport. However, the ominous clouds of war would soon overshadow the burgeoning ease of travel.

On December 7, 1941, the attack on Pearl Harbor reverberated far beyond the confines of the naval base. The surprise assault, perpetrated by the Japanese, thrust the United States into World War II and fundamentally altered the dynamics of transportation to Hawaii. With the Pacific theater of war at its doorstep, civilian travel was sharply curtailed, and the focus shifted to military logistics.

1942-1945: Restricted Skies

During the war years, civilian flights to Hawaii faced severe restrictions. The islands became a crucial military outpost, and air travel was primarily reserved for strategic and wartime purposes. The wartime blackout measures further complicated civilian transport, plunging Hawaii into a period of isolation.

1945: Post-War Resurgence

With the conclusion of World War II in 1945, Hawaii gradually emerged from the shadows of conflict. The resumption of civilian air travel saw a surge in interest and demand. The post-war era witnessed the expansion of air routes and the introduction of newer, more advanced aircraft, ushering in unprecedented accessibility to the islands.

In retrospect, the period from 1930 to 1941 reflects a transformative chapter in the history of transportation to Hawaii. From the stately voyages of steamships to the revolutionary dawn of transpacific air travel, the modes of reaching the islands mirrored the evolving tapestry of technology and geopolitics. The indelible mark left by the attack on Pearl Harbor, however, cast a long shadow over this era, disrupting the paradigms of travel and reshaping Hawaii's place in the global imagination.

1945-1959: Rebuilding and Reconnecting

In the aftermath of World War II, the post-war resurgence of civilian travel to Hawaii was marked by rebuilding and reconnection. The end of hostilities prompted a wave of optimism, and the islands became a sought-after destination for returning service members and their families. The aviation industry experienced a boom, with improved aircraft and expanded air routes making Hawaii more accessible than ever before.

In 1947, Pan American Airways introduced the luxurious "Stratocruiser" on its Hawaii route, offering passengers unprecedented comfort and style. This era saw a growing interest in Hawaiian culture, further fueled by the popularity of films and literature romanticizing the tropical paradise. The 1950s witnessed increased tourism, laying the foundation for Hawaii's future as a premier vacation spot.

1960s-1970s: Jet Age and Cultural Shifts

The 1960s brought about a revolution in air travel with the introduction of jet airliners. Boeing 707s and Douglas DC-8s began ferrying passengers to Hawaii with unmatched speed and comfort, further fueling the tourism industry. The development of Honolulu International Airport into a modern hub facilitated the influx of visitors, and airlines like United and American increased their services to meet the growing demand.

Simultaneously, the 1960s and 1970s saw a cultural renaissance in Hawaii. The global popularity of tiki culture and the music of Hawaiian artists like Don Ho added to the allure, drawing visitors seeking an exotic escape. The burgeoning popularity of Hawaii Five-O on television also played a role in casting the islands as an enticing destination.

1980s: The Age of Package Tours and Economic Growth

The 1980s marked a new phase in Hawaii's tourism industry with the rise of package tours. Travel agencies bundled flights, accommodations, and activities, making Hawaiian vacations more accessible to a broader demographic. The islands experienced an economic boom, and the tourism sector became a vital driver of the local economy.

Airlines like Aloha and Hawaiian further expanded their fleets and services, introducing more non-stop flights and connecting Hawaii to a growing number of mainland and international destinations. The allure of the islands extended beyond leisure tourism, with the business and convention sectors also contributing to the influx of visitors. As the 1980s came to a close, Hawaii had firmly established itself as a global tourism hotspot, with air travel playing a pivotal role in shaping its identity.

Wrestling in the Wake of Pearl Harbor

In the annals of history, few events have left as profound a mark on the American psyche as the devastating attack on Pearl Harbor in 1941. As the nation grappled with the aftermath of that fateful day, seeking solace and grappling with anger, the world of professional wrestling in Hawaii stood at the epicenter of a seismic shift. The reverberations of war not only silenced the roar of the crowd but also cast a pall over the squared circle, plunging the islands into a wrestling hiatus that lasted a full year. Yet, within this unexpected intermission, a complex and enduring trope began to take In the shadow of Pearl Harbor, the emergence of the villainous Japanese wrestler became an indelible chapter in the story of sports entertainment, revealing the unexpected consequences that arise when the worlds of geopolitics and professional wrestling collide. As we step into this complex narrative, we navigate the ringside shadows, exploring the interplay between history, societal dynamics, and the world of larger-than-life characters who grappled not only with each other but with the echoes of a world at war.

Pearl Harbor, Prejudice, and the Emergence of a Wrestling Trope

In the aftermath of the attack on Pearl Harbor, the subsequent internment of Japanese-Americans, fueled by wartime hysteria and xenophobia, cast a long shadow over the nation's psyche. As the echoes of war resonated, an unexpected consequence emerged within the world of professional wrestling—an enduring and, at times, troubling trope: the villainous Japanese wrestler.

1940s-1950s: A Mirror of National Sentiments

As the nation grappled with the trauma of Pearl Harbor and the ensuing war, pro wrestling became a canvas onto which societal fears and biases were projected. The wrestling ring, already a theater of exaggerated characters and storylines, reflected prevailing national sentiments. Wrestlers of Japanese descent, irrespective of their individual backgrounds or allegiances, were often cast as nefarious villains, playing upon the wartime distrust that lingered in the collective consciousness.

Promoters, ever attuned to the pulse of public opinion, capitalized on these sentiments to create compelling narratives that resonated with the audience. The villainous Japanese wrestler became a stock character, embodying the lingering anxieties and prejudices of the era.

1960s-1970s: Cold War Politics and Cultural Caricatures

The Cold War era saw the continuation of the trope, albeit with a shift in focus. With the geopolitical stage dominated by U.S.-Soviet tensions, the wrestling narrative adapted to the times. Japanese wrestlers, still depicted as cunning and deceitful, took on additional layers of caricature, often presented as agents of mysterious organizations or practitioners of mystical arts.

This period also witnessed the rise of Asian wrestling stars, such as Mr. Fuji and Mr. Saito, who were often cast as antagonists despite their talent and athleticism. The juxtaposition of their wrestling prowess with the perpetuation of harmful stereotypes reinforced the notion of the villainous Japanese wrestler in the eyes of the audience.

1980s-1990s: Cultural Awareness and Lingering Stereotypes

Even as the wrestling landscape evolved and became more diverse, the trope of the villainous Japanese wrestler persisted. The 1980s and 1990s, marked by increased cultural awareness and a push for inclusivity, saw a nuanced approach in some promotions. However, the lingering stereotypes continued to surface, reflecting the industry's struggle to fully disentangle itself from the legacy of wartime caricatures.

While some Japanese wrestlers, like Jushin Thunder Liger, were celebrated for their skill and athleticism, others were still typecast as cunning and conniving individuals, reinforcing the narrative established decades earlier.

21st Century: A Shift Towards Authentic Representation

As the 21st century unfolded, pro wrestling began to reckon with its historical portrayals of different ethnicities, including the trope of the villainous Japanese wrestler. Wrestlers like Shinsuke Nakamura and Asuka emerged as talented competitors and individuals whose characters were not defined by stereotypes. The industry, reflective of broader societal shifts, moved towards more authentic representation and diverse storytelling.

Nationalistic Villains and Societal Reflections in Professional Wrestling History

The phenomenon of casting professional wrestlers as villains based on national stereotypes and wartime animosities was not a unique occurrence with the aftermath of Pearl Harbor. The echoes of such theatrical portrayals can be traced back to the aftermath of World War I, where the wrestling canvas served as a mirror reflecting societal fears and biases. In the post-war period, the emergence of the villainous German wrestler became a compelling trope, resonating with the geopolitical climate and public sentiments.

In conclusion, wrestling's portrayal of nationalistic villains, whether German or Japanese, serves as a historical artifact reflecting the theatrical dimensions of sports entertainment and its complicated relationship with the socio-political contexts in which it unfolds. The evolution of these tropes underscores the industry's responsibility to transcend stereotypes and embrace a more nuanced and inclusive storytelling approach.

The trope of the villainous Japanese wrestler in pro wrestling, a result from the tumultuous post-Pearl Harbor era, persisted for decades. It served as a stark reminder of how historical events and societal prejudices can manifest unexpectedly within the realm of sports entertainment. The evolution of this trope parallels the broader journey of pro wrestling, reflecting both its ability to entertain and its responsibility to confront and transcend the legacies of the past.

It is crucial to remember that these tropes do not define the rich tapestry of Hawaiian wrestling. The true essence lies in the tremendous characters, indomitable personalities, and extraordinary athletes who graced the rings of this tropical paradise. Al Karasick, Lord Blears, Steve Rickard, Peter Maivia, and a legion of others—each a luminary in their own right—left an indelible mark on the history of professional wrestling in Hawaii.

In shedding light on these luminaries, it is our hope that this book becomes a beacon, guiding readers through the corridors of time to witness the triumphs, struggles, and larger-than-life stories that unfolded beneath the Hawaiian sun. It is the resilience of these wrestlers, their commitment to entertaining, and the enduring spirit of aloha that truly define the legacy of Hawaiian wrestling. Ohhh Yeahhh honors not only the athletes but also the devoted fans who turned wrestling in Hawaii into one of the greatest promotions in history. May this book stand as a tribute to the remarkable journey of professional wrestling in the Aloha State, forever immortalizing the legends in the shadows who made it a cultural phenomenon worth remembering.

The Personalities

Pampero Firpo

Real Name: Juan Kachmanian
Born:1930 Died: 2020

Pampero Firpo held the NW title on one occasion. During his career, other titles he held included The US title in Detroit four times, The Americas title in LA and The Hawaiian title. I found Pampero to be one of the most engaging people I have ever interviewed, a stark contrast to the character he often portrayed. The interview is recounted as Firpo dictated; no corrections have been made for readability.

RATNW: Talk about how you became interested in becoming a wrestler.

Firpo: This message is to the readers of Ring Around the Northwest, to anybody who knows. I was there in 1964, a brief story about Pampero Firpo, the Wild Bull of the Pampas. I practically was born in a stadium. My father was a promoter after he quit boxing. He was an outstanding amateur boxer, under the division of featherweight and then lightweight. He was pointing to the Olympics in 1936. But somehow, he had to forfeit the trip because he got married and all these things happened. Anyway, he became a promoter and opened a stadium over there. So I grew up in the stadium.

When I was six years old, my father said, OK, you can start timing the guys now. So I timed them, skipping rope and sparring. Then after that, I was practically saying to myself. I have to make a name for myself, and I went into track and field in 1944 when I was in college. So at an early age, I was in college. My first diploma was in 1943 in Piedmont Academy with cut writing and shorthand when I was 13 years old. In 1944 when I was 14 years old, I was doing very good in track and field in the 100-meter flat race and 80-meter flat face. Well, now I will try a little boxing. So I went to box and fought ten matches and won nine by knockout and one by points.
After that, I said, wait a minute, there has to be a better way to make a living. At that time, the army was calling me to do my duty in Argentina. So, I went to the military. Somebody mistook me for another big name, an Armenian name. I am originally Armenian. My name is Karach Manion. The man who was over there who was wrestling was Karapetian. I was very much in excellent physical condition. One day I was well; I might try because of the mistaken identity. In the army, a lieutenant said, I think I saw your name in the paper. I said, no, that is someone else. Yes, NO, Yes, No. Then I finally said, well, you take me to the matches, and you will see someone else. I said, well, why don't you go over there and see what is going on. The man over there was a man who, from 1933 to practically 1940 in the Eastern belt of the US from Washington to Massachusetts, has a name for himself under the promotion of Rudy Dusek. He went with a troop to Argentina with another guy named Bobby Brown and some other people. He was so much of a success over there that he liked the country that he stayed. I went to approach him, an excellent man and a great professional. He said to me, Hey, soldier. I went with my unit over there. I had a medal 2 or 3 months prior, and I had an opportunity to save several elderly people, and then the

army recognized me and put the whole troop in front of me and saluted me, and you know things like this happen when you are young.

So, he saw my medals, and he said, what do you know, we have a hero here. I said, No, I'm not much of a hero. I did what was supposed to be done. He asked if I was a wrestler. I said, No. I was a fighter, a track and field runner, and I was very good at calisthenics and good at soccer. I was good because of my speed, and I was right-wing. I was faster than the ball. I said I could try (to wrestle), and I saw one guy wink eye to another guy, and we have what we call a mark. It is no fun to be a mark anyway. I trained for half-hour and went back to the army. I just collapsed. I went to the hospital. I was three months in the hospital. After three months, I asked the lieutenant if I could train here in the army corp for one month, then I had to do a job, finish up. So after a month, I went to a stadium, Luna Park, with 22,000 people. I was in the heart of Buenos Aires. They were still practicing. What took you so long to come back? In the army, you cannot control the timing. The timing controls you. I said I would like to train a little bit with that one over there. So, the old man knew something was coming, the person who was in New York before. So, he said, all right, no one interferes; this is between two men. But I never in my life, never, do I try to use force. I believe it is very important to try and convince people without force, but sometimes you have to speak softly and carry the hard stick.

He knew what was coming, but I threw my hook and left jab and a right. Then he went on the floor. When he went on the floor, I tried to kick his head because I was so upset. I missed his head, and I went on my butt. I got up, and he said, time, that's it. So, the old man told me I would like to talk to you. I said, Yes Sir, what is it? How much do you weigh? I said 198 pounds. But I was in tremendous physical condition. So, he said, Do you like wrestling. I said I love it. He said, OK, you come Tuesdays and Thursdays when no one is here I will teach you.

So, he taught me, then when I went back, he was Olympic Champion in 1948 in England. He said I'm going to teach you how to shoot a little. I hate the term shoot because I am the shoot of a shooter.

But he says this will be a good passport for you wherever you go when someone tries to take advantage of you and let them know you are not a jabroni. I say, well, OK. Now that you mention it differently, I will try because I do not believe in violence. But when the time comes and if the circumstance pushes you, you got to do it. But anyway, to me, that term (shoot) doesn't exist. From the chin-up will always prevail more than the chin down. Wisdom is stronger than muscles. It took me 32 years, and then they told me they cannot teach me anymore. You know everything, you know self-defense, you know how to protect yourself. Here is your passport to any part of the world. You got a trade now. You are extremely smart, very witty, very fast, very conscious.

So then I started my matches. From day one, wherever I went and saw a wrestling fan, even if I make them upset, even if I make them angry, even if I make them applaud because psychology is so important, I can cause a riot, and I can cause a peace war. Make it that way; you become a headliner. In wrestling, you have four positions, preliminary, semi, special attraction, and then the main event, and above them, you have the box office attraction. So wherever I went, I was always headlining.

Now, in Oregon, it was a different chapter. I don't like to talk about it. I came there in a quick circumstance to stay awhile and let my short hair and beard grow out. Over there, I saw a young man with a great future; his name was Dean Silverstone. He's a great man, and he was a very macho, ambitious young man to go places in the journalism field. So I liked the kid, he was young, and in life, it is like a ladder when you go up, don't forget to look down and help someone to come up because later on you will go down, and no one will give you the time of day to you.

I say, what are you doing here, kid. He says I would like to make an interview with you. I said, sure, why not. What would you like to do? Well, you can come to my place. So, I went to his place, and we spent a lot of time, and we did a good interview for him, and he was very happy. I believe he sold that interview to one of the magazines. You know, the tough traveler from South America.

Wrestling for me from day one was a blessing because it fulfilled my dreams to come to this country which was the biggest dream of my life, and from there to bring my family here. My mother and father, my two sisters, two cousins, nieces and nephews, and then they come here, and the family grows up here with more kids. Some of them went on to go to Harvard with high honors. Another went to Berkeley and with high honors. Then San Jose State University with high honors. Tony from Harvard is working next to the mayor of San Francisco. Another works as a chemical engineer for NASA. My kids are a schoolteacher, a child recreation therapist, and the other was no genius, but he was up there in computers. So the family grew up now, and they are cats, birds, they are rabbits.

RATNW: When did you come to the US?

Firpo: August 9th, 1957. I came to Texas first by Brownsville by Mexico. I couldn't speak one word of English. The promoter said, Tell the kid if he wins tonight, he can stay. If he loses, he has to go back to Mexico and Argentina. I said tell the gentleman, the promoter Morris Siegel, God keep his soul, a great, great man. A great man with a good heart, a real human being. Of course, he is a promoter too. Tell this gentleman with all my respect, the only way he can send me back to these two countries he mentioned is in a pine box. My opponent this night is Don Leo Jonathan. Excellent man, tremendous physical condition, 325 pounds, 25 years old, 6'6 tall. He came from the top rope. I had to come from the bottom. It looked like the highest I could reach on his was his pectorals.

It was a very important, interesting match. He is a good friend of mine. But somehow, on August 30th, 1957, in Houston, Texas, I won the belt. (RATNW note: I verified this, Ivan the Terrible beat Don Leo Jonathan for Texas Title on this date)

From there, everything was peaches. So they sent me to St. Louis, Missouri, and from there, I went to Chicago. Then, I started hitting the big leagues. From there on, I became the champion in Nebraska, November 15th, 1964.

From there, I went to New York, and I conquered the Big Apple. I believe everyone knows what I did over there in New York. I had tremendous success with a very good supporting card. Each individual could have been a main eventer, including Johnny Valentine, Buddy Rogers, and all of them. But I was on top of them with Argentina Rocca, a fellow countryman. He was born in Italy, but he grew up in Rosario, Argentina. He was one of my idols when I was a kid. I was 14, and he was 24. When he wrestled me the first time in Omaha, Nebraska, in a tag match with Yukon Eric against Dick the Bruiser and myself, he told me your place is in New York; it is not here. I said Well, someday maybe I will get there. So, I went there, and he and I did great business for eight months.

I told the promotion I had to go to Argentina to see how my people were doing. In the meantime, I was sending money home. They had built the best home in town,12 bedrooms, 4 or 5 bathrooms. Plus, the office in the front of the house for my sister, who was going to graduate as a schoolteacher. I said one day I bought her a car. I bought her a Fiat. My other sister had a little nephew. I saw my mom with all these appliances, which was a big deal. Over there, it was around $40,000; here, it would have been 4 or 5 hundred thousand dollars. So even the toughest man on earth can show emotion. A tear rolled down my cheek. I say the place for you is America. Come to America, see the country if you love it, you stay. If not, you can come back. My father said, well, I cannot speak; I am 75% English. He was under the English flag. When he was in the orphanage. He was in Greece. The orphans were saved by Pope John 23rd, whose name was Joseph Roncalli. The Good Pope they called him. He is the one who protected 200 Armenian orphanages back in '32.

Everywhere you go, politics. I don't want to get deeper into this because I love and bless this country every day. Wherever I went, I have dual citizenship. I was born in Argentina, by choice United States, and by origin, I am Armenian. So I always put the three cultures on the same level. No better or worse. My folks came here twice, and then they decided to come back via Mexico, then they came here.

I traveled to 5 different continents, all 50 states, 21 foreign countries. I had 6,881 matches. My last was October 17th, 1986. That was the day October 17th; I left for Argentina to Chile. From the first day on, I was headlining. I was a box office attraction, and I was a gentleman in society.

Consequently, promoters could not ignore me. The only thing I can tell you is when someone did something improper, I never argued. I said you will never have me again. Step by step, professional wrestling is like an art, an unfinished theme for you to give to the people. I was hated in some places; in others, they were loving me, like Honolulu, Hawaii. I went by the name of the Missing Link. The Natives, it is hard for them to say Pampero.
I went to Honolulu, Hawaii, and there was a big name by the name of Luther Lindsay. Great wrestler, great wrestler, great person, great human being. He was in Australia with me, and he said, what can I do for you, Mr. Firpo. I said, "nothing." He said you proved you are something else. I said, well, I am just a human being. I said, where are you going now, Luther? He said I am going to Oregon, but first I am going to Hawaii. The promoter in Hawaii was a protégé of Don Owen in Oregon, Ed Francis, a good man. I said, if you are there, put a word for me. Tell them if I don't take the Island by a storm in two weeks, I will leave.

I went to Hawaii and took the Island by storm. I got hurt pretty bad in Hawaii. I was hospitalized for 56 days. I lost 56 pounds in 56 days. Had a fever of 106. The Dr. told me and said, look, your chances to live are 65 for, 35 against. I said, OK, give me a few minutes, and I will write three letters. One to my folks, saying I am sorry for hiding from you people, my situation. But if you come and all the paperwork of being an immigrant, you will become just like a tourist. Then to my sister, I said, you are the professional; take care of the papers. Then to my younger sister, who was expecting a baby in Santa Clara. I don't want to give her the bad news. Now God willing and in your hands, maybe we could pull through. Another good thing was an intern from Argentina who came to do the final test in Honolulu, and he was from the same place where Argentina Rocca was from, Rosario. His name was Ricardo LaBak. My doctor's name was James Wiliam Cherry. He had just graduated from the Mayo clinic. I said OK, doc, I am ready. They had more tests, and they said I might pull through. When they opened me, they said I looked like a kid of 18 years old, and I was 36. That showed you how I took care of my life: no drink, no smoke, no drugs, no other thing. They pronounced me dead, and they brought me back with an electric shock. When I woke up after 13 hours, my chest was in tremendous pain. I said, what did you do to me, doc? He said I saved your life, son. I gained 46 pounds in the following 56 days.

RATNW: Was it a sickness?

Firpo: It was an injury, and during the surgery, they removed a perforated part of the intestine, 1 foot long. They had a new technique.

RATNW: A injury from wrestling?

Firpo: Yes. I pulled through that and came back for the mainline in time to see my mother and father come in here. My sister was already here. The doctor gave the letters back to me, and I could throw them in the garbage. There was a big demand to see a rematch between my opponent and myself. I went to wrestle with an opening almost 2 inches in my tummy. I was still bleeding, but the doctor put something in when I went to wrestle. My opponent somehow put his finger inside of that when he put on the claw, and he busts everything again. My doctor came to see me wrestle, and when he saw me wrestle, he put his hands over his face and said, OH MY.

RATNW: Can you remember your opponent?

Firpo: Yes, Johnny Barend. He put his finger in my tummy. That was his specialty hold. The patches were just paper, so they had to take me back to the doctor and put more stitches in. The doctor said, why don't you stop. I said, well, we will see.

RATNW: You had a chance to work with Lou Thesz.

Firpo: I met him in 1964 in Salem, Oregon. I went to him, and we talked. I worried he would test me. We were fine. As good as I was, Lou Thesz was ten times better. That shows you what kind of class he had. A long time later, I saw him in 1965 in Texas, and we wrestled against each other. I said, Lou, you don't have to put the same on me again nowhere. He said, No, it is too hard. I said, Good.

From left: Firpo, Dan Manoukian, Ed Francis, Billy Whitewolf, and The Intelligent, Sensational Destroyer Dick Beyer.

Then I saw him in Honolulu, Hawaii, when he came from Japan. He said to me, Hey Mr. Firpo, please hold this for me, $60,000 cash. I said OK, no problem. He said I am going to go wrestle, and then I take a shower, and then you come with me. Charlie, who is his wife, and we go to Sammy Steamboat's father's business in Honolulu, and we have a nice meal. It was their anniversary of the Thesz's. In Honolulu, after the Governor, I was the most popular man in Hawaii.

When I was dying in Hawaii, Sammy Steamboat came to see me when I was in the hospital. There was a sign that said, don't bother this man. He left a note. He was a very quiet, typical native man—polite, humble.
Back to Lou Thesz. I will say no man in that profession, and this is from another world champion, Dory Funk JR, can fit his shoes. Only Bockwinkel carrying the belt of Thesz will carry the strap with dignity. In and out of the ring was a gentleman. He proved a point which I will not say a bad thing, and he handled himself with class.
Another friend is Bobby Managoff, another great wrestler, great gentleman. Great war champion too. Another great professional is Don Leo Jonathan, and another one is Maurice Vachon. Maurice Vachon, I will say, is not in size physically speaking, but his heart is bigger than the sky. His integrity is bigger than anything else. I have nothing but high respect for him. He is a real product of the school of the streets—good man, gutsy, witty, and lots of wisdom. When you mention witty and wisdom, I cannot ignore Bobby Heenan. Bobby Heenan is something else.

He is a walking living encyclopedia. He is always there to give you the finest talk in a short time. Nick Bockwinkel is a great professional. Angelo Poffo, I'm talking the peak. You ignore the good and bad and ugly. Ignore the bad and ugly and only mention the good ones. Long life to wrestling and long life to the wrestlers and even more yet to the wrestling fans. I am very grateful for my profession. I start facing the sun, and I left facing the sun.

That means clear, clean, cut, mind and body. I am 71 years old now, and I was born, April 6th, 1930. Wherever I go, people say I don't look my age. They say we never knew you were so handsome. I say well, that is your opinion, ladies, Penny Banner and those. Those compliments will add to my ego.

RATNW: How did your catchphrase OHHHH YEEAAHHHH come about?

Firpo: This was something else that I created In Honolulu, Hawaii. Wherever I went, people were always yelling OOOHHHH YEAAAHHH. So one day, I am in the gas station, and this lady comes running up to me and says Missing Link, Missing Link. This is my son, Gary; he is three years old. Look, listen here. Gary, who is this man?" He was a Japanese kid, and he said, "Missing Link." His mom asked him, "What's he done?" The kid just went, "OHHHHHH YEEAHHHH." It had become an institution.

Now I hear the Governor wants to see me in the palace. So I went over there to pay him a visit. We had pictures and everything. He says, "What do you know; finally, I meet the Missing Link. My grandchildren are making me crazy. Can you give me something for them? Can I give them an autograph picture or pose with me in a picture?" I say, of course, I will. We chatted and had coffee. I appreciate very much in the name of our country what you have done for our people from Viet Nam. I was visiting the hospital almost every day to the Red Cross to the Crippled Children's Hospital. I was making 75 to 1000 personal appearances a year. I will tell you this. I see how life is to be appreciated the way I do now, always.

I went to one hospital and saw one sign that said, "special, do not disturb." It was a special case, 19 years old; we just brought him in a week ago. I would like to see him even if I don't talk to him. They opened the door for 10 seconds. He was a kid with no arms, no legs from Iowa. I said, son, how do you feel. He said, "Sir, I feel fine now. You should have seen when they brought me here." Now you have to imagine a tough guy, a 19-year-old kid with no future, practically speaking. He said, thanks to the Lord, I am OK now, sir. I said God bless you, son. I want to hug him and give him all my feelings, but I just walk away. I said to myself, what do you know. I had been complaining that I didn't have any shoes and I saw my fellow man with no feet. After that, you become so small.

When I was in New York, a big special newspaperman said to me, " Mr.Firpo, what does it take to be a champion?" I said, "what you say about this belt?" He says, "yes." The belt is a symbol of supremacy. But deep down, it is a symbol of diplomacy. You see, sometimes, to avoid friction, when someone asks me a question that is deep enough to answer them wrongly, I say, "Yes, but the yes means maybe, when I say maybe, I mean no. When I say no, I am not diplomatic at all." He said he had a lot to learn. I told him I knew everything. That was a sportswriter who had a big break in TV who earned more than 10 million dollars. Walter Winchel. Never say no; this is being diplomatic.

I was lucky to speak different languages, and I was lucky to communicate with different groups. When I was away, I had to learn a new language- Samoan. I said OK. I learned 50 words in Samoan. They came to me like a man. You talk about an adopted son. I was one of them. They gave me an emblem, an honorary chief. When I greet them and tell them what I feel about Samoans, which is true because they are human and natives and they like nature. Water, the sky, and power, nothing else, no malicious intentions. Then society transforms them, especially your native countries.

I accumulated a great amount of knowledge and diplomacy. I learned a lot, and I changed points of view a lot. Always, what is good is good, and what is not good, I don't need to repeat.
I saw Muhammad Ali when I was over there in Australia. One thing they asked me what he was saying. It is important for free expression, and everybody is equal.

I make a promise to myself to fulfill my dreams, 80% to the bank, 20% to live the best I can. So, my best friends were always libraries, movies, training in the gym, and go to wrestle every day nothing else, no smoke, no drink. Sometimes people say, what are you, a bishop? I say no, you do your life, and I do my life.

Was a wrestler who went and bought a bottle of Champagne for $260. I said, why did you pay so much for it. You could pay $4.95 around the corner. He says I like to feel how it feels to have gold inside your body. So how can you change people's minds? Let everybody live their own lives. Right, wrong, or whatever, it is your opinion, that's it. I respect it.

RATNW: Did you prefer to wrestle a heel or babyface?

Firpo: Well, I will tell you one thing, in my situation, I had to be a bad guy. Wisdom, even if I didn't have long hair, I could still be a crusader and a big hero. But for my style and my vocabulary, I think as a heel, I was to be hated more than anyone else. When I switch to babyface, the fans didn't know what to do. That is when you have complete control of two different personalities. Not too many people have that gift. I am not praising myself. I say the thing I feel are true, when you are bad, and we are good, you raise your hands, and they raise up, and the people stand upfront on the chair, and when you put them down, they sit down. Then you have complete control of the crowd.

RATNW: You spent a lot of time in Detroit; anything to say about the Sheik?

Firpo: The Sheik, in my opinion, was 101 % professional. Always for the wrestling game. He was a man who took the opportunity to take the Motor City by storm. He came to Honolulu, and he said, "Please, I need you in my place." I saw him for the first time in 57 in Chicago. He was commuting between Detroit and Chicago. Family man, respectable. I never saw him doing any wrong thing; you know what I mean. I condemn adultery. I mean, I condemn adultery to myself. Anybody else can do what they want. He took on the responsibility to take care of some of his nephews because one of his sisters died very young, and he was from a large family. Many men who do not have education, you have to give credit. In my opinion, he had good intentions; then, in the profession, money is the root of all devils. Unfortunately, you can be derailed sometimes. Deep down, he was better than many people in the profession. As a wrestler, he was very colorful. As a promoter, he was very successful. I told him I believe in him, whatever you want to do with me. I went over and took The Motor City by storm. I don't need to tell you that; you know better than me. I will say, my success may have clashed a little with his position. Unfortunately, I have seen in the past; you cannot be a promoter and a wrestler at the same time. When you succeed in that, don't forget one thing, son, and you remember this from my mouth because of my experience. Success is very insolent and arrogant. You have to be tremendously diplomatic. Success being envy and jealousy. This is worse than an empty stomach. Because it is spiritual emptiness, I will not go any deeper; I believe you are smart enough to understand. I cannot condemn the man as a promoter, and I cannot condemn the man as a man. Only I say good things about him. Let's leave it that way.

RATNW: What are your hobbies, and how do you spend your time?
Firpo: Reading, movies but movies from the past. Movies from the past will be one or two sequences that will become a symbol to be found. I have the opportunity and the privilege one day to meet James Cagney. I was in Chicago and ready to take a taxi, and it was raining, typical wintertime in Chicago. The driver said, Do you mind

if we take Mr. Cagney with us. I said, Sure, why not. I said. Please, sir. May I have the honor of having you in my car? He said Oh, OK, Thank you. I said, where are you going? He said Palmer House. I said I am going to the Palmer House too. Now, this is what you call a down-to-earth man. What a gentleman he was. Polite, well-mannered, accepted around the world as a great artist. He said, What do you do for a living? I said I am a wrestler. He said, Ohhh. I know many of the wrestlers. I know Lou Thesz, Argentina Rocca because he was from New York.

We have a nice conversation, and we arrive at the Parker House and now Mr. Cagney, respecting your position and your respecting mine. I cannot be social in this society that we are in now. Thank you very much. It was a pleasure to talk to you. I wish I could talk to you more. I wish we could have a picture because I am a real admirer of your films. He said, well seems to me that we are cut from the same scissors. I said I believe nothing better than you can say about me because that is the way I feel about you. We shook hands, and I never saw him again. If it weren't for wrestling, I never would have had the chance.

RATNW: Any final thoughts, final stories?

Firpo: Only one thing I have to say, that goes for the future of wrestlers in that profession. Believe there is a future regardless of the negative information we get in the news about the air polluted, water polluted, the planet will explode. Everyone must be the owner of their destiny, not a toy for someone else. For that, you must be smart enough to stay away. Don't smoke, drink or use drugs. Try and eat the food that you need to eat. Today we are pointing to our own self-destruction by all and told to be sweet. Since I was six years old, my grandma said, now is the time to do home chores. Because someday, when you marry, and the lady is sick, you can take care of your children. Only one thing my grandma doesn't push me to sew, knit, or iron because that is for sissy people. I will learn how to wash the dishes and cook and take care of my sister. OK, we agree on that. So, I was lucky. I know how to cook. There is a future that is all up to each individual. You have to remain strong because temptations are always around. But you have to be smart because the best credit card to succeed in life is your health. I believe in longevity. I believe in a long life. There are four words I carry around, faith, love, peace, and God. That is my side of the discipline in the sporting life. On the man's side, I would say loyalty, courage, dignity, and above all the honesty. You prevail in every place. Never go after the dollar because, in the final stage of your life, the dollar remains here.

A promoter one time told me, Hey Firp, you know something, I already made 2 million dollars. I said I hope you can make 10. He said, you know you are the only person ever to wish me to be richer. I said, do me a favor if you don't get the message; next time I come to your promotion, you ask me again, and I will give it to you. Two years later, he came to Chicago, and I told him, now I hope you can make 25 million. He said, why? When you leave this world, you need to leave with one eye open. Why? So you can see who is spending your money. I will be damned; I have a lot to learn. The only thing I know is I don't know anything.

When my son was six years old, I brought this big bunch of sticks. I said, come here, son. Can you break this stick? He said that is easy, and he broke it. I gave him two sticks, and he broke them. He broke three sticks. I gave him four sticks, and it was harder to break. By the 5th stick, he could not do it. The first stick is your mother; the second stick is your father, then you and your two sisters. Because they are unified, you cannot break them. Unity makes strength.

Firpo with longtime rival The Shiek

Mary Fries

(Pampero Firpos Daughter)

Mary Fries appeared on the 6:05 podcast to talk about her father. She was such a good, articulate, and likable guest that I wanted to have her say some words about her father for this book.

Question: Your dad was one of the most intelligent people I've ever interviewed. His wrestling character was quite the contrast to that and one of the wildest characters in wrestling. Do you think he liked playing that part that was so different from who he actually was?

Mary Fries: I think that was natural for him because of his look. I asked him, "Did you like being a heel or babyface?" He kind of chuckled and said, "Oh, a heel, of course."

You know, I think he had fun with that persona. He really saw himself as a professional and he talked about how the fans

Mary with dad Firpo & her brother John

became unglued when he came to the ring as a savage. He was pretending to bite into someone like Pedro Morales at Madison Square Garden; the little old ladies and the Puerto Ricans were just coming out of their seats.

I think that part of the wild character appealed to him. He really knew how to get under the fan's skins.

I think there were times when he would get kind of defensive at how people viewed wrestlers. He would talk to me and just say, "You know I'm not a clown; I knew what I was doing. I was very successful doing this, and I made money doing this, and I'm not to be taken as like a dumb wrestler."

I don't know if he particularly got a kick out of screaming at somebody and then going into his room and reading a philosophy book.

Question: Did your family have an understanding of what wrestling was, and did he smarten up your family?

Mary Fries: You know he did not smarten up the family. In fact, I was just telling Dave Meltzer the other day, my brother told this story at our dad's funeral. My dad said that Morris Siegel had told my dad he needed to win his match with Don Leo Jonathan, or he was out of the territory. My dad said, "The only way you are going to send me out of Texas was in a pine box."

OK, so my brother said that at my dad's eulogy. I was telling Dave, you know my brother really thinks it was real. I said to Dave, "Do I smarten him up and tell him like he was going over and he wasn't gonna go home in a pine box?"

He never talked to us about wrestling. It was like a clandestine thing. He wouldn't tell us when he went to wrestle in 1986. I was 11, and I would have known. My brother was 16. When I said, "Hey, it's fake, right?" He said that is a very touchy word with me. He would tell my class, "Well, you know, don't try to do these things because we're professionals."

Being blinded by The Sheik

He would just talk about how you really do get injured, and that's part of his professional ethic. He wouldn't ever give away anything.

There's a picture of my dad after being blinded by the Sheik. My dad has these bandages; it's a really funny picture. They ran it in the Detroit magazine Body Press. My dad looks kind of white because the photos are kind of underexposed. He has these black glasses on and these white bandages under the glasses like he's been blinded. He is sitting in this chair wearing a flannel shirt and there's a nurse to the left of him and a nurse to the right of him. One of the nurses is his mom dressed in a nursing outfit and one of them is his sister Rosa. My mom said you can't tell anyone.

Question: We talked about how he recognized certain wrestlers in certain terms. You mentioned that Lou Thez was a shooter, and then Buddy Rogers, Ripper Collins, and Johnny Barend were more showmen. What did he consider himself? I feel like he had the skills to be considered a shooter, but then his character would have been more of a showman.

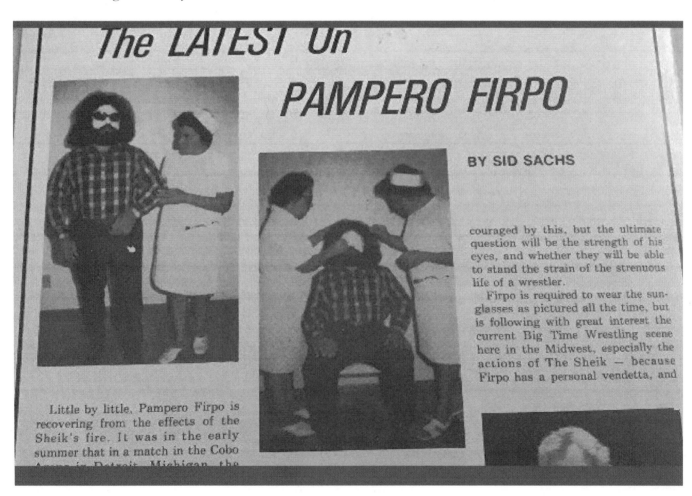

The LATEST On PAMPERO FIRPO

BY SID SACHS

Little by little, Pampero Firpo is recovering from the effects of the Sheik's fire. It was in the early summer that in a match in the Cobo Arena in Detroit, Michigan, the

couraged by this, but the ultimate question will be the strength of his eyes, and whether they will be able to stand the strain of the strenuous life of a wrestler.

Firpo is required to wear the sunglasses as pictured all the time, but is following with great interest the current Big Time Wrestling scene here in the Midwest, especially the actions of The Sheik — because Firpo has a personal vendetta, and

Mary Fries: He would have called himself a box office draw.

I think you know my dad is incredibly strong, and he knew how to fight. You said like he had the tools for that. I mean, obviously, his character wasn't doing scientific wrestling right. But I don't think he ever would put himself in the category of the showman. I think there's always this sincerity about what he was doing that he felt a certain integrity.

The other thing that came to mind was that Karl Gotch injured my dad. He would spit the name out "Gotch," and he said he tried to injure me in Hawaii. "He dropped me on my head. If it weren't for my 23-inch neck, I would become a vegetable.

Question: How did he come across the Dusek family? WrestleData has Rudy Dusek training him, but that timing doesn't sound right.

Mary Fries: He started in 1951 in Argentina and, from Argentina, went to Chile, Ecuador, and all over South America. Then, into Mexico, then into the US. So it was like early 60s he was in Omaha. He has already been wrestling for 10 years, so I'm not sure why it says that Rudy trained.

He always spoke very favorably of Joe and the Duseks. I think my dad really thought he was a man of integrity. He says, above all else, honesty, loyalty, and values were extremely important to him. It is hard to find values probably at any business, but particularly with wrestling and wrestling promoters who you know are real, true, genuine men of integrity and honesty, and he really trusted him.

Then he became friends with Joanne (Joe's Daughter) and just really respected them as a family.

He did tell me that when Ernie (Dusek) was at the end of his life and had some dementia, he wasn't able to really talk to him and communicate with people. My dad went right up to his ear and he said, "Ohh Yeah" and then Ernie said, "Firp" like he just knew it. It was so heartwarming. I know the family was just very special to him particularly.

Question: I have seen a pattern from your dad; if he couldn't say anything nice about someone, he wouldn't say anything.

Mary Fries: Yeah, he really didn't speak negatively. It took a long time to get something out of him. I told Brian Solomon on his podcast he got really angry about when The Sheik smoked him out of $8000. I said I didn't know what that meant.

Brian talked about how a lot of people have gone on the record about The Sheik. I never knew what that meant. Did my dad loan him money, or was it from payoffs? Talking to Brian, it sounded like maybe my dad was promised money for an appearance or appearances, which never came.

Question: Can you retell the Chimu story?

Mary Fries: He got Chimu when he was traveling through Ecuador. He got that from a tribal leader. It is an authentic shrunken head from the Inca tribe.

I asked him where it had come from. He said. "It was given to me as a sign of respect." I don't know if he named it or if they passed along the name of Chimu, which is their Goddess of good luck.

As an adult, I had never seen it or anything until I was an adult. I would ask him abaout it and he would always say he got it from a tribal leader as something very special and precious that they were offering him.

I asked my mom, I want to see Chimu and she would say, "Oh I think your dad had that made into jewelry." I thought, how do you make a shrunken head into jewelry?

When my brother and I were moving my dad from his apartment to assisted living, my brother found my dad's Halliburton. It had my dad's boots and jacket and things like that. Then he found this purple felt bag that looked like a Crown Royal bag. My brother found Chimu inside of it, but he didn't tell me. He put it in his front pocket of his jeans. I am sitting there talking to my sister and he says, "Oh Yeah, I have to show you something. Look what I found" and he pulls out Chimu and shoves it in my face and said "LOOK IT'S CHIMU."

It is this scary-looking thing, and it looks like it is petrified. It has stitched on its lips and white cottony hair, and then on the back, it has hair sticking out of it.

Then we think about what to do with it. I was looking online, and there is an effort to repatriate some of those artifacts back to their home countries. My kids are completely freaked out about it.

I had it on my bed, and I turned away, and the dog was going for it and trying to grab it.

Question: Can you retell the story from Hawaii 5.O?

Mary Fries: My dad was so popular in Hawaii and they just had no choice but to make him a babyface.

I got married there in 2003, and my dad came with me, and there are people who recognize my dad. There were about half a dozen people in different situations, like the rental car place or out to dinner, who recognized my dad. They would give him a hug and tell him he was a big part of their childhood. He was so popular.

I think in 1968 or 1969, he got recruited to be a part of an episode of Hawaii 5 O. It was just a small part where he was a villain in the show. Then Jack Lord (Hawaii 5.0 actor) was supposed to come and foil these villains from doing something.

My dad wasn't happy with that script and said that he wanted to rewrite it so he would be the hero in the show, foiling the villains. The producer said you know we already have a star on the show, and they just wanted him to be like a cameo in the background. He wasn't interested in doing it if he couldn't be true to his character.

Question: He had a severe injury or illness in Hawaii. Some have said it was diverticulitis; others said, in fact, Pampero said it was from a wrestling match.

Mary Fries: It's just not clear exactly how it happened; it sounds like it was just natural.

My mom just said he had a perforated intestine. I don't think it was related to wrestling, and he said he almost lost his life. He dropped a bunch of weight, and he's in the hospital for months. Then he had this long vertical scar from his sternum all the way under his belly button.

Question: I love the irony that he's working at the same post office that the Wrestling Observer comes out of. Did your dad have any thoughts about the Observer as far as it was a newsletter about the business?

Mary Fries: My dad started in the post office in, I guess, 85, and he didn't hang it up until he was 78, so that was 2008. I wish I had talked more to him about that, like how it was transitioning into this daily grind kind of situation. He just kind of kept those things very separate, like he didn't really talk about that.

There was a certain restlessness in his personality that I think wrestling satisfied. Traveling is a hard part of the business, but I think that appealed to him. Getting to travel and moving around and things like that, I think, when he was just kind of like grounded. Sometimes he would take long drives and do things like that.

Question: I know the Poffos were a really close family to your family. Was there a conversation about Randy using your dad's catchphrase and putting his twist on it?

Mary Fries: Randy really struggled with interviews at the beginning. He had the work, he had the body, but he would get stage fright or tongue-tied when he went to give interviews.

Lanny told him that if you are going to call yourself a savage, the greatest savage interview would be a cross between King Curtis and Pampero Firpo.

Randy gave it a try, "Oohhh Yeah." Lanny said he never heard Randy's normal voice again. I think my dad was really happy for Randy's success. Yeah!

Question: I love how you answered the question from the 6:05 podcast, how will he be remembered.

Mary Fries: I think that for wrestling fans, he will be remembered as somebody who made them believe. Up until his death, I would say my brother and I would probably get half a dozen letters a year from fans.

I would see people online say who the old-school wrestler who made you believe was. I would see many people say, Pampero Firpo. Many matches I saw were fake, but Firpo's matches were real. He made it believable in this ring, looking and acting wild.

Bill Apter and George Napolitano say they laugh at the bad guys these days, but nobody was laughing at you. People were genuinely scared.

He's remembered by wrestling fans like when he wrestled The Sheik, they were so bloody and crazy and unpredictable. It is that suspension of belief that is so fun.

For people in the business who knew him, he will be remembered as someone who was easy to do business with. There is so much ego involved in wrestling, and I'm not saying my dad didn't have a big ego, but I think he was able to put that aside for what was good for business.

He also drove a hard bargain. He wouldn't let himself be undercut by promoters as far as payouts. I don't think you will find too many people in the business who will say negative things about him. He was just really genuine, really sincere, a man of integrity.

I talked with Killer Brooks before he passed away in 2019, and I put him on the phone with my dad. Brooks said. "I just want to thank you for always trying to put me on the right path. I wish I would have listened a little bit more. You were always a good man, family-oriented, just a good man."

He got respect from people in the business because he was a respectful person. He tried to relate to people, he spoke multiple languages so he was able to talk to Latino wrestlers like Pedro in Spanish. He was able to talk to Bruno in Italian and the Vachons in French. He just connected with people. He had a genuine love for people.

He was really a patriarch of our family. He brought his parents and his sisters to the United States, which was their dream, living in Argentina. His sisters brought their husbands, and then everyone started with their families here. That was a real American dream. He is remembered by his family for giving them the opportunity to do that.

I said on the 6:05, apart from him being the wonderful wrestler and the fabulous entertaining character, he was a really loving dad, and I always knew that he would do anything for us. He would just crawl over broken glass to help us. We were his pride and joy. He loved being a dad, loved being a grandpa. A family was just super important to him.

My brother has a two-year-old now. He sent me a video of her eating a squeeze apple sauce packet, and she threw it on the floor, and she said, "Ohh Yeah,." My brother said I think she just channeled Dad."

Johnny Barend

Real Name: John R. Barend
Born: 1929 Died: 2011

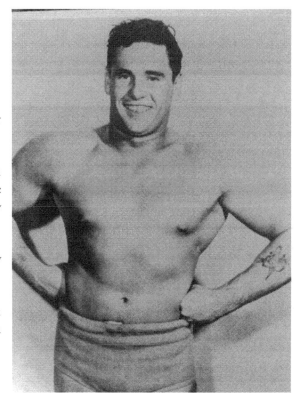

Johnny Barend started wrestling in 1948 after a very solid amateur career. He served in the Navy during World War II.

He was trained by Ed Don George. He formed a friendship with Buddy Rogers and was labeled as one of Roger's guys, someone Rogers knew he could trust. They would go into a territory together and build a feud.

In the early 60's, he was blacklisted after speaking about "shady business practices" by Vince McMahon Sr.

Barend first came to Hawaii in 1955. He had wins over Ben Sharpe, Lord Blears, and Ramon Cernandes. He teamed with Lou Thesz and Primo Carnera to lose to the Sharpe Brothers.

He would win the Hawaiian tag titles with Sandor Kovacs.

Barend would return to Hawaii in 1958 for several months.

The next time he came to Hawaii was in 1964, when Al Karasick sold the Hawaii promotion to Ed Francis. Barend has moved up the cards with this tour. He won the Hawaiian title, beating Neff Maiava.

He returned in 1966, winning the US title, beating Nick Kozak. He also had wins over Ron Reed (Buddy Colt), Pepper Gomez, Billy Whitewolf, Pampero Firpo, Neff Maivia, Mongolian Stomper, Nick Bockwinkel, and Karl Gotch. He also went to an hour-long draw with Giant Baba. He teamed with Ripper Collins to go to a ddq with Pat Patterson and Ray Stevens.

Barend had, by 1967, settled in Hawaii. He had met a local girl, and after he turned babyface, they were married in the ring on September 27th, 1967, with Jim Hady as the best man.

Hawaii Wrestling is credited with a number of characters, including Ripper Collins, Lonnie Mayne, King Curtis, and Johnny Barend. Their interviews carried the program, and Barends may have been the best.

In most of Barend's interviews, he would emerge from a coffin with a lit cigar and then take off on some wild story that often had nothing to do with the wrestling issues. Interviewer Ed Francis was often complimented as the perfect straight man. He would often take a sideways glance at the camera as a way of saying, "Are you getting this?"

Barend would often start the interview with his signature, Meeesterrrr Francisssss. The theme from Batman would be playing in the background to help give Barend an air of frenzy.

Various wrestlers traveling through Hawaii commented on Barend's interviews. "Bill Watts (from a Slam Article on Barends) commented, "Hawaii had the greatest interviews in the World. I'll never forget those interviews with Johnny Barend."

Barend would end up holding the Hawaiian tag titles eight times, the Hawaiian title twice, the Hawaiian version of the US title twice, and the North American title from Hawaii twice.

Barend's last year of wrestling was 1972. At age 42, by the results, he was still on top of his game. The amazing part is he had been in Hawaii solid for the past seven years and was still over.

In 1972, he had wins over Lonnie Mayne, Sweet Daddy Siki, Terry Funk, and Fred Blassie, and he had two nondecisions against NWA champ Dory Funk Jr.

His last match was against Dory Funk Jr. He suffered a chest injury and quietly retired. Barend was scheduled to defend his North American Championship against The Sheik on October 11, 1972, but was unable to appear due to the injury.

He moved back to Rochester, NY. John and his wife, Annie, bought the Twin Swan Motel on Routes 5 & 20 in East Avon, NY from his parents in 1971 which they operated until 1996. They lived in NY quietly until 2011, when he passed away.

Anita Barend

Wrestling in Hawaii was REALLY BIG back in the day, especially in the 60s and 70s. Yes, I was a fan. I heard about wrestling from friends who told my brother about it, so I started going to the matches w/ my sister and brother. Later, I started going w/ a friend in my class in high school. He was really into it and after a while said he wanted to become a pro wrestler. I lost touch with him after graduation and only found out a few years ago when a mutual friend got us in touch again that he did indeed get into the business on the Indie circuit.

Lots of boys would have their own matches in their backyards, each portraying their favorite wrestlers and, of course, going to the matches together and keeping up watching the televised live studio matches because of the locker room interviews.

I met Johnny at the beach in Waikiki; actually, we did kinda know each other as I had gone to an autograph session at a local department store not long before the beach, so we got to talking. I really can't remember if he was a baby face or heel at the time. Would you believe it? It was a long time ago. It must be at least 55 years now - time has a way of messing up your memory.

Johnny didn't have to smarten me up about the business; in fact, he didn't talk about it to me and I didn't ask him any questions. I thought he had a job and he was in charge of it and I had a supporting role, if any. Besides, long before I met him, my parents explained it to us kids.

Johnny and Curtis Iaukea were the guys who really started the whole interview thing; he really came up with entertaining interviews. He did use some props. For example, for Halloween, he did an interview in an upright coffin holding a Jack-o-Lantern. All around the coffin were spiderwebs! I remember one instance when they did an interview with me, and as I was talking, Freddie Blassie came up to us (me & Ed Francis) and scared me so much that I had to be helped offstage. That was fun! As I stated previously, Johnny didn't speak to me about

wrestling, so he just used his imagination as to how he was going to do it. In those days, there was some getting together to discuss what was going to happen in general, and the guys did their part to elaborate.

There was indeed a unique group of wrestlers in Hawaii, and it was a really great, relaxed atmosphere to live (obviously) and work. Many of the guys wanted to come back here to live after retirement. Billy Whitewolf was one; he was living here and I kept in touch w/ him. Don Muraco is back here, too, and we drop a line now and then. Ripper Collins never left here; he liked it that much! We had such good times on the neighboring islands, like when we went to see the volcano on the Big Island of Hawaii. It was erupting and we were scheduled to work there but on the very day we were to fly there, it stopped! We went anyway and still had some great sights to see.

Getting married in the ring was an unforgettable experience; I have to thank my parents for being so supportive in those days when something like this was unheard of in my family, especially since I wasn't even 21 yet! I was just shy of it... Anyway, my poor dad was more nervous than I was on the big night; I was a little nervous but more excitedly looking forward to this new experience in my young life. People were so nice, and we even got a few gifts. Leonard's Bakery, a very popular and well-known establishment, made and delivered in the ring a beautiful wedding cake, some people threw rice, and someone took pictures of the wedding and put them in a pretty album delivered it to Ed's office a few days later! We did not know who did this very nice thing as there was no note with it, and Ed wasn't in the office when it was delivered.

Johnny did have an injury, but it wasn't his leg. He couldn't get it pinpointed until he moved back to New York and finally found that he had torn his sterno-claido muscle. It's on the side of the neck, coming down from the skull, and attached to the collarbone. He did have quite a bit of pain from that and at one point thought he was having a heart attack!

He didn't seem to have any problems retiring from wrestling, but if he did, he didn't tell me. I was homesick, of course, and it was really culture shock for me. We did have a business to work at; we had a small motel just south of Rochester, N.Y., which his parents were operating while he was wrestling, and we took over after being back in N. Y. I lived there for 42 years. And made a life together with Johnny and moved back here after he passed away to be with my family, as we didn't have children and plus that I was sick of winter!

After a lot of years of being out of touch with the guys, Johnny was able to get back in touch with several people when Greg Oliver provided us with contact information to Beauregard, Dean Higuchi and Don Leo Jonathan. Johnny regularly corresponded with Lord Blears; I keep in touch with his son and daughters. We also kept in touch with Johnny Powers, Lanny Poffo and we would hear from Neff Maiava now and then. I also keep up with Don Lewin's widow and Curtis', as they live here in Hawaii, also Neff's daughter. I did get to meet Ata Johnson, the Rock's mom, at a Cauliflower Alley reunion in 2014. I never had the opportunity until then to meet her although I had met Rocky Johnson and Peter Maivia previously. Now, the only person to meet is the Rock himself! I was so glad I was able to see Nick Bockwinkel (he passed away not long after) at the reunion and meet his wife and she told me how they met, which was quite humorous. This was in the 70's - she was at a restaurant in the Ilikai Hotel with some co-workers when Nick approached her, introduced himself and eventually asked for her number and a date. She gave him the brush-off. Later, when she mentioned that a "Nick Bockwinkel" asked her for a date to her mother, who by the way was a rabid wrestling fan, Her mom got really excited and said "YOU turned down Nick Bockwinkel??? !! YOU go back there and accept a date with him!!" She listened to mom and the rest is history!

Postcard from the Twin Swan Motel the Barends managed after retiring.

TWIN SWAN MOTOR COURT

Ed Francis

Real Name: Edmund Francis
Born: 1926 Died: 2016

Ed Francis had a wonderful career in wrestling and may be the most important person in relating to wrestling in Hawaii. He started wrestling in 1950. He had a variety of alias's including Bobby Lyons and Daffy Daniels.

He won the NWA World Junior Heavyweight title in 1952. At the time this was a very prestigious title. He would win a variety of territorial titles including the Texas title, The NW title 5 times, The Pacific Coast Heavyweight title, the NW tag titles many times as well.

He first came to Hawaii in 1959 and won the Hawaiian championship.

In 1961 Francis bought the Hawaiian wrestling territory from Al Karasick. He also started wrestling there first as a heel and then turned into a babyface. He feuded with Al Lolotai, Sam Steamboat, King Curtis and Mad Dog Vachon. He stopped wrestling at the end of 1961 to concentrate on promoting. In the interview he talks about getting Hawaiian wrestling on TV and how important that was to the promotion.

He doesn't wrestle again for 8 years, returning in 1969. He sells his promotion in 1974 and wrestles a little in the NW. His sons Bill & Russ Francis break into wrestling and he helps them and tags with them at times. Francis used the sleeper hold as a finisher. It was the first time I had seen that hold and it had a mystique about it. It also lent excitement to the matches if he could use the hold for a win.

Francis lived near Las Vegas and Kansas. He passed away in 2016 at age 90. I had chased Francis for this interview for years. He finally agreed to do just prior to his own book coming out. His book, Ed Francis presents 50th State Big Time Wrestling is a beautiful Coffee Table book on his promotion in Hawaii.

RATNW: Had you been a wrestling fan growing up?

Francis: Well, when I was growing up, I was already a wrestling amateur in Chicago. The first matches I went to were in Chicago at the Marigold Gardens. Fred Kohler was the promoter there. They had Billy Goeltz, Walter Palmer, and a bunch of guys.

RATNW: Who trained you and helped you get into the business?

Francis: In the amateurs, it was Lou Talaber, Frankie Talabers dad, a pro wrestler in Ohio. Then a fellow named Carl Pujillo in Chicago. He came from Europe. He was the manager of the French Angel and Jim Londos, the World Champ. He started teaching Johnny Valentine and me some professional wrestling moves.

RATNW: Do you remember your first match, year, place, and opponent?

Francis: Karl promoted some towns there, and I went to Green Bay, Wisconsin, and Rock Isle, Illinois. Those were the first matches.

RATNW: What year did you start?

Francis: Gee, I don't remember, probably right after WWII. I was in the North Atlantic in the Second World War. I came back and was in a Mr. America contest with Steve Reeves and all those guys.

RATNW: I know in '56 you won the Worlds Junior Heavyweight title, a prestigious title for lighter weight wrestlers. You beat Baron Leone for the title in Tulsa. Talk a bit about the politics of a title change that prestigious, and who was pushing for you to get the title?

Francis: I had a manager called Al Ventres. Al thought I would be the perfect guy to have the JR Heavyweight title. He called and talked to Leroy McGuirk, who handled the JR Heavyweight title for the NWA. Leroy had me come in there and liked what he saw. He brought Leone in, and I defeated him.

RATNW: I know in '59 you wrestled in Calgary. At that time, Stu Hart was the promoter. How was the Calgary territory way back then? Calgary has always featured great workers.

Francis: I loved him. That is where I became the Canadian Open Heavyweight Champion, that was in 1961, I think. From there, I went to Hawaii and started promoting.

RATNW: I know while in Calgary you were the International tag champs with Luigi Macera. Talk about Macera as a tag partner.

Francis: Luigi and I wrestled all over Canada. We went to Montreal and wrestled for Eddie Quinn there. Luigi was there with me because I couldn't speak French. He could speak French and Italian. They didn't like Americans. I remember some crazy guy who had all kinds of gimmicks. He had a duffel bag, and he took out this big leather thing, and he strapped it on like a hunchback and a fake mustache and a wart. They couldn't beat him because they couldn't pin his shoulders down. Crazy guys, I'll tell you.

RATNW: I was familiar with Hawaii from 1959 on. What kind of territory was it before that, and was there much of a wrestling tradition?

Francis: I was first in Hawaii in about 1955 wrestling there.

RATNW: Do you remember what year you started promoting?

Francis: 1961

The Francis family: Bill, Ed, and Russ

RATNW: You spent a lot of time working for Don Owen. How would you describe him as a promoter, and was he good to work for? **Francis:** He was a wonderful man and a wonderful friend of mine. He was the one who gave me the money to buy the Hawaiian promotion from Al Karasick. I paid him back. It took about a year or so. But he was a wonderful man.

RATNW: When you became a promoter in Hawaii, what were some of the things you had seen other promoters do that you wanted to incorporate as far as the mechanics of running a promotion?

Francis: I had to start from the ground up. When I brought Lord Blears in, he had been on TV in Las Angeles, so he knew something about it. Then I got a contract with the ABC affiliate. It was a studio show. So there was a low ceiling in there. I had to build a ring that was lower so they could wrestle. We would have 80 or 90 people in there.

RATNW: When you took over from Karasak, were there any visible changes to the fans?

Francis: Al didn't have TV. In one of the first matches I had in Hawaii, I was sweating it out because the arena held almost 6,000 people, and I had 600 to 800 people in there. I had to build it from there. It took me about a year to get TV. I had some friends who had a TV show, and she used to put me on once a week on her show and talk about wrestling.

RATNW: I look at some of those cards you had in Hawaii; such fantastic talent. Are there any stories that you can remember?

Francis: We had one big riot there, King Curtis and Neff Maiava, and they just tore the place up. It was terrible. Luigi was there that night. During the riot, they had to send for the Metro squad. They came over and had police dogs. Some of the Samoans with chairs had the police and me pinned up against the ring. We had to punch our way out of there. A funny thing, they arrested a bunch of the Samoan fans there. Neff Maiava came in the next morning, he is a very quiet guy, and he sat around for a while, and then he asked if I had any handcuff keys. I said yes, we used some handcuffs for some of the wrestling matches. I said, what do you need the keys for? Maiava said, One of my friends was arrested and ran out of the arena. He went into the parking lot and hid under the car. The next day the guy still had the handcuffs on.

RATNW: Was it fun to promote? You had all that talent. Was it fun to try and bring forth a better card?

Francis: Well, we had to, to keep the business going. We brought the midgets in and Victor the Wrestling Bear.

RATNW: I know Honolulu was once a week, but did you go to other places in Hawaii, and how many times a week did you wrestle?

Francis: We went to all the other Islands. We went to the Big Island and Kauai, Maui, Molokai. We would wrestle 4 or 5 times a week. We would skip around to different places. I also promoted in Guam.

RATNW: Did you make the booking for the territory? Did you have any assistants that worked with you?

Francis: Well, Lord Blears worked for me. I brought him in, and he did all the announcing on television. He was great.

RATNW: I interviewed him about 15 years ago.

Francis: Poor guy is flat on his back now, and he can't get out of bed. He is in the hospital. He has been in there about a year. Great guy and great worker, I'll tell you now.

RATNW: What was the TV situation for your promotion? Was it a strong TV?

Sharing a laugh at a Dean Silverstone reunion

Francis: We had the number 1 rating of any show in Hawaii for almost 12 or 14 years. I was on an ABC station, to begin with. I switched to a CBS outlet when they made an offer.

Big Bill Francis

RATNW: In the mid 60's you didn't wrestle much but became more active in the early '70s in Hawaii and Oregon. Did you start wrestling more as Bill entered the sport?

Francis: I started Bill and Russ both in wrestling in Hawaii. Bill and I were one-time tag partners, and Bill and Russ had the Hawaiian tag titles.

RATNW: What is Bill doing now?

Francis: He still lives in Hawaii. He is in the security business at schools, and he also has some things he does with the government, taking prisoners from one place to the other.

RATNW: I am going to give you some names and your thoughts on them. Sam Steamboat

Francis: Sammy was a good wrestler and quite a shooter.

RATNW: King Curtis

Francis: Curtis was one of my number 1 attractions. Quite a guy. He was a football player. He played in the Canadian Football League, and I think he played a couple of seasons for the Detroit Lions.

RATNW: Lonnie Mayne

Francis: Lonnie Mayne was a crazy guy. He used to eat glass.

RATNW: Ripper Collins

Francis: Ripper was great, people hated him, but they enjoyed him. He liked to get on the interviews and pronounce all the Islands wrong.

RATNW: Do you have any idea of what happened to the belts you used in Hawaii?

Francis: When Neff Maiava was the Hawaiian Champ, he lost the Hawaiian belt. It was the Ring Wrestling Magazine Gold Belt. Nat Fleischer gave that belt to Al Karasick. It was the championship belt for Hawaii. They never did find it.

GENTLEMAN ED FRANCIS
ALWAYS AMONG THE TOP TEN

RATNW: You had tag belts also?

Francis: I don't know what happened to those belts.

RATNW: I know that Mr. Fuji ranks as one of the biggest ribbers around. Talk about ribs and any you can recall, or some of the most memorable ones you may have seen during your career.

Francis: Curtis knew Fuji, and he started him on television as his sidekick. Every TV show, he would have Curtis sit with him back to the audience. Then Curtis would yell, "Fuji do your thing." Curtis would hold three boards, and Fuji would break the boards. All the boards had to have the grain going the same way. Curtis took the board in the middle and turned it the other way so you couldn't break it. Fuji tried about 3 or 4 times his knuckles were bleeding.

RATNW: When did you stop promoting in Hawaii, and what was the reason? Did you sell the promotion, or did you just stop promoting?

Francis: I sold the promotion to a guy in NZ, Steve Rickard. I think they were still going in 79 and 80.

RATNW: Was it still strong when you sold it?

Francis: It was reasonably strong. I just wanted to get out because I had bought a cattle ranch in Oregon near Don Owen. I had all the kids over there. I went into the cattle business for a while.

RATNW: Wild Bill Savage once told me that once or twice in a man's career in the ring, he has a wrestling match that is unflawed and perfect for both wrestlers. For a three-fall match, that's unheard of, but in one match, every

high spot, every false finish, every move was perfect. That's the only perfect match out of 4,000 matches, and that was with Ed Francis. Do you recall that match, or did the odds just catch up with Wild Bill?

Francis: He was a great performer. I guess it just clicked. He was a great guy. When I was up in Calgary, I was helping Stu Hart do the booking. I brought Bill in under a mask. I also brought in Gino Morella (Gorilla Monsoon), Luigi, and a few other guys.

RATNW: I have Bill Savage's mask in my room.

Francis: He was a tough wrestler. There is a difference between plain wrestlers and shooters. They don't have any shooters today. They are all showmen and take a lot of steroids and stuff like that. It is a different business all together now.

RATNW: Did you suffer any serious injuries during your career?

Francis: Yeah, I had two hip replacements, broken nose 5 or 6 times, dislocated shoulder. Plenty of injuries.

RATNW: What have you been doing since you retired from wrestling?

Francis: I have been working on a website my daughter got me set up with, and she got me started writing a book.

James Blears

Born: 1923 Died: 2016

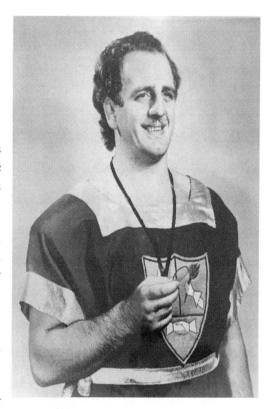

Lord Blears was born in 1923 in England.
In 1940 Blears had enlisted in the Navy and during World War II his Dutch merchant ship the SS Tijisalak was captured by a Japanese Sub. He managed to escape. This adventure was written about in an incredible article.

In 1946 Blears moved to New York where he shared an apartment with Sandor Kovacs and Stu Hart. The next few years saw Blears wrestle as a heelish Englishman. He would win a number of tag titles primarily with Gene Kiniski and Lord Layton as his partners.

Blears found his way to Hawaii in 1955. He would win the Hawaiian title once and the tag titles on many occasions. Ed Francis asked Lord Blears to come work with him to be the booker and TV announcer.

Blears also had a interest in surfing and would do commentary for surfing.

Blears needed hip surgery but declined it and for many years he was bedridden. He passed away in 2016 at the age of 92. I was fortunate enough to have this interview with Blears. I had been such a fan of Hawaiian wrestling and I repeatedly asked him questions about how special it was to the point he was getting a little annoyed with me. His main point was it was the locals who drew the money and the guys flying in were the icing on the cake.

RATNW: Was there anyone who took you under their wing while you were breaking into the business?

Blears: Carl Van Wurden, a Canadian wrestler working and living in Great Britain. Also, Billy Riley of Wigan Lanes. My dad was born in Wigan, and he was an International Rugby player. I was born in Tyldesley, 2 miles from Wigan and 4 miles from Manchester, England.

I started wrestling pro for money when I was 17 years old in 1940. During the war, 1939-45, I traveled the world as a British radio officer in the Merchant navy. I managed to get matches in Argentina, Australia, India, Canada, and the US in New York and Tampa for Nick Gulas. The promoters would always make room for you on the card. I also wrestled in Great Britain when home on leave and France after the Germans were driven out of France.

Wrestlers who helped me when I finally came to the US were Angelo Savoldi, Milo Steinborn, who was the booker in New York for Toots Mondt's office, Gino Garibaldi, Jumping Joe Savoldi, and Tony Marrelli. Also, Antone Leone. I guess the Italians were taking care of me because I was married and still am to a Caracciolo from Naples, Italy. (laughs). Others that I can recall that helped me were Kola Kwariani and Ivan Kameroff.

RATNW: You've mentioned that you roomed with Stu Hart and Sandor Kovacs. Any good memories about them?

Blears: We were all single, young, and we worked out every day at George Bothner's gym in Times Square. We would wrestle anyone who wanted to work out. Sandor Kovacs was the best man at my wedding.

RATNW: I am familiar with the Hawaii territory from 1959 on. What kind of territory was it before that, and was there much of a wrestling tradition? How far back does wrestling go in Hawaii?

Blears: I believe it started in 1930. I know Al Karasick promoted well before 1939. His top man then and during the late '30s was Ted Travis, also known as Ted Christy, brother of Vic Christy. Vic was the Masked Executioner for us for many years. The boys traveled by ship to Hawaii, Australia, and New Zealand. No planes yet.

"LORD" JAMES BLEARS

RATNW: Talk a little about Al Karasick. Was he a wrestler before promoting? How was Hawaii prior to Ed Francis promoting?

Blears: Al was from Russia. He traveled all the way across Russia and came into the US over the China border. I made my first trip to Hawaii with Gene Kiniski as the NWA World tag champs in April of 1955. We stayed ten months. I went back, along with my family, of course, each year for Al Karasick. I helped him get talent etc.

RATNW: Talk about Ed Francis as a promoter, and when he took over, I believe in 1961. Was there any significant difference to the fans concerning the promotion? Also, were there any significant changes for the boys when he took over?

Blears: Ed Francis bought Hawaii Wrestling Mid-Pacific Promotions in 1961. He called me in LA and asked if I would like to come in and do the booking. Up to this time, there was no TV. So Ed and I sniffed around and got Channel 4, ABC to put on the live studio show Saturdays. We got over big and asked the station for a contract. The owner said, "You don't need a contract."

Then we went to channel 2, NBC and signed a contract. He had one and half hours live every Saturday afternoon and outdrew ABC Wild World of Sports in their time slot. We also ran all the islands. Taped one hour of the Wednesday house show and showed that at 10:30 Friday night. We ran Hilo on Monday, Maui on Tuesday, Honolulu on Wednesday. Saturday, we ran Kauai Island and local TV Sunday at Scofield barracks. Every other Sunday, we ran Bloch Arena at Pearl Harbor. I did the narration of the matches and wrestled also. Ed and I split the interviews. The Civic Auditorium held 5,200 fans, and the HIC, now the Blaisdell Arena, held 8,732 seats.

RATNW: How and where did you know Ed Francis before calling you to book Hawaii?

Blears: I met Ed in Ohio in 1950. I wrestled Ed in Hawaii when Al Karasick was the promoter in the late '50s.
RATNW: Describe how Ed Francis was to work with?

Blears: Ed and I got along well together. What can I say? For twenty-one years, we were compatible. We looked at the boys we had and put them together the best we could to draw a house and make money for everybody. And we did. That's the bottom line.

RATNW: Talk about Hawaii as a promotion. You mentioned that the fans had to know the wrestlers before they could draw. Talk about other specifics of Hawaii as a territory.

Blears: I tried to explain to my friends and good wrestlers to take a paid vacation once a year and live the good life for a two- or three-month period, and it worked.

RATNW: What was the attendance like at the Blaisdell arena? Did you often sellout?

Blears: We ran the Civic every week, and on the fourth week, we would run the Blaisdell. For a couple of years, we would sellout every show. In recent years, cards put on by the WWF and WCW drew from 300 to 1,500 tops. They haven't been here for a couple of years.

RATNW: Were there any other assistants for Ed Francis in the office?

Blears: No.

RATNW: Did Francis have input on booking, or would he leave it up to you?

Blears: We exchanged views and ideas. I did all the narration of all the TV shows. Ed did interviews for many years. Then after a while, we split the interviews. Our interviews lasted a half-hour every show.

RATNW: I know you did some or all of the TV announcing for the promotion. Could you talk about when you started announcing and how often TV came on? What was the show like?

Blears: I mentioned this earlier. Remember, we had ten wrestlers to juggle around and not show them too much on TV, or people wouldn't pay to see them. We did an hour and a half show with two

matches and about thirty minutes of wrestling. Primarily interviews, and at the show's opening, we did fifteen minutes of "wrestling workouts." I would MC this in the ring with, let's say, Jim Hady and a rookie. Hady would show amateur holds, or it would be Karl Gotch or Billy Robinson. People in Hawaii like the first part better than anything. I also did a 10-minute spot called "Tallyho's Tales" and answered people's mail on the air.

RATNW: It appeared that Hawaii had the cooperation of west coast promoters and nearly every promoter in the country. Talk of the cooperation of promoters sharing talent with Owen, Kovacs, Shires, and LaBelle.

Blears: We developed our territory and made our own stars. We only asked for help when we needed one or two guys to put on at the NBC Arena. Shire came in opposition and used a tape on another channel in the Stevens and Patterson era. They just ran Blaisdell arena.

They started with 5,000 people their first show. We ran the same night at the Civic four blocks away and sold out 5,200 with Neff Maiava, King Curtis, Freddy Blassie, etc. However, it was too much hype for both sides. I flew to San Francisco and met with Shires at the San Francisco airport. We talked for one hour, and then I flew back. We used three or four of his talents on our cards at NBC. He stopped using his tape, and within nine months, we stopped using his men, and everything was back to normal.

We did not fly guys in and out each week. Never. Only the occasional two men on the big show once a month to present a bigger card.

RATNW: How was the transportation cost of the wrestlers handled? I noticed one random week; there were seven new wrestlers from the previous week. Three of these guys were Jerry Monti, Chuck Karbo, and Johnny Kace. Not to discredit any of these men, but these were not people who would help draw your card. How could the promotion afford to fly in this many people?

Blears: You got me there. Jerry Monti, we brought in if there was a man short at the Blaisdell Arena for our big show. He would be on the first match and catch the 11 pm flight back to California. The other two guys, maybe I'm getting Alzheimer's, but I don't remember them. Remember, someone was trying to promote Singapore and Malesia around then. They must have been passing through.

Blears with Gene Kiniski
as World Tag Team Champions

RATNW: If wrestlers were stopping over on their way to and from Japan, would the promotion kick in and help with transportation?

Blears: Once in a while, we would catch a guy going to Japan. But as I have explained, if the fans in Hawaii do not know them, it wasn't worth it. When wrestlers were heading home from Japan, they were tired and wealthy! HA HA. They wanted to get home. I talked Wilbur Snyder into staying two days en route home. He was an asset to the card. He had great matches, but not many people in Hawaii knew of him, and he left the next day. We had to concentrate on the guys who were here.

RATNW: I have a fascination with title belts. The title belts used with the Hawaiian promotion were the Hawaiian title, The Hawaiian tag titles, and the US title, which later, I believe, became the North American title. Am I correct in the Hawaiian title was also known as the Ring Magazine title? Do you know the whereabouts of these belts now?

Blears: I don't know who has or what became of any belts. The Ring Magazine belt was from Al Karasick's era. It was presented by Ring Magazine editor Nat Fleisher and became the Hawaiian title belt. The US Championship belt started in the early '60s and was first held by Nick Bockwinkel.

RATNW: Does any match or card come to mind in all those fantastic cards you presented as being something extra special?

Blears: King Curtis (Hawaiian) and Neff Maiava (Samoan) were naturally a sellout in Hawaii at the Civic and caused a riot, which never helps a town. Johnny Barend vs. Jim Hady was a sellout at the NBC arena, and we raised prices. Kiniski vs. Hady for the NWA World title. Kiniski and I against Great Togo and Tosh Togo for Karasick in 1956 was memorable.

RATNW: I looked at the cards from 1964 to 73, and on paper, they were unbelievable with all the available talent. Do you think it was fun to promote wrestling with all those tools? Did you attempt to better each card with the talent?

Blears: Talent does not equal big houses unless they are in your territory for a while. You can put on a card with all the big names you want, but that does not mean big houses. As I said before, the people in Hawaii had to get to know the wrestlers. It is hard to explain. Many of the biggest names on the mainland were not known in Hawaii. We would catch one or two guys going to or coming back from Japan, but the program we worked on for about four weeks would draw the house.

An example would be Wilbur Snyder. He stopped by one time, was a great name, and had a good match. But as far as bringing people into the matches, they didn't come to see Wilbur Snyder; they came to see the program we had been building for four weeks on TV. If he could have stayed for four to six weeks, he would have made money for us.

RATNW: Was there a feeling that something was very special about what was being presented? Did you try and outdo yourself?

Blears: When you draw 5,000 each week at the Civic Auditorium and once a month 8,732 fans week in and week out, you must be doing something right.

RATNW: Who had the longest-running, biggest money-making feud or program in Hawaii? What made that feud so special?

Blears: Handsome Johnny Barend in the '60s and up. I brought Johnny in from Buffalo, NY, where I knew him from 1951-52, along with Jim Hady, who died at age 39 in the ring of a heart attack. Others were Don Leo Jonathan, Neff Maiava, King Curtis, Billy Robinson, and Nick Bockwinkel.

RATNW: Mr. Fuji ranks as one of the biggest rib artists around. Talk of some of the more memorable ribs you may have seen during your career.

Blears: Mr. Fuji left the Islands many years ago, and I have only seen him twice since then. The only good ribbers I remember were Vic Christy and Antone Leone.

Gene LaBelle called me today and said that finally, Vic Christy got into the Motion Picture Hospital Home. He didn't have enough points or hours to get in, but finally, LaBelle got him in. He had been trying to get in for ten years, and now he will be comfortable.

RATNW: What injuries did you suffer during your career?

Blears: I broke my nose seven times, had two front teeth knocked out, cracked my neck, and broke my leg in Bakersfield, California, in 1947.

RATNW: What memories do you have of Lonnie Mayne?

Blears: The fans liked him. He wrestled his heart out every show. I did not socialize with him, so I didn't know him well outside the ring.

RATNW: Ripper Collins?

Blears: Collins found a home in Hawaii. He was always good at interviews.

RATNW: Around 1973-75, results from Hawaii become a little scarce. The results that I have show Hawaii appears to align itself with the AWA. What was happening in the area? Was attendance down? If there were just monthly shows, was there still weekly TV?

Blears: At this time, most top wrestlers who meant anything in Hawaii began flying all over the country to different spots, as territories began promoting in the big towns. We couldn't get wrestlers to stay two or three months anymore. So we used Gagne's tapes. I dubbed over the soundtrack each week. We ran the NBC every four to six weeks. The houses were fair.

RATNW: Was attendance still okay prior to switching to the AWA in 1973?

Blears: Yes

RATNW: Why did Ed decide to sell the promotion?

Blears: I never asked.

RATNW: After Ed Francis got out of the business, were you in any way involved in the others that came through, including the Rickards, Lia Maiava, or Super Fly Tui? Is there any wrestling at all on the Island now?

Blears: Steve Rickard bought Hawaii from Ed Francis. He joined Lia Maiava, and there was no wrestling for about twelve weeks. Rickard sent tapes from New Zealand, and I dubbed narration once a week on the tape. I helped Peter Maiava and did narration at NBC shows every five or six weeks. Finally, the houses went to zero, which was the end of the promotion.

RATNW: You have been president of the Pacific Wrestling Federation for Giant Baba for 34 years. What are some of your duties in that capacity?

Blears: I arbitrate any problems with talent. I help All Japan Pro Wrestling negotiate talent. Japan is like it was like in the United States in the '50s. Their style is the same as the US-style was. That is why they draw so well. I'm going to Japan next week. It is Baba's 35th anniversary in wrestling.

RATNW: You would scout guys in Portland and Vancouver to try and get them booked in Japan. Who were some of them you looked at in Portland and Vancouver?

Blears: Don Leo Jonathon and Gene Kiniski. Mainly guys would contact me from all over the world, like Dynamite Kid and Davey Boy Smith, etc.

RATNW: You mentioned that you helped get King Curtis and Don Muraco started. Who were some of the others you helped get started in the business?

Blears: Besides Muraco and King Curtis, I helped Rob Van Dam and Sam Steamboat. Muraco went to high school with my son Jimmy, and I got him into Canada with Gene Kiniski. He took off, and he was a big name all over.

King Curtis was a big card all over. He always blames me for the condition he is in now, "It's your fault, Lord." I took him off Waikiki Beach and trained him with Joe Blanchard. He was a Canadian pro football player. He got busted up really bad on the chains. They had real chains to mark off the first down. He slid on his back and nearly scalped himself. He had over 200 stitches in his head, nearly killing him. I saw this guy lying on the beach, 250 pounds, brown, real dark. I walked over to him and asked if he wanted to be a wrestler. He said, "Yeah, Yeah, Yeah."

RATNW: You also mentioned you booked Rob Van Dam. I saw him in Vegas in May, and he was very impressive. Besides the people that you book, do you still follow wrestling as it is in 1995?

Blears: Yes, I watch the matches occasionally. It comes on at noon in Hawaii. I am always out. I don't book talent anymore. I have never asked for a dime from any wrestlers I have recommended for Japan. I see a video and show it to the promotion, and Baba says Yes or No. I have been happy to help wrestlers get booked and will continue to do so.

RATNW: What are some of your hobbies?

Blears: Surfing, swimming, writing stories, and talking to my old-time friends about the great times we had back in the late '40s 50's and 60's.

Something happened last week; I got a call from the White House because I was a prisoner of war in WWII. The phone rang, and my wife answered. They said this is the White House. My wife said, which white house? There are a lot around here. This is THE White House. They invited me to an aircraft carrier, that's where the president and his wife gave a speech, and I got to meet them. I put all my medals on my coat and had one last hurrah.

RATNW: Most people who visit Hawaii say they love to visit but wouldn't want to live there as it would get confining for them. Any feelings on that since you have lived there for so long? Did you have to get used to that aspect?

Blears interviews Johnny Barend, with Billy Robinson and Friday in the ring.

Blears: I'm happy to hear that question. People who don't like Hawaii should stay away. We don't like moaners. I've heard that expression, usually on TV like Hawaii 5.0 or Magnum. Something like, "I've got to get off this rock." I think this was made up in Hollywood. The family all live on various Islands. Oahu, Maui, and Kauai. We enjoy our grandchildren.

RATNW: In closing, Lord Blears gave these random thoughts on his career.

Blears: When I arrived in New York in May of 1946, I shared an apartment with Stu Hart. Sandor Kovacs joined us two months later, and we got a bigger apartment. I became a US citizen in 1948. I had a great run in Texas for twelve weeks in 1948. I had Antonio Rocca's first match in the USA in Dallas in 1948. Also, for Primo Carnera in Dallas.

Captain Leslie Holmes was my best friend. He was a captain in the British Army in WWII in tank recovery. He was in Buffalo for two seasons, selling out the Buffalo auditorium in the summer and fall every week VS Fred Von Schott, Vic Christy, Lucky Simunovich, Great Togo, Gorgeous George, etc. We were together from 1945 to 1960, but not in Hawaii. He went into building houses.

I had some great matches with Gino Garibaldi during and after WWII. Dutch Herman Rhode (Buddy Rogers), Maurice LaChapelle of Montreal, Lou Farino (Angelo Savoldi's brother), and Benito Gardini in California. I won the World Lightweight belt in 1947 from Wild Red Berry in Phoenix.

I had great matches with Danny McShain. Now I'm up to 233, wrestling in the Heavyweight territories. I was the world tag champ with Lord Athol Layton in 1948. Then I teamed with newcomer Gene Kiniski for four years from 52 to 55 in LA, SF, and Hawaii.

Another great run was 1949-50 in Columbus, Ohio for Al Haft and Frankie Talaber. They had five towns a night. TV was such a big hit. This was when Jim Barnett began booking guys for Fred Kohler out of the Chicago office. You went on TV in Marigold Gardens, Saturday night in upstate NY, and everywhere they got that particular cable. You would have spot shows with Lou Thesz, Buddy Rogers, Ivan The Terrible, Don Eagle, and Suni War Cloud. This was probably the peak of drawing big crowds.

A War Crime at Sea....1944.

By Lord James Blears, as told to John Berger.
This article appeared in the Nov-Dec 93 issue of Command Magazine. It is reprinted with permission.

The torpedo hit right below my cabin on the port side. This ship rolled to starboard, and I was thrown out on the floor. The door to get out was suddenly the ceiling and we stayed that way for a while. After I got out of my cabin, I ran to the radio cabin to see if the first radioman was injured. I found him sending a message, but we had fragile "goal post" antennas and when the ship was hit, they'd broken, so though he was sending, it wasn't getting out.

My job, if we were attacked while I was off duty, was to go to the after gun. There was a small lifeboat there and a big metal case with a file and some ammunition and a big waterproof radio transmitter, about as big as a giant suitcase and weight 60 or 70 pounds. The ship had begun to right itself, but as I was going to the after gun, I had to swim across the well deck to get there. From the time I got my stuff, got out of my cabin and went to the radio shack and then to the after gun, the ship was back on an even keel. It sank in another 5 to 6 minutes. But I got to the gun, threw my little waterproof bag into the boat, and got the radio transmitter out of the case and put it in the boat too.

We were firing: the gun crew had spotted a periscope and was firing. Every gun position had been taken except for loading the shells, so I started passing those, but the ship had begun to list again and soon we couldn't elevate the gun high enough to shoot at anything. There was a kid on the bridge, though, who kept firing a 20 mm machine gun at where he thought he could see a periscope.

As the ship went down, another guy and I swung the boat away and got in it. While we were doing this, there was another guy, an English regular sailor, a gunner, a red headed guy I used to play cards with, who dived into the water and as he did, he hit his head and knocked himself out. So, I jumped off the boat and got him. It wasn't a big rescue or anything. I only had to swim a total of about 20 feet and then the ship was gone.

There were four lifeboats drifting. Capt. Hen had an engine on his boat, along with the chief engineer, the chief radioman, most of the officers and the Red Cross nurse. Right away all the boats started leaking because they were wood and hadn't been in water in over a year and the seams were split. So we all started bailing. All of a sudden, a periscope came up and circled us and then finally the submarine surfaced a couple hundred yards away. It was a big bugger with a small airplane hanger on deck. We could see the crew rushing to man their guns, they had some kind of twin gun mount and then one of them started yelling, "Captain? Captain?"

Finally Captain Hen identified himself and they waved him to come over toward the submarine. We watched everybody on the Captain's boat climb aboard the submarine and disappear below decks. Then the Japanese shouted for everybody else to come and we stared rowing over.

As we climbed up, I noticed all the Japanese were short, some of them so short their scabbard swords were dragging on deck as they walked. It hit me they looked exactly the way they were depicted in The Saturday Evening Post. It was the first time I'd ever seen any Japanese. They grabbed us and ripped off all our rings and watches and batted us with the flats of their swords. Some of them carried submachine guns on slings around their necks or had pistols on lanyards.

Soon, except for the officers and woman they'd taken below, they had us all, about 80 people, sitting on the foredeck ahead of the guns. I was taken forward and the guy escorting me whacked me real hard on the back of the head and I just did what everybody else was doing and squatted with my head down. There was a cameraman taking movies of the whole thing. The sub got underway and was doing six or seven knots and away we went, leaving the wreckage and our boats behind and then they started having their fun.

We had a lot of Hindus among the passengers and our crew was Indonesian with Dutch officers plus three British officers and 10 British gunners. All I could see at the time was a big mass of squatting men around me. I was mentally numb and didn't know what to do, but I was looking at the water and started trying to get myself to think. Then they grabbed one of the Indonesian guys and pushed him down all the way and they were laughing and yelling, and two Japanese crewmen held him arm up and a guy with a sword swung it and it went "zhunk!" I was watching and they cut off the top half of this Indonesian's head and it fell down and then they let him fall. He started flopping around and they kicked him overboard.

So I was thinking I had to get off that submarine. By this point we were miles away from the wreckage, but I figured my only hope was to get back there and find an empty lifeboat. But I couldn't work up the nerve to jump overboard because the Japanese with the submachine guns were all around us, keeping us covered. But every minute you'd heard their laughing from up front and then "zhunk!" The individual pistol shots started, "bang, bang": Then came a "rat-a-tat-a-tat" of a machine gun from behind us on the conning tower.

As I was trying to make up my mind what to do, the guy two people in front of me, a Hindu, jumped up, let out a scream and dived overboard. They were on him with the machine guns as soon as he hit the water and I saw him go straight down. That changed my mind about that idea.

Then a Japanese officer hit me on my back with the flat of his sword and said something. I don't know what and I stood up. As I turned, I saw our British gunners all tied together, along with a couple of our Dutch officers, standing over by the conning tower. The Japanese behind me gave another shove and they tied my hands behind my back and then tied me to Peter Bronger, our fifth officer. He was my best friend on board and they'd tied me right to him. The rope was really thick and as they tied me, I tried to keep my wrists as wide as I could. They tied the one wrist in a way I knew I couldn't get out of, but I could also feel that I could get the other free.

Then the guy started shoving all of us with his sword, wanting us to move around the conning tower. On the other side of the tower there were two more Japanese officers, one holding a sword, the other a sledgehammer. I was in the lead, and I knew the way those guys were looking at us this was it. So when they started coming at us, I. kicked with my foot and pulled my loosely tied hand out of the rope and dived, dragging Peter with me. I didn't know it at the time, but a lot more people then I'd been about to see, had already been killed and I turned out to be the fourth of only five who got away.

I hit the water and swam to get as deep as possible. The sub kept going by and I could even see her twin screws passing in the clear water. I stayed under as long as I could and then came up with my head just breaking the surface and right away, I could hear bullets splashing all around. I went back under and noticed that bullets don't keep going straight once they hit the water, they go off in all directions.

When I came up for another breath, the sub was quite a ways off and all I could see was her stern. Here were two officers sitting there in old fashioned deck chairs and they were firing rifles at whatever they spotted. So I kept diving under until I saw and heard no more firing.

Peter was kind of half under water, floating with his head down. They'd either hit him with a sword or machine gunned him as we were going over, because his back was split wide open right down to his spine and he was all covered with blood. I was in some kind of shock myself and I stayed with him for a while, but he looked dead so I finally untied my other hand, and that took another five or ten minutes and I said, "Peter, if I can find anything to come for you I will." But as far as I know he was already dead.

I guess I was aboard the sub for about 45 minutes to an hour. I didn't know how far away from our wreckage I was. If I'd known how far it was I probably would've given up, but I knew getting back there was my only shot. It turned out to be about four or five miles. There were big swells, and the water was warm, so I just started swimming in the direction opposite to where I thought the sub had been going. I swam all day. From about 8:30 AM, I swam until the sun was going down. I was in great shape, so I just kept going, figuring I wouldn't give up, but when it started to get dark, and I still hadn't found anything, I got scared that I was going to die.

Then I let the big swells lift me up and I started looking around and the second time I did that I happened to look behind me and I saw little black dots floating far off and I knew I'd found something. I'd gone past the wreckage, just missing it. I swam towards the dots and the first thing I found was a big heavy, round table that we used to play cards on when we were off duty. I grabbed that, it was the first solid thing I'd touched in six or seven hours. I hung on and then I felt strength coming back into me as my hope returned. Then I saw garbage floating and sharks thrashing away at the ship's food. The stuff that we ate had all blown out and there were things all over the place.

Then I saw a life raft, we had four on the ship. They were actually made of two big oil drums surrounded with wood and shaped into a big square. There was a hole in the center and Red Cross emergency stuff was stowed in there. Then from the raft I saw an arm waving and heard a voice calling and I let go of my table and swam over there. I'm sure I broke a world record doing that. I didn't even think to worry about the sharks. I got over to the raft and it turned out to be Chief Officer Fritz de Jong.

He was 6'6" and about 300 lbs. What had saved him was the Japanese who'd tried to kill him was so short that when he put the gun up to blow de Jongs brains out, the angle had been so steep the bullet only whacked the back of his head. He'd rolled into the water and that brought him to consciousness. They'd started with the biggest guys first, so they'd shot him early on and he'd only had to swim maybe a mile. He had a hole in the back of his head, so I opened the first aid kit and got the sulfa powder and put it on and around the wound and bandaged it and wrapped his head all around.

There was a canvas cover, so we lay down on it in the center of the raft. I was scared to death over the idea the Japanese might be circling back to get us, so I kept looking for periscopes. Then I heard another voice, and it was

Third Engineer Spuybroek. We traded stories and it turned out he'd escaped similar to me, and he was fine so that made three of us. Then I said to Spuybroek, "Let's get to the boats." Everything was still drifting and it was getting dark, but there were little lights all around because all the lifesaving equipment on the ship. Lifeboats and lifejackets that had been ripped off us and thrown overboard. They had chemical lights and they were all around. We didn't have any oars, so it took the two of us maybe half an hour to finally get to my boat. I looked inside and saw the transmitter was still there. My little waterproof bag was my ID book that showed the ships I'd served on, and I still have that.

We got de Jong moved into the boat, which by then was nearly full of water, but didn't sink because it had air tanks under the seats. One of us bailed while the other got the oars out. Once we got her bailed, we each took an oar. By this point we'd been going steadily since about six o'clock that morning. We rowed over to another boat and got all the food and water from it. Even though everything was floating around inside, it was all in watertight containers. We figured we had enough for about 40 days.

It was completely dark when we heard another voice. We rowed toward it, and it turned out to be Second Officer Jan Kekker and the same thing had happened to him as to me and Spuybroek. There was another guy with him, a Hindu name Dhange and they were floating on a hatch cover. Dhange was able-bodied. He had swum farther then I and he was the last survivor.

Dhange and the rest of us eventually gave evidence about this atrocity personally to Lord Louis Mountbatten and his staff after we made it back to Colombo. Dhange was from Bombay and had survived the sinking of his own ship earlier and was going home on a free ride when we were sunk. He testified that after the Japanese had gotten rid of the officers, they took the last 20 or 25 guys and tied them all together using one long rope, tied that rope fast to the deck of the submarine and dived. Dhange was the last guy on the rope at the tail end and as they were being towed down under the water, he managed to get loose, and he swam for it.

Anyway, after we'd gotten the mast up and started sailing, Dekker got out a little compass and figured the prevailing winds were taking us toward Java (Japanese held). We didn't want to go there so were started trying to tack, but it was difficult in that boat. We had to bail all night, so we took turns. Finally, as it started to come light. I just collapsed. I was out of it and just lay there for five or six hours. Then I came to, and we opened up some pemmican and at that, along with a dipper of water, and boy that revived me fine.

We kept trying to tack north, away from Java, but by the third day the Chief Officer started getting delirious. Dekker said to me, "Sparks, I think we have to risk transmitting a message tonight." So I got out the radio and climbed the mast and put the antenna up. I hooked up and keyed it once and everything worked OK.

It was around 4 PM and we were waiting until dark to send and we decided to have a can of peaches. Every March 29th since then I've always eaten a can of peaches. Anyway, we opened a can, and each had a big peach and drank the juice and it tasted so good. I'd memorized the coded message I'd sent, "SSS" for "attacked my submarine". When suddenly, BOOM! There was a big explosion right in front of us. Then Bang! Another shell landed a bit farther away, then one closer and that's when I figured we'd finally had it.

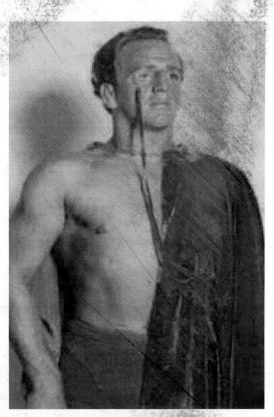

We couldn't spot anything, but I thought it was the submarine and they'd come back to find us and kill us. We tried to decide if we should jump back in the water, when we finally spotted a merchant ship. I said it was probably a Japanese supply ship for replenishing their submarines. They kept firing as they got nearer, but then they turned, and I could see it was a Liberty Ship. You could tell by the silhouette, and they stopped firing and came thundering up right alongside and threw a cargo net over.

I yelled up, "we got a wounded man that weighs 300 pounds." So, they put a crane out and hauled him up. As we were climbing the net, they were already under way again. Turns out they'd spotted us just as it was getting dark and their lookout thought our sails was the coming tower of a submarine, so they'd started firing at us. Luckily, they were bad shots.

Two guys pulled me aboard and gave me a glass of hot water mixed with whiskey. They were all standing around with machine guns and when they heard the Dutchmen talking among themselves, they thought maybe they were Germans and started getting nervous with those guns. I notice this and spoke up, "Wait! I'm English and we are on your side!"

The ship was the SS James A. Wilder, named for a member of the Wilder family in Hawaii, built in 15 days flat and on her maiden voyage to Calcutta. They were taking 14th Army Air Force pilots to fly against the Japanese in Burma. One of those pilots game me a toothbrush and some clothes and three days later we landed in Colombo. After we gave our evidence, they sent a flying boat out and found the wreckage, but no more survivors.

One night, sometime after the war ended, I woke up screaming. Rain was spattering on the skylight above me, and I guess it reminded me somehow. Since then, I've never had any kind of flashbacks or any worries about it.

King Curtis Iaukea

Real Name: Curtis Piehau Iaukea III
Born: 1937 Died: 2010

King Curtis Iaukea is pro wrestling's most prominent name to come out of Hawaii.

In the late 50s, he played in the Canadian Football League.

His father was Chief of Police in Honolulu, and his grandfather was a diplomat.

In Slam Wrestling's obituary, Curtis talks about meeting Lord Blears, saying that it changed his whole life. "He changed my whole life around. I was a football player," Iaukea said of Blears. "The Lord met me when I was surfing, out on the water, when I was a senior in high school. The Lord started me. The ring work, the Lord, he was semi-retired at the time."

He had about seven matches in Hawaii in 1959. Then, he went to the San Francisco area and returned to Hawaii in late 59.

In 1960, he had an interesting tour of Vancouver. He managed a win over former NWA champ Dick Hutton. He also teamed with future adversary Sam Steamboat.

Curtis would start traveling, but he would always return to Hawaii.

In 1961, Curtis would come to the Portland territory and work as Prince Kuhio.

Curtis would hold many titles. He would hold the Hawaiian title at least five times, the Hawaiian tag titles at least seven times, the Hawaiian version of the US title six times, and the Hawaiian version of the North American title twice.

His highest profile title may have been the WWWF tag titles with Baron Scicluna.

For years I had heard stories about King Curtis and "The Cookie". He again talked about it in the Slam Obituary.

"Did that help me in my interviews, you want to know?"

"You can't take any kind of drugs before a match, your timing is off. You're going to hurt the person you're with and yourself. You really can't take it because of the paranoia, you can't take it before you go to work either, I mean, before you're cutting interviews — that's erroneous. A good drop of acid, say a guy took it on a Sunday on his day off, it would go and keep him loaded for 10 days; any more acid that he's going to take ain't going to get him no higher, and his mind is going to really wander. But yeah, that's how he's going to come up with some far-out interviews."

Lord Blears & Curtis Iaukea

"It's been seven long years ..." and "Meeesssterrrr Francissss" were frequent lines, as he would launch into another rambling, intense interview, his back to the camera, belt over the shoulder, his words rising like lava from a volcano. His schtick wasn't that different in Hawaii in the 1970s as it was as a manager in the WWF in the late-'80s.

He credits Blears again. "The ring psychology comes from the Lord. The Lord Blears knew everything about interviews. Here in Honolulu, he's the one that told me, 'Everyone's going to be tired of pictures. You turn and put your back.'... That was my style, just the back, you go up and down. Everything from the Lord."

Despite his wild character in the ring, he was very popular with other wrestlers. No one had a bad thing to say about him.

"Gentleman" Ed Francis, ex-wrestler and promoter in Hawaii: "Curtis was the greatest, the greatest as a human being also. He was always my great friend. ... I know all the people in Hawaii really loved him. I know he did really well in New York and other places, but in Hawaii, the people really loved him. The locals called him 'Da Bull.'"

"Handsome" Johnny Barend: "He did his own thing ... He was an independent guy, he just did his own thing, nobody told him what to do. ... I knew him in Hawaii. Gosh, I spend an awful lot of time with him. I got to know him a little better. ... He liked to go to the beach, he was a beach guy. He liked surfing. ... He had a big name in Hawaii. He's pure Hawaiian, which means a lot over there, because there's not that many left."

Annie Barend, Johnny's wife and a Hawaiian: "He's like the Godfather of Hawaii."

Curtis adhered to the adage that red means green. His bloodbaths with the likes of Mark Lewin and Abdullah The Butcher both drew money and repelled fans because they often took the violence too far. He and Lewin started to get a reputation for too much blood and violence.

Again, Iaukea agreed there was a time limit to his act. "Of course, of course. Yeah, could put it right onto that. I know about the scorched earth and all that stuff. I know my reputation and Mark Lewin's, because I read the jabroni sheets, right, every week. I'll tell you, they'd only use Lewin and I when they really needed to."

One's opinion on the dual entity of Mark Lewin and King Curtis depends entirely on one's ability to cope with chaos. Lewin was often the booker of a territory, and he knew he could trust Iaukea. Their reputation was that Mark Lewin was nasty, and Curtis was an easy-going Hawaiian. "He and Lewin were joined at the hip, so wherever Lewin went, he was going to go too," said Bob Roop.

He and his wife operated a concession stand on Waikiki Beach, a catamaran business, and a carpet cleaning business in Hawaii. "If you live in Hawaii, you need more than one job," joked Jeannette. More recently, as a hobby, the primarily-house bound Iaukea raced pigeons.

King Curtis's son got into wrestling Rocky Iaukea. He wrestled often as Abbuda Dein, especially in the NW. He would also give the rambling mystical interviews with his eyes rolling up in the back of his head. Rocky Iaukea would appear in the Hawaii version of Tales of the Territories.

Curtis's carved forehead and violent ways caught up with him. In the late 70s, he caught a virus in Singapore from mats that went into his cuts. It was very debilitating and really forced him into managing rather than wrestling.

Curtis passed away in 2010 at the age of 73.

young Curtis Iaukea

KING CURTIS IAUKEA

King Curtis & Bull Ramos in Japan 1978

Curtis' great-grandfather was a diplomat

Rikidozan

Real Name: Kim Sin-rak
Born: 1924   Died: 1963

Rikidozan had an exceptional career in wrestling in Japan and was named "The Father of Puroresu" - Japanese Pro Wrestling.

He had a little trouble getting started as he was born in North Korea. In his early days of sumo, he received harassment and racial discrimination.

He was adopted by a man named Minosuke Momota, and he took the name Mitsuhiro Momota with the fictional story that he was born in Omura Nagasaki. He had a successful career in sumo wrestling. He retired from sumo amid several explanations. He suffered from a disease, and there was a heated financial disagreement, which also resulted in some discrimination.

In 1951, a business arrangement between Honolulu promotion Al Karasick, San Francisco promoter Joe Malcewicz, and Moe Lipton, a Honolulu businessman, would work with a Tokyo-based Shriners Club to arrange a Pro Wrestling Tour. Right then, Rikidozan expressed an interest in becoming a pro wrestler.

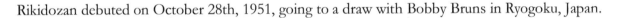

Rikidozan debuted on October 28th, 1951, going to a draw with Bobby Bruns in Ryogoku, Japan.

Rikidozan went on tour to Hawaii, where he received additional training from Oki Shikina. He debuted in Honolulu with a win over Chief Little Wolf on February 17th, 1952. He went on to rack up wins over Pete Peterson, Dick Raines, Bud Curtis, Karl Davis, Ivan Kameroff, and Lucky Simonovich.

He would split his time between San Francisco, Hawaii, Japan, and Los Angeles as his reputation and experience grew.

I find it very interesting that he spent one month in Idaho in 1957, working with Haru Sasaki, Mike Mazurki, Tosh Togo, Hardy Kruskamp, and Henry Lenz.

He would win the Hawaiian tag titles in 1953 with Bobby Bruns, in 1955 with Azumafuji, and in 1959 with Kokichi Endo.

He wrestled in Hawaii every year from 1952 to 1959.

One of the most interesting results from Hawaii was Rikidozan and Kokichi Endo beating Lord Blears and Gene Kiniski in April of 1956.

Rikidozan beat Lou Thesz for the NWA International Championship on August 27th, 1958.

He had memorable feuds with Dick Beyer, Lou Thesz, and Fred Blassie.

Rikidozan death was cloaked in controversy and mystery. He was stabbed on December 8th, 1963, by Katsushi Murata. They had begun fighting in an alley. Rikidozan had successful surgery, and he returned home.

He began eating and drinking upon returning home. He reportedly drank too much to the extent that he needed a 2nd surgery the following week. He developed peritonitis and passed away on December 15th, 1963. He was 39 years old.

He helped train Giant Baba and Antonio Inoki and also had two sons, Mitsu and Yoshi Momota, who were wrestlers.

Wrestler Rikidozan's Killer Gets 7 Years

TOKYO — UPI — The Tokyo higher court commuted to seven years the eight year prison term imposed by a lower court on a man for the slaying of professional wrestler Rikidozan, who was well known in Hawaii and California.

Katsushi Murata, 26, was convicted on manslaughter charges in the fatal stabbing of Rikidozan at a Tokyo Cabaret, December 8, 1963. He died a week later.

Murata claimed he had acted in self defense and had appealed to the higher court.

Rikidozan was a popular "villain" on the California wrestling circuit and performed numerous times in the Fresno Memorial Auditorium.

Over half a million Bee Want Ads are published every year.

Eric Pedersen

Real Name: Charles Roland Putnam
Born: 1928 Died: 1990

Eric Pedersen did not have a lot of success in Hawaiian wrestling, but he is a fascinating individual. He had a lot of success in bodybuilding. He won Mr. California in 1947 and placed in Mr. USA and Mr. Universe.

There are stories of him becoming unruly in the bodybuilding world and somewhat unconventional in the pro wrestling world.

One of the most colorful stories has Charles Putnam (Eric Pedersen) winning the Mr. California title at age 19. He wanted to enter the AAU Mr. America contest. This contest was in Chicago, and he was in LA. Pedersen stole a car in an effort to make it to Chicago. However, he was immediately caught. Somehow, Pedersen made it to Chicago and won the Most Muscular award.

Pedersen is showing off for photographers after he had been arrested on suspicion of auto theft in Los Angeles today in 1947. He and a companion named Edward Sell were busted by police inside a car belonging a third party, though both denied they were trying to steal it.

Another instance proving that he was unreliable had him earning an NWA World title shot in Portland, which was bound to be a lucrative payday. The story goes that he blew it off as he was exploring Mt. Hood with a Geiger counter.

A person wonders, with his body and good looks, why Pedersen wasn't a bigger star in wrestling. He was trained by Ed Strangler Lewis, so he knew how to work and probably how to shoot.

Pedersen had a fledgling career in acting and had a speaking part in a movie called Fighting Coast Guard.

By accounts, he was not very social, and he was not quick to make friends. This hurt him in wrestling, bodybuilding, and acting.

Pedersen wrestled in Hawaii in 1951 but surprisingly did not fare well. He had two wins in his first two weeks but then suffered losses to Ben Sherman, Kimura, and Andre Asselin. He returned in 54 and again had little success compared to how well he did in other parts of the country. He won tag titles with Fred Blassie, Bob Geigel, and Henry Lenz around the country. He won the NW and Gulf Coast singles titles. Pedersen (as Superman Apollo) wrestled Buddy Rogers eight times in 1950 while both were touring with Pfefer's group.

After wrestling, he reportedly had a career in collecting debts for the mob in Las Vegas. He passed away in 1990 from throat cancer.

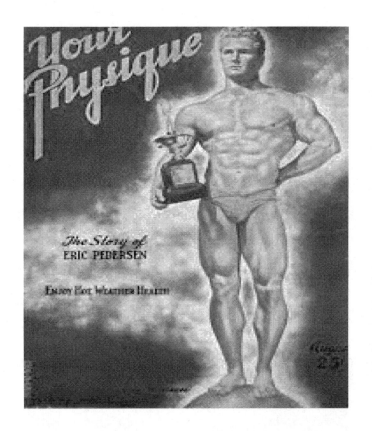

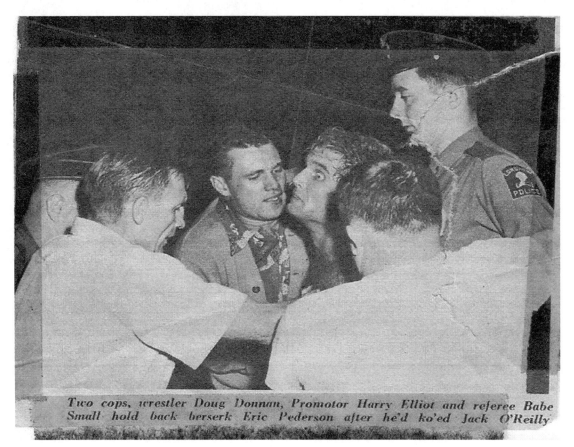

Two cops, wrestler Doug Donnan, Promotor Harry Elliot and referee Babe Small hold back berserk Eric Pederson after he'd ko'ed Jack O'Reilly

Jim Hady

Real Name: James A. Hady
Born: 1931 Died: 1969

Jim Hady became one of the most popular wrestlers in Hawaii during the boom period in the late 60's.

He was born in Pittsburgh, Pennsylvania in 1931 and grew up wrestling in the amateur ranks in school. At 20 years old, Hady decided to go pro. Hady had been wrestling since 1952. He was primarily used as a "jobber" in the Midwest territories like Detroit and Ohio. Eventually, 'Gentleman' Jim rose up the ranks and became a three time Junior Heavyweight champion in the Ohio territory.

Wrestledata credits Dutch Savage for training him, but Hady was in the business a full decade before Savage. There may have been another Dutch Savage that helped train him.

Another interesting tie is that CageMatch says that Hady used the alias Dutch Schultz, also an alias of Dutch Savage. I did not find anywhere that Hady wrestled as Dutch Schultz.

I once asked Dutch Savage who he would have liked to bring to Oregon that didn't work out, and he mentioned Jim Hady. However, I am not clear about that timing since Hady passed away in 1969, and I don't think Savage gained any say in the Portland promotion until later.

Hady had been wrestling for almost fifteen years before he came to Hawaii. In 1963, he won the International tag titles with Johnny Valentine.

In 1965, he came to Vancouver and won the tag titles twice, with Red Bastien and Don Leo Jonathan as his tag partners.

However, when he made it to Hawaii, everything just clicked. He held the Hawaiian title twice, the US title in Hawaii twice, and the tag title four times with partners Johnny Barend, Missing Link, Peter Maivia, and Billy Whitewolf.

His favorite move was the abdominal stretch.

Once, Gene Kiniski was coming to Hawaii to defend the NWA World title, and the promotion let the fans choose who his opponent would be. The bookers thought High Chief Peter Maivia was a certainty, but Jim Hady overwhelmingly won the fan's vote.

Hady's last match was in January of 1969. He was in a 6-person tag match teaming with Tex McKenzie and Lord Blears against Ripper Collins, Luke Graham, and Friday. Hady collapsed during the match and was rendered unconscious. Medical staff at the building attempted to revive Hady, but were unsuccessful. He suffered a heart attack and passed away at the height of his career and popularity.

Hady with Ed Francis

In his book, Ed Francis talked about what a great friend Jim Hady was. "Hady and I had been close friends. He was a good, solid shooter, very well-schooled in the ring, and I booked him often. Beyond that, I did more things socially with Hady than with any other wrestler. For much of the time I was in Hawaii, I owned a boat, and Hady and I would go out fishing and diving. He was a great friend to spend time with, a really nice guy, and a true gentleman."

Francis also commented that the fans stayed away from the matches after Hady's death. Francis speculated that perhaps reality infringed on the escapism of the wrestling they enjoyed.

Sam Steamboat

Real Name: Samuel K. Mokuahi
Born 1934 Died: 2006

Sam Steamboat was born in 1934. He was the prototype Hawaiian babyface. Mokuahi, translated roughly, means Steamboat.

I have to say Steamboat is such a babyface name for Sam and Ricky. It conjures images of babyface even before we knew these men. I mean, he could have been named Sam Ditchmucher or Sam Dankwhiller, and it just wouldn't have been the same thing.

He was trained by Lou Thesz and Lord Blears. He debuted in 1956, and within a month and a half, he was Hawaiian tag champs with Count Billy Varga.

In a very short time, he made his way to Texas and Montreal. He continued to travel to Los Angeles, San Francisco, Ohio, Toronto, and Buffalo.

In 1964, he would go to Florida and form a team with Eddie Graham. They would win the Florida version of the World tag titles from John and Chris Tolos. They would hold these titles on two more occasions.

Steamboat and Graham moved their team from territory to territory to win the Mid-Atlantic version of the Southern tag titles, the Mid-America World tag titles twice, the Texas World tag titles, and The Georgia World tag titles.

In 1970, Steamboat returned to Hawaii and jumped right into the main events. He would claim victories over Les Roberts (Dingo The Sundowner), Duke Savage (El Gringo), Ripper Collins, Tony Borne, Buddy Wolfe, and Kinji Shibuya. He would win the Hawaiian State title twice in 1970, feuding with Ripper Collins.

In 1971, Steamboat feuded with King Curtis and won the North American title from Curtis, then beat him in the Sicilian Stretcher loser leaves town match mentioned in the book's intro. The North American title was a little more prestigious than the Hawaiian title. Steamboat would lose the North American title to Gene Kiniski.

Steamboat finished 1971, beating Angela Mosca, The Skull, Hahn Lee, and Bob Sweetan. He would regain the North American title from Gene Kiniski on September 29th, 1971. He would also win the Hawaiian tag titles with Bearcat Wright.

Steamboat continued to blaze through 1972 with wins over Mad Dog Vachon, Jack Bence, Mighty Brutus (Bugsy McGraw), Tosh Togo, Kinji Matsuta, and Al Costello.

1973 saw wins over Ed Francis, Hard Boiled Haggerty, and Tony Borne.

By mid-1974, Ed Francis had ceased promoting in Hawaii, and it looked like Steamboat might retire from his 24-year wrestling career.

Francis reopened his Hawaii promotion in 1977. Steamboat had a handful more matches, his last being a win over Rocky Tomayo on January 25th, 1978.

Steamboat retired and then started teaching and coaching outrigger canoe paddling.

From the Slam Wrestling Obituary, wrestlers remembered Steamboat.

In February 2000, King Curtis shared his recollection of Steamboat with a Hawaiian newspaper, "He was the best-looking man I've ever seen walk across the sand of Waikiki. And now he's horrible looking — he got two cauliflower ears that look like two okoles sticking out of each side of his head, and not a hair on top of his head."

"He was a nice person, very quiet and very shy. He really was about meeting people," said Lord James Blears, who was instrumental in getting Steamboat started in wrestling.

Lord Blears stakes the claim of getting Steamboat into the grappling game, just as he would later for King Curtis Iaukea. "I started him wrestling. He was on Waikiki beach, he was a beach boy, but he had a terrific body on him, worked out surfing every day," said Blears from his nursing home bed. "I said, 'I'll teach you to wrestle if you teach me how to surf.' So he said, 'okay.' We went out every day on the board and he taught me how to surf, and we went down to the gym, and I taught him how to wrestle."

Rick Steamboat was given the surname and sometimes billed to be Sam's son or brother.

Sam Steamboat passed away in 2006 from Alzheimer's disease.

Al Karasick

Real Name: Alexander Karasick
Born: 1890 Died: 1965

Karasick was born in Bobruisk, Russia, in 1890 and was rumored to be a dancer for Anna Pavlova's ballet company in Russia before sailing to the US in 1914. He began amateur wrestling at the Olympic Club in San Francisco. He turned pro in 1921, debuting in Hayward in a carnival. Nicknamed the Russian Lion, he was a fierce light heavyweight wrestler.

Karasick wrestled from 1922 until 1936. He wrestled on the West Coast in the NW, Texas, Australia, and Arizona. In 1936, he came to Hawaii and then started promoting there.

J Michael Kenyon had some notes on Karasick. He was convinced that Karasick had wrestled as George Michaeloff in Walla Walla, Washington in 1933. He was also believed to have used the names Alexander Karasick and Jim Prokus.

THE WRESTLER — AL KARASICK
Light Heavy-Weight Champion of Russia. Expert in Headlocks and well-known to Listeners of 3 LO Melbourne.

The one thing I was taken with as I went through the timeline of Hawaiian wrestling was how much of a hustler Karasick was. In the wake of Pearl Harbor, Karasick promised that wrestling would return and kept it in people's minds. He worked with the military to be able to promote precisely one year after Pearl Harbor. Considering the conditions, he couldn't hold cards at night due to curfew and had to be very careful about using Japanese and even Hawaiian wrestlers. The cultures on the Island didn't trust each other as it was a very unstable time.

Paul Boesch had a tidbit about Al Karasick from his autobiography, "Hey, Boy? Where Did You Get Them Ears!"

Boesch explained in the book the Australian term "Fair Dinkum," which means on the level. Boesch tells the story. "One day, Al Karasick was in a taxi in Australia, and the driver asked Karasick, "Do you wrestle fair dinkum?" Karasick replied, "No, but if he'll make my weight I'll be glad to take him on."

Boesch describes Hawaii in 1939, "Hawaii, in September of 1939, was truly a paradise. At Waikiki Beach, there were two hotels. The Moana and the Royal Hawaiian. Down the beach a short distance was the Princess Liliokalani."

"We found a cottage for rent, a half-block behind the Moana Hotel. We had to shell out only 40 dollars a month to get it! When the ships were not in port, it was a delightful community where most people had little to do; some did nothing and had all day in which to do it. I soon learned that the charm of Hawaii was not in Waikiki, which, as a beach, is overrated. But Waikiki, at that time, as a way of life, was incomparable, unforgettable."

"Which leads me to a dilemma in describing wrestling there at that time. I can recall reaching for my bag each Tuesday night and walking to Kalakaua Avenue to catch the bus to the Civic Auditorium. Sometimes it was the only thought I gave to wrestling the entire week, and yet, as I recall it was the time I wrestled with the most enthusiasm. I never entered a gym during my stay in the Islands, yet, I was in better shape, sharper and more eager than at any other time in my career."

"I spent hours of every day with Sam Mokuahi, who was better known as Sam Steamboat because that is how his name was translated from Hawaiian into English."

"I may have been responsible for the fact that his son, Sam Jr, became a wrestler a generation later."

Karasick would eventually hold wrestling and, at times, double book his venue with a 2nd form of entertainment like a dance or "derbies." Derbies were different forms of entertainment, similar to Vaudeville.

Karasick was the pioneer in opening American wrestlers working in Japan. He, along with Bobby Bruns, made that happen.

April 13th, 1948, Karasick suffered a heart attack while visiting Los Angeles.

Danno O'Shocker remembers Karasick: "Al was a tough little guy, big cauliflowers and very friendly. He had a good staff with Bobby Bruns as booker, Betty Diamond on the staff and right hand man who knew everyone and had connections. I did not know Al that well, but he told me to get out on the beach and get in shape. I was indignant as I'm always in shape, but he meant get a tan. I had been working in the Midwest and Canada, so I was real white. You have to go easy on that sun as it can put you into the hospital in one day. Al must have been a good promoter as he kept running for years and always had an angle going and all the top boys wanted to work there. Even flying in from Japan or Hong Kong was a long way on those three ruddered constellations, regular prop drive, not the fast smooth jets of today. He had the guys flying through, stop for two weeks, run a good angle, come back and sell out at the old King Street auditorium. I found it small compared to HIC and whatever it is called now. Have not been back for a couple of years, but still love the Islands."

He sold his promotion in Hawaii in 1961 to Ed Francis. He passed away in 1965.

Colorful Al Karasick dies of heart attack

By PAUL W. LOVINGER

Al Karasick, the Russian ballet dancer who became a champion wrestler and later a successful sports promoter in Hawaii, died of a heart attack yesterday in Queen's Hospital. He was 75.

He was stricken with chest pains at the Civic Auditorium, taken to a doctor at the Straub Clinic, and then immediately hospitalized at 12:15 p.m. He died at 4:30 p.m.

At his bedside were his wife, Wilma, and his son-in-law and daughter, Mr. and Mrs. Randolph Diamond.

His other child, Rabbi Joseph Karasick, of Cincinnati, Ohio, was expected to fly here today.

He is also survived by a brother and three sisters, all on the Mainland, and two grandsons.

Funeral services are tentatively set for tomorrow afternoon at Williams Mortuary. Burial will follow at Nuuanu Cemetery.

The family requests that flowers be omitted. Contributions in his memory may be made to the Temple Emanu-El.

Won world title

Born in Bobruisk, Russia, Karasick danced as a young man with the Pavlova ballet troupe.

He wrestled about 15 years all over the Mainland and promoted wrestling and other sports events in Hawaii for 25 years after that, retiring in May, 1961.

In December, 1925, he won the world's light heavyweight wrestling title from Ted Thye. Two years later he became a heavyweight and won about 90 percent of his bouts. He battled the top wrestlers of his day.

As a wrestler he was known as "The Russian Lion." Later they called him "Gentleman Al."

Before he sold his interest to Ed Francis four years ago this month, he headed Al Karasick Promotions while managing the Civic Auditorium.

Since then, the stocky, balding gentleman took it easy: playing pinochle in the Civic Auditorium office, telling funny stories in his Russian accent and regaling meetings of civic clubs, or attending sports events.

Last Saturday afternoon he attended the Hawaii A.A.U. track meet at Punahou School. He loved baseball and spent the last two evenings of his life watching the Islander games at Honolulu Stadium.

Karasick was also a member of the State Board of Private Detectives. Following the May 10 shotgun death of an unlicensed private investigator, he said, "I think every man who works for a private detective agency should be licensed. I'm going to recommend this at the next meeting."

He maintained a desk at the Civic Auditorium and occasionally assisted Francis in the latter's public relations.

Karasick is said to have danced the lead opposite the great ballerina Pavlova while the top male dancer was laid up.

Half a century ago, he came to the United States on a ballet tour via the Far East quit the troupe and settled on the West Coast.

In Oakland he went to work as a welder for the Southern Pacific Railroad. He first saw Wilma Green playing basketball in San Francisco.

"She couldn't play basketball worth a lick, but she was beautiful," Karasick

Al Karasick

later recalled. So he married her.

He later explained how he got interested in wrestling: He was working out at the Olympic Club in San Francisco when someone asked him if he would be interested in wrestling for the club. He did so for five years as an amateur and then turned pro.

He admitted he had a few pro bouts under the name of Jim Prokus while still an amateur.

His first match for money, by his own account, was in Hayward, California, where some carnival operators were paying $1 a minute to anyone wrestling with their champ.

"I beat the guy in eight minutes and that was . . . my first $8 from wrestling," Karasick said in an interview.

Not long after he got $600 for a bout in Susanville, California.

"When I brought that money home, my wife, Wilma, thought I had robbed a bank. We had never seen that much money."

He drew his top purse, about $5,000, in Sydney, Australia, in 1928.

In 1925 he first came to Hawaii. He was headed for Australia but his ship developed trouble and he was stuck here three weeks,

wrestling during that time. Karasick himself told this story: While in Australia, a newspaper reporter asked him, "Do you wrestle fair dinkum?" (An Australian expression meaning honestly or on the level.)

Karasick replied, in essence: "I don't know that guy, but put him in the ring with me and I'll beat him!"

He said that Feodor Chaliapin, the famed Russian opera singer, was his honorary second in an Australian bout in 1925, and Pavlova was so in 1926.

His last bout was with "Jumping Joe" Savoldi in August, 1936, in Honolulu.

Several wrestling tours here convinced him Hawaii was for him.

In 1936 he leased the Civic Auditorium and began promoting wrestling events.

Over the years he also promoted boxing, basketball, novelty acts, dance bands, and even opera here.

Every year he would put on a charity match for the benefit of Christmas funds (the Star-Bulletin's among them).

He said his most successful venture was a roller derby that ran for 10 weeks and grossed $200,000.

The least successful event was a rickshaw race. As he told it:

"Some fellows from the Orient came into town with this idea. It goes over big in the Orient.

"In it, there are two men to each rickshaw. One pulls for four hours and the other sits in the cart. Then they change places.

"It didn't sound good to me, but I leased the fellows the auditorium. After much ballyhoo that went on for weeks, they finally opened.

"They sold exactly eight tickets the first night—and then closed down.

"As payment for rental, I now own two rickshaws."

Television had cut wrestling crowds in half and Karasick said "TV is killing Honolulu as a sports town."

2 previous attacks

He predicted that the day might soon come when all wrestling and boxing matches would take place in television studios.

Karasick suffered a coronary thrombosis in Los Angeles in 1948 and another heart attack in 1952.

In his hospital room at Cedars of Lebanon Hospital in 1948, he wrote in a letter to this newspaper that six months earlier he would have said Thrombosis was a Greek wrestler.

He didn't think it was right for the doctors to charge for their advice when he gave his away for free.

"I'm going to miss this hospital, particularly that flower each morning from my blonde nurse, Jackie," he wrote.

"I've finally convinced her that it's an old Hawaiian

custom for one to accompany a flower with a kiss."

In 1962 Karasick ran as a Democrat for the State House of Representatives from the 15th District. Receiving 7,223 votes, he placed 10th in a field of 11 candidates from the Manoa-Waikiki areas.

His campaign literature said, "At 72, I'm no spring chicken. But I'll guarantee to throw any other legislator or anyone upstairs in the Palace, for that matter."

His platform included physical fitness, better housing, medicare, and elimination of juvenile delinquency.

Talking of delinquency, he claimed to have known the famous Russian author Maxim Gorky. "When I knew him Gorky was about 18 years old, hanging around the Odessa waterfront with a bunch of no-good bums. Five years later he published his first book, 'The Lower Depths.'"

He explained why he ran for office, "Hawaii has done a lot for me. I came here broke in 1932. I want to do something for the people."

It was said that the first time Karasick rented the auditorium for a basketball game, he had a bright idea. He painted the sidelines three feet inside the regulation ones. He wanted to do the basketball fans a favor by making room for two extra rows of seats.

Later he gained a deeper understanding of the game of basketball.

In 1950, during a controversy over whether there should be a City sports arena, concert hall, or combination, Karasick declared, "I think they need a concert hall." He said that only once, during the war, did he ever have an overflow crowd at the Civic.

The following year Karasick applied for a permit to carry a revolver. He said he had been threatened by a rival promoter.

Karasick said that although he was at one time called "the Russian Lion," at other times he was called "the lyin' Russian."

But if Karasick had any foes, they could be counted on a couple of fingers.

On June 24, 1964, his close friends gave him a surprise 75th birthday party at Ala Moana Banquet Hall. Over 100 attended, including Governor John A. Burns, who presented Karasick with a Hawaii crest medallion.

"He was the kindest, sweetest, most considerate gentleman in the world." E. Walker Chapman, director of Royal Theatres, said last night.

"I don't think he ever had an enemy in the world."

Said Ed Francis, Karasick's successor, "Everybody knew what a great job he did. All the wrestlers loved him.

"Al was a real man's man."

Mr. Fuji

Real Name: Harry Masayoshi Fujiwara
Born: 1934 Died: 2016

Harry Fujiwara was born in Honolulu, Hawaii, and was of Japanese and Native Hawaiian descent.

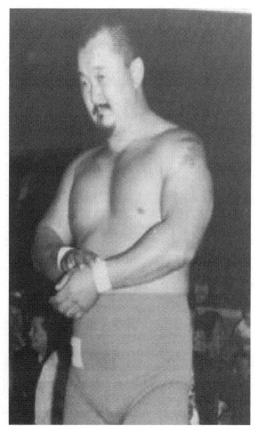

Mr. Fuji debuted in Hawaii in 1962. He started as an undercard wrestler, where victories were very few and far between. That continued into 63 and 64.

In 1964, he started teaming with King Curtis, and they captured the Hawaiian tag titles. Despite holding the tag titles, single wins were still rare.

In 1966, Fuji made his first trip outside of Hawaii and ended up in Portland. He started winning and was quickly in the main events. He had wins over Paul Jones, Pepper Martin, and Rene Goulet. He would capture the NW tag titles twice, once with Haru Sasaki and once with Tony Borne.

He would return to Hawaii for most of 67 thru 69. He did make a month-long tour of Australia in 1967.

In 1969, he teamed up with Toru Tanaka in Hawaii several times. They would have success in the WWWF in a few years, winning the tag titles there.

In 1970, he returned to Portland and took his place as the number one heel of the promotion. He again teamed with Haru Sasaki and won the tag titles and the NW title, beating Lonnie Mayne.

Fuji would claim wins over Mayne, Tony Borne, Stan Stasiak, and Johnny Kostas.

Interestingly, it was the same thing in Hawaii, rarely winning a match whenever he returned.

His career would ramp up upon debuting in the WWF in June 1972. He would win the tag titles with Toru Tanaka, beating Jay Strongbow and Sonny King.

Fuji would hold the Georgia tag titles with Toru Tanaka in 1975.

His biggest singles run would start in the Bay Area in 1976. In February, he beat Pat Patterson and won the US title.

He would defend the title against Peter Maivia, Patterson, Ray Stevens, Rocky Johnson, Tony Garea, Moondog Mayne, and Pepper Gomez. Fuji and Promoter Roy Shire would have a falling out despite getting this mega push.

Fuji was scheduled to meet Pat Patterson in a Roman Gladiator Match. Patterson claimed he would wrestle masked, as he occasionally did to hide a foreign object. It was said that Fuji also claimed that he would masked. However, it wasn't Mr. Fuji that was masked. It was Toru Tanaka.

The Commission was very strict in those days, and giving fans a main event match that essentially tricked the fans was a no-no. Shire claimed no knowledge of the switch, and Tanaka and Fuji were fined. Fuji was suspended in California for several years.

IN 1978, he returned to Hawaii and worked for Ed Francis after he had restarted Hawaiian wrestling. He won the tag titles there with Karl Von Steiger.

Fuji would continue to win tag titles with Toru Tanaka in various territories and again win the WWF Tag titles with Masa Saito in 1981 and 82.

In 1985, Mr. Fuji retired from wrestling full-time and became a manager. He still wrestled at times up until 1992. He managed Demolition, Yokozuna, and Don Muraco, among others.

A story about Mr. Fuji would not be complete without mentioning the ribs. Fuji may be the most notorious ribbers in wrestling history. Fuji's ribs ranged from playful to horribly stiff.

Bobby Jaggers was very bitter at Fuji for the stiff ribs he pulled on him. Once, Fuji painted the windshield of Jaggers's car black. Jaggers mentioned that Fuji was someone who liked to hurt people and didn't give a damn about anyone but himself.

Fuji ribs included laxatives in other wrestlers' drinks, changing their travel reservations, and peeing on them. The stiffest rib might have been against his tag partner, Toru Tanaka. Although they were tag partners, Fuji felt Tanaka was going behind Fuji's back to the office.

Fuji invited Tanaka over for dinner one night. After dinner, Fuji said I have a surprise, and he lifted a platter dome to show Tanaka that he had just eaten his own dog.

Once in a while, people got even with Fuji. In Fuji's Slam Obituary, Jules Strongbow said he found out that Fuji's feet were ticklish. Strongbow said he worked his feet over for ten minutes, and Fuji never bothered him again.

Dutch Savage, in his RATNW interview, told one of the best ribs I had heard. Fuji, Lonnie Mayne, and Savage were driving to Medford (a long drive). Fuji was drinking Southern Comfort, and he was passed out when they got back to Portland. They undressed Fuji, put him and a shotgun in a blowup raft, and pushed him out into a pond next to a retirement center. Police were called about the naked man floating in the raft with a shotgun.

Fuji retired to Knoxville, Tennessee. He worked in a movie theater as a ticket taker.

He passed away in 2016 at the age of 82 of natural causes.

Ripper Collins

Real Name: Roy Lee Albern
Born: 1933 Died: 1991

Ripper Collins may have been the best heel I have ever seen. There are many different styles of heel, the giant killer heel like King Curtis, Bull Ramos, Mongolian Stomper, and Black Angus, where size is the factor as well as attitude.

Then there is the cowardly heel. The one that takes the shortcuts and is afraid when he is about to get his comeuppance. This heel will beg off and run away.

Then there is everything in between. I feel that Collins had so much going for him in so many layers.

1. He was out of shape; to put it bluntly, he was fat and not very athletic. This leads to a person being unpopular in wrestling.

2. He did have size and a brutalness to him. In Oregon, he is remembered for filing his teeth, something he probably borrowed from Fred Blassie. His finishing hold The OPU drop was brutal and cowardly simultaneously. A simple knee drop to the groin.

3. His Southern accent in the Hawaiian Islands did not do him any favors. He would mispronounce Hawaiian towns and Islands, making him very unpopular.

4. He, in real life, was gay and, at times, promoted that image in his interviews. He had a very strange mix of brutality and effeminate demeanor. Remembering the time in society when Collins worked, being gay was generally frowned upon.

He started wrestling in 1959 and worked under the names Don Scarbo, Roy Nelson, Pretty Boy Collins, and Ripper Collins.

He came to the West Coast originally in 1964 in Vancouver. He had some success with wins over Enrique Torres, Dory Funk Jr, and Mike Sharpe.

Collins originally came to Hawaii in 1965 and, at first, was not very successful. Finally, in 1966, he was able to capture the Hawaiian title eight times. He would hold the Hawaiian tag titles thirteen times with various partners like King Curtis, Moondog Mayne, Johnny Barend, and Johnny Valentine.

Different wrestlers remember Collins:

Bull Ramos, "Ripper Collins and I never had much to do with each other. Ripper Collins was always a gentleman to me. I used to respect him because he had adopted two baby girls. He was a real family man, and that is why I respected him. He was a nice, nice guy."

Mickey Doyle, "I made a lot of trips with Ripper and I never had a problem. He was a funny man and at the time I was married so he never put me in a awkward position. I liked the old Ripper."

HE CALLS HIMSELF KING

RIPPER COLLINS

Beauregard, "Oh Ripper Roy Collins, The Southern Gentleman. He is the one that gave me the name Beauregard. When I first started wrestling in the Philippines, I was using the name Eric The Golden Boy. When I got back to Honolulu, they wanted someone to be a manager or valet for Ripper. I was still green, I had only been wrestling for 4 or 5 months. So they asked if I wanted to be Ripper's valet. We were trying to think of a name. He had this money that he used to pass out. This confederate money. It was signed by General Beauregard. He looked at me and said, Beauregard. I said, Oh ******, that is a ******* name. He said no, listen to me. He said, Fabian, Liberace alot of great people only have 1 name and you will remember better then 2 names. Beauregard is a Southern Gentleman's name, and I like it. I said OK. That's how the name I got Beauregard."

Ed Francis: "Ripper was great, people hated him, but they enjoyed him. He liked to get on the interviews and pronounce all the Islands wrong. "

Collins was married to lady wrestler Barbara Baker. They met in a diner in West Virginia and would occasionally team up in Hawaii.

As Collin's wrestling career slowed, he often served as a wrestling commentator for the different promotions.

Collins also indirectly provided a NW legacy. Dean Silverstone and his wife Ruth were visiting Hawaii, and Dean got in contact with his old friend, Ripper Collins. Collins had always been very charismatic, and Ruth was quite taken with him. Later, she asked Dean if there were other people from wrestling that she would enjoy meeting. That provided the inspiration for Deans reunions. Over the years, Dean hosted wrestlers as Lou Thesz, Johnny Valentine, Ray Stevens, Ivan Koloff, Kinji Shibuya, Neff Maiava, Shoulders Newman, Dean Higuchi, and many others.Collins passed away in 1991 at the age of 58. He passed away from melanoma skin cancer.

LORD BLEARS AND
RIPPER COLLINS

Lucky Simunovich

Real Name: Zivko Sreco Milos Simunovich
Born: 1919 Died: 1995

Lucky Simunovich was born in Yugoslavia and moved to Hawaii in the 1930's. He was trained for wrestling by Al Karasick and debuted in the mid-40s. The first that Wrestledata had a record was in 1946.

Lucky became a Honolulu Police Department motorcycle officer, assigned to the Hotel Street red light district because of his size and strength, said his son Dorian. One day he stopped Al Karasick, the wrestling promoter for a traffic violation. Karasick, impressed with Lucky's six foot 2, 225 pound frame, invited him to the Civic Auditorium for a tryout.

I had gotten Lucky Simunovich and Great Malenko mixed up at times. Someone had told me that they were one and the same. They look similar; both are billed or come from the Eastern block, and their last names are similar. Larry Simon and Lucky Simunovich. However, the rest of their bios look different, such as date of birth, date of death, and the places they wrestled.

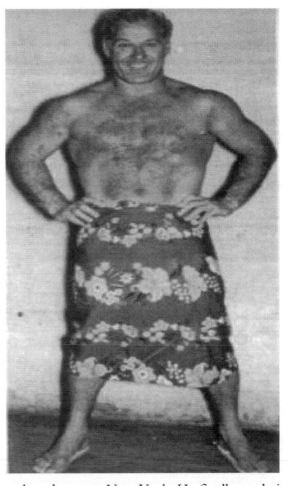

Lucky debuted in Hawaii in 1946 with a long succession of victories. In 1947, he started hitting the territories, including San Francisco, Los Angeles, Phoenix, Texas, Ohio, Kansas City, Montreal, and upstate New York. He finally made it back to Hawaii at the end of 1951.

The competition had improved in Hawaii by 1951, and Simunovich was still winning. He claimed wins over Earl McCready, Pete Peterson, Dick Raines, Chief Little Wolf, Harold Sakata, Abe Kashey, and Red Scorpion. He won the Hawaiian title for the first time in 1952. He would also win the Hawaiian tag titles with Bobby Bruns in '52.

Simunovich would win the Hawaiian title twice in his career and the tag titles four times, three with Bruns and once with Gino Garibaldi.

He was spending more and more time in Hawaii, all of 59 and 60, as well as significant portions of most years.

He was still claiming wins over some of the top wrestlers in the area, including Don Manoukian, Luigi Macera, Stan Kowalski, Michiaki Yoshimura, King Curtis, Shoulder Newman, and Mr. Fuji.

In 1965, he finished in Hawaii and took a tour of Great Britain. In 1966, he took a tour of Japan for Tokyo Pro Wrestling.

Simunovich's wife, June, was a cosmetologist and into hair design. She owned salons in Hawaii and was Don Ho's personal hair stylist. June was born in Portland, Oregon before moving to Hawaii to marry Simunovich.

He passed away in 1995 in Honolulu.

Al Lolotai

Real Name: Alo Leilani

Born 1920 Died 1990

Al was born in 1920. After being trained by Hawaii promoter Al Karasick, he started wrestling in 1945 in Hawaii. He wrestled there for five years straight before he would head off to any other territories.

During these years, he would wrestle only part-time as he played for the Washington Redskins in the NFL and the LA Rams in the AFL. He was the first Samoan and non-white player to play in the NFL.

In 1950, he wrestled in the Kansas City area and changed his name to Alo Leilani. He would win the Central States title in 1951, beating Jim Coffield. He would hold that title for a month before losing it to Bob Orton Sr.

For the next few years, he would hit many different territories, centering around the Midwest. In 1954, he reached West Texas and the Los Angeles area.

In 1955, he returned to Hawaii, where he won the Hawaiian State title three times. He would become very popular since he was from the Islands. He would feud with Gene Kiniski, Billy Varga, Tom Rice, King Curtis, Don Manoukian, Shoulders Newman, and Ed Francis.

One thing I found very interesting is that Al Lolotai never won the Hawaiian tag titles. He teamed at times with Neff Maivia, and that team was a natural. He also teamed a few times with Sam Steamboat, which would have been a natural team. Records show that in March and April of 1961, Steamboat and Lolotai met in several matches, one in which Lolotai was disqualified.

There is no record of him wrestling in 1962, but he does come back in '63 and 64 for a handful of matches.

Here comes some confusion about aliases and name borrowing. In 1978, a wrestler by the name of Alo Leilani wrestled in Calgary. This was not the same wrestler that we have highlighted in this biography. This wrestler also worked by the name Ati Tago and possibly Tama Samoa. However, later in his career in Hawaii, Ati Tago teamed with a Tama Samoa.

There is one YouTube video of Alo Leilani from a match in Chicago against Carl Meyer dated 11/19/51.

The original Alo Lolotai. He passed away in 1990.

Bobby Bruns

Robert H. Bruns
Born: 1914 Died: 1983

Bobby Bruns is genuinely one of the pioneers of wrestling that significantly impacted the business for years to come. Hawaii becomes a very big part of that story as well.

Bruns was born in 1914 in Chicago and began wrestling in 1931. Bruns would be the first Mid-West World Champion (MWA) based out of Kansas City. He would hold the title on at least two occasions.

Bruns and Orville Brown were involved in a horrible car accident on November 1st, 1949. Bruns was able to return after a couple of months. Brown had a handful of matches after about a year of recovery.

Bruns originally came to Hawaii in 1951. He worked behind the scenes to book for Al Karasick, the Hawaiian promoter. In 1951, Karasick would send Bruns and five other American-based wrestlers to Japan. On September 30th, 1951, this debut card changed Japanese wrestling forever. Bruns was Karasick's point person in Japan. Interestingly, there were no Japanese wrestlers on these initial cards. Rikidozan and Koichi Endo would start to appear a month or so after the debut.

9/30/51 Tokyo: Bobby Bruns drew Ovila Asselin, Harold Sakata beat Casey Berger, and Dr. Len Hall beat Andre Adoree.

Three years later, the JWA would debut, and Bruns, the Sharpe Brothers, and Bob Mumphrey would be the Americans in that debut. Karasick would be the booking agent for US wrestlers heading to Japan.

Bruns would appear in Hawaii from 1951 to 1955. He would hold the Hawaii title once and the tag titles seven times, three times with Lucky Simonovich, and once each with Rikidozan, Luther Lindsay, Bobby Managoff, and John Paul Henning. Bruns would move back to the Midwest in 1956 and wrestle until 1962. He would be one of the primary bookers in St. Joseph, Kansas City, and St. Louis.

In an interview, Rocky Montero talks about Bobby Bruns, who took him under his wing in St. Louis. Montero relates, "Bobby Bruns in the St. Louis area kind of took me under his wing. I thought I was in good shape, and I went out for my first St. Louis match and went to a 15-minute draw. I was tired, but it was a decent match. When I got back to the dressing room, there was Bobby Bruns, "I want you in the gym tomorrow morning." We went through 10 hours of drilling and I tell you he beat the living crap out of me. I came back for my next match at the Keil and let me tell you I was lean, mean and hungry. I went from 242 to 217. I went out for my match with some big fat guy. I don't remember his name, and I blew him up in two minutes. When he got back to the dressing room, they chewed him out and said there is no place for you in this area; pack your bags, and we are not paying you. Get your territory to pay you. Lou Thesz was in the dressing room and he said, "Hey kid, I don't think I could do to you what I did before.""

Bruns passed away in 1983.

Peter Maivia

Real Name: Fanene Leifi Pita Maivia
Born: 1937 Died: 1982

Peter Maivia started wrestling in England as early as 1960. He was born Fanene Pita Anderson, and he spent his first twenty years in Samoa and then moved to New Zealand. He received early training from Steve Rickard.

In 1964, he won his first title, the New Zealand title. He also won the Australasian title in 1964.

Maivia came to Hawaii for the first time in 1968 and immediately made a name for himself. Aligning himself with Hawaiian legend Neff Maiavi. They billed themselves as cousins due to the similar spellings of their last names. He would win the Hawaiian title, The Hawaiian tag titles three times with Jim Hady, Billy Whitewolf, and Sam Steamboat.

Maivia would have an outstanding career in other territories as well. He won the US title (San Francisco version) two times, The World tag titles (San Francisco version) two times with Pepper Gomez and Ray Stevens, The Americas title, and The Texas title, as well as other belts.

Maivia has been associated with an urban legend in a fight with Billy Robinson in Japan in 1968. The myth is that during a fight, Maivia threw Robinson through a window and pulled out his eye.

When different historians examined the story, and Robinson chimed in as well, the story seemed debunked, at least as the eye part. Robinson had suffered an eye injury when he was 11. Maivia and Robinson did get into a fight where Maivia threw Robinson through a window. Robinson was then able to hold Maivia at bay with some holds when Maivia bit through Robinson's cheek. Robinson reportedly did not miss any Japan dates from his injury.

Robinson and Maivia had met as early as 1963 and even teamed as late as 1978. Despite their times overlapping in Hawaii at times, they never wrestled or teamed together there.

Maivia was in the James Bond movie You Only Live Twice in 1967.

In 1979, Ed Francis sold the Hawaiian promotion to Steve Rickard. Rick Martel indicates that Peter Maivia was a partner from the onset. He indicated while he (Martel) was booking, he could not get on the same page as Maivia and Martel left.

Later, Rickard seemed to leave Hawaii. Mixed reports have Maivia buying him out or Maivia encouraging him to leave. Interesting because they did have a prior relationship dating back to Maivia's initial training.

Maivia is credited with promoting in Hawaii starting in 1980. The promotion appears a little erratic. Maivia's appearances were rare. He was diagnosed with an inoperable cancer, and he refused doctoring. It was rumored that his tattoos may have been a contributing cause of the cancer. He passed away in 1982 at the age of 45.

Peter's wife Lia Maivia continued to promote wrestling in Hawaii and has been remembered in Dwayne Johnson's show, Young Rock.

Maivia's son-in-law was Rocky Johnson, which makes Maivia Dwayne "The Rock" Johnson's grandfather.

The main character in the animated movie Moana was created to resemble The High Chief Peter Maivia.

Peter Maivia had two sons who wrestled, Peter Maivia Jr and Toa Maivia (1 recorded match).

Mr. Moto/Young Shiranuhi

Real Name: Masaru "Charlie" Iwamoto
Born: 1915 Died: 1991

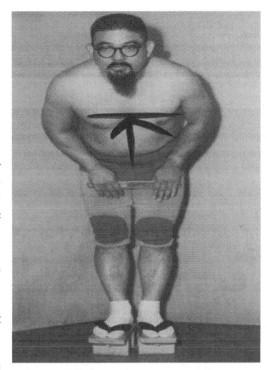

Young Shiranuhi started in 1939 in Hawaii. He had somewhat of a slow start, definitely paying some dues. Then Pearl Harbor derailed his career for three years; he was a victim of his surroundings and his heritage. When wrestling started back up, Shiranuhi had a subtle name change. Young was replaced by Charley.

Shiranuhi was a part-time wrestler in Hawaii for the next five years. He was gaining experience, but he was not featured at all.

In 1948, Charley went to the Los Angeles territory. In 1949, he went to Detroit and Chicago.

In 1950, he went to the Central States, Omaha, and Chicago and picked up a new name, The Great Moto.

From 1951 to 1964, he traveled the country to many different territories.

In 1964, he returned to wrestle in Hawaii for a week. It was the first time wrestling in Hawaii since 1950.

He again took a subtle name change in 1955, calling himself Mr. Moto instead of Great Moto.

He started appearing in the Los Angeles territory more and more, starting in 1956. He would venture off to another territory briefly but always return to LA.

Starting in 1963, besides Japan, Los Angeles had definitely become home base. He started working in the office.

Jeff Walton started working in LA at the Olympic in 1967. He remembers Moto, "I attended the weekly meetings there. He never spoke to me at all. After about two months, we were alone, and I said, "Charlie, I'm getting married in a few weeks." He looked at me through his glasses and said, "Are you crazy?" I started to laugh, and he did too. That broke the ice. As I got up to leave, he got up too. Reaching in his pocket he gave me a $20 bill. "Buy something for your future wife." From then on, we were friends. It didn't hurt that Blassie, who was very close friends with Moto, also told him I was a good guy."

Wikipedia also has a story that when Moto was wrestling The Destroyer, Kurt Beyer ran up to the ring and hit Moto in the foot with the timekeeper's hammer. Kurt insists that the story is true.

Moto worked as an agent for Giant Baba and All Japan Wrestling. He married his wife, Violet, in 1943. Walton mentions he liked to gamble with cards and often went to card clubs. He wasn't fond of bodybuilders or ex-football players. He did not like outsiders, as he was very protective of the business.

Moto was in a couple movies, Mask of Dragon in 1951 and Wagon Train in 1957.

Tom Rice/Red Scorpion

Real Name: Thomas C. Rice
Born: 1914 Died: 1996

Tom Rice was born in Bozeman, Mont., and attended high school in Visalia, in the San Joaquin Valley. He graduated from USF in 1939.

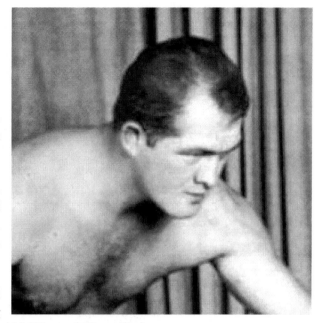

Tom Rice started wrestling in 1940. During his career, he often appeared as a masked wrestler. He wrestled as The Red Phantom, The Red Mask, The Red Hangman, and, in Hawaii, The Red Scorpion. Bonus Trivia question...What was Tom Rice's favorite color?

The Red Scorpion first came to Hawaii in 1952. The masked wrestler got over immediately with several big wins, including Bobby Bruns, Earl McCready, Rikidozan, Lucky Simonovich, Al Mills, and Gene Dubuque.

He won the Hawaiian title, beating Lucky Simonovich in May 1952. He met his match on August 31st when Lou Thesz unmasked the Red Scorpion, and it proved to be Tom Rice. Three weeks later, he lost the Hawaiian title to Bobby Bruns.

Rice was still around in '53 but did not win as often. However, he did win the Hawaiian tag titles with Abe Kashey beating Bobby Bruns and Rikidozan.

Rice left Hawaii in May of 53 and returned in September of 56. He very quickly won the Hawaiian title, beating Tosh Togo. Rice would get wins over Jack Claybourne, Don Beitelman, Al Costello, and Lucky Simonovich. As the results go and looking at his opponents, it appears Rice is now a babyface.

In 1957, Rice started teaming with Bill Savage. In his RATNW interview, Savage mentioned Rice, "Tom Rice was another good friend. He was my skin-diving buddy."

In 1993, I mentioned to Savage that I was headed off to Cauliflower Alley, and he told me that if I saw Tom Rice, I should say hello to him. In 1993, I wasn't sure I had even heard of Tom Rice. However, the first night, I was in line to enter, and I read the name tag of the person in front of me and it was Tom Rice. I struck up a conversation and told him Bill Savage said to say Hello.

When Rice wasn't in Hawaii, he wrestled on the West Coast, either in LA or San Francisco. Rice continued wrestling in Hawaii through 1960. In fact, in '60, he would find himself the tag champs again in Hawaii with Shoulders Newman.

He would retire in 1961. He became an insurance executive and was a big booster for the University of San Francisco, where he played college football. Rice swam in San Francisco Bay every day, and when he was 63 he towed a 200-ton sailing vessel several hundred yards. At the age of 67 he was strong enough to pull a 120-ton San Francisco tour boat 200 yards using a backstroke and a harness. The boat was loaded with USF alumni; it was a stunt for the school's annual fund drive.

Rice passed away in 1996 after a series of strokes.

Masahiko Kimura

Real Name: Masahiko Kimura
Born: 1917 Died: 1993

As I worked on the 1951 Hawaiian wrestling history, I was surprised at how several judo competitors took over the wrestling scene.

I underestimated just what a big deal Masahiko Kimura might have been.

He is considered one of the greatest judo competitors of all time. He did not lose a judo match from 1936 to 1950 and only four matches in his lifetime. His training regimen was legendary. He often did a thousand push-ups and practiced for nine hours a day.

In 1949, he toured Brazil and met Helio Gracie in a match. The bout took place before 20,000, including the President of Brazil. In a very tough contest, Kimura grabbed a hold and rotated Gracie's arm until it broke. Gracie still refused to give up. Kimura twisted the arm further and broke it again. Finally, Kimura was about to twist a third time when Gracie's corner threw in the towel. This armlock technique has since been referred to as the Kimura Lock and is used today.

Kimura went to Japan and founded the Kokusai Pro Wrestling Association. He also was an early member of the Japan Pro Wrestling Association.

Kimura met Rikidozan in a high-profile match, but according to Kimura, it didn't go as planned. It may be an early example of a shoot. This match was supposed to go to a draw and set up a series of rematches that never happened. Rikidozan attacked Kimura, striking him in the neck using full force. Kimura went unconscious, and Rikidozan started to kick him. Kimura never received a rematch.

Kimura wrestled in Hawaii in a limited capacity in 1951 and 52 and remained undefeated there.

He passed away in 1993 from lung cancer.

Kimura vs Rikidozan

Siva Afi

Real Name: Max Taogaga
Born: 1949

A Hot Summer Night in Aloha Stadium on August 5th, 1985, was the highlight of Siva Afi's wrestling career. He went to a draw with NWA World Champ Ric Flair. He proved to be a very good draw in Hawaii on this night. This was an opportunity he had not received before or after.

Afi was born Max Taogaga in 1949 in Samoa. He later moved to New Zealand. Siva went to Steve Rickard and Peter Maivia, who trained him for two years for his debut in 1974.

In 1979, he came to Stampede Wrestling. He also won the Hawaiian title in 1979.

In 1980, Afi went to Portland, where I had a chance to see him wrestle. He grabbed initial wins over Fidel Cortez, Rocky Deleserra, Tiny Anderson, Eric Embry, Ricky Hunter, and even Rip Oliver.

However, his push seemed to slip quickly, and he was stuck in the preliminaries.

He married Portland Wrestling sponsor Tom Peterson's daughter and homesteaded in the Northwest for a number of years.

At one point, I worked at a convenience store across from Tom Petersons. Siva would come in during lunchtime and buy one beer.

SIA AFI TAOGAGA

In 1986, he made it to the WWE and was in preliminaries. Jimmy Snuka left WWE, and Siva was moved up and given the name Superfly Afi, which seemed like a good move up. However, the fans turned on him, knowing he was a Jimmy Snuka knockoff. To his credit, he did notch wins over Bret Hart and Hercules Hernandez.

In 1997, Siva was arrested for acting as a getaway driver for a burglary and kidnapping in Ohio. After a series of appeals, he was released from prison in 2007 and deported back to Samoa.

In 2008, he published his autobiography "Reign of Fire." It is available from Amazon.

POLYNESIAN PACIFIC CHAMPIONSHIP
WRESTLING

Promoter Lia Maivia Goes To:

Aloha Stadium   7:30 pm   Saturday, August 3, 1985

'85 WORLD INVITATIONAL WRESTLING SPECTACULAR
(Hot Summer Night)

NWA WORLD CHAMPIONSHIP
— VS —

Champion
RIC FLAIR
U.S.A.

Challenger
SIVA AFI
Samoa

Polynesian Pacific Heavyweight

CHALLENGER
LARS ANDERSON

VS

CHAMPION
BAD NEWS ALLAN

Polynesian Pacific Tag Team
Winner take all.
No Disqualification

— VS —

CHAMPION
"The Soul Patrol"
ROCKY & RICKY JOHNSON
New York

CHALLENGERS
THE DIRTY WHITE BOYS
Tennessee

WWF Jr. World Championship

VS

CHAMPION
THE COBRA

CHALLENGER
SUPER FLY TUI

NWA NATIONAL HEAVY-WEIGHT CHAMPIONSHIP

VS.

CHAMPION
BLACK BART

CHALLENGER
MANNY FERNANDEZ

Jimmy "Superfly" Snuka

Larry Sharp

USA vs RUSSIA

VS

Challengers
"The American Dream" DUSTY RHODES & MAGNUM T.A.

World Champions
NANITA KOLOFF & KRUSHER KRUSCHEV

AWA LIGHTWEIGHT WORLD CHAMPIONSHIP

VS

CHAMPION
STEVE REGAL

CHALLENGER
MIGHTY MILO

4 MAN TAG MATCH

VS

KENGO KIMURA

GENE LEWIS

VS

TATSUMI FUJINAMI   GARY FULTON

The Family vs Sullivans Army

$20,000 to any wrestler that can slam SUNNY

VS

"The Family"
Andre the Giant & Steve "The Kid" Collins & "Big & Nasty" Angelo Mosca

"The Army"
King Kong Bundy & Kevin Sullivan & "Maniac" Mark Lewin

4 MAN TAG MATCH

VS

"The Samoan Connection"

"Texas Outlaws"

MATCH OF THE CENTURY

ANTONIO INOKI
Japan

— VS —

BRUISER BRODIE
New Mexico
U.S.A.

8 MAN TAG MATCH

VS

Seiji Sakaguchi

Matt Borne

Tonga Kid   Sam Anai

All eight men in the ring at the same time

— VS —

$8,000 to winning team

Afa & Sika

Dick Murdoch   Adrian Adonis

Ricky Steamboat   Alexis Smirnoff

Rickie Magnett

VS

Gypsy Joe

The Mighty Midgets

PANCHO BOY

VS

MEAN LITTLE KEVIN

Women's Street Fight
"Answer to a Challenge"

DEBBIE COMBS

VS

THE FALLEN ANGEL

TICKET PRICES: 20.00   15.00 & 12.00 Reserved   9.00 Gen. Admission   6.00 Senior Citizen & Children 5 years to 12 years

TICKETS ON SALE NOW at at FENWAY OUTLETS 942-9696 and ALOHA STADIUM 468-7731

Oki Shikina

Real Name: Morio Shikina

Born: 1904 Died 1983

The original Oki Shikina was born in 1904 in Japan. He came to Hawaii at age five to join his father, who was working on a plantation in Maui.

As he was growing up, he participated in Judo and Sumo. In 1925, he won a Sumo tournament.

He met the original Taro Miyake, a Japanese Judo teacher who had become a professional wrestler. In 1929, he went to New York to train to become a wrestler.

J Michael Kenyon, the Godfather of Wrestling historians, wrote that Shikina was to work for Miyake at a salary of $100 monthly for three years.

In 1935, Shikina returned to Hawaii and had some immediate success with wins over Wildcat Pete, Jack Morgan, and Jim Meeker. He even went to a draw with Gus Sonnenberg.

In 1937, Shikina returned to Hawaii and won the Hawaii Junior Heavyweight title from Rusty Westcoatt. He would hold this title until January of 1939. He would lose it for three months and then regain it.

During this run, he had victories over some more recognizable names, including Dick Raines, Dean Detton, Lee Henning, Danny Dusek, Lofty Blomfield, George Zaharias, and Chief Thunderbird. He had several matches with Jim Londos as well.

Oki Shikina is credited with training Rikidozan, one of the top Japanese wrestlers ever. He worked exclusively in Hawaii from 1948 to 1952. Shikina then returned in 1955 before retiring.

In the 1950s, Shikina opened the Sportsman Bar in Honolulu.

He later became a referee in Japan.

He passed away in 1983.

Vic Christy

Real Name: Vic Christy
Born: 1912 Died: 1995

Christy was born in Glendale, CA and was a star basketball player and wrestler.

Vic Christy had a 42-year wrestling career and spent a good part of it in Hawaii. His career started in 1931, and he came to Hawaii in 1936, just as Al Karasick started promoting.

He had wins over Kiman Kudo, Harry Kent, Reb Russell, and Danny Dusek. Also, he wrestled Jim Londos and Strangler Lewis through the late 30s.

Christy traveled to different territories for many years and returned to Hawaii in 1949. He teamed with his brother Ted Christy for a match in Honolulu on March 27th, 1949, beating Kenny Ackles and Bob Ford.

He came back in 1954 for a month. Several of his stays in Hawaii look like just a nice month-long working vacation.

In 1961, he came to Hawaii as the Masked Executioner. He beat Lord Blears on December 13th, 1961, to capture the Hawaiian title. His brother Ted also came to Hawaii during this time and worked as Ted Travis.

He was pushed strongly during this time. He feuded with Lord Blears, Neff Maivia, Mad Dog Vachon and Dick Beyer, Billy Whitewolf, King Curtis, and others.

In the early 60s, he split his time between Hawaii and Los Angeles. In 1964, he returned in February and had wins over Buddy Austin, Antonio Inoki, Lucky Simunovich, and Cowboy Cassidy.

In 1965 and 66, his booking in Hawaii seemed to lessen. Records show he was not wrestling in any other territories.

During this time, his acting career started to take off with some minor roles. He appeared in Get Smart as a guard, The Big Valley as a train passenger, I Spy as a guard, The Virginian and Bonanza as a townsperson, and several other TV spots.

In 1967, he came in for a month to Hawaii, but the wins were getting fewer and farther between.

He finished his wrestling career with a month in Hawaii in 72 and a few matches in 73.

Christy grew too old to constantly wrestle so he found a job as the stunt double for Mike Mazurki on various productions including It's About Time and in Batman. He would frequently be cast with his brother as an extra in films and ended up a staple of western film sets because of his sense of humor. It wasn't uncommon for him to put his fellow extras in wrestling hold and for him to just joke around with everybody.

By the late 1970s, his brother had passed away and Vic decided to retire where he passed away at the Motion Picture Retirement Home.

Wrestlers often talk very fondly of Vic Christy. He was a fantastic ribber. He is often complimented for his ribs because they took time to lay out, and they were of the harmless variety.

In the Slam Wrestling tribute to John Tolos, a Vic Christy rib was mentioned. Tolos had gotten a job as a car salesman. One day, Christy called him with an accent and acted irate, telling Tolos that he sold him a lemon and was coming down there so they could have it out.

Christy parked so he could see the car lot and watch Tolos for 2 or 3 hours. Finally he got out and approached Tolos and shouted that he sold him a lemon.

When I had a chance to ask Tolos if he was a ribber he said, "Yeahhh, I was a ribber because I was taught by the greatest ribber of them all, Vic Christy. Vic and I were tremendous friends and he was a raw ribber and I was a raw ribber too. But I could take a rib. Blassie was a good ribber too. I was taught with the old pros. But I ain't saying anything. I'm taking all my ribs to the grave with me.

Vic's ribs would never hurt anyone, but they were colossal. They would embarrass you, but they wouldn't hurt you. Now his brother Ted was a hurtful ribber. There was a guy by the name of Sandor Szabo here in the 50's. They say the reason that Sandor Szabo passed away so young was because of Vic Christy ribbing the ******* out of him. He couldn't take a rib. Vic was unreal. he passed away when he was about 84, I guess. I cried that day, he was my good friend. HEY I even had a tear when my friend Blassie passed away. I lost two good buddies right there, good ribbers, a lot of fun and they were both terrific guys.

Jules Strongbow was the big promoter here in the golden era. They had TV out of Hollywood. Strongbow was a heavy set guy and he was losing weight because he was taking these pills called Tafon. Tafon was a big sponsor of the TV show. Tafon spelled backwards was No fat. Vic Christy came in from the East Coast and Jules wanted him to do a interview in the middle of the ring and tell them that Jules was losing weight. So Vic came in the ring and Strongbow says, "Well Vic you had a very successful tour of the East Coast. Welcome back to the West Coast and your fans missed you here and we are glad you are back. Do you notice anything different?

Vic looked at him and said, "Geez, yeah, you have lost weight. Jules said, Yes, I have all because of Tafon. What do you think of that?

Vic said, "Well I'll tell you what Jules, when I left here you were just one great big fat slob. Now you are just half a slob." This is on live TV, and I guess Jules went crazy. Sweating like a pig. But Jules loved Vic. But I'll tell you what: Vic wasn't booked for the first couple of weeks as a penalty."

Another Vic Christy rib I heard about was when he picked up King Curtis in LA, and they headed off for a show. Christy drove for about six hours before they arrived at the show. Christy told Curtis that he wasn't able to give him a ride back after the show and he should get a ride with someone else.

Curtis's ride home that night was about an hour long.

Lars Anderson

Real Name: Larry Heiniemi
Born: 1939

Lars Anderson began his career in 1965 under his real name, Larry Heiniemi. In 1966, he changed his name to Anderson and became the 3rd Anderson Brother with Ole and Gene.

Interestingly, Anderson had only been in the ring with Peter Maivia four times, all in tag matches in 1972. Yet after Peter Maivia passed away, Lia Maivia hired Anderson to book the promotion.

This run as booker did not leave Anderson in a good light. He kept himself champion for a good period of time. In fact, there is a story that a very young ROCK took exception to Anderson refusing to lose the Polynesian title to Bad News Allan.

Pat Patterson reportedly stated that Anderson was only happy when he had a belt. Also, more reports of the young Polynesian wrestlers didn't like Anderson and, on one occasion, beat him up.

Anderson was able to avoid the problems that closed down Lia's pomotion. He had one more run in wrestling, starting the World League Wrestling in 1986.

Anderson is still alive and is 84 years old.

Wally Tsutsumi

Real Name: Wallace Tsuneto Tsutsumi
Born: 1915 Died: 2015

Wally Tsutsumi was one of the main referees for 50th State Wrestling. He started wrestling in 1945 at the age of thirty. He wrestled primarily in Hawaii from 1945 to 1962. He did make a two-month tour to the Northwest in 1952.

When Ed Francis started promoting Tsutsumi became a permanent referee even through the reopening until 1979

He was a Hawaii State Judo Champion in the early 50s.

He was also a concrete cement truck driver.

He passed away in 2015 at the age of 100.

Kimon Kudo

Real Name: Kaimon Kudo
Born: 1906 Died: 1993

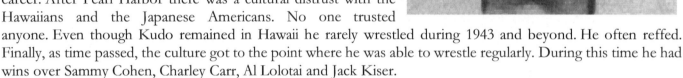

Kimon Kudo was born in Fukushima, Japan in 1906.

Two years after debuting in Seattle, Kudo came to Honolulu in August 1935. He had four matches, including a loss to promoter Al Karasick.

He returned to Hawaii in 1940 and won the Hawaii Junior Heavyweight title somewhere along the line. During this time, he had wins over Steve Nenoff, Whitey Walberg, and Billy Venable.

Kudo came back in 1941 but real life interfered with his career. After Pearl Harbor there was a cultural distrust with the Hawaiians and the Japanese Americans. No one trusted anyone. Even though Kudo remained in Hawaii he rarely wrestled during 1943 and beyond. He often reffed. Finally, as time passed, the culture got to the point where he was able to wrestle regularly. During this time he had wins over Sammy Cohen, Charley Carr, Al Lolotai and Jack Kiser.

In 1948, he started wrestling in other territories and retired in 1952. The Hawaii Junior title looks like the only title he held during his career.

There are some YouTube matches of his online.

Kimon Kudo passed away in 1993.

Lou "Shoulders" Newman

Real Name: Reino Nyman.
Born: 1913 Died: 2001

Lou "Shoulders" Newman was one of the stalwarts of Hawaiian wrestling through the 50s and the 60s. Shoulders is one of the all-time great nicknames.

He was born in British Columbia, and his uncle Waino Ketonen wrestled from 1910 to 1934. Reino would go to the matches in Victoria that his uncle was wrestling at. He would act as a gopher.

Newman started wrestling in 1937. He wrestled much of his career as a masked wrestler.

Shoulders Newman debuted in Hawaii in February of 1953 as MR. X. He lost his mask to Hans Schnabel in May of 53. He then started working under the name Lou Newman.

Interestingly enough, he started teaming with Hans Schnabel, and they won the Hawaiian tag titles in 1954 and again in 1960. Newman would hold the Hawaiian tag titles three more times, once with Tom Rice and two times with Ted Travis.

Orville Brown gave Newman the nickname "Shoulders."

He would work in Hawaii off and on through the 50s. Starting in 1960, he settled in Hawaii and worked there for the next seven years, retiring in 1967, marking a 31-year career.

He worked as an auto salesman in Honolulu and later moved to Washington State. He passed away in 2001 from a stroke.

50thStateBigTimeWrestling.com

I visited with Bill Atkinson, who has this tremendous Hawaii Wrestling Web Site. He has worked with the late George Beppu and his photos. He has put together a wonderful tribute to wrestling from Hawaii. The tabs on the website include History, where there is an overview of wrestling during the Ed Francis era. There are sketches of numerous wrestlers who wrestled in Hawaii. Classic Matches, with photos from Beppu's collection and Atkinson's memories, transports you to that night's action. Results from 1966 to 1978 and collectibles that feature a variety of things associated with wrestling in Hawaii.

During a conversation, Bill Atkinson talks about wrestling in Hawaii.

"I just started following wrestling in 1967, and that was when Jim Hady and Johnny Barend were partners, and they broke up. I graduated high school and joined the military in 1975, but I remember everything between that time."

I asked Bill how good wrestling was then and if he recognized how good it was?

"What happened is that my dad was in the military, and we would go down to the clubhouse to watch wrestling. I loved the way they talked in the interviews. It was really a big thing in Hawaii."

"I used to go to every other week at Block Arena, and then I went to the Civic a couple of times. Then my dad refused to take me because at the time they had a big riot."

"One memory that really sticks out was a match on July 10th, 1968, and it was a grudge match between Ripper Collins and Curtis Da Bull. Just going into that arena was like a big event."

"Another time in September of 1970, the buses were on strike, and someone dropped us off at the studio for the matches. The Destroyer was there, and he ran to the ring and put the figure four leg lock on someone. Then he ran out of the studio and caught a cab."

"After the matches, we found out there were no buses, and we had to walk home about 6 miles, a 13-year-old kid. Man, we got into trouble."

I asked Bill about King Curtis, and even though he was a heel most of his run in Hawaii, was he still popular?

"Since he was Hawaiian, he did have people cheering for him, especially when he would wrestle mainland wrestlers."

He remembered one time when Lia Maivia was promoting, "Ric Flair was on the card, but the first two matches were the Samoan rookies, who weren't very good. The crowd started getting rowdy, and we thought that maybe they were going to have a riot. Dusty Rhodes came out and had to get on the mic and tell the people to give Lia their respect. Michael Hayes came out as well.

I asked Bill about the Lonnie Mayne/Bearcat Wright racial angle where the loser had to be painted black or white, depending on the loser.

He told me he was talking to a wrestling fan unfamiliar with this match or the stipulations. The fan didn't believe this could be true until Bill showed him the clipping. He replied, "You are telling the truth!"

I asked Bill if he had ever met any of the wrestlers personally. He mentioned that after he had set up the website, he met King Curtis and his family. Bill mentioned that he had worked as a prison guard for 30 years, and Rocky Iaukea applied there and met him. He had met Tor Kamata's grandson and kept in touch with Anne Barend.

I asked Bill if he watched when Super Fly Tui took over. He mentioned that Super Fly Tui is a sergeant in a prison.

He said that Superfly Tui started doing shows on the military bases. The problem was it was just the local wrestlers and a few mainland guys.

I also asked Bill if there was wrestling currently in Hawaii. He mentioned that there was wrestling recently, but it ceased with the pandemic.

Atkinson finished the conversation by saying, "Everybody at school talked about wrestling. It was really a big thing."

"I will tell you this: A lot of people who went to the Hawaiian wrestling over here never had anything bad to say about it when Francis was running the show."

Billy Darnell

Real Name: William Lester Darnell
Born: 1926 Died: 2007

Billy Darnell had been wrestling for sixteen years when he worked in Hawaii for two shows in 1958. On his debut he defeated Wild Bill Savage on February 2nd and followed that with a tag team victory, teaming with Lucky Simunovich to defeat George Bollas and Tom Rice by DQ in 40-minutes.

Early in his career, Darnell was booked by Jack Pfefer as Billy Rogers, the brother of "Nature Boy" Buddy Rogers. Buddy wore sequined capes to the ring while Billy donned the leopard-skin outfit he became famous for wearing.
In 1961, Darnell beat Ali Pasha (Alexander Vieira Fontes) in a television match. Pasha died of a heart attack after being slammed down during the match.

Billy Varga

Real Name: William Joseph Varga
Born: 1919 Died: 2013

Billy Varga was trained in wrestling starting at the age of five by his father, who wrestled as Count Joseph Varga in Europe. Upon moving to California, Varga continued to learn wrestling at the YMCA, turning professional in 1937. He quickly found success, winning a version of the NWA Worlds Lightweight Championship in 1941.

Varga wrestled in Hawaii for seven months in 1956, winning the Hawaiian tag team championships with Sam Steamboat and the Hawaiian Heavyweight Championship, defeating Al Lolotai.

Since 1949, Varga split time between the ring and in Hollywood. In 1964, Varga appeared on The Munsters, working as "Strangler Murphy", wrestling Herman Munster, who was billed as The Masked Marvel.

Varga passed away in 2013 from complications related to Alzheimer's.

Bing Ki Lee/White Avenger/Avenger/Hahn Lee

Real Name: Felipe Ham Lee
Born: 1932 Died: 2011

Hahn Lee appeared with four different gimmicks in Hawaii, starting in 1968. He worked under two different masks, as the White Avenger and in a dark mask as The Avenger. Without a hood, he worked as Bing Ki Lee and Hahn Lee.

In his debut match in Hawaii, he was teamed (as Hahn Lee) with Pepper Gomez in a losing effort against the top tag team of Ripper Collins and Ray Stevens. Lee would have some of his best success in Hawaii in 1970, winning the Hawaiian tag championships with Pedro Morales.

For years, he was the head of the Box y Lucha commission in the Distrito Federal, and he also was the original trainer of Canek and Villano III. According to his daughter, Eliza Hahn, his name was Philip Lee Hahn. It was changed to Ham to simplify things.

As The Avenger with Lord Blears

Taking a chair from King Curtis

The Magnificent Maurice/Gene Dubuque/Gene Darval

Real Name: Eugene Earl Dubuque
Born: 1927 Died:1974

Only three years into his career, Dubuque appeared in Hawaii for the first time in 1952, working as Gene Dubuque for three months. He would return to Hawaii seven years later, in 1959, going by the name Gene Darval. This time he stayed for a short six-weeks.

It would be another nine years before he returned to Hawaii, this time working as The Magnificent Maurice. Having previously teamed with Johnny Barend on the mainland with great success, they found themselves teamed up once again. They would win the Hawaiian tag team championships in 1968.

During the last few years of his life, he had a career in Hollywood. On March 13, 1974, Dubuque and a crew went out to the Mammoth Lakes area in California to shoot for the film Primal Man. Their plane, carrying 31 members of the production crew and 5 airplane staff, crashed into a White Mountains ridge, killing all aboard, including Dubuque. He was only 46 years old.

Ray Eckert

Real Name: Floyd Ray Eckert
Born: 1917 Died: 1996

Ray Eckert debuted in pro wrestling in 1935, winning titles throughout the United States, with his greatest success in Pacific Coast/San Francisco area. He won the Hawaiian Heavyweight Championship on July 16th, 1950, defeating Arjan Singh. Eckert was a transitional champion, losing the title the next week to Terry McGinnis.

He would return in 1953 for a NWA #1 Contender Tournament, winning the tournament, but losing to World Champion Lou Thesz in a title match.

After retiring from wrestling in 1954, with his wife, Dorothy, he owned and operated the Western Auto Store in the town of California, Missouri, from 1958 to 1988. He drowned in an accident on his farm in Missouri in 1996.

Sandor Kovacs

Real Name: Sandor Kovacs
Born: 1920 Died: 2004

Sandor Kovacs was born in Hungary, before moving to Canada in 1930. In WW2, he joined the Royal Canadian Navy, where he met Stu Hart. After the war, Kovacs moved to New York, rooming with Hart and James Blears, and became proficient in pro wrestling.

In a Slam Wrestling obituary, it was noted, Sandor Kovacs was definitely different than the average muscle-bound grappler. "He might have been a little bit of an elitist, compared to the other guys. He loved opera, ballet. He was more of a classical guy," his wife Betty said, adding that he would often go to the opera with the likes of Lou Thesz and Yukon Eric.

In 1955, Kovacs would win the Hawaiian tag titles, teaming with Johnny Barend. He stayed in Hawaii, working there through 1956. He would return for quick bouts in 59 and 69, and single bouts in 70, 72, and 73.

He passed away from Alzheimer's in 2004.

Dingo the Sundowner

Real Name: Les Roberts
Born: ?
Died: "The reports of my death are greatly exaggerated." Mark Twain

Worked Hawaii for three months in 1970, going to five draws, seven loses, and no wins. He had only had a handful of matches before debuting in Hawaii, so he was truly just getting started. The boys, including Earl Maynard, said Les worked pretty stiff. Legit tough guy.

It's been reported for years on the net that Les Roberts died in an auto accident in 1997, but Roberts turned up at a wrestling reunion in Melbourne as was amused to find out that he was supposedly dead. He lives in Tasmania now. He reportedly hung with a biker gang when he was wrestling and from all accounts, he was a real hard man but nice guy.

Wrestled in Australia, Detroit, Los Angeles, Texas, Hawaii and Canada. Defeated Rocky Johnson in 1970 in Los Angeles to win the "Beat the Champ" TV title. Wrestled Dory Funk Jr for the NWA World title in Texas in 1972.

Ron Reed/Buddy Colt

Real Name: Ron Reed
Born: 1936 Died: 2021

Ron Reed was born in Maryland, and grew up watching wrestling on tv, and dreaming of becoming one. Reed would say, "I was a little skinny kid, so I'd look at the wrestlers on TV and I would fantasize about being a professional wrestler, but think, 'Well, I'm too little and too skinny and I'd never be big enough.'" Reed got into weightlifting and body building, eventually meeting Joe Mercer (Otto Von Krupp) in Houston and his training began. He debuted in 1962 and quickly moved up cards.

He ventured to Hawaii in late 1965, and defeated Luther Lindsay for the Hawaiian championship in January of 1966. Reed would drop the title to Ripper Collins in two weeks, and head to the Central States territory.

On February 20, 1975, Colt was the pilot of a plane which crashed in water near Tampa Bay, resulting in the death of Bobby Shane. Colt and passengers Gary Hart and Austin Idol were seriously injured. Reed retired from wrestling due to broken ankles. He remained in Championship Wrestling from Florida as a color commentator.

Historian Mike Mooneyham wrote that Colt "might have been the greatest performer to have never held the world heavyweight title."

Klondike Bill/The Brute

Real Name: Bill Soloweyko
Born: 1931 Died: 2000

Bill was trained by Stu Hart in Calgary after a very successful amateur wrestling career. In the *Calgary Sun, Hart recalls* that Klondike was "a nice, sweet guy … but it'd take a pretty big man to take him down off his feet. I never met anybody stronger than him."

Soloweyko had a clean-shaven look early in his career and worked in Hawaii in 1963 as The Brute. His strong amateur background made him a good talent for guys like Nick Bockwinkel, Lord Blears. However, being new to pro wrestling, he was kept mostly in tag matches.

He would return in 1968, as Klondike Bill and a grizzled bearded look. Less than two weeks after returning, he would win the Hawaiian Heavyweight title, defeating King Curtis. He would go on to feud with Curtis, Pampero Firpo, Peter Maivia, and Luke Graham. He would leave Hawaii for the Central States in November of 68 for a short run before returning to Canada.

Soloweyko retired from wrestling in 1987. He passed away in 2000 and his death was a result of a neuromuscular disorder that took away the use of his tongue and left him speechless for the last months of his life.

Abe Jacobs

Real Name: Abner Robert Jacobs
Born: 1928 Died: 2023

Abe Jacobs is said to have wrestled over 4,000 matches. However, his very first pro match was on November 23, 1958 in Hawaii, with a win over Jerry Gordet. His stay would be uneventful, lasting until January 21, 1959.

His career would skyrocket, and Jacobs became a major star in the NWA. He was often billed as the "Jewish Heavyweight Champion" and wrestled in high-profile matches against NWA World Champions Thesz Kiniski Rogers Hutton, and O'Connor.

Kay Bell/Samson

Real Name: Kay Dee Bell
Born: 1914 Died: 1994

Kay Bell played NFL football for five seasons from 1937-1942, after graduating from Washington State where he earned All-American honors. He started his pro wrestling career in 1938 and worked mainly in California for the first seven years. He would find success in the New York market later in his career. Bell retired from wrestling in 1954.
Bell had short runs in Hawaii in 1949 and 1951 and returned for two matches in 1960.

His ring name of Samson came from being the stunt-double for Victor Mature (as Samson) in the 1949 classic movie Samson and Deliah.

Steve Strong

Real Name: Stephen Cepello
Born: 1949

Strong began his wrestling career in late 1974. He defeated Roddy Piper in the second and third matches of his career in 1975. Strong would find success working in Hawaii in 1977-78, often paired as a strongman tag team with Jesse Ventura. He would win the Hawaiian tag team titles six times with partners Ventura, Chris Markoff, and John Tolos.

Cepello is a gifted artist, and after retiring from wrestling was chosen to paint the official portraits of former Minnesota Governor Jesse Ventura for the Minnesota State Capitol and Governor's Mansion.

Russ Francis

Real Name: Russell Ross Francis
Born: 1953 Died: 2023

Russ Francis did a little wrestling, but his number one thing was football. He was a 3-time pro bowler playing for New England and San Francisco in the NFL.

His first match was in Portland, teaming with his father Ed to beat Dale Lewis and Kurt Von Steiger. He often teamed up with his father and brother Bill. He even had a win over Bob Remus. He was protected because of his high profile. He also worked his off-season's in the AWA, where I don't believe he lost a singles match.

In 1978 he and his brother Bill won the Hawaiian tag titles.

His wrestling career would have been much more significant if his football career hadn't been so successful.

Russ passed away in a plane crash on October 1, 2023 in Lake Placid, New York at the age of 70.

Bill Francis

Real Name: Bill Francis
Born: 1962

Bill Francis was a wrestler who seemed to have many things going for him. He had the size, lineage, and athletic ability to have made a promising career for himself as a wrestler. However, Francis didn't seem to put everything together for a successful career in wrestling.

Francis debuted in 1969 in Hawaii on Christmas night, teaming with his dad Ed to defeat King Curtis and Friday Allman. The newspaper exclaimed they "brought the house down."

He would be declared the Hawaiian Heavyweight Champion in July 1977, a title vacant since July 1974, when wrestling in Hawaii went on hiatus. Francis would win the Hawaiian Tag Team championships with long-time rival John Tolos in November of 77 and with brother Russ in 1978.

After retiring from wrestling in 1979, Bill entered law enforcement in Dallas, Oregon. I did my student teaching at Dalles High School. I remember a staff member coming into the lounge and telling people that Bill Francis was in the weight room.

From the debut match: Collins, second from right, holding back Bill
Francis as Friday Allman has Ed Francis in a hammer lock.

Bill Francis Interview
(conducted 2024)

RATNW: I was always drawn to those cards in the late 1960s and early 1970s that I thought were just unbelievable. There was so much talent, and Lord Blears made sure that I understood that it was the local guys who were drawing the house, and the guys who were passing through were just icing on the cake. I kept asking him just how special the cards were, and to the point where he started to get just a little annoyed with me, he kept telling me that it's the locals that draw the house.

Bill Francis: Yeah, that's true, and all those guys are gone.

RATNW: How special were those cards in the late 1960s and early 1970s? I looked through those cards, and in hindsight, they were just unbelievable.

Bill Francis: Yes, the people, the residents of the islands, were just fascinated with the way that Lord Blears and my father put together the wrestling programs.

What was very important was that every Saturday, they would have some little wrestling matches on the TV down the KHVS. The most important thing on Saturdays was the locker room interviews, and then Wednesday night we got the locker room interviews. Those stand out and make history for the promotion not only in Hawaii.

Vince JR himself told my brother Russ how important our father's influence was when he started promoting.

Many of the wrestlers who worked with my father and Lord Blears carried those same sentiments back to different promotions throughout the United States and perhaps some in Australia and Japan.

RATNW: I never saw wrestling in Hawaii, but I get the feeling the Hawaiian fans might have been more rabid than other territories, considering the number of riots they had.

Bill Francis: You know, I'm not sure if they were or not, but I know that when we had our highlight events, they didn't like Ripper Collins at all. At the same time, they couldn't help but like him.

RATNW: I know King Curtis was a heel most of the time, but I still get the feeling that he was very popular with him being Hawaiian.

Bill Francis: No matter how angry he got the people, they loved the brother. He had the lineage of Colonel Curtis, who was in the court of Kalakala. King Curtis's father was an inspector for the Honolulu Police Department, OK, so there's a lot of Royal and civil history.

RATNW: Did you know Al Karasick at all? You probably would have been too young.

Bill Francis: Yes, I've met him. At that time, children were to be seen and not heard.

But yeah, I wasn't privy to any conversations that they had other than being introduced to him. That is as far as it went for me.

I have received some stuff from my dad and my mother. I have a letter in which Al Karasick offers the promotion to my father. I have that letter; it still survives. I believe one other letter that doesn't really tell much other than my father agreed to purchase the promotion. At the time he bought the Hawaii promotion, he was in Calgary working for Stu Hart, and he was booking. He was highly respected as a ring general.

RATNW: Do you remember any ribs that were played? I know with Fuji on your crew, there were bound to be some humorous ones.

Francis: The story with Fuji and Curtis and the breaking of the boards. Fuji was going to do his karate and bust the boards. This was done on Saturday afternoon TV, which was shown live.

What was going to happen was Fuji was going to these boards that Curtis was holding up in front of him. Fuji would strike, punch, and break the boards.

The two boards put up one with the vertical facing grain, but the board in the back had a horizontal grain. He broke the first one easily, but he couldn't break the 2nd because the grain was going the wrong way. Curtis had set them up that way. He made a fool of himself because he couldn't break the board.

I can't remember if he broke his hand or severely injured it. Curtis laughed and laughed, and I'm sure, of course, Fuji never forgave him for that.

I was very fortunate to get in at a time when I had some very fine men teaching me the profession. I went through high school and did high school wrestling, but one of my professional trainers was Karl Gotch. If you know about Karl, he was a fantastic wrestler—what we used to call a shooter. He was brutal. He was an excellent wrestler, Nothing to do with showmanship or anything to do with that.

Another one was Billy Robinson. He was more of a showman, but he was also from Wigan, Manchester, England, and he was fantastic.

RATNW: When you came to Portland, did any of the guys there press you to try to get you to get them booked into Hawaii?

Francis: Yeah, there were a number of different wrestlers who did that. The one I will mention is Jesse Ventura. Jesse is a very good gentleman. I think very highly of him. I remember his service in the US Navy as well. He was a Seal and, as we say in the military, a four-square stand-up guy.

He had asked me if there was a possibility that I could get him booked in Hawaii. He actually got in there because of Lord Blears, and of course, my father agreed. Jesse's history goes on from there. He went to many different places before he ended up in New York. His roots were still in Minnesota. He is still a very good friend. His wife is also very, very kind.

RATNW: I know that Hawaii closed down a little bit for a few years there in 74 and 75 and then reopened, I believe, in 77. Did it just pick up right from where it left off, or was it a little bit harder to get going at that point?

Francis: It was a little bit harder to get going, and my father only ran for a couple of years. After that he returned back to Oregon where we owned property. I was on the road quite a bit at that time.

RATNW: I know that your dad sold to Steve Rickard from New Zealand, and Peter Maivia became involved at some point. My understanding at this moment in Hawaii is a little murky. It is unclear if Maivia bought in or just worked his way in.

Francis: The information that I have and I cannot definitely say. Peter and his wife Lia who was also a very strong force in that promotion. They lasted a few years before it collapsed.

I don't know for sure what the situation was there. I stick to the adage, "If I need to know, I will be told, and if I want to know, I will find out." I never really found out what the real truth was.

RATNW: Any Ripper Collins stories?

Francis: (Laughs), Roy Collins what a character. As we've mentioned he was a villain, and he was a hero.

He was an avid bowler; I don't recall what league he was in. The people loved him. Outside the ring, he was very kind and very courteous, and the people loved him, and at the same time, they hated him. He was quite the character. I wrestled him many times.

RATNW: Final thoughts and memories.

Francis: Of course, here in about two weeks, my sister and my daughter and a bunch of other people are going to Hawaii for Russ's and my dad's celebration of life. I am sure it's going to be quite an event, so I'm told.

I'm still in mourning for the loss of my brother. I dealt with the loss of my father, who passed away in 2016, but I'm not quite too ready to let go of my brother. I didn't want to participate in this because I felt so strongly that that we should leave my brother alone and let him rest. Everybody tells me this is an honor, and I know they're going to do a real good job. I know some of the dignitaries will be there, and that's wonderful.

I tell my daughter, if you have any questions ask your father the same with the other survivors. I said, please ask me as soon as you can before I start to forget these things.

My dad had a book; I don't know if you heard about that.

RATNW: Oh, I have that book, and it is wonderful. I want to plug your book in my book.

Francis: That is my sister's thing. She takes care of father's books.

I'm the family genealogist. My father was Edmund Charles Francis the Third. My youngest brother is Edmund Charles Francis the Fourth. It goes all the way back to where my great grandfather had a Hayden green building in Chicago. He had property in the old country and property down and, I believe in Nicaragua or Costa Rica, pre-Depression. Everything went away after the depression because people who had bought on credit in Chicago didn't feel the need to pay back their debts.

My dad recalled a time when my grandfather's car, a Marmon, was sitting in the backyard loaded with trash. A Marmon at that time was equal to the Duesenberg.

Great Grandpa had a really strong business going, but it all turned around after the depression. He ended up dying of gangrene. He had a blister on his heel, and he had black socks, and the dye always washed out of your socks, and it got infected. He was a stubborn German and wouldn't get medical attention.

Hawaii was a wonderful time. When my father first took over the promotion, we were soon to be a state, but we weren't quite a state yet. So I saw a lot of things change from the territorial times and statehood, the boom of the 1970s and 1980s. I wish I could say I would like to go back home to Hawaii, but it has changed so much, like so many other places people have grown up in.

Neff Maiava Promo Pictures

The Link   The Chief   The Prince

Neff Maiava

Real Name: Neff Alfred Maiava
Born: 1924 Died: 2018

Neff Maiava was born in American Samoa and moved to Hawaii when he was two years old.

Neff Maiava was trained by Al Karasick and debuted in Hawaii in 1952 under the name Auteaga Maiava. He continued in Hawaii until 1953, and then he began touring the territories. He went to Los Angeles and San Francisco, West Texas, Montreal, the East Coast, Texas, Vancouver, Calgary, Chicago, Buffalo, Toronto, the Maritimes, and other places.

In late 1958, he returned to Hawaii. With his experience of the previous five years, he was moving up the cards working with the likes of Stan Kowalski, Tiny Mills, and Don Manoukian and teaming with Al Lolotai and Lord Blears.

He finished 1958 with another stop around Calgary, Vancouver, Idaho, and Los Angeles, returning to Hawaii for the first part of 1959.

1960 was again making stops around the country, including New York, Florida, and Phoenix.

In 1961, he returned to Hawaii, moved to the top of the ladder, and stayed there for the next eight years.

He won the Hawaiian State title six times and held the Hawaiian tag titles six times, with Lord Blears four times and Billy Whitewolf and Pampero Firpo once each.

Being on top in Hawaii meant that you were meeting some of the top competition. Maiava would defeat such wrestlers as Shoulders Newman, Masked Executioner, Mad Dog Vachon, Dick Beyer, Tosh Togo, Don Manoukian, Hard Boiled Haggerty, Don Leo Jonathan, Fred Blassie, Ripper Collins, Mr. Fuji, and Bill Dromo.

Then there was the feud to top them all: King Curtis. They met on August 16th, 1961, when Maiava defended his Hawaiian title against Curtis in front of a crowd of 2,000. A little racial tension between the Samoans and the Hawaiians and a heel win caused a riot. Eight people were arrested, and nine people, including several officers, were injured. This story is recounted elsewhere in this book.

Maiava often did fire dances or walked on a bed of nails. He was managed by Coconut Willie who sent messages to Maiava by drums beats. He also beat Maurice Vachon in a hair match.

Peter Maivia took a similar name to Neff Maiava, and they became a tag team, winning the Hawaiian belts.

By 1969 Maiava was slowing down. He didn't have any matches in Hawaii in 1970. In 1971, he had a handful of matches and won over Lonnie Mayne.

After retiring, he ran a tree-trimming company.

He passed away in 2018 at the age of 93. At the time, it was thought he was the second-oldest living wrestler.

Dean Higuchi

Real Name: Dean Kiyoshi Higuchi
Born: 1949 Died: 2021

Dean Higuchi was one of the most popular wrestlers in Hawaii and, in fact, anywhere he wrestled. He was popular inside the ring and probably even more popular outside the ring.

At age 16, he won the Hawaiian Islands competition and finished 6th in the Mr. America competition.

He opened a gym in 1957, which was the spot for both bodybuilders and wrestlers.

He started wrestling in Portland in 1962 and worked there and in Hawaii between 1962 and 1969.

In Hawaii, Dean was never really on top, but he was always popular. It was probably the hometown boy when things didn't go his way.

When he moved to Vancouver, Canada, his career started to heat up. He held the Canadian tag titles on four occasions between 1969 and 1971.

He had a successful tour in Texas and held the tag titles there twice with Fritz Von Erich and Red Bastien.

One of his higher-profile title reigns was teaming with Tony Garea, and they won the WWWF tag titles. On this run, he changed his name to Dean Ho.

He also won the US title in the San Francisco territory on two different runs, which was probably his highest-profile singles reign.

For a while, Higuchi wrestled in Portland as Dean Kallani and claimed he was honoring his mother by using his mother's maiden name.

Higuchi was a regular at Dean Silverstone's wrestler reunion. Every year, when Higuchi walked in, Ed Wiskowski shouted, "Mr. Fuji is here." Higuchi, obviously enjoying the rib, would grouse, "I am not Mr. Fuji."

I had a chance to form a friendship with Dean, and I would receive wonderful handwritten letters that were so gracious and detailed.

Dean passed away in 2021 from CTE.

Don Muraco

Real Name: Don Muraco
Born: 1949

King Curtis may have had the most success in Hawaii, and Don Muraco may have been the most successful wrestler from Hawaii.

Muraco started wrestling in April 1970 in the Northwest. He was trained, at least in part, by veteran Jack Bence. Dean Higuchi, Mr. Fuji, Lonnie Mayne, Tom Andrews, and a few others are also credited with some training. He wrestled Bence five times in that first month as he broke into the business. He also wrestled Gene Kiniski four days into his career. Despite Muraco's being very skinny (which is hard to believe), they must have seen something in him because he got a few wins that first month over Bence, Moose Morowski, Bud Rattal, and Pierre LeGrande.

Muraco primarily worked on the West Coast in the first few years of his career. He also worked a little in the AWA. He was given a more prominent spot when he returned to Hawaii in 1973. He went to a draw with Ray Stevens and teamed up with Billy Robinson to beat Dusty Rhodes and Billy Robinson.

He gained size and moved around the country to territories like Florida and Georgia. He ended up in WWE through the 80s decade and evolved into one of the biggest stars in the business. He would come back to Hawaii when Ed Francis reopened it from 78-80. He wrestled regularly until 1995. He moved back to Hawaii, worked as a longshoreman, and now retired.

Local Boy Who Made Good but...

Bill Kwon

"I'm a villain everywhere I go. I was when I left here. I enjoy it."

So the villainous Don Muraco, "Magnificent Muraco," if you will, will be the bad guy in tomorrow night's pro wrestling main event against world champion (at least third world) Bob Backlund at the Blaisdell Arena.

What Muraco doesn't appreciate is the lack of recognition by Hawaii's fans for a hometown boy who makes good. Good money, at least.

Muraco, now in his 13th year as a professional wrestler, made more than $100,000 last year, putting him in the upper 10 percent income bracket for those in the trade.

"I'VE SOLD OUT MADISON Square Garden three times, sold out the Capital Centre (in Maryland) and the Spectrum (in Philadelphia) and set an attendance record (18,000) in the Hartford Convention Center," Muraco said during a workout yesterday at the Clark Hatch Fitness Center in the Amfac Building downtown.

"Here, I don't know what we will draw," he said. But he won't be disappointed.

"Pro wrestling has been on the decline here and you can't blame the fans. If you don't have the top wrestlers, they won't come out. You can't fool the public. People in Hawaii are used to seeing first-class entertainment.

"I would like to see it come back but on a true professional level. But it'll take a lot of money," he said. "And you have to put back what you take out of the sport."

He didn't mean only in terms of money, but also educating the fans, giving them more of a wrestling background and supporting amateur wrestling, especially on the high school level. He thinks there is a need to get more kids—and better athletes—involved and interested in the sport.

MURACO AND BACKLUND ARE fighting tomorrow night (the card starts at 8) to stimulate the sport and help Peter Maivia's Polynesian Promotions get off to a solid start in bringing big-time pro wrestling back. Whether it'll succeed or not remains to be seen.

Muraco just happened to be home for the winter before going on a four-week tour of Japan and then the South Seas with Maivia, while Backlund, the current World Wrestling Federation champion (one of three recognized in the world—the other two are Rick Flair, National Wrestling Alliance, and Nick Bockwinkel, American Wrestling Association), is here to help Maivia out.

"Hey, it's no phony match. If I win, I'm the (WWF) champion and will assume all his title matches," Muraco said. They've fought to eight, one-hour draws last year so they're not following any "script" as some skeptics believe.

"It's for real but you have to entertain to be successful since most pro wrestlers are independent and have individual contracts with promoters," Muraco said. "You have to promote yourself."

MURACO ADMITS THAT SOME of his opponents can be dogs so he has to liven things up occasionally.

"Otherwise, it might not be exciting on TV, or to the fans. If I 'carry' anyone, it's to entertain myself. I'm selling myself at the expense of another guy's body. But, sometimes I'm not in the mood. I got rid of two guys in 59 seconds."

Muraco isn't an Andre The Giant in size as pro wrestlers go. He is 6-foot-3, 248 pounds, only about three pounds more than his high school days when he was an all-star tackle and the state prep wrestling champion for Punahou in 1966-67. One of his teammates on the Buffanblu line was Henry Kaaihue, who's in another line of entertainment as singer "Kapono" of C&K fame.

Because he isn't so villainous—nor grotesque-looking, Muraco has to work at being a bad guy.

"There's a love-hate relationship with my fans," he said. Obviously, they don't know whether to cheer him or boo him.

MURACO DESCRIBES HIMSELF as a wrestler with rough-house tactics . . . a lot of activity and up-and-down style to his way of fighting. Also, for effect, he tries to sound conceited and arrogant, especially for those mandatory TV promos.

"I guess I was always talkative and a leader in football," Muraco said, not trying to sound conceited.

Born in Honolulu and adopted during infancy by an Italian-Portuguese family, Muraco is half-Irish, and one-fourth Hawaiian and one-fourth German. After playing football at Punahou, he won all-California junior college honors at Glendale and Santa Monica.

"But I could never get into the academic system. I never had the grades, so I didn't continue," he said.

He surfed a lot—he still does when he's home—and one of his first surfing buddies was Jim Blears, whose dad, Lord "Tally Ho" Blears, was into wrestling. And so the Lord saw to it that Muraco took up wrestling.

HIS FIRST PRO MATCH wasn't in Honolulu but in Vancouver, B.C., against then world champion, Gene Kiniski.

"It was on TV and pretty horrifying . . . I lost," said Muraco, who hasn't lost many matches since. Last year he wrestled 200 times during his eight months on the circuit. A lot of the matches are made-for-television shows. He said he'd film six shows in two days, three and three, for cable-TV which has been a boon for pro wrestling.

The travel gets to Muraco, even though the money's good. He has since gotten married—here last New Year's Eve. He and his new bride—Sharon, whom he met in Florida—live on the North Shore and call Hawaii home, although they will live in West Haven, Conn., when he's on tour.

"It gets frustrating when you don't get the recognition in your own hometown. But I'm used to it. I won't be disappointed if we don't draw well in our match here.

"I remember once wrestling in the Garden (Madison Square Garden) one day and then going to a New Jersey high school gym the next. That's the nature of the wrestling business."

Harold Suga

One unsung hero that lent so much to the excitement of the TV show was Harold Suga. According to the excellent website 50thstatebigtimewrestlingcom, Suga was the artist that created the excellent lineups that were shown each week during the interview sessions on the Hawaii show.

George Atkinson mentioned that Suga used three sheets of mat board and hand painted the lineups and then attached the photos of the wrestling in the proper place. To the diehard fans, seeing the lineups each week was definitely an exciting addition to every show.

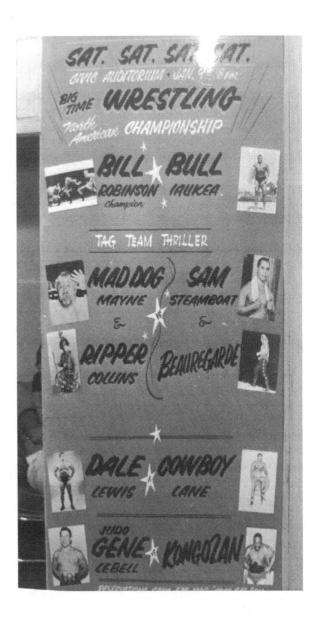

Rocky Johnson

Real Name: Wade Douglas Bowles
Born: 1944 Died: 2020

Born on August 24, 1944, as Wayde Douglas Bowles, Rocky Johnson's journey into wrestling began in Canada in 1965.

Rocky Johnson's first journey to Hawaii was a short month-long run in November of 1970. He would not return to Hawaii until 1979, where he would feud with Don Muracao.

Johnson returned to Hawaii in 1984, teaming with his brother, Ricky Johnson. They would win the Polynesian Tag Team Championship twice, beating The Dirty White Boys, Len "The Grappler" Denton and Tony Anthony.

Johnson's family connections added a unique dimension to his legacy. His marriage to Ata Maivia, the daughter of wrestling legend Peter Maivia, intertwined his story with the rich tapestry of Samoan wrestling heritage. This familial link laid the groundwork for the emergence of one of the most celebrated wrestling dynasties—the Anoa'i family.

Rocky Johnson's son, Dwayne "The Rock" Johnson, would become a megastar in his own right, both in the ring and in television and movies. The Anoa'i dynasty, with roots in Hawaii, has become synonymous with wrestling excellence.

Rocky was inducted into the WWE Hall of Fame in 2008. He passed away in 2020 from a pulmonary embolism at the age of 75.

Yearly Summaries

The very beginning 1907-1917

The first pro wrestling record in Hawaii was on June 25th, 1907. John Pappas is in Honolulu with the 10th infantry, claiming to be "the lightweight champion of Massachusetts", and he issued a challenge to meet the best wrestler in Honolulu for a $100 side bet. That wrestler turned out to be James Spencer, who was considered the champion of Honolulu.

Pappas won 2 straight falls in the Greco-Roman style. There were several other matches, and there was a small crowd of primarily soldiers who bet on their favorites.

In February of 1908, things start to heat up. Hans Froelicher, who claims to be the 168-pound wrestling champion of the World, is in Honolulu seeking matches. He came to Hawaii to challenge some Japanese sumo champions.

It appears there is a lot of hype around potential matches, and negotiations go back and forth between various competitors. Some include Frank Kanae, a champion thrower of the Islands and an all-around strong man. Mitsuka is a jiu-jitsu expert, and Kid Tate is another involved in the mix.

Finally, on April 18th, Hans Froelicher beat Frank Kanae in 2 straight falls.

These contests were probably shoots, and the line is fuzzy when wrestling evolved from legit contests to worked contests. These challenges heated up and continued through 1908. Dr. B.F. Roller was vacationing and training in Hawaii for a rematch with Frank Gotch.

In August of 1908, Freddie Smith promoted a boxing card in Honolulu and hoped to have Dr. B.F. Roller in a preliminary. Matches featuring Roller all fell through as the other wrestlers failed to post their bonds for guarantee. Roller gave various lectures and made some appearances but left Hawaii in October 1908.

By 1910, Joe Cohen had emerged as a promoter. Sailor Roberts is considered the Hawaiian Champion. On April 2nd, Roberts beat Big Bill Dettmers.

On July 22nd, Joe Thomas, from Michigan, appeared as part of a vaudeville program and challenged all comers in a catch-as-catch-can-match.

On July 27th, Thomas beat Sailor Roberts in 3 minutes. Thomas weighed in at over 200 pounds and outweighed Roberts by a considerable margin.

The next night, Joe Thomas beat John Froelicher in 12 minutes.

It is now 1912, and it is certainly a different time. One of the entertainment choices was Leon Morris and his wrestling ponies, which is a comedy act. John Hedge attempts to throw three Shetland ponies. There is also Dolly the Monkey, who is involved in some way. The act proves to be popular.

In 1913, George McCloud came to Hawaii and seemed the next big thing. Wild Cat Derby was billed as the Hawaiian Islands Champion.

On July 17th, McCloud beat Montague Stanford in two straight falls. Both competitors weighed in the 130's.

1914 seemed like a lot of wrestling talk, but contestants, more often than not, could not come to terms with having a match.

In 1915, Sam Searle beat Husky Willis 2 falls out of 3.

Sam Searles made it to Hollywood and, in 1920, played the lead in The Son of Tarzan. He served in World War 1 and passed away very young in 1924.

In February 1916, the wrestling bear, John Brown, took on all comers. Later in the book, we wonder about getting a wrestling bear to Hawaii. What about in 1916? Imagine what was involved in that excursion.

The original Taro Miyaki started making waves in Hawaii around 1916.

On September 30th, Miyaki beat Frank Kanae in 2 straight falls.

The promoter's name for this match was S. Shikata.

On October 13th, Miyaki beat Elbert Williams in a Jiu-Jitsu.

On November 30th S. Fuji beat F. Fukai. Fuji and Fukai were battling for the championship of Oahu. They also had boxing matches and a battle royal. This must be one of the very early examples of a battle royal.

On December 9th, Miyaki beat William Lager in a Jiu-Jitsu boxing mixed match.

On January 6th, 1917, Taro Miyake beat Young Santell (William Lager) in a Jiu-Jitsu contest.

On January 30th, Ad Santell, a claimant to the World Light-Heavyweight title, hoped to come to Hawaii to wrestle. He also said that he hoped that "Young Santell" would drop that name and go be his real one.

March through June, Young Santell had a series of matches with Edosakura. Santell won all the matches. He won so fast in one match that he agreed to continue wrestling to give the crowd their money's worth. Santell did say that Edosakura was a better wrestler than Taro Miyaki.

There were just a handful of cards later in 1917 featuring wrestlers who had not wrestled in Hawaii.

1907-1916 Wrestling Ads & Pictures

(Top L) Dr. Roller (Top R) Hans Froelecher (Bottom L) Frank Kanae   (Bottom R) Sailor Roberts

Tuesday Evening, June 25, 1907

Greco-Roman Wrestling Match
JOHN PAPAS,
Champion 148 Pounds Catch as Catch
can Wrestler
Versus
J. O. SPENCER
Local Champion.
Best 2 Falls out of 3.

HEAVY WEIGHT CONTEST.
Catch as Catch Can.
CHASTER A. PERRY
VS.
JAMES H. SNELL

OTHER PRELIMINARIES.

Admission: Reserved Seats 50c, 75c
and $1.00. Gallery 25c.

WRESTLING MATCH HAS BEEN ARRANGED

SOLDIER AND CIVILIAN ASPIRANTS FOR HONORS ON MAT WILL MEET TOMORROW NIGHT.

The much-talked-of wrestling bout between John Papas, of Company L, 10th Infantry, and J. O. Spencer, a well known local amateur wrestler, has finally been arranged and will be pulled off on Tuesday evening at the Orpheum. The details of the match were arranged yesterday after a conference of the two athletes. The match will be according to Greco-Roman rules, and the wrestling is for 60 per cent of the door receipts, the amount, in case Spencer wins to go to some charity, as he is strictly an amateur.

There will be a preliminary bout between C. A. Perry and J. H. Snell, two heavyweights from the 10th Infantry, which will also be interesting. The match will be refereed by Harry Cobb.

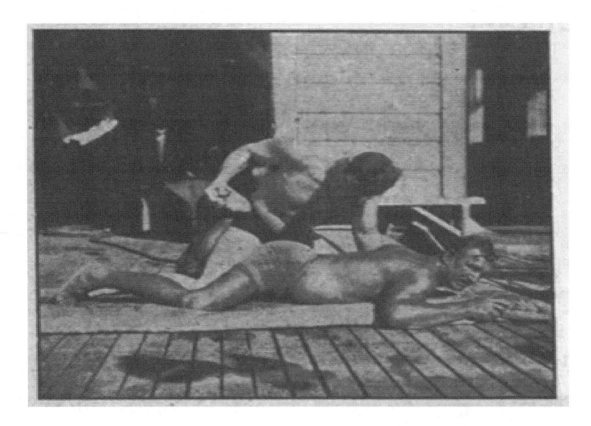

B.F. Roller demonstrating the Gotch Toe-Hold on trainer Pete Barron

JACK YOUNGER AND HANS FROELICHER, WHO ARE TO WRESTLE MAY 17.

Frank Gotch, Farmer Burns, Ole Marsh aka Joe Carrol

ED SEARLE.

SAMUEL SEARLES.

"JOHN BROWN." EDDIE FERNANDEZ' WRESTLING BEAR, CHALLENGING AT AALA PARK SHOW

112

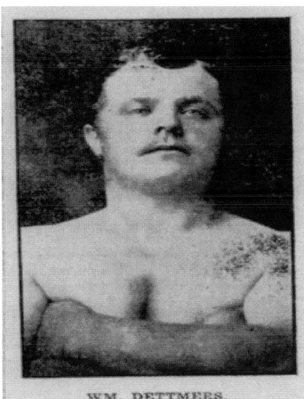

WM. DETTMEES.

MITSUKA
The giant Japanese wrestling champion of Hawaii, matched with Sailor Roberts for May 2.

Champion Wrestler of All
Japan Here With Comrades

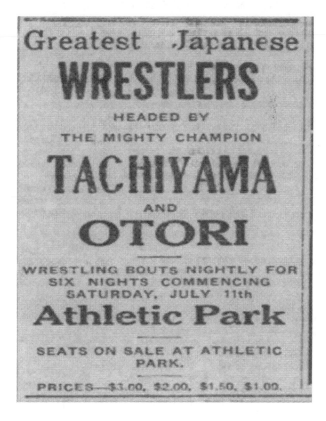

Greatest Japanese
WRESTLERS
HEADED BY
THE MIGHTY CHAMPION
TACHIYAMA
AND
OTORI

WRESTLING BOUTS NIGHTLY FOR
SIX NIGHTS COMMENCING
SATURDAY, JULY 11th
Athletic Park

SEATS ON SALE AT ATHLETIC
PARK.

PRICES—$3.00, $2.00, $1.50, $1.00.

1917-1919

The wrestler who came out of 1917 and into 1918 was Pvt. Louis Espetvedt, who weighed in at 175. He was based at Fort Ruger and challenged anyone in Hawaii. Plans start to pit Espetvedt against Young Santell fall thru.

On June 20th, Louis Espetvedt beat Pvt. J.F. Jones. Jones was a soldier at Fort DeRussey and claimed to be the former middleweight champ of Iowa.

Finally, on September 7th, Louis Espetvedt beat Young Santell in two straight falls.

In late 1918, Kinjo Ikeda emerged. Ikeda was a Japanese American who had trained in sumo. He also learned jiu-jitsu and catch-as-catch can and picked up the Samoan art of slipping out of an opposing wrestler's grasp.

On December 14th, Ikeda beat Louis Espetvedt and won the Hawaiian title. The match lasted an hour and was "the greatest encounter of the game ever staged in Hawaii, bar none." It drew a packed house.

In March of 1919, Kinjo Ikeda beat William Berne and went to a draw with C.C. Williams.

On May 7th, Louis Espetvedt was scheduled to wrestle Leo Poaha; however, Espetvedt was not allowed to wrestle because he was accused of biting his last opponent.

On July 1st, Kinjo Ikeda went to a draw with Louis Espetvedt.

There seemed to be random cards popping up around Hawaii with different grapplers. Most of the shows had service members as their wrestlers.

KINJO IKEDA

On August 14th, Louis Rego went to a draw with Alfred Pali. The card drew 400 people, and the match lasted 2 hours and 14 minutes before being ruled a draw. With the length of this match and a rapid result earlier, I am speculating that we have not yet reached the era of worked matches.

On August 22nd, Kinjo Ikeda beat Sailor Ferris in 2 straight falls. The match drew 1,800.

On November 11th, Leo Poaha beat Kinjo Ikeda to win the Hawaiian title. A hint that this could have been a work was Ikeda announced that he would be touring the mainland soon.

1919 Wrestling Ads & Pictures

The Dance Around the Pacific Club
WILL PRESENT ITS FIRST NIGHT OF
Hula Hula and Oriental Dancing and Music

An original and unique entertainment illustrating the favorite pastimes of the peoples of lands bordering the Far Eastern shores of the broad Pacific.

Hawaii is the hub around which our side of the world revolves and naturally takes the lead in this wonderful night of unusual and interesting fun. Interspersed between these Hula Hula numbers will be Hindu, Egyptian, Chinese, Japanese and Siberian dances by natives of those countries, as well as by dancers of local reputation.

At Moiliili Ball Park TONIGHT, 8 p. m., and Friday, August 23rd
—CHAMPIONSHIP WRESTLING—
HADDOCK, *Champion of Pacific Fleet* vs. KINJU IKEDA *for* $2,000 purse
ADMISSION 50 CENTS, including war tax

WILLIAM BERNE
Champion of New York

BIJOU THEATER
SPECIAL WRESTLING MATCH
Monday Night Only—March 3rd
William BERNE vs. Louis ESPETVEDT
BEST TWO FALLS OUT OF THREE—TIME LIMIT ONE AND ONE-HALF HOURS

Also An Array of Preliminaries

PRICES: General Admission .... 50 Cents
Reserved Seats .... $1.00 and $1.50
Ringside Seats $2.00

—SEATS NOW ON SALE—
Box Office open from 10 a. m. to 9 p. m.
PHONE 3837

The Sporting Event of the Season at the
ARMORY TONIGHT, MARCH 15th
KINJO vs BERNE
Catch-As-Catch-Can—Two Falls Out of three
THREE FAST PRELIMINARIES BY
C. C. Williams vs Leo K. Poaha
and Two Other Wrestling Teams—to a Finish

DOORS OPEN 7:00 P. M.
REGULAR ADMISSION $1.00

PRELIMINARIES BEGIN AT 8:15 P. M.
RESERVED RINGSIDE SEATS $2.00

Advance Tickets on Sale at Gunst Cigar Store and Bijou Theater

Sailors and Soldiers in uniform, admission 50c. • • • • • • • • • • • • • Ladies Invited

1920

Kinjo Ikeda turned around and regained the Hawaiian championship with a two-straight fall win over Leo Poaha on February 7th.

On March 12th, a match between Louis Espetvedt and Alfred Naeole went to a 3-hour and 22-minute draw. Most of the time, they were on their feet, as Espetvedt did not want to go to the mat.

They had a rematch on April 16th, with Poaha winning two falls over Espetvedt.

On July 3rd, Kinjo Ikeda beat Leo Poaha in two straight falls.

On September 20th, Kinjo Ikeda beat Bennie Finn on dq. This may be the first dq finish I have noticed in Hawaii. Finn was from the USS New Mexico and claimed to be the champion of the US Navy. He was disqualified for continually ramming his arm into Ikeda's throat.

On September 25th, Louis Rego beat Senzan in two straight falls. Someone named Chillingworth was the promoter.

Kinjo Ikeda finished the year with December wins over Louis Rego and three wins over Aukai.

1920 Wrestling Ads & Pictures

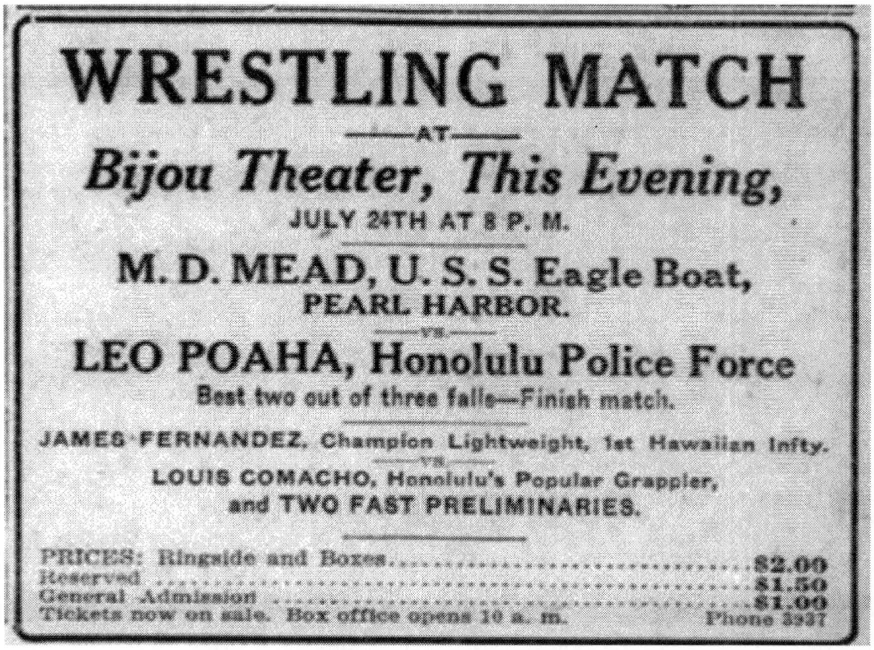

WRESTLING MATCH
—AT—
Bijou Theater, This Evening,
JULY 24TH AT 8 P. M.

M. D. MEAD, U. S. S. Eagle Boat,
PEARL HARBOR.
—vs.—
LEO POAHA, Honolulu Police Force
Best two out of three falls—Finish match.

JAMES FERNANDEZ, Champion Lightweight, 1st Hawaiian Infty.
—vs.—
LOUIS COMACHO, Honolulu's Popular Grappler,
and TWO FAST PRELIMINARIES.

PRICES: Ringside and Boxes.............................$2.00
Reserved $1.50
General Admission $1.00
Tickets now on sale. Box office opens 10 a. m.   Phone 3937

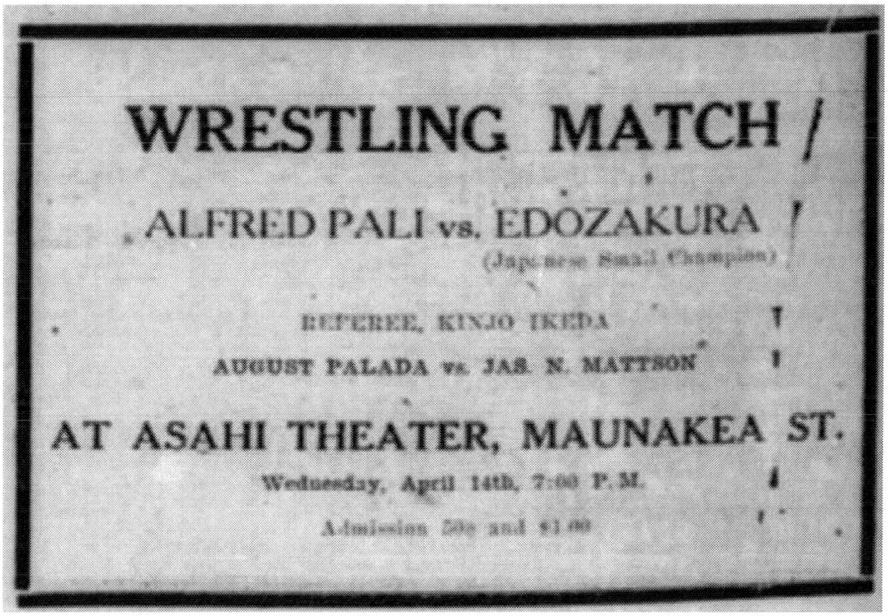

WRESTLING MATCH /

ALFRED PALI vs. EDOZAKURA
(Japanese Small Champion)

REFEREE, KINJO IKEDA

AUGUST PALADA vs. JAS. N. MATTSON

AT ASAHI THEATER, MAUNAKEA ST.

Wednesday, April 14th, 7:00 P. M.

Admission 50c and $1.00

Leo Poaha   Kinjo Ikeda   Doc Hess

Championship Wrestling Match TONIGHT at 7:30

J. F. BUTLER
Champion Wrestler of the U. S. N.,
Pacific Fleet

This event will positively be the greatest of
its kind ever staged in Hawaii

MAIN SHOW
Butler vs. Ikeda

PRELIMINARIES

J. FERNANDEZ — vs. —   AUGUST CAMACHO
JACOB AKIONA — vs. —   F. FERNANDEZ

AND OTHERS

ARMORY---Doors Open 6 o'clock

PRICES: Ringside . . . $2.00
Reserved . . . $1.50
General $1.00

REF. EDDIE SEARLE

KINJU IKEDA
Champion Wrestler of
the Hawaiian Islands

Don't Forget the Date TOMORROW NIGHT At the Armory

Tickets at Consoli Cigar Store and White Palace Billiard Parlor

CHAMPIONSHIP
Wrestling
Match

Kinjo Ikeda
Champion of Hawaii

vs

Bennie Finn
Champion—U. S. Navy

IN A FINISH BOUT
The Fastest Card of Preliminaries Ever Played

LEO POAHA vs. SAILOR BEDNER
Former Champion of Hawaii   U. S. S. New Mexico

LOUIS COMACHO vs. JIMMIE FERNANDEZ
and others.

N. G. Armory
Tomorrow Night

Kinjo Ikeda

Bennie Finn

BIJOU THEATER
Championship Wrestling Match
Saturday Night, July 3d, 8 o'clock

KINJU IKEDA, Champion of Hawaii
vs.
LEO POAHA, Former Champion

David Kaleikini (180 lbs.) of Honolulu, vs. Ed. Smith (180) of San Francisco.

James Fernandez vs. Louis Comacho, 150 lbs.

Wright Brothers, Bantamweight

PRICES....Ringside, $2.00; Reserved, $1.50; General Admission, $1.00
Tickets now on sale at Bijou Box Office. ———— Phone 3937

Goldie Rogers (above) was billed as the former the
former welterweight and middleweight champion
of San Francisco's Olympic Club

1921

Like today, Kinjo Ikeda had to have a real job for many wrestlers. He was a car salesman.

Maneul Barboza is Ikeda's manager and is getting ready to promote wrestling.

On March 12th, 1921, Sam Clapham came to Hawaii from Britain. Clapham will wrestle Kinjo Ikeda on March 19th as one of Barboza's first cards. On that card, the stipulation was that Clapham would beat Ikeda twice in 75 minutes. Clapham won a fall in 46 minutes. Clapham had won in a toehold when Ikeda began thrashing and accidentally kicked Clapham in the jaw. Ikeda quickly grabbed him in an armlock and got a pin. In this match, Ikeda suffered a torn ligament in his leg, which will keep him out of action for a while.

That rematch finally came on November 30th, and Clapham beat Ikeda when Ikeda was unable to continue. Ikeda did not return to the ring after losing the first fall. The card drew 7,000.

The last card of 1921 saw Sam Clapham beat Bull Montana in two straight falls. Clapham defended the Hawaiian title and captured the Pacific Coast title.

1921 Wrestling Ads & Pictures

Bull Montana (left) in an exhibition wrestling match with heavyweight boxing champion Jack Dempsey, as part of the training for his fight with Georges Carpentier.

TOMORROW NIGHT

"Bull" Montana vs. Sam Clapham

FAMOUS MOVIE STAR AND PACIFIC COAST CHAMPION — in a — THE BRITISH LIGHT-HEAVYWEIGHT CHAMPION

WRESTLING MATCH

For the Light-Heavyweight Title of the Pacific Coast—the main go on an extraordinary card offered at

MOILIILI FIELD 8:00 P.M. SHARP,

Tickets now on sale at the WHITE PALACE Billiard Parlors, YAMASHIRO HOTEL, and by J. A. Beaven—$1.10, $2.00, $3.00

THREE OTHER GOOD CONTESTS

CHAMPIONSHIP
Wrestling

Moiliili Field, Wednesday, Nov. 30
8 P. M.

Sam Clapham vs. Kinjo Ikeda
British Champion   Champion of Hawaii

Young Barbosa v. Joe Jannel—115 pounds.
Louis Camacho v. Young Gardini—145 pounds.
Lee K. Puahi v. Jack Lemberg—180 pounds.
Ex-Champion   Champion of
of Hawaii   Omaha, Neb.

Prices: General Admission 50c to bleachers; $1.10 to grand stand. Reserved Seats. Grand circle and corner chairs, $4.00. Ringside chairs: first row, $5.00; next five rows, $3.00.

Sam Clapham has arrived in Honolulu…he claims to be a Lord Lonsdale belt holder, emblematic of the British light-heavyweight title…Clapham will meet Hawaiian champ Kinjo Ikeda in the first of Manuel Barboza's wrestling cards on 3/19

1922

Professor S. Takahashi came to Hawaii with a big reputation. He was billed as the best Japanese wrestler in the world at the modern style of mat work. Takahashi had been wrestling on the mainland for several years. He was also billed as the champion jiu-jitsu wrestler, an army self-defense instructor, and an operator of two jiu-jitsu academies.

After that buildup, Sam Clapham beat Takahashi in two straight falls on March 4th, 1922. The promoter was J. Ashman Beaven.

They had a rematch in a mixed jiu-jitsu and catch as catch can, which Takahashi won and captured the Championship of Hawaii.

Another match was set up between Clapham and Takahashi, and again Takahashi won, but Clapham claimed he had been fouled by a finger thrust to the throat. This was held on 3/31 in Hilo.

On April 8th, Kayo Morris, a boxer, knocked out Takahashi. The bout only lasted a little over a minute. Takahashi claimed his poor eyesight was a hindrance in judging punches and reaction time.

Takahashi got some revenge on Kayo Morris in a mixed contest on May 6th in Honolulu.

July 1st saw Kinjo Ikeda dispute Professor S. Takahashi's claim as to who the best Japanese wrestler was. Ikeda beat Takahashi in two straight falls.

1922 Wrestling Ads & Pictures

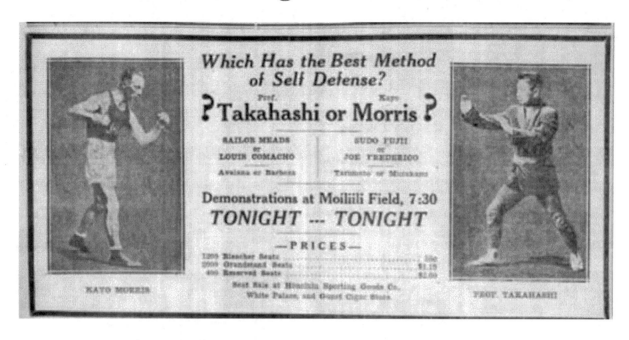

(L-R) Kayo Morris, promoter J. Ashman Beaven, Professor
S. Takahashi

Jiu-Jitsu Wrestling Match

FOR CHAMPIONSHIP OF HAWAII
THE BIGGEST MATCH OF THE SEASON

Tomorrow Night at 8 o'Clock

At Downtown Arena, next to Liberty Theater

Prof. S. Takahashi vs. Sam Clapham

TWO FAST PRELIMINARIES

Reserved seats now on sale after 10 o'clock—Downtown Arena, corner
Nuuanu and Pauahi streets; White Palace Billiard Parlor, M. A. Gunst, Honolulu Sporting Goods, Hawaiian Drug Company.

PRICES: $1.00, $2.00, $3.00 (Including Tax)

Feg Murray cartoon in the Los Angeles Times for a Taro Miyake/Walter Miller match;
6/30/22. The depiction of Charley Keppen predicting a "JAP-O-LAAC" finish

1923

Wrestling continued on through '22 and 1923 with numerous cards. Ted Thye, the promoter from the Northwest and Australia, wants to come in. It is a somewhat uninspiring time. Many of the matches are mixtures in style or primarily Jiu-Jitsu.

On May 11th, Professor Takahashi beat Leo Poaha and Alfred Caliu in a mixed handicap match.

Once again, at the end of the year, Ted Thye sent a challenge to wrestle Kinjo Ikeda in 1924. The article noted that wrestling has died down in the islands considerably. There has been a void since Sam Clapham, Bull Montana, and Prof Takahashi left the Islands.

1923 Wrestling Ads & Pictures

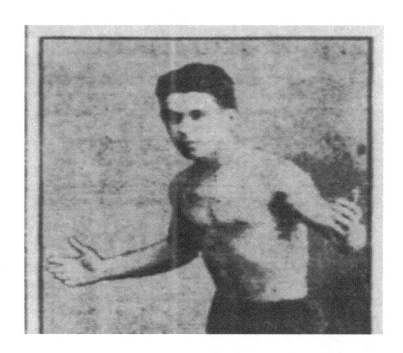

Sam Serpa – "The Honolulu Bear"

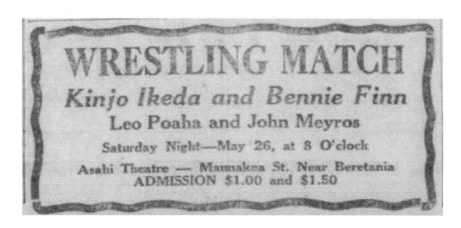

1924

Wrestler and boxer Tommy Dawson was arrested and charged with violation of the Volstead Act during alcohol raids. Dawson reportedly worked as a bartender in one of the "booze joints." Dawson was reported to have recently been hospitalized after attempting suicide.

I wondered if Prohibition hit Hawaii as it was not a state yet. Research told me that National Prohibition started earlier and lasted longer in Hawaii. It started in 1918 and was repealed in 1934.

There is little or no wrestling during 1924.

1925

March 15th was the first match in 1925, with Professor Tsutao Higami beating Pete Sauer in a jiu-jitsu match. J. Ashman Beaven was the promoter.

On June 20th, Professor Tsutao Higami drew Ad Santel in a mixed contest. Santel toured Hawaii and had a win over Hagami, and he went to a draw with Manuel "Kahuku" Rodrigues.

In November, Al Karasick passed through Honolulu, returning from Australia. Karasick would later become a significant figure in Hawaiian wrestling.

Manuel Rodrigues, an all-around athlete and strong man, was called 'The Jim Thorpe of Hawaii.' In 1930, in a terrible flood, Rodrigues was said to have single-handedly saved twenty-five people. He was said to have bested John Brown, a wrestling bear, somewhere along the line. Among other feats attributed to him were besting a horse in a tug-of-war. His son Abel Rodrigues also became a well-known local wrestler. He had two other sons who became professional baseball players. Rodrigues passed away in 1947.

HELD FOR THREATENING

H. K. Dawson, also known as Tommy Dawson and to the police as Tomi-Tomi, was arrested in the judiciary building this morning by Detective Kanjiro Noda and Officer John G. Burke after complaints had been made that he had threatened to blow up and otherwise annoy his wife's family.

Dawson was charged Friday with passing bad checks and was released pending trial. Earlier in the week while he was being held in the city jail he attempted "suicide" by drinking a bottle of ink. The police report that Dawson has made similar attempts in the past when he was under their care, but has never met with success.

NEW WRESTLING CHAMPION

Wayne ("Big") Munn, who last night defeated Ed ("Strangler") Lewis and won the heavyweight wrestling championship of the world. Munn started his career by being a boxer but found that he was easy pickings for smaller men.

1925 Wrestling Ads & Pictures

Tsutao Higami, Jujitsu Expert

CATCH-AS-CATCH-CAN AND JIU JITSU

Wrestling Matches

AT MOILIILI FIELD
2:30 p. m.—TOMORROW—2:30 p. m.
First Event
KID LEE vs. TARUMOTO at 118 lbs.
Catch-As-Catch-Can
Second Event
MURAKAMI vs. MENDONCA
at 125 lbs.
Catch-As-Catch-Can
Third Event
TANAKA vs. YAMASHIRO
at 130 lbs.
Jiu Jitsu Exhibition
Special Event
POAHA vs. NAEOLE (Heavyweights)
Catch-As-Catch-Can

MAIN EVENT

TSUTAO HIGAMI
Of Los Angeles, Cal.
— vs. —
PETE SAUER
Of Phoenix, Arizona
Finish Match—Jiu Jitsu—
Two-Out-Of-Three Falls

Grandstand and Ringside Bleachers $1.00
Ringside Chairs—Reserved $1.50
Box Office Open 10 A. M.   Phone 89746

THE PHOENIX WHIRLWIND

Pete Sauer (Ray Steele)   "Rubberman" Higami   Manuel "Kahuku" Rodrigues

READY TO MEET ANYBODY, ANY PLACE, ANY STYLE, SAYS SANTEL
SANTEL HAS WRESTLED MANY TIMES IN JAPAN AND TOSSED THEM AS FAST AS THEY CAME—
SANTEL HAS GREAT POWER IN HIS ARMS—AND KNOWS HOW TO USE IT—
AD IS DEVELOPING HIS 3 YEAR OLD SON FOR A TRAINING PARDNER.
AD SANTEL
LIGHT HEAVY WEIGHT CHAMPION OF THE WORLD—

1926

On June 9th, Stanislaus Zbyszko wrestled Frank Judson in an exhibition. They were on their way to Australia. Doc Adams was the promoter.

1927

On March 18th, Al Karasick stopped off in Honolulu and discussed holding a light heavyweight tournament with promoter J. Ashman Beaven in August. It appears that this tournament did not take place.

1928

Johnny Solomon is now advertised as the Hawaiian Champion.

1929

Very little is even mentioned in the year.

1930

J. Ashman Beaven hopes to start promoting wrestling at the Honolulu Stadium in the fall.

On July 1st and 2nd, Heishimo Ishiyama's troupe of Japanese women wrestlers appear in sumo wrestling matches. The show also featured musical and dancing performances. Kaname Kano is promoting the shows.

The advertisement says twenty-six women wrestlers are advertised.

1931

Wrestling is finally revived in May of 1931 with promoter J. Ashman Beaven. Jacques Manuel beat Harry Demetral by a decision on May 15th. These are two well-known wrestlers of the time. This card is billed as 1931 style. 1931 style meant they wrestled in rounds.

They returned two weeks later with Al Karasick beating Harry Demetral, who could not continue. These matches were held at Honolulu Stadium.

Joe Neves takes over as promoter, and I bet there is a story there. He had been promoting boxing at the Houston Arena in Honolulu.

On June 16th, Al Karasick beat Jacques Manuel. The referee for this match was Ed Raetch. This name is important because his name, listed as Ed Ratsch, comes up as the initial promoter in Hawaii. In Mark Hewitt's research, this is the first time his name has come up.

A great wrestler named The Man in the Black Mask has emerged in Hawaii. He main events the August 4th card and beat Toby Wallace. The top men of Al Karasick, Jacques Manuel, and Harry Demetral were not on this card. Without those wrestlers, the cards look a little lacking.

On August 11th, Al Karasick beat The Man in the Black Mask. The masked man was unmasked, and it was Tom Ray from Omaha, and he was said to be a Farmer Burns protégé.

By August 28th, Maurice Gomberg, an auto dealer, had taken over the wrestling promotion at Honolulu Stadium. Ed Raetch is listed as the matchmaker.

The only other thing known about Ed Raetch is that he did promoting in San Antonio in 1918. He had to have some connections because the cards improved from this point on. With that nod to him, Ed Ratsch is a name that is lost to history.

The main event on September 15th has Gus Sonnenberg, who has probably just lost a World title, beating Al Karasick. The attendance isn't listed, but the paper says this is the largest crowd ever to turn out to see a wrestling event in Hawaii.

On September 23rd, Sonnenberg beat Bull Montana on dq. Al Karasick and returning Taro Miyake are introduced to the crowd.

On 9/27, in Maui, Bull, Montana beat Tiny Heitsman, a substitute for Taro Miyake, who could not wrestle due to a boil outbreak.

Ahh, Yes, the old excuse of a boil outbreak. Warning! Do not Google 'boils'; please just take my word for it. I am sorry that I took one for the team on this one. I am glad Taro did not wrestle on this night. For God's sake, where is Kayfabe in this story?

On September 30th, Sonnenburg beat Karasick on decision.

On October 23rd, Taro Miyake beat Harry Demetral.

On November 6th, Al Karasick beat Taro Miyake, and in a top-notch semi-main event, Jacques Manuel beat Harry Demetral. The paper mentions that Miyake and Karasick are great showmen.

Cards stop at the end of November. Karasick is going back to the mainland. There is report of Kenneth Dixon getting ready to promote in January of 1932.

In June of 1931, Karasick underwent an eye operation. He had been suffering from eye problems for several months. It was reported he had been nearly blind for many of his matches prior to the operation.

With no proof at all, I feel we have entered the era of worked matches. We are ten years removed from the three-hour matches and the Jiu-Jitsu contests. In December of 1931, there was an article in the Honolulu Star-Bulletin titled Promoters Have Exhausted Dramatic Ideas. This was geared more to the National audience than the local Hawaiian scene.

PROMOTERS HAVE ABOUT EXHAUSTED DRAMATIC IDEAS

Edgren Writes That Wrestling Promoters Are On the Verge of Panic

By ROBERT EDGREN

Wrestling promoters all over the country are in a panic. Wrestling is showing signs of becoming a "flop."

Nothing could be more natural. Old time wrestling used to have an on the level contest once in a while, to keep up interest. A modern "wrestling match" is purely a circus performance, a carefully planned series of stunts, laughable or startling, with the "winner" of each fall scheduled in advance. It isn't a contest and it isn't on the level, except as a bit of entertainment. So, when the entertainment begins to lose novelty there's nothing left to draw the crowds. And the novelty has to wane.

Wrestlers can't get up new torture holds, new flying falls, new dives out of the ring, airplane spins, new funny complications like getting sore at the referee and rolling him in the resin, for each weekly show.

Drew Big Crowds

Big crowds have been going to wrestling shows for a couple of years or more. They paid at the gate, yelled, laughed and enjoyed themselves as long as there was some novelty to provide excitement. As a novelty it was hot stuff. But nobody pays to see the same show over and over again, with merely a change in the actors.

If there was some element of a contest even this freak wrestling might last a while longer. But by this time everybody knows it's all a show—no real contest at all. There isn't, at this time, a real wrestling champion. How could there be, without real contests?

Work Same Line

There are thousands of wrestlers, all working along the same line, trying to be original. The number of stunts that can be pulled in a wrestling match is rather limited. Of late some of the boys have tried to introduce such humorous novelties as kicking an opponent in the stomach, swinging punches at an opponent, missing and accidentally socking the referee, pretending to bite an opponent, etc. It just shows how hard up they are for ideas. And they have to put on new stuff or people won't pay to see them. It's a tough spot, lads.

Torture Holds

Frank Gotch was first to use a "torture hold" that had nothing to do with wrestling, the object of which always had been to put an opponent on his back. Gotch invented the "toe hold."

With it he wrenched an opponent's ankle until he quit. Gotch always seemed to think there was a fine bit of humor concealed somewhere in this performance. I once saw him wrestling a tall young German in Chicago. The German was no match for Frank as a wrestler, so to put a little pep into the match Frank sat on him, got his toe hold, and very slowly bent his ankle back until it was nearly broken.

The German wrestler, unable even to roll over on his back, screamed.

This was before the days of grunt and groan wrestling, and it was a real scream.

The crowd piled into the ring and pulled Gotch away. Frank got up and walked around, grinning. The German was carried out. I heard afterward his ankle was actually broken, and six months later he was still partly crippled.

The Headlock

After Gotch, Strangler Lewis developed his "head-lock," a mauling grip supposed to be very painful and to render an opponent so groggy that when Lewis was ready to let go he could easily flop the victim over on his shoulderblades. Papers were full of pictures of Lewis practicing his headlock on a wooden block, developing a grip that could dent a human skull like a watermelon.

Stecher had his "body scissors," locking his strong legs around an opponent's middle and putting on the squeeze until he gave up. Another torture hold.

Munn Starts New Era

But it was big Wayne Munn who revolutionized wrestling and made it what it is today. Knowing nothing of wrestling, he picked up Strangler Lewis and threw him over the ropes, giving him such a bump that he was through for the evening. They've all been chucking each other out of the ring ever since. It's a regular stunt.

For a long time people went to wrestling shows hoping to see some beefy behemoth dumped into somebody's lap at the ringside—which was a great laugh getter.

Then Sonnenberg came along with his flying tackle. He butted them out of the ring, or just for variety he missed and went head first through the ropes into somebody's lap himself. That was so entertaining that he was made champion.

Then came airplane spins—just a modernizing of the way Hackenschmidt threw Jenkins over 20 years ago—and new "torture holds," and tickling, and jiu jitsu nerve pressure, and one "doctor" wrestler is supposed to use hypnotism. And in the last wrestling show I saw the bout ended in a fight, and the referee disqualified one of the grapplers for slugging, and the grappler grabbed the referee and they wrestled for five minutes before the referee put the grappler down and

And the Rasslers Wonder Why This Town Doesn't Fall For Their Stuff

If You Want a Good Laugh, Read "The Lion of the Bronx" In the Satevepost; Mainland Crowds Getting Wise To Wrestling Racket; Why Spend Money When Zoo Free?

Rasslers who have been dropping in on Honolulu of late are complaining that somehow this town doesn't get excited over their presence. The fans aren't all het up over a wrestling "contest."

That's right. Sports fans down here have heard enough of the way the wrestling racket has been developed on the mainland to make them wary of these grunt-and-run "champions" who now want to show their stuff in this city.

Honolulu is a first class sporting town—full of red-blooded fans. But they want bona fide contests, real battles, whether it's the wrestling ring, the boxing ring, on the gridiron or on the baseball diamond.

Just imagine two teams of football players grunting and gyrating around a gridiron, sweating and shouting and making faces—and not really trying to beat each other! How long would football last under those conditions?

Or imagine a baseball game—to which money is charged—with the pitcher out there on the mound merely putting on a show—all his windup exaggerated, his pitches accompanied by grimaces and gestures; the batter taking healthy cuts at the ball but not really trying to drive out safe hits! Imagine two teams going through nine innings of motions and tossing away chances to score, merely to keep the score close!

How long would the great American games of football and baseball last under these conditions?

Wrestling is a good sport—when honestly conducted with honest competition—but the way it is being conducted on the mainland is no recommendation for anybody to fall for it in Honolulu. And mainland audiences, gypped too often, are now turning from the wrestling performances. The grass is getting short in mainland pastures—and is not as green as it was a couple of years ago.

Sport flourishes when it's "on the square." No sport built up on ballyhoo and bluff can survive—or should survive.

And the rassler who complains that Honolulu doesn't go in for wrestling in a big way is paying this town and the people of it a high compliment.

Honolulu isn't falling for the wrestling because of what Honolulu has heard of the wrestling racket on the mainland.

If you want to get a good laugh out of this whole wrestling racket, read in a recent issue of the Saturday Evening Post "The Lion of the Bronx." There a first class fiction writer who follows sports closely has told, in fiction form, how wrestling "contests" are carried on.

The rasslers who are coming to Honolulu in such numbers needn't complain if the fans of Honolulu won't put up money to see them clown about the ring. Why spend money on aboriginal antics when you can go to the zoo for nothing?

1931 Wrestling Ads & Pictures

EDUCATIONAL   (SOMETHING NEW)

JIU JITSU and WRESTLING

Sponsored by Burns Post No. 388 Veterans of Foreign Wars

ST. JAMES AUDITORIUM
Friday, Dec. 11
8:15 P. M.

MAIN BOUTS
PROF. TAKAHASHI
135 lb. Jiu Jitsu King and World Lightweight American Style
Champion.

— vs. —

"TUFFY" LEROY SCHMALFUS, 190 lbs., Merrill
"PEANUTS" REINHARD WIEMAN, Wausau
AL. JONAS, 198 lbs., Wausau
ERWIN WENDT, Wausau
"GORILLA" JOHNSON, 220 lbs., Michigan

Strong Man
Exhibition by
"Peanuts"
Wieman

Before the match Prof. Takahashi
will demonstrate nerve control by
forcing hatpins and knives through
his arms. Jiu Jitsu is the most
scientific method of self defense.
Ladies should see and know about
this system.

ADMISSION
50c and $1.00
Children Half Price.

Seats on Sale at Smitty's,
Jones' Cafe and Marathon
Billiard Hall.

ASSAULT!!
Spectacle of mayhem and manslaughter at Honolulu
Stadium Tomorrow Night, Sept. 23—8 o'clock—The
Great "Dynamite" Gus

SONNENBERG
vs.

"BULL" MONTANA
"Ingagi" of the Movies & Plug-Ugly
of the Wrestling World

Eight 10-Minute Rounds—1931 Style

A real fight, boys! Would you care to take
either man's place for just one round?

PRICES: 75c — $1 — $1.50 — $2
MORE THAN 2,000 COVERED GRANDSTAND SEATS

GRAND DOUBLE WINDUP
ALL ACTION WRESTLING CARD
STADIUM TONIGHT

8:00 O'CLOCK

JACQUES MANUEL **ALEX LUNDIN**

Portuguese Champion Bone Crushing Finn

vs. vs.

FIREMAN YAMASHITA **TINY HITESMAN**

Makiki Terror The Wrestling Gob

Also Jack Freitas vs. Johnny Potter

Jiu Jitsu Style

Kazuto Miura vs. Junichi Uyeda

Kiyoto Okada vs. Midori Yamashiro

TICKETS 50c-75c AND $1.00—ON SALE AT HONOLULU STADIUM DOWN-
TOWN OFFICE, 1112 BISHOP ST., UP TO 4 P. M. THIS AFTERNOON.
AT THE HONOLULU STADIUM FROM 4:30 ON.

 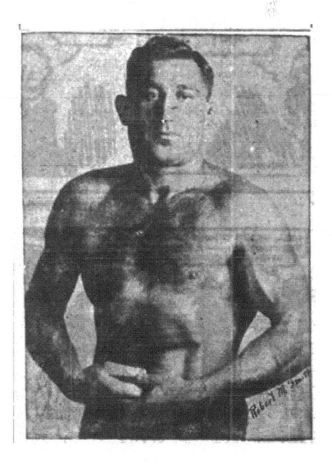

Tiny Hitesman (L) "Pride of the Navy" Jacques Manuel (R)

HARRY DEMETRAL

Joe Neves – Honolulu Promoter

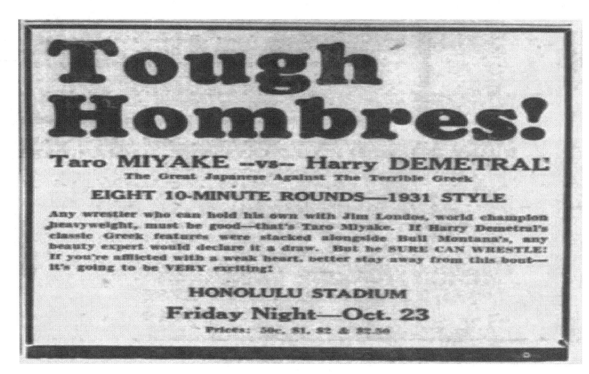

Tough Hombres!

Taro MIYAKE --vs-- Harry DEMETRAL
The Great Japanese Against The Terrible Greek

EIGHT 10-MINUTE ROUNDS—1931 STYLE

Any wrestler who can hold his own with Jim Londos, world champion heavyweight, must be good—that's Taro Miyake. If Harry Demetral's classic Greek features were stacked alongside Bull Montana's, any beauty expert would declare it a draw. But he SURE CAN WRESTLE! If you're afflicted with a weak heart, better stay away from this bout—it's going to be VERY exciting!

HONOLULU STADIUM
Friday Night—Oct. 23
Prices: 50c, $1, $2 & $2.50

136

THIS IS AL'S FAVORITE POSE, GUS!

This is the way Al Karasick, the Russian Lion, disposes of wrestlers who attempt to put headlocks or face chancerys on him when they are on their feet. Al sticks his head down, humps his shoulders and rears back on his heels, dumping the unfortunate grappler on his own head on the mat behind Al's feet. Nice trick, what?

1932

At the start of the year, Maurice Gomberg was nowhere to be found, and the yoyoing of promoters continued. Now, Joe Neeves and Kenneth Dix have teamed up. Their first show was on January 5th, 1932.

The main events were Wild Bill Beth beating Joe Ferguson and Ted Cox drawing with Herman Hellwig. The notes say that a number of the wrestlers were sent to Hawaii by Hutch Hutchinson of San Francisco.

Historian Rock Rims has this to say about Charles "Hutch" Hutchinson. He was from San Francisco and was a boxing manager before turning to boxing promoting in San Jose. Rims believes that Hutchinson had no connection to wrestling before coming to Hawaii, and certainly was not a booking agent. He may have presented himself in that manner to put him over.

The next match on January 12th saw Ted Cox beat Herman Hellwig.

On January 16th, Kenneth Dix resigned as matchmaker.

On January 26th, Tom Alley beat Paul Wilkins, and Harry Demetral beat Herman Hellwig. Hutch Hutchison was the referee for the main events.

Al Karasick was reported to be coming back to Hawaii.

Tom Alley had emerged as one of the top talents in Hawaii. He had wins over Paul Wilkins and Ted Cox. Then he beat them both in one night.

Alley then challenged Al Karasick to a $2500 challenge.

By February 19th, Tom Alley, Harry Demetral, and Paul Wilkins had all left Hawaii.

Gomberg restarts his promotions in August at Honolulu Stadium. A crew new to Hawaii features Joe Gardinier going to a draw with Cowboy Pete Axtman and Ray Lyness beating Reed Detton.

The following week, on 8/19, Ray Lyness beat Joe Gardinier on DQ, and Reed Detton went to a draw with Pete Axtman.

Maurice Gomberg hoped to restart in 1933. However, there was no wrestling until June of 1933, under Ed Ratsch's promotion.

1932 Wrestling Ads & Pictures

Tom Alley Offers Al Karasick $2,500 to Meet Him On the Mat

Tom Alley, recognized light heavyweight wrestling champion of the United States (and he has a belt to prove it), has issued a formal challenge to Al Karasick, the Russian Lion, who will arrive here next Thursday. He backs up his challenge with a check (certified) for $2,500 which he states will be turned over to Karasick if the Russian Lion can throw him, best two out of three falls in a local ring.

"I am not betting on myself, do not ask Karasick to post a similar check, and it is not a gambling proposition," says Alley, "but I know I can beat him and only want to get him to meet me in a local ring with a competent referee."

Alley has the money and tomorrow will post his forfeit at The ADVERTISER. He is sincere in this proposition and wants to prove all local wrestling fans that he can beat Karasick.

THE NEW SENSATIONAL 1932

Wrestling
TONITE!

JOE GARDINEER vs. PETE AXTMAN
RAY LYNESS vs. REED DETTON

Each bout, Six 10-Minute Rounds

And a hot prelim:

JACK FREITAS vs. SAILOR MINCE

Six 5-Minute Rounds

Rougher than football! Faster than boxing! A thrill
a minute! Anything short of mayhem goes!

Show Starts at 8 P. M.

LADIES INVITED FREE! (Pay tax only, if escorted by ticket-
holder.) Prices, ringside $1.10; general admission 55c. On
sale at Dimond-Hall's—or at Stadium after 5 p.m.

HONOLULU STADIUM

LET HIM COME, I'M READY

JOE GARDENIER
Welterweight wrestler from St. Louis, Mo., who meets Pete Axtman of
Great Falls, Montana, in one of the feature bouts on the Stadium pro-
gram tonight.—Al Williams photo

SEE THIS NEW 1932 STYLE WRESTLING

rough–fast punishing!

Battles of brute strength, stamina and skill that keep you tense with excitement every minute—make you sit on the edge of your seat and howl! Pick your favorites:

MAIN EVENT—Ray Lyness, who beat Detton last week, meets Joe Gardineer in six 10-minute rnds.

SEMI-FINAL—Reed Detton of Salt Lake City vs. Pete Axtman, the cowboy; five 10-minute rnds.

SPECIAL EVENT — Fireman Yamashita, local boy, meets Tarzan Knight, newcomer from New York; five 5-minute rnds.

OPENER—Jack Freitas of Kaimuki vs. Sailor LaPorte of the Navy; four 5-minute rnds.

Tomorrow Night

Ladies Free (pay tax only) if escorted by ticket holder.

HONOLULU STADIUM

Ringside Reserved............$1.10;   General Admission.........55c

TICKETS ON SALE AT DIMOND-HALL'S

1933

Wrestling does indeed return on June 6th, 1933. The main event is Wildcat Pete beating Reed Detton.

The next card a week later sees Wildcat Pete beat Des Anderson.

On June 20th, Pete beats Joe Kirk.

On July 4th, Norman "Rusty" Westcoatt debuted, beating Ted Shores. Westcoatt is a protégé of Wildcat Pete. The paper seemed to indicate he was rather green.

On July 16th, a sportswriter stated that Honolulu seems to have taken to wrestling like a duck takes to water. So, this incarnation is proving to be popular.

July 17th has Sammy Kohen beat Wildcat Pete. Billy Weidner beats Des Anderson. With Kohen and Widner, there are a couple of wrestlers who have had experience in other places.

On August 17th, Tetsuo Rubberman Higami arrives in Honolulu. Higami is referred to as the greatest Japanese in the rasslin' business today.

On August 22nd, Higami beats Wildcat Pete. The following week Higami gets a win over Billy Weidner.

On September 12th, Rubberman Higami beat Sammy Kohen, and Wildcat Pete beat Johnny Fraga. This card drew over 5,000 people. This is billed as the largest crowd in Hawaiian history for Pro Wrestling.

We thought we had heard the last of Joe Neves, but no. He draws 400 people on September 22nd using heavyweights. Wong Bock Cheung beat Herman Swede Olson, and Everett Kobbons drew Walter Sirois. They return on October 5th, and Wong Bock Cheung again beats Swede Olsen, but this time by DQ.

Switching back to the Ed Ratsch promotion, Johnny Nemanic goes to a draw with Billy Weidner on October 10th.

On October 19th, it was announced that Wildcat Pete was leaving Hawaii as his mother was ill in Eugene, Oregon.

On October 24th, Rubberman Higami beats Billy Weidner. Baseball player Babe Ruth was in attendance on this card. He had been barnstorming Hawaii, playing in various all-star games.

On October 31st, Rubberman Higami beat Johnny Nemanic. Big Ed Ratsch resigned as the Civic Auditorium promoter. The venue owner, Manuel Calhau, will start promoting.

As of November 7th, Manuel Calhau emerges as the only promoter in Hawaii as Joe Neves has disappeared and Ratsch has resigned.

On December 26th, the main event saw Joe Gunther beat Billy Spendlove and Bobby Bylund beat Des Anderson.

1933 Wrestling Ads & Pictures

Promoter Big Ed Ratsch standing behind recent arrivals Joe Gunther (left) and Billy Spendlove

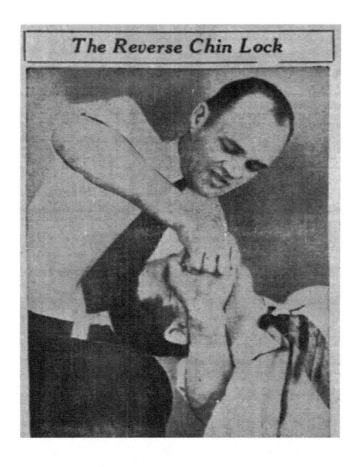

The Reverse Chin Lock

Wildcat Pete demonstrating reverse chin lock

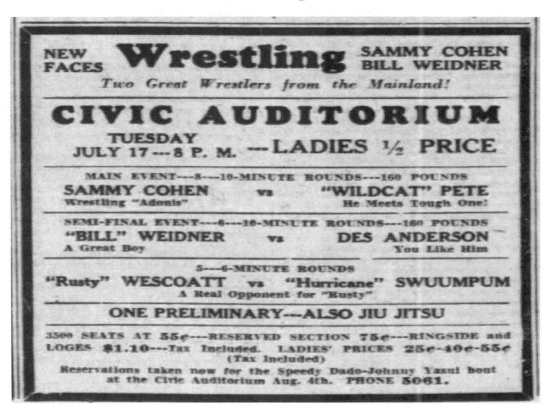

WRESTLING—Houston Arena
THURSDAY, OCT. 12, 1933, 8 P. M.

HEAVYWEIGHT   MAIN EVENT   6 10-MINUTE ROUNDS

Wong Bock Cheung   vs.   Ernie Andrade
Sensational Chinese   One of Hawaii's Best

HEAVYWEIGHT   SEMI-FINAL   6 10-MINUTE ROUNDS

Everett Kibbons   vs.   Young Aguinaldo
Oklahoma A. & M. Star   Filipino Sensation

HEAVYWEIGHT   SPECIAL   5 10-MINUTE ROUNDS

J. L. Solomon   vs.   "Kahuku" Rodrigues
Former Cop   Former Detective
A Real Crowd Pleaser   Hawaii's Strong Man

WELTERWEIGHT   PRELIMINARY   4 5-MINUTE ROUNDS

Marion Freitas   vs.   Jackie Freitas
Punchbowl Whirlwind   Kapahulu Cowboy

PRICES: Ringside **75c**   General Admission **40c**   Children **25c**
Ladies, accompanied by an escort, TAX ONLY
Tickets on sale now at the Hawaiian Drug, Bethel and Hotel Sts.
Phone 3316 for reservations or at the Houston Arena Box Office
PHONE 8477

"BULL" TOYAMA

Wrestling Card Civic -- Auditorium
TUESDAY, NOVEMBER 28 · · · 8 P. M.

MAIN EVENT—8 10-Minute Rounds

"RUBBERMAN" HIGAMI   vs.   JOE GUNTHER

SEMI-FINAL—6 10-Minute Rounds

SAMMY KOHEN   vs.   JOHNNY NEMANIC

SPECIAL EVENT—6 5-Minute Rounds

"BULL" TOYAMA   vs.   JOE KIRK

OPENING BOUT—4 5-Minute Rounds

BILL WEIDNER   vs.   "SWEDE" OLSEN

NO ADVANCE IN PRICES — LADIES HALF PRICE

3,500 Seats at **55c** — Reserved Section **75c** — Ringside and
Loges **$1.10**—Tax Included—Ladies Half Price—Phone 5061

1934

On January 9th, Johnny Nemanic beat Tetsuo "Rubberman" Higami. This was Higami's first loss since coming to Hawaii in August 1933.

On January 11th, Big Ed Ratsch announced he would again start promoting light heavyweight wrestling at Honolulu Stadium.

On January 15th, Joe Carroll Marsh of Seattle, who handles the affairs of all the middleweight wrestlers appearing in the Civic Auditorium, will be coming to Honolulu at the invitation of promoter Manuel Calhau. Marsh will be bringing Gust Johnson, who is reported to be the 2nd best middleweight in the United States.

Over the rest of January, Tetsuo Higami collects wins over Bill Weidner, Sammy Kohen, Bobby Bylund, and Joe Gunther.

On February 6th, Higami beat Johnny Nemanic to gain revenge on his only loss. Gust Johnson and Herb Parks were introduced to the crowd.

February 13th saw Gust Johnson beat Billy Spendlove and Herb Parks beat Hugh Adams.

On March 6th, Tetsuo Higami beat Herb Parks, giving Parks his first Hawaiian loss.

Higami and Parks had a rematch on March 13th, with Park's Canadian Light-Heavyweight title on the line. This match went to a draw.

On March 20th, Higami beat Parks and was awarded the Canadian title.

On April 9th, Al Karasick arrives in Honolulu ready to appear for a match for Ed Ratsch's promotion. There is talk about matching up Rubberman Higami and Karasick even though they work for rival promotions.

April 16th is the first show of the year for Ed Ratsch at Honolulu Stadium. The main event has Al Karasick beat Danny Winters, and Wong Bock Cheung beat Jack King in the semi-main event.

Karasick went on a tear, beating Jack King and Rusty Westcoatt.

In the Westcoatt match on April 21st, Karasick refused to break a Boston Crab hold, which left Westcoatt injured. Karasick started brawling with the referee. Then he finally screamed to the crowd, "Bring all the Filipinos into the ring, and I will throw 'em all. I am Russian and proud of it."

On April 28th, Gust Johnson challenged Al Karasick with a side bet for charity. This is interesting because they do wrestlers for rival promotions.

Karasick accepted the challenge and promised to throw Johnson, Bobby Bylund, Bobby Samson, and Rubberman Higami on the same night.

There seem to be a lot of promos on Karasick and Johnson's match, with Ratsch claiming Johnson must first prove himself.

On May 2nd, there was an announcement that Manuel Calhau is bringing back Joe Carroll Marsh to run wrestling while Calhau wants to concentrate on boxing.

May 12th saw Tetsuo Higami beat Herb Parks in another battle between these two; this match was in Kauai.

Joe Parelli makes his debut on May 22nd, beating Herb Parks. Parelli claims to be the World Middleweight Champ.

Parelli gets another win on May 29th, beating Bobby Bylund.

On May 31st, Jack Manuel upsets Al Karasick. This night is for a Junior Police Benefit, and the show draws 5,000.

On June 14th, Karasick beat Jack Manuel to get his win back.

On June 19th, Joe Parelli went to a draw with Gust Johnson.

On June 28th, Walter Achiu is in town visiting his parents. Achiu had played pro football and was now wrestling.

Jack Reynolds, who was the World Welterweight champion, and Lord Lansdowne arrived in Hawaii. They will be appearing for Calhau and Marsh at the Civic Auditorium.

On July 10th, Joe Parelli beat Tetsuo Higami by decision in a tremendous match. Lord Lansdowne beat Gorilla Cassu on decision.

On July 17th, Joe Parelli beat Gust Johnson, and Lord Lansdowne beat Herb Parks.

July 31st saw Gust Johnson beat Joe Parelli and Jack Reynolds beat Mike Caddock.

On August 7th, Tetsuo Higami beat Joe Parelli.

On August 14th, Jack Reynolds beat Higami in a non-title match.

This promotion is doing a great job rotating Joe Parelli, Gust Johnson, Higami, Jack Reynolds, Herb Parks, and Lord Lansdowne to have interesting matchups.

On September 1st, Joe Carroll Marsh left Hawaii.

On September 2nd, Walter Achiu commented that he had refused to wrestle while the Civic Auditorium was under Marsh's control. Achiu claimed that Marsh had demanded a percentage out of Achiu's purse. With Marsh out of the picture, Manuel Calhau plans to book Achiu on upcoming cards.

On September 11th, the card was full of wrestlers who had been in main events. Jack Reynolds beat Lord Lansdowne, Steve Nenoff beat Joe Parelli, and King Tut drew Herb Parks. Gust Johnson was to wrestle Jack Manuel, but Manuel backed out of the match. Manuel said that he would appear for Big Ed Ratsch soon.

On September 16th, Joe Marsh reportedly instructed all the wrestlers under his management to return to Seattle. Joe Parelli, Jack Reynolds, and Steve Nenoff have all left. Gust Johnson remains behind to briefly look after Marsh's interests.

On September 18th, Walter Achiu debuted and beat Herb Parks, and Tetsu Higami beat Lord Lansdowne.

On September 21st, Manuel Calhau announced he was no longer associated with Joe Marsh and would now be working with Texas Promoter Josh McIntosh to book wrestlers. Calhau said that Marsh demanded 10% of every gate and 10% of the purse of every wrestler appearing. Marsh later denied that he had ever extracted 10% from the payoffs of the wrestlers.

On September 24th, Ed Ratsch announced he would be the matchmaker for the Pan Pacific Athletic Club. He would be holding matches at the Honolulu Stadium. The group is financed by a group of Japanese businessmen.

The debut card for Honolulu Stadium finally took place on October 1st. The main event saw Shinichi Shikuma beat Jack Manuel in a jiu-jitsu contest. This was Shikuma's pro wrestling debut. Tetsuo Higami drew with Rocky Brooks.

They returned a week later, and Shikuma beat Rocky Brooks, and Tetsuo Higami beat Lord Lansdown.

On October 9th, the Civic Auditorium group had Don Hill beat Reed Detton and Tiger Lou Miller, upsetting Walter Achiu. This group seemed to have had to totally redo their rooster.

On October 15th at the Stadium, Shinichi Shikuma beat Jack Manuel in a catch-as-catch-can match, and Tetsuo Higami beat Mike Golden.

On November 8th, one of the biggest names comes to Hawaii in Dangerous Danny McShain, and he beats Don Hill on his debut.

Joe Marsh is still sending his point of view to the sports editor of the Honolulu Advertiser and is working to get back into Hawaii. Marsh had been a barnstormer with Farmer Burns and Frank Gotch. In 1909, he was arrested and convicted as a sports gambling con man and served a year in Leavenworth. He died in 1952 at 84 years of age.

On November 20th, a big match saw Danny McShain beat Walter Achiu. One thing I will mention about the year as a whole is that it seems like there were a lot of matchups and expected matchups that did not occur. I think both promotions left money on the table during the year.

On December 4th at the Civic, Tommy Cowboy Heinz beat Danny McShain, and Jack Curtis beat Walter Achiu.

Towards the end of December, McShain and Tommy Heinze returned to the mainland.

A giant card was scheduled for December 27th with Gus Sonnenberg to meet Tony Felice. The card had to be postponed due to heavy wind damage to the stadium's canvas covering.

1934 Wrestling Ads & Pictures

Joe Marsh (top left) with his crew in Honolulu, 1934; (l-r standing)
Jack Reynolds, "Rubberman" Higami, Lord Lansdowne,
(l-r kneeling) Johnny Nemanic, King Tut.

Wrestling Card -- Civic Auditorium
TONIGHT—8 O'CLOCK

MAIN EVENT—8 10-Minute Rounds
"Rubberman" HIGAMI   vs.   BOBBY BYLAND

SEMI-FINAL --- 6 10-Minute Rounds
COWBOY ADAMS   vs.   BOB CUMMINGS

SPECIAL — 6 5-Minute Rounds
BULL TOYAMA   vs.   BILLY BARTON

OPENER — 4 5-Minute Rounds
CARL MARTIN   vs.   BILLY SPENDLOVE

NEW ADMISSION PRICES FOR LADIES — DUE TO TAX
General Admission.........................Gents—55c, Ladies—30c
Reserved Section.........................Gents—75c, Ladies—50c
Ringside and Loges.........................Gents—$1.10, Ladies—60c
Tax included—Phone 5061 for reservations

Rival Attractions for Rival Wrestling Shows

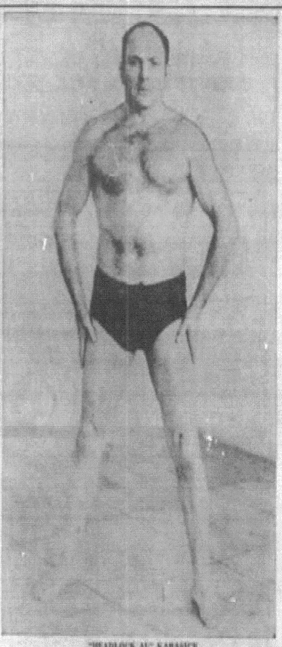

桶上菖雄

"PROFESSOR" HIGAMI
Who meets Gus Johnson in main bout at Civic Auditorium Tuesday night.

"HEADLOCK AL" KARASICK
Features opening card of heavyweights tonight in Honolulu Stadium. His opponent will be Donor Winters.

RATSCH OF STADIUM ACCEPTS CHALLENGE OF GUST JOHNSON

Honolulu, Hawaii,
April 30, 1934.

Red McQueen, The Advertiser:

It is very interesting to sit on the side lines and listen to all this controversy about the challenge of Gust Johnson, who has posted $250 with The Advertiser, and is willing to meet Al Karasick.

I believe that Johnson, as challenger, is a little out of order in specifying where the match will be held. The challenged always dictates the terms, weight, referee, place, etc., and I am afraid it will have to be so in this case.

In checking up Johnson's record of his wrestling matches since he arrived in Honolulu, I can't say that it is very impressive, as the majority of his matches were special events, and semi-finals. His defeat of Higami and lesser middleweights, is nothing to boast of when you stop to consider that Johnson is a light-heavyweight.

I would be only too glad to accommodate Johnson with a match with Karasick, providing of course, that he can prove his ability to beat the lesser lights than Karasick at the Honolulu Stadium, and work himself up to the main event, and the match with Al Karasick. One defeat, of course, will put him out of the running. These conditions are only fair to the public, the challenged and the promoter.

If Johnson has the ability, and I am told (as I do not know him) that he is a very fine chap and a wonderful wrestler, he should in no time prove that he is entitled to this match with Karasick.

Negotiations have been started to have Mr. Karasick remain here for an indefinite period, or until the time that Mr. Johnson can be accommodated. This is final.

Yours,

EDWARD A. RATSCH.

Gust Johnson Challenges Al Karasick To Match At the Civic Auditorium

TO GENTLEMEN "AL" KARASICK:

I have seen in the local papers that "Al" Karasick has challenged to wrestle Higami. I don't see why he wants to wrestle Higami when I have already defeated Higami.

Although Karasick weighs 200 pounds, I am willing to give him a weight advantage of 40 pounds, and I will wrestle him two best out of three falls at the Civic Auditorium.

I will place $250 with any one sports writer as may be designated, a like amount to be placed by Karasick. Should I fail to win over Karasick, my $250 goes to him. In the event that I win a decision over Karasick, I will donate $250 of the joint purses to any form of local charity as may be designated by one of our local sports reporters.

GUST JOHNSON.

Gust Johnson

Manuel Calhau, Civic Auditorium owner

Calhau welcomes Joe Parelli to Hawaii

Rubberman Higami with
Junior Championship Belt

Joe Carrol Marsh

Shunichi Shikuma

Wrestling Card -- Civic Auditorium
TONIGHT—8 o'clock

FIVE BOUTS —— DOUBLE MAIN EVENT
WALTER "SNEEZE" ACHIEU vs. TIGER LOU MILLER
DON HILL vs. REED DETTON
Eight—Ten-Minute Rounds

SPECIAL ATTRACTION—"BATTLE ROYAL"
Six men in the ring at one time. First two losers wrestle opening bout. Next two losers wrestle in the second preliminary. Last two men in the ring wrestle in the special bout. The wrestlers are: Marine Brown, Jack Freitas, Curley Freedman, Marian Freitas, Augie Ornellas and Charles T. Hamp of Schofield Barracks. First time in Honolulu. Don't miss it. Royal battles are huge successes in the mainland. No advance in prices.

General Admission	Gents 55c	Ladies 30c
Reserved Section	Gents 75c	Ladies 50c
Ringside and Loges	Gents $1.10	Ladies 60c

Tax Included—Phone 5061 for reservations.

Danny McShain   Ref Ernie Andrade   Tommy Cowboy Heinz

Mr. and Mrs. Jack Reynolds arrive in Hawaii

How Pachyderms Looked In Opening Show

Close to 3,000 saw Ed Raisch's first card at the Stadium Monday night. Here are some of the highlights of the card. The impressions are the work of Les Grimes, Australian grappling star, who showed in one of the feature bouts of the card. Versatile people, some of these grapplers.

How Rasslers Looked at Schofield

"—retaliated by messing up the indignant Tetsura's face."

"—spluttering involved, oriental invectives."

SOME RINGSIDE IMPRESSIONS

HIGAMI-KOHEN MATCH.

SCHOFIELD BOWL January 27, 1934.

"—grabbed a Kohen ankle—"

"—sat down hard on Sammy's midriff."

1935

The first big card of the year took place on January 4th, 1935. This was the card that was postponed from late 1934. Gus Sonnenberg beat Tony Felice and Tetsuo Higami beat Einar Lindberg.

Ed Ratsch was the matchmaker for the Pan Pacific Athletic Club. He got a court order to attach the gate receipts, claiming he was owed back salary. Not surprisingly, Ed Ratsch was fired from his position as matchmaker.

On January 9th, The Pan Pacific Athletic Club and Manuel Calhau reached an agreement to hold cards at the Civic Auditorium. The politics going on in Hawaii at this time must have been crazy.

On January 11th Gus Sonnenberg beat Freddie "Do " Meyer, and Shinichi Shikuma beat Tony Felice.

On January 15th, Gus Sonnenberg beat Shinichi Shikuma, who could not continue.

Gus Sonnenberg beat Tetsuo Higami on January 22nd.

On January 29th, Gus Sonnenberg went to a draw with Oki Shikina. Sonnenberg is going through the roster.

Einar Lindberg passed away on January 29th due to pneumonia. He was only 28 years old. Very sad, but how do you get pneumonia in Hawaii.

February 12th's card was a benefit for the widow of Einar Lindberg to cover hospital and funeral expenses. Tetsuo Higami beat Lou Mueller in the main event.

February 13th Advertiser pulls back the curtain on the state of wrestling in Hawaii. The Civic Auditorium wrestling shows have been suffering. The Auditorium is in financial arrears and has been put on auction several times, but no one has bid the asking price of $65,000. Promoter Calhau has combined promotions on the Island to help get all the wrestling fans on the Island rather than divide them.

Man Mountain Dean is rumored to be coming to Hawaii.

April 23rd saw Wildcat Pete beat Tetsuo Higami for the Junior Middleweight title.

Ed Ratsch has announced that he has financial backing to purchase the venue or build a new one. Ratsch is credited for introducing "modern pro wrestling" to Hawaii.

Toots Estes beat Wildcat Pete for the Junior Middleweight title. The title changed hands twice in two weeks.

May 18th has Joe Marsh back in Honolulu on his honeymoon. Rumors have he and Ed Ratsch are teaming up to run a promotion. Matches through late spring and early summer are not very appealing.

On July 20th, Tetsuo Higami beat Ack Meyers in a junior heavyweight title match. This card drew 3000 people at the Stadium.

On August 5th, Shinichi Shikuma beat Man Mountain Dean in a mixed-style match; Tetsuo Higami beat The Masked Marvels. This show drew 7,500 and was promoted by Tetsuo Higami.

Don Sugai debuted on August 13th, beating Wildcat Pete, and Fred Kimball beat Norman Mack in the main event.

Tetsuo Higami and Shunichi Shikuma have left Hawaii for a tour of the mainland, and their absences are showing.

Joe Gunther goes on a winning streak, beating Don Sugai, Wildcat Pete, Jack Morgan, and Tug Wilson.

On November 16th, Manuel Calhau and four wrestlers were involved in a car accident. Calhau passed away 4 days later. Wildcat Pete, Don Carlos Vigario, and Don Sugai were others in the car. Calhau was born in the Azores in 1978 and immigrated to Hawaii with his family at a young age. Calhau's son Ernest will continue the promotion.

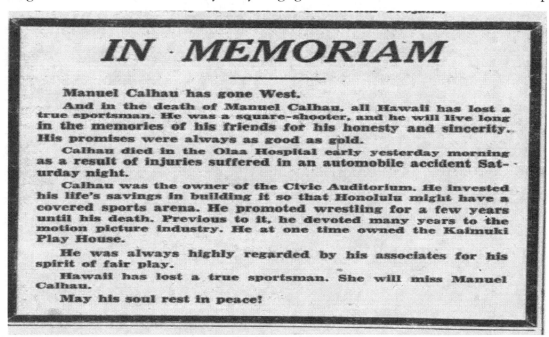

IN · MEMORIAM

Manuel Calhau has gone West.

And in the death of Manuel Calhau, all Hawaii has lost a true sportsman. He was a square-shooter, and he will live long in the memories of his friends for his honesty and sincerity. His promises were always as good as gold.

Calhau died in the Olaa Hospital early yesterday morning as a result of injuries suffered in an automobile accident Saturday night.

Calhau was the owner of the Civic Auditorium. He invested his life's savings in building it so that Honolulu might have a covered sports arena. He promoted wrestling for a few years until his death. Previous to it, he devoted many years to the motion picture industry. He at one time owned the Kaimuki Play House.

He was always highly regarded by his associates for his spirit of fair play.

Hawaii has lost a true sportsman. She will miss Manuel Calhau.

May his soul rest in peace!

1935 Wrestling Ads & Pictures

Shinichi Shikuma and Tetsuo Rubberman Higami

Man Mountain Dean promo

Dean puts Higami in a headlock

WRESTLING
HONOLULU STADIUM
Monday, August 5---8 P.M.

Main Event---Heavyweight Bout

"Man Mountain" DEAN

217 POUNDS

— vs —

Prof. SHIKUMA

NO TIME LIMIT — 2 out of 3 Falls

Semi-final---8 10-Minute Rounds

"Rubberman" Higami vs. John Williams

And 2 other Bouts

ADMISSION............CHILDREN 25c — GENERAL 35c
RESERVED SEATS............75c & $1.10 (Tax Included)
PHONE 2400 FOR RESERVATIONS
SPONSORED by EDWARD K. YUASA

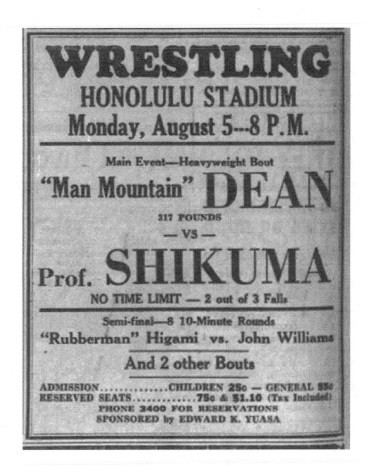

WALTER KING
New Referee

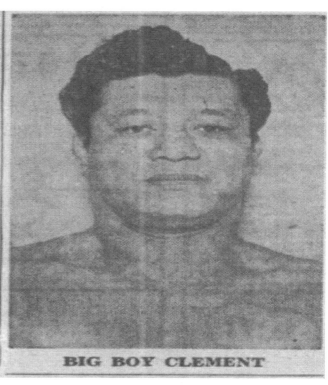

BIG BOY CLEMENT

HEADLINERS ON WRESTLING CARD

Left to right: "Professor" Higami, Shikuma, Gus Sonnenberg who will appear in Civic Auditorium next Tuesday night. (Advertiser Photo)

Wrestling at Civic Auditorium

TONIGHT AT 8 O'CLOCK

MAIN EVENT—8 10-Minute Rounds

Joe Gunther
-- vs --
Oki Shikina

SEMI-FINAL—6 10-Minute Rounds

DON SUGAI vs. "BULL" TOYAMA

SPECIAL—6 5-Minute Rounds

Jack Morgan vs. Gust Steele

OPENER—4 5-Minute Rounds

Charles Keene vs. Big Boy Clement

Bring your "Calhau Fund Drive" receipts and exchange them for wrestling tickets at the main ticket office window.

For Reservations Call 5061

Wrestling at Civic Auditorium

Tuesday, Nov. 19, 8 P.M.

MAIN EVENT—8 10-Minute Rounds

Jack Morgan
-- vs --
Don Carlos Vigario

Semi-Final 6 10-Minute Rounds

Don   Wildcat
Sugai   vs.   Pete

Special—6 5-Minute Rounds

Oki   Chas.
Shikina   vs.   Keene

Opener—4 5-Minute Rounds

Benny   Curley
Kim   vs.   Freedman

Bring your "Calhau Fund Drive" receipts and exchange them for wrestling tickets at the main ticket office window.

FOR RESERVATIONS call 5061

1936

1936 opens with a main event of Joe Gunther beating Don Sugai on January 7th.

Following the show, a publicity stunt starts. Wrestler Jack Morgan is shackled to the steering wheel of a car, A Willys "77" sedan, and begins a 7-day endurance test. He is to drive continuously for seven days and nights, ending the stunt by immediately engaging in a wrestling match the following week.

Why do I love this so much? The practical person in me says, "That is not safe for Mr. Morgan or anyone he might pass on the following Thursday."

The person in me who loves wrestling says, "I want Mr. Morgan to succeed and get out there the following week and wrestle." (Let's see what happens). Fans are invited along to ride with Morgan for portions of his ride. Brilliant! Fan participation!

Well, the 14th comes along, and the notes say that Morgan ended his driving stunt, entered the ring, and beat Charlie Keene.

Also, on the 14th, Wildcat Pete returned from the auto accident that killed Manuel Calhau and beat Dick Craddock.

Jack Morgan took part in a boxing card on February 21st and was knocked out in the first round by Pietro Georgi.

February 25th saw Sheik Mar Allah beat Jack Terry, and Joe Gunther beat Wildcat Pete.

The following week, on March 3rd, Sheik Mar Allah beat Joe Gunther.

On March 26th, the aforementioned Pietro Georgi is seeking to meet a wrestler in a mixed match. Wildcat Pete is considering the challenge.

April 21st has Sheik Mar Allah beat Al Szasz. Another boxer, Tony Roccaforte, on this card, challenged Jack Terry to a mixed match. They actually brawled a little to work towards an actual match.

On May 5th, Jack Terry beat Terrible Tony Roccaforte in a challenge contest.

Terry knocked him down with a hard right and then secured a hammerlock and forced him to concede.

On May 21st, Virgil Hamlin, a promoter from Portland, Oregon, comes to Hawaii with Sam Leathers, Bob Kruse, and Babe Zaharias; they are on their way to New Zealand.

On May 26th, Bob Kruse beat Sam Leathers in a heavyweight contest. Also Sheik Mar Allah beat Al Szasz.

June 2nd saw Pancho Aguirre beat Sheik Mar Allah, giving the Sheik his first loss in Hawaii. Aguirre is able to repeat his victory the following week.

On June 16th, Kimon Kudo made his Hawaiian debut and beat Sheik Mar Allah. Kudo goes on a winning streak, beating Wildcat Pete, Al Szasz, Jack Terry, and Pancho Aguire.

There is a report on June 27th that Lou Daro, a leading promoter on the Pacific Coast, asserted that Man Mountain Dean deliberately "stunk up" his appearance last year in Honolulu on orders from an unnamed party who wanted to "kill the game" on the Island. Virgil Hamlin had told the same story.

Daro reportedly was planning on establishing a Japan-Hawaii-mainland pro wrestling circuit. Interesting that plans were already being made to utilize Japan as a territory even though there is no known official pro wrestling there. Obviously, real life will intercede in these plans.

July 21st, Al Karasick arrives in Honolulu.

On the July 21st card, Totem Anderson is married in the ring to Vera Vance. Anderson suffered a loss to Jack Terry. (Couldn't they give him a win on his wedding day!)

On July 28th, a significant match saw Al Karasick go to a draw with Kimon Kudo.

This was Ernest Calhau's last card. Al Karasick is taking over the Civic Auditorium in association with Ted Thye and Virgil Hamlin. They will bring heavyweights to Hawaii.

August 4th has Karasick beating Kimon Kudo and wins the opportunity to meet Jumping Joe Savoldi.

On August 6th, M.K. Choo and Al Karasick make arrangements to partner to book cards around the Hawaiian Islands.

August 12th has Joe Savoldi beating Al Karasick, and Vic Christy comes in to beat Harry Kent.

August 18th has Ed Don George beating Joe Savoldi. Karasick's influence is being seen immediately with higher-profile wrestlers.

September 15th has Strangler Lewis beating Ed Don George, Vic Christy beating Reb Russell, and Sam Leathers going to a draw with Babe Small.

The Lewis/George match was described as very scientific, with no leapfrog stunts, exaggerated facial grimaces, and no slapstick comedy. Just technical holds of the profession.

September 22nd was Strangler Lewis beating Vic Christy.

September 29th had Chief Chewacki beating Vic Christy. There was reportedly a riot, and twenty fans came into the ring to attack Chewacki. Police cleared the ring, and the match continued.

On October 14th, Rusty Westcoatt had acute appendicitis and was rushed to the hospital for an operation.

November 11th saw the debut of Chief Thunderbird. He got a win over Jack Holland; the following week, he beat Harry Demetral and then Holland again.

The Red Scorpion debuted on December 15th, beating Tommy Mead. Scorpion had a masked manager who signaled him throughout the match using playing cards. Scorpion was Jack McCarthy.

Scorpion finishes out the year beating Jack Holland and Rusty Westcoatt.

1936 Wrestling Ads & Pictures

RASSLERS MIX TUESDAY NIGHT

An all-star rassling card will be staged tomorrow night at the Civic auditorium by Ernest Calhau.

Headlining the performance will be a return tussle between Don Sugai, sturdy Japanese grappler from Portland, Ore., and Noel Franklin, a fine showman who also hails from the northwest.

Sugai beat Franklin with his famous dropkick in their initial meeting.

The semi-final brings Joe Gunther against Isao (Bull) Toyama, local boy who is rapidly developing into a convincing showman. Jack Morgan, the tough one who is on a seven day automobile driving endurance run, will get out of the car to take on Charlie Keene in the special. Morgan had no trouble subduing Keene last week, but may encounter difficulty this time.

The opening affair will see Wildcat Pete's return to action following the automobile accident that took Manuel Calhau's life. He tackles Dick Craddock.

Wrestling at Civic Auditorium

TONIGHT
8 P. M.

MAIN EVENT—8 10-Minute Rounds

NOEL FRANKLIN
-- vs --
JOE GUNTHER

SEMI-FINAL—6 10-Minute Rounds

"WILDCAT" PETE vs. DON SUGAI

SPECIAL—6 5-Minute Rounds

Totem   Dick
ANDERSON   vs.   CRADDOCK

OPENER—4 5-MINUTE ROUNDS

Charles   "Bulldog"
KEENE   vs.   AYRESMAN

Bring your "Calhau Fund Drive" receipts and exchange them for wrestling tickets at the main ticket office window.

FOR RESERVATIONS call 5061

163

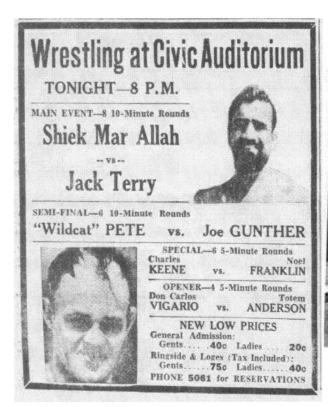

Joe Savolodi

Chief Thunderbird

Al Szaz

164

The Red Scorpion

Introducing, ladies and gentlemen, the latest addition to Al Karasick's wrestling troupe at the Civic Auditorium, a 245-pound gentleman who is known as the Red Scorpion and who has recently been taking the Mainland by storm. He's another masked marvel and meets Tom Meade in the main event of next Tuesday's card.

Battle Royal Is Arranged For Tuesday

Wrestling Extravaganza to Feature Red Scorpion At Auditorium

AL KARASICK, wrestling impresario, announced yesterday that he will put on a great wrestling extravaganza next Tuesday night in the Civic Auditorium.

He has arranged a battle royal that promises to be one of the wildest and most hectic and sensational ever staged locally.

In addition to this gruelling battle royal, Karasick will introduce a new comer to local fans. He is the Red Scorpion who will meet Tommy Mead in the main event. The Scorpion arrived from the Mainland on the Niagara and reports are that he is a tough hombre.

Mead will have his hands full.

The battle royal will be worth the price of admission in itself. Arjan Singh, the powerful Hindu, who arrived several weeks ago from India enroute to San Francisco, Harry "Baldy" Demetral, Jack Holland, Chief Thunderbird, Rusty Westcoatt, and Dr. Dan O. McKenzie will be the principals in the battle.

The first two wrestlers to be eliminated will clash over four five-minute rounds, the second two dragged out will meet in a bout over five rounds of six minutes each, while the last two will come to grips for a 45-minute-time-limit bout, with victory going to the one gaining two falls out of three.

In the opener, Walter King meets Totem Anderson.

AL KARASICK presents

WRESTLING

DEC. 29—TUES.
CIVIC AUDITORIUM

DOUBLE MAIN EVENT—1-HOUR TIME LIMIT EACH

RED SCORPION vs. RUSTY WESCOATT
HARRY DEMETRAL vs. CHIEF THUNDERBOLT

Ladies, Res., **60¢**; Children, **30¢**; Gen. Adm., **55¢**
Reserved **$1.10** — Tax Inc. — Phone **2002**

1937

The Red Scorpion is the hot new wrestler as the new year starts. He goes to a draw with Arjan Singh on January 5th.

On January 12th, Chief Thunderbird beat Red Scorpion, who had to unmask and proved to be Jack McCarthy.

Al Karasick always seems to have rotating top wrestlers and thus compelling main events each week.

February 9th has Chief Thunderbird beat Rusty Westcoatt.

AL KARASICK PRESENTS
WRESTLING TONIGHT
JAN. 5th, 8 P. M. — CIVIC AUDITORIUM

DOUBLE MAIN EVENT
1 hour time limit—best 2 out of 3
Red Scorpion vs. Arjan Singh

Second Main Event
45 minutes—best 2 out of 3
Chief Thunderbird vs. Dan O. McKENZIE

Semi-final—30 minutes—1 fall
Harry "Baldy" Demetral vs. Tommy Mead

Special—20 Minutes—1 fall
Jack Holland vs. Rusty Wescoatt

Referees:
Big Boy Clement & Bull Campbell

Admission: RESERVED, Gents, $1.10; Ladies, 60c. GENERAL ADM., 55c; Children under 12, 30c (Tax Included). Phone 2002.

February 16th, Arjan Singh beat Chief Thunderbird. This show drew 2,000.

On March 18th, a note in the paper mentions that Al Karasick's wife and daughter have arrived in Honolulu.

On March 30th, some new wrestlers debut. Tony Felice beat Hal Rumberg, Bob Kruse beat Jack Forsgren dq.

On April 6th, Arjan Singh went to a draw with Bob Kruse.

April 13th saw a partial riot as Bob Kruse beat Tony Felice on DQ. The ref, spectators, ushers, and police officers all became involved.

April 20th saw Ted King Kong Cox's debut, beating Jack Forsgren.

April 27th saw Ted Cox beat Tony Felice, and Big Boy Naumu beat Harry Demetral. Naumu was the Hawaiian Islands Sumo champ. He was trained by Al Karasick.

June 15th saw Chief Little Wolf beat Big Boy Naumu.

Strangler Lewis returned to Hawaii on June 29th to beat Ray Richards.

Oki Shikina (pictured right) returns to the Islands and starts racking up wins over Dan McKenzie, Ernie Petersen, Herb Freeman, Tommy Mead, and Vic Christy.

October 27th saw wrestling at Schofield Barracks and drew 11,000. The main event was Jack Gacek beating Ernie Petersen and Vic Christy beating Dan McKenzie on DQ.

On November 16th, Oki Shikina beat Rusty Westcoatt for the Hawaiian Championship in a tournament. Shikina is the first title holder, and the history of the title extends over 40 years.

Oki Shikina defended the Hawaiian title, beating Jack Gacek on December 14th. This card drew 3,000.

1937 Wrestling Ads & Pictures

Ed "Strangler" Lewis arrives in Hawaii
with new wife Bobby Lee

Count Fouche (top) & Ray Richards (bottom)
are Lewis opponents

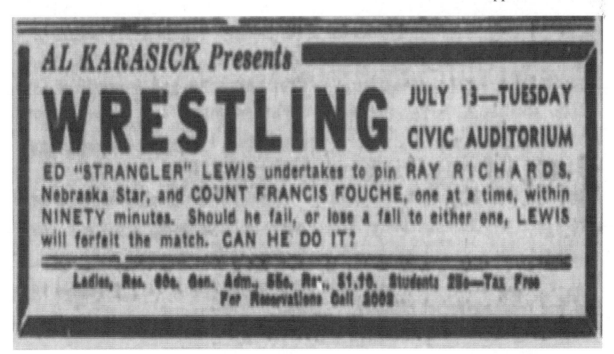

AL KARASICK Presents

WRESTLING

JULY 13—TUESDAY
CIVIC AUDITORIUM

ED "STRANGLER" LEWIS undertakes to pin RAY RICHARDS,
Nebraska Star, and COUNT FRANCIS FOUCHE, one at a time, within
NINETY minutes. Should he fail, or lose a fall to either one, LEWIS
will forfeit the match. CAN HE DO IT?

Ladies, Res. 60c. Gen. Adm., 55c. Rr., $1.10. Students 20c—Tax Free
For Reservations Call 2003

Fight Riot Casualties

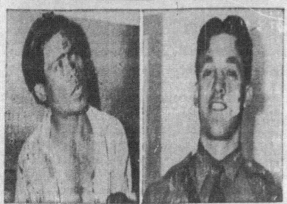

Upper photo, from left, Olimpio Nunes, 29, of 661 Iwilei Rd.; Venancio Rosario, 32, of Ewa, and Geriaco Domingo, 29, of Waipahu, injured in riot at Civic auditorium Friday night. Lower left, Donisio Labis, 21, of Aiea. Daniel Toomey, lower right, one of seven officers injured.—Star-Bulletin photos.

CHARGES FILED AGAINST 8 FOR RIOT AT FIGHTS

Police Officer In Hospital With Broken Jaw; Two Firemen Blamed

OAKLAND, Cal., May 1. (AP)— Four persons were undergoing treatment today for painful wounds received in a melee at wrestling matches last night featuring an unidentified "Red Phantom." Spectators said the Phantom, who was aided by his manager, angered the fans, who opened a barrage of whisky bottles. Hundreds participated in the fighting before police restored order.

Nine men were charged today with affray as the result of a riot at the Civic auditorium which sent 13 persons to the hospital Friday night during the boxing matches.

Police Officer William Centeio is confined to Queen's hospital with a broken jaw and cut lips received in the melee. An X-ray was taken today to determine if he has a fractured skull. Officer Centeio, who played football for McKinley high school and the Town team, was conscious today and reported "slightly improved."

Bond was set at $100 each for these men, charged with affray:

Rufo Oujon, 29, of 116 Kamanuwai lane; Venancio Rosario, 32, of Ewa; Donisio Labis, 21, of Aiea; Pedro Abrina, 26, of 445 Buckle lane; Olimpio Nunes, 29, of 661 Iwilei Rd.; Timotio Molena, 27, of Waialua; Vilrnls Blas, 25, of Waimanalo; Vidal Sabala, 37, of 1274-B Hall St. and Geriaco Domingo, 29, of Waipahu.

When the riot broke out just before the final bout on the boxing program, the air was filled with flying chairs, bottles and pipes. Blame for starting the disturbance that led to the riot was placed by police on two firemen, Jonah Wise and William Blaisdell.

Fans Start To Boo

Dissatisfied with the decision in the semifinal bout in which Anton Rego was given the nod over Dommy Ganzon of Manila, the Filipino

(Continued on Page 5, Col. 3)

EIGHT CHARGED IN FIGHT RIOT

(Continued from Page 1) fans began booing. At this point, police reports state, Wise was seen to grab a Filipino.

Another Filipino shoved Wise. Then Blaisdell, police reports say, went to the aid of Wise. The fight exploded into a riot.

Filipinos hurled chairs into the pit where the ringside seats were, threw pop bottles, and tore up pipe railing to swing as clubs. Chairs were broken and used as cudgels.

Crowd Downs Officer

Two uniformed policemen and about six offduty officers in plain clothes were among the 4,500 spectators. Officer Centeio tried to grab a man to arrest him. Fifteen others descended on him. A chair sailed through the air, struck the officer's cheek. He went down.

A riot call was sent to the police station. Meanwhile the officers managed to quiet the rioters. Suddenly the fighting broke out again.

Whenever an officer tried to arrest a fighter, 20 others would rush the officer. Only with the arrival of reinforcements with long riot clubs were police able to begin the work of clearing the auditorium.

Many Hit By Chairs

Scores of persons were struck by flying chairs but only a few went to the Emergency hospital for treatment. Six officers, besides Officer Centeio, who were injured were:

Reginald Field, black eye; John Dickson, deep scalp wound; Daniel Toomey, cheek gash; Walter Liu, bruised and cut forehead; Arthur C. Lum, scraped finger; Andre Padaken, scrapes and bruises to his leg. All were treated and discharged.

Maximo Sevilla, 52, local Filipino journalist, of 532 S. Queen St. was treated for a gash on his forehead, received when a chair struck him. John Thomas, 21, of Pearl Harbor was cut on the head and chin.

Four of the fans who were charged received cuts to their heads from police clubs. They were Nunes, Rosario, Labis and Domingo.

They Will Meet for Hawaiian Wrestling Title

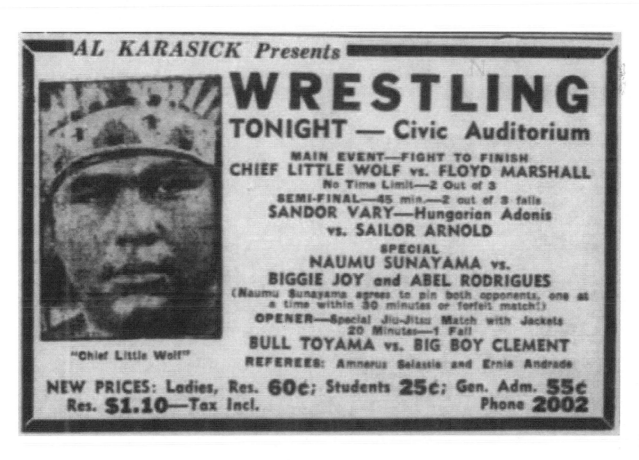

169

Big Boy Naumu   Al Karasick

The Red Scorpion was red hot. The following were all front page stories.

Al Karasick's Fan Mail

Honolulu, T.H.

Dear Mr Karasick:

Will you please enlighten me and a group of my friends as to the identity of the enclosed picture. I say it is Harry Demetral but the others say it is either you or the Red Scorpion's manager.

Please answer.

A wrestling fan.

P.S.

I forgot to put down my name and address.

The above letter and picture was sent to Al Karasick, wrestling promoter at the Civic Auditorium, through the mail last Thursday afternoon. Instead of feeling hurt, Al thought it was a good laugh—a swell publicity gag. But it's a different story with Handsome Harry Demetral—he's furious. Karasick, who is the only one who has seen the Red Scorpion's manager, wouldn't say whether there was any resemblance between the two.

'Tiser Cameraman Sneaks Up On Scorpion

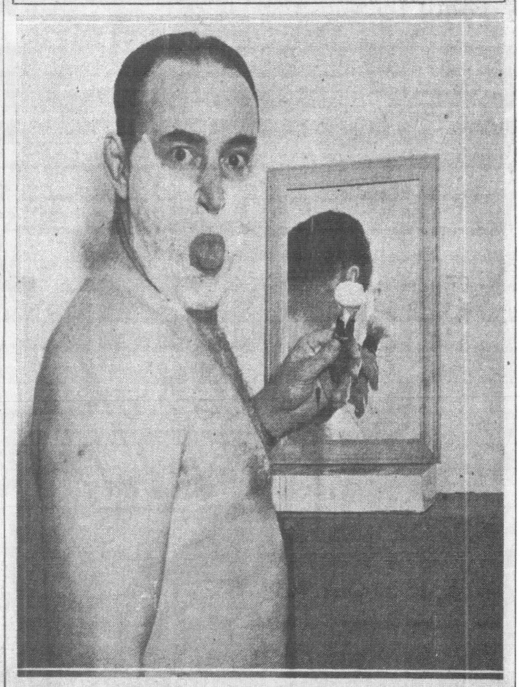

For more than a month, the identity of a wrestler, variously known as the Red Scorpion, Masked Marvel, Hooded Hoodlum et cetera, because he makes his appearance both in public and in the ring garbed in a red outfit that conceals his features, has had the Island grappling public in a quandary. Allan Campbell, Advertiser staff photographer, has a wager that he will get a shot of the mysterious one, unmasked. Campbell snuck up on the Scorpion as he disrobed to shave yesterday morning, but all he got for his efforts was a lusty Bronx—as the picture shows. The Scorpion's identity may be disclosed when he faces the Indian Chief Thunderbird next Tuesday night.

Red Scorpion Unmasked By Indian Chief

Mysterious One Beaten, Turns Out To Be Jack McCarthy

THE Red Scorpion can finally come out for a little air. Hidden under a red mask ever since his arrival while he proceeded to take the measure of the outstanding grapplers doing business at Al Karasick's wrestling emporium, the mysterious one was finally beaten last night by Chief Thunderbird, following which his features were disclosed to a jubilant audience for the first time. He turned out to be Jack McCarthy of Spencer, Iowa.

After 43 minutes and 47 seconds of brutal grappling, the Chief finally forced the Scorpion into submission with his famous Indian death lock. This was the only fall of the match, which was scheduled to travel 60 minutes.

Inasmuch as he was thrown but once instead of the required two out of three falls, the Scorpion refused at first to be unmasked. He was finally forced back into the ring for the unveiling ceremonies.

RUSTY WINS

In the first half of the double-main event, Rusty Wescoatt won from Dr. Dan O. McKenzie. McKenzie secured the first fall with a body press, 16 minutes and 36 seconds after the opening bell. Rusty came back eight minutes and 41 seconds later to even the score with a back body press. McKenzie was unable to resume hostilities after this fall and the bout was awarded to Wescoatt.

Jack Holland won the special event from Harry Demetral when the latter was disqualified for unnecessary roughness after 10 minutes of milling.

HINDU TRIUMPHS

ArJan Singh took but seven and a half minutes to dispose of Tommy Mead in the opening melee. A leg clip and a body press brought victory to the Hindu.

Walter King and Big Boy Clement acted as referees with Tony Faria as timer.

A crowd estimated at 2,000 witnessed the card.

Ex-Red Scorpion Peaceful Citizen When Not In Ring

By LOUI LEONG HOP

It's a tough life being a rassling villain but it's twice tougher to be a masked wrestler.

Where nobody loves a "villain," the hooded mystery man of the mat is in constant danger of physical injury of the infuriated fans and also he must always be on the alert to keep from being identified.

This bit of preliminary, of course, introduces one Jack McCarthy, who has been entertaining local groan and grunt followers for nearly a month, masquerading as the big bad Red Scorpion.

When Chief Thunderbird exposed him the other night, it was the second time in his long and strange career that McCarthy was unmasked.

"When you have been wrestling on and off as a masked marvel under one name or another for 19 years," McCarthy chuckled knowingly, "you sort of get used to things. But even then you can't be too careful. People will go to the limit to find out things for themselves.

"Take my trip to your fair Honolulu, for instance. I had to use an assumed name in booking passage here. I used the name of Don Nolan. This was the same name I put on my door of the place I'm living.

"People scanned the steamer arrival lists, followed me to my room, watched me come out, looked over my shoulder when I'm sorting out the mail to see which one I claim and slip into my pocket.

"Well, it's funny, I had things prearranged so that the letters would come under one name. Then I would carefully leave the envelopes around so the inquiring eyes could see.

"That's the reason why I think Promoter Al Karasick received over 50 of the 700 letters he received identifying me as positively Don Nolan.

"Unintentionally, I threw a terrific scare into two girls the first two days I came to Honolulu. Al and I were going to a theater for an appearance. On our way I spotted something interesting to look at in a shoe store. Of course, I had my costume on.

"We edged to the show window which at the moment had occupied the attention of two young women. When they turned around and saw me they let out a terrific yell. I would have been arrested if I

JACK McCARTHY
Red Scorpion in the flesh
(Peaceful citizen outside ring)

hadn't secured approval of your police department to wear the mask."

In civilian clothes one would little suspect McCarthy a wrestler. Just a peaceful citizen minding his own business. He wears spectacles, has a pleasing smile and talks softly. He has practically no scars to show for his 1,400 mat bouts.

His right ear, which is slightly cauliflowered, may be the give away of his profession.

McCarthy is 36 years of age . . . weighs 235 pounds . . . comes from a sturdy Irish family . . . being born and raised at Spencer, Iowa.

His father knew Frank Gotch, the peerless champion, and taught Jack wrestling before he was knee high to a grasshopper.

Started out in life as a mining prospector . . . found wrestling for money on the side more profitable than prospecting . . . now has given up the latter although the urge sometimes has caused him to go back to it until he runs out of dough and he has to return to rassling . . . Has met some of the best heavyweights in the business, including Joe Stecher, Earl Caddock, Charlie Hansen and Martin Pestana, the Dusek brothers and others of top-notch ability and showmanship.

1938

1938 started with Matros Kirilenko as the hot new star on the islands. He beats Jack Gacek on January 4th and goes to a draw with Hawaiian Champion Oki Shikina on January 11th.

Shikina seems to be ducking a rematch with Kirilenko and is threatened to be suspended if he doesn't agree to a rematch by February 15th.

On February 15th, Brother Jonathan debuts and goes to a draw with Matros Kirilenkio. Brother Jonathan is the father of Don Leo Jonathan.

On February 22nd Gus Sonnenberg beats Count Otto Von Buesing.

Al Karasick announces there is a rematch of Kirilenko and Shikina forthcoming.

That rematch comes on March 1st, and Shikina gets the win. Also, on the card, Gus Sonnenberg beats Harry Demetral, and Brother Jonathan goes to a draw with Count Otto Von Buesing. The card draws 4,000. Another notch in the Karasick bag of tricks makes the fans wait for what they want.

On March 8th Martos Kirilenko beat Gus Sonnenberg on DQ. The paper calls this a huge upset. It must mean they had different thoughts on a DQ finish and still see it as a legitimate win.

Shikina goes to a draw with Sonnenberg on March 15th.

On March 29th, Sonnenberg beat Kirilenko in only his 2nd loss since coming to Hawaii.

On April 5th, Brother Jonathan beat Gus Sonnenberg.

On April 12th, Arjan Singh returns and beats Sonnenberg, who is going through a rough patch.

On April 20th, there was an announcement that World Champion Bronko Nagurski would be coming to Hawaii. However, he will not be defending his title.

Matros Kirilenko "The Terrible Cossack" (above)   Brother Jonathan (below)

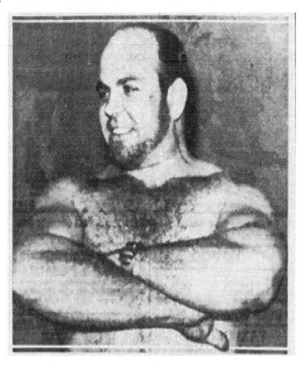

The following week, there were continued negotiations to try to get at least one title match from Nagurski. They had disagreements on who the ref would be. They finally agreed to use Don McDonald from California.

On May 3rd, Bronko Nagurski beat Brother Jonathan in a non-title match.

May 10th saw Bronko Nagurski defeat Oki Shikina in a title contest. A clip from the newspaper showed the substantial size difference. The card drew 6,000. Another tip of the cap to Al Karasick for laying out the story that Nagurski would not defend the title. Shikina did take a fall with a Japanese reverse arm bar. They reported that was the first fall Nagurski had lost since he became champ. He was quoted as saying that it was his toughest match; he had never had to face Ju-jitsu before and did not want to meet it again.

LONG HOPS • WITH LOUI

They're taking rassling out of wrestling.

For years the grappling fanatics have been demanding that the boys (and girls, too) quit their hippodroming, clowning and amateur acting and produce some honest to goodness wrestling.

Now they're going to get it.

The above information was offered your Long Hops the other day by Don McDonald, Long Beach stock and bonds broker, who is here to referee world's champeen Bronko Nagurski's matches.

BRONKO NAGURSKI (BACK) (World's Wrestling Champion)	
Neck	19
Chest	46
Biceps	17
Waist	37
Thigh	26½
Calf	18
Ankle	10½
Forearm	13½
Wrist	8
Height	6-2
Weight	222
Age	29
Reach	73½

OKI SHIKINA (FRONT) (Hawaiian Champ and Challenger)	
Neck	19
Chest	46
Biceps	16½
Waist	37
Thigh	25½
Calf	17
Ankle	9½
Forearm	13
Wrist	7½
Height	5-8
Weight	218
Age	30
Reach	69

On May 31st, Vincent Lopez beat Gus Sonnenberg. Also, Arjan Singh went to a no contest with Brother Jonathan, and Big Boy Naumu went to a draw with Lee Henning. Karasick began billing Henning under the name Joe Palooka as fans thought he resembled the cartoon character.

Joe Tonti, a protégé of Jimmy Londos, comes to Hawaii. On June 23rd, he performed a strength stunt by pulling a ton and a half milk truck down the street with his teeth while walking on his hands. Karasick had a $25 bet with him.

On July 12th, Andre Adoree (Al Baffert) beat Bobby Roberts. Adoree is a protégé of Stanislaus Zbyszko. Baffert was a movie stuntman and actor. Also, on this car, Pat McKay beat Lee Henning in a no-rules, no-referee match. They both had their fists taped.

On August 23rd, Al Pereira beat Andre Adoree in a tournament final to see who would meet Bronko Nagurski in the future. Pereira had attacked the referee after the first fall, and Karasick came to finish reffing duties.

Nagurski sent word that he wouldn't meet Pereira under any circumstances despite his agreement to meet the tournament winner.

Nagurski, in fact, canceled his trip to Hawaii. Pereira started calling himself the champion of the world.

On September 3rd, it was announced that Oki Shikina was in a financial dispute with promoter Al Karasick. Shikina had not made an appearance in Hawaii since June 14th.

On September 29th, they still had not reached an agreement. Karasick said that the title would become vacant if Shikina didn't make arrangements by October 4th.

Rudy LaDitzi had come to Hawaii and started to make an impression. On the October 4th card, Rudy LaDitzi beat Billy Hanson. The paper had a big ad featuring LaDitzi calling him the World's Most Colorful Wrestler and title claimant.

On October 11th, Billy Hanson beats Rudy LaDitzi, and Oki Shikina returns to action and beats Jack Gacek.

Oki Shikina defends the Hawaiian title, beating Billy Hanson on October 18th. The card draws 5,000.

On October 22nd, former boxing champ Max Baer came to Hawaii for a series of fights. He beat Andre Adoree in a boxing exhibition in Hilo. Max Baer again faced Adoree on October 31st in Kauai.

Leo Numa came to Hawaii and beat Rudy LaDitzi on his debut on November 1st.

Laditzi beat Oki Shikina on DQ on November 8th in a non-title match. That's a surprising booking since Numa beat LaDitzi the week before.

November 29th saw Dick Raines beat Leo Numa in the main event. Why do I picture that as a knock-down affair?

Rudy LaDitzi beat Oki Shikina by decision. However, the title does not change hands; Dick Raines beat Jack Holland. These matches took place on December 6th.

December 21st saw Dean Detton draw Dick Raines.

The last card of the year saw Dean Detton beat Rudy LaDitzi and Dick Raines beat Swede Olsen, and he was awarded the "rough house championship cup." Why do I think of something like the Hardcore title of the 30's? Lofty Bloomfield was also on this card, beating Jack Gacek.

Brother Jonathan is coming in 1939 to challenge Bloomfield.

1938 Wrestling Ads & Pictures

Bunny Martin   Leonardo "Young Bolo" Garcia   Duke Kahanamoku

They're Primed For Title Wrestling Bout

Oki Shikina, Hawaiian champion (center), and Bronko Nagurski, heavyweight wrestling champion of the world (right), expressed themselves as being in condition for their match Tuesday evening at the Auditorium. Nagurski's title will be at stake. In the above picture, Leo Fleiding, former Navy star halfback, is measuring Shikina's chest which is 46 inches. Nagurski has the same measurements.

Gus Sonnenberg locks up Count Von Buesing

Max Baer (below L)   (below R) Baer & brothers Ancil Hoffman (C) and Buddy (R) arrive in Hawaii.

Vincent Lopez body slams Armand Emanuel

HOOMALIMALI
"Kid 'em along"
By RED McQUEEN

THE GREAT NAGURSKI'S FINALLY HERE

Bronko Nagurski, heavyweight wrestling champion of the world and the greatest fullback of all time, moved into town yesterday for a series of wrestling matches at the Civic Auditorium. He makes his debut tonight meeting the super-dreadnaught of Al Karasick's stable, the bewhiskered Brother Jonathan.

Karasick tried for months to get Nagurski here and succeeded only after guaranteeing him $2,500 and transportation for three performances. This seems like a lot of sugar but I can't see where Al has anything to worry about. Honolulu grappling enthusiasts will surely flock to see the Nag, considered the greatest athlete since Jim Thorpe.

Nagurski gained the world's wrestling title in Minneapolis on June 29, 1937 by beating Dean Detton. Up to the time no one had considered him much of a grappler. However, he had appeared in 259 bouts and had learned the rudiments of the grappling game from Tony Stetcher, whose brother Joe was twice champion, and several other veterans before meeting Detton.

1939

Dick Raines beat Lofty Bloomfield on DQ on the first card of 1939. There is also a battle royal, and Rudy LaDitzi beats Bunny Martin in the royal finale on January 3rd.

On January 17th, Oki Shikina beat Dean Detton and defended the Hawaiian title. Brother Jonathan went to a draw with Dick Raines. The card drew 4,000.

Dean Detton won the Hawaiian title, beating Oki Shikina on January 24th.

Detton defended the Hawaiian title, going to a draw with Lofty Bloomfield on January 31st. Danny Dusek also debuted, beating Jack Gacek.

Dettons title reign did not last long, as Dick Raines won the Hawaiian title on February 7th. Also, Oki Shikina beat Lee Henning, and Brother Jonathan went to a draw with Danny Dusek.

Lofty Blomfield of New Zealand, British Empire Heavyweight Champion

There was an announcement on February 13th that World Champ Jimmy Londos would appear in Hawaii. Hawaiian crowds saw a series of elimination matches to see who would face Londos.

On February 28th Dick Raines beat Oki Shikina on DQ.

On March 7th, Lofty Bloomfield beat Dick Raines, and Oki Shikina beat Danny Dusek in top matches. The Bloomfield match was a non-title win.

Jim Londos was expected to arrive in Honolulu on April 3rd and had agreed to two matches. He was traveling with promoter Lou Daro.

Oki Shikina beat Dick Raines in the finals of the elimination to see who would face Jim Londos. This also was a non-title match, and Raines continues to hold the Hawaiian title.

It seems Jim Londo's appearance has fallen through as he claimed he had transportation issues and had taken a booking in Philadelphia for the date he was coming to Hawaii.

Oki Shikina regained the Hawaiian title with a win over Dick Raines on April 4th.

May 2nd had several newcomers making their mark in Hawaii. George Zaharias beat Barto Hill in the main event. Curtis Chartier beat Floyd Marshall on DQ. Danny Dusek and Brother Jonathan were also on this card.

Babe Didrikson, an Olympic champion and all-around athlete and George Zaharias's wife were introduced. She would be taking part in a golf match exhibition while in Hawaii.

Oki Shikina beat George Zaharias in a Hawaiian title defense on May 16th. The paper said it was one of Shikina's best matches.

June 20th saw Chief Thunderbird beat Danny Dusek. Al Getz beat Barto Hill on the same card.

Chief Thunderbird beat Brother Jonathan on July 4th. Oki Shikina captured another victory, this time over Danny Dusek. Tony Felice was announced from the crowd.

July 19th, an article in the paper talking about wrestlers in Hawaii and how many of them have 2nd jobs.

HONOLULU ATTRACTIVE TO BEHEMOTHS

Has it ever occurred to you that there are 10 first-rate heavy-weight wrestlers making their homes in Honolulu at the present time. There seems to be something about Hawaii that attracts the behemoths for former world champion Dean Detton intends to settle here next year, while George Zaharias, Dick Raines, Rudy La Ditzi and several others all claim they will return to live here one of these days.

Gentleman Al Karasick, one of the game's greats and now the local promoter, heads the list. Other members of the Karasick Alumni Association are:

AL PEREIRA: former European champion, now owns Al Pereira's Tavern.

BALDY DEMETRAL: the "Fierce Greek," now owns a newsstand at Waikiki.

SAILOR JACK ARNOLD: former Navy champ, now works at trade of machinist.

COUNT OTTO HANS VON BUESING: still wrestles but local masseur.

FLOYD MARSHALL: still wrestles but local masseur.

NAUMU SUNAYAMA: local star and works here, wrestles occasionally.

OKI SHIKINA: Hawaiian champion, native of Maui, very active now.

BROTHER JONATHAN: giant Mormon star, still wrestles, raises rabbits on big scale here.

WONG BUCK CHEUNG: Present champion of the Orient, still wrestles but is in restaurant business here.

July 25th has Shikina beating Tony Velice. The semi-final had Dick Lever beating Barto Hill. After the match, the wrestlers, referee, and some fans got involved in a wild free-for-all.

Al Karasick has announced he has made another offer to Jim Londos. Londos finally appears in Hawaii for his honeymoon and two matches.

The first match occurred on August 22nd, and he beat Vic Christy in a non-title match. This card drew 4,000.

On August 29th, Londos beats Oki Shikina in a title match. This card draws 6,000. Londos won the only fall and, at the bell, was trapped in a Japanese arm bar. The paper again does a tale of the tape photo and dimensions and Shikina is very much outsized.

On September 5th, Londos agreed to another match, beating Chief Thunderbird. The card was a benefit for the Pacific Aquatic Carnival. This card drew 5,000. London was certainly a draw.

Londos was scheduled to travel to Australia, but that tour was cancelled with the start of World War II. Londos agreed to stay in Hawaii for a while longer.

September 12th saw Londos beat Oki Shikina again.

It has also been reported that Londos has been absent from the mainland. Sandor Szabo and Pantaleon Manlapig have both claimed to be world champions.

Chief Thunderbird beat George Pencheff in an Australian rules match. This type of match has six 10-minute rounds. These rules had been used in Hawaii previously, especially with the lighter-weight wrestlers.

October 3rd is an interesting group of wrestlers. Jim Londos beat George Pencheff in the main event.

The undercard had three wrestlers who would become incredible promoters. There was Paul Boesch, who had the reputation of being one of the fairest promoters in the history of wrestling; Paul Jones, who owned The Georgia promotion from 1944 to 1974, and Ignacio Martinez, who would be better known as Pedro Martinez and would promote in upstate New York.

I once shared a silent cab ride with Martinez in Las Vegas, returning from Cauliflower Alley. As I left, I respectfully said, "Goodbye, Mr. Martinez."

A card at Scofield Barracks took place on October 19th. Jimmy Londos beat Chief Thunderbird, who was unable to continue. This card drew 9,000.

October 24th saw Oki Shikina go to a draw with George Zaharias. Rube Wright debuted on this card and was scheduled to appear in the opener. He refused that spot, and they moved his match to 2nd on the card. He beat Curtis Chartier. Such a simple angle had to get heat on Wright. Why do I find this so brilliant?

Ignacio Martinez upset Rube Wright on November 7th, winning the right to meet Shikina for the Hawaiian title.

On November 14th, Martinez beat Paul Boesch, who was a substitute for Shikina, who was out with pneumonia.

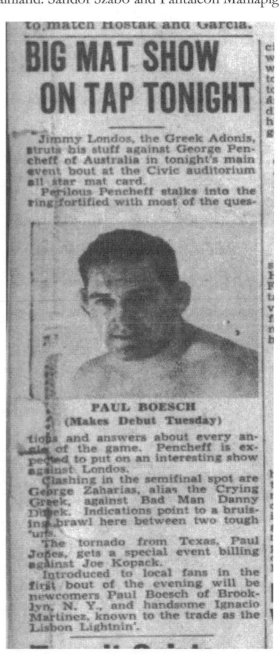

BIG MAT SHOW ON TAP TONIGHT

Jimmy Londos, the Greek Adonis, struts his stuff against George Pencheff of Australia in tonight's main event bout at the Civic auditorium all star mat card.

Perilous Pencheff stalks into the ring fortified with most of the ques-

PAUL BOESCH
(Makes Debut Tuesday)

tions and answers about every angle of the game. Pencheff is expected to put on an interesting show against Londos.

Clashing in the semifinal spot are George Zaharias, alias the Crying Greek, against Bad Man Danny Dusek. Indications point to a bruising brawl here between two tough 'uns.

The tornado from Texas, Paul Jones, gets a special event billing against Joe Kopack.

Introduced to local fans in the first bout of the evening will be newcomers Paul Boesch of Brooklyn, N. Y., and handsome Ignacio Martinez, known to the trade as the Lisbon Lightnin'.

A few days later, Karasick announced that he and Oki Shikina had parted ways, and Shikina was heading to the mainland. Karasick accused Shikina of being afraid of wrestling Ignacio Martinez, who was now champion by default.

183

On November 28th, Paul Jones beat Ignacio Martinez for the Hawaiian Championship. Also, on this card, Young Shiranuhi debuted and beat Dr. Ed Kowarsky. Shiranuhi was billed as Oki Shikina's prize protégé. Shiranuhi would later become one of the world's top wrestlers and be known as Mr. Moto.

December 5th saw a team match, which was very rare. Paul Boesch and Henry Graber beat Ignacio Martinez and Wong Buck Cheung

On December 28th, Jack Gacek beat Ignacio Martinez with Jack Dempsey as the referee. A brawl started in the 3rd fall, and Martinez started to attack Dempsey. Dempsey landed four shots on Martinez, and then Gacek was able to earn an easy victory. Dempsey reportedly earned 50% of the gate.

<u>1939 Wrestling Ads & Pictures</u>

Oki Shikina signs to defend Hawaiian Heavyweight title against Dean Detton.
Promoter Al Karasick in the middle.

AL KARASICK presents

WRESTLING

CIVIC AUDITORIUM
TONIGHT

FOR THE CHAMPIONSHIP OF THE WORLD

JIM LONDOS

WORLD'S HEAVY-
WEIGHT WRESTLING
CHAMPION.

VERSUS

HAWAIIAN
CHAMPION

OKI SHIKINA

JIM
LONDOS

George Pencheff.........vs.....Irish Jack Donovan
Wong Buck Cheung....vs............Vic Christy
Chief Thunderbird....vs.........Danny Dusek
Doc Barto Hill.........vs.........Al Getzewich

Make Your Reservations Immediately as
seats are going fast.

PRICES: Reserved ringside $1.65, 1st 10 rows in
balcony $1.10, General admission $0.75

PHONE 2002

AL KARASICK presents

WRESTLING

CIVIC AUDITORIUM
TUESDAY, SEPT. 12

RETURN MATCH BY POPULAR DEMAND
FOR THE CHAMPIONSHIP OF THE WORLD

JIM LONDOS

WORLD'S HEAVY-
WEIGHT WRESTLING
CHAMPION.

VERSUS

HAWAIIAN
CHAMPION

OKI SHIKINA

2 out of 3 falls to an hour time limit or decision. Make Your Reservations
Immediately as seats are going fast.

POPULAR PRICES: Reserved ringside $1.10, General admission $.75,
Students $.55. PHONE 2002.

(L-R) Judges Prof. Henry Okazaki, Louie Abrams, champion Jim Londos, referee Ernie Andrade, promoter Al Karasick, KGU radio announcer Bob Glenn, challenger Oki Shikina. Karasick reviews the rules for the title contest.

(Below: Shikina works a head lock on Londos, and both men shake hands after the match.

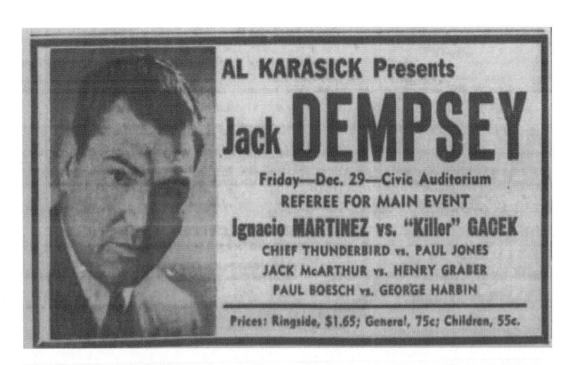

AL KARASICK Presents
Jack DEMPSEY
Friday—Dec. 29—Civic Auditorium
REFEREE FOR MAIN EVENT
Ignacio MARTINEZ vs. "Killer" GACEK
CHIEF THUNDERBIRD vs. PAUL JONES
JACK McARTHUR vs. HENRY GRABER
PAUL BOESCH vs. GEORGE HARBIN
Prices: Ringside, $1.65; General, 75c; Children, 55c.

Jimmy Londos, judge Louie Abrams, auditorium announcer Jimmie Camacho, Al Karasick, judge Freeman Lang, KGU sports announcer Harry Mitchell, Chief Thunderbird w/second.

(L-R) Announcer Jimmie Camacho, Gacek's second, Jack Gacek, Jack Dempsey, Al Karasick, Ignacio Martinez, KGU sports announcer Harry Mitchell

1940

The new decade starts, one that will change Hawaii and the world forever. The first card on January 3rd, is held at the Civic Auditorium.

The main event is Al Pereira beating Ignacio Martinez and Paul Boesch beating Jack McAndrew. Paul Jones is the Hawaiian champ, and he beats Jack "Killer" Gacek; George Harben beats Chief Thunderbird. The referee is Henry Graber.

During 1940 there were such stars as Wong Buck Cheung, Whitey Walberg, Steve Nenoff, and Billy Venable.

On February 14th, a card was rearranged due to the death of Wong Bock Cheung's wife, Dorothy. She was 24 years old. Paul Jones beat Jack Gacek on DQ. Jones was leaving and left the Hawaiian title with promoter Karasick and promised to be back.

On July 3rd, Tetsuo Rubberman Higami beat Billy Venable for the Hawaiian JR Heavyweight title. Jack Benny was in the audience for this match.

The newspaper also mentioned that wrestler/promoter Ted Thye was in attendance for the 7/3/40 show. He was on his way to Australia. It also mentioned that he works with Al Karasick to help book wrestlers into Hawaii.

Mike "Whiskers" London came to Hawaii for a time. He was billed as the NWA Worlds Lightweight Champion and defended that title several times in Hawaii.

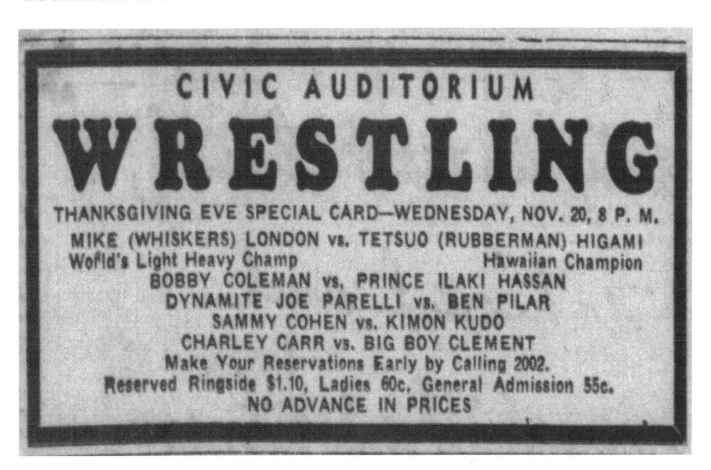

Ben Pilar was very popular in the Hawaiian Islands, and several times, the newspaper talks about his Filipino fans storming the ring. It appears there were several near riots during this time when Pilar was wronged.

Towards the end of the year, there was a card at the Schofield Barracks Bowl. The first card there in a year, and it drew 7,500 fans. Balk Estes beat Prince Iiaki Hassan, Sammy Cohen and The Red Shadow (Cyclone Mackay) beat Kimon Kudo and Tetsuo Higami, Ben Pilar drew Charley Carr, and David Gomez beat Doc Kowarski.

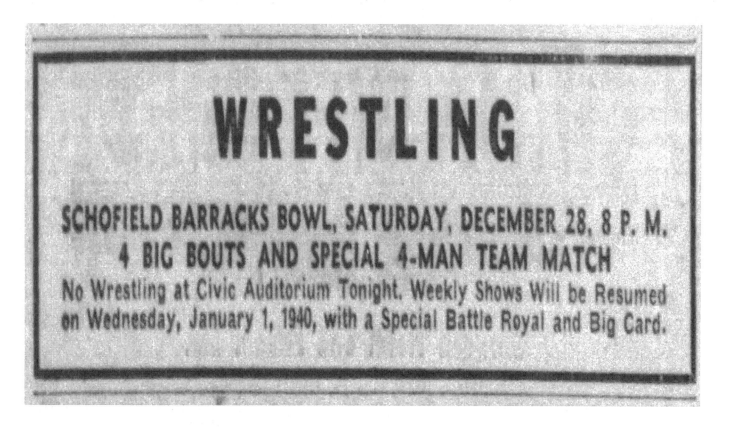

1941

The Red Shadow had an undefeated streak going and, on the first card of 1941, beat Tetsuo Higami. Also, on this card, George Wagner drew Balk Estes. Wagner would later become Gorgeous George. Wagner, at this time, was a scientific wrestler.

On January 22nd, Ben Pilar beat Tetsuo Higami for the Hawaiian Junior title.

On January 29th, The Red Shadow beat Balk Estes. During this match, Estes ripped the mask of Shadow, but he was wearing a 2nd mask underneath.

February 12the card saw George Wagner beat The Red Shadow on decision. Shadow had promised to unmask if he lost a match but not on a decision.

Danny Savich debuted on this card. He began his career in 1935 and became a football star at Utah. Savich was a tremendous draw in Texas through the 40s and 50s. Savich went through Ernie Powers, George Wagner, Balk Estes, Sammy Cohen, and Kimon Kudo in successive weeks.

March 12th saw Red Shadow beat Ben Pilar, who was unable to continue. He reportedly suffered a broken collarbone in this match.

On April 1st, an article in the Hawaiian Advertiser states that The Hawaiian Territorial Boxing Commission is trying to gain control over pro wrestling. Their efforts were primarily to participate in the receipts realized at the wrestling matches.

On April 2nd, Ben Pilar was able to regain his Hawaiian Junior title, and The Red Shadow was unmasked as Cyclone Mackey.

On May 14th, George Wagner beat Ben Pilar in a non-title match. Tony Morelli is the next big thing to hit the Islands, and he is billed as the NWA Eastern States Champ.

On May 30th, it was announced that Doc Kowarski, after being in Hawaii for fifteen years, had returned to Detroit due to his wife's health.

On June 11th, Tony Morelli beat Sammy Cohen in a Texas rules match, and Gene Blackley beat George Wagner. Attendance for the card was 4,000, but there was a bonus. After the card was a "derbie". A derbie was a popular attraction similar to a dance marathon or roller derby. Couples would wear helmets and knee pads and compete in "dynamite sprints." They had a troupe of competitors that traveled with the show. Still, challengers were welcome, and there was a $100 prize. After that explanation, I still don't know what this is. The ad says 2 Master of Ceremonies, 3 trainers, 1 nurse, and 1 dietician.

On June 14th, Al Karasick had a quote that said he had resisted booking "the Angel, woman wrestlers, lady referees, matches in Poi, battle royals in mud, and so forth. My boys are out to give a show, but they are never permitted to forget to wrestle to the best of their ability."

Matches in Poi are the 40's version of exploding barbed wire death matches. Make no mistake, Karasick was having none of that.

The June 25th show had the Derbie show after, and the advertising included this, 'Maxine Lang of Silver Springs, Maryland will be FROZEN ALIVE in a 1400 lb cake of ice. She will attempt to break the world record of 21 minutes 40 seconds, which Miss Reila Finney was unable to do.' (OK, now the burning question of this book is what exactly happened to Miss Reila Finney?)

July 2nd had Gene Blackley draw Tony Morelli, and Dutch "Hillbilly" Hefner beat Charley Carr. This was Jimmy Hefner, the brother of heavyweight Ernest Dutch Hefner.

July 30th card had Dutch Hefner beat Gene Blackley, and Kimon Kudo beat Sammy Cohen on DQ. The big news was that Brother Jonathan was a ref on this card.

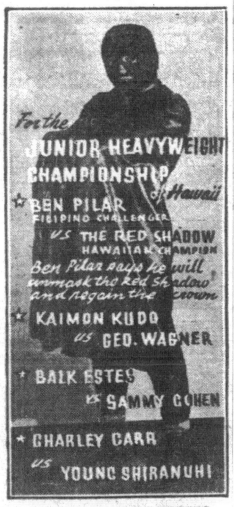

THE CIVIC AUDITORIUM
WRESTLING
WEDNESDAY, APRIL 2—8 P.M
THE YEAR'S GREATEST MAT CARD

For the
JUNIOR HEAVYWEIGHT CHAMPIONSHIP of Hawaii
BEN PILAR
FILIPINO CHALLENGER
vs THE RED SHADOW
HAWAIIAN CHAMPION
Ben Pilar says he will unmask the red shadow and regain the crown

KAIMON KUDO vs GEO. WAGNER

BALK ESTES vs SAMMY COHEN

CHARLEY CARR vs YOUNG SHIRANUHI

NO ADVANCE IN PRICES
Call 2002 for Reservations:
Reserved Ringside, $1.10; Ladies 60c; General Admission, 55c

On August 6th, a match between Dynamite Goodwin and Tennessee Wade on the undercard was listed as the Red Hills Hard Rock Mine championship. The Red Hills Hard Rock Mine was a secret defense project for underground fuel tank storage. It was connected by a tunnel to Pearl Harbor. It began in 1940 and employed 3,000 workers. It was described as an impenetrable, bomb-proof reserve of fuel for the military.

The word secret is in the definition, but with 3,000 employees and a wrestling championship named after it, it doesn't appear too secret.

A little more on this history. This would store up to 250 million gallons of fuel. It consisted of 20 steel-lined underground storage tanks encased in concrete and built into the cavities mined inside Red Hill.

In 2014, there was a fuel spill after a 3-year maintenance upgrade. However, there was a 27,000-gallon jet fuel loss. The spill was caused by faulty work and poor quality control. In 2021, there was another fuel leak.

As recently as March 7th, 2022, the planned closure of the Red Hill facility was announced.

At any rate Dynamite Goodwin won this title over Tennessee Wade.

On the August 13th card, Taro "Bull" Ito debuted, beating Charley Carr. Ito was a Japanese American from Oregon who had played football at Oregon State University. It was trained by Tetsu Higami. He was better known as The Great Togo.

On September 10th, Ito beat Gene Blackley but brawled with referee Brother Jonathan following his match. This card drew over 4,000.

GIL KNUDSEN
Meets Kaimon Kudo

Big Crowd Is Expected At Show Tonight

Tonight's wrestling card at the Civic auditorium with five bouts and a special added attraction promises to attract another capacity house.

In the top spot Tony Morelli takes on Dutch Heffner. Morelli has never been beaten here. His toughest bout was against the Tennessee mountaineer. It will be two out of three falls to an hour.

Gil Knudsen meets Kaimon Kudo in the semifinal. Knudsen made a big hit in his debut last week.

A special added attraction is the Red Hill hard rock miner's championship bout between A. V. (Dynamite) Goodin and Tennessee Wade. The big miners won the two elimination tourneys conducted at the Red Hill defense project. The winner will receive the Red Hill trophy posted by the hard rock miners. It will be one fall to a finish.

Sammy Cohen takes on Gene Blackley in a special event. Charley Carr and Young Shiranuhi meet in the opener. Brother Jonathan, heavyweight grappler, will again referee.

October 13th was scheduled to be Higami Day to celebrate the 20th anniversary of Higami's wrestling career. The card was postponed when Higami suffered a knee injury.

November 12th saw Billy Weidner beat Tony Morelli for the Hawaiian Junior Heavyweight title.

November 19th was the rescheduled Prof Tetsuo Rubberman Higami day. He went to a draw with Dutch Hefner. The attendance was 4,000.

On December 3rd, Billy Weidner beat Dutch Hefner on DQ. Joe "Kayo" Berry was scheduled to meet with Wild Bill Sinclair in a boxer vs. wrestler match. Berry was a no-show. Also, Dr. Kildare drew David Gomez. Dr. Kildare was a series of movies at the time, later to be a TV series.

The Pearl Harbor Bombing took place on December 7th. The card scheduled for December 10th was Billy Weidner VS Gust Johnson, Taro Ito VS Dutch Hefner, Wild Bill Sinclair VS Charley Carr, and Johnny Berkowitz VS Chester Hayes. The ref was scheduled to be Kimon Kudo.

Al Karasick offered the Civic Auditorium as a dormitory or any other purpose needed by the military or government.

We understand the significance of the Pearl Harbor Bombing, but I did not realize the long-term effects.

Hawaii was under Martial Law until 1944. The Hawaiian Islands were basically a naval and army base. The Military dictated everything on the islands, both military and civilian. During martial law, no lights could be on at night, which was a total blackout. They eventually evacuated people back to the mainland states if they wanted to. Tourism was done, and the Islands were populated by service members. This was a considerable controversy because Hawaiian businesses relied on tourism. However, martial law circumvents the local laws.

This period sounds complicated and difficult; very much distrust between people of Japanese and Hawaiian descent. Also, it was very hard to tell the two cultures apart, which only added to the distrust.

English was the only language allowed, and Japanese schools were closed.

They were considering internment camps, but 160,000 people of Japanese descent made this impossible, so they theoretically turned all of Hawaii into detention centers.

1941 Wrestling Ads & Pictures

George Wagner pre Gorgeous George

TARO (BULL) ITO
(Meets Blackley Tonight)

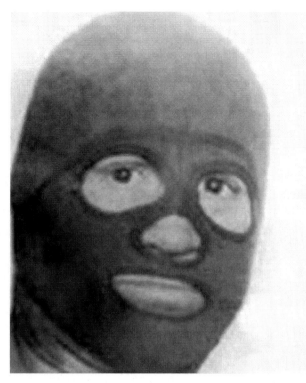

Red Shadow & unmasked as Cyclone Mackey

Danny Savich   Gene "Big Bertha" Blackley

DERBY SHOW
STARTS TONIGHT—6:30
TILL 1 A. M.

Beyond all question the most fascinating show of its kind, since the memory of man runneth not to the contrary.

Where stars shine and records fall.

IT FEATURES:

40 PERFORMERS
2 MASTER OF CEREMONIES
3 TRAINERS
1 NURSE   1 DIETICIAN

CARL HICKERSON
Director and
Producer

TO THE WINNING COUPLE
$1,000.00

A complete change of show nightly of myriads of new and novel features.

CONTINUOUS MUSIC BY BOBBY KAAI AND HIS TROPICAL ISLANDERS

Sponsored by Oahu County Council American Legion

Hear Danny Bramer, Derby Show Commentator, over KGU at the following broadcasts: Tonight—6:30 p. m.
Monday, Tuesday, Thursday, Friday—4 p. m. and 9 p. m.
Wednesday and Saturday—5:15 p .m. and 9:30 p .m.
Sunday—3:15 p. m. and 10:00 p. m.

CIVIC AUDITORIUM

OPENS TONIGHT—6:30 P. M.

Every Day—1:00 p. m. to 1:00 a. m.
Every Sunday Evening—6:30 p. m.
PRICES: 20c MATINEES, 40c NIGHTS

1942

There is a note that as of 2/6/42, Al Karasick plans to start his promotion at some point.

Bulldog Atkinson and Ernie Powers have both enlisted in the army.

Al Karasick starts holding dances at the Civic to improve the morale of the armed forces.

In the Honolulu Star-Bulletin of June 23rd, 1942, Al Karasick plans to start pro wrestling back up "in association with military officials for the recreation and morale purposes of both defense workers and Uncle Sam's armed forces."

On August 17th, 1942, there is a note that Al Karasick issued a call for all former pro wrestlers now in the military or on the Island to get in touch with him to appear on upcoming cards. He hopes to get permission for mainland wrestlers to travel to Hawaii. Part of the problem has been lining up sufficient talent for weekly shows.

On September 20th, there is a military boxing tournament final and one 20-minute pro wrestling exhibition. No word on who wrestled.

On October 6th at Waikakaluah Gulch, the first match since Pearl Harbor took place. It looks like a match just to test the waters. Chester Hayes drew Harry Martin, and Johnny Metsler beat Victor Koleman. It sounds like it is a very out-of-the-way venue.

Al Karasick ran an ad in the paper in December of '42 asking for any wrestlers or members of the armed forces to fill out the cards.

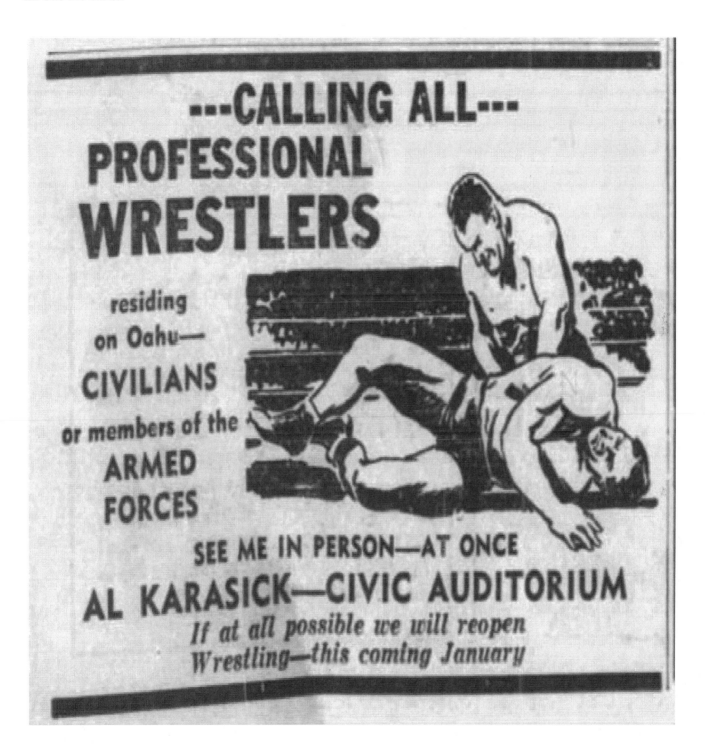

1943

Finally, on January 3rd, 1943, working with military officials on the problems of wartime travel restrictions and curfews, Al Karasick was able to revive pro wrestling in Hawaii. They drew 4,000 people, probably due to there being no entertainment options for quite some time.

The matches for this show saw Chester Hayes beat Ben Pilar and Bucky King Kong O'Neill drew Charley Carr. Only a handful of these wrestlers had worked before. Bucky O'Neil, Chester Hayes, Stan Hackney, and Charlie Carr. Young Shiranuhi was a ref and will be better known as Mr. Moto.

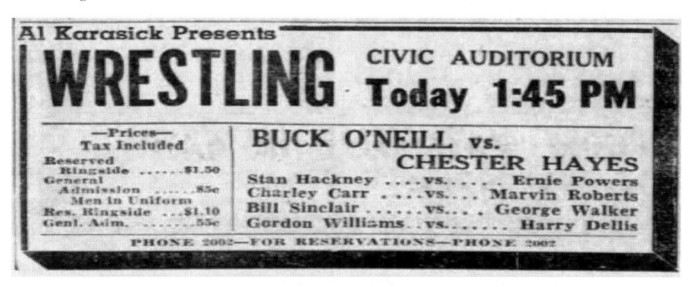

On January 18th, Ring magazine publisher Nat Fleischer will offer a gold belt to the winner of a Junior Heavyweight Tournament. It will initially be called the Ring Magazine Hawaiian Jr Heavyweight title. Later, it will be called the Hawaiian State title. It is said that Fleischer hopes "to encourage the wrestlers in their efforts to entertain and bolster the morale of war workers and servicemen in the islands."

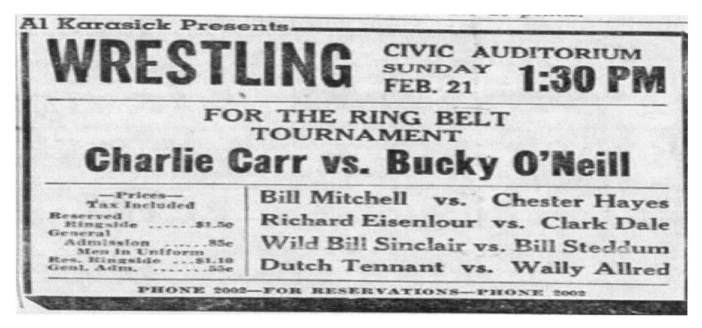

On April 25th, Kahuna Lupe debuts and beats Clark Dale. The paper says that Lupenu is said to be Hawaii's first full-blooded native to take a fling at pro wrestling.

May 7th saw the year's first nighttime show as Bucky O'Neil beat Blackie Roberts. Curfew was still around the area, so this show started at 6:15.

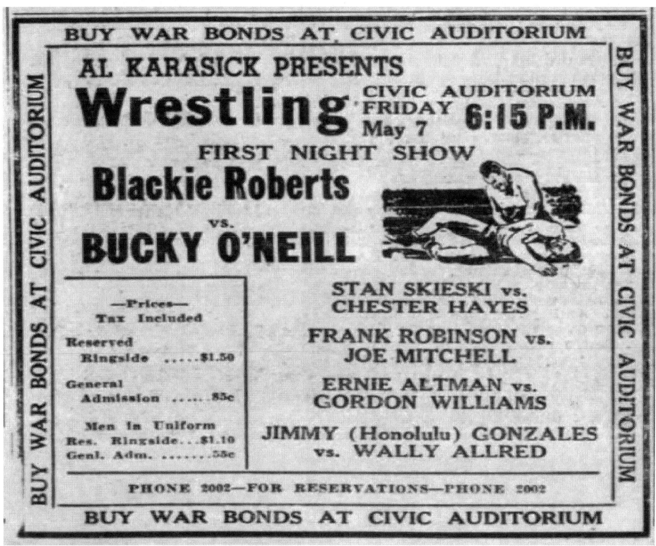

On June 20th, Bucky O'Neill, who sounds like the top heel, was in a match with Chester Hayes, had Hayes trapped in a Boston Crab, and refused to release the hold. Promoter Al Karasick entered the ring and got into a fight with O'Neill.

July 16th drew 13,000 to Schofield Barracks Bowl. Usual attendance was around 3,000 per show. This venue may have been the draw, especially for the service members.

By August, Elmer Davis and Bill Kaiser had started wrestling in Hawaii. Elmer Davis went on to have a 15-year career. Kaiser wrestled for five years, all in Hawaii.

By November, Axel Madsen had come to Hawaii. He had been wrestling since 1934 and settled in Hawaii for the last five years of his career.

One wrestler working in Hawaii doesn't have any facts listed in Wrestledata. His name was Doug Corregidor. He had wrestled before in Hawaii before this time, and his name was Cerco Viernes.

The name Corregidor had several connections to WWII. The USS Corregidor was an aircraft carrier stationed at Pearl Harbor for a time. My father was stationed on this carrier. It was named for an area in Alaska. There was also a Battle of Corregidor near the Phillippines that the USS Corregidor was not part of.

On October 12th, another show at the Schofield Barracks Bowl again drew 13,000. Charley Carr beat Chester Hayes for the Hawaiian Junior title. This was the debut of this title. It was mentioned earlier, sponsored by The Ring Magazine.

October 31st was the debut of Kelly Cox, who was billed as the brother of Ted King Kong Cox. During his match, he went "berserk" and was disqualified against Leo McCallister.

Heading into 1944, this makeshift crew was devoid of actual wrestling stars. Reading the reports from the shows from 1940 prior to Pearl Harbor and when wrestling resumed, I am convinced that Al Karasick was a very good promoter. He presented matches that involved and appealed to the service members that were now his audience.

1943 Wrestling Ads & Pictures

 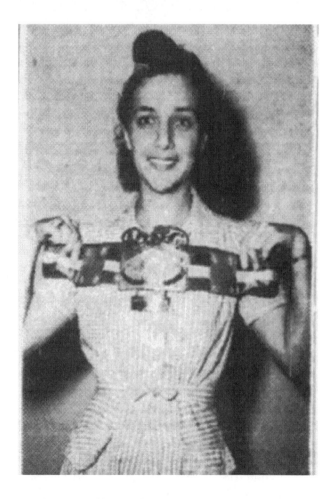

Ring publisher Nat Fleischer & Elizabeth Maloney of Star Bulletin shows Ring magazine belt

Charley Carr (Ring Mag champ)   Stan Skieski "The Russian Bear"   Bucky "King Kong" O'Neil

BLACKIE ROBERTS   FRANK ROBINSON (The Golden Terror)   JIMMY GONSALVES

1944

For the next two years, Al Karasick continued to promote using the same core group of wrestlers. There was not much of a turnover in talent as World War II still had its effect on Hawaii.

On February 6th, the card drew 5,400 to see Sammy Cohen beat Chester Hayes.

The main event on March 5th saw Axel Madsen go to a draw with Sammy Cohen. The match was stopped by promoter Karasick due to a cut above Madsen's eye.

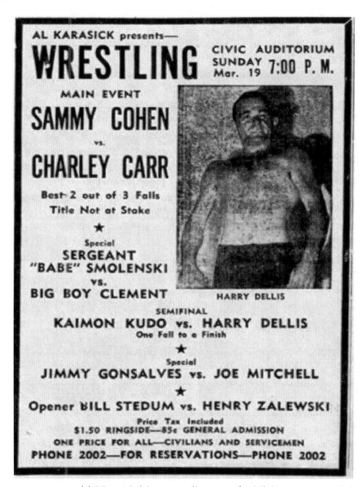

AL KARASICK presents—
WRESTLING
CIVIC AUDITORIUM
SUNDAY
Mar. 19 **7:00 P. M.**

MAIN EVENT
SAMMY COHEN
vs.
CHARLEY CARR
Best 2 out of 3 Falls
Title Not at Stake
★
Special
SERGEANT "BABE" SMOLENSKI
vs.
BIG BOY CLEMENT

HARRY DELLIS

SEMIFINAL
KAIMON KUDO vs. **HARRY DELLIS**
One Fall to a Finish
★
Special
JIMMY GONSALVES vs. **JOE MITCHELL**
★
Opener **BILL STEDUM** vs. **HENRY ZALEWSKI**
Price Tax Included
$1.50 RINGSIDE—85c GENERAL ADMISSION
ONE PRICE FOR ALL—CIVILIANS AND SERVICEMEN
PHONE 2002—FOR RESERVATIONS—PHONE 2002

On March 7th, Babe Small debuted, beating Joe Mitchell.

March 19th saw attendance climb to 6,000 as Charley Carr beat Sammy Cohen on DQ, and Kaimon Kudo beat Harry Dellis. This was Kudo's first match in three years. He frequently refereed during that time. He was raised in Seattle and lived in the US all of his life, but he was of Japanese descent, so his career was put on hold.

On April 4th, they had a tournament with all wrestlers who were servicemen. Sgt. Babe (Small) Smolenski beat Elmer Davis for the trophy.

On May 28th, Charley Carr beat Samy Cohen. This bout was billed as the greatest championship wrestling match ever staged in Hawaii. This card drew 6,500.

On June 18th, Ring magazine reported that Honolulu "is now the hotbed of professional wrestling."

On June 25th, Axel Madsen beat Sgt. Babe Smolenski. This was Smolenski's first defeat on a local card.

On July 8th, The US Navy announced that they would no longer allow any of their enlisted personnel to appear on Al Karasick's wrestling cards. This was surprising as Karasick had been providing cards at The Schofield Bowl and The Royal Hawaiian Hotel, which was used as a Navy center, without any compensation. Several of his current stars were sailors. Elmer Davis and Lou Franco were with the Navy.

On July 13th Seabees Athletic Association "Smoker" was held. Bruns was a well-known pro wrestler and was serving with Seabees. Seabees were the Naval Construction crew. Bruns beat The Green Hornet. Al Karasick was not involved in this card. Bruns and Karasick would become partners in the future.

August 15th show at the Schofield Barracks Bowl drew 9,500, with Babe Smolenski beating Jimmy Gonsalves on DQ. Elmer Davis drew Harry Dellis. Naval officials relented on their decision to prohibit personnel from participating in wrestling matches.

They returned to Schofield Barracks with a card that drew nearly 9,000. The main event had Sgt. Babe Smolenski going to a draw with Chester Hayes.

Martial law officially ended in Hawaii on October 24th, 1944. This should allow more accessible travel in and out of Hawaii.

Again, on November 14th, the Navy stopped its personnel from appearing on wrestling shows. This affected Elmer Davis and Lou Franco. The show from the Schofield Barracks drew over 9,000. The main event saw Axel Madsen beat Harry Dellis.

On December 10th, the main event saw Sgt. Babe Smolenski beat Charley Carr on a decision. Shin Miyashiro made his debut, beating Tiger James. Miyashiro was a protégé of Kudo and Higami. His real name was Shin'ich Stanley Mayeshiro, and he wrestled under the names Great Kato and Oyama Kato.

BABE SMOLENSKI

1944 Wrestling Ads & Pictures

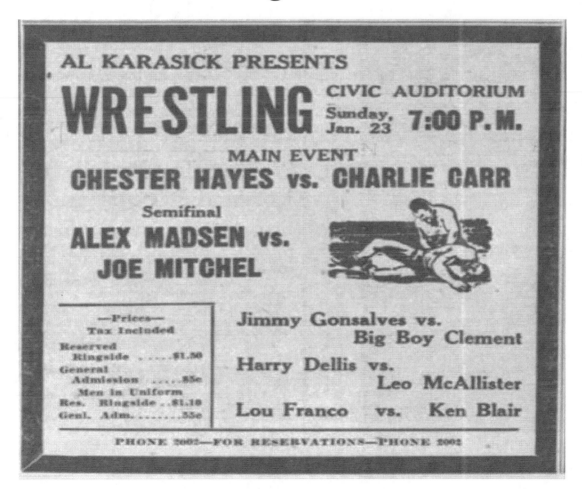

AL KARASICK PRESENTS

WRESTLING CIVIC AUDITORIUM
Sunday, Jan. 23 7:00 P.M.

MAIN EVENT
CHESTER HAYES vs. CHARLIE CARR

Semifinal
ALEX MADSEN vs. JOE MITCHEL

—Prices—
Tax Included
Reserved
Ringside $1.50
General
Admission 85c
Men in Uniform
Res. Ringside .. $1.10
Genl. Adm. 55c

Jimmy Gonsalves vs.
Big Boy Clement

Harry Dellis vs.
Leo McAllister

Lou Franco vs. Ken Blair

PHONE 2002—FOR RESERVATIONS—PHONE 2002

ALL-SERVICE WRESTLING TROPHY—While Post athletic officer Lt. Harry Collins displays the new Schofield Barracks All-Service wrestling trophy four of the top soldier grapplers "sweat it out." Left to right they are Staff Sgt. Henry Zalewski, Pvt. Robert (Soldier Bob) Bohach, Sgt. Broni (Babe Small) Smolenski and and Sgt. Ken Blair. The trophy was presented by promoter Al Karasick and belongs exclusively to Schofield Barracks where professional mat shows are staged every third Tuesday night.

Sgt. Babe Smolenski

BULLDOG JOHNSON

AXEL MADSEN

FRANK CUTLER.

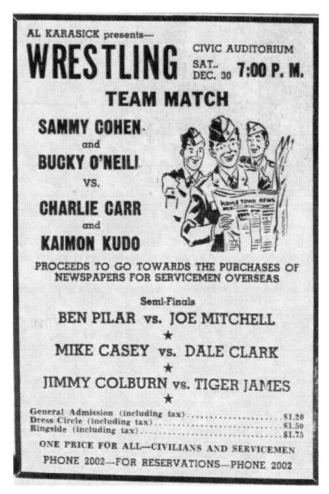

AL KARASICK presents—

WRESTLING

CIVIC AUDITORIUM
SAT., DEC. 30 7:00 P. M.

TEAM MATCH

SAMMY COHEN
and
BUCKY O'NEILL
vs.
CHARLIE CARR
and
KAIMON KUDO

PROCEEDS TO GO TOWARDS THE PURCHASES OF
NEWSPAPERS FOR SERVICEMEN OVERSEAS

Semi-Finals

BEN PILAR vs. JOE MITCHELL
★
MIKE CASEY vs. DALE CLARK
★
JIMMY COLBURN vs. TIGER JAMES
★

General Admission (including tax) $1.20
Dress Circle (including tax)..$1.50
Ringside (including tax) $1.75

ONE PRICE FOR ALL—CIVILIANS AND SERVICEMEN

PHONE 2002—FOR RESERVATIONS—PHONE 2002

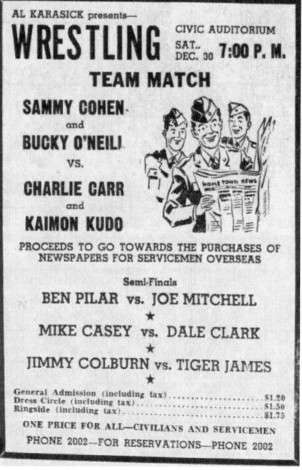

AL KARASICK presents—

WRESTLING

CIVIC AUDITORIUM
SAT., DEC. 30 7:00 P. M.

TEAM MATCH

SAMMY COHEN
and
BUCKY O'NEILL
vs.
CHARLIE CARR
and
KAIMON KUDO

PROCEEDS TO GO TOWARDS THE PURCHASES OF
NEWSPAPERS FOR SERVICEMEN OVERSEAS

Semi-Finals

BEN PILAR vs. JOE MITCHELL
★
MIKE CASEY vs. DALE CLARK
★
JIMMY COLBURN vs. TIGER JAMES
★

General Admission (including tax) $1.20
Dress Circle (including tax)..$1.50
Ringside (including tax) $1.75

ONE PRICE FOR ALL—CIVILIANS AND SERVICEMEN

PHONE 2002—FOR RESERVATIONS—PHONE 2002

1945

As 1945 stars, Mark Hewitt's notes indicate Honolulu is still under Martial Law. Full control of Hawaii was not returned to civilians at that time; the US Army still controlled Hawaiian labor.

Jack Dempsey with Al Karasick

On March 11th, Chester Hayes beat Sammy Cohen in the main event, which drew 6,000. Boxing Champ Jack Dempsey reffed the Hayes/Cohen match. During the match, Cohen swung at Dempsey, who responded with a punch that set up Cohen for the pin.

On March 18th, Kimon Kudo beat Chester Hayes. Also, Vilai Su'a made his debut. Su'a was a local football star and had been training for six weeks.

April 11th has another big Schofield Barracks Bowl card, which drew 9,500. There are some new faces on the card. The main event saw Irish Mike Casey beat Vic Bulldog Rancourt, who was billed from Boston. Jimmy Gonsalves beat Vincent Ramos, who is from Argentina.

On April 25th, All Karasick announced he planned to book Woody Strode and Raymond Sheffield on upcoming cards. Strode, the better-known of the two, had started in wrestling career in 1940.

On May 1st, the Army followed suit and banned their employees from participating in the wrestling show as well as boxing and baseball. The wrestlers affected by this ruling were Axel Madsen, Sgt. Babe Smolinski, Ralph Teague, Little Ali Baba, Nick Nichols, and Frank Merrill. This talent was allowed to wrestle on the Schofield Barracks shows.

Al Lolotai appeared on this show and went to a draw with Don Martin. His official debut would take place later in May at the Civic Auditorium. Lolotai would also wrestle under the name Alo Leilani. He would become a very big name and draw in Hawaii.

June 10th Wallace (Wally) Tsutsumi debuted to beat Tiger James. Tsutsumi would have an outstanding career and become the main referee during Ed Francis's promotional run in the 60's.

The card billed for June 24th, 1945, was billed as Al Karasick's 53rd Birthday Anniversary card. Originally scheduled on the card was a match between Al Lolotai and Vilai Su's. However, it was canceled when Mormon officials protested holding the bout as both wrestlers were Mormons, and they feared it would cause unrest among the community.

July 22nd saw Blackie Adachi beat Stan Miyashiro. Adachi was billed as the Honolulu Indian. He was also an amateur and judo star.

Al Karasick is on the mainland doing business and sent back word that he had signed Lee Grable to some matches. Al's son Joe was handling the cards while his dad was away.

They reported Karasick had met with Ted Thye, Joe Malcewicz, and Hugh Nichols and planned to meet with Tony Stecher, Tom Packs, and Al Haft.

The story also talked about trying to book a series of billiards contests between billiard champions; however, one of them, Willie Hoppe, couldn't be booked.

World War II was winding down. The war in Europe ended with Germany surrendering on May 8th, and Japan surrendered on September 2nd. Life would slowly return to normal.

1945 Wrestling Ads & Pictures

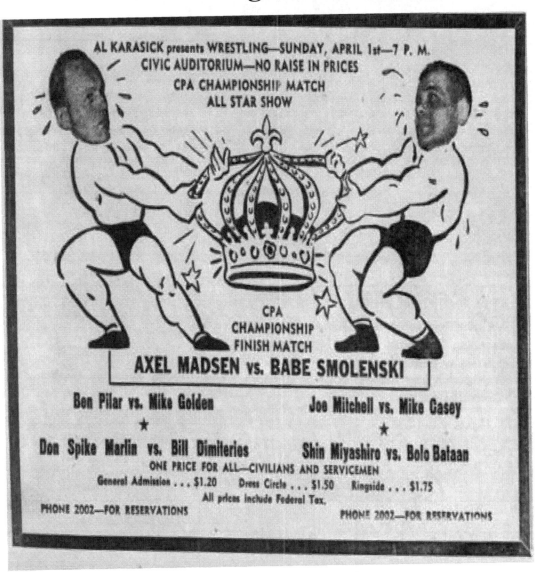

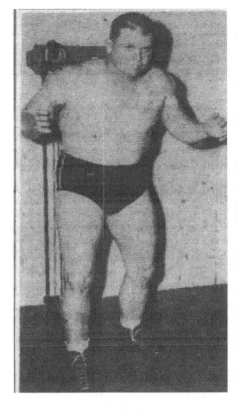  

Ralph Teague   Francis "Sonny Rawlins   Ray "Sea Wolf" Higgins

Chief Arnich   Vilai Su'a "The Samoan Strongman"   Joe Mitchell

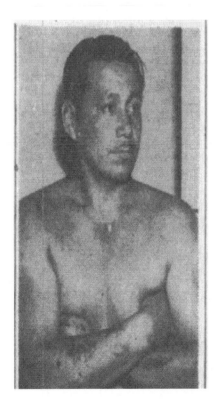 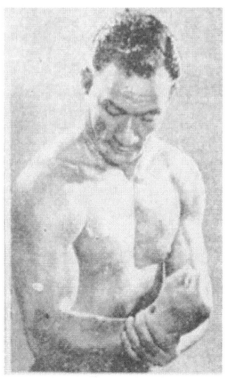 

1946

Al Karasick continues to build Hawaii back up as a promotion.

On January 8th, a masked wrestler debuts billed as The Scarlet Pimpernel. He is the master of the pile driver. Despite being masked, his match is described as someone who used some holds seldom seen in Hawaii. He beat Kimon Kudo on his debut.

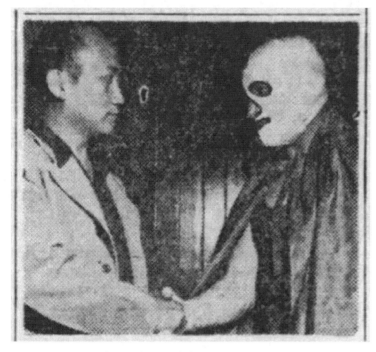

The Scarlet Pimpernel shakes Ben Pilar's hand.

Tex Porter

On February 2nd, The Scarlet Pimpernel beat Ben Pilar, and Al Lolotai returned to Hawaii after playing football for the Washington Redskins. Wladek Zbyszko was introduced to the crowd on his way to Japan for a USO tour.

On March 24th, Jimmy Gonsalves went to a draw with Billy Venable. This was a non-title match, as Jimmy Gonsalves holds the Hawaiian Jr title.

On March 30th, Lee Grable made his debut and beat Charley Carr. Grable is billed as the Pacific Coast Light Heavyweight champion.

On April 18th, at the Schofield Barracks show, Ben Pilar beat Wimpy Wellington, and Charley Shiranuhi beat Leo MacAllister dq; this show drew over 10,000, but admittance was free.

May 12th saw Lee Grable beat Al Lolotai, and Billy Venable beat Charley Carr. This card drew 5,000 fans.

May 16th saw Simon "Lucky" Zvko's (Simonovich) debut in wrestling, beating Buck Lee. Simonovich had been in Hawaii since 1941 and had been an amateur wrestler and weightlifter, a merchant marine, a semi-pro football player, and a Honolulu policeman before starting a wrestling career.

May 19th saw the outstanding matchup of Scarlet Pimpernel beating Lee Grable on DQ when Grable wouldn't release a stranglehold.

On May 26th, the Hawaiian Jr Championship went to The Scarlet Pimpernel, who beat Jimmy Gonsalves.

On June 9th, Tex Porter made his debut in Hawaii. He beat Wimpy Wellington. In other matches, Scarlet Pimpernel beat Stan Skieski, and Lee Grable beat Vilai Su'a.

On June 23rd, Lee Grable beat Tex Porter, and Kimon Kudo beat Billy Venable. Kudo had been injured much of the past year. Lucky Simonovich beat Buck Lee in his Civic Auditorium debut.

On July 28th, Scarlet Pimpernel beat Tex Porter, and Lucky Simunovich beat John Starkey.

Al Lolotai is getting ready to go back to football. This year, he is scheduled to play for the LA Dons. Bob Hope is part-owner of the Dons. Actor Edward G. Robinson is in attendance for this show.

On September 22nd, Lee Grable beat Scarlet Pimpernel to win the Hawaiian Jr title. Pimpernel was forced to unmask, revealing Ben Sherman. Ben Sherman had wrestled a lot in the Northwest and was also a Yale graduate.

Ken Tsutsumi helps hold up the stunned Ben Sherman as referee Charley Shiranuhi pulls of his mask.

Gorilla Poggi also debuted in Hawaii during this time. Gorilla Poggi spoke 5 languages.

Sherman continued to wrestle in Hawaii, and on September 29th, he beat Jimmy Gonsalves.

On October 8th, the newspaper mentioned that Al Karasick is again on the mainland looking for new wrestling talent and has booked Jack Kaiser for a tour. Karasick is also considering buying new equipment for the Civic Auditorium, including new chairs.

On November 3rd, Jack Kaiser made his debut. Kaiser was a Northwest mainstay. He beat Charley Carr on his debut. The main event that night saw Jacques Manuel beat Ben Sherman. This event drew 4,000.

November 10th saw a tag team main event. There had been tag matches before in Hawaii, but this may have been one of the more critical matches with top talent. Lee Grable and Jack Kiser beat Jacques Manuel and Gorilla Poggi.

The talent has improved towards the end of the year with Grable, Sherman, Poggi, Jack Kaiser, and Simonovich. More recognizable talent and not relying on one or two people to draw the houses is another nod to Karasick as a promoter.

On December 15th, Karasick brought in Jimmy Londos, who had The World Championship (a precursor to the NWA World title). Londos would beat Abe King Kong Kashey in a top heavyweight matchup. This card drew over 5,000. Lee Grable put up a challenge to Londos.

They kept Londos busy while he was in Hawaii as he beat Jacques Manuel on December 18th on a Schofield Barracks show that drew 11,000.

On December 22nd, Londos beat Lee Grable. Grable was unable to continue due to bleeding too badly.

It doesn't look like Hawaii is shy on the blade. Many of the match recaps from the paper indicate there are more than a fair share of matches that have blood in them.

The last card of the year had a battle royal. The last 2 in the ring were Kimon Kudo and Jack Kiser. Kudo got the win for this match.

Londos and Abe "King Kong" Kashey

1946 Wrestling Ads & Pictures

New Year's Greeting
from
AL KARASICK
Your Wrestling Promoter
WRESTLING CIVIC AUDITORIUM
SUN. JAN. 6 — 7:30 P. M.
MAIN EVENT

Charley
CARR
VS.
Kaimon
KUDO

Semi-Final

Chester
HAYES VS. Wimpy **WILLINGTON**

Whitey (Gorilla)
GLOVER VS. Count **VON BUESING**

Bob
McALISTER VS. Francis **RAWLINS**

ADACHI VS. **TAKASE**

General Admission (including tax) $1.20
Dress Circle (including tax) $1.50
Ringside (including tax) $1.75
PHONE 2002—FOR RESERVATIONS—PHONE 2002

LEE GRABLE
In Honolulu Debut Tonight

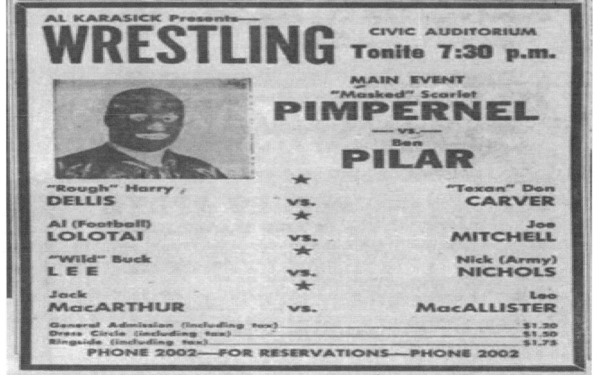

AL KARASICK Presents—
WRESTLING CIVIC AUDITORIUM
Tonite 7:30 p.m.
MAIN EVENT
"Masked" Scarlet
PIMPERNEL
vs.
Ben
PILAR

"Rough" Harry
DELLIS VS. "Texan" Don **CARVER**

Al (Football)
LOLOTAI VS. Joe **MITCHELL**

"Wild" Buck
LEE VS. Nick (Army) **NICHOLS**

Jack
MacARTHUR VS. Leo **MacALLISTER**

General Admission (including tax) $1.20
Dress Circle (including tax) $1.50
Ringside (including tax) $1.75
PHONE 2002—FOR RESERVATIONS—PHONE 2002

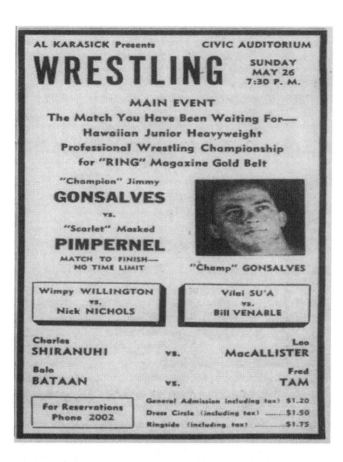

Mr. & Mrs. Tex Porter arrive in Hawaii

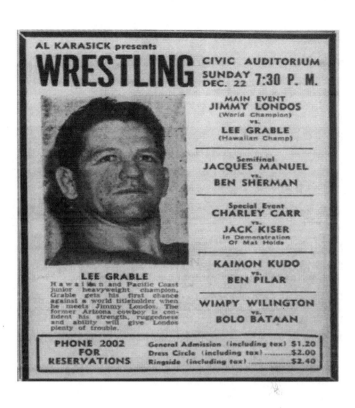

Londos shows off his belts.

JACK KISER

JOHN STILES

"LUCKY" SIMUNOVICH

George Temple   Billy Venable   Harry Dellis

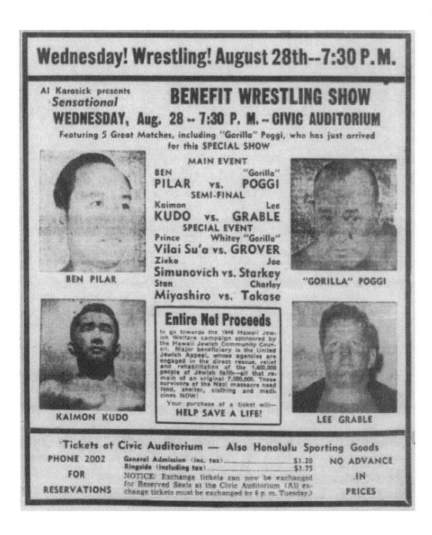

SCARLET PIMPERNEL

1947

Al Karasick continues to build back his promotion after World War II as he procures an increasingly talented roster. He promotes weekly shows at the Civic Auditorium and monthly shows at Schofield Barracks that draw very well.

The first Schofield show was on January 9th, and the main event saw Jack Kiser beat Charley Shiranuhi. This show drew over 9,000.

Al Lolotai has returned from his football season.

Mildred Burke contacted Al Karasick about wrestling in Honolulu. However, Karasick was said to have frowned on women's wrestling.

On February 3rd, Al Lang announced that he planned on promoting pro wrestling at the Honolulu Stadium, and his shows would feature heavyweight wrestlers from the mainland. He was also hoping to bring lady wrestlers in as well.

Al Karasick commented on this and said lady wrestling was "a disgrace to the high ideas of womanhood." A local religious newspaper, The Catholic Herald, started editorializing against it, labeling it "jaded and vulgar" and "a debased type of entertainment."

Art Lang's first show was at the Honolulu Stadium on February 20th, 1947. George Temple Jr beat Alex Kasaboski, Vilai Su'a beat Whitey Glover, Al Lolotai beat Henry "Bomber" Kulkovich by a decision, Terry McGinnis beat Frank Cutler when he was unable to continue, and Andre Adoree drew Francis Rawlins. The attendance was over 2000.

Su'a, Lolotai, and Rawlins left Krausnicks stable to wrestle for the new promotion.

Karasick attempted to get a restraining order to keep Su'a from appearing on the card, claiming he had him under contract. This shows that this promotional war was contentious.

Art Lang came right back a week later, on February 27th, at the Honolulu Stadium. George Temple beat Whitey Glover, Henry "Bomber Kulkovich beat Terry McGinnis, Vilai Su'a beat Frank Cutler, Al Lolotai beat Alex Kasaboski, Andre Adoree beat Francis Rawlins, Kulkovich and Kasaboski beat Cutler and Glover in a tag match. The ref was Wong Bock Cheung. No attendance was listed for this card.

Honolulu Stadium opened in 1926 and was the primary sports venue in Hawaii before Aloha Stadium. It could hold about 25,000 fans.

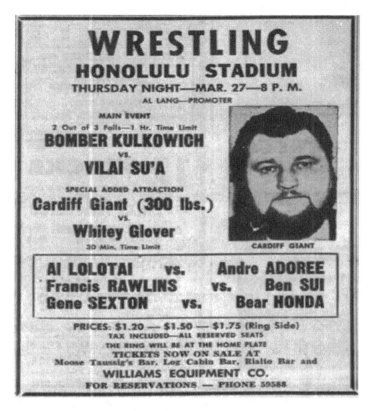

WRESTLING

HONOLULU STADIUM

THURSDAY NIGHT—MAR. 27—8 P. M.

AL LANG—PROMOTER

MAIN EVENT

2 Out of 3 Falls—1 Hr. Time Limit

BOMBER KULKOWICH

vs.

VILAI SU'A

SPECIAL ADDED ATTRACTION

Cardiff Giant (300 lbs.)

vs.

Whitey Glover

30 Min. Time Limit

CARDIFF GIANT

AL LOLOTAI	vs.	Andre ADOREE
Francis RAWLINS	vs.	Ben SUI
Gene SEXTON	vs.	Bear HONDA

PRICES: $1.20 — $1.50 — $1.75 (Ring Side)

TAX INCLUDED—ALL RESERVED SEATS

THE RING WILL BE AT THE HOME PLATE

TICKETS NOW ON SALE AT

Moose Taussig's Bar, Log Cabin Bar, Rialto Bar and

WILLIAMS EQUIPMENT CO.

FOR RESERVATIONS — PHONE 59588

Sticking with the Lang promotion on March 7th, Henry "Bomber" Kulkovich beat Andre Adoree, Vilai Su'a beat George Temple Jr, and Al Lolotai beat Whitey Glover. Wrestling will be off for a few weeks due to baseball games.

On March 26th, the legislature introduced a bill prohibiting women's wrestling and boxing matches from being held in Hawaii.

March 27th was the next Al Lang show. In the main event, Henry Bomber Kulkovich beat Vilai Su'a, The Cardiff Giant debuted and beat Whitey Glover. Mitsugu "Bear" Honda beat Gene Sexton. Honda was a Hawaiian AAU welterweight, middleweight, and light heavyweight title holder. He made it to the 1936 Olympic tryouts.

The April 3rd Lang show saw The Cardiff Giant beat Bomber Kulkovich, and Al Lolotai drew Andre Adoree.

April 10th saw Al Lolotai go to a no-contest with The Masked Terror, Bobby Stewart beat Henry Bomber Kulkovich, and The Cardiff Giant went to a draw with Andre Adoree. This card sounds like it got out of hand when a spectator came to the ring to attack Whitey Glover, who was seconding The Masked Terror. The fan was removed, but other fans began throwing chairs into the ring.

April 17th saw The Cardiff Giant go to a no-contest with the Masked Terror. Lang had planned to have Mildred Burke meet Mae Weston on this card but was forbidden to present a women's wrestling bout by the Honolulu Stadium Board of Directors.

The May 1st card was postponed due to rain with a scheduled main event of Al Lolotai VS The Masked Terror.

They returned a week later, and Lolotai and Masked Terror went to a draw.

This was Lang's last card in Hawaii as he wanted to concentrate on matchmaking for a boxing card scheduled for May 30th.

Circling back to Karasick's promotion, on January 12th, Lee Grable drew Ben Sherman, and this card drew 3,500.

A little more on Ben Sherman, The Wrestling Fans book published in 1952 says that Ben Sherman graduated from Yale University. He spent a lot of time wrestling in England, South Africa, and India.

A YouTube video of Ben Sherman vs. Jack Pye captures the style of the day (probably the 30s) with a frantic, awkward style that sometimes looks legitimate.

Karasick did an excellent job of building his entire crew. He had ten or so wrestlers who were taken seriously and could main event.

January 26th saw Jack Kiser beat Lee Grable in a non-title match that also drew 3,500.

On February 9th, Lee Grable turned back Jack Kiser's challenge when Kaiser could not continue. This card drew 5,000 fans. Incredible, really, the jump in the crowd from two weeks previous.

TED TRAVIS

Ted Travis debuted on February 16th and beat Axel Madsen. Travis was Ted Christy, and he would become a fixture in Hawaii off and on for the next fifteen years. Travis is billed as the Junior Heavyweight Champion of America.

Interesting to really look at the Karasick cards from this point on, as he was involved in a promotional war. It doesn't look like he really hot-shots his promotion; he just continues to use his regular crew with good matches.

On February 23rd, Ted Travis beat Jacques Manuel, and Ben Sherman beat Ben Pilar.

March 2nd saw Lee Grable go to a draw with Ted Travis in a non-title match. George Pencheff debuts beating Ben Sherman. Pencheff is billed as the Australian Jr Heavyweight champ.

March 9th sees George Pencheff set himself up for main events as he beats Lee Grable on a decision.

March 16th saw Ted Travis beat George Pencheff, and Leo Wallick debuted, beating Ben Sherman.

On April 3rd, it was reported that Al Karasick met with officials from the Philippines to hold matches in Manila.

On April 20th, Lee Grable beat Ben Sherman in a title match. This card drew 5,000.

On May 25th, Ted Travis beat Ben Sherman, and Lee Grable beat Leo Wallick by decision.

On May 30th, Karasick sent word he had signed Jimmy Londos to defend his World title during the summer. He had also signed Pantaleon Manlapig from the Philippines.

June 8th saw Pantaleon Manlapig beat Bob Corby in two straight falls. Ben Sherman also went to a draw with Leo Wallick.

July 13th saw Ted Travis beat Leo Wallick, and Ben Sherman beat Frank "Speedy" Moscato. This card drew 4,000.

July 20th saw Mike Nazarian debut, going to a draw with Leo Wallick. Pantaleon Manlapig beat Lee Grable in a non title match.

On August 3rd, Ted Travis won the Hawaiian JR Heavyweight title, beating Lee Grable.

August 11th saw Sandor Szabo stop off in Honolulu on his way to Australia. He hopes to appear in Hawaii on his return.

August 17th saw Vilai Su'a return to the Karasick promotion after appearing with the rival promotion earlier in the year. Ted Travis went to a draw with George Pencheff in the main event.

September 7th saw Pantaleon Manlapig beat George Pencheff, and Pete Peterson beat Mike Nazarian.

"PETE" PETERSEN

Petersen was discharged from the army in March and received a Purple Heart for his service. He had been a wrestler since 1935.

On September 14th, Ted Travis beat Sammy Stein. Stein was a movie actor and former pro football player. He was on his way back from Australia.

September 21st saw a crowd of 5,700 watch Pantaleon Manlapig and Pete Peterson beat Ted Travis and Jacques Manuel in a tag match.

By the end of October, Julius LaRance had come into the area and beaten George Pencheff and Jacques Manuel. Ali Hassan had also come to Hawaii.

On November 2nd, Sandor Szabo came to Hawaii and defended his world title against Pete Petersen. Interestingly, this card only drew 3,500, which seems lower than usual.

November 23rd saw Maurice Lachapelle come into Hawaii and beat Ali Hassan.

On November 30th, Maurice LaChappelle beat Julius LaRance in the main event. LaChappelle also won a battle royal. Ivan Kameroff debuted and beat Jacques Manuel. Kameroff was the first wrestler before this that I had personally seen. Kameroff wrestled until the early 1970's and settled in the NW.

On December 6th was the annual Shrine Aloha Bowl to benefit disabled children. Wrestling was part of the halftime show. Jimmy Gonsalves won a battle royal. A member of the University of Hawaii football team was Bob Shibuya, who later was better known as Kinji Shibuya. He played center.

December 7th saw Maurice LaChappelle go to a draw with Ivan Kameroff and Pantaleon Manlapig beat Ali Hassan. Jack Sherry, an old timer with a claim to a world title, issued a challenge to Pantaleon. Sherry would have been 54 years old.

Despite arriving in Hawaii on December 5th, Sherry did not wrestle here in 1947. He is introduced to the crown on the 12/28 card.

There is a show on December 18th that is not a Karasick card. It is held at a Marine Air Station in Ewa, Hawaii. It is speculated that it is run by Whitey Glover. Glover had been in Hawaii since 1944 and had appeared on Karasicks and Langs cards.

There are no results for this card listed, but The New Masked Blue Beetle was scheduled to wrestle Dale Clark, Francis Rawlins VS Al Camacho, Gene Sexton VS Ted Sanders, and Bear Honda VS Fred Tam.

1947 Wrestling Ads & Pictures

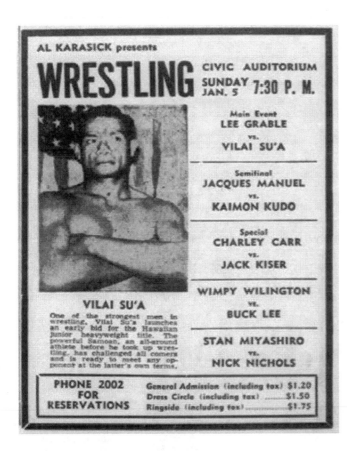

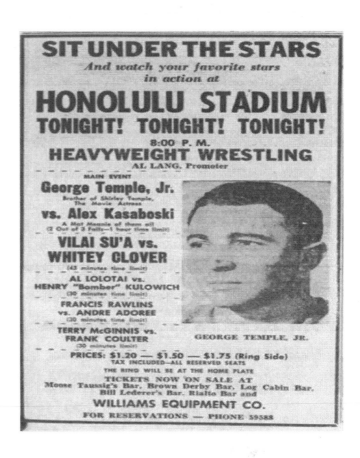

GEORGE TEMPLE, JR.

THE MASKED TERROR

ALI HASSEN

Julius LaRance

Sammy Stein

Frank "Speedy" Moscato

BATTLE ROYAL!

Six Wrestlers,
Two Referees
Featuring
**MAURICE CHAPPELLE
ALI HASSEN
IVAN KAMAROFF
JACQUES MANUEL
JULIUS LARANCE
BEN SHERMAN**

First two eliminated return
for 20 minute match—sec-
ond pair clash over 30
minutes, and last two survivors meet in main event.

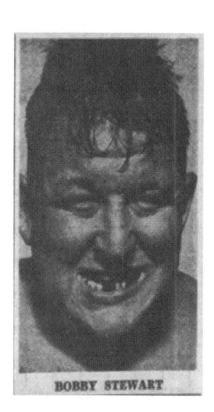

Al Karasick signs Pantaleon Manlapig   SF promoter Joe Malcewicz behind Karasick

1948

1948 starts with a show on January 4th. Jack Sherry beat Julius LaRance, and Maurice LaChappelle drew Ivan Kameroff.

Interestingly, the paper mentions that Al Karasick is reluctant to book Jack Sherry. The paper even calls him an old "shooter." They are working to get Strangler Lewis to meet Jack Sherry, and they have agreed to a match on January 25th.

On January 10th, Al Karasick talks about the upcoming Jack Sherry/Strangler Lewis match. He mentions he doesn't know how the match will get over. He even claims he is not proud of staging this match. He warns the public that this match will not compare in speed, agility, and thrills compared to their regular matches.

223

On January 11th, Ted Travis beat Ivan Kameroff in the main event, and Pantaleon Manlapig beat Ali Hassan in the semi-main event.

Jack Sherry comments on Al Karasick's comments, saying if he is too old, he will wrestle anyone from Karasick's stable. He even goes as far as saying he will wrestle four wrestlers on the same night. Despite all the banter, Jack Sherry no shows this match and announces he will be working for a new promotion run by Whitey Glover. Karasick had a feeling the Sherry/Strangler Lewis match would not materialize, and he booked Butch Levy as a backup match. Strangler Lewis got the win in his very last match.

Al Lolotai also returned on this January 25th show. The show drew 2,500 with increased ticket prices.

On February 8th, Ted Travis went to a draw with Ivan Kameroff.

Veteran wrestler Dude Chick was introduced to the crowd. He was in town with the Hopalong Cassidy Wild West Show.

Another chapter in this new promotional war took place on February 13th when the board of directors of the Honolulu Stadium turned down Whitey Glover's application to hold pro wrestling at this venue. Glover accused Al Karasick of exerting his influence to stop a rival promotion.

February 5th saw Maurice LaChappelle beat Ivan Kameroff, and Pantaleon Manlapig drew Dude Chick.

On February 16th, Gene Sexton and Francis Rawlins formed the Hawaii Wrestling Association and will promote cards in opposition to Karasick. No mention if Whitey Glover will be involved in this promotion.

Sexton's first show was at the Schofield Barracks. Jack Sherry beat Jimmy Gonsalves, who has apparently jumped promotions as well.

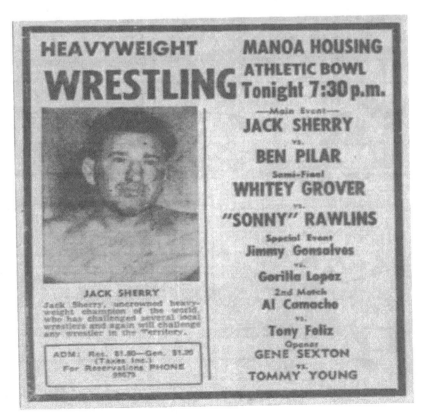

February 28th saw the HWA have another show. Jack Sherry beat Ben Pilar, and Sonny Rawlins beat Whitey Glover. This was a junior police benefit show.

Karassick's wrestlers went to Kauai for two shows, and the listed promoter was Tom Kanemoto.

On Feb 29th Ted Travis beat Pantaleon Manlapig.

On March 10th, Oki Shikina returned to Hawaii after a 9-year absence.

On March 17th, Shikina had his first match and captured a win over Ali Pasha Fontes.

March 18th and another HWA show saw Spider Al Galento beat Jimmy Gonsalves, and Jack Sherry beat Al Camacho.

On March 24th, it appears that Galento has jumped to the Karasick group as he gets a win over Mike Casey. Oki Shikina picks up another win over Bob Corby.

On March 28th, Shikina got another win over Ivan Kameroff, and Galento beat Kimon Kudo.

JACK CLAYBOURNE

On April 4th, Oki Shikina beat Ted Travis in a non-title match; Jack Claybourne debuted and went to a draw with Maurice LaChappelle. Claybourne was billed as the Negro Champion of the World. He had previously appeared in Hawaii in 1937 under the name Juan Selassie Amnerus, The Black Panther.

April 11th, Ted Travis beat Jack Claybourne in a non-title match, and Ivan Kameroff beat newcomer Red Vagnone.

On April 13th, Al Karasick suffered a heart attack while in Los Angeles and was hospitalized. He was recruiting wrestlers and negotiating to bring in an ice skating revue.

April 18th saw Ted Travis beat Oki Shikina and Tony Morelli beat Maurice LaChappelle.

On May 2nd, Lee Grable returned and regained the Hawaiian title, beating Ted Travis.

On May 23rd Leo Wallick beat Lee Grable in a non-title match, and Pantaleon Manlapig beat Whitey Whittler on dq.

After an absence, the HWA had a card at Schofield Barracks and drew 3,000. Gene Sexton beat The Blue Beetle in the main event.

June 6th is the last wrestling card at the Civic Auditorium until mid-July. The Ice Vogues will be using the Auditorium in the meantime. Karasick is still recovering from a heart attack and has not returned to Hawaii yet.

Wrestling resumed on July 18th as John Swenski beat Lee Grable in a non-title match. Kimon Kudo and Martin Tanaka beat Jimmy Lott and Tony Ross.

Swenski was a friend of Al Jolson. He also had discovered oil on his property which was very lucrative.

Tanaka would have a long career and be better known as Duke Keomuka.

Al Karasick is back in Hawaii.

On July 30th, Jimmy Gonsalves issued a challenge to any wrestler in Hawaii and would like the match to take place for Al Karasick's promotion. Gonsalves trained under Karasick but had skipped over to the rival promotion and was now ready to return to work for Karasick. Karasick said he held no grudges and was more than willing to give Gonsalves another chance to wrestle on his cards.

August 8th saw Hisao Tanaka (Duke Keomuka) beat Lee Grable and win the Hawaiian title,

On September 5th, Bud Curtis beat Hisao Tanaka on DQ. Ben Pilar returned to the Karasick promotion and went to a draw with Harry Dellis.

On September 7th, Gene Sexton beat Earl Rasmussen to win the HWA title.

Jimmy Gonsalves beat Lee Grable on a decision on September 26th. The main event saw Red Vagnone beat Hisao Tanaka in a non-title match.

October 24th saw a big card as Hisao Tanaka beat Jimmy Lott, Jack Claybourne drew Oki Shikina, and Bud Curtis beat debuting Brother Frank on DQ (Frank Jares).

On October 31st, Jack Claybourne beat Hisao Tanaka for the Hawaiian Championship.

November 7th saw Jack Claybourne beat Chief Little Wolf in a non-title match, Oki Shikina drew Brother Frank, and Dick Raines beat Bud Curtis. Al Karasick is starting to use a few heavyweights for his cards.

December 2nd, it was reported that Al Karasick contacted the NWA to discuss the legality of using head butts in pro wrestling matches. There has been some controversy about Claybourne using head butts.

December 5th saw Jack Claybourne beat Chief Little Wolf, Leo Wallick beat Dick Raines on DQ, and Seelie Samara beat Brother Frank. Samara, who has worked as Ras Samara, is one of the top wrestlers in the world. Samara accused Claybourne of not defending the Negro Championship against him.

December 12th saw Jack Claybourne and Seelie Samara team up to go to a draw with Dick Raines and Brother Frank.

December 26th saw Seelie Samara beat Dick Raines, and Henry Bomber Kulkovich beat Jack Claybourne on DQ. Kulkovich had worked for rival promotions in the past year.

AL KARASICK presents SUNDAY NOV. 28 7:45 P.M.

WRESTLING

CIVIC AUDITORIUM

Double Main Event
2 out of 3 falls

JACK CLAYBOURNE
vs.
BROTHER FRANK

CHIEF LITTLE WOLF
vs.
DICK RAINES

—Special Event—
OKI SHIKINA
will attempt to pin
Jimmy Gonsalves
and Bucky O'Neill
within 30 minutes

One Fall Opener
EARL RASMUSSEN
vs.
ABEL RODRIGUES

CHIEF LITTLE WOLF
Famed Navajo Indian star, Chief Little Wolf is a veteran of pro wrestling. He is rough and tough and specializes in the Indian deathlock, a hold he originated. Chief Little Wolf wants a title match after his battle with Dick Raines.

FOR RESERVATIONS PHONE 55002

Reserved ringside $1.75
Reserved dress circle 1.50
General admission 1.20
(Prices Include Tax)

1948 Wrestling Ads & Pictures

Jack Sherry

Sherry with a Half Boston Crab
(aka Japanese Leglock) on Pat McGill

Ed "Strangler" Lewis

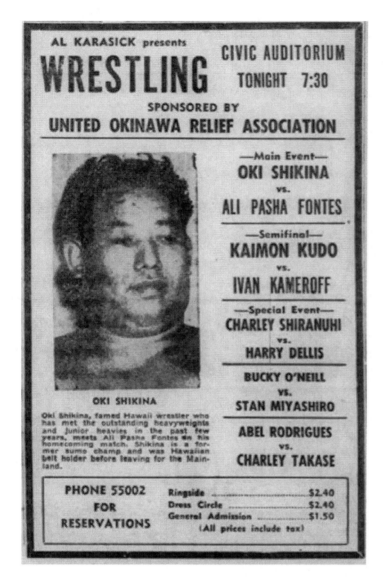

AL KARASICK presents

WRESTLING

CIVIC AUDITORIUM TONIGHT 7:30

SPONSORED BY
UNITED OKINAWA RELIEF ASSOCIATION

—Main Event—
OKI SHIKINA
vs.
ALI PASHA FONTES

—Semifinal—
KAIMON KUDO
vs.
IVAN KAMEROFF

—Special Event—
CHARLEY SHIRANUHI
vs.
HARRY DELLIS

BUCKY O'NEILL
vs.
STAN MIYASHIRO

ABEL RODRIGUES
vs.
CHARLEY TAKASE

OKI SHIKINA

Oki Shikina, famed Hawaii wrestler who has met the outstanding heavyweights and junior heavies in the past few years, meets Ali Pasha Fontes in his homecoming match. Shikina is a former sumo champ and was Hawaiian belt holder before leaving for the Mainland.

PHONE 55002
FOR
RESERVATIONS

Ringside $2.40
Dress Circle $2.40
General Admission $1.50
(All prices include tax)

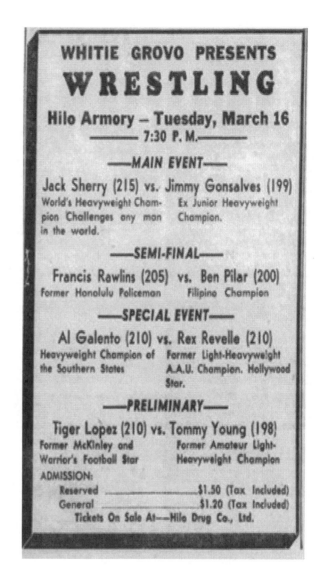

WHITIE GROVO PRESENTS

WRESTLING

Hilo Armory — Tuesday, March 16
——— 7:30 P. M.———

—MAIN EVENT—
Jack Sherry (215) vs. Jimmy Gonsalves (199)
World's Heavyweight Champion Challenges any man in the world.   Ex Junior Heavyweight Champion.

—SEMI-FINAL—
Francis Rawlins (205) vs. Ben Pilar (200)
Former Honolulu Policeman   Filipino Champion

—SPECIAL EVENT—
Al Galento (210) vs. Rex Revelle (210)
Heavyweight Champion of the Southern States   Former Light-Heavyweight A.A.U. Champion. Hollywood Star.

—PRELIMINARY—
Tiger Lopez (210) vs. Tommy Young (198)
Former McKinley and Warrior's Football Star   Former Amateur Light-Heavyweight Champion

ADMISSION:
Reserved ....$1.50 (Tax Included)
General ....$1.20 (Tax Included)
Tickets On Sale At—Hilo Drug Co., Ltd.

1949

1949 opens with an even better roster of wrestlers, with many fresh matchups to look forward to.

On January 9th, a very interesting match saw Jack Claybourne beat Seelie Samara for the Worlds Negro Heavyweight title.

On January 30th, Henry "Bomber" Kulkovich beat Jack Claybourne on DQ. Malkovich had a badly cut eye due to Claybourne's headbutting.

February 27th saw Jack Claybourne beat Johnny Sepeda. Also, Al Lolotai came back from football season. He beat Basher McDonald.

March 6th saw Vic Christy return to beat Bomber Kulkovich, and Jack Claybourne beat Kenny Ackles on decision.

On March 20th, Jack Claybourne turned back the challenge of Vic Chrisy, Lofty Bloomfield came in from Australia to beat Bomber Kulkovich, and Lee Grable returned to beat Johnny Sepeda.

March 27th saw Ted Travis return and team with his brother Vic Christy to beat Kenny Ackles and Bobby Ford.

March 28th saw the official announcement that the Hawaiian Wrestling Association had folded. This promotion was run by Gene Sexton and Francis "Sonny" Rawlins.

April 10th saw Jack Claybourne beat Ted Travis, and Antone Leone beat Vic Christy.

April 17th saw Ben Sherman return to Hawaii. He was billed as the Pacific Coast Jr Heavyweight champ. Sherman went to a draw with Jack Claybourne.

Pantaleon Manlapig beat Jacques Manuel. This would be Manlapig's last match. Five days later, Al Karasick announced that he was removing Pantaleon Manlapig for being unfit to compete in a wrestling match. He was found to have high blood pressure and a heart condition.

Antone Leone beat Jack Claybourne in a non-title match on May 1st.

On May 8th, Antone Leone beat Ben Sherman, and Ray Daong debuted, beating Pierre LaSalle. Daong had wrestled in other places as Ray Duran.

On June 5th, Antone Leone drew Kenny Ackles, and the Bat debuted and beat Charley Shiranhi. The Bat was African American Don Kindred.

On June 15th, there was an announcement that Olympic Weightlifting medalist and bodybuilder Harold Sakata was being trained by Ben Sherman as a wrestler.

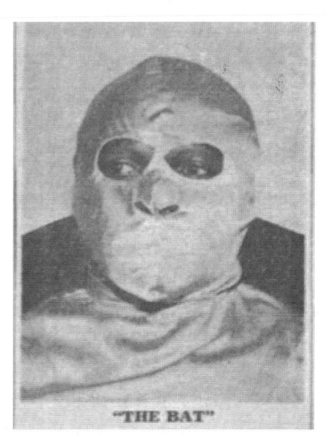

"THE BAT"

On July 17th, a big card saw George Pencheff beat The Bat. The Bat congratulated Pencheff and removed his mask, revealing Don Kindred. Sailor Tiger Joe Marsh drew Kay "Samson" Bell.

Kay Bell may be the first person up to this point that I have written about that I met in person at a Dean Silverstone reunion. Bell and Red Bastien would rib each other about being their favorite wrestler when they were kids. I can still hear Bastien's big booming laugh.

On July 31st, Jack Claybourne beat Kay Bell on DQ, George Penchoff beat Sailor Joe Marsh, and Pete Managoff debuted and beat Red Vagnone.

On August 7th, Jack Claybourne beat Kay Bell, and George Pencheff drew Pete Managoff.

On August 28th, Jack Claybourne drew George Pencheff. Pete Managoff beat Sailor Tiger Joe Marsh. This card's highlight was Harold Sakata's debut as he beat Earl Rasmussen.

On September 4th, another big name came to Hawaii, and Ray Gunkel beat Jack Claybourne on DQ. Gunkel was a former Purdue football player and 2-time AAU National Wrestling Champion.

On September 12th, Ray Gunkel captured a non-title win over Jack Claybourne. Bobby Manogoff beat George Pencheff.

Manogoff was a former NWA World Champ. Karasick spelled his name with an O to show that he and Pete Managoff were unrelated. As World Champ, Manogoff was correctly spelled Managoff.

On September 18th, Bobby Manogoff beat Pete Managoff in two straight falls. I guess that is a good way to differentiate those two guys.

On October 9th, Jack Claybourne's lengthy title reign came to an end at the hands of Bobby Manogoff as he captured the Hawaiian title. Pat Fraley had come to Hawaii and beat George Pencheff, and Ray Gunkel beat Sonny Kurgis.

October 30th saw an interesting tag match as Tommy O'Toole and Earl McCready beat Bobby Manogoff and Ray Gunkel.

On November 6th, Earl McCready beat Bobby Manogoff by a decision. These were two of the highest-rated wrestlers in the country at this time.

On November 20th, Bobby Manogoff beat Dirty Dick Raines, and Dean Detton beat Ray Gunkel. Brother Reed Detton had been in Hawaii since 1934 wrestling and became an amateur coach.

December 4th saw Dean Detton go to a no-contest with Bobby Manogoff. Ray Gunkel beat Ben Sherman, and Martin Tanaka returned and beat Jimmy Gonsalves.

On December 11th, Dean Detton won the Hawaiian title, beating Bobby Manogoff. Dean Detton did not hold the title very long; the next week, Hans Schnabel debuted and won the title on 12/18.

Christmas night, Fritz Schnabel joined his brother Hans. Fritz went to a no-contest with Ken Kenneth. That night, Hans Schnabel beat Mickey Gold.

1949 Wrestling Ads & Pictures

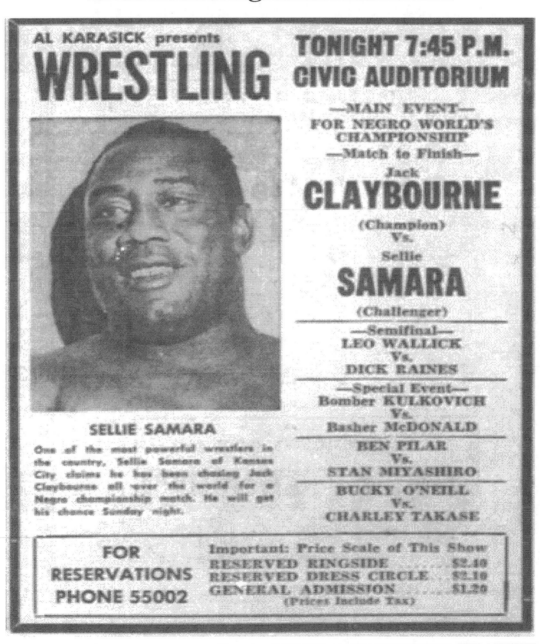

Curly Connors
"Champion of the Orient

"Dirty" Dick Raines

Rocco Toma

TARZAN WHITE

PETER MANAGOFF

"SAILOR" TIGER JOE

Harold Sakata

Tommy O'Toole

Daoang and manager EA Taok

Newlyweds Vic and Patty Christy
arriving in Honolulu

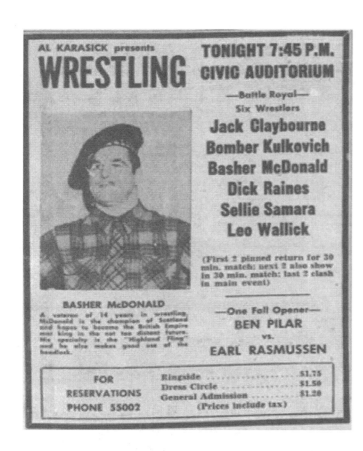

AL KARASICK presents

WRESTLING

TONIGHT 7:45 P.M.
CIVIC AUDITORIUM

—Battle Royal—
Six Wrestlers

Jack Claybourne
Bomber Kulkovich
Basher McDonald
Dick Raines
Sellie Samara
Leo Wallick

(First 2 pinned return for 30 min. match; next 2 also show in 30 min. match; last 2 clash in main event)

BASHER McDONALD

A veteran of 14 years in wrestling, McDonald is the champion of Scotland and hopes to become the British Empire mat king in the not too distant future. His specialty is the "Highland Fling" and he also makes good use of the headlock.

—One Fall Opener—
BEN PILAR
vs.
EARL RASMUSSEN

FOR RESERVATIONS PHONE 55002	Ringside $1.75
	Dress Circle $1.50
	General Admission $1.20
	(Prices include tax)

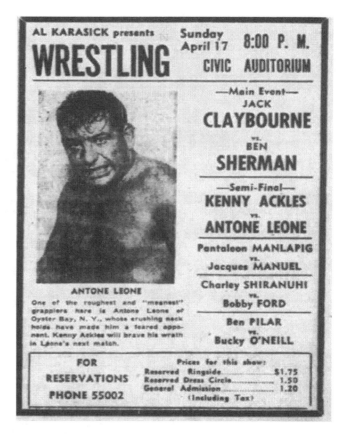

AL KARASICK presents

WRESTLING

Sunday April 17 8:00 P. M.
CIVIC AUDITORIUM

—Main Event—
JACK
CLAYBOURNE
vs.
BEN
SHERMAN

—Semi-Final—
KENNY ACKLES
vs.
ANTONE LEONE

Pantaleon **MANLAPIG**
vs.
Jacques **MANUEL**

Charley **SHIRANUHI**
vs.
Bobby **FORD**

Ben **PILAR**
vs.
Bucky **O'NEILL**

ANTONE LEONE

One of the roughest and "meanest" grapplers here is Antone Leone of Oyster Bay, N. Y., whose crushing neck holds have made him a feared opponent. Kenny Ackles will brave his wrath in Leone's next match.

FOR RESERVATIONS PHONE 55002	Prices for this show:
	Reserved Ringside $1.75
	Reserved Dress Circle 1.50
	General Admission 1.20
	(Including Tax)

Reed Detton with brother Dean

234

1950

The new decade of the 50s starts, and there are some exciting things to note about the crew that starts the decade off in Hawaii.

Fritz and Hans Schnabel

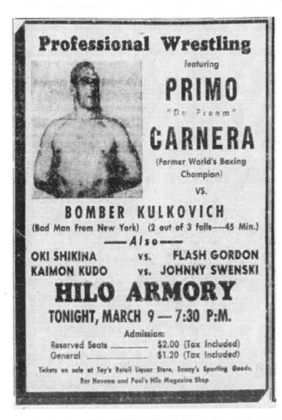

Fritz and Hans Schnabel look like the top heels in the area. 1950, and doing a German gimmick looks a little dicey. Hans started in 1934, and Fritz started in 1936. They were real-life brothers, and even though they are of German descent, it doesn't look like they pushed it to the Nazi level.

On January 1st, The Schnabel brothers beat Ken Kenneth and Martin Tanaka. Tanaka would be better known as Duke Keomuka. He started wrestling in 1944. Tanaka was billed from Hawaii. In the opener, Charley Shiranuhi went to a draw with John Swenski. Who knew these two would be in the office and promotions for years? Charley Shiranuhi would later become Mr. Moto and be one of the main bookers in LA. John Swenski would be one of the leading promoters in the Bay Area.

On January 22nd, Primo Canera came to Hawaii and beat Hans Schnabel.

On February 5th, Sandor Szabo came in and won the Hawaiian Junior Heavyweight title, beating Hans Schnabel. This was even, at this point, called the Ring Wrestling title.

On February 12th, Jack Claybourne came in to beat Flash Gordon. Claybourne had been the Hawaiian Champion in 1948. This Flash Gordon was Joe Gordon, and by 1950, he had been wrestling for twelve years.

The February 19th show drew a big crowd of 5,000 to see Jack Claybourne beat Flash Gordon.

On March 12th, Primo Carnera came in to beat Jack Claybourne. This seemed to be a huge matchup.

We think of Hawaii from the mid-60s on as these fantastic matchups and dream cards. Things did not change. These matchups in Hawaii in 1950 were some of the top stars in the country, and they rotated in and out quickly to get continuous great matchups.

March 26th has Sandor Szabo and Primo Carnera fight to a draw. Also on the card are top hands Antone Leone and Bomber Kulkovich.

April 16th has Sandor Szabo beat Jack Claybourne.

On May 7th, the French Angel (Maurice Tillet) beat Bomber Kulkovich. The Angel was a traveling attraction, much like Andre The Giant in the future.

Sandor Szabo got a big win over The Angel on May 14th.

On May 28th, Sandor Szabo beat Antone Leone. Also on the card was Rey Urbano, who would later become the original Great Kabuki.

Arjan Singh would come to Hawaii in June of 50 and get a non-title win over Szabo on June 4th and then win the Hawaiian title on June 18th. This was the only title he ever won. He started in Hawaii in 1936 and had been to the Islands a number of times. In 1950, he was just finishing his career.

Ray Eckert was the latest to come to Hawaii, and he beat Arjan Singh for the Title on July 16th. However, Eckert's title reign only lasted one week, and he was beaten by Terry McGinnis.

McGinnis would go on a run and get wins over Eckert, Juan Humberto and Bill Sledge. He would lose the title back to Sandor Szabo on September 3rd. McGinnis was in a movie in 1950 called Jiggs and Maggie Out West. In March of 1952, McGinnis suffered a heart attack and passed away at the age of 41.

The October 22nd main event had Charro Azteca beat Flash Gordon on DQ. Earl McCready had also come to Hawaii.

At this point, it is unclear if wrestling took a 6-month break or if results were unavailable during that time.

AL KARASICK presents
WRESTLING
Sunday May 7   8:00 P. M.
CIVIC AUDITORIUM

—MAIN EVENT—
Introducing
MAURICE **TILLET**
(The French Angel!)
VS.
BOMBER **KULKOVICH**

—SEMIFINAL—
ANTONE LEONE
VS.
JESSE JAMES

Joe Benacaso vs. Armand Tanny

Ben Pilar vs. Earl Rasmussen

MAURICE TILLET
THE FRENCH ANGEL — Here is a wrestler you have to see to believe—Maurice Tillet, the sensational French Angel!

PHONE 55002 FOR RESERVATIONS
PRICES FOR THIS SHOW
Reserved Ringside.........$2.40   General Admission.........$2.10
Reserved Dress Circle........2.10   (Taxes Included)

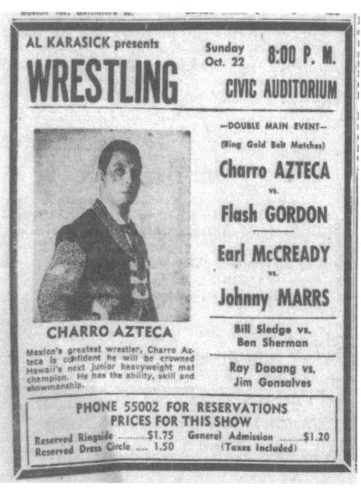

AL KARASICK presents
WRESTLING
Sunday Oct. 22   8:00 P. M.
CIVIC AUDITORIUM

—DOUBLE MAIN EVENT—
(Ring Gold Belt Matches)
Charro AZTECA
vs.
Flash GORDON

Earl McCREADY
vs.
Johnny MARRS

Bill Sledge vs. Ben Sherman

Ray Daoang vs. Jim Gonsalves

CHARRO AZTECA
Mexico's greatest wrestler, Charro Azteca is confident he will be crowned Hawaii's next junior heavyweight mat champion. He has the ability, skill and showmanship.

PHONE 55002 FOR RESERVATIONS
PRICES FOR THIS SHOW
Reserved Ringside.........$1.75   General Admission.........$1.20
Reserved Dress Circle.....1.50   (Taxes Included)

1950 Wrestling Ads & Pictures

PRIMO CARNERA
Former World's Heavyweight Boxing Champion

To Appear at Paseo de Susana
Monday, March 20th   **7:30 p. m.**

Primo Carnera Former Heavyweight Boxing Champion	vs 45 minutes	"Bomber" Kulkovich Sensational Honolulu Matman
	Supporting Boxing Card	
Eddie Pettegrew	vs 6 rounds	Young Quintin
Baby Arogones	vs 4 rounds	Small Landrino
Jesse Stein	vs 1 rounds	Norberto Diaz
Zamorra Kid	vs 4 rounds	Romeo Iral
Anasticio Martinez	vs 4 rounds	Shorty Domingo

Flash Gordon & his wife

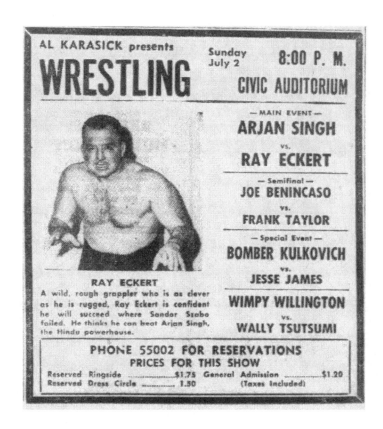

AL KARASICK presents
WRESTLING
Sunday July 2 — 8:00 P. M.
CIVIC AUDITORIUM

— MAIN EVENT —
ARJAN SINGH
vs.
RAY ECKERT

— Semifinal —
JOE BENINCASO
vs.
FRANK TAYLOR

— Special Event —
BOMBER KULKOVICH
vs.
JESSE JAMES

WIMPY WILLINGTON
vs.
WALLY TSUTSUMI

RAY ECKERT
A wild, rough grappler who is as clever as he is rugged, Ray Eckert is confident he will succeed where Sandor Szabo failed. He thinks he can beat Arjan Singh, the Hindu powerhouse.

PHONE 55002 FOR RESERVATIONS
PRICES FOR THIS SHOW
Reserved Ringside .... $1.75   General Admission $1.20
Reserved Dress Circle .... 1.50   (Taxes Included)

Sandor Szarbo

1951

1951 became a very strange year with many ups and downs.

I asked historian Mark Hewitt if he knew what this Hawaiian wrestling hiatus was about. He mentioned that he didn't find a good explanation for this. Karasick did say that he was scouting and recruiting wrestlers to bring to Honolulu.

During this period, there were a lot of ads and stories about judo and how popular it had become. Karasick made use of its appeal in his promotions. However, it doesn't make sense to abandon wrestling for judo competitions.

Wrestling picks up on March 4th. The opening crew looks more like junior heavyweights with Gordon Hessell, Glen Detton, Sugy Hayamaka, and Stan Miyashiro from Hilo Hawaii. Miyashiro would later be known by a number of aliases, including Great Kato, Omaya Kato, and Kato Yama.

April 8th saw Jack Claybourne and Woody Strode beat Bobby Bruns and Gordon Hessell. I believe this is Bobby Bruns's debut, and he will play an essential part in Hawaiian wrestling history.

April 22nd saw Masahiko Kimura beat Ben Sherman in a judo match. This was Kimura's debut as a wrestler.

April 29th saw Kimura beat Eric Pedersen in two straight falls, one fall a regular catch wrestling and the 2nd fall in a judo jacket fall. Toshio Yamaguchi beat Woody Strode.

May 6th saw Kimura beat Joe Benincasa in a straight American-style match, and Toshio Yamaguchi beat Ted Travis in a judo match.

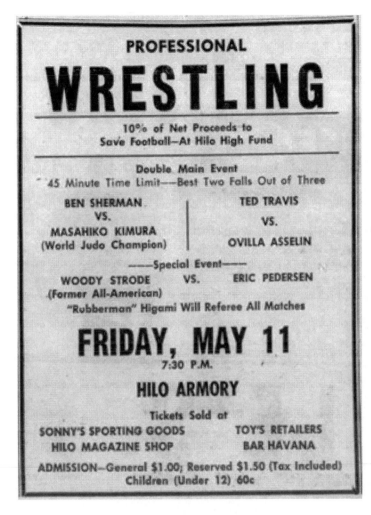

PROFESSIONAL

WRESTLING

10% of Net Proceeds to
Save Football—At Hilo High Fund

Double Main Event
45 Minute Time Limit——Best Two Falls Out of Three

BEN SHERMAN
VS.
MASAHIKO KIMURA
(World Judo Champion)

TED TRAVIS
VS.
OVILLA ASSELIN

——Special Event——
WOODY STRODE   VS.   ERIC PEDERSEN
(Former All-American)

"Rubberman" Higami Will Referee All Matches

FRIDAY, MAY 11
7:30 P.M.

HILO ARMORY

Tickets Sold at
SONNY'S SPORTING GOODS   TOY'S RETAILERS
HILO MAGAZINE SHOP   BAR HAVANA
ADMISSION—General $1.00; Reserved $1.50 (Tax Included)
Children (Under 12) 60c

This is interesting because, at least on paper, these judo guys are killing the American wrestlers in both judo and catch as catch can. Kimura is really a big deal and will carve out his place in wrestling history. However, during this time, it seems like they could be hurting the credibility of some of their top talent.

However, by June 3rd, Kimura and Yamaguchi are gone; they will go to Brazil for a wrestling tournament.

It will be interesting to see how wrestling fares the rest of 1951 after the late start and the invasion of the judo/wrestlers who dominated the cards in the first part of 51.

June 3rd has Andre Adoree and Andre Asselin beat Buddy Jackson and Woody Strode, and Ted Travis beat Joe Benincasa. These wrestlers, at least on paper, do not appear to have long-term appeal.

July 9th, Mike Mazurki makes his debut, beating Andre Adoree. The following week, he beats Andre Asselin.

On the first show in August, some new wrestlers, including Earl McCready, Wally Dusek, and Dave Levin, debut.

On August 19th, Terry McGinnis beats Ted Travis for the Hawaiian title. McGinnis runs off a series of victories over Wally Dusek, Dave Levin, Laverne Baxter, Abe Kashey and Kay Bell.

On September 10th, Bobby Bruns was on the card, losing to Kay Bell. The main event saw McGinnis beat Laverne Baxter. Bruns was the son of opera singer Lotta Gunter. He participated in the 1932 water polo Olympics. Bruns had passed the bar exam and was eligible to be a lawyer.

The Hawaiian scene appeared a little shaky in 1951, but there was big news. Al Karasick would send a crew to Tokyo, changing Japanese wrestling forever with the first American tour. Bobby Bruns was Karasick's point man. September 30th was the first card in Tokyo to feature American wrestlers. In fact, in that initial card, there were no Japanese wrestlers. However, after about a month, Rikidozan and Koichi Endo would start to appear.

That first card on September 30th had Bobby Bruns go to a draw with Ovila Asselin, Harold Sakata beat Casey Berger, and Dr. Len Hall beat Andre Adoree.

Karasick would continue to be the booking agent for US wrestlers heading to Japan. That would make Hawaii an even more attractive workplace, knowing a favorable nod might lead to work in Japan.

October 1st saw a significant wrestler debut. Hawaii native Bob Shibuya beat Buck O'Neil. He would later work as Kinji Shibuya and have a very successful career.

On October 22nd, Abe Kashey beat Terry McGinnis for the Hawaiian Title. Earl McCready was along on this card, beating Bob McCune.

On November 5th, Lucky Simonovich would return to Hawaii, last appearing there six years prior. He would rack up wins over Earl McCready, Pete Peterson, and Dick Raines. He would become a fixture in Hawaii over the next decade.

1951 Wrestling Ads & Pictures

JUDO STARS SIGN — Masayuki Kimura (seated) and Toshio Yamaguchi (standing), two of Japan's greatest judo wrestlers, yesterday signed with Promoter Al Karasick to appear on his pro mat cards at the Civic auditorium. Kimura and Yamaguchi will be featured on this Sunday night's card. (Jack Matsumoto photo.)

ON BENEFIT MAT CARD—Three of the eight "main event" wrestlers who will appear on Sunday night's pro wrestling show for The Advertiser's Christmas Fund are pictured above. They are, left to right, Lucky Simunovich, Bob McCune and Abe Kashey. The card headlines a match for the Ring magazine gold belt, with Kashey defending it against Simunovich. McCune takes on Dick Raines in the semifinal. (Advertiser photo.)

MAT HEADLINER—Bobby Bruns, internationally famous mat star, arrived yesterday morning and will team with Gordon Hessell for a tag team battle against Jack Claybourne and Woody Strode tonight at the Civic auditorium. Bruns is pictured above (United Air Lines photo.)

1952

1952 begins with Bobby Bruns, Lucky Simonovich, Abe Kashey, and Dick Raines on top.

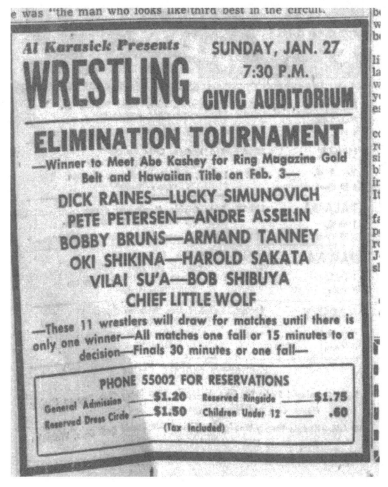

On January 27th, there is a big tournament to see who will meet Abe Kashey for the Hawaiian title. Bobby Bruns wins the tournament and, along the way, beats Dick Raines, Pete Peterson, and Andre Asselin.

The following week, Kashey turned back the challenge of Bruns. Also on that card on February 4th, The Red Scorpion debuts and goes to a draw with Lucky Simonovich.

February 17th has Rikidozan beating Chief Little Wolf and Abe Kashey beating Dick Raines on dq.

February 24th, Dick Raines beat Lucky Simonovich, Bobby Bruns went to a draw with Abe Kashey, and Rikidozan beat Andre Asselin.

On March 30th, Lucky Simonovich beat Abe Kashey to win the Hawaiian title.

April 6th has Karl Davis and Red Scorpion beating Rikidozan and Oki Shikina. Rikidozan is very early in his career and has not reached the level where he is main eventing most of the cards. It is still important to note how he is used on these early cards.

April 13th has Bobby Brun, and Lucky Simonovich beat Red Scorpion and Hans Schnabel, and Bud Curtis beat Jim Mitchell (Black Panther). Mitchell has been wrestling since 1931. Mitchell may be injured in this match as he does not wrestle again for six months.

The promotion seems to be rolling again with compelling matchups and good talent.

April 20th has Red Scorpion beat Earl McCready in a very important match that is 3rd from the top. The main event has Fritz and Hans Schnabel beating Bobby Bruns and Lucky Simonovich. The 2nd main event has Rikidozan beating Ivan Kameroff.

On May 4th, Rikidozan moved right into the main event, getting a win over Lucky Simonovich.

On May 11th, The Red Scorpion (Tom Rice) beat Rikidozan in the main event.

The following week, Red Scorpion won the Hawaiian Title, beating Lucky Simonovich.

Red Scorpion repeated his victory over Rikidozan on June 1st.

On June 8th, Bobby Bruns and Lucky Simonovich were the first holders of the Hawaiian tag titles. They beat The Red Scorpion and Bud Curtis to win the titles. Albert Mills also debuted on June 8th, beating Johnny Senda.

Leo Nomellini had come in for a few weeks, teaming with Lucky Simonovich to get wins over Red Scorpion and Bud Curtis and then going to a draw with Red Scorpion and Albert Mills. Seelie Samara returned to be on the undercard and went to a draw with Bud Curtis.

On paper, Hawaii is now on a roll with good talent revolving every few weeks.

Baron Leone showed up on July 6th to go to a draw with Bobby Bruns. Leone got a win over Bruns the following week.

Other matches on 7/13 saw Kimura return and go to a draw with Johnny Sepeda, and Red Scorpion go to a draw with Seelie Samara.

On July 20th, Gene Dubuque debuted and beat Bud Curtis on DQ. Interesting because, over the years, he would use three different names in Hawaii. In 1952, he worked as Gene Dubuque. In 1959, he would return as Gene Darval; in 1968, he would return as Magnificent Maurice. He would team with Johnny Barend and win the Hawaiian tag titles.

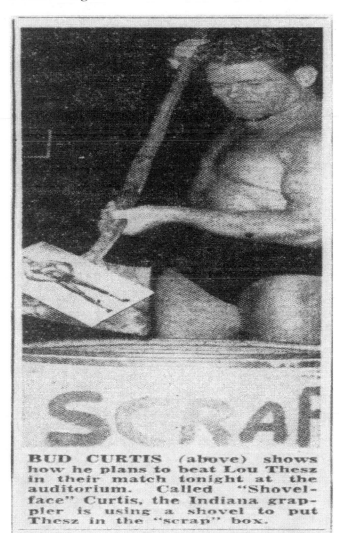

BUD CURTIS (above) shows how he plans to beat Lou Thesz in their match tonight at the auditorium. Called "Shovel-face" Curtis, the Indiana grappler is using a shovel to put Thesz in the "scrap" box.

On July 27th, Kokichi Endo debuted in Hawaii. He had just a handful of matches under his belt in Japan. On this date, he beat Ray Daoang on DQ.

Endo also wrestled under the name Kintaro Oki.

On August 24th, Lou Thesz came to the Islands and beat Bud Curtis in an NWA world title defense. Bobby Bruns and Dave Levin beat Bob Legs Langevin and Red Scorpion in a tag match.

Langevin started wrestling in 1934. He stays in Hawaii for four months.

August 31st has some interesting bookings as NWA champ Lou Thesz wins the Hawaiian Championship from Red Scorpion. Scorpion then unmasks as Tom Rice.

Thesz's commitment to the NWA title forces him to vacate the Hawaiian title.

On September 7th, there is a tournament for the Hawaiian title. The night ends with Tom Rice and Bobby Bruns ready to meet for the title on the next card, September 14th.

Bruns is able to beat Rice for the title.

On October 5th, Ben and Mike Sharpe come to Hawaii to defend the NWA World tag titles. They beat Tom Rice and Bud Curtis. The Sharpes stay until December and carry the territory for the next two months.

The Sharpes beat Bobby Bruns and Gino Garibaldi in the following two weeks.

On November 2nd, Primo Carnera comes in to be Gino Garibaldi's tag partner, and they go to a draw with the Sharpes.

The tag titles that were won in June by Bobby Bruns and Lucky Simonovich have become vacant. That problem was solved on November 9th as Gino Garibaldi and Lucky Simonovich beat Bob Langevin and Tom Rice for the vacant tag titles. Also, on that card, Mike Sharpe beat Primo Carnera in a battle of big-time names.

November 16th saw Gino Garibaldi and Lucky Simunovich battle the Sharpes and Gino and Lucky won on DQ.

The Sharpes won the rematch on the following week, November 23rd.

Lou Thesz returned to Hawaii on December 7th to beat Mike Sharpe.

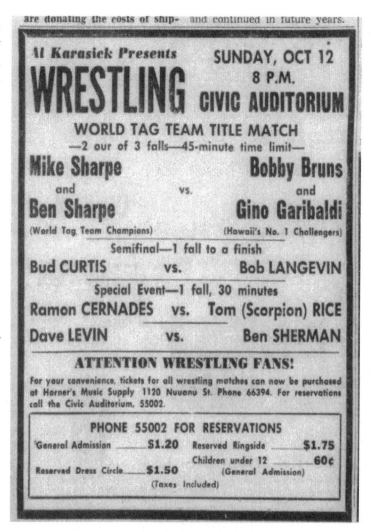

Bobby Bruns and Lucky Simonovich, the original Hawaii tag title holders who were never beaten, wrestled the Sharpes on December 14th. The Sharpe's came away with another victory.

At the end of 1952, Gorgeous George came to Hawaii. George was in his prime and one of the most famous people on television.

George beat Lucky Simonovich on December 21st and returned on the last card of the year to lose to Bobby Bruns the following week.

The hiatus at the beginning of 1951 seems to be well in the past. 1952 ends with some of the top stars in the country wrestling in Hawaii. Talent like The Sharpe's, Gorgeous George, Bobby Bruns, Gino Garibaldi, and Rikidozan makes everyone notice what is happening in Hawaii.

1952 Wrestling Ads & Pictures

MAT CHAMPION SIGNED—Promoter Al Karasick (seated, right) smiles happily after signing National Wrestling Alliance-recognized world champion Lou Thesz (left) for appearances in Honolulu. The signing took place in San Francisco last week. Looking on is Ed (Strangler) Lewis, oldtime great of the mat sport. Thesz arrived in Honolulu Friday night and will meet Bud Curtis on tonight's card at the Civic auditorium.

TITLE MATCH SIGNED—Abe Kashey (right) is shown signing "under protest" a contract to defend the Hawaiian mat belt Sunday night against Dick Raines of Dallas, Tex. Looking on as Kashey scribbles his signature are, left to right, Raines, Attorney Robert Hogan and Promoter Al Karasick (standing). The Kashey-Raines match will be the main event of Sunday night's card at the Civic Auditorium.

TOP BENEFIT CARD—Lou Thesz, left, and Mike Sharpe, headline tomorrow night's wrestling card at Civic Auditorium. Part of the proceeds will be turned over to Christmas Charities. Thesz, recognized world champion by the National Wrestling Alliance, will defend those laurels against Sharpe. —Jack Matsumoto Photo.

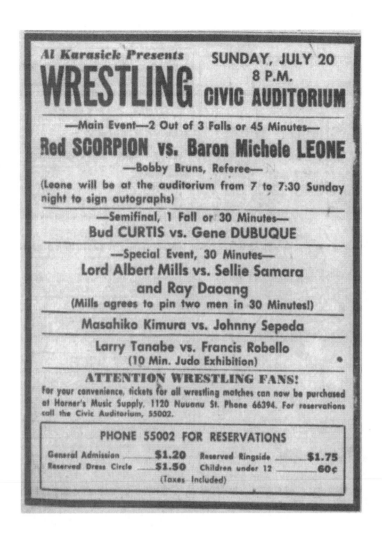

Al Karasick Presents

WRESTLING

SUNDAY, JULY 20
8 P.M.
CIVIC AUDITORIUM

—Main Event—2 Out of 3 Falls or 45 Minutes—

Red SCORPION vs. Baron Michele LEONE

—Bobby Bruns, Referee—

(Leone will be at the auditorium from 7 to 7:30 Sunday
night to sign autographs)

—Semifinal, 1 Fall or 30 Minutes—

Bud CURTIS vs. Gene DUBUQUE

—Special Event, 30 Minutes—

Lord Albert Mills vs. Sellie Samara and Ray Daoang

(Mills agrees to pin two men in 30 Minutes!)

Masahiko Kimura vs. Johnny Sepeda

Larry Tanabe vs. Francis Robello

(10 Min. Judo Exhibition)

ATTENTION WRESTLING FANS!

For your convenience, tickets for all wrestling matches can now be purchased
at Horner's Music Supply, 1120 Nuuanu St. Phone 66394. For reservations
call the Civic Auditorium, 55002.

PHONE 55002 FOR RESERVATIONS		
General Admission $1.20	Reserved Ringside $1.75	
Reserved Dress Circle $1.50	Children under 12 .... 60¢	
(Taxes Included)		

DEFENDS MAT TITLE—Abe Kashey (above), veteran grappler from New Jersey, is defending the Ring magazine gold belt and Hawaiian mat title tonight at the Civic auditorium. His opponent will be Lucky Simunovich.

1953

1953 starts out with a battle royal that is won by Mario DeSouza. Mario DeSouza had a great look. He wrestled for about seven years and didn't win any titles. He started out with the win in a big battle royal. He got a win over Tom Rice and a draw with Rikidozan, but that was the extent. DeSouza spent most of 1953 in Hawaii.

On January 11th, Bobby Bruns and Dennis Clary beat Mario DeSouza and Tom Rice. Clary had come to Hawaii in late 1952. He was nicknamed Mr. California, so it figures that he was well-built. He had a 7-year career that included being World tag champs with Rikidozan in the San Francisco area.

On January 18th, Bobby Bruns beat former tag partner Gino Garibaldi.

On January 25th, Verne Gagne debuted and beat Jack Terry. The following week, he would go to a draw with Bobby Bruns. Verne would not wrestle in Hawaii again for eighteen more years.

A peek at Gagne's February shows how he traveled the country and made a name for himself. In February, he appeared in Honolulu, San Francisco, Amarillo, Chicago, Syracuse, Minneapolis, Jacksonville, Cleveland, Montreal, and other places.

The following week, on February 8th, Rikidozan beat Tom Rice in the main event.

On February 15th, Bobby Bruns and Rikidozan went to a draw with Abe Kashey and Tom Rice.

In a preliminary, Auleaga Maiava, who had started quietly in 1952, was starting to make more and more appearances. He would be better known in Hawaii as Neff Maiava.

WRESTLING PROGRAM
Civic Auditorium—8:00 P.M.

First Match—1 Fall 20 Min.

Larry TANABE _____ vs. _____ Auleaga MAIAVA

Semifinal—1 Fall to a Finish

Bearcat WRIGHT _____ vs. _____ Jack HADER

Tag Team Match
2 Out of 3 Falls—45 Min.

BOBBY BRUNS and BOBBY MANAGOFF
VS.
EL HOMBRE MONTANA and TOM RICE

Mr. X would debut, beating Dennis Clary. Mr. X would spend a lot of time in Hawaii, and once he was unmasked, he would be known as Shoulders Newman.

On March 1st, Abe Kashey and Tom Rice beat Bobby Bruns and Rikidozan to win the once again vacated Hawaiian tag titles. It isn't clear why there has been such a problem with the tag titles.

On March 15th, Abe Kashey drew with Mr. X in the main event. Bearcat Wright beat Jack Hader in one of the preliminaries. Bearcat is very early in his career. He stays in Hawaii for about two months and doesn't get into main events.

On March 22nd, Bobby Managoff came back to beat Tom Rice. In the following weeks, he teamed with Bobby Bruns and won the Hawaiian tag titles from Tom Rice and Abe Kasehy on April 5th.

On April 12th, Mr. X got a singles win over Bobby Bruns.

On April 19th, Hombre Montana debuted teaming with Tom Rice to beat Bobby Bruns and Bobby Managoff.

Hombre Montana (325 Pounds) To Show Here

EL HOMBRE   TOM RICE

On May 10th, Hans Schnabel returned to go to a no-contest with Hombre Montana. Also, on the same card, Bobby Bruns and Bobby Managoff beat Tom Rice and Mr. X.

Hans Schnabel picked up wins over Hombre Montana. Bobby Managoff and Hombre Montana unmasked Mr. X as Shoulders Newman in consecutive weeks.

On June 7th, Schnabel beat Bobby Bruns to win the Hawaiian title. Lee Grable also returned and beat Sonny Kurgis. Jim Mitchell had also returned to Hawaii.

Two weeks after unmasking Mr. X and revealing Shoulders Newman, Hans Schnabel and Newman teamed up. They lost, however, to Bobby Bruns and Jim Mitchell on June 14th.

June 28th saw Leo Nomellini return to Hawaii and beat Hans Schnabel on DQ.

On July 19th, Bobby Managoff beat Hans Schnabel to win the Hawaiian title. The following week, Ray Eckert returned and had his way with Hans Schnabel.

Brother Frank Jares had come to Hawaii. He debuted by beating Sonny Kurgis.

Lou Thesz came to Hawaii on August 9th to beat Bobby Managoff. The following week beat Ray Eckert on DQ.

The Hawaiian title changed hands again on August 23rd as Ben Sharpe beat Bobby Managoff. That's interesting because Mike Sharpe had always been the more successful brother as far as winning singles titles. Ben Sharpe captured the Pacific Coast title twice, and this Hawaiian title, to go with his many tag titles, reigns with his brothers.

Suddenly, by mid-September, much of the talent had disappeared. Tom Rice, Ray Eckert, and The Sharpes went to San Francisco. Hans Schnabel, Shoulders Newman, and Rikidozan went to Japan. Bobby Managoff went to the Midwest. Bobby Bruns was left with a couple of newcomers, Tommy O'Toole and Jack Witzig, on top of the cards.

We make it to October 18th and Gorgeous George comes back to Hawaii. He beats Pat McGill and then loses to Jack Witzig on DQ the following week.

November 1st sees Frank Valois come to Hawaii and debuts with a win over Jack Witzig. Valois is better known as the initial handler for Andrew The Giant in the early 70's. Valois was the person for that job because he spoke French.

By the end of November, things were back on track. Newcomers include Sammy Berg and Al Lovelock. Rikidozan returns, and Lou Thesz comes back to the Islands.

In fact, on December 6th, Lou Thesz beats Rikidozan. If you had thought about dream matches from the 50s, this match would have had to be the most wished for.

This was the first time they ever met. They met a number of times in Japan, and they had one other match in the US in Los Angeles.

On December 13th, Lou Thesz beat Frank Valois, and Rikidozan beat Al Lovelock.

1953 Wrestling Ads & Pictures

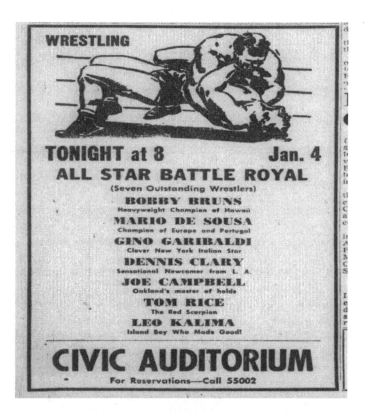

MARIO DE SOUSA

LEO KALIMA

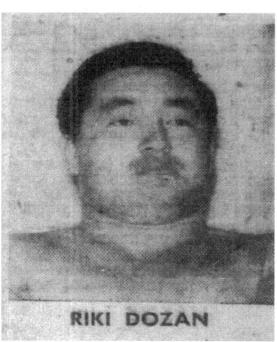

RIKI DOZAN

NO HOLDS BARRED — Lou Thesz (center), heavyweight wrestling champion, takes a stranglehold from traditional Hawaiian leis as he disembarks from a Pan American plane at Honolulu Airport. Also arriving last night was Dr. John Bonica, director of anesthesia at Tacoma General Hospital and Pierce County Hospitals in Tacoma, Wash. They were greeted at the airport by Promoter Al Karasick (right). Both will be on Sunday night's card at the Civic Auditorium. Thesz will defend his title against Riki Dozan. Dr. Bonica is here to give three lectures and at the same time indulge in some wrestling which, as he puts it "is my hobby." (Pan American Airways photo.)

ALL SET FOR WORLD TITLE BOUT—Principals in the world's heavyweight wrestling championship bout to be held at the Civic Auditorium Sunday night for the benefit of The Advertiser Christmas fund go over details for the match with Lorrin P. Thurston, president and general manager of The Advertiser Publishing Co., Ltd. Left to right, Challenger Frank Valois of Montreal, Mr. Thurston, Promoter Al Karasick and World Champion Lou Thesz. Promoter Karasick will turn over a part of the proceeds to The Advertiser Christmas fund for the needy. (Advertiser photo)

1954

1954 starts with the tag titles vacant again. I'm not sure if it is poor planning or if the tours in and out of Hawaii are so fast the tag titles just don't get a chance to change hands.

Luther Lindsay and Bobby Bruns win the titles in a tournament, beating Al Lovelock and Frank Valois in the finals on January 10th.

On February 14th, Al Lovelock beats Ben Sharpe for the Hawaiian Title. Sharpe had been absent from Hawaii since September of '53.

LOGGER LARSEN

Logger and Elmer Larsen had come in to make a team. Ed Gardenia, Larry Moquin, and Rey Urbano were other newcomers. Urbano later had success as The Great Kabooki.

In hindsight, March looks like a downtime. Al Costello came in and had several matches with Larry Moquin.

Karl Von Schober came in April. He had been here in 1950 under his real name, Lou Sjoberg. He debuted on April 4th with a win over Pat McGill.

On April 11th, Bobby Bruns and Larry Moquin teamed up to beat Al Costello and Pat McGill.

The last we knew, Al Lovelock was the Hawaiian champ, but he hadn't been seen since the night he won the Title. Back in the day, you would have wrestlers say they were going to win the Title and take it back to wherever they were from. Evidently, that is what Lovelock did.

Larry Moquin beat Karl Von Schober for the now-vacant Hawaiian Title on May 23rd.

Newcomers are Jungle Boy, John Paul Henning, Pedro Godoy, and Eric Pedersen, who also returned.

On June 6th, Larry Moquin went to a draw with Lou Thesz for the NWA World title.

The next week 6/13, Thesz beat Karl Von Schober.

The following week, Thesz met Moquin again, and this time was able to get the win.

On July 11th, Karl Von Schober beat Larry Moquin to win the Hawaiian Title.

Also, on July 11th, Danno O'Shocker debuted, beating Jim Szikszay.

I interviewed Danno O'Shocker many years ago and asked him about working in Hawaii.

O'Shocker: "I thought it was paradise. After years sailing the North Atlantic and down around the Horn, to see all that white sand and warm water with surf. We only worked one night a week, sometimes a spot show in Hilo.

Caught a few big guys coming in from Japan, where the Sharpe's were champs. People were the friendliest I had ever met anywhere. I worked out three days a week and got in the best shape I had ever been. Couldn't get rich but had a good guarantee. I had to send half home to the wife and baby. They had paid my way over, but not the family. The population is mostly in Honolulu, so you have to get known there with the locals. The paper did a good job with publicity and featured the guys every day. Lou Burnsner of Primo Beer sponsored the matches and dropped around the taverns to push his beer and be friendly with the locals. He was very generous even if the beer was lousy (green beer), lots of gas! Al Karasick told me to get out on the beach and get in shape. I was indignant as I'm always in shape, but he meant get a tan. I had been working in the Midwest and Canada, so I was really white. You have to go easy on that sun as it can put you into the hospital in one day.

I spent four months there and really loved it. I did not have my family there and my daughter was four years old. I really missed them and was getting antsy when I came back to Toronto. Even paradise is to much with out the loved ones."

On August 1st, Bobby Bruns and John Paul Henning beat Karl Von Schober and Pedro Godoy for the tag titles. Not certain, but it looks like they have been vacant again.

On August 8th, Wladek "Killer" Kowalski came to Hawaii and beat Rocky Brown.

The following week, Kowalski went to a draw with John Paul Henning. Rocky Brown beat Karl Von Schober in another important match.

Rocky Brown

On August 22nd, Killer Kowalski beat Karl Von Schober in a battle of the villains, and Rocky Brown also beat the returning Mike Sharpe.

John Paul Henning beat Karl Von Schober on August 29th to win the Hawaiian Title. On the same card Killer Kowalski went to a draw with Mike Sharpe.

On September 12th, Bobby Bruns and John Paul Henning defended their tag titles against Pedro Godoy and Killer Kowalski.

Newcomers now include Don Arnold, Jack Pesek, Bob Corby, and returning Vic Christy.

Hans Schnabel and Shoulders Newman had been teaming up in Japan in August and September. They returned to Hawaii and immediately won the Hawaiian tag titles on October 10th.

October 17th saw the debut of The Zebra Kid. He went to a draw with Bobby Bruns. He had come from the Toronto area.

November 7th sees Roger Mackay debut with a win over Bobby Bruns. The following week Mackay gets a win over John Paul Henning.

Mackay wins the Hawaiian Title on November 21st with another win over John Paul Henning.

On November 28th, Roger Mackay and Don Bettleman (who will be better known as Don Curtis) won the Hawaiian tag titles with a win over Shoulders Newman and Hans Schnabel.

Lou Thesz returns to the Islands on December 5th and gets a win over Dick Raines. The following week, he beats Ed Gardenia and then goes to a draw with Zebra Kid facing two opponents on December 12th.

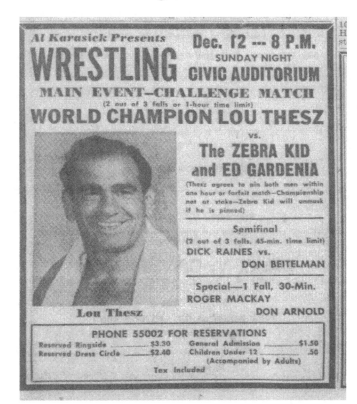

Zebra Kid   Ed Gardenia

1954 Wrestling Ads & Pictures

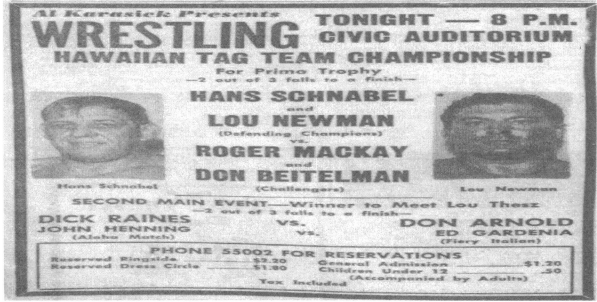

Kowalski arrives in Hawaii

Luther Lindsay

"Frogman" John Paul Henning

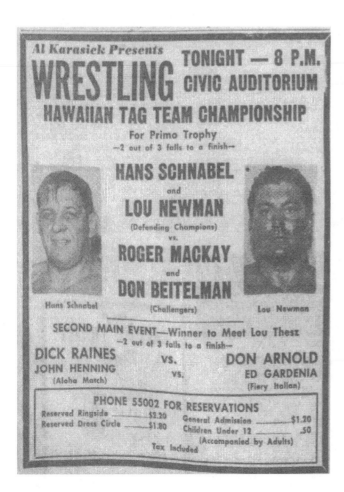

Al Karasick Presents

WRESTLING

TONIGHT — 8 P.M.
CIVIC AUDITORIUM

HAWAIIAN TAG TEAM CHAMPIONSHIP

For Primo Trophy
—2 out of 3 falls to a finish—

HANS SCHNABEL
and
LOU NEWMAN
(Defending Champions)
vs.
ROGER MACKAY
and
DON BEITELMAN

Hans Schnabel   (Challengers)   Lou Newman

SECOND MAIN EVENT—Winner to Meet Lou Thesz
—2 out of 3 falls to a finish—

DICK RAINES   vs.   **DON ARNOLD**
JOHN HENNING   vs.   **ED GARDENIA**
(Aloha Match)   (Fiery Italian)

PHONE 55002 FOR RESERVATIONS

Reserved Ringside ....$2.20   General Admission $1.20
Reserved Dress Circle ....$1.80   Children Under 12 50
                                  (Accompanied by Adults)
Tax Included

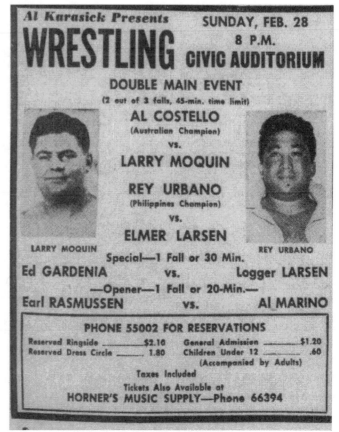

Al Karasick Presents

WRESTLING

SUNDAY, FEB. 28
8 P.M.
CIVIC AUDITORIUM

DOUBLE MAIN EVENT

(2 out of 3 falls, 45-min. time limit)

AL COSTELLO
(Australian Champion)
vs.
LARRY MOQUIN

REY URBANO
(Philippines Champion)
vs.
ELMER LARSEN

LARRY MOQUIN   REY URBANO

Special—1 Fall or 30 Min.

Ed GARDENIA   vs.   **Logger LARSEN**

—Opener—1 Fall or 20-Min.—

Earl RASMUSSEN   vs.   **Al MARINO**

PHONE 55002 FOR RESERVATIONS

Reserved Ringside ....$2.10   General Admission $1.20
Reserved Dress Circle ....1.80   Children Under 12 60
                                  (Accompanied by Adults)
Taxes Included
Tickets Also Available at
HORNER'S MUSIC SUPPLY—Phone 66394

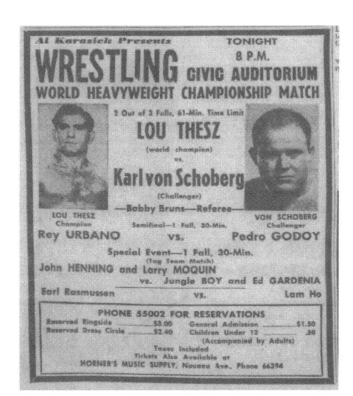

Al Karasick Presents | TONIGHT 8 P.M.

WRESTLING

CIVIC AUDITORIUM

WORLD HEAVYWEIGHT CHAMPIONSHIP MATCH

2 Out of 3 Falls, 61-Min. Time Limit

LOU THESZ
(world champion)
vs.

Karl von Schoberg
(Challenger)

—Bobby Bruns—Referee—

LOU THESZ
Champion

VON SCHOBERG
Challenger

Semifinal—1 Fall, 30-Min.

Rey URBANO   vs.   Pedro GODOY

Special Event—1 Fall, 30-Min.
(Tag Team Match)

John HENNING and Larry MOQUIN
vs.   Jungle BOY and Ed GARDENIA

Earl Rasmussen   vs.   Lam Ho

PHONE 55002 FOR RESERVATIONS

Reserved Ringside _____ $3.00   General Admission _____ $1.50
Reserved Dress Circle ____ $2.40   Children Under 12 _____ .50
(Accompanied by Adults)

Taxes Included
Tickets Also Available at
HORNER'S MUSIC SUPPLY, Nauana Ave., Phone 66294

CHAMPION LOU THESZ   CHALLENGER DICK RAINES
They will battle in main event of Christmas Fund wrestling show tonight

Christmas Fund Mat Show

Thesz Defends Mat Title Against Raines Tonight

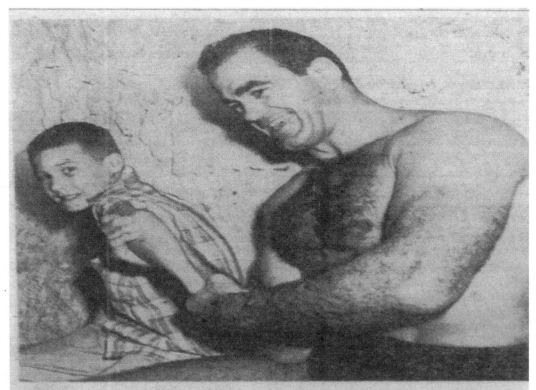

RELAX, THIS WON'T HURT A BIT—Lou Thesz, world's heavy weight wrestling champion, demonstrates one of his pe holds for a youthful fan, Charles Guard Jr., of 2329 Sonom Street. Thesz will take on two foes, the Zebra Kid and E Gardenia, in the unique main event of next Sunday's ma card at the Civic Auditorium. Part of the proceeds will g to The Star-Bulletin-Salvation Army Christmas Fund.

1955

The new year starts off with the debut of Tosh Togo. Harold Sakata has wrestled in Hawaii before, but Tosh Togo has not.

He starts with a win over Al Warshawsky and Don Beitelman and wins a battle royal.

He continues his ways in the following weeks, beating Buddy Lenz (Henry Lenz), Roger Mackay, Bobby Bruns, and Ed Gardenia.

Lucky Simonovich will end Tosh Togo's winning streak on February 6th.

On February 13th, Lucky Simonovich beat Roger Mackay to win the Hawaiian title.

Simonovich and Bobby Bruns win the Hawaiian tag titles the following week, beating Don Beitelman and Roger Mackay.

Gene Stanlee comes to Hawaii on March 20th and beats Ed Gardenia on his debut. The following week, he beat Roger Mackay, landing him in the main event with Lucky Simonovich on April 3rd. Stanlee lost on DQ.

On April 10th, Zebra Kid won the Hawaiian title, beating Lucky Simonovich. Rikidozan was on this card, beating Roberto Pico. He brought Azamafuji with him, who beat Don Beitelman.

On April 17th, Rikidozan and Azamafuji won the tag titles, beating Lucky Simonovich and Bobby Bruns. Azamafuji also wrestled as Kin'ichi Inoue.

On May 8th, Zebra Kid beat Rikidozan on DQ. Zebra Kid was unmasked by Rikidozan.

"LUCKY NUMBER"—Lucky Simonovich says he isn't superstitious as he points to number 13 on the calendar. Today is the 13th and Lucky feels it will be his good luck date because he claims he will regain the Hawaiian heavyweight wrestling title tonight. Simonovich will battle Roger Mackay, the defending champion, for the title at the Civic Auditorium this evening.

The following week, May 15th, George Bollas, who had wrestled as Zebra Kid, appeared.

On May 15th, Bollas went to a draw with Nick Roberts. By this time, a few new wrestlers, including Doc Gallagher and Tony Angelo, were in the area.

The Hawaiian Promotion took a break for the summer of '55. Not sure of the reason. The crew prior to the hiatus seemed like one of the weaker crews that had been assembled. I don't know if they were not drawing well then or if there was another reason.

Wrestling started back up on September 11th with a different crew. The main event saw Ben and Mike Sharpe beat Johnny Barend and Clyde Steeves. The Sharpe Brothers had been around Hawaii before. This was Johnny Barend's debut, and he would be one of the biggest names in Hawaii over the years.

On September 25th, Lou Thesz beat Ben Sharpe, and in the semi-main event, Mike Sharpe beat Clyde Steeves.

K. Shimogaki

Carnera at the beach

Carnera Here On 4th Trip; Likes Hawaii

The following week, October 2nd, Ben and Mike Sharpe beat Lou Thesz and Johnny Barend. A rare tag team match with Thesz.

On October 9th, Primo Carnera came to Hawaii and beat Clyde Steeves. Johnny Barend beat Ben Sharpe. Some interesting wrestlers were on the undercard, with Ricardo Gattoni beating Hardy Kruskamp and Mike Sharpe beating Frank "Gorilla" Monsoon.

The Sharpes were on a roll and added Primo Carnera and Johnny Barend to the victim list on October 16th.

On October 23rd, Johnny Barend and Sandor Kovacs beat The Sharpes. The following week, these same tag teams went to a draw.

On October 30th, George Bollas came back to beat Mike Sharpe in the main event. Bollas was in Hawaii back in May.

On November 13th, Johnny Barend and Sandor Kovacs beat George Bollas and Tony Vagnone to win the vacant tag titles. Lord Blears also debuted on this date. Blears would be a fixture in Hawaii.

I have heard the story that Sandor Kovacs, Lord Blears, and Stu Hart all roomed together before and as they were getting into the business. So Blears coming here following Kovacs makes sense.

On November 20th, Johnny Barend beat Lord Blears. Al Lolotai came back to Hawaii and beat Tony Vagnone. Lolotai last appeared here in 1949.

On December 4th, Lord Blears and Gene Kiniski beat Johnny Barend and Sandor Kovacs to win the tag titles. Kiniski and Blears already had success and had claimed the World tag titles in Vancouver and San Francisco. More irony in this match, Kiniski and Kovacs would later become partners in owning the Vancouver promotion.

On December 16th, Al Lolotai beat George Bollas to win the Hawaiian title.

The last match of the year saw Leo Nomellini beat George Bollas and Lord Blears, and Gene Kiniski beat Kokichi Endo and Tosh Togo.

1955 Wrestling Ads & Pictures

Gene Stanlee

Rikidozan

Hardy Kruskamp

The Nomellinis smile on arrival

250-Pound Nomellini Here To Play Football, Grapple

Leo Nomellini, 6-3 250-pound powerhouse tackle of the San Francisco 49ers, opens a wrestling engagement at the Civic Auditorium tonight.

Here to play in the Hula Bowl January 8, Nomellini is combining wrestling with football.

He will meet George Bollas, 240-pound former masked Zebra Kid who played football at Ohio State University. Their match will be the two-out-of-three-falls, 45-minute time limit main event of Promoter Al Karasick's year-end mat show.

Sharing main event billing will be a non-title tag team match pitting Kokichi Endo of Japan and Tosh Togo of Hawaii against Lord Blears and Gene Kiniski, the National Wrestling Alliance's team titleholders.

Togo is Hawaii's Hal Sakata, who gained fame as a weightlifter in Olympic and national meets.

Al Lolotai, local Samoan star, battles Sandor Kovacs in a one-fall, 30-minute semifinal. Lolotai's Hawaiian belt will not be at stake.

Doug Dawkins of Texas and Earl Rasmussen have been paired for a special event which opens tonight's card at 8.

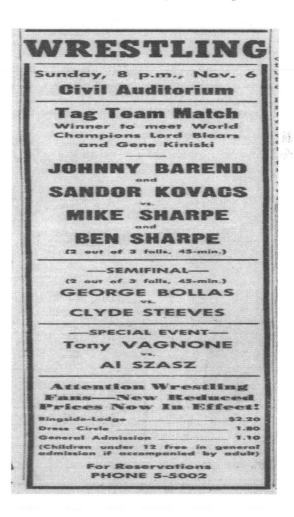

WRESTLING

Sunday, 8 p.m., Nov. 6
Civic Auditorium

Tag Team Match
Winner to meet World Champions Lord Blears and Gene Kiniski

JOHNNY BAREND
and
SANDOR KOVACS
vs.
MIKE SHARPE
and
BEN SHARPE
(2 out of 3 falls, 45-min.)

—SEMIFINAL—
(2 out of 3 falls, 45-min.)
GEORGE BOLLAS
vs.
CLYDE STEEVES

—SPECIAL EVENT—
Tony VAGNONE
vs.
Al SZASZ

Attention Wrestling Fans—New Reduced Prices Now In Effect!

Ringside-Lodge	$2.20
Dress Circle	1.80
General Admission	1.10

(Children under 12 free in general admission if accompanied by adult)

**For Reservations
PHONE 5-5002**

Al Karasick Presents

WRESTLING

TONIGHT — 8 P.M.
JANUARY 30, 1955
CIVIC AUDITORIUM

DOUBLE MAIN EVENT

(2 out of 3 falls, 45-min. time limit)

BOBBY BRUNS

vs.

TOSH TOGO

LUCKY SIMUNOVICH

vs.

ZEBRA KID

Special Event

ROGER MACKAY

vs. BUDDY LENZ

Added Attraction

DON BEITELMAN

vs. ED GARDENIA

TOSH TOGO

PHONE 55002 FOR RESERVATIONS

Reserved Ringside	$2.20	General Admission	$1.10
Reserved Dress Circle	$1.80	Children Under 12	.50
Tax Included		(Accompanied by Adults)

Wrestling Program

Civic Auditorium—8 P.M.

First Match—1 Fall, 30-Min.

JOHNNY BROWN vs. RAMON CERNANDES

Special Event—1 Fall, 30-Min.

RICARDO GATTONI vs. CLYDE STEEVES

Semifinal—1 Fall, 30-Min.

TONY VAGNONE vs. FRANK MARCONI

Main Event—Tag Team Match
(2 Out of 3 Falls, 61-Min. Time Limit
For World's Tag Team Championship)

MIKE SHARPE and BEN SHARPE

VS.

LOU THESZ and JOHNNY BAREND

WRESTLING PROGRAM

Civic Auditorium—8 P.M.

First Event—1 Fall

JOHNNY CABRAL—vs.—AL MARINO

Special Event—1 Fall

GEORGE BOLLAS vs. KOKICHI ENDO

Semifinal—1 Fall

AL LOLOTAI vs. SANDOR FOZO

Main Event—Tag Team Match
—2 out of 3 Falls or 45-Min. Time Limit—

LORD BLEARS and GENE KINISKI

VS.

JOHNNY BAREND and SANDOR KOVACS

260

Zebra Kid Unmasked; Is Bollas

The Zebra Kid was unmasked last night and his identity revealed, as George Bollas, former Ohio State University athlete.

Riki Dozan, of Japan, did the unmasking in the main event of Promoter Al Karasick's wrestling card at the Civic Auditorium.

Although he delighted the crowd with the unmasking, he performed it illegally and was disqualified by Referee Frank Merrill. Azumafuji, 310-pound sumo star, held the Zebra Kid's arms while Riki Dozan removed the mask.

* * *

Bollas won the first fall of the match in 20:35 with body slams and a press. Riki Dozan evened it up 9:30 later with judo chops and throws and a press. The disqualification followed 5:20 later.

* * *

Azumafuji took only 9:01 to flatten Doc Gallagher in the semifinal, using bear hugs to subdue his 240-pound opponent.

Handsome Nick Roberts made his Isle debut with Bobby Bruns as his partner in a special tag team match. They held Roberto Pico and Tony Angelo to a 30-minute draw

Roberts looked good in the match and showed plenty of class and ability.

Tinei Sua and Earl Rasmussen tussled to a draw in the opener.

Wally Tsutsumi alternated with Merrill as referee. Tony Faria was timer and Stan Anderson the announcer.

THE ZEBRA KID

GEORGE BOLLAS
The Zebra Kid without his mask

Unmasked' Zebra Kid

261

1956

1956, at least on paper, is starting off like gangbusters. Local favorite Al Lolotai is on top with the Hawaiian title and has many worthy challengers on the cards.

On January 6th, Lolotai beat Tosh Togo to win a battle royal. Also on the card, Leo Nomellini beat Gene Kiniski on dq,

January 20th has Lord Blears and Gene Kiniski beat Al Lolotai and Dick Beyer.

Beyer was just starting in the business and would later wrestle as the Sensational Intelligent Destroyer and Dr. X in other territories. Hans Schnabel had also returned.

Hans Schnabel and George Bollas beat Lord Blears and Gene Kiniski in a battle of the heels on January 27th.

On February 19th, Lord Blears and Gene Kiniski went to a draw with Sandor Kovacs and Count Billy Varga, who debuted. Also, Al Lolotai beat Kokichi Endo.

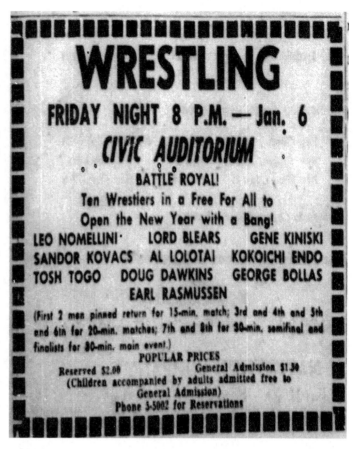

February 24th saw a huge card with Hans Schnabel beat Gene Kiniski in a match that sounded like a Texas Death Match. They had six falls each, and Kiniski refused to continue after midnight, so they gave the match to Schnabel. Billy Varga beat Dick Beyer, and Al Lolotai went to a no-contest with Lord Blears.

On March 16th, Count Billy Vargo beat Al Lolotai and won the Hawaiian title; Lord Blears and Gene Kiniski went to a draw with Sandor Kovacs and Hans Schnabel. Somewhat stranger of a match in Schnabel teaming with Kovacs. The following week, he was teaming with Kiniski and Blears.

On April 1st, The main event saw Gene Kiniski beat Hans Schnabel.

April 9th saw a dream match of Rikidozan and Kokichi Endo beating Lord Blears and Gene Kiniski. They had a rematch the following week, with Kiniski and Blears coming out on top.

April 29th saw Great Togo and Tosh Togo upset Gene Kiniski and Lord Blears to win the Hawaiian tag titles.

On May 27th, Lou Thesz came to team with Count Billy Varga to beat Tosh Togo and The Great Togo.

The following week, on June 3rd, Lou Thesz drew with Leo Nomellini.

Great Togo and Tosh Togo suffered losses to a couple of top tag teams in consecutive weeks.

On June 10th, they lost to Leo Nomellini and Billy Varga; on June 17th, they lost to the Sharpe Brothers.

On June 24th, Sam Steamboat debuted, going to a draw with Zack Malkov. The main event that night saw Billy Varga beat Tony Morelli.

On July 29th, Tosh Togo won the Hawaiian title from Billy Varga.

On August 5th, Sam Steamboat and Billy Varga won the Hawaiian tag titles, beating Tosh Togo and Tony Gardenia. The Great Togo had been the other tag champ with Tosh Togo, but he had apparently left Hawaii.

There seemed to be a lot of turnovers as fall came. Now, main eventing included Pedro Godoy, Vic Christy, Jack Claybourne, Aldo Bogni, Mike Mazurki, and Lord Layton. Tom Rice had returned.

In fact, Rice won the Hawaiian title, beating Tosh Togo on October 7th.

On October 28th, Jack Claybourne teamed with Pat O'Connor to beat Tom Rice and Lord Layton.

SAM STEAMBOAT, JR.

Pat O'Conner was still a few years away from being a World champ, but he went on a winning streak in Hawaii. He beat Tom Rice, Lord Layton, and Gorgeous George.

On December 9th, another dream match occurred as Pat O'Connor went to a draw with Whipper Billy Watson.

On the last card of the year, Lou Thesz defended his world title against the Great Zorro. Zorro had many aliases, but his best-known would probably be Hans Mortier. In fact, he would return to Hawaii in 1967 as Hans Mortier.

1956 Wrestling Ads & Pictures

MIKE MAZURKI

LORD LAYTON

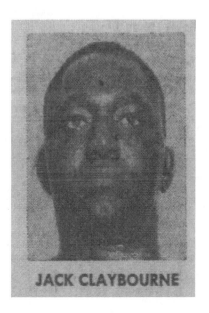

JACK CLAYBOURNE

263

WRESTLING CIVIC AUDITORIUM
SUNDAY-8 P.M. FEB. 19

TAG TEAM MATCH

KOVACS

Billy VARGA
and
Sandor KOVACS
Vs.
Gene KINISKI
and Lord BLEARS

VARGA

Al LOLOTAI vs. Kokichi ENDO | Hans SCHNABEL vs. Dick BEYER

POPULAR PRICES—Phone 5-5002 for RESERVATIONS — CHILDREN UNDER 12 FREE

WRESTLING
CIVIC AUDITORIUM FRIDAY 8 PM FEB. 24

MAIN EVENT—CHALLENGE MATCH
30 MINUTES TO A FINISH!

GENE KINISKI vs. HANS SCHNABEL

(This match is 30 falls to a finish unless one wrestler scores 3 CONSEC-UTIVE falls. At end of 30 falls, wrestler with the most falls will be declared the winner. Keep your own boxscore of falls in adjoining columns)

BILLY VARGA vs. DICK BEYERS
AL LOLOTAI vs. LORD BLEARS
SANDOR KOVACS vs. KOKICHI ENDO

Phone 5-5002 for Reservations

——Popular Prices——

SCHNABEL

KINISKI

AL KARASICK PRESENTS

WRESTLING

TONIGHT, 8 P.M.
CIVIC AUDITORIUM

FOR RESERVATIONS
PHONE 5-5002

LOU THESZ

Lou Thesz
vs.
Leo Nomellini
(Winner to be matched with World
Champion Whipper Watson
for title)
2 Out of 3 Falls
Or
45-min. to Decision
Semi Final Tag Team
TOGO BROS. vs.
DOUG HAWKINS
JERRY CHRISTY

TONY MORELLI vs.
BILLY VARGA
RAYMOND CERNANDES
vs. EARL RASMUSSEN

PRICES
$3.50 $2.50 $1.50
Children Under 12 Free
in general admission
when accompanied by
adults.

LEO NOMELLINI

WRESTLING
CIVIC AUDITORIUM—SUNDAY—8 P.M.

PAT O'CONNOR
POPULAR PRICES
Reserved ———— $2.40
Gen. Admission ———— $1.50
(Children under 12 — FREE in
General Admission if accom-
panied by adults.)
PHONE 5-5002
for reservations

British Empire
Heavyweight Title Match
PAT O'CONNOR
vs.
BILLY WATSON
** ALL STAR CARD **
TOM RICE vs.
DON BEITELMAN

LORD LAYTON vs.
SAMMY BERG

JACK CLAYBOURNE
vs. JOE MITCHELL

KOKICHI ENDO vs.
WONG BUCK LEE

265

WRESTLING

CIVIC AUDITORIUM
SUN., DEC. 30 8 P.M.

PROMOTER AL KARASICK
PRESENTS

WORLD'S HEAVYWEIGHT CHAMPIONSHIP MATCH

(2 out of 3 falls or 61-Minute — time limit)

LOU THESZ
(World Champion)

Vs.

The Great Zorro
(European Champion)

All-Star Supporting Card

●

TOM RICE
Vs.
DON BEITELMAN

LORD LAYTON
Vs.
JOE BLANCHARD

KOKICHI ENDO
Vs.
SAMMY BERG

PRINCE CHARMING
Vs.
JOE MITCHELL

CHAMPIONSHIP PRICES

Ringside and Loge	$3.00
Center Dress Circle	$2.40
General Admission	$1.50

Children Under 12 FREE

(Tax Included)

FOR RESERVATIONS TELEPHONE
5-5002

1957

The first card of 1957 had Lou Thesz beating Tom Rice.

I came across my interview with Lou Thesz; he had this to say about Hawaii, "I would go there every chance I could, but there really was no money there. I might make a thousand and spend five hundred. I enjoyed it very much. Al Karasick was a good promoter. It was a vacation. I would go over there and pick up a couple grand, and it was a big party."

This seemed like another time of turnover with guys returning to Hawaii after an absence, Al Costello, Lord Layton, Joe Blanchard, and Johnny Walker.

On February 10th, Tom Rice got a win over Al Costello.

On February 17th, Rikidozan returned and beat Al Costello. Lord Layton and Tom Rice beat Kokichi Endo and Joe Blanchard in the main event.

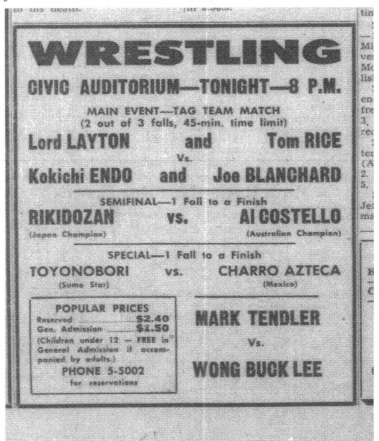

February 24th, Rikidozan, Kokichi Endo, and Toyonobori beat Charro Azteca, Lord Layton, and Tom Rice. Toyonobori made his Hawaii debut on this night.

March 3rd saw the debut of Bobo Brazil, who beat Sammy Berg. Rikidozan also went to a draw with Lucky Simonovich.

The turnover since the beginning of the year was significant. March 17th saw Bobo Brazil beat Lord Layton, while Kokichi Endo and Toyonobori beat Jan Gotch and Tom Rice.

On March 31st, Jack Claybourne and Bobo Brazil teamed up to beat Lord Layton and Tom Rice.

On April 7th, Toyonobori and Kokichi Endo beat Bobo Brazil and Jack Claybourne. Sam Steamboat was also on the card, beating Wong Buck Lee.

On April 28th, Lord Layton and Tom Rice won the vacant Hawaiian tag titles, beating Al Lolotai and Lucky Simonovich. In another match on this card, Jack Claybourne beat Kokichi Endo.

On May 19th, Al Lolotai beat Tom Rice for the Hawaiian State title. This was his 2nd reign as champ.

On May 26th, Lou Thesz came to Hawaii again to beat Bobo Brazil in another one of the exciting matches.

The following week, on June 2nd, Thesz beat Toyonobori. Also on this card Al Lolotai beat Hans Schnabel.

Lou Thesz stayed one more week to go to a draw with Al Lolotai. Interesting booking as Thesz beat Brazil and Toyonobori but went to a draw with the wrestler they were really investing in. This card drew 5,000 and was probably the biggest drawing card of the year.

One of the first challengers for Lolotai was Toyonobori. They went to a draw on July 14th, and then Lolotai won on July 21st.

Gorgeous George came to Hawaii on August 4th and beat Lucky Simunovich on DQ.

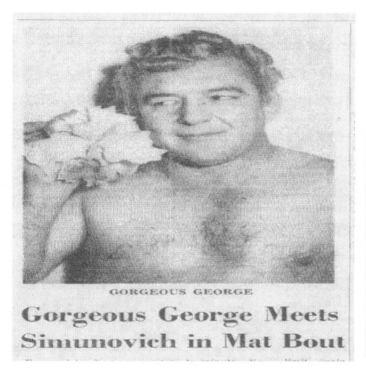

GORGEOUS GEORGE

Gorgeous George Meets Simunovich in Mat Bout

"WILD BILL" SAVAGE

Wild Bill Savage debuted on August 4th with a win over Jim Wright.

Savage remembered his time in Hawaii, "Waikiki Beach when I knew it was heaven on earth in the early 60's. The International Market Place had all grass to walk on. You could see coral in the surf. You could see lobsters 600 yards out from the Outrigger."

The following week Lucky Simonovich got the win over Gorgeous George. One thing about Gorgeous George was he was never shy about doing a job because he knew he would not lose his heat and could get it back at any time.

On August 25th, Bill Savage beat Al Lolotai on COR; Herb Freeman debuted and teamed with Lucky Simonovich to go to a no-contest with Tom Rice and Shoulders Newman.

On September 22nd, Lord Blears returned and teamed with Tom Rice beat Lucky Simonovich and Dick Hrstich. Hrstich may be better known in territories as Ray Gordon.

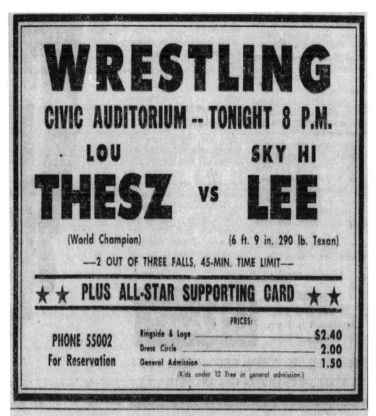

On October 20th, Sky Hi Lee came to Hawaii. Lee was 6'9, and he suffered from acromegaly, which is one of the reasons he grew so tall. He was a colorful wrestler who was known to be a heavy drinker. He also participated in boxing and had a record of 11 and 5. He also appeared in 3 movies, playing the big villain in most.

On October 27th, Lou Thesz beat Sky Hi Lee. The next week, they went to a draw in peculiar booking.

On November 10th, Ricky Waldo debuted in Hawaii. He started off with a big push, beating Sky Hi Lee. The following week, he teamed with Lucky Simonovich to beat Lord Blears and Shoulders Newman. The next week was a singles win over Newman.

On December 6th, there was a tournament to see who would face Hawaiian Champion Al Lolotai, who had been absent since August. Lolotai probably had football season. They allowed him to keep the Hawaiian title.

The tournament winner was Lucky Simonovich after beating Lord Blears and Ricky Waldo.

On December 11th, Lolotai was able to handle Simunovich.

1957 Wrestling Ads & Pictures

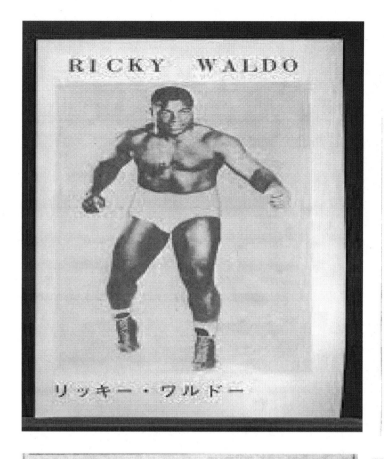

RICKY WALDO

リッキー・ワルドー

Bobo Brazil in Action

Non-Title Match

Lou Thesz to Battle Sky Hi Lee Tonight

World heavyweight wrestling champion Lou Thesz tonight faces one of the toughest matches of his long and brilliant career.

The 6 ft. 3 in. 225 pound champion from St. Louis, Mo., will meet Sky Hi Lee, 6 ft. 9 in. 290 pound giant from Texas, in a non-title two out of three falls, 45-min. time limit match.

Lee announced after signing for the match that he would claim the title if he beats Thesz.

Thesz, who defended his title successfully against Rikidozan before 50,000 in Tokyo earlier this month, is not concerned at the Texan's announcement.

He pointed out that as champion he is the target of every opponent he meets and for that reason, he always has to be at his best.

Sky Hi is as rough as he is strong and combines aggressiveness with a sound knowledge of fundamentals.

Thesz will bank on his skill and speed to keep his bigger opponent off balance.

George Pencheff of Australia and Lord Blears of England meet in a two out

LOU THESZ

of three falls or 45-min. time limit semifinal. This is another in a series of elimination matches to determine a challenger to meet Al Lolotai for the Hawaiian belt.

Tom Rice and Lou Newman will pit their power and rough tactics against Herb Freeman and Dick Hrstich in a special one fall, 30-min. tag team match.

Dr. John Bonica and George Kongozan will open the card at 8 p—.

TOYONOBORI

Three Japan Wrestlers In Team Match Tonight

Three of Japan's top professional matmen, headed by Rikidozan, will be featured in a six-man tag team wrestling main event tonight at the Civic Auditorium.

Toyonobori, 255 pound powerhouse, and judo expert Kokichi Endo, a 233 pounder, will team up with Rikidozan, 246 pound former sumo star. Rikidozan is the professional wrestling champion of Japan.

Opposing the Japanese wrestlers will be Lord Layton, 260, Tom Rice, 232, and Charro Azteca, 235. This is an international team as Layton hails from Canada and Azteca is from Mexico. Rice is the Hawaiian heavyweight champion.

Promoter Al Karasick said the team match will be two out of three falls to a one hour time limit. The extended time limit should give all six wrestlers plenty of opportunity to see action.

As in any team match, two matmen on one side must be pinned before a team can win the match before the time limit expires. If there are no falls or if both sides have one fall apiece, the referee's decision will decide the match.

Lucky Simunovich and Joe Blanchard will clash in a one fall to a 30-minute time limit semifinal that should have fans in a dilemma. Both Lucky and Blanchard are great favorites here, so the fans will be "on the fence" when it comes to rooting for one of them.

Simunovich has set a "win at all cost" pattern as he wants a title match with Tom Rice and is out to establish himself the No. 1 contender. He is expected to set the tempo of tonight's match.

Mark Tendler of New York and Johnny Brown of Honolulu will open the card at 8 p.m. Both are action wrestlers and should give the fans a run for their money.

1958

1958 starts, and on top are Lord Blears, Tom Rice, Bill Savage, George Bollas, Nelson Royal, and Lucky Simunovich. Al Lolotai is still the Hawaiian Champ despite being absent for the first few months.

On February 2nd, Billy Darnell beat Bill Savage. It looks like it was two matches for Darnell, here and the 9th. Also, George Bollas and Tom Rice beat Lord Blears and Kokichi Endo in a top tag match.

On March 2nd, Luigi Macera debuted and beat Ricky Waldo on DQ.

On March 9th, Tosh Togo would beat Tom Rice, and George Bollas went to a draw with Kokichi Endo.

On March 16th, Al Lolotai had his first match of the year and went to a draw with Tosh Togo.

On March 30th, Tosh Togo beat Luigi Macera in the main event.

Luigi Macera

On April 6th, Kokichi Endo beat Ricky Waldo, and an interesting tag match had two debuts as Jack Bence and George Bollas beat Nick Kozak and Luigi Macera. Bence was the prototypical journeyman wrestler. He would later have a hand in training Don Muraco. Nick Kozak was the other person who debuted.

On April 27th, Sky Hi Lee returned and beat Tosh Togo in the main event. Lucky Simunovich beat Luigi Macera.

On May 7th, Al Lolotai came in for only his 2nd match of the year and beat Sky Hi Lee. Leo Nomellini was also on the card and beat Ricky Waldo.

On May 11th, Sky Hi Lee went to a draw with Leo Nomellini.

On June 2nd, Charley Kalani makes his Hawaiian debut, beating Mark Tendler. He would be better known as Toru Tanaka.

On June 8th, the main event was a 6-person tag match, and Stan "Big K" Kowalski & Sky Hi Lee & Tom Rice beat Kokichi Endo & Jerry Gordet & Lucky Simonovich.

Another 6-person tag match took place on July 6th with Rikidozan & Kokichi Endo & Toyonobori beating Stan Kowalski & Sky Hi Lee & Tom Rice.

On August 3rd, Tiny Mills debuted with a win over Bob McCune. The main event saw Rikidozan and Toyonobori beat George Bollas and Sky Hi Lee.

On August 10th, the team of Tiny Mills and Stan Kowalski began. This team would later be known as Murder Incorporated, and this was their 2nd time teaming. They would go on to hold the AWA World tag titles on two occasions.

Things started looking up in late August of 58 as Don Leo Jonathan came in and Johnny Barend returned. Barend teamed up with Toyonobori on August 24th to beat Stan Kowalski and Tiny Mills on dq.

Jonathan debuted on the 31st and went to a draw with Lucky Simonovich.

Hard Boiled Haggerty came to Hawaii on October 5th and beat Juan Humberto. The following week, he beat Lucky Simonovich. Then Haggerty beat Tiny Mills on DQ. His next victim was Kowalski.

November 9th was one of those cards everyone would have liked to have attended due to the talent all through the card. Hard Boiled Haggerty went to a draw with Sky Hi Lee in the main event, Don Leo Jonathan beat Tiny Mills, Johnny Barend beat Stan Kowalski, and in a tag team affair, Joe Blanchard and Lord Blears beat Jerry Gordet and Lucky Simonovich on dq.

Another big show on November 12th saw Al Lolotai beat Hard Boiled Haggerty as he defended the Hawaiian title.

On November 16th, Don Leo Jonathan beat Hard Boiled Haggerty in a battle of the big men.

On December 14th, the NWA title had passed on to Dick Hutton, who came and defended it against Don Leo Jonathan. The following show had Hutton beating Al Lolotai on December 17th.

On the 20th, Hutton wrestled Don Leo Jonathan again, and that match went to a draw.

1958 Wrestling Ads & Pictures

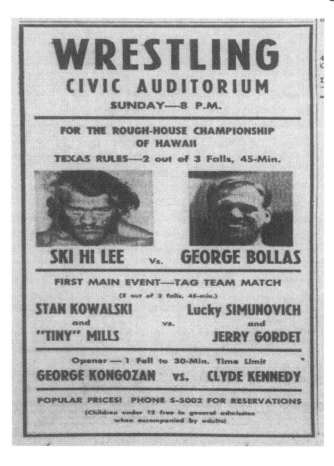

Charley and Deloris Kalani (above), Charley at University of Utah in 1951 (below right)

Kalani to Wrestle as Pro

Charley Kalani, well known Honolulu football player and heavyweight amateur wrestling champion, is turning professional.

The Hawaiian athlete will make his pro wresting debut on Sunday night's card at the Civic Auditorium. He will meet Mark Tendler in a one fall match.

Kalani played football at Iolani School and later won all-Skyline Conference honors at Utah. He also played in the Hula Bowl game here.

Promter Al Karasick has matched an outstanding card for Sunday. Kokichi Endo meets Ski Hi Lee and Lucky Simunovich takcles Ricki Waldo in two out of three falls matches.

One fall matches include Tom Rice vs. Jerry Gordet and Kongozan vs. Charro Azteca in addition to Kalani's joust with Tendler.

1959

As 1959 starts, the talent level will ratchet up even more. King Curtis Iaukea debuted on January 7th. Curtis will become the top Hawaiian wrestler ever, certainly the most recognized Hawaiian wrestler. He will pay some dues here in 59, but there is no doubt about his talent.

January 7th had Don Leo Jonathan and Bob "Kinji" Shibuya win a battle royal and then team up to lose to Lord Blears and Al Lolotai. Curtis debuted with a win over Al Marino.

On January 14th, Al Lolotai beat Don Leo Jonathan, who was probably working as a heel this early in his career.

Don Leo remembers his time in Hawaii, "Ed Francis always drew money, and another guy who always treated me right. I was with him in New York in 50 or 51, and he got his shoulder separated, and I remember riding with him in the car, and he was holding his shoulder and trying to prop himself up so he wouldn't move too much. He couldn't get his shoulder set until we got back to New York, and he was hurt somewhere in Pennsylvania that he got hurt.

From there, he went and said, I got to find something else to do; this business is killing me. It was shortly after that he took over Hawaii. But I used to work for Al Karasick before Francis had Hawaii. I spent quite a bit of time in Hawaii. I used to fly in the late 50's and 60's. I used to fly in from LA. The time I worked there for him, I was on a diving job on the Island of Kauai. We were building the underwater structures of the Wailuwa Bridge.

When I was diving, of course, in those days, you only wrestled once a week or so, and I would jump on the plane and the next morning jump on another plane back in the morning and back to work. I never got to hang around Honolulu very much, a night here and there if I couldn't get a plane out. Ed had some good men, as long as he had to fly them in. He could fly in what he needed."

On February 18th, Bob Shibuya handed Al Lolotai a rare loss.

Lolotai got the win back on March 4th, beating Shibuya.

On March 11th, Lolotai had a big win over Primo Carnera. This was Carnera's first match in Hawaii since 1955. This was also his last match in Hawaii. His career would last another three years.

March 22nd saw Lord Blears and Joe Blanchard defend the Hawaiian tag titles against Clyde Steeves and Kinji Shibuya. The Hawaiian tag title situation is never a clear one.

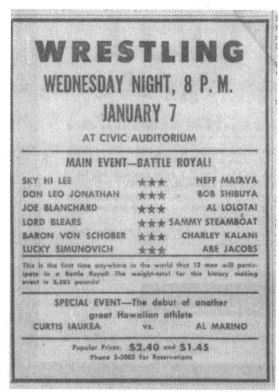

WRESTLING
WEDNESDAY NIGHT, 8 P. M.
JANUARY 7
AT CIVIC AUDITORIUM

MAIN EVENT—BATTLE ROYAL!

SKY HI LEE	★★★	NEFF MAIAVA
DON LEO JONATHAN	★★★	BOB SHIBUYA
JOE BLANCHARD	★★★	AL LOLOTAI
LORD BLEARS	★★★	SAMMY STEAMBOAT
BARON VON SCHOBER	★★★	CHARLEY KALANI
LUCKY SIMUNOVICH	★★★	ABE JACOBS

This is the first time anywhere in the world that 12 men will participate in a Battle Royal! The weight-total for this history making event is 3,203 pounds!

SPECIAL EVENT—The debut of another great Hawaiian athlete
CURTIS IAUKEA   vs.   AL MARINO

Popular Prices: $2.40 and $1.45
Phone 5-5002 for Reservations

Advertisement
TAG TEAM WRESTLING CHAMPIONSHIP

Clyde Steeves   Bob Shibuya

Jolting Joe Blanchard and Lord "Tally Ho" Blears are in for a rugged and rough work-out.

They have accepted a challenge match for the Hawaii State tag team wrestling championship and will battle Bob Shibuya and Clyde Steeves Sunday night, March 22, at the Civic Auditorium.

Blanchard and Blears hold the Hawaiian tag team crown and also the Pacific Coast championship. They form a great team.

Shibuya, probably the top-ranking American-Japanese wrestler in the world today, and Steeves believe they will be crowned the new champions—the first since Hawaii became a state of the union.

Prince Neff Maiava, the Samoan powerhouse, collides "head on" with Baron Karl von Schober, the Teuton dynamite, in the special event. All we can say if this is, Wow!

Reg Parks, Mr. Canada himself, and Curtis Iaukea, a local boy headed for big things in football and wrestling, clash in the special event.

Kokichi Endo and Charley Kalani will show in a judo elimination match to open the card at 8 p.m.

Don't forget, folks, wrestling is SUNDAY night this week and March 29 due to the Cherry Blossom Festival activities at the auditorium. Phone 5-5002 for information and reservation.

Ed Francis made his Hawaiian wrestling debut on March 29th and defended his NWA Junior Heavyweight title, beating Reggie Parks.

Ed Francis won the Hawaiian title on May 19th, beating Al Lolotai.

On June 24th, the main event is full of irony as Lord Blears beats Ed Francis by dq. These two will be in charge of Hawaii and putting on fantastic cards in just a few years. Neff Maivia goes to a draw with George "Catalina" Drake.

On July 8th, Al Lolotai beat Ed Francis to regain the Hawaiian title. Before this, Lolotai had held the title for over two years. He regains it and will hold it another year and a half. A tremendous title reigns in a territory.

On August 12th, Enrique Torres debuts. Torres has had tremendous success in the Bay Area. He teams with Lord Blears and Neff Maivia to beat Tiny Mills and Stan Kowalski and Carl Schoberg. Don Manoukian has also debuted.

On October 7th, Bill Savage returns and teams with Don Manoukian to beat Toyonobori and Yoshimura.

On December 2nd, the NWA World title passed from Dick Hutton and ended up with Pat O'Connor. O'Connor meets Lou Thesz and wins the match.

The following week, O'Connor beat Al Lolotai, and Lou Thesz beat Toyonobori.

The Great Bolo comes into the area and is unmasked as Al Lovelock. He lost to Yoshimura. Bolo and Lovelock have lost their masks at least eight times during his career.

The Great Bolo and unmasked as Al Lovelock

Ed Francis Debuts

Francis Makes Isle Mat Debut Tonight

"Gentleman" Ed Francis of Chicago makes his Honolulu wrestling debut on tonight's card at the Civic Auditorium.

Recognized by the National Wrestling Alliance as the world's junior heavyweight champion, Francis arrived yesterday and reported himself in top shape.

The newcomer will meet Reg (Mr. Canada) Parks in a two out of three falls, 45-min. time limit main event. Francis' title will not be at stake in the match.

BOB SHIBUYA and Lord James Blears are billed for the semifinal, a one fall grudge battle. Shibuya was booked to leave for the mainland but postponed the trip to tackle Blears in a challenge match.

Neff Maiava, rugged Samoan star, and Clyde Steeves clash in the special event, a one fall to 30-min. sizzler. Steeves has stamped himself as a real tough grappler and is gunning for Al Lolotai and the Hawaiian belt.

Jolting Joe Blanchard and

ED FRANCIS

Baron Karl von Schober come to grips in the first special event.

In the finals of the professional judo tournament Kokichi Endo and Wally Tsutsumi will trade holds in a one fall to finish joust. Both are undefeated.

The judo match opens the card at 8 p.m.

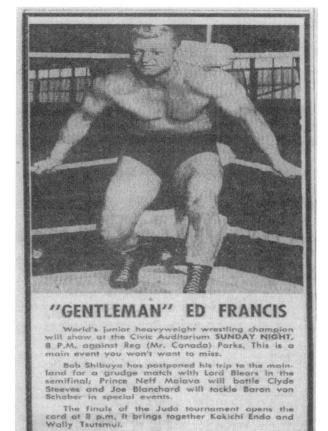

"GENTLEMAN" ED FRANCIS

World's junior heavyweight wrestling champion will show at the Civic Auditorium SUNDAY NIGHT, 8 P.M. against Reg (Mr. Canada) Parks. This is a main event you won't want to miss.

Bob Shibuya has postponed his trip to the mainland for a grudge match with Lord Blears in the semifinal; Prince Neff Maiava will battle Clyde Steeves and Joe Blanchard will tackle Baron von Schober in special events.

The finals of the Judo tournament opens the card at 8 p.m. It brings together Kokichi Endo and Wally Tsutsmui.

WRESTLING SUNDAY NIGHT

Phone 5-5002 for reservations.

Francis Pins Parks; Dozan on Next Card

Ed Francis of Chicago, world's junior heavyweight wrestling champion, last night made a rough Civic Auditorium debut by defeating Reg Parks.

Weighing 220 pounds, Francis won the first and third falls of the match. He used a Boston crab in 15:20 for the first fall, yielded to Parks' spin-press 4:45 later, then came back to score the clincher in 3:39 with a backdrop.

Francis was impressive and displayed a world of talent despite his rough tactics.

* * *

IN THE semifinal Bob Shibuya and Lord Blears tussled to a rousing 30-minute draw. This was Shibuya's aloha match for the year as he plans to campaign on the Mainland.

Neff Maiava won on a disqualification from Clyde Steeves in a wild and woolly special event. The match lasted 12:05.

Joe Blanchard and Baron von Schober tussled to a draw in their match.

Kokichi Endo of Japan won the professional judo championship of Hawaii by using an arm bar to subdue Wally Tsutsumi in 5:08.

Riki Dozan, heavyweight wrestling champion of Japan, was an interested spectator at last night's matches. He will headline Wednesday night's card, pairing with Maiava for a tag team match against Steeves and Parks.

276

1959 Wrestling Ads & Pictures

ED FRANCIS   GEORGE DRAKE   NEFF MAIAVA

Clyde Steeves   Bob Shibuya   YOSHIMURA

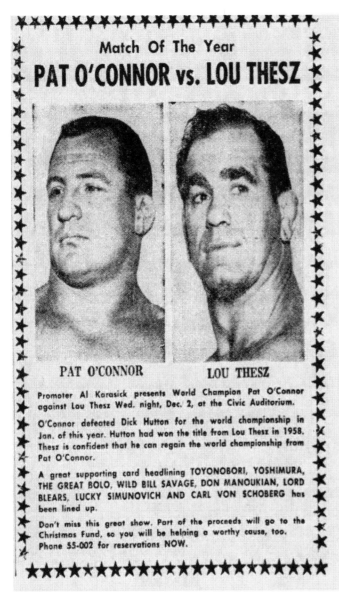

Match Of The Year

PAT O'CONNOR vs. LOU THESZ

PAT O'CONNOR   LOU THESZ

Promoter Al Karasick presents World Champion Pat O'Connor against Lou Thesz Wed. night, Dec. 2, at the Civic Auditorium.

O'Connor defeated Dick Hutton for the world championship in Jan. of this year. Hutton had won the title from Lou Thesz in 1958. Thesz is confident that he can regain the world championship from Pat O'Connor.

A great supporting card headlining TOYONOBORI, YOSHIMURA, THE GREAT BOLO, WILD BILL SAVAGE, DON MANOUKIAN, LORD BLEARS, LUCKY SIMUNOVICH AND CARL VON SCHOBERG has been lined up.

Don't miss this great show. Part of the proceeds will go to the Christmas Fund, so you will be helping a worthy cause, too. Phone 55-002 for reservations NOW.

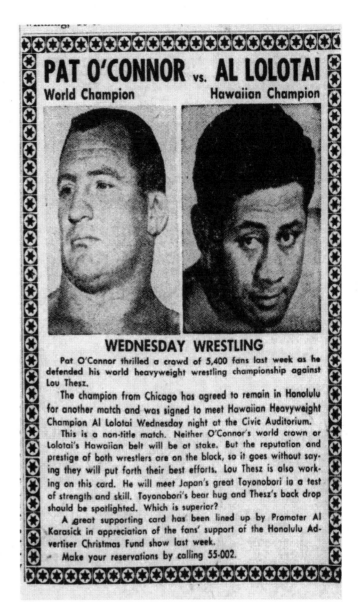

PAT O'CONNOR vs. AL LOLOTAI

World Champion   Hawaiian Champion

WEDNESDAY WRESTLING

Pat O'Connor thrilled a crowd of 5,400 fans last week as he defended his world heavyweight wrestling championship against Lou Thesz.

The champion from Chicago has agreed to remain in Honolulu for another match and was signed to meet Hawaiian Heavyweight Champion Al Lolotai Wednesday night at the Civic Auditorium.

This is a non-title match. Neither O'Connor's world crown or Lolotai's Hawaiian belt will be at stake. But the reputation and prestige of both wrestlers are on the block, so it goes without saying they will put forth their best efforts. Lou Thesz is also working on this card. He will meet Japan's great Toyonobori in a test of strength and skill. Toyonobori's bear hug and Thesz's back drop should be spotlighted. Which is superior?

A great supporting card has been lined up by Promoter Al Karasick in appreciation of the fans' support of the Honolulu Advertiser Christmas Fund show last week.

Make your reservations by calling 55-002.

1960

As The new decade starts, Hawaii has a very nice crew. Al Karasick is still the promoter but is getting to the end of his run.

Al Lolotai has emerged as the top star in Hawaii and is the Hawaiian Champ.

Others in the territory are Lord Blears, Toyonobori, King Curtis, Bill Savage, Don Manoukian, Hard Boiled Haggerty, and a few more.

On January 6th, Al Lolotai won a battle royal. He also teamed with Toyonobori to beat King Curtis and Carl Von Schoberg.

On January 20th, a preliminary match featured Dr. Jerry Graham beating Angelo Savoldi. Both Graham and Savoldi were headed to Australia. Also, on this card, Hard Boiled Haggerty beat Lucky Simonovich.

On January 27th, Bill Savage and Hard Boiled Haggerty beat Jerry Gordet and Lord Blears to win the Hawaiian tag titles. Toyonobori beat King Curtis, who is still very young, in another top match.

Savage and Haggerty defend their tag titles against Toyonobori and Yoshimura, Lord Blears and Jerry Gordet, and Lucky Simonvich, and Yoshimura.

They finally lost the tag titles on March 9th to Herb Freeman and Lord Blears.

On March 23rd, probably one of the top matches that could have been made, saw Al Lolotai beat King Curtis.

On April 6th, Hard Boiled Haggerty beat Al Lolotai in a non-title match. Butcher Vachon had come to Hawaii, and he got a win over Herb Freeman on DQ.

April 13th saw Butcher Vachon and Hard Boiled Haggerty beat Lord Blears and Herb Freeman to win the tag titles.

April 22nd saw Al Lolotai beat Butcher Vachon, and Nick Kozak and Jerry Gordet beat King Curtis in a handicap match. I always think it is strange when the single person loses the handicap match.

May 4th was a big card because Al Lolotai beat Hard Boiled Haggerty to avenge the previous loss.

On May 11th, Jerry Gordet and Nick Kozak beat Butcher Vachon and Hard Boiled Haggerty to win the tag titles.

I am always a little puzzled by the career of Butch Vachon. He is one of the most imposing people ever. He is Mad Dog Vachon with size. However, his career did not explode like Mad Dog's did.

On May 18th, Leo Nomellini came in and beat Hard Boiled Haggerty in a top-notch main event. Elliott Hardy debuted and beat King Curtis. Hardy was better known as Stan Neilson or Stan Lisowslki.

On May 25th, Leo Nomellini beat King Curtis in a single match. Nomellini, Elliott Hardy, and Al Lolotai came back to beat Curtis, Bob Orton Sr and Hans Herman. There is a definite pattern of Curtis paying his dues early in his career.

The first part of the summer in Hawaii seems to have been dominated by the midgets, Brown Panther and Pancho Lopez against Sky Low Low and Fuzzy Cupid. Their run was over a month, which was much longer than usual. Perhaps the reason the midget's run was so long was that Haggerty, King Curtis, Bob Orton, and Ronnie Etchison, who had been there before the midgets came, were at least temporarily gone.

July 27th has Al Lolotai beat Nick Kozak in a babyface match. Interestingly, they had another

BROWN PANTHER   PANCHO LOPEZ

match on August 10th, and again, Lolotai beat Kozak. It seemed like Kozak remained a babyface, but he was gone shortly.

On August 17th, Hans Schnabel and Shoulders Newman won the tag titles, beating Nick Kozak and Jerry Gordet.

On September 21st, Al Lolotai beat Hans Schnabel to defend the Hawaiian title. Shoulders Newman beat Seymour Koenig, Utica Panther and Bill Wright also teamed up to beat Sammy Berg and Carl Von Schoberg.

PRO WRESTLING

TONIGHT'S WRESTLING CARD
Civic Auditorium—8 P. M.

★ ★ ★ SIX-MAN TAG TEAM MATCH ★ ★ ★
(2 out of 3 falls, 1 hr. time limit)
LEO NOMELLINI and AL LOLOTAI and ELLIOT HARDY
Vs.
HANS HERMAN and CURTIS IAUKEA and BIG BOY ORTON

★ ★ Semifinal—1 Fall, 30-Min. ★ ★
NICK KOZAK . . . . Vs. . . . . PAUL VACHON

★ ★ First Match—1 Fall, 30-Min. ★ ★
JERRY GORDET . . . . Vs. . . . . . . TOSHI TAKAMURA

AL LOLOTAI   ELLIOT HARDY

On September 28th, Bill Wright and Utica Panther won the tag titles, beating Shoulders Newman and Hans Schnabel. Bill Wright ended up as Billy Red Cloud. No idea who Utica Panther was. Wright came from the AWA, and they came in on the same day, so perhaps Panther is someone from AWA, but I have no idea who.

As we head into October, it looks like a low period of the year on paper.

On October 5th, Al Lolotai beat Sammy Berg.

On October 12th, Wild Red Berry was on the card teaming with Shoulders Newman and Sammy Berg, losing to Utica Panther, Bill Wright, and Vili Ava. Berry was returning from Australia.

Tom Rice returns and starts teaming up with Shoulders Newman. They beat Vili Ava and Al Lolotai on October 19th.

On November 2nd, Newman and Rice won the tag titles, beating Utica Panther and Bill Wright.

On November 9th, Ed Carpentier beat Sammy Berg, defending a world title. Carpentier is now the Montreal version of a World title and also The American Heavyweight title from Los Angeles.

The following week, Carpentier beat Shoulders Newman.

On November 23rd, business picks up as Leo Garibaldi beats Gorgeous George. Al Lolotai beats Tex McKenzie, and King Curtis returns to beat Bill Wright.

On November 30th, Lou Thesz came to town and beat Al Lolotai. The following week, he beat Sandor Szabo.

There was a massive card on December 14th. Ed Carpentier beat Lou Thesz on DQ, Sandor Szabo went to a draw with Al Lolotai, and Sam Steamboat beat Sammy Berg on DQ.

1960 Wrestling Ads & Pictures

PAUL VACHON   HERBIE FREEMAN

Paul Vachon and Herbie Freeman clash in a grudge match Wednesday night at the Civic Auditorium. It's a wrestling battle of bearded toughies.

Loser will have his beard shaved in the ring by Tony (The Barber) Faria, veteran Civic Auditorium timer, and must leave town the next day!

Vachon claims Freeman assisted Al Lolotai in Friday night's match. Freeman was referee and was challenged by Vachon. They'll go hammer and tongs at each other Wednesday.

Curtis Iaukea teams up with Hard-Boiled Haggerty to battle Nick Kozak and Jerry Gordet in a tag team headliner.

Toshi Takemura of Japan meets Lord Blears and Lucky Simunovich tackles Von Schoberg in one-fall matches.

The opener is at 8 p.m. Phone 5-5002 for reservations!

**LEO   BOB
NOMELLINI   ORTON**

Nearly a ton of human dynamo will be in the ring Wednesday night at the Civic Auditorium when six wrestlers and two referees work a six-man tag team battle.

Promoter Al Karasick has lined up Leo Nomellini, Elliot Hardy and Al Lolotai for one side. The other team will be made up of Hans Herman, Big Bob Orton and Curtis Iaukea.

The team battle will have a one-hour time limit, with two out of three falls to decide the winners. There will be plenty of slambang action, bone-crushing spills and exciting thrills.

Nick Kozak and Paul Vachon clash in the semifinal and Jerry Gordet tackles Toshi Takamura in the opening match. Both will be one fall to 30-minute.

Phone 5-5002 for reservations. Don't miss this big card.

 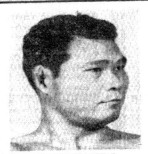

DON MANOUKIAN   YOSHIMURA

Hard-Boiled Haggerty, a wrestling dynamo who was suspended a year ago in Honolulu for being too rough; Jerry Graham, who sold out Madison Square Garden two weeks ago, and Angelo Savoldi, son of Jumping Joe Savoldi, headline next Wednesday night's card at the Civic Auditorium.

Haggerty meets Lucky Simunovich and Savoldi takes on Graham in a double main event, both 2 out of 3 falls to 45 minutes.

Lord James Blears engages Taro Miyaki while a tag team match, Toyonobori and Yoshimura vs. Wild Bill Savage and Don Manoukian opens the big all-star card at 8 p.m.

Phone 55-002 for reservations.

**HARD-BOILED   LUCKY
HAGGERTY   SIMUNOVICH**

Hard-Boiled Haggerty, a wrestling dynamo who was suspended a year ago in Honolulu for being too rough; Jerry Graham, who sold out Madison Square Garden two weeks ago, and Angelo Savoldi, son of Jumping Joe Savoldi, headline next Wednesday night's card at the Civic Auditorium.

Haggerty meets Lucky Simunovich and Savoldi takes on Graham in a double main event, both 2 out of 3 falls to 45 minutes.

Lord James Blears engages Taro Miyaki while a tag team match, Toyonobori and Yoshimura vs. Wild Bill Savage and Don Manoukian opens the big all-star card at 8 p.m.

Phone 5-5002 for reservations.

1961

1961 rolls around, and Al Karasick is looking to sell the promotion. Ed Francis speaks to Don Owen and asks to borrow $10,000 to buy the promotion. Owen agrees, and it looks like Francis will be the owner by April.

Leading up to April, the promotion has Al Lolotai, Sam Steamboat, King Curtis, Leo Garibaldi, and Dick Hutton. This was an excellent crew even before Francis began to work his magic.

On January 11th, Dick Hutton wins a tournament to face Al Lolotai for the Hawaiian title. Hutton beats Maurice LaPointe and Leo Garibaldi along the way and wins a coin flip over Sam Steamboat.

On January 18th, Hutton wins the Hawaiian title with a win over Lolotai. The following week, a match that was a natural had Sam Steamboat beat Hutton for the Hawaiian title, avenging the coin flip loss.

On February 22nd, Steamboat beat Curtis. This is a feud that would last for years. Al Lolotai beat Clyde Steeves to position himself for a title shot at Steamboat.

On March 1st, Steamboat beats Lolotai in a match with the top babyfaces on the Island.

Ed Francis debuts on April 26th with a win over Mitsu Yoshimura. Francis had been in Oregon up to two days prior.

May 18th is the official start date of 50th State Big Time Wrestling.

Francis worked in Hawaii through 1961, mainly as a heel. Interestingly, he removes himself from the equation, as he doesn't wrestle again for eight years.

Ed Carpentier came to the Islands in April and won over Clyde Steeves and John De Silva.

On May 24th, Antonio Rocca comes and beats Karl Von Schoberg and Shoulders Newman by DQ in a handicap match.

On June 14th, Billy Whitewolf comes to the area for the first time. Whitewolf is a friend of Francis's from the Portland area. Whitewolf gets a debut win over Shoulders Newman.

Luigi Macera had emerged with the Hawaiian title on that same card but lost it to Neff Maivia.

Two weeks later, on June 28th, Whitewolf and Maivia won the tag titles, beating Ted Travis and Shoulders Newman.

The main event on July 5th saw Whitewolf beat King Curtis. This was a feud that would last for years.

CRAZYMAN TRAVIS

On July 19th, Ted Travis and Shoulders Newman would regain the tag titles, beating Whitewolf and Maivia. Another interesting booking of a match saw Wally Tsutsumi and Kenny Ackles upset King Curtis in a handicap match.

On August 2nd, Maivia and Whitewolf would beat King Curtis and Haru Sasaki. Sasaki's debut in Hawaii is another of Francis's connections with wrestlers from the NW.

Sasaki and Curtis would team up in the Portland area and win the tag titles there in 1962.

August 16th was one of the most important days of the fledgling promotion. On this night, the heat that the promotion had created in a feud with King Curtis and Neff Maivia would boil over. The storyline of Hawaiian (Curtis) VS Samoan (Maivia) would result in a full-blown riot. I interviewed both Francis and Blears, they mentioned this night.

Francis, "We had one big riot there, King Curtis and Neff Maivia and they just tore the place up. It was terrible. During the riot, they had to send for the Metro squad. They came over and had police dogs. Some of the Samoans with chairs had the police Sgt and me pinned up against the ring, and we had to punch our way out of there. A funny thing, they arrested a bunch of the Samoan fans there. Neff Maivia came in the next morning. He is a very quiet guy and he sat around for a while and then he asked if I had any handcuff keys. I said, yes, we used some handcuffs for some of the wrestling matches. I said what do you need the keys for? He said, "One of my friends was arrested and ran out of the arena, he went into the parking lot and hid under the car. The next day, the guy still had the handcuffs on."

Lord Blears remembers the riot and puts it in perspective. "King Curtis (Hawaiian) and Neff Maiava (Samoan) was naturally a sellout in Hawaii at the Civic and caused a riot which never helps a town."

The 50th State Big Time Wrestling site has this recollection of the match. "During the match, Maivia, who was the champion, attempted to headbutt Iaukea, who was backed up against the ring post. Iaukea, however ducked and Maivia hit his head, was knocked unconscious for at least fifteen minutes, was counted out, and lost his Hawaiian title to Iaukea. Wearing his championship belt, Iaukea was walking back towards the locker room when wrestling fans tried to knock him down; Iaukea ran inside the locker room and slammed the door.

Wrestling fans, upset, tried to break into the locker room, fought with police, and a riot broke out. Many fans and police were injured, and the event made front-page headlines in the Honolulu Papers."

The TV show Tales From The Territories added a couple of details. Included in the panel was Rocky Iaukea, King Curtis's son. He mentioned that when Maivia ran into the turnbuckle, it opened him up, and his blood sprayed the audience. He also said that King Curtis had tied Maivia's hair into the ropes and then slipped Neff an Alka Seltzer, which caused him to foam from the mouth. He also convulsed, selling his injury. While some of those details may have been exaggerated, there is no doubt the heat blew the top off the building. An inaccuracy in the TV show was that Peter Maivia came to make the save, but Maivia had not started wrestling yet.

They waited three weeks for a rematch to allow things to cool off while still promoting a match the fans wanted to see. Maivia got the win for this one on September 6th.

Mad Dog Vachon debuted on September 6th, losing to Billy Whitewolf. Francis is again bringing in a NW wrestler who will draw a lot of money over the years in Hawaii.

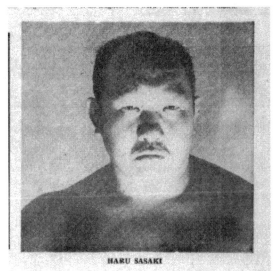

HARU SASAKI

The following week, on September 13th, King Curtis and Haru Sasaki beat Ted Travis and the debuting Lord Blears. Blears had worked in Hawaii regularly for the past six years. However, this time, Blears came into Hawaii as a wrestler, booker, and shortly the TV announcer.

Blears talks about how the partnership and booking were split up. "We exchanged views and ideas. I did all the narration of all the TV shows. Ed did interviews for many years. Then after a while we split the interviews. Our interviews lasted a half hour every show."

On October 25th, Lord Blears beat King Curtis Iaukea for the Hawaiian title. Also, on this card, Neff Maivia beat Mad Dog Vachon, where Vachon's head was shaved.

On November 1st, Lord Blears and Neff Maivia would beat Ted Travis and Shoulders Newman for the tag titles.

On November 15th, Fred Blassie would make his Hawaiian debut defending his WWA world title against George Drake. Blassie's wild style fits perfectly with the Hawaiian style that Francis and Blears cultivated. Also on this card for the 15th saw a Maivia and Curtis rematch and Lord Blears battling Mad Dog Vachon to a draw. The cards were getting stronger and stronger. Any of those matches alone could have main evented a card.

On November 22nd, The Masked Executioner debuted. The Masked Executioner was Vic Christy. Ted Christy was also in the area working as Ted Travis. Vic Christy had worked in Hawaii dating back as far as 1936. Executioner debuted by beating Luigi Macera.

The Mysterious EXECUTIONER

1st MAIN EVENT

The Executioner's manager Mr. X contacted promoter Francis quote: "The Executioner has mastered catch as catch can—Greco Roman—Judo—and the art of Karate. Match him with your best." Unquote.

The Mysterious

EXECUTIONER

VS.

LUIGI MACERA

2 out of 3 falls 45 min. time limit

★ ★ ★ ★ ★ ★ ★ ★

2nd MAIN EVENT

Also making his 1961 debut was Don Manoukian. Manoukian was a solid wrestler who had only been wrestling for three years. He had worked in Hawaii before, so he was known to the fans.

Manoukian was also known as The Bruiser, and he remembers his time in Hawaii, "I worked in Hawaii from 1959 off and on through 1955. My first son, Dirk, was born there in December of 1963. I had a disc jockey show there called The Bruiser Hour. I also attended graduate school at the University of Hawaii."

Fred Blassie returned in December and went to a ddq with Lord Blears in Hilo on the 10th. He then beat Neff Maivia in Honolulu on the 13th. Also, on the 13th, the Executioner beat Lord Blears to win the Hawaiian title.

1961 Wrestling Ads & Pictures

WRESTLING
TONIGHT—8 P.M.
CIVIC AUDITORIUM—Phone 581-002
★ ★ ★ ★
ALL STAR CARD—TRIPLE MAIN EVENT
INTRODUCING
"THE MONGOL"
Vs.
LEO GARIBALDI
★
Sam STEAMBOAT
Vs.
MICHIAKI YOSHIMURA
★ ★ ★ ★
NEFF MAIAVA vs. **CURTIS IAUKEA**
One-Fall Special Events
CLYDE STEEVES vs. **LUCKY SIMUNOVICH**
★ ★ ★ ★
MAURICE LA POINTE vs. **PRINCE MERETANA**
Popular Prices—Phone 581-002

CURTIS IAUKEA

Maiava Will Risk Mat Crown Tonight

Neff Maiava, popular Samoan mat star, puts his Hawaiian heavyweight title and Ring magazine goldbelt on the block tonight against big Curtis Iaukea at the Civic Auditorium.

The championship match headlines Promoter Ed Francis' weekly pro wrestling card. The title match will go two out of three falls to a one hour time limit.

AN UNUSUAL angle of the match is that Maiava, the champion, challenged Iaukea —using his Ring belt as the bait to lure the giant Hawaiian into accepting the challenge.

White Wolf, the Oklahoma Indian, and Luigi Macera clash in a two out of three falls, 45-minute time limit semifinal.

A special added attraction features Hogan Wharton, 245-pound Houston Oilers guard, in a one-fall battle with Ted "Crazyman" Travis. Wharton couldn't have signed to meet a rougher matman than Travis.

Haru Sasaki and Ken Ackles meet in the one-fall opener at 8 p.m.

NEFF MAIAVA

Sports Events

TONIGHT

(Wrestling)

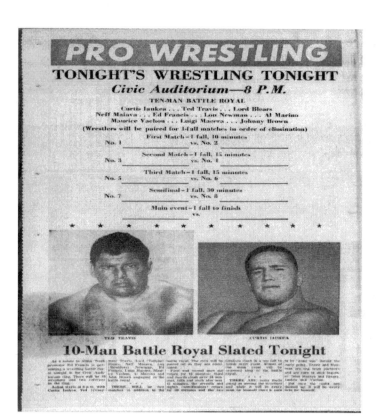

Val Valentine

Promoter Ed Francis is shown with wife Arlene and sons Russ, Bob, Jim and Bill.

Promoter Is Family Man

The Honolulu Advertiser

10¢

WEDNESDAY, SEPTEMBER 6, 1961

PRO WRESTLING

WINNER TAKE ALL

Curtis Iaukea applies headlock on opponent as referee Wally Tsutsumi watches.

NEFF MAIAVA

MAURICE VACHON

Anything Can Happen In Iaukea-Maiava Match

1962

To start off 1962, another new face entered the area as Dick Beyer, later known as the Intelligent, Sensational Destroyer, debuted.

His first match on January 3rd had him beating Mad Dog Vachon.

On January 24th, Fred Blassie returned to defend his WWA World title by beating Dick Beyer. These two would have a tremendous feud later in the Los Angeles area.

The talent level on these cards is growing and growing. The January 31st card featured Neff Maivia, Lord Blears, Fred Blassie, Ray Stevens, Mad Dog Vachon, and Dick Beyer.

In late February, the Masked Executioner and Mad Dog Vachon began a feud, temporarily turning Mad Dog into babyface. On March 14th, Vachon teamed with Lord Blears and Neff Maivia to face Dick Beyer, Masked Executioner, and Shoulders Newman.

On April 4th, Neff Maivia recaptured the Hawaiian title from Masked Executioner and unmasked him, revealing Vic Christy. Nick Bockwinkel also debuted as a young babyface, beating Ted Travis. Bockwinkel debuted a new title that would be defended in the area. They proclaimed him the US Champ.

April 11th, Fred Blassie returned to defend the WWA World title against Neff Maivia again. Also debuting that night was Eric The Red, who was better known as Larry Hennig.

April 18th had Lord Blears, Neff Maiava, and Bockwinkel beat Dick Beyer, Maurice Vachon, and Ray Stevens. It is hard to imagine much better talent anywhere assembled in a single match. Also, a little irony: Bockwinkel and Ray Stevens, who would later be known as one of the best teams in history, were on opposite sides for this match.

On May 2nd, King Curtis returned from an absence and beat Mad Dog Vachon. If I had to choose one match from all of the history of Hawaii, this would undoubtedly be in the top 5.

Carnera, Midgets To Show Tonight

Ten midget wrestlers and former heavyweight boxing champion Primo Carnera will headline a special mat card tonight at the Civic Auditorium.

Promoter Ed Francis arranged the special card to give local fans a chance to see the greatest number of midgets ever to appear here in one match. They are en route to Japan.

All 10 midgets will show in a battle royal, with Carnera serving as referee. The midgets are Fuzzy Cupid, Brown Panther, Irish Jackie, Little Beaver, Sky Low Low, Tiny Tim, Farmer Pete, Lord Littlebrook, Pancho Lopez and Andy Moore.

Carnera is a 6 ft. 7 in. 260-pound giant while the midgets average around 46 inches in height and weigh between 90-110 pounds.

A tag team match featuring regular heavyweights and several individual midget matches round out the card. Action starts at 7:30 p.m., a half hour earlier than usual.

Francis announced that the regular Wednesday night card will feature a U.S. heavyweight title match with Nicky Bockwinkel defending his crown against Indio Azteca.

On May 8th in Hilo, an all-midget card was presented. The card drew 2,000, one of Hilo's better drawing cards. Imagine what this card would have meant to them, a whole card dedicated to them rather than just the special attraction. Sky Low Low and Fuzzy Cupid won the battle royal. Lord Littlebrook and Little Beaver beat Sky Low Low and Fuzzy Cupid, Sonny Boy Cassidy beat Brown Bomber, and Tiny Tim beat Irish Jackie. Primo Canera, 6'7" was the special referee.

On May 23rd, Dean Higuchi debuted in a preliminary match. Also, Cowboy Cassidy had entered the area. By the name, you would have imagined him as a babyface. However, he started feuding with Bockwinkel and teaming up with King Curtis.

On June 6th, King Curtis beat Nick Bockwinkel for the US title.

1962 marked the debut of the 50th state wrestling TV show. Francis and Blears knew that TV was the key to really having success in wrestling in Hawaii. Francis related how vital TV was to the promotion. "We had the number one rating of any show in Hawaii for almost 12 or 14 years. I was on an ABC station to begin with. I switched to CBS outlet when they made an offer."

Blears also talked about the format of the TV show, "Remember we had ten wrestlers to juggle around and not show them too much on TV or people wouldn't pay to see them. We did an hour-and-a-half show with two matches and about 30 minutes of wrestling. Mostly interviews and at the opening of the show we did 15 minutes of "wrestling workouts." I would MC this in the ring and say, Jim Hady and a rookie. Hady would show amateur holds, or it would be Karl Gotch or Billy Robinson. People in Hawaii like the first part better than anything. I also did a 10-minute spot called "Tallyho's Tales" and answered people's mail on the air."

Tosh Togo had come into the area and was moving up the cards. Togo would become very famous later when he got a part in the James Bond movie Goldfinger, playing the part of Odd Job. Harold Sakata (Tosh Togo) would remain a fixture in Hawaii rings for years.

Gil Ane

On July 11th, Killer Buddy Austin debuted. Austin would jump to main events shortly as well.

Billy Whitewolf returned to Hawaii on August 15th and captured a win over Buddy Austin in a main event match.

King Curtis and Cowboy Cassidy had a falling out that culminated in a match in Hilo and ended in a double DQ. It appears they both stayed heels.

Billy Whitewolf scored a big win over King Curtis in an Indian Death Match on October 17th.

Also, Jerry Christy had started appearing. Christy was the nephew of Ted (Travis) Christy and Vic (Masked Executioner) Christy.

Local Hawaiian wrestler Gil Ane started in late 1962. He was talked into getting into the business by his friend King Curtis. Ane wrestled for four years until he became part of the Police Department. He spent most of 1963 in the Northwest. For the rest of his time, he wrestled in Hawaii. He also served as a bodyguard for Governor George Ariyoshi from 1974 to 1985. Ane became very involved in canoeing and the construction of canoes. He started a horse ranch in Waimanalo, Hawaii. He passed away in 2006.

On November 14th, journeyman Gorilla Marconi stopped off in Hawaii on his way back from Japan. He lost to King Curtis.

Billy Whitewolf won the US title from King Curtis on November 21st. However, Curtis regained the US title on December 12th. Art Boom Boom Mahilik debuted on this card, beating Luigi Macera.

1962 Wrestling Ads & Pictures

WRESTLING

WEDNESDAY — CIVIC AUDITORIUM — 8 P.M.

World's Champion Fred Blassie

Blassie says, "I'll send Maiava back to Samoa on a stretcher this time, and Blears with him."

in a

TAG MATCH

2 out of 3 falls 1 hour

Neff Maiava and **Lord Blears** vs. **Fred Blassie** and **Executioner**

SEMI FINAL

2 out of 3 falls 45 min. time limit

DICK BEYER vs. "Nature Boy" STEVENS

SPECIAL EVENT

1 fall with a 30 min. time limit

MAURICE VACHON vs. TIGER TRAVIS

FIRST MATCH

1 fall with a 20 min. time limit

CATALINA DRAKE vs. JONNY BROWN

POPULAR PRICES: General $1.55 Ringside $2.50

Maiava Tackles World Titlist

Neff Maiava, who regained the Hawaiian heavyweight wrestling title last week, goes after the Worldwide Wrestling Association belt tonight at the Civic Auditorium.

* * *

FRED BLASSIE, the world champion, is defending his jeweled belt against Maiava in a two out of three falls, one hour time limit main event.

U.S. heavyweight champion Nicky Bockwinkel takes on newcomer Duke Hoffman in a one fall to finish semifinal.

Maurice Vachon and Eric the Red tackle Lord Blears and Luigi Macera in a two out of three falls tag team special event.

Dick Byer meets Nature Boy Stevens and Catalina Drake takes on Shoulders Newman in other matches. Action starts at 8 p.m.

MAIAVA

BIG TIME WRESTLING

ED FRANCIS PRESENTS AT THE CIVIC

WED. 8 P.M.—11 WRESTLERS—2 REFEREES in a

TEXAS BATTLE ROYAL

(Over the top ropes elimination—Last man in ring wins)

3,057 LBS. OF BEEF ALL IN THE RING

Men signed for this match are as follows:

- CURTIS IAUKEA
- KILLER BUDDY AUSTIN
- LUIGI MACERA
- NEFF MAIAVA
- SHOULDERS NEWMAN
- NICKY BOCKWINKEL
- LORD TALLYHO BLEARS
- COWBOY CASSIDY
- TOSH TOGO
- PAT MATTSON

and the return of CHIEF BILLY WHITE WOLF

PLUS 5 OTHER BIG MATCHES

Prices: Ringside $2.50   Gen. $1.55   Res. 581-002

East's Tom Kiyosaki and team captains Gil Ane (left) and Alex Kane map out strategy for Friday's benefit game against the West All-Stars.—Star-Bulletin Photo.

GIL ANE

Gil Ane To Make Pro Mat Debut

Gilbert Ane, former Southern California and Punahou football star, will make his professional wrestling debut next Wednesday night at the Civic Auditorium.

Promoter Ed Francis said Ane has been working out with wrestlers here for the past eight months and is ready for his debut. He has been teamed up with Chief Billy White Wolf and Lord Blears for a six-man tag team battle.

This trio will oppose Curtis Iaukea, Tosh Togo and Cowboy Cassidy in a two out of three falls, one hour time limit match.

Shoulders Newman has been matched with Samoan Neff Maiava for the two out of three falls semifinal.

Young Jerry Christy meets Luigi Macera in the special match and Rocky Hunter tackles Tosh Togo in a special opener at 8 p.m.

1963

As 1963 opens, Whipper Watson comes to the Islands to team up with Lord Blears to beat King Curtis and Tosh Togo.

In February, Gene LeBell comes to the Islands, but Billy Whitewolf beats him in an Indian Deathmatch on Feb.13th

March 14th, a couple of newcomers show up. Dino Lanza won a battle royal and beat George Drake. Lanza is better known as Tony Marino.

Also debuting that night was The Brute, better known as Klondike Bill. He debuted by beating Dean Higuchi.

Brother Jonathon Wrestles Tonight

Brother Don Leo Jonathon, a 6 ft. 8 in. 305-pounder, makes his return debut tonight against Dino Lanza in the main event of the weekly professional wrestling card at the Civic Auditorium.

Lanza arrived here two weeks ago and already is a big favorite with his classy style. Although he will be outweighed by nearly 75 pounds, Lanza has the speed and skill to hold his own.

* * *

NEFF MAIAVA and Luigi Macera will team up to meet The Brute and Cowboy Cassidy in a two out of three falls, 45-min. time limit tag team battle.

Maiava and Macera will be giving away weight to their opponents but they are not worried. The Samoan's head butts should be potent enough to fell even the 340-pound bewhiskered "Brute."

Tosh Togo and Lord Blears clash in the special event. They are rivals of long

JONATHAN

standing, so their match should be a torrid one.

Gene (Judo) LeBell tackles Catalina Drake in the first match at 8 p.m. Drake is the more experienced but LeBell's judo skill will be tough to top.

On March 27th, Don Leo Jonathan debuted in Hawaii, beating Dino Lanza. This led to the April 10th match between King Curtis and Don Leo Jonathan, which Curtis won. I can fully commit to this being my number one dream match in Hawaii. This is the match that I wish I could go back in time to see.

In the meantime, Gene LeBell won the Hawaiian title but lost it back to Neff Maivia on April 24th.

On May 29th, the next chapter in the King Curtis-Neff Maivia feud occurred, with Curtis defending the US title.

King Curtis and The Brute had been teammates in some tag matches, but there must have been some miscalculations because it appears they got into a feud. King Curtis beat The Brute on June 5th in Honolulu and June 10th in Hilo.

The next significant challenger to come to the Islands was Gorilla Monsoon. Monsoon beat King Curtis on DQ on June 20th. Curtis beat Monsoon on July 4th in Hilo. Interesting to think about different matches in different matches. Thinking of Curtis and Monsoon in WWWF in 1973 would be appealing, but Curtis and Monsoon in 63 in Hawaii is way more exciting.

Don Manoukian returned to Hawaii and captured the US title from King Curtis in July.

Manoukian defended the US title against Nick Bockwinkel on September 4th.

Sonny Cooper (Don Jardine) came to Hawaii, beating Tosh Togo on September 18th, but lost to Curtis on September 25th.

Hilo was a monthly stop on the circuit. I have been to Hilo, a small coastal town. The population today, 2024, is about 45,000. In the early 60s, they would draw anywhere from 1,000 to 3,500 people.

'Haystack' Calhoun prepares his breakfast

The one card I want to highlight for Hilo is October 22nd, 1963. The night's main event saw Giant Baba beat King Curtis on DQ, Lord Blears and Dean Higuchi drew Don Manukian and Tosh Togo, and Togo also beat Higuchi. Only six wrestlers for this card, but what an unbelievable card for this small little town.

King Curtis beat Don Manoukian to win the US title on November 6th.

Hard Boiled Haggerty, Luther Lindsay, and Fred Blassie came to the Islands in mid-November. Lindsay beat Curtis on November 13th to cement himself in the main events.

Blassie went to a draw with Lindsay on November 20th in Honolulu.

Haystacks Calhoun won a battle royal on December 11th. Calhoun and Billy Whitewolf teamed up to go to a draw with Curtis and Cowboy Cassidy on DQ, and they went to a draw on December 18th. Curtis and Cassidy have been the tag champs since August 1st.

Neff Maivia beat Fred Blassie on Christmas night, defending the Hawaiian title.

1963 Wrestling Ads & Pictures

DINO LANZA

THE BRUTE

MANOUKIAN

293

Whipper Watson On Next Pro Mat Card

WATSON

Whipper Billy Watson, former world's heavyweight champion, will show on next Wednesday night's wrestling card at the Civic Auditorium.

Watson, who hails from Montreal, will team up with his old partner, Lord Tally-ho Blears, for a tag team match against Curtis (The Bull) Iaukea and Tosh Togo.

* * *

BLEARS AND Watson held the British Empire tag team championship in 1955. Now a resident of Honolulu, Blears is co-holder of the Hawaiian tag team trophy with Neff Maiava.

The tag team main event will go two out of three falls to a one hour time limit.

The masked Executioner and Luigi Macera have been matched for another main event. This will also go two out of three falls to an hour.

Neff Maiava vs. Cowboy Cassidy and Dean (Mr. Ha- waii) Higuchi vs. Chief Billy White Wolf round out the card. The first match goes on at 8 p.m.

Lebell To Tackle Billy White Wolf

GENE LEBELL

Gene Lebell, 235-pound former National AAU judo champion, and Chief Billy White Wolf have been paired for an unusual wrestling main event next Wednesday night at the Civic Auditorium.

They will meet in an Indian death match, with both men chained at the wrists. They will wear judo jackets.

* * *

LEBELL IS A judo expert and believes that by wearing regulation judo jackets he can offset White Wolf's skill in Indian death matches. The match will go to a finish.

Samson Burke and Lord Blears team up to battle Cowboy Cassidy and Shoulders Newman in a two out of three falls, 45-min. time limit tag team match.

Neff Maiava engages Ca- talina Drake, who is making a return showing here, and Tosh Togo meets Dean Higuchi in one fall matches.

★ ★ ★ ★ ★ ★ ★ ★
WRESTLING
sponsored by Hilo Promotional Enterprises, Ltd.
TUES., OCT. 22— 7:30 p.m.
HILO CIVIC
Battle Of The GIANTS

GIANT BABA
from Japan
vs.

CURTIS IAUKEA
the Hawaiian Giant
IN THE MAIN EVENT
2 out of 3 falls, 1 hour time limit

WRESTLING
sponsored by Hilo Promotional Enterprises, Ltd.
SPECIAL ATTRACTION
GIANT BABA
world's largest wrestler direct from Japan, over 7' tall—325 lbs.
1 APPEARANCE IN HILO
VS. THE BRUISER
U.S. Heavyweight Champion
in the FIRST MAIN EVENT
2 out of 3 falls with 1 hour time limit

TUESDAY
OCT. 8, 1963
7:30 P.M.
HILO CIVIC

SECOND MAIN EVENT—
TAG TEAM MATCH
2 out of 3 falls—45 minutes time limit
NEFF MAIAVA & SONNY COOPER
Vs.
CURTIS IAUKEA & TOSH TOGO
FIRST MATCH
1 fall with a 20 min. time limit
SONNY COOPER VS. TOSH TOGO
Admission:
Ring ...... $2.25   Gen. $1.75
Students $1.25
tax included
Children Under 12 Yrs. ...... 50¢

1964

1964 came, and 50th State Wrestling was rolling along, but they would have a challenge during the year that they may not have been expecting.

The year opened with a bang, with King Curtis defending the US title, beating Fred Blassie.

SAMSON BURKE

Sammy Burke was finishing up his career that started in 1948. He had an upset win over King Curtis on January 8th. Curtis would get the win back on January 29th over Burke, defending the US title.

Hard Boiled Haggerty, one of the greatest names in wrestling history, had come to the Islands at the end of 63. He racked up wins over Lord Blears, Gil Ane, and Lucky Simonovich. He then won the Hawaiian title from Neff Maivia on February 5th.

King Curtis defended the US title against Haggerty on February 12th, going to a draw.

On March 4th, Billy Whitewolf beat Haggerty on a night when wrestling drew 4,000.

King Curtis beat Kanji (Antonio) Inoki by DQ the next week to defend the US title.

I have to mention the March 23rd Hilo card only because the Hilo cards often had only six wrestlers. On this night, you had Masked Executioner beat Inoki, Billy Whitewolf beat King Curtis on DQ, and Lord Blears beat Haggerty on DQ. For such a small town, you had some of the best wrestlers in the world.

April 3rd had Giant Baba come and beat Hard Boiled Haggerty. Interesting, as Baba was here a week after Inoki. Inoki was heading off for a tour of North America.

On April 8th, Neff Maivia regained the Hawaiian title from Hard Boiled Haggerty. Also, on the card, King Curtis went to a draw with Billy Whitewolf.

Billy Whitewolf talks about his time in Hawaii in his RATNW interview, "I could fill a book about it. It got me to Japan many times. The Promoter, Ed Francis, was a real promoter and friend. He and I thought of doing the finger thing which is good will. Good luck to you like Snuka and other Islander types used."

Robert Duranton came into the area in May and got some main events. He beat Curtis by DQ and won the tag titles, teaming with Luther Lindsay to beat Curtis and Cowboy Cassidy. Duranton started wrestling in 1952 and was towards the end of his career. He would wrestle only part-time in the 60s, taking all of 1961 and '65 off from wrestling.

Jay York, The Alaskan, also came in, arriving in late May. I was always surprised that Jay and Mike York didn't win more titles than they did with their size and look. From the results, it appears that York was sometimes a babyface teaming with Maivia and Duranton and at other times teaming with Shoulders Newman against Blears and Duranton. York did get one main event against King Curtis, which Curtis won on June 10th.

Gene Kiniski came to the Islands and won the Hawaiian title, beating Neff Maivia on July 16th.

One of the main stories of the Hawaiian territory is about to start in the summer of 1964.

50th State Wrestling and previous promotions had used the Civic Auditorium for years. A new venue, The Honolulu International Center, was about to open up. This was a bigger venue that Francis had his sights set on to perhaps have bigger shows at. However, a person by the name of Dallas Western (which sounds like a wrestling name if there ever was one) won the bid to start promoting at the HIC. He was the frontman for Aloha Promotions, backed by Roy Shire and Big Time Wrestling out of San Francisco.

THE ALASKAN

Aloha Promotions had been running a TV show, and they debuted on July 28th with a packed card. Ray Stevens beat Ed Carpentier with their version of The US title, and Pepper Gomez and Jose Lothario beat Stan Neilson and Karl Von Brock in the semi-main event. Quite a number of the wrestlers were familiar with the Island fans. They drew 8,700 fans to the new arena for the new promotion.

Francis also promoted a show the same night with an 18-person battle royal won by Luther Lindsay; Neff Maivia also went to a draw with Kiniski. This show sold out to the tune of 5,300 people. Honolulu drew 14,000 people to local wrestling on this night. Ed Francis ran a show the following night in Honolulu with King Curtis-Luther Lindsay main event that also sold out.

The two promotions ran head to head from September through December. The details of Aloha promotions folding get a little murky. In early 65, there was a lawsuit concerning payment from the talent agency he used to fly in wrestlers from the West Coast.

Dave Meltzer elaborates on this situation in his Ed Francis obituary issue. Francis and Shire had worked together in the 50's in Ohio. Francis thought Shire was "annoying as hell." Francis admitted to playing nasty in the promotional feud. He put in a call to the airlines, and they lost some of the wrestler's luggage.

Francis reportedly met with Shire in an elevator at the NWA convention. Francis approached Shire and said, "Listen, let's work together instead of bumping heads. Why don't you share your wrestlers with me, and we'll make it work as a team without Dallas Western."

Lord Blears addresses this situation in his interview in RATNW, "I flew to San Francisco and met with Shires at the San Francisco airport. We talked for one hour, and then I flew back. We used three or four of his talents on our cards at NBC, and he stopped using his tape, within nine months we stopped using his men, and everything was back to normal.

Without Shires' wrestlers, Dallas Western's group was doomed. Francis was able to get the rights to promote in the HIC in 1965.

Johnny Barend debuted in early September with a win over Lucky Simonovich. Barend would take Hawaii by storm and spend the better part of the next eight years in Hawaii. Barend would come in as a heel teaming with King Curtis.

Ed Francis tells a story of meeting Barend in the Bay Area. Francis was dismayed because the local Commission charged wrestlers $50 to get their license. Barend loaned Francis the money, and a friendship was born.

King Curtis beat Toyonobori on September 16th. Toyonobori and Yoshimura were two top hands in Japan and had worked semi-regularly in Hawaii.

On October 8th, Johnny Barend won the Hawaiian title from Neff Maivia.

On November 14th, in another big card, King Curtis beat Don Leo Jonathan, a young Bobby Shane beat Shoulders Newman on DQ, and Johnny Barned drew Shag Thomas.

On December 4th, Johnny Barend and King Curtis started the first chapter of their feud.

On December 12th, Enrique Torres won the US title from King Curtis. Curtis didn't go beltless for very long, as he won the Hawaii title from Nick Bockwinkel on December 18th.

Iaukea Tops Mat Show

Johnny Barend tussles with Curtis Iaukea, 355-pound Hawaiian, in the top match of tonight's professional wrestling card at the Civic Auditorium. T h e program gets under way at 8.

Promoter Ed F r a n c i s' weekly card also features a tag t e a m match billed for the international championship. It sends Neff Maiava and Lord Blears against The Mighty Ursus and Tosh Togo.

The Iaukea-Barend match will be under the "anything goes" Texas rules.

Enrique Torres takes on Fuji Fujiwara, Nicky Bockwinkel m e e t s Shoulders Newman and Gil Ane tackles Bobby Shane in one-fall matches.

1964 Wrestling Ads & Pictures

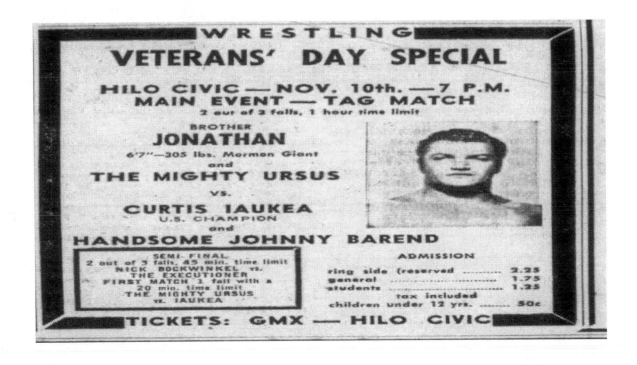

Negro Wrestler In Main Event

Luther Lindsey, one of the top Negro wrestlers in the country, meets the Masked Executioner in one of three pro wrestling main events tonight at the Civic Auditorium.

Curtis Iaukea, 355-pound Hawaiian who holds the United States heavyweight belt, tackles Frenchman Robert Ray Duranton and Hard-Boiled Haggerty battles Lucky Simunovich in the other main events.

All three matches have been signed to go two out of three falls to one-hour time limits.

Lindsey is making a return appearance in Honolulu. The Charlotte, N.C., star first appeared here in 1954 and has made several trips to Hawaii since then.

Samson Burke and Cowboy Cassidy meet Neff Maiava and Lord Blears in a one-fall tag team match which opens the card at 8 p.m.

Club 100 Golf

The Club 100 golfers have scheduled a special tournament for Sunday at 1:10 p.m. at Ala Wai course.

EXECUTIONER

1965

1965 sets up for 50th State Wrestling to continue to grow. The promotional war is just about over. They have secured the rights to the HIC for big shows each month, and things are rolling along.

Enrique Torres is the US champ. The Von Stroheim's and The Mongols came into the territory.

The next to the last Aloha Promotions match was on January 9th. The main event was Kinji Shibuya beating Mark Lewin and Bearcat Wright beating Mitsu Arakawa.

On February 15th, King Curtis went to a double count out with Nick Bockwinkel. Soldat Gorky, also known as the Wolfman debuted, but he lost to Enrique Torres.

On February 24th, Hard Boiled Haggerty beat Enrique Torres for the US title.

The last Aloha match was on February 25th, with Pepper Gomez and Ricky Romero beating Pat Patterson and Don Manoukian.

March 19th was the first HIC show for the Ed Francis promotion. They presented quite a card, which had King Curtis going to a draw with Giant Baba in the main event, Hard Boiled Haggerty beating Enrique Torres, Fred Blassie beating Leo Nomellini, and Nick Bockwinkel going to a draw with Masked Executioner were all the top matches.

On April 2nd, Hard Boiled Haggerty beat Fred Blassie, and Enrique Torres drew King Curtis. Also, Ripper Collins made his Hawaii debut. Collins would spend much of the rest of his career here in Hawaii.

In 1964 we touched on the bids that earn the right to promote at the HIC. Aloha promotions had folded, this was the first card that Francis would promote at HIC. For some reason, Portland promoter Don Owen was listed as the promoter on the clipping. Historian Rock Rims has some thoughts on this. "The longer the promotional war went on, the more it would have cost Ed because the population was too small to support two promotions for any real length of time. It is possible that Ed was thinking of taking on Don as a partner, possibly getting more talent from Don to hopefully finish off Shire. Maybe getting assistance and or talent and money to branch out a little more." Then Rims drops a shocker. Francis had applied for a promoter's license in Northern California. So the questions are: Was Shire's infiltration partly inspired by Ed looking to run a competition in NorCal? Or had Francis already gotten wind of Roy's plans to start up in Hawaii and was firing a response? Or was the response incidental, and Ed had hoped to branch out to Northern California and maybe even beyond?

On that first card at HIC on April 30th, Lou Thesz defended the NWA title for the first time in Francis' promotion. He beat Hard Boiled Haggerty. Enrique and Alberto Torres teamed up on this card to beat Ripper Collins and Shoulders Newman.

A-14 Honolulu Star-Bulletin Wed., May 19, 1965

Arena wrestling rights to go to one promoter

One wrestling promoter will be given one year's exclusive use of the Honolulu International Center Arena for matches under a new policy set yesterday by the City Council.

The new rental policy, recommended by Byron Trimble, director of the Center, calls for a 12-month contract for between 12 and 18 wrestling matches.

Promoters will bid for the contract. The exclusive contract plan resulted from incidents of unfair competition between wrestling promoters, Trimble said.

Under the present system, promoters make arrangements for a performance at a time. It has resulted in instances when, for example, one promoter will wait until a competitor has set a date, then will ask for the preceding night and get the better crowd.

"I don't think bidding is a good thing. I never heard of it before," said Ed Francis, a local wrestling promoter, who spoke to the Council.

He said that most other cities only have one wrestling promoter.

Francis said that in spite of large crowds, it is hard to "make the Center pay" because it costs a minimum of $8,000 to put on a match there.

Thesz would spend the week in Hawaii and wrestled at least two more times, beating Haggarty again in Hilo and Luther Lindsay on May 7th.

Enrique and Alberto Torres won the Hawaii tag titles, beating King Curtis and Mr. Fuji on May 28th. Victor The Bear beat Hard Boiled Haggerty, and Fred Blassie beat Dean Higuchi.

Greg Oliver and I discussed the effort it would take to get Victor The Bear to Hawaii. Probably not on a plane! Probably on some sort of boat.

Here, you have Victor in Honolulu on the 4th and Hilo on the 6th, beating King Curtis. So again, some sort of transportation had to ensue.

On June 23rd, Hard Boiled Haggerty beat Hercules Cortez to defend the US title. Also, on this card, King Curtis beat Chief Red Cloud.

Even though this period is interesting, it is a little transitional, with the Torres Brothers and Haggerty on top and even Luther Lindsay on top. These are not the wrestlers you associate with Hawaii, so it makes an interesting time.

On July 14th, Pat Patterson and Ray Stevens defended their World tag titles, beating Alberto and Enrique Torres. This is the first example of Roy Shire wrestlers working with the Ed Francis promotion since the promotional war.

Ricky Hunter

On August 11th, another big show saw Kinji Shibuya go to a draw with Hard Boiled Haggerty. Lord Blears enjoyed putting two heels against each other to ensure some wild main events.

Also, on this show, Ray Stevens beat Bearcat Wright, and King Curtis beat Jack Lanza (before he became Blackjack Lanza). These shows that are starting now with the San Francisco wrestlers are bringing up the quality of the shows a notch, if that is even possible.

On August 25th, King Curtis won a battle royal. A bevy of undercard newcomers, including Seymour Koenig, Ricky Hunter, and McRonald Kamaka, better known as Tor Kamata, were on this card.

Ricky Hunter noted: "Ed Francis was the promoter there, and he always had the best wrestlers on his cards. He would get wrestlers as they came to and from Japan and Australia. There was a constant supply of wrestlers because they had to change planes in Hawaii. They would come in for a couple of weeks and Ed would keep them there a month.

Jim Barnett did the booking in Australia, and Steve Rickard did the booking in New Zealand. When you were through, you would call Hawaii and tell them you were coming through. They would say, well, we have you booked Wednesday night. A lot of times I would come in for a couple weeks and stay a couple months.

This is where my wife and I met. I finished a tour of Australia, and Ed Francis always used me. It was kind of like a working vacation. When you went to Australia, you worked six nights a week for three months and were really tired. When you were in Hawaii, you only had to work three shows a week.

I just fell in love with Hawaii; it was such a neat place to be. I have a lot of fond memories of Hawaii.

I have to tell you how I met my wife. A lot of people would go to the Royal Hawaiian Motel. They had a lot of beach frontage, and they had white garbage cans. In black letters, it had, please deposit in garbage cans. I was leaning on one of these cans. I had a couple hours to tan. Sherri (my wife) and her girlfriend were sitting 10 or 12 feet away from me. Sherri said to her girlfriend, "I'm going to meet that fellow over there. I don't know how." I always tell people she had the pick of the litter.

I started talking to the girls, and I asked them if they would be down on the beach the next day. That night, Sherri and I went out to a famous place called Chuck's Steak House. I knew when I saw her, I thought, "God what a great gal." and she turned out to be my wife. It was a real romantic place to meet your wife."

Pepper Martin came in August and feuded with Hard Boiled Haggerty and King Curtis. Johnny Kostas also made some appearances and had wins over Soldat "The Russian Wolfman" Gorky and Ripper Collins.

The next big card was on September 15th, with King Curtis beating Hard Boiled Haggerty, Bearcat Wright and Luther Lindsay beating Pat Patterson and Ray Stevens, and Wilbur Snyder beating Juan Sebastian.

On September 29th, Luther Lindsay beat King Curtis for the Hawaiian title. Also on this card, Killer Kowalski and Bobby Graham made their debut.

Kowalski began feuding with Lindsay, getting a win on October 6th and a no-contest in Hilo on October 9th.

Beauregard debuted in Hawaii on October 13th, teaming with Ripper Collins.

Beauregard talks about how he got into wrestling, "I was going to the University of Hawaii and on a wrestling scholarship. The gym I worked out at was Dean Higuchi's, who also wrestled as Dean Ho. All the wrestlers worked out at Deans gym because it was close to the Civic Auditorium. One of the wrestlers, Neff Maivia, was going to the Philippines. He wanted to train a couple new wrestlers. I was at the gym, and I had wrestled at the college, and they asked me if I wanted to turn pro. But at that time, I was about 179 pounds. They said I had to bulk up to 200 to at least be in the ballpark. Back then, in the 60s, the average wrestler wasn't even 250 pounds. Some of the bigger guys were 280, but a majority of the guys were 210 or so.

They were going to try to open the Philippines as a territory. Neff was going to be the pioneer. He didn't have enough money, and we didn't draw enough money, and he ran out of money, and they had to quit."

Beauregard also talks about Ripper Collins and how he gave him his name. "Oh, Ripper Roy Collins, The Southern Gentleman. He is the one who gave me the name Beauregard. When I first started wrestling in the Philippines, I was using the name Eric The Golden Boy. When I got back to Honolulu, they wanted someone to be a manager or valet for Ripper. I was still green. I had only been wrestling for 4 or 5 months. They asked if I wanted to be Ripper's valet. We were trying to think of a name. He had this money that he used to pass out. This confederate money. It was signed by General Beauregard. He looked at me and said, Beauregard. He said, Fabian, Liberace, a lot of great people only have one name, and you will remember better than two names. Beauregard is a Southern Gentleman's name, and I like it. I said OK. That's how the name I got, Beauregard."

October 22nd was another great card, topped by Killer Kowalski beating Don Leo Jonathon, King Curtis beating Pepper Gomez, and Pat Patterson and Ray Stevens going to a draw with Luther Lindsay and Bearcat Wright.

On November 3rd, Killer Kowalski beat King Curtis to win the US title.

Killer Kowalski started feuding with Joe Scarpa (Jay Strongbow) and Red Bastien.

On December 22nd, Bearcat Wright won a big battle royal, Killer Kowalski beat Pepper Gomez, Karl Gotch went to a draw with Joe Scarpa, Neff Maivia & Luther Lindsay beat Pat Patterson and Ray Stevens by dq. Any of those four matches could have been a main event, and the undercard had Ron Reed (Buddy Colt), Kinji Shibuya, Ripper Collins, and Mr. Fuji.

Thesz defends title tonight

One of pro wrestling's all-time greats, Lou Thesz of St. Louis, headlines tonight's all-star card in the Honolulu International Center Arena. The program starts at 8.

Thesz meets Hard-Boiled Haggerty in the main event of Promoter Don Owens's first local promotion. It is billed for the world's heavyweight belt held by Thesz.

Crusher Staisiak, a 325-pound newcomer, tackles Curtis Iaukea, the 350-pound Hawaiian, in another featured match.

Making their first appearance together in a tag team match will be Enrique Torres and Alberto Torres of Mexico. The latter arrived last night to join his brother.

Wild Bill Savage, Luther Lindsey and Ripper Collins will be among the matmen showing in supporting matches.

Action begins at 8 p.m.

Thesz Keeps Mat Crown

Lou Thesz retained his world heavyweight wrestling championship when Hard Boiled Haggerty was disqualified in the third and deciding fall of last night's professional wrestling main event at the Honolulu International Center arena.

After Thesz took the first fall in 25 minutes, Haggerty evened matters at six minutes of the second fall. He was disqualified at 2:29 of the deciding fall for using a claw hold outside the ring.

In the semifinal match, Curtis Iaukea also won on a third fall disqualification over The Crusher.

The Crusher, who won the first fall with a bear hug, was disqualified at 2:29 of the third fall when he threw Iaukea over the top rope. Iaukea used a big splash to take the second fall.

Luther Lindsey also used the big splash and body press to subdue Fuji Fujiwara in their special one-fall match.

The Torres brothers, Enrique and Alberto, won the tag team match over Shoulders Newman and Ripper Collins.

In a pair of 20-minute time limit marches, Lord Blears won over The Bandit and Nicky Bockwinkel defeated Gilbert Ane.

1966

On the first card in 1966, both singles titles changed hands, with Ron Reed beating Luther Lindsay to win the Hawaii title and Killer Kowalski losing the US title to Nick Kozak.

If you took wrestling historians and said there would be a match between Killer Kowalski and Nick Kozak, probably 95 to 100% of them would imagine that Kowalski would win due to the pecking order and drawing ability.

After a four-month vacation in Hawaii, Kowalski headed back to Australia.

It shows that Blears and Francis would take a chance on someone to elevate them. To be clear, Kozak looked great.

Scott Teal has an interview with Ron Reed (Buddy Colt) in his book Wrestling Archive Project Vol. 1. This book is available from www.crowbarpress.com.

Reed talked about working in Hawaii: "On the way back from Australia, we stopped in Honolulu, and I stayed there for about three months. I had made arrangements with the promoter, Ed Francis before I left Australia. He put me over Luther Lindsay for the Hawaiian title. Luther was a good worker. Francis gave me a guarantee good enough that I could make it a paid vacation. My wife flew over and met me there, and we stayed in an efficiency condo about two blocks from Waikiki Beach. I was paid good money to live in Hawaii and be on the beach every day. Nick Bockwinkel and Nick Kozak came to Hawaii while I was there. Joe Scarpa and I were riding around with Kozak one day when we saw Bockwinkel riding towards us on his rented 125 motorcycle. Kozak stopped the car, and Bockwinkel pulled up beside us so we could talk. I was in the back seat of the driver's side. While Kozak was talking to Bockwinkel, I reached out and slid Bockwinkel's keys out of the ignition. We finished our chat, said our goodbyes and Kozak drove off, leaving Bockwinkel there to figure out where his keys went. We drove around the block and took the keys back to him, but he gave us a good cursing."

Johnny Barend returned to Hawaii on January 10th and went to a no-contest with Nick Bockwinkel.

One interesting preliminary match occurred on January 26th, with Dean Higuchi going to a draw with Mr. Fuji. Higuchi and Fuji would have a career that dovetailed each other over the years, with both starting early in Hawaii. Wrestledata says they faced each other over 100 times.

Fast forward 40 years at a Dean Silverstone reunion. Dean Higuchi enters Silverstone's home and Ed Wiskowski would deadpan, "Hey Mr. Fuji is here!!!!!" Higuchi would always play along, replying, "I am not Mr. Fuji."

Barend would win the US title from Kozak on February 2nd.

On February 16th, Lou Thesz would come to the Islands and defeat Don Manoukian on DQ. Ray Stevens and Pat Patterson also were on this card, beating Bill Watts and Rene Goulet.

Two weeks later, on March 2nd, Thesz wrestled again and went to a draw with Luther Lindsay.

March 16th saw Giant Baba return and go to a draw with Johnny Barend. Dale Lewis also debuted and went to a draw with Lindsay.

The following week, on March 23rd, another big card was held with Pat Patterson and Ray Stevens going to a draw with Ripper Collins and Johnny Barend. Also on this card, Dale Lewis went to a draw with Joe Scarpa, Bill Watts beat Kinji Shibuya by DQ, and Neff Maivia and Dean Higuchi beat Tosh Togo and Beauregard in tag team action.

The regular crew was a little down before April 6th; however, on this date, one of the most captivating characters would debut in Hawaii, The Missing Link, Pampero Firpo. He would beat Joe Scarpa on his debut. He was given the name Missing Link because the office didn't feel like the locals would be able to pronounce Pampero Firpo.

FIRPO

Don Chuy and Joe Carollo got a push as a tag team. They beat Ripper Collins and Beauregard and went to a draw with tag champs Ripper Collins and Johnny Barend.

On April 27th, one of the big cards saw Pat Patterson and Ray Stevens finally beat Ripper Collins and Johnny Barend, Bill Watts beat Don Duffy, and Nick Kozak drew Cyclone Negro.

After only being in Hawaii for about a month as a heel, Missing Link turned from heel to babyface. He won battle royals on May 4th in Honolulu and May 9th in Hilo. He would grab singles wins over Beauregard and Mr. Fuji.

Sam Steamboat would also return to the area and feud with Ripper Collins over the Hawaiian State title.

On May 3rd, King Curtis and Ripper Collins would beat Johnny Barend and Hans Mortier to win the tag titles. Mortier refused to tag Barend and, after the match, helped Curtis and Collins attack Barend. Jim Hady made the save.

June 29th was another huge card, with Johnny Barend beating Missing Link. This match becomes a very big question mark. In his interview, Pampero Firpo talks about having a stomach injury. This is the last match he will wrestle for three months. In his RATNW interview, he said, "I got hurt pretty bad in Hawaii. I was hospitalized for 56 days. I lost 56 pounds in 56 days. I had 106 fever. The Dr. told me and said, "Look, Your chances to live are 65 for, 35 against." During the surgery, they removed a perforated part of the intestine, one foot long. They had a new technique.

When Firpo came back in October, he wrestled Barend again. Firpo remembered, "There was a big demand to see a rematch between my opponent and myself. I went to wrestle with an opening almost two inches in my tummy. I was still bleeding, but the doctor put something in when I went to wrestle. My opponent somehow put his finger inside of me when he put on the claw and he bust everything again. My doctor came to see me wrestle and when he saw my wrestle he put his hands over his face and say, OH MY.

Johnny Barend. He put his finger in my tummy. That was his specialty hold. The patches were just paper so they had to take me back to the doctor and put in anothers stitches in. The Doctor said, Why don't you stop? I said, well, we will see."

Also, on June 29th, Pat Patterson and Ray Stevens beat Billy Whitewolf and Red Eagle, and Gorilla Monsoon drew Nick Bockwinkel. This also marked the debut of Jim Hady, who went to a draw with The Masked Executioner. Hady would become very big in Hawaii. This, however, was just a one-off match. Hady and Monsoon came from the Bay Area for this shot.

Kongozan was appearing; he had also wrestled as Taro Miyaki, Professor Hiro, and Professor Hito. He held several tag titles, including the NW tag title with Tony Borne as Professor Hiro.

KONGOZAN

MONGOLIAN STOMPER

Bill Dromo came in from Australia and stayed for about three months. Dromo debuted teaming with Ripper Collins and Johnny Barend, beating Sam Steamboat, Nick Bockwinkel, and Neff Maivia. On his way home from Japan, Killer Kox was also on this card, losing to Billy Whitewolf.

The next big card was July 27th, with the main event being Johnny Barend, Ripper Collins, and Gorilla Monsoon beating Ray Stevens, Pat Patterson, and Haystacks Calhoun.

The Mongolian Stomper Archie Gouldie was the next big name to come into the area in early August. He stayed about three months, coming from the Kansas City area. He started with wins over Dean Higuchi and Red Eagle and went to draws with Nick Bockwinkel and Sam Steamboat.

On August 20th, another new promotion debuted. Promoters Jimmy O'Brien and Augie Curtis used wrestlers from Arizona. This was this group's only show. The main event was Arman Hussian beating Don Arnold on DQ. Tito Montez, Gorgeous George Jr, and Bruce Kirk were some of the wrestlers on the card.

On August 24th, Neff Maivia beat Ripper Collins for the Hawaii title. Also, on 8/24 saw the debut of Charlie Kalani, who would be better known as Toru Tanaka.

The next massive card was on August 31st. The main event saw Billy Whitewolf beat Johnny Barend in an Indian Death Match, Pat Patterson and Ray Stevens beat Kinji Shibuya and Cyclon Negro, and Bill Dromo and Mongolian Stomper beat Nick Bockwinkel and Sam Steamboat.

If there was one thing that I didn't care for in the booking of Hawaii wrestling, there were a lot of 6, 8, or 10-man tag matches, especially in some of the main events. It may be a personal pet peeve, but I never felt like a 6-man tag match was a match that should really draw or further the issues. I felt like it was just too many people involved. Obviously, there are a lot of matches listed where there is so much talent, and that is the only thing that really appeals to me with that type of match.

An example of that is the main event of the September 21st card. Ray Stevens, Pat Patterson, and Billy Whitewolf beat Johnny Barend, Ripper Collins, and Gorilla Monsoon. In other top matches on the card, Hard Boiled Haggerty drew with The Mongolian Stomper, and Bobo Brazil makes his 2nd Hawaii debut, beating Bill Dromo.

The September 26th card in Hilo had a top-notch main event, with Johnny Barend beating Mongolian Stomper in a Texas Death Match. Stomper must have had an issue with Barend, as now Stomper is a babyface.

On October 12th, Missing Link is back in the area. He beats Ripper Collins, Johnny Barend, Mighty Atlas, Karl Gotch, and Mongolian Stomper. Atlas had an impressive body. He also wrestled under various names, including Chuck Bruce and Chuck Fish. He did not achieve very much success in wrestling.

On October 19th, Ripper Collins regained the Hawaii title by beating Neff Maivia. Also, Pat Patterson and Ray Stevens beat Pepper Gomez and Victor Rivera, and Missing Link beat Johnny Barend.

On October 26th, Jim Hady came to Hawaii for a regular tour. He seemed to get over big and had initial wins over Tony Sheppard, Beauregard, Ripper Collins, Crybaby Cannon, Mike Paidousis, Mighty Atlas, and Skull Murphy.

On Wrestledata, it mentions that Dutch Savage was the trainer of Hady, but that can't be true because they have Hady debuting in 1951. Savage didn't debut until 1961. Savage and Hady apparently were friends. In Dutch Savage's defunct website, he mentioned it was Hady's idea to drop the Hawaiian State title to Savage. Savage, in his RATNW interview, mentions that Jim Hady was someone he wanted to bring to the NW.

At any rate, Hady proved to be one of the most popular wrestlers in Hawaiian history.

Neff Maivia and Pampero Firpo won the Hawaiian tag titles on November 2nd, beating Ripper Collins and Johnny Barend.

Hawaiian title match tonight

Karl Gotch, who claims the European title, takes on Ripper Collins for the Hawaiian heavyweight wrestling belt at the Civic Auditorium tonight.

Collins is making his first defense of the Ring belt since he regained it from Neff Maiava recently.

The title-billed match is one of three main events lined up for the card. Other headliners are Johnny Barend versus Bob Boyer and Man Mountain Cannon versus The Missing Link.

Jim Hady takes on Mighty Atlas in one of two special events. The other sends Mike Paidosus against Billy White Wolf in the first match at 8.

On November 23rd, the main event was very interesting, with Ripper Collins wrestling Karl Gotch. Despite being one of the most respected shooters in wrestling history, Gotch never really figured into the main events in Hawaii. In Japan, he was known as The God of Wrestling.

On the other hand, you had Ripper Collins, who I have often thought of as one of the best heels I have ever seen. Certainly not the best wrestler, but one of the best heels. It would have been interesting to see the contrast in that match. Collins won on DQ.

November 30th saw Johnny Barend beat Pampero Firpo in another chapter of their feud. Also on the card was Bill Watts going to a draw with Ripper Collins, Karl Gotch beat Sonny Meyers, Johnny Valentine beat Mike Paidousis, Tarzan Tyler and Cyclon Negro went to a draw with Pepper Gomez and Jim Hady.

On the last card of the year for '66 on December 25th, Johnny Barend beat

Ripper Collins on DQ after their team collapsed after losing the tag titles. Also on the card, Pat Patterson and Ray Stevens beat Missing Link and Jim Hady, Billy Whitewolf dcor Cyclone Negro, and Karl Gotch drew Tarzan Tyler. This card drew over 7,000.

1966 Wrestling Ads & Pictures

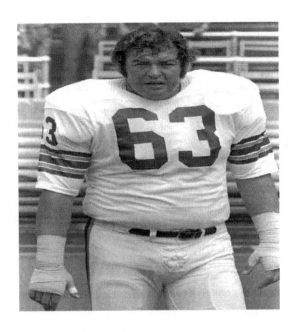

Joe Carollo #63
Don Chuy #62

In Civic Auditorium
Pro Grid Stars Headline Wrestling Show Monday

Two Los Angeles Rams football stars, Joe Carollo and Don Chuy, will make their Hilo wrestling debut Monday night here in the Civic Auditorium.

They will meet Handsome Johnny Barend and Ripper Collins in a two-out-of-three falls, one-hour time-limit tag team battle. Barend is the United States champion and Collins holds the Hawaiian belt.

Carollo, 265, starred at Notre Dame and was the Rams' second draft pick in 1963. Chuy, 256, played at Clemson and was a fifth draft choice of the National Football League club. Both are lineman, Carollo holding sway at tackle and Chuy at guard.

The "Missing Link," who also answers to Pampero Firpo, will be introduced to Big Island fans in a semifinal with Nick Kozak, the Texan who is after Barend's U.S. belt. The wild-haired Missing Link is as rough as they come and is just as tough.

Lord Tallyho Blears and Beauregarde are matched for the first match. Beauregarde is Collins' valet and protege and has picked up many of his master's tactics. He will need them against the veteran and experienced Blears, former British Empire heavyweight champion and twice co-holder of the world's tag team belt.

HIC ARENA — HIC ARENA

"INTERNATIONAL ALL STAR WRESTLING"

8:00 P.M. **SAT. AUG. 20th** 8:00 P.M.

H.I.C. ARENA --- H.I.C. ARENA --- H.I.C. ARENA

the ASSASSINS
WORLD TAG TEAM
CHAMPIONS
vs.
RAY GORDON ★ ★ ★
EUROPEAN CHAMPION
&
★ ★ ★ TITO MONTEZ
ARIZONA STATE CHAMPION

the ASSASSINS

CHAMPIONSHIP
DON ARNOLD, U.S.A. CHAMPION
vs.
ARMON HUSSAN, Champ of Sudan
THE GOLIATH HEAVYWEIGHT CHAMPIONSHIP

WAHINES! WAHINES! WAHINES!
CAROL LYNN VS. MARIA PIZZA
ROCKY STORM VS. JIM GRABMEIR
BRUCE KIRK VS. FIDEL GRIMO

FOR RESERVATIONS CALL 513-731
Res. Seats $3.00 & $4.00 Gen. $2.00 CHILDREN $1.00 (Gen'l Adm.)

DON ARNOLD
OPEN 10-6 DAILY

HIC ARENA ★★★★★ HIC ARENA

Promoters O'Brien & Curtis only show

STEAMBOAT BAREND

WRESTLING

Sponsored by Hilo Promotional Enterprises, Ltd.

MON., MAY 9th—7:30 P.M.—CIVIC

GIGANTIC TEXAS "OVER THE ROPES" BATTLE ROYAL

$50.00 ENTRY FEE—JACKPOT OF $400.00
TO THE LAST MAN IN THE RING

• SAMMY STEAMBOAT   • THE MISSING LINK
• DON CHUY   • RIPPER COLLINS
• JOE CAROLLO   • JOHN BAREND
• NICK KOZAK   • BEAUREGARDE

PLUS 4 OUTSTANDING MATCHES

tickets available at Hilo Civic and at AMA-PRO Sporting Goods	ADMISSION	
	Ring	2.25
	General	1.75
	Students	1.25
	tax included	
	children under 12 years	50c

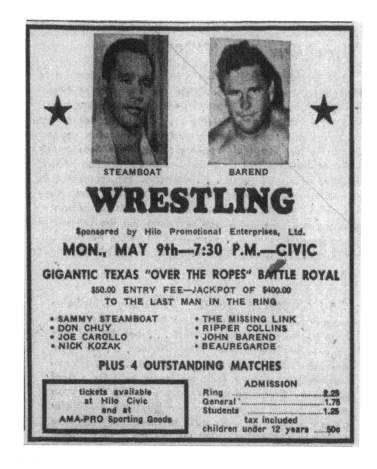

STEAMBOAT BAREND

WRESTLING

Sponsored by Hilo Promotional Enterprises, Ltd.

MON., MAY 9th—7:30 P.M.—CIVIC

GIGANTIC TEXAS "OVER THE ROPES" BATTLE ROYAL

$50.00 ENTRY FEE—JACKPOT OF $400.00
TO THE LAST MAN IN THE RING

• SAMMY STEAMBOAT   • THE MISSING LINK
• DON CHUY   • RIPPER COLLINS
• JOE CAROLLO   • JOHN BAREND
• NICK KOZAK   • BEAUREGARDE

PLUS 4 OUTSTANDING MATCHES

tickets available at Hilo Civic and at AMA-PRO Sporting Goods	ADMISSION	
	Ring	2.25
	General	1.75
	Students	1.25
	tax included	
	children under 12 years	50c

Former Champ
Lou Thesz, who lost his world's heavyweight mat title last month, makes his HIC debut to-morrow night. He meets Dick the Bruiser.

Nick Kozak Battles Barend Tonight

Nick Kozak of Texas meets Johnny Barend of New York in the main event of tonight's pro wrestling card at the Civic Auditorium.

Barend wrested the U.S. heavyweight belt from Kozak several weeks ago but tonight's match is not for the title.

Ripper Collins and his valet, Beauregarde, take on Joe Scarpa and Lord Blears in a tag team semifinal. Scarpa is from New Jersey and Blears is a former British Empire champion.

Luther Lindsay and Tosh (Oddjob) Togo are billed for the special event.

Neff Maiava, popular Samoan mat star, and Fuji Fujiwara clash in the opening

KOZAK

Kozak Tackles Ripper Collins

Newly crowned mat champions are featured on tonight's pro wrestling card at the Civic Auditorium.

Nick Kozak of Houston, Texas, who dethroned Killer Kowalski as the U.S. champion, meets Ripper Collins in one of the main events. Collins will have his valet, Beauregarde, with him in the ring.

Johnny Barend of New York goes up against Ron Reed of Baltimore, Md., the new Hawaiian champion, in the second main event.

Both are non-title matches scheduled for two out of three falls to one-hour time limits.

Popular Nick Bockwinkel of California returns to the auditorium, teaming up with Lord Blears for a tag team battle against The Bandit and Fuji Fujiwara.

BOCKWINKEL

Neff Maiava meets Joe Scarpa in the opener at 8 p.m.

1967

1967 opened with a few newcomers, including Hans Mortier and Eddie Morrow. Mortier beat Nick Bockwinkel on Jan 11th.

Morrow had started overseas in Germany. Mortier was twenty years into a journeyman career. With the debut win over Bockwinkel, it was clear that he was lined up for a push.

On January 25th, Mortier went to a draw with Jim Hady. Hady was fast becoming one of Hawaii's favorite sons. Ray Stevens, Pat Patterson, and Ripper Collins beat Johnny Barend, Bill Watts, and Cyclon Negro. Interesting as Collins and Barend were feuding with Patterson and Stevens for a period of time in 66.

On February 1st, Mortier and Barend won the tag titles over Missing Link and Neff Maiava.

King Curtis had been gone for about a year with a tour of WWWF and England. He returned on February 15th with a win over Kongozan.

February 20th saw another Hilo show that drew 1,000 people to see some of the best wrestlers in the world. King Curtis beat Karl Gotch, and Johnny Barend beat Jim Hady by DQ. Also on the card were Mortier, Collins, Blears, and Executioner.

New Mat Stars Show

Hans Mortier and Eddie Morro, two newcomers to local wrestling, will be featured in promoter Ed Francis' first mat card of 1967 Wednesday night at the Civic Auditorium.

They will be among 16 matmen in a Texas battle royal.

Johnny B a r e n d, Ripper Collins, Jim Hady, B i l l y White Wolf, Karl G o t c h, Mighty Atlas, Beauregarde, Low Newman, Lord Blears, Neff Maiava, the Missing Link, Fujiwara, Steve Stanlee and Kongozan are the others in the battle royal.

TO WRESTLE HERE—Paul Diamond, one of professional wrestling's top drawing attractions all over the world today, makes his Hilo debut Monday night in a match against Ripper Collins in the Civic Auditorium. Diamond stands 6-2 and weighs 235 pounds. Collins lost his Hawaiian heavyweight champion title Wednesday night in Honolulu to Jim Hady in a title match there. The first of four bouts gets under way at 7:45 p.m.

On March 1st, King Curtis beat Johnny Barend for the US title. This is another example of heel vs heel; you know this had to be a wild match.

Also, on the 1st, Ray Stevens and Pat Patterson beat Jim Hady and Eddie Morrow, and Ripper Collins beat Cyclon Negro.

On March 15th, Jim Hady beat Ripper Collins for the Hawaiian title.

On March 20th, Paul Diamond debuted in Hilo. Diamond was a good-looking, preliminary babyface.

The big card of the month was on March 29th and saw Pat Patterson and Ray Stevens beating Missing Link and Nick Bockwinkel. King Curtis went to a draw with Johnny Barend. Mongolian Stomper returned and beat Jim Hady.

April 12th saw Dory Funk Jr go to a draw with Paul Diamond. The main event saw Johnny Barend team with Beauregard to beat King Curtis and Mr. Fujiwara. (Fuji).

King Curtis beat Dory Funk Jr on 4/19. This was still two years before Dory became the NWA champ. Also, a strange appearance by Tojo Yamamoto. This looks like a one-off, as Yamamoto moved from Memphis to The Mid-Atlantic area.

On May 3rd, King Curtis and Ripper Collins beat Johnny Barend and Hans Mortier to win the Tag titles. I can only imagine the interviews leading up to this match.

Let's talk for a moment about exactly how much the promotion invested in the power of the interview. They reportedly had two shows, one that was 90 minutes long and featured two matches from the Civic Auditorium from the previous week's wrestling. It also featured about 30 minutes of interviews, building the matches for the following week.

The 2nd show was a studio show featuring two matches, often a display of wrestling holds, and a large part of the program to interviews.

King Curtis had a lot of natural charisma. Still, he credits Lord Blears with pushing the envelope as to the interview style. Blears urged Curtis to do his interview with his back to the camera. Then, with his big booming voice, he would deliver his interview.

In a Slam Wrestling interview, Curtis talked about partaking in the "cookie" (acid). ""You can't take any kind of drugs before a match; your timing is off. You're going to hurt the person you're with and yourself. You really can take it because of the paranoia; you can't take it before you go to work either, I mean, before you're cutting interviews — that's erroneous. A good drop of acid, say a guy took it on a Sunday on his day off, it would go and keep him loaded for ten days; any more acid that he's going to take ain't going to get him no higher, and his mind is going to really wander. But yeah, that's how he's going to come up with some far-out interviews."

"It's been seven long years ..." and "Meeesssterrrr Francissss" were frequent lines, as Curtis would launch into another rambling, intense interview, his back to the camera, belt over the shoulder, his words rising like lava from a volcano. His schtick wasn't that different in Hawaii in the 1970s as it was as a manager in the WWF in the late-'80s.

He credits Blears again. "The ring psychology comes from the Lord. The Lord Blears knew everything about interviews. Here in Honolulu, he's the one that told me, 'Everyone's going to be tired of pictures. You turn and put your back.'... That was my style, just the back, you go up and down. Everything from the Lord."

Johnny Barend also had a great interview style. He might emerge from a Tepee or a coffin, complete with a lit cigar. He would, at times, not make any sense, but that was the charm and the attraction.

Ripper Collins had interviews that would rub the Islanders the wrong way. He would mispronounce Hawaiian towns wrong. He had a Southern accent, and with his out-of-shape body, he was a heat machine.

May 10th saw Johnny Barend beat former partner Hans Mortier. Mortier had helped attack Barend after their tag title loss, and Jim Hady had made the save. Jim Hady went to a draw with Ripper Collins to continue their feud.

Unusual Rassling In Civic Tonight

An unusual double main event will headline the professional wrestling card here tonight in the Civic Auditorium.

United States champion Curtis Iaukea and Hawaiian titleholder Jim Hady are billed for one match. They have signed for what looms as an old fashioned Pier 9 brawl. Clashing in an "anything goes" match, they will wear boxing gloves and go 10 2-minute rounds. They can punch, wrestle or do anything as long as they keep their gloves on.

The second main event brings together Johnny Barend and Ripper Collins in a Texas death match. The two bitter oppon-ents, once the friendliest of pals, keep wrestling until one man is no longer able to continue.

Two other matches will be presented as preliminaries on what shapes up as the most exciting card of the year.

First match starts at 7:45 p.m.

Gimmick matches were somewhat rare in Hawaii; however, in Hilo on May 15th, there were two gimmick matches to settle some scores. Jim Hady beat King Curtis in a Pier 9 Brawl, and then Ripper Collins beat Johnny Barend in a Texas Death Match.

On May 17th, Johnny Barend and Jim Hady made friends enough to team up to face King Curtis and Ripper Collins in a cage match in which Barend and Hady won.

On June 14th, Ernie Ladd made an appearance in Honolulu and beat Hans Mortier on DQ. The night's main event was King Curtis and Ripper Collins beating Johnny Barend and Jim Hady to win the tag titles.

On June 28th, King Curtis beat Don Leo Jonathon in a US title defense. This was at least the 3rd time they had faced each other in the past few years, and I don't believe Jonathan has a win over Curtis.

I looked up the records of Curtis vs. Jonathon. DLJ never got a win anywhere in the world, including matches in Los Angeles, Japan, and Hawaii. They teamed up once in Louisville, Kentucky, a surefire trivia question winner. King Curtis and Don Leo Jonathan teamed up one time in their career; what city was it? Louisville may be the last guess anyone might have.

July 5th was one of those cards that were filled with so me top fly-ins, including Ray Stevens, Pepper Gomez, Art Neilson, and Cyclone Negro. It had been March since some of the Bay Area wrestlers had flown in.

On July 12th, Dutch Schultz debuted, teaming with Hans Mortier. They lost to Jim Hady and Johnny Barend. Schultz would be better known as Dutch Savage.

Another big card on August 3rd saw Billy Whitewolf beat King Curtis in an Indian Deathmatch, Ray Stevens and Pat Patterson beat Johnny Barend and Jim Hady by DQ, Ripper Collins drew With Pat O'Connor, Pedro Morales beat Hans Mortier, and Dutch Schultz beat Beauregard. Irony here as Schultz and Beauregard would be future NW tag champions.

On August 9th, Curtis, Collins, and Schultz beat Barend, Hady, and Blears. The heels would be known as The Rat Pack.

Savage remembers, "We were the original members of the rat pack. We were the first group to start a rat pack. There was Ripper Collins, King Curtis, Mr. Fuji and myself. Then there was Johnny Barend, Jimmy Hady, Billy Whitewolf. All we did was work the big Island and Maui and a few other spots. We worked HIC once a month Civic Auditorium four times a month, and the outer islands once or twice a month. We had a big vacation for almost two years."

Haystacks Calhoun would win a battle royal in late August and team with Hady to beat Curtis and Dutch Schultz.

On September 13th, Curtis beat Bill Watts, and Barend and Hady beat Dutch Schultz and Ripper Collins. More irony, Dutch and Collins would have a tremendous feud in Oregon six years in the future.

October 18th saw Pat Patterson and Ray Stevens beat King Curtis and Dutch Schultz on DQ, Bockwinkel returned, Fritz Von Goering and Dory Funk Jr, Angelo Poffo, and Victor The Bear were all on this card.

Victor The Bear Smashes Dutch Schultz

Victor the Great, the versatile wrestling bear, used his brute strength and weight edge to great advantage to pin wrestler Dutch Schultz with a vicious body press to cop the duke in the special "man versus beast" match in last Thursday night's pro wrestling card in the Civic.

The one-sided, one fall match ended 4:45 after the opening bell.

In the evening's main bout, rough and tough newcomer Angelo Poffo and popular Nick Bockwinkel grappled to a draw after exchanging one fall apiece.

Jim Hady captured the last two falls to defeat Tank Morgan in the special event match and Chief Billy White Wolf and Curtis (the Bull) Iaukea grappled to a draw in their 20-minute time limit curtainraiser.

On October 19th in Hilo, Victor the Bear beat Dutch Schultz. Dutch had some memories of this match, "Oh Yeah, I was the only one to go for the bear. Curtis wouldn't even mess with the bear. No, Brothers, I'm fine, I ain't going with no animal. I know the bear got part of my finger, and he still has it. He wore a muzzle but he had those gums in there and they still had roots in there. Luckily they declawed him but they didn't file anything down and they were rough and ragged and the scratched the living shit out of you."

On November 15th, one of the preliminary matches saw Billy Whitewolf beat Killer Kowalski. The main event saw Hady defend the Hawaiian title against Dutch Schultz.

On November 27th in Hilo, Jim Hady and Johnny Barend beat Pat Patterson and Ray Stevens. Stevens and Patterson did not have the World Tag titles in San Francisco during this period.

On December 25th, Johnny Barend beat King Curtis for the US title. Barend's tag partner, Jim Hady, came to congratulate Barend, but for some reason, Barend pushed Hady to the ground, splitting up their team. Giant Baba beat Dutch Schultz by DQ, Fred Blassie beat Billy Whitewolf, Kinji Shibuya and Ripper Collins beat Victor Rivera and Pepper Gomez.

1967 Wrestling Ads & Pictures

BIG TIME WRESTLING
PROMOTED BY ED FRANCIS
WED. CIVIC NOV. 1st
PIER 9 BRAWL
15 — 2 min. rds.
with/gloves

HANDSOME JOHNNY **BAREND**
Vs.
Dutch Schultz

TAG THRILLER

Iaukea & Poffo
Vs.
HADY & WOLF

Alaskan Vs. Kozak

Morgan Vs. Bock

$1.75-$2.75 KIDS 50 CENTS
RES. CIVIC Phone 581-002

BIG TIME WRESTLING
PROMOTED BY ED FRANCIS
WED. CIVIC MAY 3RD.
HAWAIIAN CHAMPIONSHIP

BAREND & MORTIER
CHAMPIONS
vs
IAUKEA & COLLINS
U.S. CHAMP   THE KING

SEMIFINAL

JIM HADY
vs
ODD JOB TOGO

PLUS 2 BIG MATCHES
$1.75-$2.75 KIDS 50 CENTS
PHONE 581-002

BIG TIME WRESTLING
Promoted by Ed Francis
WED. CIVIC MAY 24TH
TEXAS TEXAS BATTLE ROYAL
"OVER THE TOP ROPES"
OVER 3,000 LBS.

ENTRIES:	LBS.
Curtis Iaukea	367
Baby Blimp	305
Ripper Collins	301
Johnny Barend	247
Jim Hady	245
Hans Mortier	244
Catalina Drake	235
Paul Diamond	236
Beaureguarde	225
Lord Blears	226
Kongozan	245
Fujiwara	240
Dean Higuchi	246
Frank Merrill ref.	325
Tony Shephard ref.	210
W. Tsutsumi ref.	165

RULES:
* $2000 JACKPOT
* LAST MAN IS WINNER
* ANYTHING GOES
* 3 REFEREES

Plus 5 Big Matches

THE BABY BLIMP

Phone
Res.
581-002
$1.75 - $2.75
KIDS 50c
CIVIC
WED. 8 pm

1968

As 1968 came along, Johnny Barend had turned back into a heel and was set to feud with Jim Hady again.

That first match occurred on January 17th, with Hady picking up the win. Also on this card, Killer Kowalski and Angelo Poffo went to a draw with Pedro Morales and Pepper Gomez, Fred Blassie and Ripper Collins drew Missing Link and Neff Maivia, and Bearcat Wright went to a draw with Dutch Schultz.

January 17th was Schultz's last match in Hawaii. In his RATNW interview, Savage might have hinted at the reason, "Tally Ho Blears will remain a Prima Donna until the day he dies."

February 12th on Hilo saw Hady again beat Barend. Also, Curtis drew Missing Link, and Killer Kowalski beat Bill Miller.

On February 21st, Missing Link and Jim Hady beat Ripper Collins and Johnny Barend to win the tag titles. Bearcat Wright and Art Thomas beat King Curtis and Fred Blassie in other matches.

On February 28th, King Curtis beat Jim Hady to win the Hawaiian title.

On March 6th, in a preliminary match, Peter Maivia would beat Angelo Poffo. Maivia would be a massive player in Hawaii wrestling for years to come and would actually do promoting in the future.

On March 13th, Missing Link beat Ripper Collins in a hair match. Collins would wear a mask after this loss to prevent people from seeing his bald head. He would do exactly the same thing in Oregon six years later. King Curtis went to a draw with Killer Kowalski in the semi-main event.

March 27th had a great lineup, with Peter Maivia winning a battle royal and getting a singles win over Harley Race. Giant Baba beat King Curtis by DQ in another match.

On April 3rd, Peter Maivia and Neff Maiiva beat Johnny Barend and King Curtis. On another night, the fans would riot and throw rows of chairs into the ring.

On April 8th, in Hilo, Peter Maivia would get a win over King Curtis. Maivia's push was very strong.

On April 24th, Jim Hady beat Johnny Barend for the US title, Peter Maivia beat King Curtis by DQ, and Ray Stevens drew Bearcat Wright.

At this time, there is no doubt that the wrestling was still hot. The wrestlers were talented, but on paper, King Curtis, Johnny Barend, Jim Hady, Ripper Collins, Neff Maiava, and Missing Link had been on top for most of the past two years. Peter Maivia is a newcomer to the top of the cards. From this point on, we will see if things shake up.

On May 15th, Ray Stevens beat Jim Hady to win the US title. Stevens had been on many cards in Hawaii but had always been one of the fly-ins and had often been in tag matches with Pat Patterson.

The tag titles changed hands on May 22nd, with Jim Hady and Peter Maivia beating King Curtis and Ripper Collins.

On May 29th, on a previous TV show, Ray Stevens said he would never face Jim Hady for a rematch. On the show that night, Ripper Collins told Hady that Stevens would defend the US title against Hady in Tampa the next night. Knowing that he couldn't make the travel on that short notice, Hady took out his frustration on Collins, turning the now-masked wrestler into a bloody mess. King Curtis and Harry Fujiwara had to come to the ring and throw in the towel.

On June 5th, Jim Hady beat Killer Karl Kox, who was returning from Australia. King Curtis beat Missing Link, also Billy Whitewolf and Little Beaver beat Ripper Collins and Sky Low Low. I also think it is interesting in mixed tags when the midget and the big-person gimmicks are the same.

June 12th saw a huge card as Jim Hady regained the US title from Ray Stevens and King Curtis went to a draw with Peter Maivia. Magnificent Maurice debuted with a win over the Missing Link, Pedro Morales beat Pat Patterson, and Billy Whitewolf beat Killer Karl Kox in five matches that could have main evented anywhere.

On June 26th, Billy Whitewolf and Peter Maivia beat Ripper Collins and King Curtis for the Hawaiian tag titles. After the match, Collins and Magnificent Maurice attacked Curtis and, briefly, turned Curtis into a babyface.

On July 3rd, Jim Hady went to a draw with Gene Kiniski for the NWA World title. Other huge matches saw King Curtis beat John Tolos, Peter Maivia went to a draw with Ray Stevens, Pepper Gomez and Pedro Morales beat Ripper Collins and Fred Blassie.

July 10th saw former partners Ripper Collins and King Curtis battle, with Collins coming out on top.

July 17th saw Magnificent Maurice and Johnny Barend win the tag titles, beating Billy Whitewolf and Peter Maivia.

On August 21st, Jim Hady and King Curtis beat Johnny Barend and Magnificent Maurice in a cage.

On August 28th, Klondike Bill beat King Curtis for the Hawaiian title, Fred Blassie and Ripper Collins beat Pepper Gomez and Pedro Morales, and Billy Whitewolf beat Johnny Barend in a chain match. Jim Hady beat Mr. Saito to defend the US title.

Jim Hady and Whitewolf would defeat Johnny Barend and Magnificent Maurice in a double chain match on September 25th. Luke Graham also debuted that night, beating Hahn Lee, who also wrestled as Bing Ki Lee.

WED. BIG TIME WRESTLING JUNE 12TH
PROMOTER ED FRANCIS PRESENTS AT
HON. INTER. CENTER
U.S. CHAMPIONSHIP
Vs.
RAY STEVENS vs. JIM HADY
(CHAMPION)
HAWAIIAN CHAMPIONSHIP
BULL IAUKEA vs. PETER MAIVIA
NO DISQUALIFICATION IN EFFECT
Moreles vs. Patterson   Maurice vs. Link
K.K. Kox vs. Wolf   J. Bull vs. H. Lee
COLLINS vs. MAIAVA
PRICES $2-$3-$4
KIDS ½ PRICE GENS
RES. PHONE H.I.C.
513-731

On October 9th, Luke Graham beat Klondike Bill to win the Hawaiian title. This battle was between two wrestlers that were relatively new to Hawaii.

On October 16th, Jim Hady and Billy Whitewolf beat Johnny Barend and Magnificent Maurice in a cage match for the tag titles.

On October 23rd, Johnny Barend beat Peter Maivia in a match where they both wore suits.

On November 6th, Ripper Collins and Luke Graham beat Hady and Whitewolf for the tag titles. Graham and Collins would tag up in many different territories.

November 13th saw Giant Baba return to Hawaii and beat Johnny Barend on DQ.

On November 27th, Gene Kiniski beat Jim Hady for an NWA title defense. Also, Giant Baba drew Bill Miller on this card, and Johnny Barend beat Nick Bockwinkel by DQ.

December 4th was a unique card with ten ladies in a battle royal. Included in the battle royal were Fabulous Moolah, Donna Christanello, Toni Rose, and Barbara Collins.

December 11th saw Jim Hady and Red Bastien go to a double countout with Toru Tanaka and Johnny Barend.

On Christmas night, Toru Tanaka beat Jim Hady to win the North American title. Also, on this card, Ray Stevens drew Tex McKenzie; Red Bastien beat Buddy Austin.

1968 Wrestling Ads & Pictures

Kiniski Out Of Action

Big Gene Kiniski, who was held to a draw by Jim Hady in Tuesday night's wrestling main event before a record crowd of nearly 8,000 at the H.I.C. Arena, will be out of action for several weeks.

He suffered a cut on his forehead which required 22 stitches. He was treated at Kaiser Medical Center after his match.

Promoter Ed Francis returns to the Civic Auditorium next Wednesday night with Ripper Collins meeting Bull Iaukea in the main event.

Magnificent Maurice and Masa Fujiwara take on Jim Hady and Billy White Wolf in a team match. Peter Maivia vs. John Bull and Rocky Hunter vs. Neff Maiava round out the card.

WED. BIG TIME WRESTLING JAN. 17TH.

Promoter Ed Francis Presents at

HON. INTER. CENTER
U.S. CHAMPIONSHIP

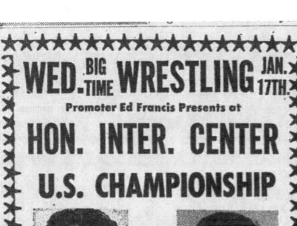

VS.

Johnny BAREND VS. Jim HADY

CHAMPION   CHALLENGER

WORLDS CHAMPIONSHIP

 **VS.**

MORELES & GOMEZ VS. KILLER & POFFO

TAG TEAM THRILLER

  VS.

BLASSIE & COLLINS VS. LINK & MAIAVA

Bearcat vs. Schultz   Shibuya vs Williams

PLUS 1 OTHER MATCH H.I.C. WED. 8 P.M.
$2 - $3 - $4. KIDS ½ PRICE GENS PH. 513-731

WED. BIG TIME WRESTLING AUG. 28th

PROMOTER ED FRANCIS PRESENTS AT

HON. INTER. CENTER
INDIAN DEATH MATCH

 **VS**

JOHNNY BAREND   BILLY WHITE WOLF

(Wrestlers Will Be Chained In The Ring Wrist To Wrist)

U.S. CHAMPIONSHIP

 **VS**

JIM HADY   MR. SAITO

CHAMPION   JAPANESE OLYMPIC STAR

HAWAIIAN CHAMPIONSHIP

 **VS**

BULL IAUKEA   KLONDIKE BILL

388 LBS.   377½ LBS.

 **VS.**

Blassie & Collins VS. Gomez & Moreles

MAURICE & FUJI
VS
Maiava & Higuchi

WED. H.I.C. 8 P.M.
$2-$3-$4
KIDS ½ PRICE GENS.
NO PHONE RESERVATIONS

Battle Royal Wednesday

A women's Texas battle royal headlines Wednesday night's pro wrestling card at the Civic Auditorium.

There will be 10 women in the battle royal and the last one in the ring is the winner. They are Princess Little Cloud, Toni Ross, Patti Neilson, the Fabulous Moolah, Linda Carroll, Barbara Owen, Betty Bouchet, Lucille Dupree, Donna Christiantano and Barbara Baker Collins.

Miss Bouchet and Princess Cloud meet in a preliminary match.

Ripper Collins vs. Pat Barrett, Johnny Barend vs. Neff Maiava, Luke Graham vs. Jim Hady and Red Bastien vs. Mr. X round out the card. Action starts at 8 p.m.

Mixed Tag Bouts Slated

A combination of two women and one man will be on each side of a six-man tag team wrestling main event tonight at the Civic Auditorium.

The unusual match features Betty Nicalli and Barbara Collins teaming up with Ripper Collins against Kathy Starr, Jean Antone and Jim Hady.

Hady and Miss Starr hold U. S. wrestling belts and give their side a lot of prestige. Ripper and Barbara Collins are a husband-wife duo.

Tosh (Oddjob) Togo returns to action in one of three special events, meeting Curtis Iaukea.

The other matches are Johnny Barend vs. Billy White Wolf and Magnificent Maurice vs. Peter Maivia. Action starts at 8 p.m.

1969

Wire Fence For Mat Men

A ring surrounded by a wire mesh fence will keep Ed Francis and Ripper Collins from "chickening out" in their return match tonight.

They headline a talent-loaded pro mat card in the H.I.C. Arena. "This is a match to a finish," Francis declared.

Prof. Tanaka puts up his North American heavyweight belt against Ray Stevens in a second main event.

Tex McKenzie and Nick Bockwinkel battle Kenji Shibuya and Mr. Saito in a tag team match. Promoter Francis said the National Wrestling Alliance has sanctioned this for the world tag team crown.

1969 starts with Ed Francis coming out of an eight-year retirement to beat Ripper Collins on January 1st. In other matches, future WWWF tag champs Toru Tanaka and Mr. Fuji beat Red Bastien and Paddy Barrett, and Tex McKenzie beat Fred Blassie.

On January 22nd, Ripper Collins got some revenge, beating Ed Francis in a cage match. In other matches, Toru Tanaka beat Ray Stevens, Mr. Saito and Kinji Shibuya beat Tex McKenzie and Nick Bockwinkel, and Wahoo McDaniel debuted and beat Mr. X.

On January 29th, Tanaka continued his winning ways and beat Bockwinkel.

February 12th, Nick Bockwinkel won a battle royal. Very interesting to note that King Curtis, Johnny Barend, Jim Hady, and Missing Link have left. A new crew, including Bockwinkel, Wahoo McDaniel, Toru Tanaka, Tex McKenzie, and Gene Kiniski, sit atop the cards.

On February 19th, Gene Kiniski beat Toru Tanaka for the North American title. This was scheduled to be a NWA World title match, but Kiniski lost the title to Dory Funk Jr on February 11th. King Curtis returned and beat Nick Bockwinkel. Curtis has no recorded matches since September of 68.

On February 22nd, Luke Graham and Ripper Collins went to a draw with Wahoo McDaniel and Billy Whitewolf. King Curtis beat Bobby Shane, and Toru Tanaka drew with Nick Bockwinkel.

On March 12th, Bobby Shane and Nick Bockwinkel beat Luke Graham and Ripper Collins for the tag titles. The undercard was full of great matches and talent, with Tex McKenzie beating Toru Tanaka in a Texas Death Match and Wahoo McDaniel beating King Curtis.

March 19th saw an upset as Rocky Montero beat Nick Bockwinkel. Montero always used a boxing gimmick in his matches. However, in his RATNW interview, he clarified, "I had been a boxer; that was no gimmick." This upset wasn't sustained in the territory; however, this wasn't the first victory for Montero that would seem out of place. He would get pushed at times.

On March 26th, the main event was Tex McKenzie going to a draw with Gene Kiniski. The wrestlers at Dean Silverstone's reunion always ribbed McKenzie. They mentioned that he was an awkward wrestler who would, at times, give out some potatoes because he just wasn't a great worker. However, they all gave McKenzie his due that he could draw some money. That looks exactly like what he was getting to do in Hawaii in 1969: draw some money. In other matches, King Curtis beat Wahoo McDaniel, Nick Bockwinkel and Paul Jones beat Ripper Collins and Luke Graham.

On April 2nd, Pedro Morales started to become more of a regular, and he was going to get his push. Morales teamed with Bockwinkel and McKenzie to go to a draw with Curtis, Buddy Austin, and Ripper Collins.

April 16th is another dream matchup between King Curtis and Gene Kiniski. This match went to a draw. Killer Buddy Austin and Ripper Collins beat Bobby Shane and Nick Bockwinkel to win the tag titles.

On April 23rd was another chapter in the King Curtis-Don Leo Jonathan feud. Curtis wins again,

On May 7th, two newcomers would make their mark. Dory Dixon won a battle royal and also beat Mr. Fuji. Billy Robinson also debuted and went to a draw with Nick Bockwinkel.

Pedro Morales would beat King Curtis for the Hawaiian title on May 21st, and Billy Robinson beat Tom Andrews.

On June 4th, Gorilla Monsoon would go to a draw with Pedro Morales. Ironically, Monsoon would act as an advisor for Morales in his WWWF championship run several years later. Also on this card, Billy Robinson beat Killer Austin, and King Curtis and Rocky Montero beat Bobby Shane and Tex McKenzie.

On June 11th, the main event saw Bobby Shane beat Ripper Collins, and the team of Gorilla Monsoon, King Curtis, and Rocky Montero go to a draw with Dory Dixon, Pedro Morales, and Nick Bockwinkel. Montero again got a great spot and pushed harder than he had before.

On June 18th, Pedro Morales beat Gene Kiniski for the North American title, and King Curtis beat Don Leo Jonathan in a boxing match. Ray Stevens brought his feud with Pat Patterson to the Islands from San Francisco, winning this match.

On July 2nd, Ed Francis put on the trunks again to team with Pedro Morales to go to a draw with King Curtis and Gorilla Monsoon. Billy Whitewolf also gained a win over Buddy Austin.

July 9th saw a card filled with talent. Rocky Montero, who had been given a push, was the lowest-rated person on the entire card besides the special attraction of the little people. Working the card were Pat Patterson, Ripper Collins, Killer Austin, Ray Stevens, Ed Francis, Peter Maivia, Pedro Morales, Gene Kiniski, Gorilla Monsoon,

King Curtis, Nick Bockwinkel, Dory Dixon, Billy Whitewolf, Karl Gotch and Montero. This card is the perfect example of my fascination with the cards that 50th State Wrestling presented.

On July 23rd, Kurt and Karl Von Steiger debuted, going to a draw with Pedro Morales and Dory Dixon. Dixon won another battle royal.

On July 30th, King Curtis and Gorilla Monsoon met in a grudge match after their partnership went haywire. Interestingly, prior to the start of their match, Pedro Morales came to ringside and said the winner of this match would receive a North American Title shot. Both Monsoon and Curtis attacked Morales, bloodying him up. Monsoon won this match on a countout.

August 6th seemed like the upset of the year as Rocky Montero beat Billy Whitewolf in an Indian Death Match. The Indian Death Match was Whitewolf's way to settle a grudge. He had beaten many of his foes in this type of match, and I believe this was his first loss in his specialty. Interestingly, the loss was to Montero, whom I mentioned here, during '69. He was getting a push like he had never received before.

von Steiger brothers in battle royal

Germany's famous wrestling brothers, Kurt and Karl von Steiger, are the headliners in Wednesday night's Texas battle royal at the Civic Auditorium.

"There will be 14 wrestlers in the battle royal," stated promoter Ed Francis. "Each man posts a $100 entry fee and the winner takes home the jackpot," he added.

In addition to the battle royal there will be a full slate of individual matches featuring the top matmen currently appearing in Honolulu. Action starts at 8 o'clock.

Kurt and Karl Von Steiger are getting a little run, getting a chance to go over Billy Whitewolf and Ricky Hunter, Jerry and Bobby Christy, and Dory Dixon and Nick Bockwinkel.

On August 27th, Dory Funk defended the NWA title against King Curtis, and they went to a draw. Pedro Morales beat Gorilla Monsoon and Billy Whitewolf.

On September 3rd, King Curtis beat Jerry Brisco. On September 10th, he beat Billy Robinson. He really just keeps winning his matches and is a fantastic villain. You wonder what it would have been like if the promotion put all their chips in on him as a babyface in Hawaii. I think it would have worked with him because the Hawaiian people would have recognized his toughness.

I asked Dean Silverstone if he felt Ripper Collins could have been a successful babyface. Dean, always ever thoughtful, finally said, "I think Ripper could do anything he set his mind to….but it wouldn't have been easy."

The Von Steiger Brothers beat Pedro Morales and Ed Francis to win the tag titles on September 10th.

Giant Baba came for a few days, beating Buddy Austin in Hilo on September 15th and teaming with Missing Link and Pedro Morales to beat King Curtis, Ripper Collins, and Buddy Austin on the 17th.

September 24th saw the first appearance of The Sheik, and he was disqualified against The Missing Link, with whom he had worked on numerous occasions. Giant Baba went to a draw with Gene Kiniski in another top match. King Curtis beat Pedro Morales to win the North American title.

October 1st saw Pedro Morales and Ed Francis regain the tag titles from The Von Steiger Brothers.

On October 15th, King Curtis beat Ray Stevens, Pedro Morales and Bing Ki Lee beat Stan Neilsen and The Alaskan, and The Sheik beat Missing Link.

Bing Ki Lee, also known as Hahn Lee, is another wrestler who really didn't get much of an opportunity in other territories. He had the most success in Mexico.

On November 26th, a big card had Pedro Morales beating the Sheik on DQ when Sheik threw a fireball. Don Leo Jonathon went to a draw with Fred Blassie, and Bing Ki Lee beat King Curtis in an upset. Johnny Barend returned after a year's absence, beating Bobby Shane.

On Christmas night, Johnny Barend beat Pedro Morales for the North American title. The fans of Hawaiian wrestling gave Morales a watch. Morales gave the watch to Bing Ki Lee to keep it safe. In the 3rd fall, Bing Ki Lee came stumbling to the ring a bloody mess. As Morales went to check on him, Barend attacked Morales and got the pin to win the title.

Later, Bing Ki Lee related that Ripper Collins and Friday attacked him and stole Morales's watch.

Bill Francis, the son of Ed Francis, made his Hawaiian debut teaming with his dad to beat Ripper Collins and Friday Allman. Also, Giant Baba and Seiji Sakaguchi beat Tank Morgan and Jack Bence.

1969 Wrestling Ads & Pictures

1970

As the new decade rolled around, Hawaii wrestling was still going strong.

The year's first show saw Johnny Barend and Ripper Collins beat Giant Baba and Seigi Sakaguchi, and Danny Hodge went to a draw with Missing Link. Jack Bence, a journeyman wrestler, went to a draw with Pedro Morales, showing that the bookers in Hawaii were always a little more forgiving and cautious with their talent. Using Bence and giving him a draw helped him much more than the win that Morales would have gotten, especially if Bence is here for more than a few cards.

The midgets come in for the next few weeks, which seems like it slows the regular proceedings down just a bit, but January 21st is another big card. Ripper Collins, Gene Kiniski, and Johnny Barend went to a double DQ with Hahn Lee, Pedro Morales, and Haystacks Calhoun. Don Leo Jonathon went to a draw with Tank Morgan. Peter Maivia and Ray Stevens beat Pat Patterson and The Masked Gladiator. Gladiator was Ricky Hunter.

Hunter talks about the Gladiator gimmick in his RATNW interview, "On the international circuit when they saw the Gladiator. The promoters would start bidding for you. They wanted the Gladiator in different territories. It was a uniquely different gimmick. I wore the wrestling singlet and the mask, and I never threw a punch. The most I threw was an elbow. I wrestled either Greco Roman or Catch as Catch can. I would force a man into the ropes and back off, then throw a sharp elbow in the stomach or something. People were expecting a masked man to be very rough. We kept reversing the psychology in wrestling, and that is what enchanted the people. It was a gimmick that worked out so well. As I say, it was something I was so glad they hung on me."

On February 4th, Ripper Collins beat The Missing Link to win the Hawaiian title.

On February 17th, Dory Funk Jr drew with Johnny Barend in an NWA World title match. Pedro Morales went to a draw in another top match.

On March 4th, Pedro Morales and Hahn Lee won the tag titles from Johnny Barend and Ripper Collins.

On March 18th, Pedro Morales and Hahn Lee beat Kinji Shibuya and Mitsu Arakawa, defending the tag titles. Les Roberts went to a draw with Bad Boy Shields (Bull Bullinski). Roberts was also known as Dingo The Sundowner.

On March 25th, Pedro Morales beat Johnny Barend in a stretcher match. Morales used a sleeper to put Barend out for the ride on the stretcher. Cyclone Negro and Spiros Arion beat Kinji Shibuya and Mitsu Arakawa for the International tag titles.

Rene Goulet had come into the area and feuded with Ripper Collins, but Collins was able to turn Goulet back on March 25th and April 13th in Hilo and they went to a draw on April 14th in Maui.

It was mentioned before that the number of six men or bigger tag matches were booked. They also, at times, booked mixed tag matches that didn't look like they would work. For example, Johnny Barend, Ripper Collins, Mighty Atom, and Lord Littlebrook beat Pedro Morales, Bing King Lee, Wee Willie Wilson, and Cowboy Lang.

You have the top heels and the top baby faces, along with the touring midgets, in a match. So you have the serious feuds and the matches that will draw you the money along with the midgets. One might argue that at this time, midgets would draw money. It is strange to lump them together in a match like this on April 15th.

On April 29th was another one of the big shows featuring Ray Stevens and Peter Maivia beating Johnny Barend and The Sheik on DQ, defending the World tag titles. Also, on this show, Kinji Shibuya beat Pedro Morales.

On May 13th, Bing Ki Lee (Hahn Lee…It is a little unclear which name he used here as he is often listed as both) and Pedro Morales beat Ripper Collins and Johnny Barend for the Hawaiian tag titles. Sam Steamboat returned to the Islands to beat Les Roberts.

On May 27th, Morales and Bing Ki Lee defended the tag titles, beating Hard Boiled Haggerty and Kinji Shibuya. Sam Steamboat beat Duke Savage, who wrestled in many places as El Gringo.

THE CONVICT IS 7'1" TALL & 460 LBS

On June 10th, Steamboat beat Ripper Collins for the Hawaiian title. Pedro Morales beat The Convict, which was Plowboy Frazier, in prison garb. Remember how big Frazier was; he could draw money in places before his lack of talent was exposed.

Billy Robinson had come into the area and must have been a heel. His early matches were against Steamboat, Bing Ki Lee, and Pedro Morales.

On June 24th, Ripper Collins regained the Hawaiian title, beating Steamboat.

On July 1st, the strange team of Billy Robinson and Johnny Barend beat Pedro Morales and Bing Ki Lee for the tag titles.

Dory Funk Jr came to defend the NWA World title on July 15th. He beat Ripper Collins. Billy Robinson beat Killer Karl Kox in another top match.

Sam Steamboat beat Ripper Collins to regain the Hawaiian title on July 29th.

On August 5th, Pedro Morales beat Johnny Barend for the North American title; Billy Robinson went to a draw with Ray Stevens, and Eddie Graham and Sam Steamboat reformed their very successful Florida team, only to lose to Ripper Collins and Kinji Shibuya.

On August 12th, Steamboat, Morales, and Ed Carpentier beat Johnny Barend, Ivan Koloff, and Billy Robinson in another example of a match with so much talent. Kinji Shibuya beat Nick Kozak, and Jack Armstrong appeared on the undercard.

On August 18th in Maui, Pedro Morales beat Ivan Koloff. In six months, Morales would beat Koloff for the WWWF championship in Madison Square Garden.

On August 26th, Dory Funk Jr went to a draw with Billy Robinson for the NWA title; Johnny Barend beat The Sheik in a stretcher match.

On September 30th, The Masked Destroyer beat Pedro Morales for the North American title. Billy Robinson beat Abdullah The Butcher. The Sheik and Ed Francis beat Johnny Barend and Ripper Collins in a very strange-sounding match.

At some point in September, Billy Robinson started teaming with other babyfaces and made the turn that was probably more suited to him.

It was noticeable in October the overall cards were not as strong as earlier in the year. Wrestlers like Soldat Gorky, Jack Armstrong, and Bill Francis were reaching the upper parts of the card.

October 28th saw a strong main event of The Destroyer beating the Sheik on DQ. Billy Robinson and Ed Francis won the tag titles, beating Ripper Collins and Johnny Barend.

November 11th saw an intriguing main event: Billy Robinson beating John Quinn. Destroyer beat Johnny Barend on DQ. Rocky Johnson debuted by beating Soldat Gorky, and Frankie Laine also debuted, going to a draw with Bing Ki Lee.

On December 9th, Johnny Barend and Ripper Collins split up again, and Barend won the Hawaiian title from Collins. King Curtis returned and teamed with the Destroyer to beat Sam Steamboat and Frankie Laine.

On December 13th in Maui and the next night in Hilo, Victor The Bear returned to the Islands to beat The Destroyer. Victor did not work in Honolulu on this trip.

The last card of the year was a good one as Billy Robinson beat The Destroyer to win the North American title, King Curtis also beat Bing Ki Lee, Frankie Laine and Sam Steamboat teamed to beat Bob Windham (Blackjack Mulligan) and Larry Hennig who were both returning from Japan.

1970 Wrestling Ads & Pictures

Russ star on mat card

Ivan Koloff, the new "Russian Lion," makes his local wrestling debut Wednesday night at the Civic Auditorium.

"We haven't signed an opponent for him yet, but he'll definitely be on the card," said promoter Ed Francis.

Tag team matches headline the card. Miss Moolah and Fran Gravette team up against Viki Williams and Toni Rose in a women's match while Sam Steamboat and Tank Morgan tackle Johnny Barend and Billy Robinson.

Pedro Morales vs. Kenji Shibuya and Hahn Lee vs. Ripper Collins round out the card. Action begins at 8 o'clock.

Rip Collins faces bear

Victor the Great is a wrestler, a wrestling bear weighing 500 pounds, and it will be featured in tonight's pro mat card at the H.I.C. Arena.

Mat fans are familiar with Victor, who first showed here in 1967, and its formidable "bear hug." Ripper Collins will face Victor tonight.

In regular matches Billy Robinson goes after the Masked Destroyer and the North American belt in a two-hour time limit match.

Big Bob Windham, former New York Jets tackle, and Larry Henning, both 300 pounds plus, gang up on Johnny Barend and Sam Steamboat in a team battle.

Curtis Iaukea vs. Beauregarde, Rocky Montero vs. Dale Lewis and Wolfman vs. Cowboy Lane wind up the card. First match goes to the post at 8 p.m.

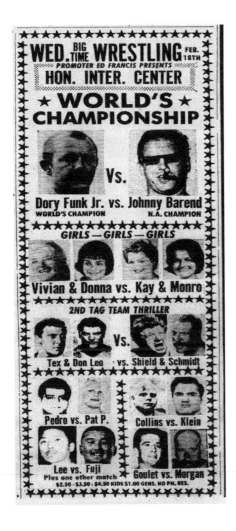

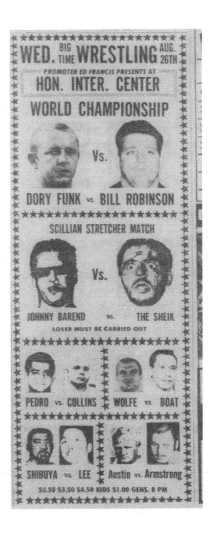

1971

1971 starts with King Curtis, Sam Steamboat, Billy Robinson, and Ripper Collins filling out the tops of the cards. Dale Lewis and Frankie Laine are other top stars in the mid-card. Lonnie Mayne debuts on January 9th, and Don Muraco, eight months into his career, makes his Hawaii debut on January 2nd.

King Curtis beat Billy Robinson for the North American title on January 9th. Lonnie Mayne teamed with Ripper Collins on his debut to lose to Sam Steamboat and his former tag partner from Oregon, Beauregard.

On January 16th, Billy Robinson and Frankie Laine would beat Lonnie Mayne and Ripper Collins in the main event. Mayne and Laine had also been tag champs in Oregon. In a preliminary match, Don Muraco drew with Mr. Fuji in another match between two wrestlers that would be linked together in the future, as Fuji would manage Muraco in the WWE.

January 23rd saw Dory Funk Jr come to town to defend the NWA World title, beating Don Leo Jonathan. King Curtis beat Billy Robinson, and two wrestlers filled out the card that certainly seemed out of place in Tojo Yamamoto and Jerry Jarrett. Interestingly, they were not headed to or from Japan; they just took a quick trip to Honolulu together.

Frankie Laine beat Ripper Collins to win the Hawaiian title on February 6th. King Curtis went to a draw with Verne Gagne.

Verne Gagne will be one of eight grapplers in the Texas battle Royal in the Civic Feb. 17.

February 17th in Hilo saw an interesting match with Ripper Collins and Lonnie Mayne beating Verne Gagne and Sam Steamboat. Steamboat also won a battle royal here. Again, there is so much talent on a Hilo card, Gagne, Curtis, Mayne, Steamboat, Collins, Muraco, Robinson, and others.

Sam Steamboat beat King Curtis for the North American title on February 24th, and Mad Dog and Butcher Vachon beat Verne Gagne and Billy Robinson.

There is an interesting side note here. The Vachon's were AWA tag champs and "lost" the belts to the Von Steiger Brothers the day before in Portland. They would head to Japan and come back and regain the titles in Portland on the way back to the AWA. Kurt and Karl Von Steiger won the tag titles in a title change that was never acknowledged in the AWA. Mad Dog Vachon confirmed the AWA tag title change in his RATNW interview, "Yes, we lost the title to the Von Steiger's for one week. We lost it and went to Japan for one week. We then came back to Portland and won it back a week later."

The Vachon's face Verne Gagne and Billy Robinson the next night. I imagine Gagne was probably ok with them losing the belts for a short period.

On March 6th, Billy Robinson beat King Curtis in a Pier 9 brawl on top.

We are in a stretch again where the matches in Hawaii are fantastic; each and every week, the matchups are great.

March 13th saw Verne Gagne beat Mad Dog Vachon in an AWA title match, Lonnie Mayne drew Mil Mascaras, and King Curtis beat Bobby Shane, who had been away from the Islands for a few years.

March 24th was the match that was detailed in the intro of this book; Sam Steamboat beat King Curtis in a Loser Leaves Town Sicilian Stretcher match. Lonnie Mayne and Ripper Collins went to a no-contest with Ray Stevens and Peter Maivia. Billy Robinson beat Gene Kiniski in another top match.

April 10th saw Bearcat Wright win a battle royal, and The White Avenger debuted. Avenger had worked in Portland and now Hawaii. His identity was Bing Ki Lee, and he was well-known in Hawaii.

On April 17th, Neff Maiava returned in his first match in almost a year to beat Lonnie Mayne in a lights-out match.

On April 28th, Ripper Collins and Lonnie Mayne beat Peter Maivia and Ray Stevens, defending the Hawaiian tag titles, and Steven Little Bear beat Bill White.

Gene Kiniski had emerged with the North American title, and he defended it against Bearcat Wright on May 19th. Also, on that card, Lonnie Mayne beat Haystacks Calhoun by DQ.

Foes Not Awed By Haystack's Size

Maddog Mayne, 275, and Angelo Mosca, 287, aren't awed by the size of Haystack Calhoun, who must be the world's biggest wrestler at 621 pounds.

Mayne, who holds the Hawaiian championship, and Mosca are meeting Calhoun and Bearcat Wright in a tag team wrestling main event Monday night here in the Civic Auditorium.

While Calhoun's 621 pounds make him hard to handle, Wright will also be a threat to their opponents. Wright is 6 feet 7 inches tall and weighs 279 pounds.

Sam Steamboat Mokuahi, 235, and The Skull, 236, are matched for the semifinal. Mokuahi needs no introduction to local fans. He played football at Roosevelt and followed famed beachboy Sam Steamboat, his father, as a surfer before taking up pro wrestling.

The Skull is Bill Steele, a tough opponent for any man.

Ripper Collins, 245, and the masked Avenger clash in a special event. The masked man, 225, is a tough, ringwise matman who should give the rough Collins all he can handle.

Don Muraco, the former Punahou gridder, and Rocky Montero clash in the opener. Muraco is 225 and Montero is 10 pounds heavier.

May 24th was a card in Hilo that saw Haystacks Calhoun and Bearcat Wright beat Lonnie Mayne and Angelo Mosca. This team would be entitled Murder Incorporated in the Bay Area in a few years. Sam Steamboat beat Mighty Brutus, who would also be known as The Skull in Oregon, The Brute in British Columbia, and Bugsy McGraw in other places.

June 16th saw Bearcat Wright beat Gene Kiniski in a Sicilian Stretcher Match. Kiniski usually didn't participate in many gimmick matches. Suni War Cloud and Steven Little Bear beat Ripper Collins and Lonnie Mayne for the tag titles.

On June 30th, Bearcat Wright beat The Sheik by DQ, and Lonnie Mayne and Ripper Collins regained the tag titles by beating Steven Little Bear and Suni War Cloud. Gene Kiniski beat Sam Steamboat, defending the North American title.

Lonnie Mayne beat Bearcat Wright for the Hawaiian title on July 7th.

On July 14th, a big tag match saw The Sheik and Gene Kiniski go to a draw with Pedro Morales and Bearcat Wright. Danny Hodge returned to the Islands to beat the Gladiator.

Sam Steamboat and Bearcat Wright beat Lonnie Mayne and Ripper Collins for the tag titles on July 21st. Bulldog Brown also made an appearance on this card.

The August 4th cards drew 8,000 people to see Lonnie Mayne beat Ripper Collins in a grudge match between former partners. Also, a rematch saw Gene Kiniski and The Sheik beat Bearcat Wright and Pedro Morales.

August 11th saw a unique match where Eddie Morrow won a hooded battle royal. Interestingly, a match a month prior saw Ed Francis return to Portland after a long absence and win a hooded battle royal. However, Francis was the special guest, so fans could recognize him; he was not hooded, which helped him win. Interesting to think if this was The Oregon promotions idea or if, in both cases, it was Francis's idea.

Also this is a fascinating time as Francis has moved to or is in the process of moving to Eugene, Oregon. He starts wrestling in the Oregon area, at least in Portland. I'm unsure if he was traveling back to Hawaii on show nights. In his book, he addresses this situation: "I was still flying back and forth to the Islands for the TV shows, and Lord Blears was handling the rest of the business when I wasn't there. It was a lot to expect of him, and I knew it couldn't continue that way."

A Hilo show on August 23rd saw Man Mountain Mike beat Lonnie Mayne.

On August 25th, a huge upset saw Eddie Morrow beat Gene Kiniski for the North American title. Morrow was an exciting wrestler, but this will be the high point of his career. This is a giant upset. The Sheik beat Bearcat Wright in an African Death Match. I'm not sure what the rules were, but I bet that match would probably not fly today.

Also, Lonnie Mayne beat Ripper Collins in a rematch on this card in a loser-leaves-town match. Collins is headed to the Bay Area.

September 8th saw Bearcat Wright beating Lonnie Mayne, which gave Wright the chance to paint Mayne black. I wish I could have heard the interviews that led up to this. I am sure fast-forwarding 50 years, they were cringeworthy. I know I actually had a question about this racial match framed for either Francis or Blears in their interview. At any rate, I didn't have the courage to ask it.

Bearcat cops Mayne event

Bearcat Wright defeated Maddog Mayne in the main event of a professional wrestling show last night at the Honolulu International Center Arena.

As a result of his victory, Wright was given the right to paint Mayne black.

Gene Kiniski beat Eddie Morrow in two out of three falls to regain the North American championship.

The Sheik defeated Stevens Little Bear on a fall; Bull Iaukea and Masa Fujiwara won a tag-team match over Dino Lanza and Hahn Lee, taking two out of three falls; Sam Steamboat chopped down Spoiler No. 2, and Rick Rinaldo downed Pancho Lopez.

In other matches, Kiniski regained the North American title from Eddie Morrow.

September 18th saw King Curtis and Bull Ramos team up in a great team to beat Sam Steamboat and Bing Ki Lee. Bearcat Wright beat Lonnie Mayne in a boxing match.

On September 29th, Sam Steamboat beat Gene Kiniski to win the North American title; the Sheik went to a draw with Peter Maivia, and King Curtis went to a draw with Lonnie Mayne. This was a bloody, bloody match.

1971 Wrestling Ads & Pictures

Lane, Mayne show spurs

Frankie Lane and Maddog Mayne will wear cowboy boots with spurs attached into the ring tonight for their wrestling main event at the Civic Auditorium.

Promoter Ed Francis is billing the match as "the battle of spurs."

A mixed tag team match with a woman teaming up with a male wrestler is another feature. Vivian Vachon has Bearcat Wright, a 6-6 giant, as her partner while Betty Niccoli will have Ripper Collins in her corner.

Don Muraco battles "the Professional," a masked man. Bill Robinson takes on Sam "Steamboat" Mokuahi and Rocky Montero engages Beauregarde.

Wright wins main event

Bearcat Wright knocked out Maddog Mayne in 19 seconds of the seventh round of a scheduled 15-rounder in a special boxing match on last night's wrestling card at the Civic Auditorium.

In other matches, Curtis "Bull" Iaukea and Bull Ramos won two out of three falls from Sam Steamboat and Hahn Lee while Eddie Morrow and Dino Lanza also took two of three from Rocky Montero and Rick Rinaldo in tag team events.

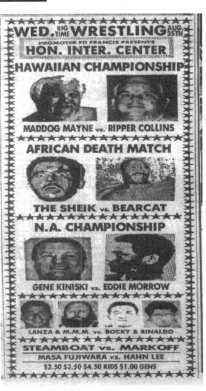

battle royal with masks

Pro wrestling's first "blind man's buff," a battle royal with all matmen wearing hoods, will headline Wednesday night's card at the Civic Auditorium.

Last man in the ring collects a $2,400 jackpot, promoter Ed Francis announced.

Lined up for the battle royal are Bearcat Wright, Sam Steamboat, Ripper Collins, Maddog Mayne, Chris Markoff, Jerri Monti, Rick Rinaldo, Hahn Lee, Rocky Montero, Pancho Lopez, Dino Lanza and Masa Fujiwara.

"There will be a mystery wrestler in it, too," the promoter stated.

Several matches will precede the battle royal. The first match starts at 8 p.m.

1972

1972 opens with a lot of talent, but only two names that have long-standing runs in Hawaii, and those are Sam Steamboat and Johnny Barend. Steamboat puts a notch in his resume with a win over Mad Dog Vachon on January 1st. Lonnie Mayne went to a draw with Jimmy Snuka. Johnny Barend teamed with Don Muraco, who, despite being very skinny, is recognized as someone with talent.

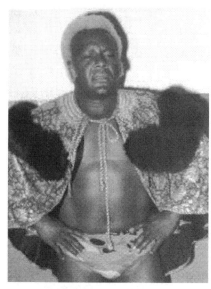

Sweet Daddy Siki

On January 26th, Dory Funk Jr came in and defended the NWA World title against Sweet Daddy Siki; Johnny Barend and Jimmy Snuka beat Mad Dog Vachon and Lonnie Mayne. Mayne and Vachon had a long-standing feud in Oregon, so it is strange to see them team up.

On February 16th, Gene Kiniski won the Hawaiian title, beating Ed Francis. Also, Johnny Barend and Bobo Brazil went to a draw with The Sheik and Sweet Daddy Siki. Lonnie Mayne beat Mad Dog Vachon, so that team did not last long.

March 8th saw a very strong card with Dory Funk Jr beating Johnny Barend in an NWA World title match, Gene Kiniski beating Ed Francis, Ripper Collins returning and restarting his feud with Lonnie Mayne, and Sweet Daddy Siki beating King Curtis.

March 11th saw an event that would change Hawaiian wrestling. The Civic Auditorium that had held wrestling for years and years was shut down. This would turn the territory of Hawaii into a place where wrestling would be held once and sometimes twice a week into a territory where matches were held once a month. It would also no doubt have an effect on the promotion's bottom line and the talent that would be available. Once-a-month cards would not be feasible for wrestlers to come to Hawaii for a few months or longer, depending on wrestling to make a living.

On March 22nd, Johnny Barend beat Sweet Daddy Siki to win the North American Title and send Siki packing in a loser-leaves-town match. Siki would return to Toronto before heading off to Australia.

Also on this card, Gene Kiniski beat Sam Steamboat, Lonnie Mayne went to a draw with Ed Francis, and Bulldog Brower, returning from Japan, beat Pat O'Brien. The very unique team of Billy Graham and Sputnik Monroe (also returning from Japan) lost to Jimmy Snuka and Manny Soto.

Now, monthly shows were loaded but at the cost of flying most people in. Steamboat, Barend, and Snuka were the only ones staying on the Islands. Mayne had gone back to Oregon and Curtis to WWWF.

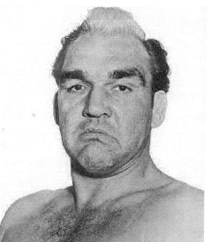

Sputnik Monroe

Staring at the April shows, they were absolutely packed, but profits would no doubt be down.

April 12th saw Johnny Barend beat Terry Funk to defend the North American title, The Sheik beat Bobo Brazil, and Kiniski and Fred Blassie teamed to beat Steamboat &and Fred Curry.

May 3rd saw Gene Kiniski beat Billy Robinson to defend the Hawaiian title, Ed Francis went to a draw with Fred Blassie, The Sheik beat Bobo Brazil, and King Curtis drew Jimmy Snuka.

June 14th saw Fred Blassie beat Sam Steamboat in a lights-out match, and the Sheik beat Fred Curry in the top two matches.

July 12th saw Johnny Barend defend the North American title, beating the Fred Blassie.

July 26th saw Johnny Barend again beat Fred Blassie, Fred & Bull Curry beat The Sheik & Abdulla Farouk.

August 2nd saw Fred Curry beat Gene Kiniski to win the Hawaiian title, Haystacks Calhoun and Johnny Barend beat The Sheik and Fred Blassie. Despite the overall card quality being down, the main events were always top-notch.

August 30th saw the cards start to take a little more AWA flavor. Nick Bockwinkel and Ray Stevens, old Hawaii favorites, defended the AWA tag titles against Wahoo McDaniel and Fred Curry, Lonnie Mayne beat Jimmy Snuka, and Johnny Barend went to a draw with Dory Funk, who was defending the NWA title. I am sure this may be the only card that saw the NWA Worlds title and the AWA tag titles being defended.

September 20th saw more unique matchups. Nick Bockwinkel and Ray Stevens, AWA champs, went to a ddq with WWWF champ Pedro Morales and Wahoo McDaniel. Ed Francis beat Fred Blassie in a cage match, Fred Curry beat John Quinn, and Giant Baba went to a ddq with the Sheik.

On November 15th, Dusty Rhodes made his Hawaiian debut and won the North American title from Sam Steamboat. Ed Francis and Billy Robinson beat Ray Stevens and Nick Bockwinkel, and Giant Baba beat Bulldog Brown.

On December 13th, Don Muraco won a battle royal. Verne Gagne beat King Curtis to defend the AWA title, and Nick Bockwinkel and Ray Stevens beat Red Bastien and Don Muraco.

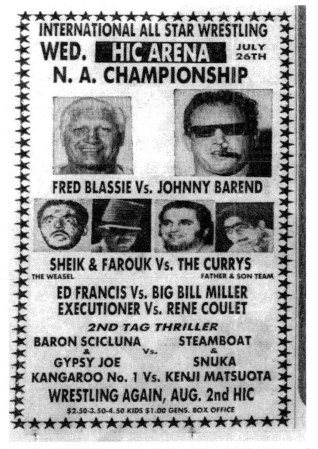

1972 Wrestling Ads & Pictures

WED. BIG Time WRESTLING JAN. 26TH
PRESENTED BY ED FRANCIS AT
HON. INTER. CENTER
WORLDS CHAMPIONSHIP
DORY FUNK vs. SWEET DADDY
TAG THRILLER
VACHON & MAYNE vs. BAREND & SNUKA
FRANCIS vs. BRUTUS   BOAT vs. BENCE
WOLFMAN vs. O'BRIEN   DINGO vs. TOGO
$2.50 • $3.50 • $4.50   KIDS $1.00   GENS. 8 PM START

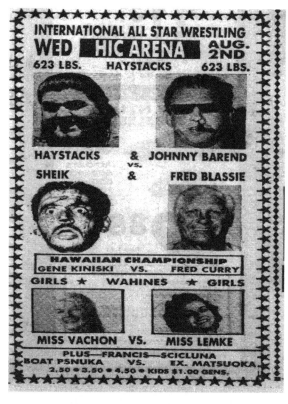

INTERNATIONAL ALL STAR WRESTLING
WED HIC ARENA AUG. 2ND
623 LBS. HAYSTACKS 623 LBS.
HAYSTACKS & JOHNNY BAREND
vs.
SHEIK & FRED BLASSIE
HAWAIIAN CHAMPIONSHIP
GENE KINISKI vs. FRED CURRY
GIRLS ★ WAHINES ★ GIRLS
MISS VACHON vs. MISS LEMKE
PLUS—FRANCIS—SCICLUNA
BOAT PSNUKA vs. EX. MATSUOKA
2.50 • 3.50 • 4.50 • KIDS $1.00 GENS.

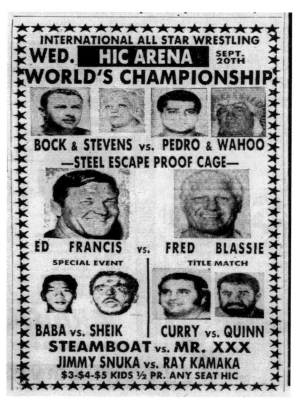

INTERNATIONAL ALL STAR WRESTLING
WED. HIC ARENA SEPT. 20TH
WORLD'S CHAMPIONSHIP
BOCK & STEVENS vs. PEDRO & WAHOO
—STEEL ESCAPE PROOF CAGE—
ED FRANCIS vs. FRED BLASSIE
SPECIAL EVENT   TITLE MATCH
BABA vs. SHEIK   CURRY vs. QUINN
STEAMBOAT vs. MR. XXX
JIMMY SNUKA vs. RAY KAMAKA
$3-$4-$5 KIDS ½ PR. ANY SEAT HIC

INTERNATIONAL ALL-STAR WRESTLING
WED., HIC ARENA NOV. 15TH
WORLD'S CHAMPIONSHIP
BOCK & STEVENS vs. FRANCIS & BILLY R.
N.A. CHAMPIONSHIP
DUSTY RHODES vs. STEAMBOAT
BABA vs. BROWN   MAYNE vs. CARSON
TOUGH TONY BORNE vs. RAY GLENN
$3 — $4 — $5; KIDS ½ PRICE ANY SEAT

1973

1973 continued with the monthly shows that boasted the best main events in the world. January 13th saw Dory Funk Jr beat Billy Robinson, and Ed Francis beat The Sheik to win the Hawaiian title.

On March 7th, The Sheik beat Dory Funk Jr on count-out; therefore, the NWA title did not change hands. Ed Francis beat Haru Sasaki, who made a rare appearance in Hawaii.

April 18th saw Wahoo McDaniel beat Billy Graham, and Ed Francis drew Sam Steamboat. The rest of the undercard was weak.

The May 16th show was Wahoo McDaniel beating Billy Graham in an Indian Deathmatch. Dusty Rhodes beat Billy Robinson on DQ. They were using AWA TV to hype the cards, along with localized interviews.

The June 6th show saw Billy Robinson win the North American title, beating Dusty Rhodes. Jimmy Snuka, Tony Borne, and Peter Maivia filled out the undercard.

Sam Steamboat beat Ed Francis in a stretcher match on June 20th. Francis had turned heel at this time, which was unusual. Billy Robinson went to a draw with Billy Graham.

July 25th saw Verne Gagne beat Billy Graham on DQ, Ray Stevens and Nick Bockwinkel beat Ken Patera and Billy Robinson, and Ripper Collins and Ed Francis beat Peter Maivia and Sam Steamboat to win the vacant tag titles. The tag titles had been vacant for about a year. Interesting matches on the undercard saw Bill Francis go to a draw with Bull Ramos and Hard Boiled Haggerty beat Ric Flair.

On August 22nd, WWWF champ Pedro Morales went to a draw with Ed Francis.

September 12th saw Ed Francis beat Sam Steamboat for the Hawaiian title, and The Crusher beat Billy Graham.

On November 14th, Verne Gagne beat Ed Francis, defending the AWA title. The cards were becoming less exceptional because you were seeing established AWA matches. The matchups were always so intriguing in Hawaii, so unique.

On November 28th, Ripper Collins and Greg Valentine came from Oregon to win the Tag titles from Sam Steamboat and Peter Maivia. Billy Robinson beat Fred Blassie in a North American title defense.

Dave Meltzer wrote that the Holiday show was on December 19th, a rainy night that only drew 5,000, was a disappointment. Meltzer also wrote the oil crisis of 1973-74 caused the prices of airline tickets to rise. The external costs were taking a toll on the promotion.

On the Holiday show, Ken Patera won a battle royal. Giant Baba, Sam Steamboat, and Peter Maivia beat Ripper Collins, Greg Valentine, and Billy Graham.

1974

The first card of 74 saw Billy Graham win the Hawaiian title from Ed Francis. Pak Song was on the undercard going to a draw with Ripper Collins.

Billy Robinson's feud with Verne Gagne was a good draw in Hawaii. Robinson is listed as winning matches on February 13th and March 27th. No indication that these were title matches.

Flash forward twenty years; I was at Cauliflower Alley around 1991. I noticed Verne and Robinson coming out of a doorway, and they needed to go down a couple of steps. Robinson was in worse shape than Gagne. Verne offered his arm to help Robinson. Robinson had a salty reputation, and I overheard him mutter something about being dismayed that Verne had to help him.

Pak Song

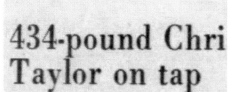

434-pound Chri[s] Taylor on tap

Chris Taylor has lost weight but there's no danger of missing him.

Taylor a bronze medal winner at the 1972 Olympics in Munich and former Iowa State star, will tip the scales at about 434 pounds when he steps into the ring at the H.I.C. Feb. 13 on the professional wrestling card.

He is training under the eye of former pro great Verne Gagne.

On the February card, Chris Taylor beat Butcher Vachon, Peter Neff Maivia and Sam Steamboat beat The Hollywood Blondes Dale Roberts and Jerry Brown.

The March show had seen the Ripper Collins and Ed Francis team dissolve, and they went to a draw.

There was almost a 3-month hiatus between the March and June 19th, 1974 show. The main event saw Gene Kiniski get some revenge over Dory Funk Jr.

The very last card during this time period was July 17th, 1974. The main event saw Verne Gagne beat Gene Kiniski; Ivan Putski was the only other fly-in besides a midget tag team match.

Thanks to Rock Rims we learn that Roy Shire tried to take advantage of wrestling going dark in Hawaii. He started sending his TV show to Hawaii starting November 9th.

They ran a show on December 25th at the HIC Arena. Moondog Mayne VS Peter Maivia for US title, Karl Von Brauner VS Pat Patterson, Kurt Von Brauner VS Raul Mata, Pepper Martin VS The Brute, Kinji Shibuya VS Earl Maynard, Terry Garvin VS Reno Tuufuli.

They returned on January 15th in 1975 with Moondog Mayne VS Peter Maivia no dq, Von Brauners & Gerhart Kaiser VS Pat Patterson & Raul Mata & Mr. Wrestling, The Brute VS Earl Maynard, Reno Tuufuli VS Rick Hunter.

SF last TV show was January 25th, 1975. These cards had a good main for Hawaii with Mayne VS Maivia. The rest of the cards were nothing special. I am sure flying the whole crew over did not make for a money making proposition.

1974 Wrestling Ads & Pictures

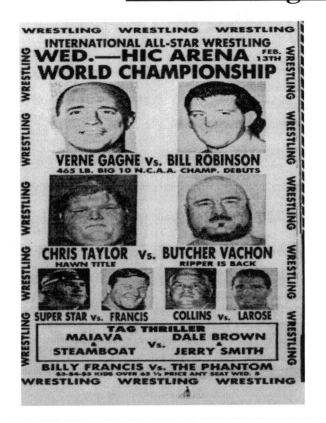

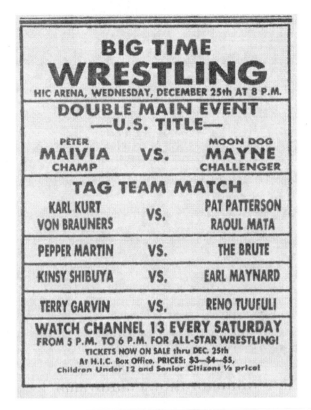

1975-1976

There is no wrestling results for these years until 1977.

1977

Ed Francis decided to reopen the Hawaii promotion on June 7th, 1977. To reopen the promotion, they brought in Andre The Giant for his first appearance on the Islands. Andre teamed with Don Muraco and Bill Francis to beat Big John Studd, Buddy Rose, and Chris Markoff. John Tolos was also on the card, beating Baron Scicluna. They drew 7,600 for this opening show.

On reopening, Francis had established an interesting crew. Billy Whitewolf and John Tolos are established veterans. His sons Bill and Russ Francis are in as the heroes to probably be the faces of the company. Jesse Ventura and Steve Strong have the potential to be the main eventers.

They were able to go back to the old formula with weekly shows at the Bloch Arena and then monthly shows at the Blaisdell Arena. They would have TV based on the weekly show.

June 22nd saw some interesting matches, with Giant Baba beating Lonnie Mayne. Also, Bill and Russ Francis beat Gene Kiniski and Apache Gringo.

The following week, Giant Baba beat Gene Kiniski, John Tolos and Steve Strong beat Bill and Russ Francis. It was evident that the promotion still hoped to present very special matches.

July 20th saw Nick Bockwinkel come back to the Islands to beat Billy Whitewolf.

On July 27th, John Tolos beat Nick Bockwinkel. Also, Steve Strong and Jesse Ventura beat Billy Whitewolf and Sam Steamboat to win tag titles.

On August 3rd, the main event saw Bill Francis beat John Tolos with a sleeper hold. Ed Francis was the first person I had seen use the sleeper hold. It was explained that the hold cut off the oxygen to the brain, rendering the opponent unconscious. It was a severe hold that only a few held the knowledge to use successfully. I had seen Ed Francis use the hold, and when the ref realized the opponent was unconscious, the match was stopped immediately. Other times, I saw Francis complete the match with a pin. The more severe side of this was waking the opponent. Francis would massage the neck muscles and then drive an elbow into the neck. This would jar the opponent awake. The opponent usually had no idea the match was over and was ready for the match to continue. This is the first time I have heard Bill Francis use the sleeper hold.

On August 17th at Pearl Harbor, Bill Francis beat Steve Strong for the Hawaiian title. Francis appears to be the first title holder upon the reopening.

On August 31st, Jesse Ventura won over Bill Francis, the two emerging as the most viable wrestlers on the top of the cards.

On September 7th, Jesse Ventura and Steve Strong beat Sam Steamboat and Nick Kozak in the main event. In the most explicit fashion, this match shows the potential stars of the future and the stars of the past.

On September 14th, Strong and Ventura got another tag win over Bill Francis and Buck Zumhoff.

On September 18th, Steve Olsonoski teams with Sam Steamboat to beat John Tolos and Jesse Ventura, while Steve Strong gets a singles win over Bill Francis.

September 28th saw a new version of some of those super cards Francis used to have in the late '60s. His son Bill got a DQ win over Nick Bockwinkel, the AWA World champ at the time. Greg Gagne and Jim Brunzell defended the AWA World tag titles against Jesse Ventura and Steve Strong; Sam Steamboat beat John Tolos for the North American title, and Missing Link returned after a 7-year absence to beat Steve Lawler.

On October 2nd, Steve Strong and Jesse Ventura beat Missing Link and Bill Francis, defending the tag titles.

On October 19th, Andre The Giant returned and split a battle royal with Buck Zumhoff. This result is a little strange. Zumhoff would appear ready for a push with the rub from a battle royal win with Andre. It just never really materializes.

They start holding spot shows on Maui. The first recorded one is on October 21st, with Andre The Giant winning a battle royal and teaming with Bill Francis and Missing Link to beat Tor Kamata, Jesse Ventura, and Steve Strong. It was not clear if they were running Hilo, which had always been a stop in the past.

October 26th saw Andre and John Tolos beat Steve Strong and Jesse Ventura, and Steamboat beat Billy Robinson.

On November 2nd, Ed Francis came out of retirement to beat Tor Kamata. Kamata started in Hawaii in 1965 as McRonald Kamaka and has not returned since.

On November 9th, Tor Kamata beat Sam Steamboat for the North American title.

November 23rd saw a pretty big card with Bobby Heenan coming to the Islands. Heenan teamed with Nick Bockwinkel to lose to Missing Link and Bill Francis. In other matches, John Tolos beat Steve Strong, Tor Kamata went to a no-contest with Billy Whitewolf, and Sam Steamboat went to a no-contest with Jesse Ventura.

On December 14th, Don Muraco returned to Hawaii, beating Duke Savage. The main event saw Nick Bockwinkel go to a draw with Missing Link, Bill Francis and John Tolos beat Steve Strong and Jesse Ventura. Tolos had become a babyface, and Francis and Tolos had captured the tag titles somewhere along the line.

On December 21st, Sam Steamboat beat Jesse Ventura, Tor Kamata and Rocky Tomayo beat Don Muraco and Billy Whitewolf. Chris Markoff appeared on opening night on June 7th and has now returned for a run in Hawaii starting on December 21st.

1977 Wrestling Ads & Pictures

Wednesday, June 22, 1977   Honolulu Star-Bulletin   G-3

Baba Is Big, Too

Giants come in different sizes, which should make Shoei Baba, better known as "Giant Baba", feel just like one of the boys when he faces up with 7-foot-4 Andre the Giant tonight in the Blaisdell Center ring.

The 7-foot-1 Baba, along with Andre, is entered in the highlight of pro wrestling's return to Hawaii under Promoter Ed Francis—the Texas Battle Royal—a smorgasbord of bodies (15 men in the ring, last man wins) which could prove to be the best argument yet against overpopulation.

"Baba has a devastating drop kick," warned Lord "Tallyho" Blears, who wouldn't say, however, whether it was Baba's kick or the impact of his 325-pound frame meeting the mat after the kick which did the most damage.

BLEARS, WHO WILL resume calling the blow-by-blow action on KGMB's televised matches each Friday night, claims that Baba is the most popular pro wrestler in Japan right now."

A one-time National Wrestling Association heavyweight champion, Baba will be in the ring for the Battle Royal, as well as a peliminary match against Mad Dog Mayne, when wrestling makes its first appearance in the Islands in three years.

Also on the card, which gets underway at 8, is a tag-team match between the Francis brothers—Russ, a tight end with the New England Patriots, and Bill—who take on Gene Kiniski and Apache Gringo.

In other preliminaries, Chief Billy White Wolf makes his return appearance against Tony Borne; Big John Tolas is pitted against German Erik Frolich, and Superstar Steve Strong faces Rocky Hunter.

Ed Francis

Wrestling's on Way Back...O-o-o-h Yeah

By Paul Carvalho
Star-Bulletin Writer

Larry, the lane's wrestling addict, would have a lot of pals come Saturday afternoon. He was the only one in the neighborhood who had Pedro Morales' "Sleeper Hold" down pat. . .and would use it without warning.

It became a matter of survival, gathering in his house to watch Big Time Wrestling on TV. He'd sit there, taking it all in, while we sat there, wondering which of Nick Bockwinkle's 1,000 holds he would try on us after the show. But it was better to be there than to have him come looking for you.

"Pro wrestling is all a fake," some would say. There were times, however, when it was much too real.

FOUR YEARS AGO, Big Time Wrestling collapsed under the weight of something more devastating than a Haystack Calhoun body smash. It was caught in an even fiercer grasp than that of the Masked Executioner's "Claw."

Even ketchup-filled blood-caps and midget wrestlers couldn't help. They just weren't making much money any more.

"When they tore down the old Civic Arena (which had been the home of Big Time Wrestling from 1961 through 1973) we couldn't afford to put on shows in the HIC on a weekly basis," Ed Francis recalled, as he relaxed in his Kaneohe Bay-front home where he lives with his wife and son, Russell Francis, the New England Patriots' star tight end.

"WE STARTED BRINGING in wrestling films from the Mainland, but they didn't go over as big, because the people couldn't relate to them," he said. "And we couldn't do lockerroom interviews in the studio, because the atmosphere just wasn't there."

Francis stopped reminiscing for a while and started looking ahead. Big Time Wrestling, you see, hadn't gone down for the three-count at all. After an absence of four years, which he spent on his ranch in Oregon, Francis is back— and many of the names on next week's card at the Blaisdell Center have a familiar ring to them.

FAMILY ACT—Bill Francis, who like his brother Russ, starred in football at Kailua, is on next week's card.

THE FEATURED TEXAS Battle Royal, for example, will have Andre the Giant, a 7-foot-6, 475-pounder who threw boxer Chuck Wepner out of the ring in the preliminary (via closed-circuit TV) match to Muhammad Ali's non-fight with wrestler Antonio Inoki.

There also will be Giant Baba, 7-foot 1 and 325 pounds, as well as Gene Kiniski and Chief Billy White Wolf.

All told, there will be six matches and, two nights later, the first televised Big Time Wrestling ruckus in four years will be aired, at 10 p.m. on KGMB.

Already, Francis has planned weekly cards, with the bulk of them taking place at Bloch Arena, where filming for the Friday night shows also will be done. You guessed it, Lord "Tallyho" Blears will be at ringside and Wally Tatsumi is bound to be the official gifted with enormous amounts of oversight.

"THE TIMING IS right for pro wrestling," Francis says, perhaps looking at the success of Honolulu martial arts programs in recent months. "I think it will go over. Now, more than ever, since nostalgia is going so strong.

"I'm amazed at how much people in Hawaii remember. It's interesting that they have such long memories for something like this. The kids, especially, who grew up watching the Saturday afternoon and Friday night shows, remember more than I do. They can recall specific matches that I've forgotten."

Francis rattled off a list of other former stars who won't be on Wednesday's card but who may be making appearances before long. Most of the old wrestlers have remained active in the Midwest, Australia, New Zealand and England, where the shows still go over big.

JOHNNY BAREND. . ."He owns some motels in Rochester, New York, now and was here in April. He's just as goofy as he ever was," said Francis, who had hoped to present a card last April with Barend as the main draw—until Barend took back off for the Mainland without notice.

"I remember that Johnny was a great wrestler, but he was also a weird guy. One time I wanted to interview him but he locked himself up inside his private room in the lockerroom and wouldn't let anyone in," Francis recalled.

"When we finally opened the door, Johnny had crawled into a long cardboard box and all you could see was his cigar sticking out. No matter what I asked him, the answer was always Yes, yes, Mr. Francis'," he said, imitating Barend's gravel-toned voice.

PAMPERO FIRPO. . .that one didn't click. . ."The Missing Link," said Francis. O-o-o-h Yeah. "He may be down here in the near future."

Chief Billy White Wolf, who will be here Wednesday. . .remembered for his Indian Death Match, but Francis swears he was the first one to use the "Shaka" sign in his weekly interviews.

"I never thought of it until I can back to Hawaii a couple of months ago, but then I saw that even the Mayor was doing it," Francis said, holding up a clenched fist save for his thumb and little finger.

"Now that I think of it, Billy White Wolf did that on every telecast."

Neff Maiava. . ."Halawa prison, how about that?" Francis said.

RIPPER COLLINS. . ."I haven't heard from him in the four months I've been back. I wonder if he's still mis-pronouncing the Hawaiian Islands and saying 'Lor Nu Lau'," Francis said.

There will be a few new names, too, though not many.

Russ Francis, his brother, Bill, will wrestle Wednesday night and, possibly, in the future, ex-Olympians Chris Taylor and Ken Patera will climb into the ring.

"For some reason, there aren't many new wrestlers coming through the ranks these days," Francis said. "The old stars are still the best. . .the ones people still go out and support.

"But then, I guess it's been proven that a guy 30 or 40 years old can still be a good athlete. Look at pro football. No one would have thought a guy could be playing that game when he's 40, but it's been done."

There was no peace in the ring during last night's "battle royal" at Blaisdell Center. The eventual winner, 7-foot-6 Andre the Giant, is taking on four foes in the skirmish at right.

Advertiser Photo by T. Umeda

More than 7,600 fans

Full, howling house for wrestling's return

AT IT AGAIN—Ed Francis, promoter of Big Time Wrestling and father of Russ Francis, the New England Patriots' tight end who will make his first appearance in Hawaii as a pro wrestler, shows off his first wrestling card in four years.—Star-Bulletin Photos by Jack Titchen.

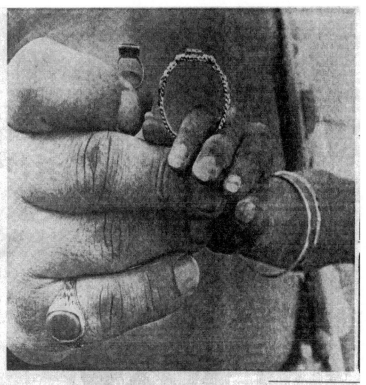

Giant-Size Difference

It may be difficult to imagine just how big a 7-foot-4, 472-pound man is but a comparison of ring sizes could give you a good idea. Reporter Grace Feliciano who is 5-4, found room to spare when she tried on Andre the Giant's favorite ring, while her own size-4 ring seems only about as big as the professional wrestler's thumbnail. Andre will be in action tomorrow night at Bloch Arena.—Star-Bulletin Photo by John Titchen.

1978

1978 starts up, and it looks like Hawaiian wrestling is back on track with a pretty good crew and stability in the promotion.

Rick Martel makes his debut on January 11th. Martel would eventually make two different runs in Hawaii. He talks about his first run in his RATNW interview: "I went there on a meeting on the first run. I was in Hawaii on vacation, coming back from New Zealand. I saw in the paper Andre The Giant was wrestling and Andre and I were friends because of the language, of course. I called different hotels to see if the wrestlers stayed there, and I lucked out. One of them I called said yes. I got in touch with Andre, and he said. "Meet me tonight. We have a meeting, but come, and I'll introduce you to the promoter." Finally, I met Ed Francis, the promoter. Ed said, "Well if you are not doing anything, how about coming back in January?" That was December 77.

I went there and had a great run wrestling guys like Tor Kamata. I did really well in Hawaii. I got over big time. I got over because Tor was champion and he was starting a restaurant in LA, a teriyaki restaurant, and he told Francis last minute about it. Ed had to put the strap on someone right away. His son Bill was already tag champion and finally they said we will put it on Rick for a while. So they put the strap on me. Finally, after about a week or two, his restaurant deal fell through and he stayed. Now Francis didn't trust him to give him the belt back anymore. I loved it in Hawaii, and the people are so nice there. I have great memories of that territory."

On that January 11th card, Martel debuted and beat Rocky Tomayo, Jim Brunzell and Greg Gagne beat Blackjack Lanza and Bobby Duncum, Steve Strong beat Missing Link, and Tor Kamata beat Billy Whitewolf.

On February 1st, John Tolos beat Steve Strong for the Hawaiian title.

On February 13th, Nick Bockwinkel came in and beat John Tolos. Steve Strong and Chris Markoff beat Russ and Bill Francis in another very good match. Also, Rick Martel beat Tor Kamata on DQ.

On March 22nd, Ed, Bill, and Russ Francis's team beat Nick Bockwinkel, Chris Markoff, and Steve Strong. Also, on this card, Rick Martel beats Tor Kamata again.

April 5th is a crucial date because it may be the only singles loss that Russ Francis had in his wrestling career. He wrestled many tag matches teaming with his father Ed or brother, Bill. He had many more tag matches than singles as a way to protect him. However, on this night, John Anson got the win. It shows they obviously had plans for Anson. Buddy Rose also wrestled here that night, beating Billy Whitewolf.

April 12th shows the new blood, with Rose, Anson, and John Studd definitely sprucing up the cards. Rose drew with Bill Francis, John Studd beat Duke Savage, and Rick Martel beat John Anson.

On April 19th, Tor Kamata beat a debuting George Wells, Russ and Bill Francis beat John Anson and John Studd.

April 26th was a massive card. George Wells won the Hawaiian title, beating John Anson, and Rick Martel beat Nick Bockwinkel by DQ in an AWA World title defense. Martel would have to wait another day to hold the AWA title.

Ed Francis beat Bobby Heenan by DQ in a Pier 9 brawl. Billy Whitewolf would beat Tor Kamata in an Indian Deathmatch. Stipulations for this match: Kamata was supposed to kiss Whitewolf's feet since he lost. He refused, so Ed Francis set up a future loser-leaves-town match. The last big match on this card saw Buddy Rose go to a draw with Russ Francis.

May 3rd saw Ed, Bill, and Russ Francis go to a no-contest with John Studd, Tor Kamata, and Rocky Tomayo. Rick Martel beat Buddy Rose, and they would bring this feud to Oregon in the future.

May 14th saw John Studd beat Rick Martel to win the North American title. However, the title was held up because Studd won by underhanded methods. Interesting since this card was held in Maui.

May 17th saw Tor Kamata beat Billy Whitewolf in a loser leaves town match. Nick Bockwinkel would beat Rick Martel.

On May 24th, Buddy Rose beat George Wells to win the Hawaiian title. Wells was headed off to work in California. John Tolos helped Russ Francis win a pole battle royal.

On June 4th in Maui, Andre The Giant returned and teamed with Bill Francis and Don Muraco to beat John Studd, Buddy Rose, and Chris Markoff with the same result a few nights later in Honolulu.

On June 18th, Ed Francis returned from retirement for a lights-out match with Chris Markoff, where Markoff failed to beat Francis in 5 minutes.

On June 21st, Mr. Fuji returned to the Islands and teamed with Tor Kamata, but they were dqed against Bill Francis and Mickey Doyle.

On June 28th, Andre returned to Hawaii for the 2nd time in June to team with John Tolos to beat John Studd and Buddy Rose.

July 19th saw another big card as Nick Bockwinkel defended the AWA title against Tor Kamata, who was disqualified. King Curtis returned after a 6-year absence. Curtis went to a draw with Missing Link.

On August 23rd, Andre The Giant beat Nick Bockwinkel, and Mr. Fuji beat Missing Link. Peter Maivia returned to go to a draw with John Studd, and Mike Cunningham, John Tolos, and Steve Strong beat Mr. Fuji, Toru Tanaka, and Karl Von Steiger.

September 20th saw Jim Brunzell and Greg Gagne defend the AWA tag titles against Karl Von Steiger and Mr. Fuji. Missing Link went to a draw with John Studd, and Don Muraco beat Tor Kamata.

October 18th saw Bill and Benny McGuire come to Hawaii to beat Karl Von Steiger and Mr. Fuji, and Nick Bockwinkel beat Don Muraco. Ripper Collins returned after a long absence; he beat Bill Francis.

November 22nd saw a very interesting result, with Ricky Morton beating Randy Alls on DQ. I once had a car ride with Ricky Morton, who mentioned that his first match was in Hawaii. Ricky Morton in Hawaii sounds out of place, but here it is, and he beat Randy Alls on DQ.

Rick Martel also returned on this card to team with Don Muraco to beat Mr. Fuji and Karl Von Steiger. Ripper Collins also beat Steve Strong.

The next huge card on December 20th saw Andre The Giant beat Nick Bockwinkel in a cage. Andre in a cage was unusual because it never had to come to that for Andre. Don Leo Jonathan also returned to Hawaii and beat Tor Kamata.

As 1978 ended, the promise of the beginning of the year faded somewhat. Don Muraco is the top star, and then Ripper Collins, Karl Von Steiger, Tor Kamata, and Bill Francis, at least on paper, were a little stale as most had been here most of the year and even longer. The booking of Lord Blears still makes the territory compelling.

Looking ahead to 1979, wrestling will unexpectedly change in Hawaii.

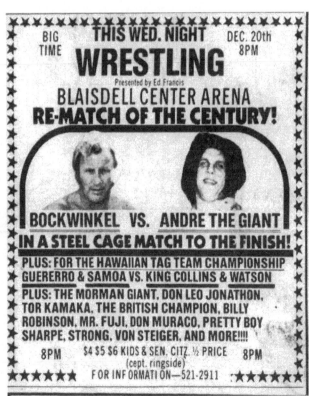

341

1978 Wrestling Ads & Pictures

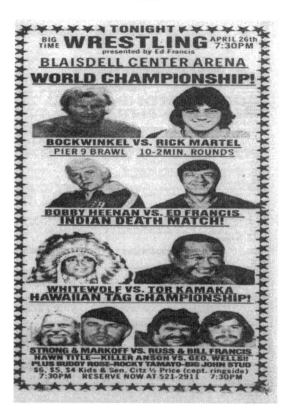

THE McGUIRE TWINS, Benny, left, and Billy, each tipping the scales at 720 pounds, will appear here Saturday in a big professional wrestling card starting at 7:30 p.m. at Hilo Civic Auditorium. The brothers will perform in a tag team thriller.

McGuire twins on mat card Saturday

Billy and Benny McGuire, the heaviest twins in the world as recognized by the Guinness Book of World Records, will headline the biggest professional wrestling card of the year Saturday night at Hilo Civic Auditorium.

The twins, each weighing over 700 pounds, will appear in a tag team main event match against Ripper Collins and Whipper Watson.

Born in 1946, the McCreary twins have appeared as tag team partners since 1972 under the names of Billy and Benny McGuire, and each now weighs 720 pounds.

In addition to the big match, four other special events are on the card.

The Missing Link will take on Karl Von Stieger, Super Star Steve Strong will tackle Bill Francis, Pretty Boy Larry Sharp meets Chief Billy White Wolf, and Mr. Fuji faces Don Muraco.

Tickets for the card, which begins at 7:30 p.m., may be purchased in advance at Sam's Sport Shop in the Kaiko'o Mall.

1979

The end of the Francis Promotion

Looking ahead to 1979, wrestling will unexpectedly change in Hawaii.

Steve Strong had turned into a babyface about halfway through 1978, and on the first Honolulu card of '79, he went to a draw with Tor Kamata.

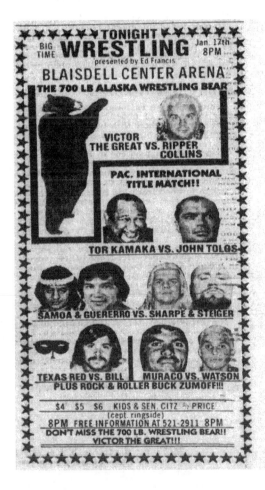

On January 17th, they presented one of the bigger monthly cards. However, those cards were not what they used to be. Headlining this card was Tor Kamata beating John Tolos on count out, Victor The Bear beating Ripper Collins, Bill Francis beating Texas Red (probably Red Bastien), Mando Guerrero and Tama Samoa beating Larry Sharpe and Karl Von Steiger.

February 14th saw another big card, and this one seems like a pretty good effort. Jumbo Tsuruta made his Hawaii debut, beating Nick Bockwinkel by DQ. Giant Baba also came in to beat Karl Von Steiger. In another long line of heels battling each other, Tor Kamata beat Ripper Collins, and somewhat of a strange babyface tag match between Bill Francis and Don Muraco went to a draw with Mando Guerrero and Tama Samoa. This Tama Samoa may very well be Cocoa Samoa.

February 21st saw Don Muraco beat Tor Kamata. Peter Maivia returned and beat Chris Markoff, who also returned. Clayton Rodriguez started wrestling and beat Whipper Watson. Rodriguez, I believe, was more known as a ref in Hawaii.

February 28th was a very good card. Harley Race defended the NWA World title, beating Peter Maivia, and Tor Kamata beat Ripper Collins in a grudge match. Former tag partners met as Don Muraco beat Bill Francis. It appears that Muraco turned heel as he only faces babyfaces from this point on.

March 7th saw Ripper Collins beat Brian Blair and Don Muraco beat Mando Guerrero.

March 21st saw Kevin Von Erich come to Hawaii and beat Whipper Watson Jr and Karl Von Steiger in two matches. Kevin would fall in love with Hawaii and eventually move there.

April 4th saw a one-night tournament to crown a new Hawaiian State Champion. Karl Von Steiger was the upset winner, beating Chris Markoff, Buck Zumhoff, and Kevin Von Erich to win the title. Also on the card was JJ Dillon.

ALL STAR ★ PRO ★ ALL STAR

WRESTLING

BLOCH ARENA—PEARL HARBOR
THIS WED. NIGHT—April 4th 7:30PM
1st NIGHT OF ELIMINATION
TOURNAMENT FOR HWN. CHAMPIONSHIP!

KING COLLINS VS. ATI-TAGO

JAMES DILLON	MARKOFF
VS.	VS.
VON ERICH	VON STEIGER
JERRY MONTI	CLAYTON RODRIGUES
VS.	VS.
TAMA SAMOA	BUCK ZUMOFF

AND

SPECIAL GRUDGE MATCH!!!!!

RESERVE NOW—CALL 474-1190
$4 Gen. Adm. $5 Reserved
Kids & Sen. Citz. $2.50 (cept. ringside)

It looks like April 4th may very well have been the last card Ed Francis promoted in Hawaii. The talent had slipped, and this card looked dismal. Karl Von Steiger beat Jerry Monti, Ati Tago and Tama Samoa beat Chris Markoff and Ripper Collins. Buck Zumhoff won two matches, beating JJ Dillon and Clayton Rodriguez.

This date is uncertain, but Dave Meltzer writes, "In April of 1979, Ed Francis sold the promotional rights to Steve Rickard, who retained Lord Blears as his front man."

Meltzer also wrote that Francis had hoped to build his own building for wrestling and hold other events. He had put a lot of work into planning, gotten some investors involved, and then the project went to local government commissioners who said it would take a $250,000 fee to keep the project going before it would be approved. That was a deal breaker.

Francis again addressed the situation in his book, "I had a little talk with myself. I said, The Civic's gone, HIC rent is high. The box office is down. TV wrestling viewers are down. Wrestlers' fees are up. Nothing lasts forever. It's time to go."

The 50th State Big Time Wrestling site notes that in June of 1979, promoter Steve Rickard promoted weekly matches at Block Arena and cards at the Blaisdell Center Arena once a month. He maintained a TV contract with KGMB TV and retained Lord Blears as his announcer.

In my RATNW interview, Francis said, "I sold the promotion to a guy in New Zealand, Steve Rickard. I think they were still going in 79 and 80." I asked Francis if it was "still going strong when you sold it?" Francis replied, "It was fairly strong. I just wanted to get out because I had bought a cattle ranch in Oregon near Don Owen. I had all the kids over there. I went into the cattle business for a while."

Lord Blears, in his interview, talked about the end of Francis's promotion:

RATNW: Why did Ed decide to sell the promotion?

Blears: I never asked.

RATNW: After Ed Francis got out of the business, were you in any way involved in the others that came through, including the Rickards, Lia Maivia, or Super Fly Tui?

Blears: Steve Rickard bought Hawaii from Ed Francis. He joined with Lia Maivia, and there was no wrestling for about twelve weeks. Rickard sent tapes from New Zealand, and I dubbed narration once a week on the tape. I helped Peter Maivia and did narration at NBC shows every five or six weeks. Finally, the houses went to zero, and that was the end of the promotion.

Steve Rickard

Francis sold the company for $80,000. However, Francis claimed he only got a small portion of the money. This is where it gets murky. It has been insinuated that Peter Maivia became involved and intimidated Rickard to leave the Islands. Others claim that Maivia purchased the promotion from Rickard. However, there is a theory that no other payments were made with Rickard off the Islands. But we are jumping ahead of ourselves.

April 11th is the date I speculate Rickard took over. There seems to be a noticeable difference in the wrestlers on the card.

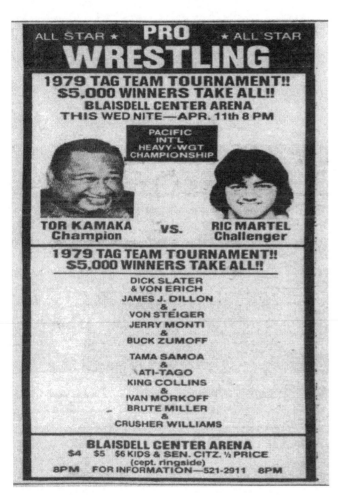

Rick Martel is in, and he becomes the booker. Also new on the cards are the Sheepherders, Kevin Von Erich and Dick Slater.

Kamata went to a draw with Rick Martel for a new title called The Pacific International Title. The Sheepherders beat Kevin Von Erich and Dick Slater.

On 4/18, Siva Afi debuted, and he would be a big player in Hawaii in the following years. He won the Hawaiian title by beating Karl Von Steiger; also, on the 18th, Martel beat Dick Slater.

These two weeks of cards in April may have been a transition period for Rickard. At any rate, there are no recorded results for two months in Hawaii. The 50th State Website mentions that Rickard starts in June.

The first card in June is June 20th. Rick Martel beats Buddy Rose, and Siva Afi goes to a draw with Brute Miller.

The next card has Siva Afi beat Buddy Rose, and The Sheepherders beat Clayton Rodriguez and Rick Martel.

With Rose, Martel, The Sheepherders, Siva Afi, and, in a few weeks, Roddy Piper, Hawaii, it looks like a dry run for one of the most successful times in Portland.

In his RATNW interview, Luke Williams talked about working in Hawaii and getting ready to head to Oregon. Williams noted, "Steve Rickard bought into Hawaii from Ed Francis. We started working for him in Waikiki. We would work four shows a week. It was just survival. We were lucky to make enough money for our overhead. We got a tour in Japan for six weeks. When we were in Hawaii, I met Roddy Piper and Buddy Rose. The tag team of Killer Brooks and Roddy Piper had just lost the tag titles, and Roddy was leaving for a while.

They need a heel tag team in Oregon. They saw us, and we called Don right away. Buddy and Roddy vouched for us and Don said as soon as you finish in Japan come on in. He gave us a starting date. We went to Japan and came back, and we had six weeks before our starting date in Oregon."

Roddy Piper debuted in Hawaii on July 11th and beat Clayton Rodriguez. There were some obscure wrestlers now like Bryan St. John from Florida, Bounty Hunter, Raul Castro, Randy Alls and the Beast. Also, on the 11th, Siva Afi and Bryan St. John beat The Sheepherders.

On the 18th, Tor Kamata returned as a babyface and teamed with Rick Martel to beat The Beast and The Bounty Hunter. The Bounty Hunter was unmasked as Mad Dog Frenchy Martin.

On August 22nd, Peter Maivia made his first appearance on cards that were promoted by Steve Rickard. Maivia beat Jay York. That becomes important in the future. Nick Bockwinkel beat Rick Martel in an AWA title match.

On September 2nd, Raul Castro beat Super Fly Tui. Tui was another wrestler who eventually built a name for himself in Hawaii. The main event saw Martel, Siva Afi, and Clayton Rodriguez beat Piper, Raul Castro, and Jay York.

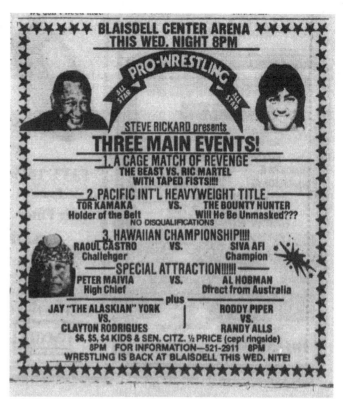

It appears that September 2nd is Martel's last night in Hawaii, and he explains it in his RATNW interview, "I was 23 years old and I loved it. (Booking), During the months that I was with Lewin in New Zealand, I learned so much. I learned his style and all that. I was pretty creative. Of course, I surrounded myself with good guys. I enjoyed doing it. I like to create something and make something happen and have an angle to it and then you have the results and it is a very satisfying job. It is a hard job, too. At 23 years old, you deal with men around you, much older guys and everyone can't win and everyone can't be in all the angles. So, of course, you get the guys who are not happy with your decisions. It is hard to juggle that.

I had a couple situations with what I was deciding. It was pretty tough at times. As a result, if you succeed, there is a big turnout, and you draw. Nobody can knock that, and I was lucky enough to have good crowds. In Hawaii, we had Peter Maivia as the other partner. Peter and I didn't see on the same wavelength. Peter had many friends from New York, and these guys weren't what I wanted in Hawaii. I wanted a bunch of young guys that could move back and forth. I brought in Roddy Piper, and we became terrific friends. I brought in a few young guys from Atlanta. So because of differences. I decided to leave. You need to be heading towards the same goal. That was my first contact with the bad side of the business where we didn't get along and I had to go. At 23, I learned another great lesson there. When you are back in the dressing room, they will knock the promoter because of money or whatever. It gave me another look at how the business works. I would never knock bookers or what they do. I understood their situation and the money situation with the promoter. I knew better to mouth off in the dressing room. I would go to the promoter and talk with them. That was the only way to settle money differences. So that gave me a good outlook."

September 19th saw Peter Maivia beat Harley Race by COR for the NWA title, Rocky Johnson beat Roddy Piper in Johnson's first appearance, Clayton Rodriguez beat veteran Al Costello, and Ripper Collins beat Siva Afi.

On September 30th, Ripper Collins beat a very young Matt Borne. Collins had his run-ins with Matt's father, Tony, in Oregon. Karl Von Steiger won over Rocky Johnson.

Andre The Giant came in on November 21st to beat Larry Sharpe and Karl Von Steiger.

By the end of 1979, Hawaii looked pretty similar to 1969 Hawaii. Billy Whitewolf, The Sheik, Peter Maivia, Mr. Fuji, Karl Von Steiger, Ripper Collins, and Mr. X (Baron Scicluna) were filling out the cards.

December 19th saw a big card as Billy Whitewolf went to a draw with The Sheik. Peter Maivia beat Ripper Collins to win the Hawaiian title, and Rocky Johnson drew Don Muraco. Ricky Rickard, Steve's son, beat Kung Fu Lee.

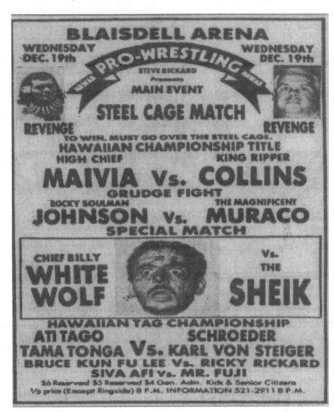

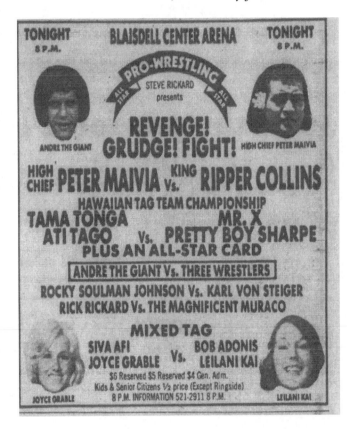

Sports Parade

Ed Francis, father of New England Patriots tight end **Russ Francis** and Hawaii professional wrestling promoter, has been named a scout for the National Football League team. The Patriots said the elder Francis will cover Hawaii and the Pacific Northwest—including the states of Washington, Oregon, Montana and Idaho.

1979 Wrestling Ads & Pictures

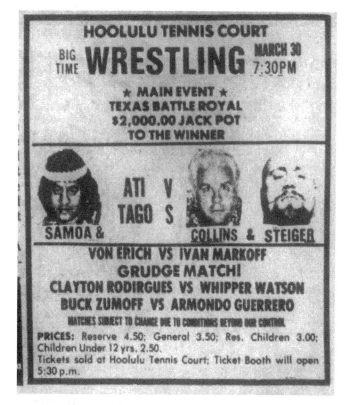

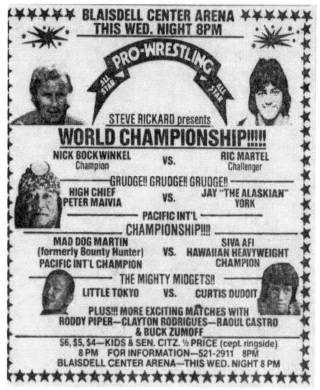

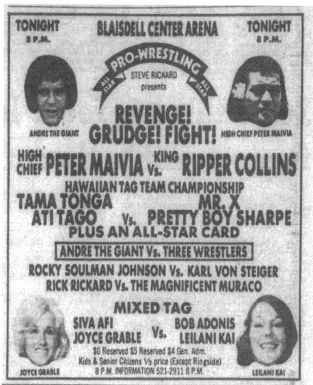

Rickard Leaves Hawaii

Rickard seems to leave Hawaii. Mixed reports have Maivia buying him out or Maivia encouraging him to leave. Interesting because they did have a prior relationship dating back to Maivia's initial training. Maivia even wrote the forward in Rickard's autobiography.

Again, examining the Rickard/Maivia partnership, there is a glimpse of how Rickard felt in a letter to New Zealand historian Dave Cameron.

Rickard said, "Johnson was lucky. I don't have anything great to say about him, at any time, or the Maivia family."

Bryan Ashby, who wrested as Bruno Bekkar in New Zealand and Australia, mentions that he doesn't know a lot about Rickards's time in Hawaii, but he "did hear he had to leave in a hurry."

Doug Wulf worked in the Polynesian office later on in the mid-80s, and we will have more on him when we get there. Lia Maivia told him that Peter had purchased the promotion from Ed Francis, and there was no mention of Steve Rickard.

Sources closer to Maivia retell it in this manner. Steve Rickard bought the promotion from Ed Francis in June of 1979. Reportedly, business was down, and Rickard thought he could turn things around. A few months into it, the business had not turned around, and Rickard was tired of the long flights from New Zealand to Hawaii.

In early 1980, Rickard sold the promotion to Maivia for pennies on the dollar and kept a small percentage for himself. Rickard agreed to come to Hawaii now and then. However, after that, he rarely returned.

Ed Francis writes in his book that the Maivia's staked their claim to promoting wrestling in Hawaii without paying any fees and essentially intimidated Rickard into leaving the Islands. Francis continues, "Not long after I'd left Hawaii, I returned on a visit. Lia Maivia called me and threatened harm to my family if I considered resurrecting our wrestling promotion business."

Doug Wulf confirms Francis's story. "When Peter died, Vince McMahon Sr told Lia he wouldn't touch her promotion. She was the only woman to have a promotion according to Lars because the "old school" didn't think they could do a good job. Later on, when we partnered with New Japan Pro Wrestling and started shows at the Blaisdell, Vince Jr told Ed Francis to come to Honolulu and take the promotion back from Lia. I walked into the office one day and Lia told me I had a good voice so I should call Ed and tell him I was going to kill him unless he left the promotion alone. Lia had called him a couple times already. Lars said that was not the way to do it, so he called Ed. Ed told Lars that if he got one more threat he would leave the island. A couple days later, I read that Ed was back on the East Coast helping his son with his restaurant. So I figured Lia made another threat."

There is giant speculation of exactly how the transfer of power went from Ed Francis to Steve Rickard to Peter Maivia. We have had testimonies and memories from many involved. I asked Australian and New Zealand wrestling historian Steve Ogilvie if he could shed any light on this situation and Steve Rickards position. He came through like a champ.

Dave Cameron is the premier historian from New Zealand and Australia. His collection of material has been stored in the Auckland, NZ library. Cameron had several letters from Steve Rickard during this time period that shed a little light at least from Rickards position. With permission from Ogilvie and Dave Cameron these letters are being reprinted.

STEVE RICKARD

NATIONAL

STEVE RICKARD

5G Jerningham Apartments
0 Oriental Terrace
riental Bay
Vellington
ew Zealand 6001

P O Box 9729
Wellington
New Zealand
6001

6th May. 2001

Dear Dave,
Thanks for your letter and info. JOHNSON was lucky. I don,t
have anything, great, to say about him, at any time, or, the MAIVIA
family.
I am sending you a few write-ups, including a little from India.
There are, also, three photos, taken in Hawaii. You can take
copies off these. However, please, return the photos to me. If
you have any problems, I will obtain copies, for you, when I return
from Australia. The achievment list, I will, also, have to look
for on my return.
Surfers Paradise will be my address for the next eight weeks. The
card, herewith, shows Tony's apartment block, where I will reside.
I will travel to Singapore, for a short time, during my Australian
stay.

Regards to you all

Steve

wrote Steve urgently.

350

Steve Rickard

15G Jerningham Apartments
20 Oriental Terrace
Oriental Bay
Wellington
New Zealand 6001

P O Box 9729
Wellington
New Zealand
6001

20th July, 2000

Dear Dave,
Thankyou for your letters and the printed material. Apart from
a few days, I was in India and Australia for nearly two months.
I am, now, home for a while.

The MAVIA story is not true. I have told you about it before.
On the 23rd January, 1979, I purchased the business, T.V. rights,
4 wrestling rings and a truck, from Ed FRANCIS. MAIVIA was to
buy in and never paid one dollar. I was left with nothing but
bills I had to pay. One day I will show you the written agreement
of sale. Anyway, that is life.

I do not know how this is operating in N.Z. I will be surprised
if the parties, advertised, have a license.

The three India promotions went off O.K. Somewhere near 10,000
at each. I had a hard time getting the money - missed some of
it - but that is India. They promised me the news media and
poster advertising. I never, even, got that.

I am enclosing written material I have received from Len HOLT
and Rex KYLE. You may not have seen it.

Kris MILLER has been in hospital, again. Heart worries. He
said he was O.K., when I last spoke to him. That was over a
week ago.

I am not sure of my next departure date but I will let you
know.

My best regards to all.

Steve

P.S. I did not know that Lofty HOUGHTON had passed on.
If you hear from The Destroyer's friend, let me know if she is
travelling to Wellington.
One Man Gang was unable to wrestle in India heart attack.

Phone : (04) 384 4694   Fax : (04) 384 4624

Steve Rickard

15G Jerningham Apartments
20 Oriental Terrace
Oriental Bay
Wellington
New Zealand   6001

P O Box 9729
Wellington
New Zealand
6001

14th Oct., 99

Dear Dave,
Thanks for the letter and news.

Glad to hear Shorty HANSEN is O.K. Say "Hello" for me.

The guy in Australia lost a lot of money and pulled the plug. I
was told that Mark didn't help much. Apparently he wanted to be
everything. He even had his wife involved and put her over as a
princess. He met her when he was with me, on a trip to Singapore.
She was, then, married to a Canadian.

Maybe it is MAIVIA'S grandson, in the Negro book. He is part negro.

MAIVIA'S wife never stayed in Hawaii. She lives in Florida. I am
not sure if she still lives with her daughter and Rocky JOHNSON or
near them. It does not surprise me that she pinched your photo
album. I have nothing good to say about any of them. JOHNSON,
his wife and son, were at a C.A.C. function in Florida where I spoke.
They did not acknowledge me and I not them. I have too many bad
memories of the MAIVIA'S and all the money they cost me. One day
I will tell you the story. It will take a considerable time.

When I get the opportunity I will send you a box of "On The Mat".

Regarding Australia T.V. I spoke with Ron MILLER when I was last
there. He, also, told me that the T.V. did not live up to their
obligations. Ron had spoken to me severaltimes before the opening.
He was asking opinions and we talked about me going to Melbourne
for a meeting with SKAPETIS. I never went. It is always to be
remembered that people have their own ideas. SKAPETIS had his.

This is it for now. Say "HI" to all.

Best regards to you and the family,

Steve

1980-82

1980 Starts with heel Don Muraco in a feud with Peter Maivia.

Tama Tonga is in the area and is better known as Haku. Tonga is just in his 2nd year of wrestling.

On January 16th, Neff Maivia comes out of retirement to team with Peter Maivia to beat Ripper Collins and Karl Von Steiger.

It appears that the formula of weekly shows and once-a-month bigger shows are still in place.

January 23rd is one of those bigger shows. Don Muraco beat Billy Whitewolf, Ati Tago and Tama Tonga beat Ripper Collins and Mad Dog Vachon, and Pat Patterson beat Tommy Rich in a strange match. Also, Bruce Hart has come to Hawaii.

On February 13th, Hawaii is starting to look like Calgary. Dynamite Kid beat Karl Von Steiger, Tama Tonga and Billy Whitewolf beat Bruce and Keith Hart, Don Muraco beat Rocky Johnson by DQ, and Peter Maivia beat Hans Schroeder.

April 2nd has a strange main event with Billy Whitewolf and Tama Tonga beating Carlos Mata and Butts Giraud.

April and May look like a giant mish-mash of wrestlers and matches. Peter Maivia and Rocky Johnson are absent during this time. Babyfaces are well represented in Siva Afi, Tama Tonga, and Billy Whitewolf. The heels appear to be Victor Rivera and Wildman Pete Austin.

Missing Link appears on the May 21st card going to a no contest with Billy White Wolf.

Peter Maivia and Missing Link teamed up on June 4th to lose to Victor Rivera and Wildman Austin.

Andre makes an appearance on June 8th to beat The Convict. This Convict is listed to be Hacksaw Jim Duggan.

At this point, the results become spotty between July and October. It isn't clear if the results were not getting reported or if wrestling went on a hiatus.

The October 15th card is so big it almost looks like a reboot. Peter Maivia VS Ernie Ladd, Ivan Putski VS Don Muraco, and Leilani Kai VS Wendy Richter. Ripper Collins is also on the card.

I have no results from November 1980 until February 1982.

The main event of the Hilo show on February 11th, 1982, saw Peter Maivia beat Victor Rivera and Bob Backlund beat Don Muraco.

From early 1980, Peter Maivia's appearances slowed down, and he made only an occasional match. We learn that he had inoperable cancer. He reportedly ignored symptoms and refused to see any doctors. He passed away on June 13th, 1982.

1980 Wrestling Ads & Pictures

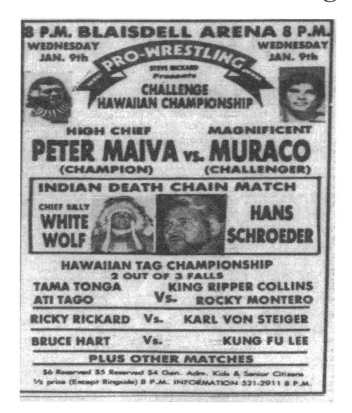

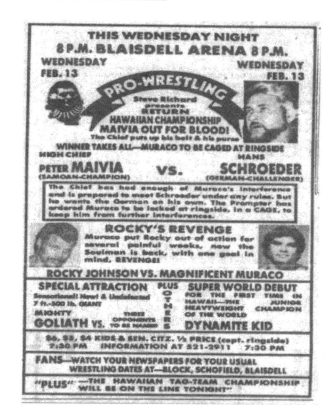

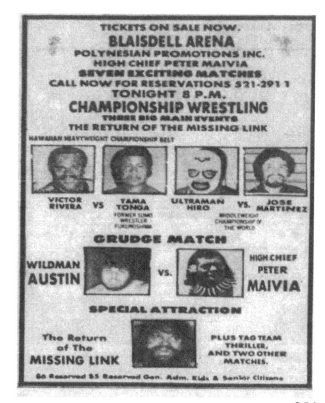

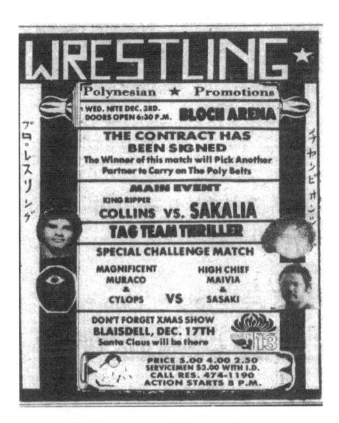

1982 Wrestling Ads & Pictures

Wrestling chiefly with ritual

New sport of kings

Ten professional wrestlers will warm up in Blaisdell Center Arena tonight for a performance before one of the few kings left in this commonplace world.

He's the king of Tonga, one of the few places that has never seen professional wrestling.

This cultural interchange will be the diplomatic triumph of paramount high chief Peter Maivia, promoter of tonight's World Wrestling Federation championship bout between Don Muraco and Bob Backlund.

No, I'm not kidding.

The wrestlers on tonight's card will head tomorrow for the South Seas to open a new chapter in Polynesian history, a new era in Pacific sports, by linking our Islands with a half-nelson and a hammerlock.

It will not be easy.

Maivia explained yesterday that he will take not only 10 wrestlers, a producer and a public relations man with two college degrees, but his own high talking chief, Talolemaanao.

"I must go prepared," he said. "It would be disrespectful to the king if I did not bring my talking chief."

Putting on tonight's card at Blaisdell was duck soup compared to the political pitfalls of bringing professional wrestling to Tonga, he said.

Fortunately, Joe Mataele, the opposition leader of the Tongan Parliament, is a former boxer. "He will be co-promoter of the card," said Maivia.

Even so, it took an act of Parliament

bob krauss

Advertiser columnist

before Maivia could schedule the matches in the Teufaiva open-air rugby park which seats more than 5,000 spectators.

"The whole kingdom will turn out because the king will be there and it's the first time they will get a chance to see professional wrestling," Maivia explained.

In Samoa, the promotion of wrestling is very time-consuming because of Maivia's status as a paramount high chief.

"When I visit a village, there must be a kawa ceremony," he said. "This takes one or two hours, depending on how many get up to make speeches to me. Then I must answer through my talking chief."

Another small worry is rioting.

Maivia said he tested his dream of bringing professional wrestling to the South Seas by taking some local champions to American and Western Samoa over Christmas.

Since Maivia is the most famous athlete Western Samoa has ever produced, his fans naturally tend to get excited.

"The wrestling was very successful," he

See Bob Krauss on Page D-3

Bob Krauss

from page D-1

said. "But there was a small riot." "The people picked up rocks and chairs," added Lia, his wife.

The same thing happened in 1968 when Maivia returned from a triumphal tour of Europe to wrestle in Western Samoa's open-air park. "That was the biggest riot I ever witnessed," he said.

How does he handle the exuberance of his fans?

"The police do not help much," he admitted. "Last Christmas, a policeman was sitting there during the riot. I asked him why he didn't do something. He said, 'What can I do?'"

As a paramount high chief, Maivia took charge himself.

"I got up in the ring and said, 'What do they say in Europe if they see this? We are trying to put our good name out in the world, to show people we are not barbarians.' Then everybody sat down."

Maivia said he plans to make a South Seas wrestling tour about every other month.

The tours, first of their kind in sports history, will start in Honolulu, go to Hilo, then American Samoa, Western Samoa and Tonga. South Pacific Airlines is sponsoring the tours, he said.

Maivia said he hopes to add Guam, Saipan, Fiji, Nauru, New Caledonia and New Zealand to the itinerary.

He said he is already sending tapes of his Saturday afternoon wrestling show on television to these islands so they are now linked to Hawaii through wrestling.

"Wrestling is a Polynesian sport," he said. "It is very popular on all the islands. I am proud to be the Polynesian to bring wrestling to the South Pacific."

Maivia has held many of the world's wrestling titles at one time or another during a 20-year career in the ring.

He said he grew up in Western Samoa and was educated in New Zealand where he began wrestling.

Obituaries

Peter Maivia

Funeral services will be held at 1 p.m. Friday at Borthwick Mortuary for Samoan High Chief Peter F. Maivia, 45, of 1617 Kapiolani Blvd., a well-known professional wrestler and wrestling promoter, who died Sunday in Kuakini Hospital.

Friends may call at the mortuary from 6 to 9 p.m. tomorrow and after 8 a.m. Friday.

Burial will be in Diamond Head Memorial Park.

Chief Maivia was president and founder of National Wrestling Alliance Polynesian Pro Wrestling Promotions. He was born in Western Samoa and began his wrestling career in New Zealand. He later wrestled all over the United States, in the Far East and in Europe, and had won several titles. Most recently, he was promoting wrestling matches in Hawaii and the South Pacific.

Through his wrestling reputation, he was picked to play a fight scene in the James Bond movie "You Only Live Twice," filmed in England.

Gus Hannemann, a leader in the Samoan community here, said, "His death is a great loss not only to the professional wrestling world, but even a greater loss to Samoans in the community."

"He was truly a giant," Hannemann said.

He is survived by his wife, Ofelia; a daughter, Mrs. Rocky (Ata) Johnson of Florida; and one grandchild.

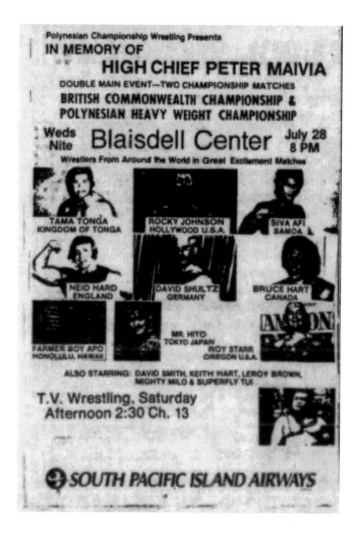

1983

Wrestling starts in 1983 in March. This is a total restart. Lia Maivia is now in charge and has hired Lars Anderson as her booker.

Professional wrestling scheduled at civic

Polynesian Promotions is returning to Hilo for a professional wrestling card at 8 p.m. Saturday at Hilo Civic Auditorium.

The main event will feature Lars Anderson against Sifa Afi a "Samoan Street Fight." The rules will be much the same as those which, in other parts of the world, are referred to as "Lumberjack Rules," "Suicide Brawls," "All-in Battles," and other names that really add up to the same thing—"No Rules At All."

The semifinal is a non title tag team match featuring Hawaii champions, Farmer Boy Ipo and Lee Roy Brown against Bruiser Stevens and Ripper Collins. The match will be two-out-of-three falls, with a one hour time limit.

The midgets are also returning. Mean Little Kevin will face Coconut Willie in a one fall 20 minute match.

Opening matches will pit Mighty Milo against Tony Hall of New Mexico in a one fall, 30-minute bout, and Magnificent Mandingo against Super Fly Dewey in a one fall, 20-minute scrap.

Lia Maivia, widow of the late High Chief Peter Maivia, is credited in bringing the sport back here.

All matches are sanctioned by the National Wrestling Association of Hawaii.

Tickets are $4, $5 and $6. Children under 12 will be admitted at half price.

The cards are filled with Polynesian wrestlers like Farmer Boy Ipo, Leroy Brown (That's Polynesian Leroy Brown), Superfly Tui, Super Samoan Sakalia, Mighty Milo, Super Fly Tui Selinga, and more. More recognizable names that did appear include Scott Casey, Tully Blanchard twice, and Tor Kamata. This was a total reorganization of local wrestlers who had just been trained.

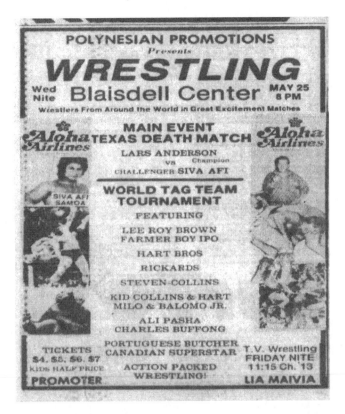

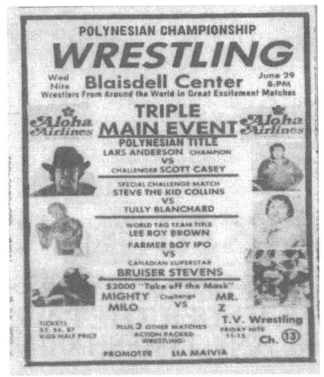

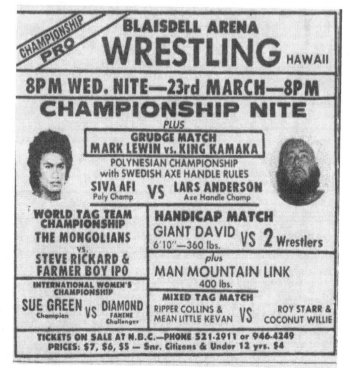

1984

1984 has a regular slate of cards for the entire year. January 27th looks to be the first card of the year. Jay Youngblood is the biggest name, and he goes to a no-contest with Superfly Tui. Lars Anderson beat Leroy Brown, and rookie Ritchie Magnett made his debut.

Pro wrestling at civic Sunday

Polynesian championship professional wrestling returns here Sunday night with a big card lined up at Afook Chinen Civic Auditorium. The first of five matches will start at 7 p.m.

Lars Anderson of Minnesota, the current Polynesian heavyweight champion, will defend his title against King Tor Kamaka of Hawaii.

In a world class grudge match, Jay Youngblood, shareholder of the N.W.A. world tag team championship belt, meets The Great Kabuki.

A two - out - of - three falls semifinal pits Farmer Boy Ipo and Roy Starr of Oregon.

In a special featured match, Sakalia of Hilo goes up against Mad Dog Vachone of Algeria.

The one-fall opening bout will see Mighty Milo of Hawaii take on Oregon's Richie Magnett.

Advanced tickets are available at Na Pua O Kahee, Da Store on Kilauea, or by calling Gerry at 935-1384. Prices are $5 for reserved seats, $4 for general admission, and $3 for children 12 and under and senior citizens.

Polynesian wrestling in Hawaii is promoted by Lia Maivia.

The next card is February 25th, and Lars Anderson beat Mad Dog Vachon by DQ in the main event. Farmer Boy Ipo beat Roy Starr. (Ok, I found a YouTube video of a match between these two. You should find it. Ipo went to the ropes, which were too saggy and would not support his weight, so he went for a bottom rope splash. Both were very green).

On March 10th, Lars Anderson beat Robert Toronto. I was able to find a few lines on Robert Toronto. He was a Viet Nam Vet, and it said at times he legitimately lost his temper in his matches.

Ritchie Magnett was 19 years old here in 1984. He ended up being one of the most respected veterans in the NW. A very quiet, standup guy was getting his initial training in Hawaii.

Hoagie Young was a good-looking youngster who owned his own gym. He was trained in Hawaii by Lars Anderson and Ritchie Magnett. He had done some modeling work since he had a Tarzan look about him. After about a year, he passed away after a night of heavy partying. It was revealed that he had a heart condition that, on top of steroid use and partying, led to his death.

June 29th was a pretty big card that featured out-of-town talent. Kevin Von Erich beat Michael Hayes, Seigi Sakaguchi beat Bad News Allen on DQ, Tatsumi Fujinami beat Rip Oliver, and Lars Anderson beat Roy Starr to win the Hawaiian title.

On August 16th, Lars Anderson and Seigi Sakaguchi beat Superfly Tui and Super Samoan Sakalia to win the tag titles. Kevin Von Erich beat Michael Hayes in the other main event match.

On October 3rd, the promotion amped up the outside talent. Don Muraco returned to the Islands for a no-contest with Mark Lewin. Superfly Tui and Super Samoan Sakalia beat Lars Anderson and Seiji Sakaguchi to regain the tag titles. Siva Afi beat Bad News Allan on DQ, Kerry Von Erich beat Missing Link, Rocky Johnson beat Masked Superstar on DQ, plus all the regulars for a massive card.

November 14th saw Terry Gordy beat Killer Kahn on DQ, Lars Anderson beat Mark Lewin on DQ, and Don Muraco beat Kevin Sullivan on DQ. Interesting booking in that all the top three matches had a DQ finish.

On December 19th, the size of the cards expanded to 29 wrestlers on the card, including Andre The Giant, who won a battle royal. Talent that was flown in saw Jimmy Snuka beat Tiger Toguchi (Kim Duk), Don Muraco beat Bad News Allen, Siva Afi and Lars Anderson beat Kevin Sullivan and Mark Lewin, Kevin Von Erich beat Chris Adams, and Seiji Sakaguchi and Tatsumi Fujinami beat Super Samoan Sakalia and Superfly Tui.

1984 Wrestling Ads & Pictures

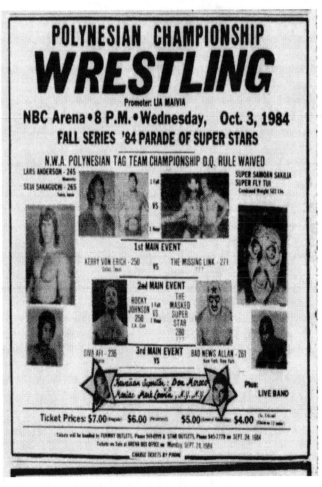

Blaisdell Wrestling Card Will Honor Peter Maivia

A Polynesian Championship Wrestling extravaganza dedicated to the memory of Peter Maivia, the late promoter of professional wrestling in Hawaii, is scheduled for Wednesday, Dec. 19, at the Blaisdell Arena.

Thirty-one pros, including legendary Andre The Giant, have agreed to appear on the card, billed as an "International Tribute to High Chief Peter Maivia" and promoted by his widow, Lia.

Other prominent names include Kevin Von Erich of Dallas; Hawaii's Don Muraco, a regular on New York's Madison Square Garden shows, and Superfly Snuka of Fiji.

There will be 11 bouts, including a 20-man battle royal and a "Tribute Match" pitting the tag team of Siva Afi (Samoa) and Lars Anderson (Minnesota) against the tandem of Mark Lewin (New York) and Kevin Sullivan (Boston).

The opening match is scheduled for 8 p.m. Tickets are priced at $8 (ringside), $7 (reserved), $6 (general admission) and $4 (senior citizens and children 12-and-under. They are on sale at the Blaisdell box office and at Funway (949-6999) and Star (945-7770) outlets.

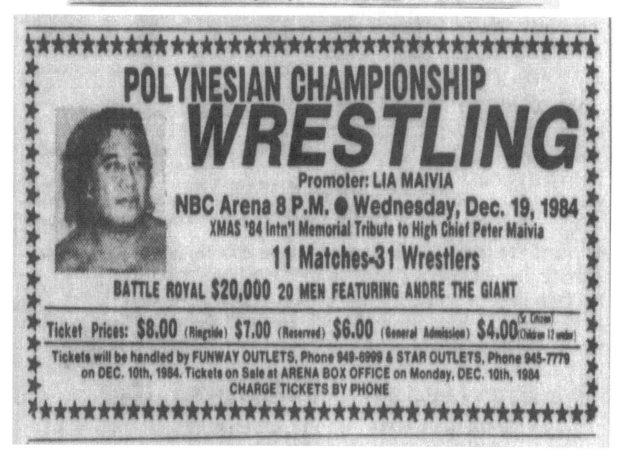

360

1985

It now appears that the shows are monthly, with cards with big names on them, but are they really desirable to the crowds? I am not sure about the angles that made Ed Francis' promotion so viable and cards that fans don't dare miss. I don't think that feeling exists because the fans are not invested in the wrestlers.

February 13th saw Ric Flair go to a draw with Kerry Von Erich, Antonio Inoki beat Hacksaw Higgins, Lars Anderson and Siva Afi beat Mark Lewin and Kevin Sullivan, and Tatsumi Fujinami beat Super Strong Machine.

During this time, Doug Wulf, a fan from Albany, Oregon, now living in Honolulu, came to the matches. Used to the matches in Oregon, he arrived an hour early. He was greeted by Lia Maivia herself, and they visited as they waited for the matches to start. She invited him to lunch.

Lia Maivia and Lars Anderson were at lunch. They visited and talked about wrestling. They asked Wulf if he would like to invest in the promotion. He paid $2,500 and would work unpaid for one year for the promotion. At the end of the year, he would start getting paid. Wulf said he worked on publicity, writing magazine articles, doing a lot of homework work, and even became a ref for a while. He was also the commissioner to make matches and lay down rules. At the end of the year, Wulf was still rarely paid, and he had to sue. Despite winning, he did not collect, and then threats came, and it was time for Wulf and his wife to leave the Islands. Wulf has some writing available on Kayfabe Memories in the stories section.

The March 27th show saw Ricky and Rocky Johnson beat Adrian Adonis and Dick Murdoch, who were just about to become WWF tag champs. Siva Afi beat Mark Lewin, Lars Anderson beat Kevin Sullivan, and Bad News Allan beat Strong Machine I.

The April show on the 17th saw Alexis Smirnoff beat Samoan 3 on DQ, Siva Afi beat Buck Robley, and Angelo Mosca Sr and Lars Anderson beat Kevin Sullivan and Mark Lewin.

May 22nd top matches saw Bruiser Brody, Angelo Mosca, and Siva Afi beat Buck Robley, Kevin Sullivan, and Mark Lewin in a barbed wire match. Bad News Allen beat Lars Anderson for the Polynesian Pacific title. Lynn Denton & Tony Anthony (The Grapplers and/or The Dirty White Boys) went to a double DQ with Ricky and Rocky Johnson.

The June show saw Lars Anderson beat Bad News Allen on DQ, Ricky and Rocky Johnson beat The Dirty White Boys, Angelo Mosca beat Mark Lewin on DQ in a stretcher match, and Siva Afi beat Kevin Sullivan in a blindfold match. Bruiser Brody beat Buck Robley in a Texas Death Match, and Alexis Smirnoff beat Sam Anoia in a Russian Chain match.

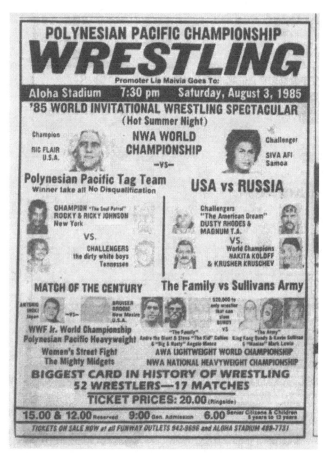

This brings us to A Hot Summer Night - the most successful night of wrestling in Hawaii's history. It was held at Aloha Stadium in Honolulu. It was reported to draw 15,000, which made a gross gate of over $100,000. Another report had attendance at 12,533. While this show drew very well, expenses were high, including rent for the Stadium and 44 wrestlers who appeared on the card. These included Andre, Ric Flair, Bruiser Brody, Antonio Inoki, and Dusty Rhodes. One has to wonder how profitable this show was.

The main matches saw Ric Flair ddq Siva Afi for the NWA World title and Antonio Inoki dcor Bruiser Brody in a match that was one of the hottest feuds in the world at the time.

Ricky and Rocky Johnson beat The Dirty White Boys to win the Polynesian Pacific tag titles, Andre The Giant, Angelo Mosca, and Steve Collins beat King Kong Bundy, Mark Lewin, and Kevin Sullivan, Dusty Rhodes and Magnum TA beat Nikita Koloff and Krusher Khrushchev. Other matches featured Jimmy Snuka, Tatsumi Fujinami, Manny Fernandez, Seiji Sakaguchi, and many others.

Speculation was that New Japan helped sponsor this show, at least with payoffs to their wrestlers.

The next listed result isn't until November, so it is unclear if there was a break or if we don't have results from August until November.

The highlights of the November 13th show saw Ricky and Rocky Johnson beat Scott and Bill Irwin, Lars Anderson beat Kevin Sullivan, Siva Afi beat The Russian Exterminator, and Jerry Lawler beat Anoaro Atisanoe.

On December 18th, the last card of the year saw Andre The Giant team with Antonio Inoki to beat The Deaton Brothers. Lars Anderson went to a no-contest with Bad News Allen, Rocky and Ricky Johnson went to a draw with Kevin Sullivan and Bob Roop. Jimmy Snuka won a battle royal.

1985 Wrestling Ads & Pictures

Hot, Heavy Wrestling at Stadium

By Dave Reardon
Star-Bulletin Writer

Lia Maivia

Sports Illustrated devoted half an issue to it recently. It's scheduled to dominate one "Saturday Night Live" show each month this fall. It has been embraced by college students and hard hats, as well as celebrities and rock groups making videos for MTV.

It's professional wrestling, and it's hot.

Polynesian Pacific promoter Lia Maivia likes it hot, as in "Hot Summer Night." That's the billing for her 1985 World Invitational Wrestling Spectacular. The mammoth card includes more than 15 fights tomorrow night at Aloha Stadium, beginning at 7:30.

Hulk Hogan, Cyndi Lauper and Sargeant Slaughter won't be there, but there will be something for every pro wrestling fan.

A WORLD championship will be at stake, with Ric Flair defending his title against Siva Afi. There also will be a bout between "The Mighty Midgets" (Pancho Boy and Mean Little Kevin) and a "Women's Street Fight" pits Debbie Combs against The Fallen Angel.

Tag team matches include "The Soul Patrol" (Ricky and Rocky Johnson of New York) against Tennessee's "Dirty White Boys."

Dusty Rhodes, Andre the Giant and Adrian Adonis are three of the card's bigger names.

Rhodes, aka "The American Dream," teams with Magnum T.A. against Nakita Koloff and Krusher Kruschev in a battle that could start World War III. Polynesian Pacific's promotional poster bills it as "USA vs. Russia."

ANDRE THE GIANT leads a trio that takes on King Kong Bundy, Kevin Sullivan and "Maniac" Marc Lewin. If either Andre or teammates Steve "The Kid" Collins and "Big and Nasty" Angelo Mosca can body-slam the humongous Bundy, that wrestler will earn a $20,000 bonus.

Ticket prices range from $6 for senior citizens and children to $20 for ringside. General admission is $9, and tickets are available at Funway outlets and Aloha Stadium.

Wrestling card tonight

Fifty-two professional wrestlers will participate in a 17-match show tonight at Aloha Stadium. The first bout begins at 7:30.

The main event will be a match between champion Ric Flair and Siva Afi for the National Wrestling Alliance world title. There will be five other championship matches.

Also appearing will be such wrestlers as Andre the Giant, Antonio Inoki, Jimmy "Superfly" Snuka, King Kong Bundy, Dusty Rhodes, The Fallen Angel and Mean Little Kevin.

A ring has been set up in the infield, directly over home plate, and surrounded by approximately 1,000 seats. Reserved and general admission seating will be in the grandstand and along both baselines.

Tickets are $20 (ringside), $15 and $12 (reserved), $9 (general admission) and $6 (senior citizens and children ages 5 to 12). Parking is $2.

The matches:

Ric Flair vs. Siva Afi for NWA world championship; Lars Anderson vs. Bad News Allen for Polynesian Pacific heavyweight championship; The Soul Patrol vs. The Dirty White Boys for Polynesian Pacific tag team championship; The Cobra vs. Super Fly Tui for WWF junior world championship; Black Bart vs. Manny Fernandez for NWA national heavyweight championship; Steve Regal vs. Mighty Milo for AWA lightweight championship; Dusty Rhodes and Magnum T.A. vs. Nikita Koloff and Krusher Kruschev; Jimmy "Superfly" Snuka vs. Larry Sharp; Andre the Giant, Steve Collins and Angelo Mosca vs. King Kong Bundy, Kevin Sullivan and "Maniac" Mark Lewin; Kengo Kimura and Tatsumi Fujinami vs. Gene Lewis and Gary Fulton: The Samoan Connection vs. The Texas Outlaws; Antonio Inoki vs. Bruiser Brodie; Seiji Sakaguchi vs. Matt Borne; The Tonga Kid, Sam Anoai and Sika & Afa vs. Dick Murdock, Adrian Adonis, Royce Starr and Alexis Smirnoff; Richie Magnett vs. Gypsy Joe; Pancho Boy vs. Mean Little Kevin; Debbie Combs vs. The Fallen Angel.

Names have changed, but wrestling still grips crowd

By Dave Koga
Advertiser Staff Writer

An aunt who loved the sight of men beating each other senseless took me to my first professional wrestling match when I was 8 or 9.

It was, as King Ripper Collins would have put it, "at Kakapaka gym, over on the island of Kwai."

I believe the main event was a grudge match between Collins and Gentleman Jim Hady, but I can't be sure. Besides, it doesn't really matter. Names, after all, are the only things that change in this game.

What mattered — at least to my mother, who had feared the worst from the moment my aunt mentioned wrestling — was that the daily after-school death matches began in my back yard shortly thereafter.

* * *

Richie Magnett was in a foul mood — and who could blame him?

Why, not more than a minute earlier, he had been yanked about the ring by his beard, slugged in the chops while gripped in a headlock, raked across the eyes, kicked in the midsection, elbowed in the Adam's apple, kneed in the privates, and then picked up and hurled to the mat.

You and I might have packed it in at that point, or at least been in extreme pain, but Magnett clearly was made of sterner stuff.

And, ah, the tables were turned now.

Gypsy Joe, Magnett's mean-spirited opponent, was on his knees in a corner, his spine pressed against the turnbuckle, his hands pressed together in a plea for mercy.

No, no, no, no, said Joe.

Yes, yes, yes, yes, said the fans.

Magnett, who had tried to fight the clean fight until now, lashed out with an open-handed slap to the side of Joe's neck. He followed with another slap, and another, and another, and yet another.

The gypsy's head snapped back and forth like a speed bag, and the crowd howled its approval.

It was, I thought, like watching Mighty Mouse punching out Oil Can Harry, Popeye getting physical with Bluto, or Moe moldering Curly.

Well . . . maybe not exactly that.

There was no horn beep for a smash to the nose. No kettle-drum boom for a hook to the belly. No cowbell clang when a head was driven into a ring post. And no chirping birds when Gypsy Joe's eyes rolled and he teetered on his heels before crashing face first to the canvas.

But I guess you can't have everything.

Besides, the fans loved it. And, in the last analysis, I suppose that's all that matters.

About 15,000 people, some of whom had paid as much as $20 for a ticket, turned out to watch four hours of professional wrestling last night at Aloha Stadium.

The repertory company assembled for the event — call them the good, the bad and the ugly — included such luminaries as "Nature Boy" Ric Flair, Andre the Giant, Antonio Inoki, The Fallen Angel, "Maniac" Mark Sullivan, Jimmy "Superfly" Snuka, King Kong Bundy, Dusty Rhodes and Angelo Mosca.

They are some of the best in this business. From gouging to strutting to leaping off the ropes, they know their stuff.

And whatever it is they do — whether it is pandering to the basest instincts of the crowd or entertaining them with physical skill and showmanship — they do it well.

The daily after-school death matches were banned in my back yard less than an hour after The Mighty Igor put the Atomic Drop on Craig the Egg and sent him home in tears.

They returned, in the Egg's back yard, a day later.

The adults should have known better, of course. Wrestling has a life of its own. It does not go away just because you want it to.

A two-count was the best they could hope to get — this or any other day.

Advertiser photo by Carl Viti

It was high-flying action during one of 17 matches in the Polynesian Pacific Championship wrestling extravaganza. A member of the Samoan Connection prepares to administer a head butt to a member of the Texas Outlaws.

1986

Jerry Lawler beat Lars Anderson to win the Pacific title on January 25th in Singapore. However, it is not sure if this is a fictional match.

This promotion took a California tour that did not draw well. 2/13 in San Jose saw Jimmy Snuka beat Buddy Wolfe, Lars Anderson beat Jerry Lawler on dq, and Rocky Johnson beat Ciclon Negro. Tatsumi Fujinami and Kengo Kimura were in the prelims filled with California Independent guys and the prelim Hawaii guys.

Doug Wulf mentioned they had toured Samoa, New Zealand, and then the LA area, which was described as ok.

Wulf also talks about Lia and Lars's conflicts. He said that the local wrestlers did not like Lars. At one point, Toronto and Fue attacked Lars and hospitalized him. Muraco hated Lars so badly that he would not use the same dressing room. Lia once challenged Wulf to shoot on Lars.

March 26th saw Super Fly Tui beat Jerry Lawler for the Pacific Polynesian title, and Lars Anderson beat former tag partner Buddy Wolfe.

They returned on 3/28 with a card that saw Tui again beat Lawler, and Buddy Wolfe beat Lars Anderson.

April 17th saw Farmer Boy Ipo and Leroy Brown win the tag titles, beating Dave Deaton and Solo. Also, Paul DeMarco beat Lars Anderson COR. About fourteen years prior, DeMarco and Anderson were World tag partners in the Bay area.

May 21st had no fly-ins, and the main event saw Lars Anderson and Ritchie Magnett go to a no-contest with the Kinipopos, and Madd Maxx won a battle royal.

June 26th saw Ric Flair return to the Islands to defend the NWA title against Sam Anoia. Flair won on dq; the Madd Maxxes won the tag titles, beating Farmer Boy Ipo and Leroy Brown. The only other flyins were Seiji Sakaguchi beating Hans Schroeder.

Stadium wrestling features barbed-wire ring

A six-man tag-team match in a barbed-wire ring will highlight Hot Summer Night II, the second annual World Invitational Wrestling Spectacular Saturday at Aloha Stadium.

Last year's event drew an estimated crowd of 15,000.

Saturday's feature match, in which the top two ropes of the ring will be replaced by barbed wire, will pit a team of Bruiser Brodie, Tommy Rich and Jeff Magruder against Maniac Mark Lewis, Kevin Sullivan and Kamalamala.

In other top matches, Lars Anderson meets Super Fly Tui in a 16-foot-high cage for the Polynesian Pacific Heavyweight title, and the Samoan Connection takes on Mad Max and Super Max Malo for the Polynesian Pacific Tag Team title.

In all, there will be 60 wrestlers competing in 20 matches, including 14 various championships.

Tickets are on sale at Aloha Stadium. Prices are $30 for ringside, $15-20 for reserved, $11 for general admission and $7 for senior citizens and children. Inquire about a military discount.

The event, which is being promoted by Lia Maivia, will also feature entertainers Al Harrington as guest announcer and Danny Kaleikini as guest referee.

The next big show was the Hot Summer Night II at Aloha Stadium. Everything that went right with the previous year went wrong with this year's show. The 5-hour show drew 1,900 for a gate of $28,000, which reportedly barely covered the venue. There was a terrible rainstorm that covered the stadium for the entire show.

The main events saw Lars Anderson beat Superfly Tui in a cage to win the Polynesian Pacific title, Bruiser Brody and Grizzly Smith beat Mark Lewin and The Sheik in a barbed wire match, Tatsumi Fujinami and Kengo Kimura beat Kendo Nagasaki and Mr. Pogo, Bad News Allan beat Alexis Smirnoff - judo match, Keiji Muto beat Jerry Grey, Kinipopos drew Keith and Owen Hart, and Uncle Elmer beat Hans Schroeder. Sixteen matches, thirty wrestlers, and many of the matches had to be rebooked because of no-shows.

The dismal outing of Hot Summer Night II forces Lia Maivia to scale back her promotion. They went from having regular shows at the Blaisdell Center to the Iilai Hotel. In two years, this promotion would fold.

MANIAC ATTACK—Maniac Mark Lewin tries to get Keith Hart's attention during the six-man tag team finale to A Hot Summer Night II, Saturday night at Aloha Stadium.—Star-Bulletin Photo by Ken Sakamoto.

'Summer Night' Was Wet, Wild

By Dave Reardon
Star-Bulletin Writer

A Hot Summer Night II, Polynesian Championship Wrestling's event of the year, was more wet than hot at a rain-drenched Aloha Stadium Saturday night.

But a fire-bug wrestler named The Sheik supplied some heat during the main event with arson in a six-man tag team match that ended with no clear winner.

Bruiser Brodie promised redemption for a "burning" of teammate Keith Hart's face.

"The history of these guys is seeing who they can put out of the ring with career-ending injuries," Brodie said of The Sheik and Maniac Mark Lewin. "Next time, Sheik, you bring the fire. You may burn me, but you'll pay for it."

Brodie's post-match comments came after a wild end to five hours of wrestling involving 60 wrestlers battling for 14 championships. About 10,000 saw it.

THE SHEIK LIT a high flame near Hart's face about five minutes into the final match, which was contested in a ring where the two top ropes where replaced with barbed wire.

When the flame went up Hart fell back, and his face was immediately covered with a towel by teammate Bruiser Brodie, as The Sheik fled from the ring and climbed a 50-foot TV tower, where he lit more flames.

Security personnel called for a nurse. But when she went to the locker room to administer first aid to Hart, she was kept out of the area by a guard who said "the wrestling doctor is taking care of him."

PHOTOGRAPHERS AND reporters were also barred from Hart's locker room.

Who "the wrestling doctor" was, wasn't quite clear.

In the co-main event, Lars Anderson took Super Fly Tui's Polynesian Pacific heavyweight championship belt in a match that was held in a locked, 16-foot steel cage.

Other matches had Antonio Inoki over Hacksaw Higgins, Chilly Bo Dilly beating Little Kevin, and Keiji Moto topping Jerry Grey.

Also, Bad News Allen beat the Kremlin Krusher and Killer Tomato felled Spicy Williams for the Hollywood Stunt Girls championship.

Ed Francis writes in his book, "The Maivia's staked their claim to promoting wrestling in Hawaii without paying any fees and essentially intimated Rickard into leaving the Islands."

Francis continues, "Not long after I'd left Hawaii, I returned on a visit. Lia Maivia called me and threatened harm to my family if I considered resurrecting our wrestling promotion business."

Doug Wulf confirms Francis's story. "When Peter died, Vince McMahon Sr told Lia he wouldn't touch her promotion. She was the only woman to have a promotion according to Lars because the "old school" didn't think they could do a good job. Later on, when we partnered with New Japan Pro Wrestling and started shows at the Blaisdell, Vince Jr told Ed Francis to come to Honolulu and take the promotion back from Lia. I walked into the office one day and Lia told me I had a good voice so I should call Ed and tell him I was going to kill him unless he left the promotion alone. Lia had called him a couple of times already. Lars said that was not the way to do it, so he called Ed. Ed told Lars that if he got one more threat, he would leave the island. A couple days later, I read that Ed was back on the East Coast helping his son with his restaurant. So I figured Lia made another threat."

Wrestling Fun at Blaisdell

Titan Sports, the folks that bring you "entertainment" wrestling, is bringing an all-star cast of World Wrestling Federation wrestlers to the Blaisdell Arena Thursday at 8 p.m.

The turnbuckle-slamming event is being billed as a classic confrontation of the Good Guys vs. the Bad Guys—but if you're a pro wrestling fan, you already know that.

Tickets are $8 to $12 and are avaiable at the Blaisdell Center box office and all Funway ticket outlets.

WWF would promote in Hawaii in July and run the Blaisdell Center. They drew 5,000 people with a main event of Bob Orton Jr beating George Steele. Not one of the male wrestlers had ever worked for a Hawaiian promotion prior to this show.

Only two cards are remaining for 1986.

On 8/20, Super Fly Tui regained the title, beating Lars Anderson.

On November 19th, mostly all locals, Dirty White Boy beat The Medic, who is the only outsider.

Over the next two years, there are records of six cards. The last card listed looks like a Florida or WCW-based card. There are no local Hawaiian or Samoan wrestlers, and it is primarily a crew that looks like they were from Florida. It was a great card featuring Dory and Terry Funk going to a ddq with Dick Slater and Danny Spivey, Stan Hansen and Terry Gordy beating Michael Hayes and Tommy Rich. Jerry Blackwell won a battle royal. Also on the card were the Nasty Boys, Mike Graham, Johnny Ace, Scotty The Body, The Great Kabuki, and more.

Tales From the Territories, the wrestling documentary series, had an episode on wrestling from Hawaii. Guests were Downtown Bruno, Lars Anderson, Kevin Sullivan, and Rocky Iaukea.

The show detailed some of the promotion's last gasps. Lars Anderson explained that Dunbar Wakayama started booking mainland wrestlers, and he received a Lia-directed phone call from referee Sam Samson that threatened Wakayama to scare him away. Wakayama took his story to the FBI, where he helped set up a sting against Lia and Anderson for extortion and threats. Anderson finished the story with the not-guilty verdict that was delivered. All three involved, including Lia Maivia, were acquitted.

Lia Maivia and Polynesian Pro Wrestling Legal Battle

After Peter Maivia passed away, his wife Lia took over running the business and became the NWA's only female promoter. Despite challenges from other groups trying to take advantage of Maivia's death, Polynesian Pro Wrestling, or P.P.W., stayed as the top wrestling promotion in Hawaii under Lia's leadership. One of the highlights was the "A Hot Summer Night" event on August 3, 1985, which drew over 20,000 fans, setting a new record for attendance in Hawaii.

However, maintaining success was tough. Lia faced the same problems as previous promoters. There were only a few big cities in Hawaii where wrestling could be profitable, and bringing in top wrestlers from the mainland was expensive. Without regular visits from big stars, attendance dropped. Competition from other wrestling organizations like WWF, J.C.P., AWA, UWF, and World Class made things even harder.

P.P.W. got caught up in a costly lawsuit from one of its rivals. Though Lia and her team were eventually cleared of wrongdoing in court in 1989, the legal battle took its toll. By then, the damage was done, and NWA Polynesian Pro Wrestling had to shut down in 1988.

The lawsuit included Lia Maivia, Ati So'o, and Larry Heiniemi (aka Lars Anderson). The lawsuit alleged physical threats and extortion. The FBI recorded conversations and those are detailed in the news clippings attached. A jury found all three defendants not guilty.

Lia Maivia
The Lady Behind Hawaii's Pro Wrestling Revival

By Jim Easterwood
Star-Bulletin Writer

Lia Maivia, the only woman ever to promote professional wrestling in the United States, has earned the respect of those who participate in the sport.

"They know I can get into the ring if I have to," said Lia, who began promoting after her husband, Peter, died two years ago.

Peter Maivia, a former wrestler, brought the sport back to Hawaii about eight years ago with hopes of reviving the success Ed Francis' promotions had enjoyed in the 1960s.

Interest began to fade, however, with the closing of the old Civic Auditorium on King Street, which featured once-a-week wrestling shows. Francis found it too expensive to stage once-a-week cards at Blaisdell Arena and soon pulled up stakes. He returned from Portland a few years later and gave it another shot but pulled out for good when a convenient, low-rent site could not be found for regular shows.

FOR PETER MAIVIA, promoting here was an uphill battle. Unlike Francis, he didn't have a TV contract with one of the major stations to work with. His shows at Bloch Arena didn't draw well and Maivia felt it was because Pearl Harbor was out of the way for wrestling fans.

Things have turned for the better in recent months. Polynesian Championship Wrestling, using wrestlers who appear regularly on national TV wrestling shows as well as local talent, is generating interest again and doing good business for its once-a-month cards at Blaisdell Arena. Average attendance for the five shows Lia has promoted is 6,000.

"I'm trying to carry out (Peter's) dream," Lia said. "I traveled with him for 20 years

when he was a professional wrestler. We lived in New Zealand, France, England and Tokyo before settling down in Hawaii (eight years ago)."

Her ticket prices are from $4 general admission to $9 ringside.

"THE WRESTLERS tell me the prices are way too low," said Lia. "But I would rather see a lot of people there. If I lose money, I just eat coconut the next day. I want to appeal to families."

Gus Hannemann, a close friend of Lia and Peter, said the pro wrestlers have a lot of respect for Lia.

"I've seen her in action . . . she's a tough lady," said Hannemann. "She reminds people of Peter. She's not a fragile person and she commands respect. And you have to be tough in this business."

"I've seen her in action . . . she's a tough lady. She reminds people of Peter. She's not a fragile person and she commands respect. And you have to be tough in this business." —Gus Hannemann on wrestling promoter Lia Maivia, who is pictured with her late husband, Peter Maivia.

She has a scar on her leg to remind her of a 1963 brawl in Glasgow, Scotland.

"Peter was wrestling a Scot named Ian Campbell and people were yelling some bad things things like 'hey, go home Samoan, you have no shoes and you eat coconuts.' Those things hurt my pride," Lia recalled. "So I stood up and hit one guy and he pulled a knife and cut my leg. It took 12 stitches to close the wound. Peter saw what was happening and got into it. I wound up going to the hospital."

Tomorrow night's show will feature a National Wrestling Alliance world heavyweight championship match between Ric Flair, the champion, and Kerry Von Erich. Those two wrestlers recently headlined a stadium card in Texas that drew 50,000.

Pro wrestling figures face trial

By Ken Kobayashi
Advertiser Courts Writer

A man charged with extorting a wrestling promoter wasn't the caller who left a threatening message on a telephone answering machine, a defense attorney said yesterday in the opening of a federal court trial that will cover the history and inner workings of professional wrestling promotions in Hawaii.

Both the defense and the prosecution in the extortion trial of wrestling figures Lia Maivia, Larry Heiniemi and Ati So'o agreed that leaving the recorded message was an inane move by the caller.

But beyond that, the two sides disagreed on the identity of the caller and gave conflicting accounts on whether the promoter, John R. Wakayama, also known as Dunbar Wakayama, was a victim of extortion or a manipulator who wanted to throw his competitors out of business.

Maivia, 58, is president of the World Pacific Wrestling Association, a successor to the organization that has promoted professional wrestling here for years. Heiniemi, 50, the association's secretary-treasurer, is also known under his professional wrestling name, Lars Anderson. So'o, 47, a salesman, is the vice president.

Assistant U.S. Attorney Michael Burke told the jury in his opening statements that Wakayama found himself threatened when he decided to put on his own professional wrestling match at the Blaisdell Arena in November last year without engaging the services of the defendants.

Wakayama worked with promoter Tom Moffatt and others, including Brian Gallagher, a public relations writer, to write the scripts for the wrestling show, Burke said the shows are "scripted" just the same as any television program.

According to Burke, Wakayama became the target of a conspiracy by the three defendants to extort $5,000 from him in "tribute money."

Burke portrayed Maivia as a woman who demanded money from anyone putting on a professional wrestling match here, billing herself as "Hawaii's wrestling promoter."

He said Wakayama received the threatening call on his business phone recorder in October and recognized the voice as belonging to So'o. The call, riddled with expletives, tells Wakayama to stay out of the wrestling business and mentions a member of his family.

So'o's name was later repeatedly mentioned by Maivia when she and Heiniemi met with Wakayama to demand the money, Burke said.

The defense attorneys, however, characterized the dispute between Wakayama and Maivia as a "business" dispute and said Wakayama saw the threatening phone call as an opportunity to force Maivia and her associates out of business.

Wakayama also saw the threat as a way to explain away the losses that he knew would be incurred by his wrestling promotion, the defense attorneys said. The wrestling show eventually lost $66,000, according to William Brady, Maivia's attorney.

Brady said Maivia is a well-respected leader in the wrestling community who was simply trying to ensure jobs for the "local wrestlers."

He said in the professional wrestling business, the local promoters get a percentage of the gate or a flat fee for supplying wrestlers for matches.

Maivia knew Wakayama was afraid, but thought it was a general fear because Wakayama had angered "a lot of local boys" by bringing in outsiders for his wrestling show.

So'o's attorney, Brook Hart, told the jury that he will present an expert who matched the voice on the taped call with samples of So'o's voice and concluded that they aren't the same.

The expert relied on spectograms, which analyzes the energy levels from voices, according to Hart.

Hart said his client never threatened Wakayama and never made that phone call, but indicated So'o's defense will be at odds with the defenses raised by the co-defendants.

He said Maivia told So'o that the call to Wakayama was made by Faasamoa Mausali, a wrestling referee also known as Sam Samson.

But "unfortunately," Maivia, without So'o's knowledge, used So'o's name in trying to get money from Wakayama, Hart said.

Burke said the science of voice identification through spectograms is under "serious question," but said the prosecution may call its own expert to say that So'o's voice is probably the one on the tape.

Mausali, who will be called by the prosecution, and So'o are both expected to testify.

3 wrestling promoters are accused of extortion

☐ The FBI says Lia Maivia and two aides also threatened to harm a matchmaker

By Lee Catterall
Star-Bulletin

Prominent Honolulu wrestling promoter Lia Maivia and two associates are being accused by federal authorities of extorting money from a man trying to stage a wrestling match at the Blaisdell Arena next week.

Lia Maivia, 53, president of the World Pacific Wrestling Association, and the associates are charged with extorting $1,800 in expectation of getting $3,200 the next day from John R. Wakayama for allowing the Pacific Area Conference to stage a match at Blaisdell next Tuesday.

Maivia; Ati So'o, the association's vice president; and Larry Heiniemi, 40, its secretary-treasurer, were ordered held without bail yesterday by federal Magistrate Daryl Conklin. A continuation of their bail hearing is scheduled Monday.

Heiniemi also is known as Lars Anderson, the name he has used as a professional wrestler.

If convicted of the charges, the three would face maximum prison terms of 20 years.

FBI agent Joseph F. Holtslag Jr. said in an affidavit that the three defendants demanded a $5,000 "tribute" from Wakayama and said they received similar "tributes" from other promoters.

Holtslag said Wakayama was threatened with violence against him and his two children. A specific threat was made against Wakayama's 14-year-old son.

Maivia also indicated that "people die in this business," and that her husband had been killed because of his involvement in the wrestling business.

In fact, Samoan High Chief Peter Maivia, her husband, died of cancer in 1982.

Lia Maivia

According to the affidavit, Maivia and Heiniemi told Wakayama at an Oct. 24 meeting at the Pagoda Restaurant that he would have to pay the "tribute" and include two wrestlers sponsored by Maivia in her match.

The affidavit also alleges that Wakayama was told he would have to rent a wrestling ring for $1,100 and buy three commercials on Maivia's regular Saturday morning television show for $450.

The following day, So'o left a message on Wakayama's business telephone, allegedly used profanities and made the threats against Wakayama and his son and daughter, according to the FBI affidavit.

Wakayama, fearing for his family, canceled an Oct. 30 television commercial promoting the match and almost canceled the match, the affidavit says.

He then went to the FBI, agreed to cooperate in taping subsequent meetings with the Maivia group.

Assistant U.S. Attorney Les Osborne said the FBI tape-recorded a meeting later that day that included Wakayama, Maivia and Heiniemi at Kengo's Restaurant on Kapiolani Boulevard and videotaped a meeting among the three immediately afterward at Wakayama's office.

At the restaurant, according to the affidavit, Maivia and Heiniemi again made the demand for the $5,000 "tribute."

When Wakayama expressed fear and asked what he could do to save himself, Maivia responded, "Pay," it says.

In the videotaped meeting at Wakayama's office, Maivia allegedly said So'o was the kind of person who goes "bang, bang," and made shooting gestures.

Osborne said Wakayama paid Maivia and Heiniemi $1,800 in cash provided by the FBI and promised to pay $3,200 the next day.

Maivia and Heiniemi were arrested after leaving the office, and So'o was arrested later that evening at his home.

Maivia's husband, whose full name was Fanene Leifi Pita Maivia, purchased the Ed Francis promotions in 1979, and was president and founder of the National Wrestling Alliance Polynesian Pro Wrestling.

Lia Maivia assumed control of her husband's business following his death.

"I'm trying to carry out his dream," she said in a 1985 interview. "I traveled with him for 20 years when he was a professional wrestler.

Lia Maivia has told of her involvement in a 1963 brawl in Glasgow, Scotland.

After being insulted by a Scot, she said, "I stood up and hit one guy, and he pulled a knife and cut my leg. It took 12 stitches to close the wound."

---

3 accused of extortion freed on $20,000 bonds

A federal magistrate has allowed Honolulu wrestling promoter Lia Maivia and two associates to be freed on bail while facing charges that they extorted money from a man trying to stage a wrestling match.

Magistrate Daryl Conklin yesterday allowed Maivia, Ati So'o and Larry Heiniemi freed on $20,000 signature bonds.

Maivia, 53, president of the World Pacific Wrestling Association, is accused of extorting $5,000 from Jon R. Wakayama last month for allowing Wakayama's Pacific Area Conference to stage a match at Blaisdell, scheduled for tonight. So'o is the association's vice president and Heiniemi, known under his wrestling name as Lars Anderson, is its secretary-treasurer.

Reported by Star-Bulletin staff

HAWAII

Friday, October 13, 1989 ■ Star-Bulletin ●

- ■ Big wave knocks 15 off tour boat **A-4**
- ■ Image consultant warns Waikiki **A-7**
- ■ Builder backs mixed-income housing **A-14**

Court wrestles with lively extortion case

☐ **Lia Maivia faces charges of trying to put the arm on an isle promoter for $5,000**

By Charles Memminger
Star-Bulletin

The wild world of professional wrestling came to Honolulu yesterday, but the venue was a federal courtroom, not a wrestling ring.

In one corner was Lia Maivia, the "first lady of Hawaii wrestling," charged with trying to extort $5,000 from local wrestling promoter Dunbar Wakayama. In another corner was Larry Heiniemi, known in the wrestling world as the stern-faced Lars Anderson. In another corner was Maivia's former business partner Ati So'o, who claims she threw his name around in order to get money from Wakayama.

In yet another corner was Michael Burke, assistant U.S. attorney who is prosecuting the case.

Presiding over the legal battle was U.S. Judge Alan Kay and a jury of 12.

Unlike professional wrestling matches, which are scripted and winners picked beforehand, the outcome of this trial is unknown.

What is known is that sparks will fly before it comes to a close, if the opening remarks were any indication.

For one thing, So'o's attorney, Brook Hart, wants to put as much distance as possible between his client and the other defendants.

Hart told the jury that Maivia used his client's name without his knowledge in an effort to squeeze money out of Wakayama, who wanted to put on a wrestling show.

There is also no love lost between So'o and Heiniemi, Hart told the jury. When he mentioned a dispute that So'o and Heiniemi once got in, Heiniemi glared at So'o, and his attorney had to put a hand on Heiniemi's shoulder to calm him down.

The question is: Did Maivia, with the help of So'o and Heiniemi, try to extort money from Wakayama, or was she merely trying to get some local wrestlers on the program Wakayama was promoting and collect "booking" fees?

Burke told the jury in his opening remarks that Maivia had become upset when the World Wrestling Federation held a show in Hawaii in 1986.

Maivia considered herself the head of wrestling in Hawaii since the death of her husband, another well-known promoter, even though she had no exclusive contract with anyone as the island's sole wrestling promoter.

Burke referred to the WWF as the "Hulk Hogan Federation" because Hogan is one of the superstars who wrestle in that organization.

The WWF extravaganza was promoted in Hawaii by Tom Moffatt, who is better known for his concert promotions.

In 1988, Wakayama teamed with Moffatt and Florida wrestlers to put on a show in Hawaii. When Maivia found out, she was upset again, Burke said.

In October 1988, Maivia met with

Lia Maivia

Larry Heiniemi aka Lars Anderson

Wakayama and told him that she wanted two of her wrestlers on the program, Burke said. But the program already had been filled, and Wakayama told her no.

It was then that things began to get hot, according to the government. Maivia allegedly told Wakayama that So'o, who is large and heavy-set, wanted to talk to him.

Wakayama said he received a message on his telephone answering machine from So'o in which So'o threatened Wakayama's son.

Wakayama agreed to meet again with Maivia at which time she asked for a $5,000 "tribute" so he could stage the match, Burke said.

Wakayama eventually went to the FBI, and agents secretly taped conversations in which the alleged payments were discussed.

Maivia's attorney, Bill Brady, told the jury the government is off base in this case. Maivia, he said, was only trying to represent the interests of local wrestlers in her discussions with Wakayama. The money discussed was not extortion, but booking fees, he said.

"All wrestlers on this island look up to her," he said. "They call her mama."

He said Wakayama is merely trying to blame Maivia for the loss of $66,000 on his program.

"The government is simply wrong," he said. "They've been conned by the victim."

Hart said the only thing tying his client to the case is an answering machine tape recording. And that is not even his client's voice, he said.

He plans to bring in a voice analyst to prove it.

Hart described So'o as a University of Hawaii graduate who is married and has three children. So'o, who works as salesman of industrial solvents, formed World Pacific Wrestling Association with Maivia, but owned only 10 percent of the company.

Hart read the text of the answering machine tape, which included graphic profanity and sexual threats against Wakayama's son.

"He's not the kind of guy who would do that," Hart said of So'o. "And he didn't do it."

Instead, the defense contends a local wrestling referee named Sam Samson, angered that Wakayama was promoting an all-out-of-state program, made the call.

But Hart said Maivia did apparently use So'o's name in trying to get money from Wakayama.

After they were arrested, Maivia told So'o, "You're not the voice on the tape."

3 acquitted of wrestling extortion
Identity of threatening caller unclear to jury

By Ken Kobayashi
Advertiser Courts Writer

A federal jury yesterday acquitted wrestling promoter Lia Maivia and two men of all charges accusing them of extorting a man trying set up his own wrestling business in Hawaii last year.

Maivia, 57; her business partner Ati So'o, 47, and Larry Heiniemi, 50, a professional wrestler also known as Lars Anderson, were charged with extorting newcomer promoter John R. "Dunbar" Wakayama, 43, with a threatening phone call in October last year and demands of $5,000.

The jury, however, did not believe that So'o was the caller who left the threatening message on Wakayama's recording machine, according to the jury forewoman. And the jurors agreed with the defense that Maivia and Anderson were not trying to extort Wakayama, but only trying to negotiate "booking fees" from him, the forewoman said.

"I think the jury believed that there just wasn't enough evidence (for a conviction) in the case," she said.

The trial in federal Judge Alan Kay's courtroom spanned nearly six weeks. The jury deliberated more than a day and a half.

"I love the jury," said an elated Maivia, president of the World Pacific Wrestling Association. "God knows I'm a lady innocent."

Maivia   So'o

Heiniemi, the association's secretary-treasurer, said, "I did have my doubts about the criminal justice system, but it came out the only way it could have come out."

So'o, the group's vice president who testified he never made the phone call, said he was upset that the case went as far as it did. "I almost lost my belief in the system," So'o said.

The defense had maintained that professional wrestling referee Sam Samson made the threatening phone call. Samsom denied the allegation on the witness stand.

The jury heard the tape of the threatening call a number of times and listened to both So'o and Samson testifying in the case. The forewoman said the jury didn't think that it mattered who left the message after the panel determined that So'o

wasn't the caller.

Assistant U.S. attorneys Marshall Silverberg and Michael Burke handled the government's case.

Silverberg said he was disappointed because he thought the evidence was enough to convict all three.

He said he believes So'o made the call and the other defendants invoked So'o's name as a "sword over Dunbar Wakayama's head, and they did it effectively."

Maivia, who took over wrestling promotions from her husband High Chief Fanene Leifi Pita "Peter" Maivia following his death, said she holds no grudges against Wakayama.

"He knows he's wrong," Maivia said. "But he's still a friend. It's OK. I forgive him."

Wakayama had worked with Maivia as an announcer on her organization's local television wrestling show before he decided to put on his own promotion using Mainland wrestlers. He went to the FBI after he received the threatening phone message and thought it came from So'o.

Wakayama was then wired for sound by the FBI during a meeting with Maivia and Heiniemi and videotaped when he gave them $1,800 toward the $5,000 payment. The three defendants were arrested shortly afterwards.

Wakayama eventually staged the wrestling matches in November last year, but said the shows generated only a fraction of the $60,000 in costs he personally paid for the venture.

371

Yearly Results

1934

Promoter Ed Ratsch

7/5/34 Honolulu
Fred Maracci beat Al Karasick, Chief Little Wolf drew Jacques Manuel, Danny Winters beat Young Aguinaldo, Louis Mendonca beat Marion Freitas.

7/12/34 Honolulu
Fred Maracci beat Jacques Manuel dq, Chief Little Wolf beat Danny Winters, Rocky Brooks beat Larry Idzikowski, Ossie Karms beat Steve Brady.

10/1/34 Honolulu   Att 6,000
Shunichi Shikuma beat Jacques Manuel, Rocky brooks drew Rubberman Higami, Danny Winters dcor Ted Shores, Louie Mendonca beat Mike Chrisner. (Lord Lansdowns in audience challenges Higami to a title match)

10/8/34 Honolulu
Shunichi Shikuma beat Rocky Brooks, Rubberman Higami beat lord Lansdowne COR, Jacques Manuel beat Danny Winters, Louie Mendonca beat Wilfred.

10/15/34 Honolulu
Shunichi Shikuma beat Jacques Manuel, Prof Higami beat Mike Golden, Lord Lansdowne beat King Tut, Danny Winters drew Rocky Brooks.

10/22/34 Honolulu
Shunichi Shikuma beat Doc Bursan, Rocky Brooks drew Harry Johnson, Rubberman Higami beat Charlie Hamp, Danny Winters drew Larry Idzikowski, Louie Mendonca beat Antone Aguilar.

10/29/34 Honolulu
Oki Shikina beat Jacques Manuel, Rubberman Higami beat Doc Bursan, Tony Felice beat Rocky Brooks, Harry Johnson beat Steve Brady.

11/5/34 Honolulu
Tony Felice beat Oki Shikina dq, Shunichi Shikuma beat Harry Johnson, Jacques Manuel beat Rusty Westcoatt, Rocky Brooks beat Doc Burson.

11/12/34 Honolulu
Tony Felice beat Shunichi Shikuma, Rubberman Higami drew Jacques Manuel, Rocky Brooks drew Young Aguinaldo, Oki Shikina beat Harry Johnson.

11/19/34 Honolulu
Shunichi Shikuma beat Tony Felice, Herry Markus beat Rubberman Higami, Elmer Lindberg beat Rocky Brooks, Young Aguinaldo beat Harry Johnson.

11/26/34 Honolulu
Tony Felice beat Shunichi Shikuma, Rubberman Higami beat Jerry Markus, Dean Detton beat Rusty Westcoatt, Einar Lindberg beat Harry Johnson, Jim Meeker beat Doc Burson.

12/3/34 Honolulu
Tony Felice beat Jacques Manuel, Shunichi Shikuma beat Einard Lindberg, Rubberman Higami beat Jim Mekker, Jerry Markus beat Harry Johnson, Tony Aguinaldo beat Steve Brady.

12/10/34 Honolulu
Rubberman Higami beat Jerry Markus World Junior Middleweight title, Shunichi Shikuma beat Jim Meeker, Rusty Westcoatt beat Harry Johnson, Jack Manuel beat Einar Lindberg.

12/17/34 Honolulu
Tet Higami beat Jerry Markus, Shunichi Shikuma beat Jacques Manuel, Young Aguinaldo drew Einar Lindberg, Jim Meeker beat Harry Johnson, Tony Felice beat Rusty Westcoatt.

Promoter Manuel Calhau

10/9/34 Honolulu
Louie Miller beat Walter Achiu, Don Hill beat Reed Detton, Curly Freitas drew Marine Brown, Jack Freitas beat L. Jevis.

10/16/34 Honolulu
Walter Achiu beat Louie Miller dq, Augie Ornellas drew Mario Freitas, Reed Detton beat Marine Jones, Don Hill beat Ernie Andrade.

10/23/34 Honolulu
Joe Kirk drew Don Hill, Ernie Andrade beat Gust Steele, Reed Detton beat Augie Ornellas, Lou Mueller beat Walter Achiu.

10/30/34 Honolulu
Don Hill beat Lou Mueller, Jack Freitas beat Benny Kim, Reed Detton beat Gene Bothelho, Walter Achiu beat Joe Kirk dq.

11/8/34 Honolulu
Danny McShain beat Don Hill, Walter Achiu drew Louis De La Torre, Lou Mueller beat Lou Heinz dq, Joe Kirk drew Jack Curtis.

11/13/34 Honolulu
Cowboy Lou Heinz beat Jack Curtis, Mike Caddock drew Don Hill, Louis De La Torre beat Danny McShain dq, Joe Kirk beat Lou Mueller.

11/20/34 Honolulu
Joe Kirk beat Louis De La Torre, Danny McShain beat Walter Achiu, Lou Mueller drew Jack Curtis, Cowboy Lou Heinz beat Don Hill.

11/27/34 Honolulu
Danny McShain beat Cowboy Lou Heinz, Walter Achiu beat Don Hill, Joe Kirk beat Lou Mueller, Jack Curtis beat Louis De La Torre.

12/4/34 Honolulu
Cowboy Heinz beat Danny McShain, Don Hill beat Joe Kirk, Lou Mueller beat Louis De La Torre, Jack Curtis beat Walter Achiu.

12/11/34 Honolulu
Jack Curtis beat Danny McShain in the final of battle royal, Lou Mueller drew Mike Caddock, Walter Achiu beat Louis De La Torre.

12/18/34 Honolulu
Jack Curtis beat Joe Kirk, Augie Ornellas beat Al Jevins, Mike Caddock beat Walter Achiu, Don Hill beat Lou Mueller.

1935

1/12/35 Honolulu
Gus Sonnenberg beat Doc Meyers, Einard Lindberg beat Jacques Manuel, Joe Kirk beat Jim Meeker, Jerry Marcus drew Lou Mueller.

1/15/35 Honolulu
Gus Sonnenberg beat Shunichi Shikuma, Tet Higami beat Tony Felice judo jacket match, Jim Meeker beat Harry Johnson, Joe Kirk drew Jerry Marcus.

1/22/35 Honolulu
Gus Sonnenberg beat Rubberman Higami, Jacques Manuel beat Harry Johnson, Lou Mueller beat Jim Meeker, Shunichi Shikuma beat Tony Felice.

1/29/35 Honolulu
Gus Sonnenberg drew Oki Shikina, Jerry Marcus drew Lou Mueller, Joe Kirk drew Sailor Giberson, Young Daruma beat Jim Meeker.

2/12/35 Honolulu
Tsutao Higami beat Lou Mueller, Jerry Markus beat Jim Meeker, Shun'ich Shikuma beat. Young Aguinaldo, Joe Kirk beat Smoky Bowser.

2/19/35 Honolulu
Tsutao Higami beat Lou Mueller, Shun'ich Shikuma beat Ernie Andrade, Oki Shikina beat Jim Meeker, Bull Toyama drew Jerry Markus, Joe Kirk drew Young Daruma.

2/23/35 Hilo
Tsutao Higami beat Jerry Markus, Oki Shikina beat Young Aguinaldo.

2/26/35 Honolulu
Bull Toyama beat Lou Mueller, Jerry Markus drew Tsutao Higami, Joe Kirk beat Sailor Gilbertson, Jim Meeker drew Young Aguinaldo.

3/5/35 Honolulu
Tsutao Higami beat Joe Kirk, Jerry Markus beat Lou Mueller, Isao Toyama beat Sailor Gilbertson, Jim Meeker beat Smoky Bowser.

3/12/35 Honolulu
Dick Sampson beat Tsutao Higami, Wildcat Pete beat Lou Mueller, Jerry Markus drew Toots Estes, Bull Toyama drew Joe Kirk.

3/19/35 Honolulu
Dick Sampson beat Jerry Markus, Toots Estes beat Bull Toyama, Wildcat Pete beat Joe Kirk, Young Daruma beat Young Bowser.

3/26/35 Honolulu
Dick Sampson beat Jerry Marcus, Rubberman Higami drew Toots Estes, Wildcat Pete beat Bull Toyama, Joe Kirk beat Young Daruma, Augie Ornellas beat Soldier Bowser.

4/2/35 Honolulu
Tsutao Higami beat Dick Sampson COR, Jerry Markus drew Wildcat Pete, Toots Estes beat Joe Kirk, Reed Deeton beat Bull Toyama.

4/9/35 Honolulu
Toots Estes beat Tsutao Higami, Wildcat Pete beat Dick Sampson, Bull Toyama drew Joe Kirk, Bull Campbell beat Young Aguinaldo (Pantaleon Manlapig)

4/16/35 Honolulu
Wildcat Pete beat Toots Estes, Shun'ichi Shikuma beat Bull Campbell, Dick Sampson beat Joe Kirk, Bull Toyama drew Dr. Kowarski.

4/23/35 Honolulu
Wildcat Pete beat Tsutao Higami, Toots Estes beat Dick Sampson, Bull Campbell beat Ernie Andrade, Joe Kirk beat Dr. Kowarski.

4/30/35 Honolulu
Toots Estes beat Wildcat Pete, Dick Sampson beat Joe Kirk, Bull Toyama beat Dr. Kowarski, Bull Campbell drew Ernie Andrade.

5/7/35 Honolulu
Toots Estes beat Dick Sampson, Professor Higami beat Wildcat Pete dq, Bull Toyama beat Joe Kirk, Augie Ornellas drew Dr. Kowarski.

5/14/35 Honolulu
Toots Estes drew Tsutao Higami, Wildcat Pete beat Dick Sampson, Bull Toyama beat Augie Ornellas, Young Daruma beat Dr. Kowarski.

5/21/35 Honolulu
Toots Estes beat Wildcat Pete, Tsutao Higami beat Dick Sampson, Isao Toyama beat Smoky Bowser, Augie Ornellas beat Benny Kim.

5/28/35 Honolulu
Tiger Moore beat Dick Sampson dq, Tsutao Higami drew Wildcat Pete, Isao Toyama drew Reed Detton, Augie Ornellas beat Smoky Bowser.

6/4/35 Honolulu Att 1100
Tiger Moore beat Toots Estes, Fred Kimball beat Dick Sampson, Clayton Fisher beat Wildcat Pete, Augie Ornellias beat Marion Freitas.

6/11/35 Honolulu Att 1000
Clayton Fisher beat Tiger Moore, George Pete beat Fred Kimball, Dick Sampson beat Toots Estes, Big Boy Clement drew Ernie Andrade.

6/18/35 Honolulu
Clayton Fisher beat Wildcat Pete, Fred Kimball drew Toots Estes, Dick Sampson beat Tiger Moore, Judge Landis beat Augie Ornellas.

6/25/35 Honolulu Att 2000
Clayton Fisher beat Dick Sampson, Wildcat Pete beat Tiger Moore, Toots Estes beat Ernie Andrade, Fred Kimball beat Bull Toyama.

7/2/35 Honolulu
Fred Kimball beat Toots Estes, Dick Sampson beat Clayton Fisher, Tiger Moore beat L. Ayresman, Augie Ornellas beat Tony Freitas. Att 2500

7/9/35 Honolulu
Wildcat Pete beat Tiger Moore, Clayton Fisher drew Fred Kimball, Isao Toyama beat L. Ayresman, Augie Ornellas beat Dr. Kowarski.

7/16/35 Honolulu
Clayton Fisher beat Fred Kimball, Tug Wilson beat Tiger Moore, Norman Mack beat Wildcat Pete, Bull Toyama drew Ernie Andrade.

7/20/35 Honolulu. Att 3000. Al Karasick promoter debuts at Honolulu Stadium.
Shun'ich Shikuma beat Elephant Jenkins, Tsutao Higami beat Jack Myers, Shun'ichi Shikuma beat Handsome Snider, Shun'ichi Shikuma beat J P Tunney.

7/23/35 Honolulu
Tug Wilson beat Clayton Fisher, Norman Mack beat Fred Kimball, Wildcat Pete beat Big Boy Clement, Reed Detton beat Tiger Moore.

7/30/35 Honolulu
George Pete drew Tug Wilson, Fred Kimball beat Norman Mack dq, Clayton Fisher beat Ernie Andrade.

8/4/35 Honolulu
Al Karasick beat Kimon Kudo, Harry Kent beat Ernie Andrade, Don Carver beat Bob Anderson, Young Duruma beat Curly Freedman.

8/6/35 Honolulu
Wildcat Pete beat Fred Kimball, Clayton Fisher beat Norman Mack, Oki SHikina drew Tug Wilson, Reed Detton beat Big Boy Clements.

8/12/35 Honolulu
Joe Savoldi beat Al Karasick, Vic Christy beat Harry Kent, Kimon Kudo beat Don Carver, Reed Detton drew Young Duruma.

8/13/35 Honolulu
Fred Kimball beat Norman Mack, Don Sugai beat Geroge Pete, Clayton Fisher drew Oki Shikina, Tug Wilson beat Ernie Andrade.

8/18/35 Honolulu
Ed Don George beat Joe Savoldi, Vic Christy beat Harry Kent, Kimon Kudo beat Pat Hennessey, Big Boy Clement beat Don Carver.

8/20/35 Honolulu
Oki Shikina beat Tug Wilson, Don Sugai beat Norman Mack, George Pete beat Clayton Fisher, Fred Kimball beat Big Boy Clement.

8/27/35 Honolulu
Oki Shikina beat Clayton Fisher, Don Sugai drew Fred Kimball, Tug Wilson beat Big Boy Clement, Norman Mack drew Wildcat Pete.

8/25/35 Honolulu
Ed Don George beat Harry Kent, Vic Christy beat Kimon Kudo, Al Karasick drew Babe Small, Big Boy Clement beat Bob Anderson.

8/31/35 Hilo
Don Sugai beat Fred Kimball, Oki Shikina beat Young Aguinaldo.

9/1/35 Honolulu
Ed Don George drew Vic Christy, Reb Russell drew Sam Leathers, Babe Small beat Claude Davis, Don Carver beat Big Boy Clement.

9/3/35 Honolulu
Clayton Fisher beat Don Sugai, Tug Wilson beat Norman Mack, Jack Morgan drew Wildcat Pete, Fred Kimball beat L. Ayresman.

9/8/35 Honolulu
Ed Don George drew Vic Christy, Reb Russell beat Babe Small, Sam Leathers beat Bull Campbell, Walter King beat Joe Lynch.

9/10/35 Honolulu
Oki Shikina beat Tug Wilson, Clayton Fisher beat Wildcat Pete dq, ack Morgan beat Fred Kimball, Don Sugai drew Norman Mack.

9/15/35 Honolulu
Ed Lewis beat Ed Don George, Vic Christy beat Reb Russell, Babe Small drew Sam Leathers, Don Carver beat Walter King.

9/17/35 Honolulu
Jack Morgan beat Clayton Fisher, Norman Mack beat Fred Kimball, Tug Wilson drew Wildcat Pete, Don Sugai beat Augie Ornellas.

9/22/35 Honolulu
Ed Lewis beat Vic Christy, Reb Russell beat Sam Leathers, Norman Wescoatt beat Babe Small, Big Boy Clement beat eIsao Toyama.

9/24/35 Honolulu
Don Sugai beat Wildcat Pete, Joe Gunther beat Clayton Fisher, Jack Morgan drew Oki Shikina, Charlie Keene drew Tug Wilson.

9/29/35 Honolulu
Chief Chewacki beat Vic Christy, Norman Wescoatt drew Reb Russell, Babe Small beat Ernie Andrade, Big Boy Clement drew Walter King.

10/1/35 Honolulu
Joe Gunther beat Tug Wilson, Oki Shikina beat Jack Morgan dq, Charlie Keene drew Don Sugai, George Pete beat Norman Mack.

10/6/35 Honolulu
Chief Chewacki beat Reb Russell, Norman Wescoatt beat Babe Small, Don Carver drew Pat Hennessey.

10/8/35 Honolulu
Joe Gunther beat Don Sugai, Jack Morgan beat Tug Wilson, Oki Shikina beat Wildcat Pete, Charlie Keene beat Bulldog Ayresman.

10/13/35 Honolulu
Norman Wescoatt won battle royal, Chief Chewacki beat Babe Small, Ernie Andrade beat Bull Campbell, Don Carver beat Jack Holland dq.

10/15/35 Honolulu
Joe Gunther beat Wildcat Pete, Don Sugai beat Tug Wilson, Jack Morgan beat Charlie Keene, Joe Gunther & Wildcat Pete won battle royal, Ernie Andrade drew Oki Shikina.

10/20/35 Honolulu
Chief Chewacki beat Jack Holland dq, George Pete beat Babe Small, Ernie Andrade beat Gust Steele, Big Boy Clement drew Don Carver.

10/22/35 Honolulu
Joe Gunther beat Jack Morgan, Oki Shikina beat Norman Mack, Tug Wilson beat Don Sugai, Charlie Keene beat Wildcat Pete dq.

10/29/35 Honolulu
Charlie Keene beat Norman Mack, Joe Gunther beat Tug Wilson, Wildcat Pete beat Don Sugai, Charlie Keene & Norman Mack won battle royal.

11/5/35 Honolulu
Jack Morgan beat Oki Shikina COR, Joe Gunther beat Don Sugai, Don Carlos Vigario beat Charlie Keene, Wildcat Pete beat Bull Toyama.

11/11/35 Honolulu
Chief Thunderbird beat Jack Holland, Harry Demetral beat Tommy Mead, Doc Dan McKenzie beat Ernie Andrade, Young Ing beat Walter Camara.

11/12/35 Honolulu
Joe Gunther beat Don Sugai, Don Carlos Vigario beat Jack Morgan dq, George Pete beat Charlie Keene, Oki Shikina beat Reed Detton.

11/17/35 Honolulu
Chief Thunderbird beat Harry Demetral, Arjan Singh beat Tommy Mead, Doc Dan McKenzie drew Jack Holland, Walter King beat Benny Kim.

11/19/35 Honolulu
Oki Shikina beat Ernie Andrade, Jack Morgan beat Big Boy Clement, Charlie Keene drew Reed Detton, Curley Freedman beat Benny Kim.

11/24/35 Honolulu
Chief Thunderbird beat Jack Holland, Harry Demetral beat Norman Wescoatt dq, Doc Dan McKenzie no contest Tommy Mead, Big Boy Clement beat Walter King.

11/26/35 Honolulu
Oki Shikina beat Jack Morgan, Joe Gunther beat Charlie Keene, Big Boy Clement drew Bulldog Ayresman, Augie Ornellas drew Curley Freedman.

12/1/35 Honolulu
Arjan Singh beat Harry Demetral, Chief Thunderbird beat Doc Dan McKenzie, Tommy Mead beat Bull Campbell, Norman Wescoatt beat Jack Holland.

12/3/35 Honolulu
Joe Gunther drew Oki Shikina, Don Sugai beat Isao Toyama, Jack Morgan beat Gust Steele, Charlie Keene beat Big Boy Clement.

12/8/35 Honolulu
Arjan Singh beat Ernie Andrade & Doc Dan McKenzie handicap match, Jack Holland beat Tommy Mead, Norman Wescoatt beat Harry Demetral, Bob Anderson beat Young Duruma.

12/10/35 Honolulu
Don Sugai beat Joe Gunther, Dick Craddock beat Big Boy Clement, Oki Shikina beat Gust Steele, Jack Morgan beat Charlie Keene.

12/15/35 Honolulu
Red Scorpion beat Tommy Mead, Harry Demetral beat Jack Holland, Arjan Singh beat Doc Dan McKenzie, Chief Thunderbird drew Norman Wescoatt, Bob Anderson beat Walter King.

12/17/35 Honolulu
Jack Morgan beat Don Sugai, Joe Gunther beat Isao Toyama, Noel Franklin beat Big Boy Clement, Charlie Keene drew Dick Craddock.

12/22/35 Honolulu
Red Scorpion beat Jack Holland, Harry Demetral beat Doc Dan McKenzie, Arjan Singh drew Norman Wescoatt, Chief Thunderbird drew Tommy Mead, Walter Camara beat Kid Algiers.

12/23/35 Honolulu
Jack Morgan drew Joe Gunther, Noel Franklin beat Charlie Keene, Don Sugai beat Dick Craddock, Big Boy Clement drew Isao Toyama.

12/29/35 Honolulu
Tommy Mead beat Doc Dan McKenzie, Arjan Singh beat Jack Holland, Chief Thudnerbird drew Harry Demetral, Red Scorpion beat Norman Wescoatt.

12/30/35 Honolulu. Att 5000
Don Sugai beat Noel Franklin, Jack Morgan beat Charlie Keene, Joe Gunther beat Dick Craddock, Isao Toyama beat Big Boy Clement.

1936

8/4/36 Honolulu
Al Karasick beat Kimon Kudo, Harry Kent beat Ernie Andrade, Don Carver beat Bob Anderson, Young Duruma beat Curly Freeedman.

8/12/36 Honolulu Att 4000
Joe Savoldi beat Al Karasick, Vic Christy beat Harry Kent, Kimon Kudo beat Don Carver, Reed Detton drew Young Duruma.

8/18/36 Honolulu Att 6000
Ed Don George beat Joe Savoldi, Vic Christy beat Harry Kent dq, Kimon Kudo beat Pat Hennessey, Big Boy Clement beat Don Carver.

8/25/36 Honolulu. Att 2500
Ed Don George beat Harry Kent, Vic Christy beat Kimon Kudo, Al Karasick drew Babe Small, Big Boy Clement beat Bob Anderson.

9/1/36 Honolulu
Ed Don George drew Vic Christy, Reb Russell drew Sam Leathers, Babe Small beat Claude Davis, Don Carver beat Big Boy Clement.

9/8/36 Honolulu
Ed Don Geroge drew Vic Christy, Reb Russell beat Babe Small, Sam Leathers beat Bull Campbell, Walter King beat Joe Lynch.

9/15/36 Honolulu Att 4000
Ed Lewis beat Ed Don George, Vic Christy beat Reb Russell, Babe Small drew Sam Leathers, Don Carver beat Walter King.

9/22/36 Honolulu
Ed Lewis beat Vic Christy, Reb Russell beat Sam Leathers, Norman Wescoatt beat Babe Small, Big Boy Clement beat Isao Toyama.

9/29/36 Honolulu
Chief Chewacki beat Vic Christy, Norman Wescoatt drew Reb Russell, Babe Small beat Ernie Andrade, Big Boy Clement drew Walter King.

10/6/36 Honolulu Att 3500
Chief Chewacki beat Reb Russell, Norman Wescoatt beat Babe Small, Don Carver drew Pat Hennessey.

10/13/36 Honolulu
Norman Wescoatt won battle royal, Chief Chewacki beat Babe Small, Ernie Andrade beat Bull Campbell, Don Carver beat ack Holland dq.

10/20/35 Honolulu
Chief Chewacki beat Jack Holland dq, George Pete beat Babe Small, Ernie Andrade beat Gust Steele, Big Boy Clement drew Don Carver.

11/11/36 Honolulu
Chief Thunderbird beat Jack Holland, Harry Demetral beat Tommy Mead, Doc Dan McKenzie beat Ernie Andrade, Young Ing beat Walter Camara.

11/17/36 Honolulu
Chief Thunderbird beat Harry Demetral, Arjan Singh beat Tommy Mead, Doc Dan McKenzie drew Jack Holland, Walter King beat Benny Kim.

11/24/36 Honolulu
Chief Thunderbird beat Jack Holland, Harry Demetral beat Norman Wescoatt dq, Doc Dan McKenzie no contest Tommy Mead, Big Boy Clement beat Walter King.

12/1/36 Honolulu
Aran Singh beat Harry Demetral, Chief Thunderbird beat Doc Dan McKenzie, Tommy Mead beat Bull Campbell, Norman Wescoatt beat Jack Holland.

12/8/36 Honolulu
Arjan Singh beat Ernie Andrade & Doc Dan McKenzie, Jack Holland beat Tommy Mead, Norman Wescoatt beat Harry Demetral, Bob Anderson beat Young Duruma.

12/15/36 Honolulu
Red Scorpion beat Tommy Mead, Harry Demetral beat Jack Holland, Arjan Singh beat Doc Dan McKenzie, Chief Thunderbird drew Norman Wescoatt, Bob Anderson beat Walter King.

12/22/36 Honolulu
Red Scorpion beat Jack Holland, Harry Demetral beat Doc Dan McKenzie, Arjan Singh drew Norman Wescoatt, Chief Thunderbird drew Tommy Mead, Walter Camara beat Kid Algiers.

12/29/36 Honolulu
Tommy Mead beat Doc Dan McKenzie, Arjan Singh beat Jack Holland, Chief Thunderbird drew Harry Demetral, Red Scorpion beat Norman Wescoatt.

1937

Al Karasick Promoter

1/5/37 Honolulu
Arjan Singh drew Red Scorpion, Chief Thunderbird beat Doc Dan McKenzie, Harry Demetral beat Tommy Mead, Jack Holland drew Norman Wescoatt.

1/12/37 Honolulu
Chief Thunderbird beat Red Scorpion, Norman Wescoatt beat Doc Dan McKenzie, Jack Holland beat Harry Demetral dq, Arjan Singh beat Tommy Mead.

1/19/37 Honolulu. Att 1200
Arjan Singh drew Jack McCarthy, Chief Thunderbird beat Harry Demetral, Norman Wescoatt beat Jack Holland, Doc Dan McKenzie beat Tommy Mead dq.

1/26/37 Honolulu
Harry Demetral beat Jack McCarthy, Norman Wescoatt beat Tommy Mead, Jack Holland beat Doc Dan McKenzie, Big Boy Clement beat Walter King, Abel Rodriguez beat Sammy Sugai.

2/2/37 Honolulu
Norman Wescoatt beat Doc Dan McKenzie, Harry Demetral drew Jack Holland, Tommy Mead beat Big Boy Clement, Curly Freedman beat Benny Kim, Chief Thunderbird beat Jack McCarthy.

2/9/37 Honolulu
Chief Thunderbird beat Norman Wescoatt, John Wood beat Jack Holland, Arjan Singh beat Harry Demetral, Doc Dan McKenzie drew Tommy Mead, Abel Rodriguez beat Bob Anderson.

2/16/37 Honolulu. Att 2000
Arjan Singh beat Chief Thunderbird, Doc Dan McKenzie beat Harry Demetral, John Wood beat Tommy Mead, Jack Holland drew Norman Wescoatt, Don Carver beat Abnel Rodriguez.

2/23/37 Honolulu
Norman Wescoatt won battle royal, Norman Wescoatt beat Tommy Mead, Arjan Singh drew John Wood, Harry Demetral beat Jack Holland, Chief Thunderbird beat Doc Dan McKenzie, Torchy Smith beat Walter King.

3/2/37 Honolulu
Tony Felice beat Chief Thunderbird, Arjan Singh beat Norman Wescoatt, Harry Demetral beat Tommy Mead dq, Doc Dan McKenzie beat Jack Holland.

3/9/37 Honolulu
Tony Felice beat Harry Demetral, Tommy Mead beat John Wood, Arjan Singh beat Doc Dan McKenzie, Torchy Smtih beat Abel Rodriguez, Albert Carvalho drew Don Carver.

3/16/37 Honolulu. Att 2000
Tony Felice beat Arjan Singh dq, Tommy Mead beat Doc Dan McKenzie, Harry Demetral drew John Wood, Big Boy Clement beat Torchy Smith, Don Carver beat Albert Carvalho.

3/24/37 Honolulu
Tony Felice beat Arjan Singh dq, Harry Demetral beat Tommy Mead, John Wood beat Doc Dan McKenzie, Don Carver drew Torchy Smith.

3/30/37 Honolulu
Tony Felice beat Hal Rumberg, Bob Kruse beat Jack Forsgren dq, John Spellman beat Harry Demetral, Ernie Andrade beat John Wood, Walter King beat Torchy Smith.

7/6/37 Honolulu
Ed Lewis beat Count Francis Fouche, Jack Arnold beat Sandor Vary, Ray Richards beat Naumu Sunayama COR, Biggie Joy beat Black Panther.

7/13/37 Honolulu
Ray Richards beat Ed Lewis dq, Naumu Sunayama beat Sandor Vary, Jack Arnold beat Big Boy Clement, Bull Toyama drew Walter King.

7/20/37 Honolulu
Herb Freeman beat Ray Richards, Francis Fouche beat Scott Dawkins dq, Bob Jessen beat Jack Arnold, Popeye McKenzie beat Abel Rodrigues.

7/27/37 Honolulu
Herb Freeman beat Francis Fouche, Bob Jessen beat Scotty Dawkins dq, Naumu Sunayama drew Jack Arnold, Big Boy Clement beat Biggie Joy.

8/3/37 Honolulu
Herb Freeman beat Francis Fouche, Naumu Sunayama beat Scotty Dawkins dq, Bob Jessen beat Jack Arnold, Walter King beat Al Carvalho.

8/10/37 Honolulu
Scott Dawkins beat Bob Jessen, Naumu Sunayama beat Herb Freeman dq, Jack Arnold drew Francis Fouche, Biggie Joy beat Abel Rodrigues.

8/17/37 Honolulu
Herb Freeman beat Scott Dawkins, Bob Jessen drew Francis Fouche, Ernie Petersen beat Jack Arnold, Popeye McKenzie beat Walter King.

8/24/37 Honolulu
Francis Fouche beat Bob Jessen, Jack Arnold drew Naumu Sunayama, Ernie Petersen beat Scotty Dawkins, Bull Toyama beat Popeye McKenzie.

8/31/37 Honolulu
Scotty Dawkins beat Francis Fouche, Bob Jessen drew Ernie Peterson, Herb Freeman beat Naumu Sunayama, Dan McKenzie beat Jack Arnold.

9/7/37 Honolulu
Ernie Petersen beat Scotty Dawkins dq, Bob Jessen beat Francis Fouche, Walter King beat Bull Toyama, Herb Freeman no contest Tommy Mead.

9/14/37 Honolulu
Tommy Mead beat Herb Freeman, Naumu Sunayama beat Scotty Dawkins, Bob Jessen drew Dan McKenzie, Bill Sinclair beat Al Carvalho

9/21/37 Honolulu
Oki Shikina beat Dan McKenzie, Herb Freeman beat Tommy Mead, Ernie Andrade beat Biggie Joy, Ernie Petersen beat Jack Arnold.

9/28/37 Honolulu
Oki Shikina beat Ernie Petersen, Danno McKenzie beat Herb Freeman dq, Tommy Mead drew Naumu Sunayama, Big Boy Clement beat Gus Steele.

10/5/37 Honolulu
Oki Shikina beat Herbie Butch Freeman, Ernie Peterson beat Tommy Mead dq, Naumu Sunayama beat Dr. Dan McKenzie, Abelu Rodrigues beat Henry Pa, Mr. X beat Big Boy Clement.

10/12/37 Honolulu
Tommy Mead beat Ernie Petersen, Naumu Sunayama beat Herb Freeman, Sailor Jack Arnold drew Danno McKenzie, Ernie Andrade beat Manuel Rodrigues, Abel Rodrigues beat Bill Sinclair.

10/19/37 Honolulu
Vic Christy beat Tommy Mead, Ernie Peterson beat Danno McKenzie, Naumu Sunayama beat Ernie Adrade, Mr. X beat Abel Rodrigues.

10/26/37 Honolulu
Oki Shikina beat Tommy Mead, Vic Christy beat Jack Gacek, Naumu Sunayama beat Mr. X, Bill Sinclair beat Bull Toyama.

11/2/37 Honolulu
Oki Shikina beat Vic Christy, Rusty Wescoatt beat Danno McKenzie, Floyd Marshall drew Jack Gacek, Ernie Petersen beat Tommy Mead.

11/9/37 Honolulu
Rusty Westcoatt beat Naumu Sunayama, Jack Gacek beat Ernie Petersen, Floyd Marshall beat Tommy Mead, Jack Arnold beat Danno McKenzie.

11/16/37 Honolulu Att 4500
Oki Shikina beat Rusty Westcoatt First Hawaiian Heavyweight Champ, Glenn Wade beat Tommy Mead, Jack Gacek beat Jack Arnold, Floyd Marshall drew Naumu Sunayama.

11/23/37 Honolulu
Floyd Marshall beat Glenn Wade, Jack Gacek beat Ernie Petersen, Tommy Mead drew Jack Arnold, Big Boy Clement beat Bill Sinclair.

11/30/37 Honolulu
Oki Shikina beat Floyd Marshall, Glenn Wade beat Naumu Sunayama, Jack Gacek beat Tommy Mead, Ernie Petersen drew Jack Arnold.

12/7/37 Honolulu
Jack Gacek beat Oki Shikina, Glen Wade beat Floyd Marshall, Naumu Sunayama beat Ernie Petersen, Bull Toyama drew Al Carvalho.

12/14/37 Honolulu
Oki Shikina beat Jack Gacek, Matros Kirilenko beat Glen Wade, Floyd Marshall drew Naumu Sunayama, Bull Toyama beat Eddie Fushiyama, Jack Freitas beat Al Carvalho.

12/21/37 Honolulu
Oki Shikina drew Glen Wade, Matros Kirilenko beat Jack Gacek, Jack Arnold beat Ernie Petersen, Jack Freitas drew Bull Toyama.

12/28/37 Honolulu
Ernie Petersen beat Naumu Sunayama, Oki Shikina beat Glen Wade dq, Jack Gacek drew Matros Kirilenko, Ernie Petersen beat Ernie Andrade, Bill Sinclair drew Young Daruma.

1938

1/4/38 Honolulu
Matros Kirilenko beat Jack Gacek, Glen Wade beat Naumu Sunayama, Ernie Adrade drew Ernie Petersen, Torchy Smith no contest Jack Carvalho.

1/11/38 Honolulu
Oki Shikina drew Matros Kirilenko, Jack Gacek beat Glen Wade, Count Otto Hans Von Buesing beat Ernie Petersen, Bill Sinclair beat Abel Rodrigues.

1/18/38 Honolulu
Oki Shikina beat Glen Wade, Matros Kirilenko beat Count Von Buesing dq, Jack Gacek drew Naumu Sunayama, Abel Rodriges beat Torchy Smith.

1/25/38 Honolulu
Count Von Buesing beat Glen Wade battle royal, Jack Gacek beat Naumu Sunayama, Totem Anderson beat Young Tony Carrillo, Oki SHikina beat Ernie Petersen.

2/1/38 Honolulu
Oki Shikina beat Count Von Buessing dq, Matros Kirilenko drew Jack Gacek, Naumu Sunayama beat Glen Wade, Totem Pole Anderson beat Al Carvalho.

2/8/38 Honolulu
Matros Kirilenko beat Count Von Buessing, Oki Shikina beat Naumu Sunayama, Sammy Sugai beat Tony Freitas, Jack Gacek beat Ernie Petersen.

2/15/38 Honolulu
Count Von Buessing beat Jack Gacek, Brother Jonathan drew Matros Kirilenko, Ernie Petersen beat Dutch Banks dq, Torch Smith beat Totem Pole Anderson.

2/19/38 Hilo
Oki Shikina beat Ernie Peterson, Jack Gacek beat Matros Kirilenko, Eddie Kameenui drew William Matsu.

2/22/38 Honolulu
Gus Sonnenberg beat Count Von Buesing, Brother Jonathan beat Jack Gacek, Harry Demetral beat Ernie Petersen, Abel Rodrigues drew Biggie Joy.

3/1/38 Honolulu
Oki Shikina beat Matros Kirilenko, Gus Sonnenberg beat Harry Demetral, Brother Jonathan drew Count Von Buessing, Abel Rodrigues beat Bill Sinclair.

3/8/37 Honolulu
Matros Kirilenko beat Gus Sonnenberg dq, Brother Jonathan beat Count Von Buessing, Naumu Sunayama drew Harry Demetral, Big Boy Clement beat Abel Rodrigues.

3/15/38 Honolulu
Oki Shikina drew Gus Sonnenberg, Matros Kirilenko beat Count Von Buesing, Brother Jonathan drew Harry Demetral handicap match, Dutch Banks beat Big Boy Clement dq.

3/22/38 Honolulu
Matros Kirilenko beat Count Von Buessing, Gus Sonnenberg drew Brother Jonathan, Naumu Sunayama beat Bill Sinclair, Harry Demetral beat Ernie Petersen.

3/29/38 Honolulu
Gus Sonnenberg beat Matros Kirilenko, Bobby Roberts beat Count Von Buesing, Brother Jonathan beat Harry Demetral, Ernie Peterson drew Jack Arnold.

4/5/38 Honolulu
Brother Jonathan beat Gus Sonnenberg, Ernie Petersen drew Naumu Sunayama, Jack Arnold beat Count Von Buesing.

4/12/38 Honolulu
Arjan Singh beat Gus Sonnenberg, Bobby Roberts beat Harry Demetral, Lee Henning beat Jack Arnold, Ernie Petersen beat Bill Sinclair.

4/19/38 Honolulu
Arjan Singh drew Brother Jonathan, Gus Sonnenberg beat Bobby Roberts, Lee Henning drew Harry Demetral, Ernie Petersen beat Lynn Gustafson.

4/26/38 Honolulu
Oki Shikina beat Gus Sonnenberg, Al Pereira beat Count Von Buesing, Arjan Singh beat Harry Demetral, Lee Henning drew Bobby Roberts.

5/3/38 Honolulu Att 5000
Bronko Nagurski beat Brother Jonathan, Al Pereira drew Lee Henning, Jack Holland beat Bobby Roberts, Ernie Petersen beat Naumu Sunayama.

5/10/38 Honolulu Att 6000
Bronko Nagurski beat Oki Shikina, Gus Sonnenberg drew Bobby Roberts, Arjan Singh beat Count Von Buesing, Al Pereira beat Harry Demetral dq, Lee Henning drew Jack Holland.

5/17/38 Honolulu
Al Pereira beat Arjan Singh, Gus Sonnenberg beat Brother Jonathan, Lee Henning beat Bobby Roberts, Jack Holland drew Jack Arnold.

5/24/38 Honolulu
Al Pereira beat Oki Shikina dq, Gus Sonnenberg beat Lee Henning, Brother Jonathan no contest Arjan Singh, Bobby Roberts beat Ernie Petersen.

5/31/38 Honolulu
Vincent Lopez beat Gus Sonnenberg, Bobby Roberts beat Jack Holland, Arjan Singh no contest Brother Jonathan, Lee Henning drew Naumu Sunayama.

6/7/38 Honolulu
Vincent Lopez beat Al Pereira, Oki Shikina beat Bobby Roberts, Gus Sonnenberg beat Lee Henning, Brother Jonathan beat Arjan Singh.

6/14/38 Honolulu
Oki Shikina drew Vincent Lopez, Al Pereira beat Bobby Roberts, Arjan Singh beat Pat McKay dq, Joe Tonti beat Ernie Petersen.

6/21/38 Honolulu
Al Pereira beat Bobby Roberts, Lee Henning beat Ernie Petersen won battle royal, Pat McKay beat Naumu Sunayama, Brother Jonathan drew Joe Tonti, Al Caralho beat Tony Carillo.

6/28/38 Honolulu
Al Pereira beat Lee Henning, Bobby Roberts beat Joe Tonti, Pat McKay drew Brother Jonathan, Ernie Petersen beat Jack Arnold.

7/5/38 Honolulu
Al Pereira beat Brother Jonathan, Bobby Roberts beat Pat McKay dq, Joe Tonti beat Naumu Sunayama, Lee Henning beat Ernie Petersen.

7/12/38 Honolulu
Andre Adoree beat Bobby Roberts, Pat McKay beat Lee Henning, Al Pereira beat Pat McKay, Andre Adoree beat Harry Demetral, Joe Tonti beat Bobby Roberts, Lee Henning beat Naumu Sunayama, Tony Carrillo beat Johnny Wood.

7/19/38 Honolulu
Al Pereira beat Pat McKay, Andre Adoree beat Harry Demetral, Joe Tonti beat Bobby Roberts, Lee Henning beat Naumu Sunayama, Tony Carrillo beat Johnny Wood.

7/26/38 Honolulu
Al Pereira drew Joe Tonti, Vic Hill beat Lee Henning, Andre Adoree beat Pat McKay COR, Harry Demetral beat Ernie Peterson.

8/2/38 Honolulu
Al Pereira beat Bobby Roberts, Andre Adoree beat Pat McKay dq, Vic Hill drew Joe Tonti, Jack Arnold beat Ernie Petersen.

8/9/38 Honolulu
Al Pereira beat Andre Adoree, Vic Hill drew Pat McKay dcor, Joe Tonti beat Lee Henning, August Ornellas beat Tony Carrillo, Harry Demetral drew Bobby Roberts.

8/16/38 Honolulu
Al Pereira beat Vic Hill, Andre Adoree beat Pat McKay, Joe Tonti drew Bobby Roberts, Naumu Sunayama beat Lee Henning, Ernie Peterson beat Dutch Banks.

8/23/38 Honolulu
Al Pereira beat Andre Adoree, Pat McKay beat Joe Tonti, Jack Gacek beat Bobby Roberts, Lee Henning drew Vic Hill, Jack Freitas beat Al Carvalho dq.

8/30/38 Honolulu
Al Pereira beat Vic Hill, Jack Gacek beat Pat McKay, Andre Adoree beat Lee Henning COR, Joe Tonti drew Bobby Roberts, August Ornellas beat Jack Freitas.

9/6/38 Honolulu
Andre Adoree beat Jack Gacek, Vic Hill drew Harry Demetral, Pat McKay beat Bobby Roberts, Al Pereira beat Joe Tonti.

9/13/38 Honolulu
Al Pereira beat Jack Gacek, Joe Tonti beat Naumu Sunayama, Pat McKay beat Vic Hill, Andre Adoree drew Lee Henning, Don Carver beat Al Carvalho.

9/20/38 Honolulu
Andre Adoree beat Lee Henning won battle royal, Pat McKay drew Bobby Roberts, Rudy LaDitzi beat Jack Arnold.

9/27/38 Honolulu
Al Pereira beat Jack Gacek, Rudy LaDitzi beat Bobby Roberts, Andre Adoree beat Pat McKay dq, Joe Tonti drew Lee Henning.

10/4/38 Honolulu
Rudy LaDitzi beat Billy Hansen, Al Pereira beat Andre Adoree, Jack Gacek beat Lee Henning, Joe Tinti beat Bobby Roberts.

10/11/38 Honolulu
Billy Hansen beat Rudy LaDitzi, Oki Shikina beat Jack Gacek, Andre Adoree drew Joe Tonti, August Ornellas beat Reed Detton.

10/18/38 Honolulu
Leonard Garcia beat Joe Tonti, Oki Shikina beat Billy Hansen, Rudy LaDitzi drew Al Pereira, Jack Gacek drew Andre Adoree.

10/25/38 Honolulu
Leonardo Garcia beat Andre Adoree, Oki Shikina drew Billy Hansen, Rudy LaDitzi beat Naumu Sunayama, Jack Gacek beat Joe Tonti.

11/1/38 Honolulu
Leo Numa beat Rudy LaDitzi, Oki Shikina beat Jack Gacek, Billy Hansen beat Leonard Garcia 10 seconds, Joe Tonti beat Dutch Banks.

11/8/38 Honolulu
Rudy LaDitzi beat Oki Shikina dq, Leo Numa drew Billy Hansen, Naumu Sunayama beat Jack Gacek dq, Ernie Andrade beat Dutch Banks.

11/15/38 Honolulu
Oki Shikina beat Billy Hansen, Leo Numa beat Dick Raines dq, Leonardo Garcia beat Big Boy Clement, Naumu Sunayama drew Jack Gacek.

11/22/38 Honolulu
Leo Numa beat Billy Hansen, Oki Shikina beat Rudy LaDitzi dq, Dick Raines beat Jack Gacek, Leonardo Garcia beat Abel Rodrigues.

11/29/38 Honolulu
Dick Raines beat Le Numa, Rudy LaDitzi beat Jack Holland, Jack Gacek beat Leonard Garcia, Joe Toni drew Naumu Sunayama.

12/6/38 Honolulu
Rudy LaDitzi beat Oki Shikina dq, Dick Raines beat Jack Holland, Herman Swede Olsen drew jack Gacek, Joe Toni beat Big Boy Clement.

12/11/38 Hilo
Oki Shikina beat Jack Gacek, Joe Tonti beat Leonardo Garcia, Herman Olson drew Rudy LaDitzi.

12/13/38 Honolulu
Dick Raines beat Rudy LaDitzi, Oki Shikina beat Count Von Buesing, Swede Olsen beat Jack Gacek, Bunny Martin beat Joe Tonti, Al Carvalho beat Tony Carrillo.

12/21/38 Honolulu
Dean Detton drew Dick Raines, Rudy LaDitzi beat Swede Olson, Harry Demetral beat Leonard Garcia, Jack Gacek drew Bunny Martin, Jack Holland beat Joe Tonti.

12/27/38 Honolulu
Dean Detton beat Rudy LaDitzi, Oki Shikina beat Bunny Martin, Lofty Blomfield beat Jack Gacek, Dick Raines beat Swede Olsen.

1939

1/3/39 Honolulu
Dick Raines beat Lofty Bloomfield dq, Jack Gacek drew Jack Holland, Rudy LaDitzi beat Bunny Martin, Dr. Ed Kawarsky beat Al Carvalho.

1/10/39 Honolulu
Dean Detton beat Dick Raines, Lofty Blomfield beat Rudy LaDitzi, Lee Henning beat Jack Gacek, Swede Olsen drew Bobby Roberts.

1/17/39 Honolulu
Oki Shikina beat Dean Detton, Lofty Blomfield beat Lee Henning, Dick Raines drew Brother Jonathan, Jack Gacek beat Swede Olsen.

1/24/39 Honolulu
Dean Detton beat Oki Shikina win Hawaiian title, Dick Raines beat Jack Gacek, Brother Jonathan beat Lee Henning, Brother Jonathan drew Swede Olsen handicap match, Bobby Roberts beat Jack Holland.

1/31/39 Honolulu
Dean Detton drew Lofty Blomfield, Danny Dusek beat Jack Gacek, Lee Henning beat Swede Olsen, Bobby Roberts beat Jack Holland, Kid Diamond beat Ivan Andrevitch.

2/7/39 Honolulu
Dick Raines beat Dean Detton won Hawaiian Title, Oki Shikina beat Lee Henning, Danny Dusek drew Brother Jonathan, Bobby Roberts beat Bill Sinclair, Don Carver beat Augie Ornellas.

2/14/39 Honolulu
Lofty Blomfield beat Danny Dusek, Dick Raines drew Brother Jonathan, Wong Buck Cheong beat Bobby Roberts, Lee Henning drew Curtis Chartier, Abel Rodrigues beat Bill Sinclair dq.

2/21/39 Honolulu
Lofty Blomfield beat Brother Jonathan, Dick Raines beat Danny Dusek, Wong Buck Cheong beat Lee Henning, Curtis Chartier beat Bobby Roberts, Abel Rodrigues beat Blue Shadow.

2/28/39 Honolulu
Dick Raines beat Oki Shikina dq, Wong Buck Cheung drew Lofty Bloomfield, Danny Dusek beat Bobby Roberts, Lee Henning drew Red Chartier, Ed Kawarsky beat Al Carvalho.

3/7/39 Honolulu
Lofty Bloomfield beat Dick Raines, Oki Shikina beat Danny Dusek, Wong Buck Cheung beat Lee Henning, Red Charteir beat Bill Sinclair, Don Carver beat Ed Kawarsky.

3/14/39 Honolulu
Oki Shikina beat Wong Buck Cheung, Dick Raines beat Danny Dusek, Lofty Blomfield beat Lee Henning, Red Charteir beat Walter Leck.

3/21/39 Honolulu
Oki Shikina beat Lofty Blomfield, Dick Raines beat Wong Buck Cheung dq, Danny Dusek beat Red Chartier, Count Von Buesing drew Lee Henning, Al Carvalho beat Mike O'Hara.

3/28/39 Honolulu
Oki Shikina beat Dick Raines, Danny Dusek beat Barto Hill, Lofty Blomfield drew Harnan Singh, Red Chartier beat Lee Henning, jack Freitas beat Ben Younger.

4/4/39 Honolulu
Oki Shikina beat Dick Raines won Hawaiian title, Harnan Singh beat Danny Dusek, Lofty Blomfield drew Barto Hill, Wong Buck Cheung beat Red Chartier, Abel Rodrigues drew Bill Sinclair.

4/11/39 Honolulu
Harnan Singh beat Wong Buck Cheung, Danny Dusek beat Dick Raines, Barto Hill drew Floyd Marshall, Red Chartier beat Bill Sinclair, Ernie Andrade beat Abel Rodrigues COR.

4/18/39 Honolulu
Chief Little Wolf drew Danny Dusek, Oki Shikina beat Floyd Marshall, George Boujle beat Al Carvalho, Harnan Singh beat Count Von Buesing.

4/25/39 Honolulu
Oki Shikina beat Harnan Singh, Barto Hill beat Danny Dusek, Red Chartier beat Raoul Lopez, Floyd Marshall drew Wong Buck Cheung.

5/2/39 Honolulu
George Zaharias beat Barto Hill, Red Chartier beat Floyd Marshall dq, Harnan Singh drew Brother Jonathan, Danny Dusek beat Raoul Lopez.

5/9/39 Honolulu
Oki Shikina beat George Zaharias dq, Harnan Singh beat Floyd Marshall, Wong Buck Cheung drew Danny Dusek, Barto Hill beat Raoul Lopez.

5/16/39 Honolulu
Oki Shikina beat George Zaharias, Danny Dusek beat Barto Hill, Floyd Marshall beat Wong Buck Cheung, Harnan Singh beat Raoul Lopez.

5/23/39 Honolulu
Danny Dusek beat Floyd Marshall, Harnan Singh drew Barto Hill, Joe Benincassa beat Red Chartier, Raoul Lopez drew Wong Buck Cheung.

5/30/39 Honolulu
Dean Detton VS Danny Dusek, Oki Shikina VS Harnan Singh, Joe Benincassa VS Raoul Lopez, Brother Jonathan VS Barto Hill.

6/6/39 Honolulu
Dean Detton beat Harnan Singh, Joe Benincassa drew Oki Shikina, Wong Buck Cheung beat Floyd Marshall, Red Chartier beat Raoul Lopez.

6/13/39 Honolulu
Dean Detton beat Oki Shikina, Red Chartier beat Floyd Marshall, Harnan Singh drew Danny Dusek, Barto Hill beat Joe Benincassa.

6/20/39 Honolulu
Chief Thunderbird beat Danny Dusek, Al Getz beat Barto Hill, Joe Benincassa beat Raoul Lopez, Brother Jonathan drew Harnan Singh.

6/27/39 Honolulu
Chief Thunderbird beat Joe Benincassa, Danny Dusek beat Harnan Singh, Red Chartier beat Brother Jonathan dq, Al Getz beat Barto Hill.

7/4/39 Honolulu
Chief Thunderbird beat Brother Jonathan, Wong Buck Cheung beat Joe Benincassa dq final of battle royal.

7/11/39 Honolulu
Oki Shikina beat Danny Dusek, Chief Thunderbird beat Joe Benincassa, Al Getz beat Floyd Marshall, Barto Hill beat Red Chartier.

7/18/39 Honolulu
Chief Thunderbird beat Al Getz, Oki Shikina beat Joe Benincassa, Danny Dusek no contest Brother Jonathan, Bart Hill beat Floyd Marshall.

7/25/39 Honolulu
Oki Shikina beat Tony Felice, Dick Lever beat Barto Hill, Danny Dusek beat Brother Jonathan COR, Al Getz beat Red Chartier.

8/1/39 Honolulu
Oki Shikina beat Al Getz, Dick Lever beat Tony Felice, Danny Dusek drew Barto Hill, Red Chartier beat Big Boy Clement.

8/8/39 Honolulu
Chief Thunderbird beat Dick Lever dq, George Pencheff beat Al Getz, Danny Dusek beat Floyd Marshall, Barto Hill beat Wong Buck Cheung.

8/15/39 Honolulu
Vic Christy beat Danny Dusek, George Pencheff beat Dick Lever, Chief Thunderbird beat Wong Buck Cheung, Barto Hill drew Al Getz.

8/22/39 Honolulu Att 5000
Jim Londos beat Vic Christy, Chief Thunderbird beat Al Getz, George Pencheff beat Danny Dusek dq, Jack Donovan beat Barto Hill, Wong Buck Cheung beat Red Chartier.

8/29/39 Honolulu Att 6000
Jim Londos beat Oki Shikina, George Pencheff beat Jack Donovan, Vic Christy beat Wong Buck Cheung, Chief Thunderbird beat Danny Dusek COR, Al Getz drew Barto Hill.

9/5/39 Honolulu Att 4000
Jim Londos beat Chief Thunderbird, Vic Christy drew George Pencheff, Al Getz drew Tiger Joe Kapach, Barto Hill beat Jack Donovan dq.

9/12/39 Honolulu
Jim Londos beat Oki Shikina, George Pencheff beat Vic Christy, Chief Thunderbird beat Danny Dusek dq, Al Getz beat Jack Donovan, Joe Kapach drew Barto Hill.

9/19/39 Honolulu
George Pencheff drew Chief Thunderbird, Andy Moen beat Vic Christy, Billy Hansen beat Danny Dusek, Wong Buck Cheung beat Barto Hill.

9/26/39 Honolulu
George Pencheff beat Billy Hansen, Oki Shikina beat Andy Moen, Chief Thunderbird beat Joe Kopach, Danny Dusek drew Al Getz.

10/3/39 Honolulu
Jim Londos beat George Pencheff World Title, George Zaharias beat Danny Dusek, Paul Jones beat Joe Kopach, Paul Boesch drew Ignacio (Pedro) Martinez.

10/10/39 Honolulu
George Zaharias beat Chief Thunderbird, Paul Boesch drew George Pencheff, Ignacio Martinez beat Al Getz, Paul Jones beat Red Chartier.

10/17/39 Honolulu
Oki Shikina beat George Pencheff, George Zaharias beat Paul Boesch, Chief Thunderbird drew Ignacio Martinez, Al Getz beat Joe Kopach.

10/24/39 Honolulu
Oki Shikina drew George Zaharias, Rube Wright beat Red Chartier, Chief Thunderbird beat Ignacio Martinez dq, Paul Boesch beat Al Getz.

10/31/39 Honolulu
Oki Shikina beat Chief Thunderbird, Rube Wright beat Al Getz, Paul Boesch drew Ignacio Martinez, Paul Jones beat Wong Buck Cheung.

11/7/39 Honolulu
Ignacio Martinez beat Rube Wright, Paul Jones beat Paul Boesch, Wong Buck Cheung beat Chief Thunderbird dq, Jack Donovan beat Al Getz.

11/14/39 Honolulu
Ignacio Martinez beat Paul Boesch, Paul Jones beat Rube Wright, Chief Thunderbird beat Wong Buck Cheung dq, Al Getz beat Walter Leck.

11/21/39 Honolulu
Ignacio Martinez beat Chief Thunderbird battle royal, Paul Jones beat Rube Wright, Paul Boesch drew Wong Buck Cheung, Doc Kawarsky beat Bob Pierre.

11/28/39 Honolulu
Paul Jones beat Ignacio Martinez won Hawaiian title, Henry Graber beat Wong Buck Cheung, Chief Thunderbird drew Paul Boesch, Young Shiranuhi (Mr. Moto) beat Doc Kawarsky.

12/5/39 Honolulu
Paul Boesch & Henry Graber beat Ignacio Martinez & Wong Buck Cheung, Paul Jones beat Chief Thunderbird, Young Shiranuhi beat Big Boy Clement dq.

12/12/39 Honolulu
Paul Jones drew Ignacio Martinez, Paul Boesch & Chief Thunderbird beat Wong Buck Cheung & Henry Graber, Joe Dunn drew Walter Leck.

12/19/39 Honolulu
Jack Gacek beat Paul Boesch, Paul Jones beat Henry Graber, Chief Thunderbird beat Ignacio Martinez dq, Wong Buck Cheung beat Joe Dunn.

12/28/39 Honolulu
Jack Gacek beat Ignacio Martinez, Paul Jones beat Chief Thunderbird, Jack McArthur beat Henry Graber, George Harbin drew Paul Boesch.

1940

1/3/40 Honolulu
Al Pereira beat Ignacio Martinez, Paul Boesch beat Jack McArthur, Paul Jones beat Jack Gacek, George Harbin beat Chief Thunderbird.

1/9/40 Honolulu
Al Periera beat Ignacio Martinez, Paul Jones beat Paul Boesch, Jack McArthur beat George Harbin, Jack Gacek drew Henry Graber.

1/17/40 Honolulu
Paul Jones beat Jack Gacek, Jack McArthur beat Henry Graber, George Harbin beat Wong Buck Cheung dq, Young Shiranuhi drew Big Boy Clement.

1/24/40 Honolulu Starts to feature Jr. Heavyweights
Whitey Walberg beat Tony Bommerito, Paul Jones beat Jack McArthur, Steve Nenoff drew Jack Gacek, Henry Graber beat George Harbin.

1/31/40 Honolulu
Whitey Walberg beat Steve Nenoff, Tony Bommerito beat George Harbin, Wong Buck Cheung beat Henry Graber, Jack Gacek beat Jack McArthur.

2/7/40 Honolulu
Tony Bommerito beat Steve Nenoff, Jack Gacek beat Whitey Walberg, Young Shiranuhi drew Sir Nicholas Baynalis, Wong Buck Cheung beat Henry Graber.

2/14/40 Honolulu
Paul Jones beat Jack Gacek dq, Tony Bommerito beat Whitey Walberg, Steve Nenoff beat Henry Graber, Nicholas Baynalis beat Doc Kawarsky.

2/21/40 Honolulu
Kimon Kudo beat Steve Nenoff, Whitey Walberg beat Jack Gacek, Nicholas Baynalis beat Tony Bommerito dq, Young Shiranuhi beat Doc Kawarsky.

2/28/40 Honolulu
Kumon Kudo beat Tony Bommerito, Whitey Walberg beat Nicholas Baynalis, Naumu Sunayama drew Jack Gacek, Steve Nenoff beat Young Shiranuhi COR.

3/6/40 Honolulu
Kimon Kudo beat Whitey Walberg, Nicholas Baynalis beat Steve Nenoff, Jack Gacek beat Ernie Andrade, Tony Bommerito drew Young Shiranuhi.

3/13/40 Honolulu
Kimon Kudo beat Nicholas Baynalis, Whitey Walberg beat Tony Bommerito dq, Wong Buck Cheung beat Jack Gacek, Young Shiranuhi drew Steve Nenoff.

3/20/40 Honolulu
Kimon Kudo beat Whitey Walberg, Steve Nenoff beat Billy Venable, Tony Bommerito drew Kid Chapman, Nicholas Baynalis beat Young Shiranuhi.

3/27/40 Honolulu
Billy Venable beat Jack Gacek, Nick Baynalis drew Whitey Walberg, Kid Chapman beat Steve Nenoff dq, Tony Bommerito beat Fred Kimball.

4/3/40 Honolulu
Billy Venable beat Tony Bommerito, Kimon Kudo beat Steve Nenoff, Whitey Walberg beat Kid Chapman, Nick Baynalis drew Jack Gacek.

4/10/40 Honolulu
Whitey Walberg & Kimon Kudo beat Tony Bommerito & Jack Gacek, Billy Venable beat Nick Baynalis, Kid Chapman drew Steve Nenoff.

4/17/40 Honolulu
Kimon Kudo beat Billy Venable, Joe Parelli beat Kid Chapman, Whitey Walberg beat Steve Nenoff, Nick Baynalis drew Young Shiranuhi.

4/24/40 Honolulu
Billy Venable beat Kimon Kudo won Hawaii Jr heavy title, Joe Parelli beat Steve Nenoff, Whitey Walberg beat Nick Banalis, Young Shiranuhi beat Kid Champman.

5/1/40 Honolulu
Billy Venable beat Tony Bommerito, Kimon Kudo drew Whitey Walberg, Joe Parelli beat Nick Baynalis, Steve Nenoff beat Kid Chapman.

5/8/40 Honolulu
Whitey Walberg beat Billy Venable, Young Shiranuhi & Kimon Kudo beat Nick Baynalis & Steve Nenoff, Sailor Bill Proshisky drew Doc Kawarsky, Tony Bommerito beat Sailor Sam Harris.

5/15/40 Honolulu
Whitey Walberg beat Joe Parelli dq, Billy Venable beat Young Shiranuhi, Kimon Kudo beat Steve Nenoff, Nick Baynalis drew Tony Bommerito.

5/22/40 Honolulu
Whitey Walberg beat Billy Venable, Kimon Kudo drew Joe Parelli, Steve Nenoff beat Young Shiranuhi, Tony Bommerito beat Nick Baynalis.

5/29/40 Honolulu
Billy Venable beat Joe Parelli, Kimon Kudo beat Whitey Walberg, Big Boy Clement beat Tony Bommerito, Young Shiranuhi drew Nick Baynalis.

6/5/40 Honolulu
Billy Venable beat Kimon Kudo, Joe Parelli beat Tony Bommerito, Big Boy Clement beat Nick Baynalis, Auggie Ornellas beat David Gomez.

6/12/40 Honolulu
Whitey Walberg beat Kimon Kudo, Joe Parelli beat Billy Venable, Tony Bommerito beat Big Boy Clement, Young Shiranuhi beat Nick Baynalis.

6/19/40 Honolulu
Tetsuo Higami beat Whitey Walberg, Billy Venable beat Tony Bommerito, Kimon Kudo drew Joe Parelli, Young Shiranuhi beat Nick Baynalis.

6/26/40 Honolulu
Rubberman Higami beat Joe Parelli, Billy Venable beat Whitey Walberg, Kimon Kudo beat Tony Bommerito dq, Big Boy Clemment drew Nick Baynalis.

7/3/40 Honolulu
Tetsuo Higami beat Billy Venable won Hawaii Jr Heavy Title, Mike London beat Tony Bommerito, Whitey Walberg beat Joe Parelli dq, Nick Baynalis drew Ernie Powers.

7/10/40 Honolulu
Mike London beat Whitey Walberg, Tetsuo Higami & Kimon Kudo beat Joe Parelli & Tony Bommerito, Billy Venable beat Young Shiranuhi, Sailor Wes Crowther beat Nick Baynalis.

7/17/40 Honolulu
Mike London beat Kimon Kudo, Billy Venable beat Whitey Walberg, Young Shiranuhi drew Ernie Powers, Charley Carr beat Tony Bommerito.

7/24/40 Honolulu
Rubberman Higami beat Billy Venable, Whitey Walberg beat Joe Parelli dq, Charley Carr drew Kimon Kudo, David Gomez beat George Waialama.

1941

1/1/41 Honolulu
Red Shadow beat Kimon Kudo, Charley Carr beat Iiaki Hassan, Balk Estes beat Sammy Cohen dq, Rubber Higami drew Ben Pilar, David Gomez beat Ivan Matchin.

1/8/41 Honolulu
Red Shadow beat Rubber Higami, Kimon Kudo drew Ben Pilar, Balk Estes drew George Wagner, Sammy Cohen beat Charley Carr, Stanley Skieski beat David Gomez.

1/15/41 Honolulu
Balk Estes beat George Wagner, Sammy Cohen drew Red Shadow, Kimon Kudo beat Charley Carr, Ernie Powers beat Tony Madiola, Stan Skieski beat Augie Ornellas.

1/22/41 Honolulu
Ben Pilar beat Rubber Higami won Hawaiian Junior Title, Red Shadow beat Balk Estes, George Wagner beat Sammy Cohen, Young Shiranuhi beat Ernie Powers, Doc Kowarsky drew Stan Skieski.

1/29/41 Honolulu
Red Shadow beat Balk Estes, Kimon Kudo drew George Wagner, Sammy Cohen beat Charley Carr, Young Shiranuhi beat Stan Skieski, Augie Ornellas beat David Gomez.

2/5/41 Honolulu
Ben Pilar beat Sammy Cohen, Red Shadow beat Kimon Kudo, George Wagner beat Rubber Higami, Balk Estes beat Charley Carr, Augie Ornellas beat Stan Skieski dq.

2/12/41 Honolulu
George Wagner beat Red Shadow, Rubber Higami beat Sammy Cohen, Danny Savich beat Ernie Powers, Balk Estes drew Kimon Kudo.

2/19/41 Honolulu
Danny Savich beat George Wagner, Rubber Higami drew Red Shadow, Balk Estes beat Sammy Cohen dq, Fred Kimball beat Charley Carr, Ernie Powers drew Young Shiranuhi.

2/26/41 Honolulu
Danny Savich beat Balk Estes, Ben Pilar beat Kimon Kudo, Red Shadow beat Fred Kimball, Rubber Higami drew George Wagner, Young Shiranuhi beat Stan Skieski.

3/5/41 Honolulu
Danny Savich beat Sammy Cohen, Balk Estes drew Rubber Higami, George Wagner beat Red Shadow dq, Fred Kimball beat Ernie Powers.

3/12/41 Honolulu
Red Shadow beat Ben Pilar won Hawaiian Junior Title, Rubber Higami beat George Wagner, Danny Savich beat Kimon Kudo, Balk Estes drew Fred Kimball.

3/19/41 Honolulu
Red Shadow beat Danny Savich, Balk Estes drew George Wagner, Rubber Higami beat Fed Kimball, Charley Carr drew Sammy Cohen.

3/26/41 Honolulu
Rubber Higami drew Red Shadow, Sammy Cohen beat Charley Carr, Balk Estes drew Ben Pilar, George Wagner beat Kimon Kudo.

4/2/41 Honolulu
Ben Pilar beat Red Shadow won Hawaiian Junior Title, Sammy Cohen beat Balk Estes, Kimon Kudo drew George Wagner, Charley Carr beat Young Shiranuhi.

4/9/41 Honolulu
Rubber Higami beat Cyclone Mackey dq, George Wagner beat Kimon Kudo, Don Sebastian beat Balk Estes, Big Boy Clement drew Young Shiranuhi.

4/16/41 Honolulu
Ben Pilar beat Cyclone Mackey, George Wagner beat Sammy Cohen, Don Sebastian beat Charley Carr, Big Boy Clement beat Stan Skieski.

4/23/41 Honolulu
George Wagner beat Sammy Cohen, Rubber Higami beat Ben Pilar, Tony Morelli beat Charley Carr, Kimon Kudo drew Don Sebastian.

4/30/41 Honolulu
Tony Morelli beat Don Sebastian, Rubber Higami drew George Wagner, Kimon Kudo & Young Shiranuhi beat Big Boy Clement & Sammy Cohen.

5/7/41 Honolulu
Ben Pilar beat Rubber Higami, Tony Morelli beat Kimon Kudo, George Wagner beat Don Sebastian, Don Carver drew Sammy Cohen.

5/14/41 Honolulu
George Wagner beat Ben Pilar, Tony Morelli beat Sammy Cohen, Charley Carr dew Don Carver, Don Sebastian beat Young Shiranuhi.

5/21/41 Honolulu
George Wagner beat Tony Morelli, Charley Carr drew Rubber Higami, Doc Kowarsky beat Bull Yoyoma, Kimon Kudo beat Don Sebastian.

5/28/41 Honolulu
Tony Morelli beat Kimon Kudo, George Wagner beat Don Sebastian, Ben Pilar beat Charley Carr, Sammy Cohen drew Rubber Higami.

6/4/41 Honolulu
Ben Pilar beat George Wagner, Gene Blackley beat Rubber Higami, Sammy Cohen no contest Tony Morelli, Don Sebastian beat Ernie Powers.

6/11/41 Honolulu
Tony Morelli beat Sammy Cohen, Gene Blackley beat George Wagner, Rubber Higami beat Don Sebastian dq, Bob Redman beat Bob Ford.

6/18/41 Honolulu
Tony Morelli beat Gene Blackley, Ben Pilar beat Charley Carr, Sammy Cohen drew Kimon Kudo, Don Sebastian beat Young Shiranuhi.

6/25/41 Honolulu
Gene Blackley beat Sammy Cohen, Tony Morelli beat Kimon Kudo, Charley Carr drew Don Sebastian, Ernie Powers beat Young Shiranuhi.

7/2/41 Honolulu
Gene Blackley drew Tony Morelli, Jim Hefner beat Charley Carr, Cliff Olson beat Don Sebastian, Sammy Cohen drew Chester Hayes.

7/9/41 Honolulu
Tony Morelli beat Jim Hefner, Gene Blackley beat Kimon Kudo, Chester Hayes beat Charley Carr, Don Sebastian beat Cliff Olson dq.

7/16/41 Honolulu
Gene Blackley beat Jim Hefner, Chester Hayes beat Charley Carr, Tony Morelli beat Cliff Olson, Sammy Cohen beat Don Sebastian.

7/23/41 Honolulu
Tony Morelli beat Ben Pilar won Hawaiian Junior Title, Jim Hefner beat Sammy Cohen, Gene Blackley drew Chester Hayes.

7/30/41 Honolulu
Jim Hefner beat Gene Blackley, Gil Knudsen beat Don Sebastian, Charley Carr beat Chester Hayes, Kimon Kudo beat Sammy Cohen, Sailor Cox beat David Gomez.

8/6/431 Honolulu
Tony Morelli beat Jim Hefner, Gil Knudsen beat Kimon Kudo, Gene Blackley drew Sammy Cohen, Charley Carr beat Young Shiranuhi.

8/13/41 Honolulu
Gil Knudson beat Chester Hayes, Taro Ito beat Charley Carr, Jim Hefner drew Tony Morelli, Kimon Kudo beat Ernie Powers.

8/20/41 Honolulu
Gene Blackley beat Tony Morelli, Gil Knudsen beat Jim Hefner, Taro Ito beat Chester Hayes, Sammy Cohen beat Kimon Kudo.

8/27/41 Honolulu
Gene Blackley no contest Taro Ito, Jim Hefner & Gil Knudsen beat Sammy Cohen & Tony Morelli, Charley Carr drew Chester Hayes.

9/3/41 Honolulu
Tony Morelli beat Gil Knudsen, Jim Hefner beat Cliff Olson, Sammy Cohen beat Chester Hayes, Ben Pilar beat Charley Carr.

9/10/41 Honolulu
Taro Ito beat Gene Blackley, Gil Knudsen beat Sammy Cohen, Cliff Olson beat Don Sebastian, Charley Carr beat Chester Hayes.

9/17/41 Honolulu
Tony Morelli beat Gene Blackley, Jim Hefner drew Gil Knudsen, Brother Jonathan no contest Cliff Olson, Sammy Cohen beat Ernie Powers.

9/24/41 Honolulu
Taro Ito beat Sammy Cohen, Gene Blackley & Gil Knudsen beat Jim Hefner & Tony Morelli, Ben Pilar beat Chester Hayes.

10/1/41 Honolulu
Tony Morelli beat Gil Knudsen, Gust Johnson beat Sammy Cohen, Gene Blackley beat Sailor Garcia, Kimon Kudo beat Charley Carr.

10/8/41 Honolulu
Taro Ito beat Ben Pilar, Gust Johnson beat Gil Knudsen, Gene Blackley drew Jim Hefner, Chester Hayes beat Kimon Kudo.

10/15/41 Honolulu
Tony Morelli beat Taro Ito, Gust Johnson beat Gene Blackley, Jim Hefner beat Chester Hayes, Kimon Kudo drew Ernie Powers.

10/22/41 Honolulu
Gust Johnson beat Jim Hefner, Billy Weidner beat Gene Blackley, Chester Hayes drew Kimon Kudo, Ernie Powers beat Young Shiranuhi.

10/29/41 Honolulu
Billy Widner beat Gust Johnson, Taro Ito beat Gene Blackley, Jim Hefner beat Kimon Kudo, Sailor Carmach no contest Ernie Powers.

11/5/41 Honolulu
Billy Weidner beat Tony Morelli, Jim Hefner beat Kimon Kudo, Gust Johnson drew Ben Pilar, Chester Hayes beat Ernie Powers.

11/12/41 Honolulu
Billy Weidner beat Tony Morelli won Hawaiian Junior title, Gust Johnson beat Taro Ito, Kimon Kudo beat Chester Hayes, Sailor Redman beat David Gomez.

11/19/41 Honolulu
Jim Hefner drew Rubber Higami, Gust Johnson beat Kimon Kudo, Taro Ito drew Billy Weidner, Johnny Baskowitz beat Sailor Redman.

11/26/41 Honolulu
Jim Hefner beat Taro Ito, Gust Johnson drew Billy Weidner, Kimon Kudo beat Wild Bill Sinclair dq, Chester Hayes beat Bulldog Atkinson.

12/3/41 Honolulu
Billy Weidner beat Jim Hefner, Gust Johnson beat Chester Hayes, Johnny Baskowitz beat Bulldog Atkinson dq, David Gomez drew Dr. Kildare.

1943

1/3/43 Honolulu
Chester Hayes beat Ben Pilar, Charlie Carr drew Buck O'Neil, Ernie Powers beat Harry Dellis, Clark Dale beat Bulldog Atkinson dq, Walter Alred beat David Gomez.

1/10/43 Honolulu
Chester Hayes drew Buck O'Neil, Stan Hackney beat Ernie Powers, Charley Carr beat Marvin Roberts, Bill Sinclair beat George Walker, Gordon Williams beat Harry Dellis.

1/17/43 Honolulu
Buck O'Neil beat Charley Carr, Stan Hackney beat Bill Sinclair, Ernie Powers beat Marvin Roberts, Elmer Davis beat Gordon Williams, Harry Dellis beat Walter Alred.

1/31/43 Honolulu
Stan Hackney beat Charley Carr, Chester Hayes beat Buck O'Neil, Joe Mitchell beat Bill Sinclair, Elmer Davis beat Harry Dellis, Robert Callahan drew Sam Nettles.

2/14/43 Honolulu
Stan Hackney beat Chester Hayes, Buck O'Neil beat Joe Mitchell, Ernie Powers beat Clark Dale, Bill Sinclair beat Bill Steddum, Dutch Tennant beat Walter Alred.

2/21/43 Honolulu
Charley Carr drew Buck O'Neil, Chester Hayes beat Joe Mitchell, Rich Eisenbour beat Clark Dale, Bill Sinclair beat Bill Steddum, Butch Tennant beat Walter Alred.

3/7/43 Honolulu
Charley Carr drew Buck O'Neil, Stan Hackney beat Ernie Powers, Frank Robinson beat Rich Eisenbour, Harry Dellis drew Mavin Roberts, Robert Callahan beat Bill Hemmon.

3/21/43 Honolulu
Buck O'Neil beat Ernie Powers, Charley Carr drew Chester Hayes, Elmer Davis beat Stan Skieski dq, Harry Dellis beat Dutch Tennant, Bulldog Atkinson drew Rich Eisenbour.

4/4/43 Honolulu
Stan Hackney beat Buck O'Neil, Ernie Powers beat Chester Hayes, Marvin Roberts beat Harry Dellis, Joe Mitchell drew Stan Skieski, Walter Alred beat Bill Hemmon.

4/11/43 Honolulu
Charley Carr beat Stan Hackney, Ernie Powers beat Mavin Roberts, Chester Hayes beat Stan Skieski, Frank Robinson beat Buffalo Murphy, Walter Alred drew Dutch Tennant.

4/25/43 Honolulu
Charley Carr beat Buck O'Neil dq, Stan Hackney beat Chester Hayes, Marvin Roberts drew Stan Skieski, Frank Robinson beat Buffalo Murphy, Kahuna Lupe beat Clark Dale.

5/7/43 Honolulu
Buck O'Neil beat Marvin Roberts, Stan Skieski beat Chester Hayes, Joe Mitchell beat Frank Robinson, Ernie Altman beat Gordon Williams, Jimmy Gonsalves beat Walter Alred.

5/14/43 Honolulu
Ernie Powers beat Charley Carr, Stan Skieski beat Joe Mitchell, Harry Dellis beat Elmer Davis, Jim Davidson beat Bill Steddum, Jimmy Gonsalves beat Curley Freedman.

5/23/43 Honolulu
Buck O'Neil beat Stan Skieski, Chester Hayes beat Harry Dellis, Frank Robinson beat Joe Mitchell dq, Dutch Altman drew Elmer Davis, Kahuna Lupe beat Buffalo Murphy.

6/6/43 Honolulu
Ernie Powers beat Buck O'Neil, Charley Carr beat Harry Dellis, Stan Skieski beat Frank Robinson, Jimmy Gonsalves beat Bob Grimmett, Clark Dale drew Kahuna Lupe.

6/20/43 Honolulu
Charley Carr beat Ernie Powers, Chester Hayes beat Buck O'Neil, Elmer Davis beat Harry Dellis, Bob Bohach beat Clark Dale, Jimmy Gonsalves drew Gordon Williams.

7/11/43 Honolulu
Buck O'Neil beat Ernie Powers, Stan Skieski beat Elmer Davis, Harry Dellis beat Joe Bakos, Bob Bohach beat Bill Steddum, Clark Dale beat Bob Bohach, Lou Franco drew Gordon Williams.

7/25/43 Honolulu
Stan Skieski beat Charley Carr, Harry Dellis drew Buck O'Neil, Chester Hayes beat Joe Mitchell, Big Boy Clement beat Clark Dale, Jimmy Gonsalves beat Lou Franco.

8/8/43 Honolulu
Charley Carr & Chester Hayes beat Harry Dellis & Buck O'Neil, Elmer Davis beat Joe Mitchell dq, Big Boy Clement drew Stan Skieski, Bill Kaiser beat Cliff Norager.

8/29/43 Honolulu
Buck O'Neil beat Harry Dellis, Chester Hayes no contest Stan Skieski, Elmer Davis beat Big Boy Clement dq, Bill Kaiser beat Lou Franco, Dutch Altman beat Ted Skrzynecki.

9/12/43 Honolulu
Stan Skieski beat Chester Hayes, Buck O'Neil beat Charley Carr, Harry Dellis beat Dutch Altman, Jimmy Gonsalves beat Bill Kaiser, Cliff Norager beat Lou Franco.

10/3/43 Honolulu
Charley Carr & Chester Hayes beat Harry Dellis & Buck O'Neil, Big Boy Clement beat Joe Mitchell, Segundino Pascua beat Cliff Norager, Leo McAllister beat Clark Dale.

10/17/43 Honolulu
Stan Skieski beat Harry Dellis, Chester Hayes drew Buck O'Neil, Joe Mitchell beat Leo McAllister, Elmer Davis beat Jimmy Gonsalves, Ed Pitt drew Ed Silva.

10/31/43 Honolulu
Stan Skieski beat Charley Carr, Axel Madsen beat Buck O'Neil, Jimmy Gonsalves beat Joe Mitchell, Bob Bataan beat Lou Franco, Leo McAllister beat Kelly Cox.

11/14/43 Honolulu
Axel Madsen beat Buck O'Neil, Chester Hayes beat Stan Skieski, Elmer Davis drew Harry Dellis, Doug Corregidor beat Lou Franco.

11/28/43 Honolulu
Charley Carr beat Harry Dellis, Axel Madsen beat Chester Hayes, Jimmy Gonsalves beat Big Boy Clement, Bob Bataan beat Kelly Cox.

12/12/43 Honolulu
Buck O'Neil beat Stan Skieski, Elmer Davis beat Jimmy Gonsalves, Joe Mitchell beat Harry Dellis, Bob Bataan drew Bill Kaiser, Clarence Wimpy Willington beat Kelly Cox.

12/26/43 Honolulu
Charley Carr beat Buck O'Neil, Axel Madsen beat Chester Hayes, Big Boy Clement beat Joe Mitchell, Henry Zalewski beat Ken Blair, Wimpy Willington beat Doug Corregidor.

1944

1/9/44 Honolulu
Stan Skieski beat Buck O'Neil, Chester Hayes beat Elmer Davis, Jimmy Gonsalves beat Harry Dellis dq, Joe Mitchell beat Henry Zalewski, Bob Bataan drew Clarence Willington.

1/23/43 Honolulu
Chester Hayes beat Charley Carr, Axel Madsen beat Joe Mitchell dq, Big Boy Clement beat Elmer Davis, Harry Dellis beat Leo McAllister, Lou Franco beat Ken Blair.

2/6/43 Honolulu
Chester Hayes beat Sammy Cohen, Axel Madsen beat Big Boy Clement, Harry Dellis beat Bob Bataan, Bill Kaiser beat Joe Mitchell, Henry Zalewski beat Wimpy Willington.

2/20/44 Honolulu
Charley Carr beat Chester Hayes, Jimmy Gonsalves beat Big Boy Clement, Sammy Cohen beat Harry Dellis, Bob Bataan drew Henry Zalewski.

3/5/44 Honolulu
Sammy Cohen drew Axel Madsen, Harry Dellis beat Jimmy Gonsalves, Big Boy Clement beat Henry Zalewski, Bill Kaiser beat Ken Blair, Joe Mitchell beat Bill Steddum.

3/19/44 Honolulu
Charley Carr beat Sammy Cohen, Kimon Kudo beat Harry Dellis, Babe Small beat Big Boy Clement, Jimmy Gonsalves drew Joe Mitchell, Bill Steddum beat Henry Zalewski.

4/2/44 Honolulu
Axel Madison beat Charley Carr, Kimon Kudo beat Joe Mitchell, Chester Hayes beat Elmer Davis, Bob Bohach beat Bill Steddum, Wimpy Willington beat Bob Bataan.

4/16/44 Honolulu
Sammy Cohen beat Chester Hayes, Babe Small beat Joe Mitchell, Kimon Kudo beat Big Boy Clement dq, Elmer Davis drew Jimmy Gonsalves, Al Nyles beat Clarence Willington.

4/30/44 Honolulu
Charley Carr drew Kimon Kudo, Andre Adoree beat Big Boy Clement, Marvin Roberts beat Harry Dellis, Red Carter beat Henry Zalewski, Lou Franco beat Al Nyles.

5/14/44 Honolulu
Sammy Cohen beat Kimon Kudo, Chester Hayes drew Babe Small, Elmer Davis beat Harry Dellis dq, Jimmy Gonsalves beat Red Carter, Don Marlin beat Bob Bohach.

5/28/44 Honolulu
Charley Carr beat Sammy Cohen dq, Andre Adoree drew Axel Madsen, Harry Dellis beat Marvin Roberts, Charley Shiranuhi beat Bill Steddum, Albert Llewellyn beat Lou Franco.

6/11/44 Honolulu
Kimon Kudo beat Chester Hayes, Babe Small beat Frank Cutler, Elmer Davis beat Harry Dellis dq, Big Boy Clement beat Tony Blackstone, Bob Bataan beat Ken Blair.

6/25/44 Honolulu
Axel Madsen beat Babe Small, Sammy Cohen beat Harry Dellis, Jimmy Gonsalves beat Elmer Davis, Ed Hout drew Albert Llewellyn, Bill Kaiser beat Bob Bataan.

7/9/44 Honolulu
Sammy Cohen & Buck O'Neil beat Charley Carr & Chester Hayes, Kimon Kudo beat Jimmy Gonsalves, Albert Llewellyn beat Bill Kaiser, Big Boy Clement drew Bill Steddum.

7/23/44 Honolulu
Kimon Kudo beat Sammy Cohen, Chester Hayes drew Axel Madsen, Jimmy Gonsalves beat Albert Llewellyn, Charley Shiranuhi beat Big Boy Clement dq.

8/6/44 Honolulu
Buck O'Neil beat Chester Hayes, Babe Small beat Axel Madsen, Jimmy Gonsalves beat Albert Llewellyn, Charley Shiranuhi beat Big Boy Clements dq.

8/20/44 Honolulu
Sammy Cohen beat Buck O'Neil, Harry Dellis beat Chester Hayes, Bob Bataan beat Albert Llewellyn, Al Hardy drew Bobby Jones, Wimpy Willington beat Ken Blair.

9/3/44 Honolulu
Axel Madsen beat Babe Small dq, Buck O'Neil drew Ben Pilar, Jimmy Gonsalves beat Bobby Jones, Al Hardy beat Joe Mitchell, Bob Bataan beat Wimpy Willington.

9/17/44 Honolulu
Charley Carr beat Kimon Kudo, Jimmy Gonsalves beat Chester Hayes, Frank Cutler drew Babe Small, Harry Dellis beat Al Hardy, Bobby Jones beat Buck Lee.

10/1/44 Honolulu
Axel Madsen beat Sammy Cohen, Buck O'Neil beat Jimmy Gonsalves, Chester Hayes beat Bobby Jones, Al Hardy beat Mike Casey, Buck Lee beat Wimpy Willington.

10/15/44 Honolulu
Sammy Cohen drew Kimon Kudo, Ben Pilar beat Harry Dellis, Bob Bataan beat John Peters, Babe Small beat Joe Mitchell, Mike Casey beat Buck Lee.

10/29/44 Honolulu
Charley Carr beat Axel Madsen, Babe Small beat Chester Hayes, Harry Dellis drew Buck O'Neil, Joe Mitchell beat Bob Bataan, Tiger James beat Bill Kaiser.

11/12/44 Honolulu
Ben Pilar beat Buck O'Neil, Sammy Cohen beat Harry Dellis, Chester Hayes beat Joe Mitchell, Bob Bataan beat Tiger James, Bill Kaiser drew Buck Lee.

11/26/44 Honolulu
Babe Small beat Sammy Cohen, Kimon Kudo beat Chester Hayes, Jimmy Gonsalves beat Joe Mitchell, Bob Battan drew Bill Kaiser, Wimpy Willington beat Buck Lee.

12/10/44 Honolulu
Babe Small beat Charley Carr, Axel Madsen drew Buck Lee, Jimmy Gonsalves beat Bob Battan.

12/16/44 Honolulu
Ben Pilar beat Buck O'Neil, Sammy Cohen beat Jimmy Gonsalves, Kimon Kudo beat Joe Mitchell, Axel Johnson drew Wimpy Willington, Buck Lee beat Charles Dimitrios.

12/24/44 Honolulu
Axel Madsen beat Babe Small, Sammy Cohen drew Buck O'Neil, Kimon Kudo beat Clark Dale, Joe Mitchell beat Axel Johnson, Stan Miyashiro beat Buck Lee.

12/30/44 Honolulu
Sammy Cohen & Buck O'Neil beat Charley Carr & Kimon Kudo, Ben Pilar beat Joe Mitchell, Mike Casey drew Clark Dale, Jim Coburn beat Bobby Roberts.

1945

1/7/45 Honolulu
Sammy Cohen beat Ben Pilar, Axel Madsen drew Buck O'Neil, Babe Smolinski beat Clark Dale, Mike Casey no contest Joe Mitchell, Wimpy Willington beat Octopus Roberts.

1/21/45 Honolulu
Kimon Kudo beat Buck O'Neil, Chester Hayes no contest Ben Pilar, Mike Casey beat Jimmy Gonsalves, Joe Mitchell beat Clark Dale, Bolo Bataan beat Buck Lee.

1/28/45 Honolulu
Axel Madsen & Babe Smolinski beat Sammy Cohen & Buck O'Neil, Mike Casey drew Chester Hayes, Jimmy Gonsalves beat Joe Mitchell, Jimmy Colburn beat Charley Dimitrio.

2/5/45 Honolulu
Charley Carr beat Ben Pilar, Babe Smolinski beat Mike Casey, Charley Shiranuhi beat Joe Mitchell, Don Carver beat Bolo Bataan, Stan Miyashiro drew Stanley Walicki.

2/19/45 Honolulu
Sammy Cohen beat Axel Madsen, Ray Higgins beat Charley Shiranuhi, Mike Casey drew Jimmy Gonsalves, Joe Mitchell beat Jimmy Colburn, Wimpy Willington beat Stan Walicki.

2/24/45 Honolulu
Sammy Cohen no contest Ben Pilar, Chester Hayes beat Buck O'Neil, Ray Higgins beat Joe Mitchell, Little Ali Baba beat Wimpy Willington, Bolo Bataan beat Stan Miyashiro.

3/4/45 Honolulu
Kimon Kudo beat Ben Pilar, Ray Higgins no contest Axel Madsen, Don Carver drew Chester Hayes, Ralph Teague beat Clark Dale, Little Ali Baba beat Bobby Roberts.

3/11/45 Honolulu
Chester Hayes beat Sammy Cohen, Mike Casey beat Babe Smolinski, Buck O'Neil beat Little Ali Baba, Bolo Bataan drew Bill Kaiser, Tiger James beat Bobby Roberts.

3/18/45 Honolulu
Kimon Kudo beat Chester Hayes, Jimmy Gonsalves beat Ray Higgins, Vilai Su'a beat Buck Lee, Nick Nichols beat Tiger James.

3/24/45 Honolulu
Charley Carr drew Sammy Cohen, Axel Madsen beat Mike Casey, Babe Smolinski beat Charley Shiranuhi, Vilai Su'a beat Wimpy Willington, Nick Nichols beat Stan Walicki.

4/1/45 Honolulu
Axel Madsen beat Babe Smolinski, Ben Pilar beat Mike Golden, Mike Casey drew Joe Mitchell, Don Marlin beat Bill Dimitrios, Bolo Bataan beat Stan Miyashiro.

4/15/45 Honolulu
Kimon Kudo beat Sammy Cohen, Chester Hayes beat Don Carver, Jimmy Gonsalves beat Vic Rancourt, Vilai Su'a beat Bolo Bataan, Bill Kaiser drew Buck Lee.

4/29/45 Honolulu
Charley Carr beat Ben Pilar, Sammy Cohen no contest Buck O'Neil, Harry Dellis beat Mike Casey, Vilai Su'a beat Stan Miyashiro, Buck Lee beat Nick Nichols.

5/5/45 Honolulu
Charley Carr beat Chester Hayes, Jimmy Gonsalves drew Buck O'Neil, Vilai Su'a beat Joe Mitchell, Mike Casey beat Buck Lee, Tiger James beat Fred Tam.

5/13/45 Honolulu
Harry Dellis beat Buck O'Neil, Sammy Cohen beat Mike Casey, Don Carver beat Jimmy Coburn, Al Lolotai beat Buck Lee, Stan Miyashiro beat Jack Ajax.

5/20/45 Honolulu
Ben Pilar beat Harry Dellis, Sammy Cohen drew Kimon Kudo, Vilai Su'a beat Chief Arnlach, Mike Casey no contest Joe Mitchell, Wimpy Willington beat Bolo Bataan.

5/27/45 Honolulu
Jimmy Gonsalves beat Sammy Cohen, Don Carver beat Chester Hayes, Vilai Su'a beat Joe Mitchell, Francis Rawlins beat Buck Lee, Whitey Glover drew Charley Shiranuhi.

6/3/45 Honolulu
Charley Carr & Kimon Kudo beat Sammy Cohen & Harry Dellis, Chester Hayes drew Vilai Su'a, Stan Miyashiro drew Francine Rawlins, Buck Lee beat Bolo Bataan.

6/10/45 Honolulu
Harry Dellis beat Sammy Cohen, Don Carver drew Kimon Kudo, Joe Mitchell beat Buck Lee, Al Lolotai beat Stan Miyashiro, Wallace Tsutsumi beat Tiger James.

6/17/45 Honolulu
Ben Pilar beat Jimmy Gonsalves, Buck O'Neil beat Joe Mitchell, Vilai Su'a beat Charley Shiranuhi, Al Lolotai beat Whitey Glover, Francis Rawlins drew Wimpy Willington.

6/24/45 Honolulu
Kimon Kudo beat Don Carver, Vilai Su'a beat Chester Hayes, Al Lolotai drew Joe Mitchell, Stan Miyashiro beat Buck Lee dq, Wally Tsutsumi beat Doug Corregidor.

7/8/45 Honolulu
Jimmy Gonsalves beat Vilai Su'a, Buck O'Neil beat Ben Pilar, Whiley Glover beat Joe Mitchell, Al Lolotai drew Charley Shiranuhi, Bolo Bataan no contest Francis Rawlins.

7/22/45 Honolulu
Charley Carr beat Kimon Kudo, Chester Hayes no contest Buck O'Neil, Whitey Glover beat Charley Shiranuhi, Wimpy Willington beat Wally Tsutsumi, Blackie Adachi beat Stan Miyashiro.

8/5/45 Honolulu
Don Carver beat Harry Dellis, Vilai Su'a beat Chester Hayes, Joe Mitchell drew Wimpy Willington, Stan Miyashiro no contest Fred Tam, Francis Rawlins drew Wally Tsutsumi.

8/19/45 Honolulu
Harry Dellis no contest Ben Pilar, Jimmy Gonsalves drew Kimon Kudo, Buck Lee drew Francis Rawlins, Wimpy Willington beat Stan Miyashiro, Blackie Adachi beat Al Carvalho.

9/2/45 Honolulu
Vilai Su'a beat Jimmy Gonsalves, Charley Carr beat Harry Dellis, Joe Mitchell beat Buck Lee, Wimpy Willington beat Doug Corregidor, Bolo Bataan drew Stan Miyashiro.

9/9/45 Honolulu
Kimon Kudo beat Vilai Su'a, Don Carver beat Harry Dellis, Whitey Glover drew Frank Merrill, Nick Nichols beat Bolo Bataan, Fred Marco beat Joe Mitchell.

9/16/45 Honolulu
Buck O'Neil no contest Ben Pilar, Jimmy Gonsalves drew Chester Hayes, Whitey Glover drew Buck Lee, Whitey Glover beat Joe Mitchell, Fred Marco beat Wimpy Willington, Francis Rawlins beat Wally Tsutsumi.

9/22/45 Honolulu
Don Carver beat Ben Pilar, Fred Marco no contest Buck O'Neil, Harry Dellis drew Chester Hayes, Nick Nichols beat Francis Rawlins, Charles Takase beat Fred Tam.

9/29/45 Honolulu
Charley Carr beat Don Carver, Jimmy Gonsalves beat Fred Marco, Joe Mitchell beat Nick Nichols, Buck Lee drew Charley Takase, Francis Rawlins beat Bolo Bataan.

10/14/45 Honolulu
Vilai Su'a beat Harry Dellis, Joe Mitchell beat Buck O'Neil, Chester Hayes beat Buck Lee, Wimpy Willington beat Tiger James, Stan Miyashiro drew Wally Tsutsumi.

10/28/45 Honolulu
Jimmy Gonsalves beat Kimon Kudo, Ben Pilar beat Chester Hayes, Nick Nichols drew Wimpy Willington, Frank Merrill beat Billy Fredrick, Bill Kaiser beat Fred Tam.

11/11/45 Honolulu
Jimmy Gonsalves beat Charley Carr, Axel Madsen beat Joe Mitchell, Kimon Kudo beat Wimpy Willington, Frank Merrill beat Bill Dimitrious, Blackie Adachi beat Fred Tam.

11/18/45 Honolulu
Buck O'Neil beat Joe Mitchell, Harry Dellis no contest Chester Hayes, Billy Fredrick beat Frank Merrill, Don Carver drew Ben Pilar.

12/2/45 Honolulu
Jimmy Gonsalves beat Charley Carr, Kimon Kudo drew Buck O'Neil, Vilai Su'a beat Joe Mitchell, Wimpy Willington beat Charley Takase, Francis Rawlins beat Tony Allesandro.

12/16/45 Honolulu
Harry Dellis no contest Chester Hayes, Bobby Nelson beat Buck O'Neil, Don Carver beat Wimpy Willington, Frank Merrill drew Leo McAllister, Buck Lee beat Tiger James.

12/22/45 Honolulu
Bobby Nelson beat Chester Hayes, Don Carver drew Kimon Kudo, Vilai Su'a beat Leo McAllister, Whitey Glover beat Frank Merrill, Nick Nichols drew Charley Takase.

12/30/45 Honolulu
Bobby Nelson beat Harry Dellis, Vilai Su'a beat Kimon Kudo, Chester Hayes no contest Joe Mitchell, Wimpy Willington beat Buck Lee, Francis Rawlins beat Wally Tsutsumi.

1946

1/6/46 Honolulu
Blackie Adachi beat Charley Takase.

1/13/46 Honolulu
Nick Nichols beat Joe Mitchell dq.

1/20/46 Honolulu
Jimmy Gonsalves beat Bobby Nelson, Scarlet Pimpernel beat Joe Mitchell, Don Carver drew Buck O'Neil, Frank Merrill beat Leo McAllister, Tiger James beat Bill Kaiser.

1/26/46 Honolulu
Harry Dellis & Buck O'Neil beat Bobby Nelson & Scarlet Pimpernel, Scarlet Pimpernel beat Bobby Nelson, Ben Pilar beat Wimpy Willington, Jack McArthur beat Frank Merrill, Buck Lee beat Tiger James.

2/10/46 Honolulu
Scarlet Pimpernel beat Ben Pilar, Don Carver beat Harry Dellis, Al Lolotai drew Joe Mitchell, Buck Lee beat Nick Nichols, Leo McAllister beat Jack McArthur dq.

2/16/46 Honolulu
Scarlet Pimpernel beat Buck O'Neil, Jimmy Gonsalves beat Don Carver, Al Lolotai beat Jack McArthur dq, Wimpy Willington beat Buck Lee, Bill Kaiser drew Wally Tsutsumi.

2/24/46 Honolulu
Scarlet Pimpernel beat Charley Carr, Whitey Glover beat Jack McArthur, Harry Dellis beat Joe Mitchell, Buck Lee beat Charley Takase, Stan Miyashiro beat Bill Kaiser.

3/2/46 Honolulu
Scarlet Pimpernel beat Harry Dellis, Ben Pilar beat Wimpy Willington, Al Lolotai beat Joe Mitchell, Leo McAllister beat Stan Miyashiro, Francis Rawlins drew Charley Takase.

3/10/46 Honolulu
Charley Carr beat Billy Venable, Jimmy Gonsalves drew Vilai Su'a, Buck Lee beat Buck O'Neil, Nick Nichols beat Charley Takase, Buck Lee beat Buck O'Neil, Nick Nichols beat Charley Takase, Frank Merrill beat Clark Dale.

3/16/46 Honolulu
Vilai Su'a beat Scarlet Pimpernel, Billy Venable beat Joe Mitchell, Don Carver beat Buck O'Neil dq, Charley Shiranuhi beat Buck Lee, Wally Tsutsumi beat Nick Nichols.

3/24/46 Honolulu
Jimmy Gonsalves drew Billy Venable, Scarlet Pimpernel beat Ben Pilar, Harry Dellis beat Wimpy Willington, Al Lolotai beat Leo McAllister, Fred Tam beat Tiger James.

3/30/46 Honolulu
Lee Grable beat Charley Carr, Al Lolotai & Vilai Su'a beat Harry Dellis & Billy Venable, Frank Merrill beat Stan Miyashiro.

4/7/46 Honolulu
Lee Grable beat Charley Carr, Scarlet Pimpernel beat Don Carver, Harry Dellis drew Ben Pilar, Frank Merrill beat Leo McAllister, Francis Rawlins beat Wally Tsutsumi.

4/14/46 Honolulu
Lee Grable drew Vilai Su'a, Billy Venable beat Harry Dellis, Ben Pilar beat Buck Lee, Wimpy Willington beat Nick Nichols, Charley Takase beat Tiger James.

4/21/46 Honolulu
Scarlet Pimpernel beat Billy Venable, Al Lolotai beat Whitey Glover, Don Carver drew Ben Pilar, Charley Shiranuhi beat Frank Merrill, Leo McAllister beat Buck Lee.

4/28/46 Honolulu
Lee Grable beat Vilai Su'a, Jimmy Gonsalves beat Ben Pilar, Billy Venable beat Wimpy Willington, Jack McArthur beat Leo McAllister, Stan Miyashiro beat Charley Takase.

5/4/46 Honolulu
Scarlet Pimpernel beat Jimmy Gonsalves, Al Lolotai beat Billy Venable, Charley Carr beat Harry Dellis, Jack McArthur drew Charley Shiranuhi, Nick Nichols beat Stan Miyashiro.

5/12/46 Honolulu
Lee Grable beat Al Lolotai, Billy Venable beat Charley Carr, Wimpy Willington beat Harry Dellis dq, Charley Shiranuhi beat John Starkey, Bolo Bataan drew Wally Tsutsumi.

5/19/46 Honolulu
Scarlet Pimpernel beat Lee Grable, Jimmy Gonsalves beat Billy Venable, Wimpy Willington beat Harry Dellis, Leo McAllister drew Nick Nichols, Francis Rawlins beat Buck Lee dq.

5/26/46 Honolulu
Scarlet Pimpernel beat Jimmy Gonsalves, Vitali Su'a drew Billy Venable, Wimpy Willington beat Nick Nichols, Charley Shiranuhi beat Leo McAllister, Bolo Bataan beat Fred Tam.

6/2/46 Honolulu
Lee Grable beat Billy Venable, Stan Skieski beat Charley Carr, Al Lolotai beat Charley Shiranuhi, Harry Dellis beat Buck Lee, Frank Merrill drew Joe Starkey.

6/9/46 Honolulu
Scarlet Pimpernel beat Stan Skieski, Lee Grable drew Vilai Su'a, Tex Porter beat Wimpy Willington, Francis Rawlins beat Leo McAllister dq, Buck Lee beat Bolo Bataan.

6/16/46 Honolulu
Lee Grable beat Jimmy Gonsalves, Tex Porter beat Billy Venable, Al Lolotai drew Stan Skieski, Buck Lee beat Francis Rawlins, Nick Nichols drew Charley Takase.

6/23/46 Honolulu
Lee Grable beat Tex Porter, Vilai Su'a beat Stan Skieski, Kimon Kudo beat Billy Venable, Lucky Simunovich beat Buck Lee, Francis Rawlins beat Charley Takase.

6/30/46 Honolulu
Tex Porter beat Scarlet Pimpernel, Johnny Stiles beat Stan Skieski, Kimon Kudo beat Al Lolotai, Lucky Simunovich beat Frank Merrill, Leo McAllister drew Nick Nichols.

7/7/46 Honolulu
Lee Grable beat Stan Skieski, Jimmy Gonsalves beat Tex Porter, Johnny Stiles beat Wimpy Willington, Whitey Glover drew Al Lolotai, Stan Miyashiro beat Nick Nichols.

7/14/46 Honolulu
Vilai Su'a beat Tex Porter, Lee Grable beat Johnny Stiles, Ben Pilar beat Stan Skieski, Lucky Simunovich beat Leo McAllister, Buck Lee beat Nick Nichols.

7/21/46 Honolulu
Lee Grable beat Vilai Su'a, Scarlet Pimpernel beat Ben Pilar, Johnny Stiles beat Tex Porter, Wimpy Willington beat Buck Lee, Leo McAllister beat Stan Miyashiro.

7/28/46 Honolulu
Scarlet Pimpernel beat Tex Porter, Jimmy Gonsalves beat Stan Skieski, Al Lolotai drew Johnny Stiles, Lucky Simunovich beat Joe Starkey, Abel Rodriguez beat Charley Takase.

8/4/46 Honolulu
Lee Grable drew Jimmy Gonsalves, Vilai Su'a beat Johnny Stiles, Stan Skieski beat Tex Porter, Buck Lee drew Abel Rodriguez, Wally Tsutsumi beat Fred Tam.

8/11/46 Honolulu
Scarlet Pimpernel beat Vilai Su'a, Ben Pilar beat Tex Porter, Johnny Stiles beat Stan Skieski dq, Abel Rodrigues drew Lucky Simunovich, Francis Rawlins beat Wally Tsutsumi.

8/18/46 Honolulu
Ben Pilar beat Johnny Stiles, Stan Skieski beat Kimon Kudo, Wong Buck Cheung beat Joe Starkey, Francis Rawlins beat Jack McKinley, Abel Rodrigues drew Wimpy Willington.

8/25/46 Honolulu
Lee Grable beat Stan Skieski, Jimmy Gonsalves beat Ben Pilar, Vilai Su'a beat Johnny Stiles, Lucky Simunovic beat Francis Rawlins, Stan Miyashiro beat Fred Tam.

8/28/46 Honolulu
Gorilla Poggi beat Ben Pilar, Lee Grable drew Kimon Kudo, Vilai Su'a beat Whitey Glover dq, Lucky Simunovich beat Joe Starkey, Charlet Takase beat Stan Miyashiro.

9/1/46 Honolulu
Lee Grable beat Scarlet Pimpernel dq, Jimmy Gonsalves beat Gorilla Poggi dq, Whitey Glover drew Lucky Simunovich, Abel Rodriguez beat Francis Rawlins, Bolo Bataan beat Stan Miyashiro.

9/8/46 Honolulu
Gorilla Poggi beat Stan Skieski, Kimon Kudo beat Vilai Su'a, Lucky Simunovich beat Wimpy Willington, Frank Merrill drew Joe Starkey, Bolo Bataan beat Tiger James.

9/15/46 Honolulu
Lee Grable beat Jimmy Gonsalves, Kimon Kudo drew Gorilla Poggi, Lucky Simunovich beat Abel Rodrigues, Wimpy Willington beat Bolo Bataan, Buck Lee beat Charley Takase.

9/22/46 Honolulu
Lee Grable beat Scarlet Pimpernel, Vilai Su'a beat Gorilla Poggi, Abel Rodrigues beat Wimpy Willington, Wong Buck Cheung beat Stan Miyashiro, Blackie Adachi beat Fred Tam.

9/29/46 Honolulu
Jacques Manuel beat Charley Carr.

10/6/46 Honolulu
Jacques Manuel beat Kimon Kudo.

10/20/46 Honolulu
Lee Grable beat Jacques Manuel, Jimmy Gonsalves drew Gorilla Poggi, Lucky Simunovich beat Whitey Glover dq, Buck Lee drew Frank Merrill, Blackie Adachi beat Tiger James.

10/27/46 Honolulu
Vilai Su'a beat Lee Grable, Jimmy Gonsalves drew Jacques Manuel, Charley Carr beat Buck Lee, Wimpy Willington beat Bill Kaiser, Blackie Adachi beat Fred Tam dq.

11/3/46 Honolulu
Jacques Manuel beat Ben Sherman, Jack Kiser beat Charley Carr, Ben Pilar beat Gorilla Poggi, Charley Shiranuhi drew Lucky Simunovich, Nick Nichols beat Bolo Bataan.

11/10/46 Honolulu
Lee Grable & Jack Kiser beat Jacques Manuel & Gorilla Poggi, Jimmy Gonsalves beat Kimon Kudo, Wimpy Willington beat Nick Nichols, Wally Tsutsumi beat Tiger James.

11/17/46 Honolulu
Lee Grable beat Ben Sherman, Vilai Su'a beat Jack Kiser, Gorilla Poggi beat Wimpy Willington, Charley Shiranuhi drew Lucky Simunovich, Francis Rawlins beat Wally Tsutsumi.

11/24/46 Honolulu
Vilai Su'a beat Jacques Manuel, Jack Kiser beat Gorilla Poggi, Charley Carr drew Ben Pilar, Charley Shiranuhi beat Joe Starkey, Nick Nichols drew Franis Rawlins.

12/1/46 Honolulu
Jack Kiser beat Ben Sherman, Jimmy Gonsalves beat Gorilla Poggi, Jacques Manuel drew Charley Shiranuhi, Nick Nichols beat Francis Rawlins, Bolo Bataan beat Wally Tsutsumi.

12/8/46 Honolulu
Lee Grable beat Jack Kiser, Abe Kashey beat Jimmy Gonsalves, Jacques Manuel beat Lucky Simunovich, Nick Nichols drew Wimpy Willington, Frank Merrill beat Charley Takase.

12/15/46 Honolulu
Jim Londos beat Abe Kashey, Jack Kiser drew Jacques Manuel, Kimon Kudo beat Ben Sherman dq, Joe Starkey beat Lucky Simunovich, Bolo Bataan beat Blackie Adachi.

12/22/46 Honolulu
Jim Londos beat Lee Grable, Charley Carr drew Jack Kiser, Ben Sherman beat Jacques Manuel, Kimon Kudo drew Ben Pilar, Wimpy Willington beat Bolo Bataan.

12/29/46 Honolulu
Kimon Kudo beat Jack Kiser, Jacques Manuel beat Ben Pilar, Jimmy Gonsalves drew Ben Sherman.

1947

1/5/47 Honolulu
Lee Grable beat Vilai Su'a, Kimon Kudo beat Jacques Manuel dq, Jack Kiser beat Charley Carr, Buck Lee drew Wimpy Willington, Stan Miyashiro beat Nick Nichols.

1/12/47 Honolulu
Lee Grable drew Ben Sherman, Jack Kiser beat Jacques Manuel dq, Mike Casey beat Abel Rodrigues, Al Lolotai beat Joe Starkey, Bolo Bataan beat Fred Tam.

1/19/47 Honolulu
Jack Kiser beat Jacques Manuel, Jimmy Gonsalves beat Ben Sherman, Mike Casey beat Wimpy Willington, Al Lolotai beat Abel Rodrigues, Stan Miyashiro beat Bolo Bataan.

1/26/47 Honolulu
Jack Kiser beat Lee Grable, Jacques Manuel beat Mike Casey, Kimon Kudo drew Al Lolotai, Ben Pilar beat Buck Lee dq, Nick Nichols beat Abel Rodrigues.

2/2/47 Honolulu
Axel Madsen beat Jacques Manuel, Jack Kiser beat Stan Skieski, Vilai Su'a beat Mike Casey, Stan Miyashiro beat Wimpy Willington, Abel Rodrigues beat Wally Tsutsumi.

2/9/47 Honolulu
Lee Grable beat Jack Kiser, Vilai Su'a beat Ben Sherman dq, Jacques Manuel beat Kimon Kudo, Mike Casey beat Buck Lee, Bolo Bataan beat Tiger James.

2/13/47 Honolulu
Jacques Manuel beat Mike Casey, Ben Pilar beat Buck Lee, Nick Nichols drew Wimpy Willington, Joe Starkey beat Abel Rodrigues, Blackie Adachi beat Bolo Bataan dq.

2/16/47 Honolulu
Ted Travis beat Axel Madsen, Jacques Manuel & Ben Sherman beat Kimon Kudo & Charley Shiranuhi, Ben Pilar beat Mike Casey, Stan Miyashiro drew Joe Starkey.

2/23/47 Honolulu
Ted Travis beat Jacques Manuel, Jimmy Gonsalves beat Jack Kiser, Ben Sherman beat Ben Pilar, Mike Casey beat Abel Rodrigues, Bolo Bataan drew Buck Lee.

2/27/47 Honolulu
Alex Kasaboski & Henry Kulkovich beat Frank Culter & Whitey Glover, Henry Kulkovich beat Terry McGinnis, George Temple beat Whitey Glover, Vilai Su'a beat Frank Culter, Al Lolotai beat Alex Kasaboski, Andre Adoree beat Francis Rawlins.

3/2/47 Honolulu
Lee Grable drew Ted Travis, George Pencheff beat Ben Sherman, Axel Madsen beat Jacques Manuels dq, Mike Casey beat Bolo Bataan, Stan Miyashiro drew Wimpy Willington.

3/7/47 Honolulu
Vilai Su'a beat George Temple, Henry Kulkovich beat Andre Adoree, Al Lolotai beat Whitey Glover, Francis Rawlins beat Frank Culter dq, Alex Kasaboski drew Terry McGinnis.

3/9/47 Honolulu
George Pencheff beat Lee Grable, Jacques Manuel beat Jimmy Gonsalves, Kimon Kudo drew Axel Madsen, Mike Casey beat Bull Pugh dq, Wally Tsutsumi beat Nick Nichols.

3/13/47 Honolulu
Ben Sherman beat Ben Pilar, Mike Casey beat Abel Rodrigues dq, Frank Merrill drew Joe Starkey, Wimpy Willington beat Wally Tsutsumi, Fred Tam beat Ralph Merrill.

3/16/47 Honolulu
Ted Travis beat George Pencheff, Leo Wallick beat Ben Sherman, Jacques Manuel beat Charley Carr, Mike Casey beat Wally Takase, Bull Pugh beat Frank Merrill.

3/23/47 Honolulu
Ted Travis beat Lee Grable, Leo Wallick beat Axel Madsen, Ben Sherman beat Jacques Manuel dq, Mike Casey drew Stan Miyashiro, Joe Starkey beat Buck Lee.

3/27/47 Honolulu
Henry Kulkovich beat Vilai Su'a, Cardiff Giant beat Whitey Glover, Andre Adoree drew Al Lolotai, Bear Honda beat Gene Sexton, Francis Rawlins beat Ben Sui.

3/27/47 Honolulu
Jimmy Gonsalves beat Ben Pilar, Axel Madsen beat Buck Lee, Nick Nichols drew Abel Rodrigues, Fred Tam beat Charley Takase, Blackie Adachi drew Tiger James.

3/30/47 Honolulu
Leo Wallick beat Jacques Manuel, Lee Grable beat Ben Sherman, Mike Casey drew Kimon Kudo, Harry Dellis beat Stan Miyashiro, Bolo Bataan drew Bill Kaiser.

4/3/47 Honolulu
Bobby Stewart beat Whitey Glover, Cardiff Giant beat Henry Kulkovich, Andre Adoree drew Al Lolotai, Ben Sui beat Gene Sexton, Francis Rawlins beat Albert Camacho.

4/6/47 Honolulu
Lee Grable & Leo Wallick beat Jacques & Ted Travis, Ben Sherman beat Axel Madsen, Harry Dellis drew Wimpy Willington, Nick Nichols beat Abel Rodrigues dq.

4/10/47 Honolulu
Bobby Stewart beat Henry Kulkovich, Andre Adoree drew Cardiff Giant, Masked Terror beat Al Lolotai, Gene Sexton beat Albert Camacho dq, Bear Honda beat Ben Sui.

4/13/47 Honolulu
Ted Travis beat Leo Wallick, Jimmy Gonsalves drew Ben Sherman, Bob Corby beat Mike Casey, Kimon Kudo beat Harry Dellis, Buck Lee beat Nick Nichols.

4/17/47 Honolulu
Cardiff Giant no contest Masked Terror, Vilai Su'a beat Andre Adoree dq, Al Lolotai beat Whitey Glover, Albert Camacho drew Francis Rawlins, Bear Honda beat Gene Sexton.

4/20/47 Honolulu
Lee Grable beat Ben Sherman, Bob Corby drew Leo Wallick, Axel Madsen beat Jacques Manuel dq, Mike Casey beat Buck Lee, Abel Rodrigues beat Bolo Bataan.

4/24/47 Honolulu
Vilai Su'a beat Masked Terror, Francis Rawlins beat Ted Sanders, Cardiff Giant drew Al Lolotai, Bear Honda beat Dale Clark, Albert Camacho drew Ben Sui.

4/27/47 Honolulu
Ted Travis beat Bob Corby, Leo Wallick beat Jacques Manuel, Harry Dellis drew Ben Pilar, Charley Shiranuhi beat Able Rodrigues, Stan Miyashiro beat Wimpy Willington.

5/4/47 Honolulu
Leo Wallick beat Lee Grable dq, Bob Corby beat Axel Madsen, Ben Sherman beat Harry Dellis, Mike Casey drew Charley Shiranuhi, Bull Pugh beat Wally Tsutsumi.

5/8/47 Honolulu
Al Lolotai drew Masked Terror, Francis Rawlins drew Armand Tanny, Vilai Su'a beat Whitey Glover, Ted Sanders drew Ben Sui, Gene Sexton beat Albert Camancho dq.

5/11/47 Honolulu
Ted Travis beat Leo Wallick, Bob Corby beat Kimon Kudo, Charley Carr drew Ben Pilar, Charley Shiranuhi drew Joe Starkey, Blackie Adachi beat Fred Tam.

5/18/47 Honolulu
Lee Grable drew Ben Sherman, Bob Corby drew Jimmy Gonsalves, Harry Dellis drew Alex Madsen, Mike Casey beat Abel Rodrigus dq, Nick Nichols beat Tiger James.

5/25/47 Honolulu
Ted Travis beat Ben Sherman, Lee Grable beat Leo Wallick, Bob Corby beat Harry Dellis, Abel Rodrigues drew Wimpy Willington, Stan Miyashiro beat Bolo Bataan.

6/1/47 Honolulu
Ted Travis beat Lee Grable, Bob Corby drew Leo Wallick, Jimmy Gonsalves beat Mike Casey, Frank Merrill drew Joe Starkey, Bull Pugh beat Nick Nichols.

6/8/47 Honolulu
Pan Manlapig beat Bob Corby, Ben Sherman drew Leo Wallick, Axel Madsen beat Harry Dellis, Abel Rodrigues drew Wimpy Willington, Stan Miyashiro beat Bolo Bataan.

6/15/47 Honolulu
Lee Grable & Leo Wallick beat Bob Corby & Ted Travis, Jimmy Gonsalves beat Harry Dellis, Mike Casey drew Ben Pilar, Abel Rodrigues beat Buck Lee.

6/22/47 Honolulu
Leo Wallick beat Ted Travis, Lee Grable beat Bob Corby, Axel Madsen beat Mike Casey, Frank Moscato beat Wimpy Willington, Bull Pugh beat Charley Takase.

6/29/47 Honolulu
Ted Travis beat Ben Sherman, Pan Manlapig beat Axel Madsen, Jimmy Gonsalves beat Bob Corby, Frank Moscato beat Mike Casey, Buck Lee drew Nick Nichols.

7/6/47 Honolulu
Leo Wallick beat Lee Grable, Pan Manlapig beat Kimon Kudo, Harry Dellis drew Frank Moscato, Charley Shiranuhi beat Bull Pugh, Bolo Bataan beat Abel Rodrigues dq.

7/13/47 Honolulu
Ted Travis beat Leo Wallick, Ben Sherman beat Frank Moscato, Jimmy Gonsalves dew Kimon Kudo, Charley Shiranuhi beat Axel Madsen, Stan Miyashiro beat Frank Merrill.

7/20/47 Honolulu
Pan Manlapig beat Lee Grable, Mike Nazarian drew Leo Wallick, Harry Dellis drew Kimon Kudo, Axel Madsen beat Joe Starkey, Abel Rodrigues beat Wally Tsutsumi.

7/27/47 Honolulu
Mike Nazarian & Ted Travis beat Mel Peters & Leo Wallick, Kimon Kudo beat Ben Sherman dq, Axel Madsen drew Charley Shiranuhi, Buck Lee beat Tiger James.

8/3/47 Honolulu
Ted Travis beat Lee Grable, Pan Manlapig beat Mike Nazarian, Leo Wallick beat Axel Madsen, Charley Shiranuhi beat Mike Casey, Stan Miyashiro drew Bull Pugh.

8/10/47 Honolulu
Pan Manlapig beat Ben Sherman, Leo Wallick beat Lee Grable, Mike Nazarian beat Jimmy Gonsalves, Abel Rodrigues drew Wimpy Willington, Buck Lee beat Stan Miyashiro.

8/17/47 Honolulu
George Pencheff drew Ted Travis, Mike Nazarian beat Kimon Kudo, Vilai Su'a beat Harry Dellis, Axel Madsen beat Wimpy Willington, Abel Rodrigues beat Nick Nichols.

8/24/47 Honolulu
Pan Manlapig beat Mike Nazarian, George Pencheff drew Ben Sherman, Vilai Su'a beat Kimon Kudo, Harry Dellis beat Mike Casey, Wimpy Willington beat Buck Lee.

8/31/47 Honolulu
George Pencheff drew Ted Travis, Pete Peterson beat Ben Sherman, Mike Nazarian beat Vilai Su'a, Harry Dellis beat Axel Madsen, Abel Rodriges beat Frank Merrill.

9/7/47 Honolulu
Pan Manlapig beat George Pencheff, Pete Peterson beat Mike Nazarian, Jimmy Gonsalves beat Harry Dellis, Mike Casey drew Abel Rodrigues, Charley Takase beat Bolo Bataan.

9/14/47 Honolulu
Ted Travis beat Sammy Stein, Pete Petersen beat Jacques Manuel, Mike Nazarian drew Ben Sherman, Bucky O'Neil beat Mike Casey, Wimpy Willington beat Charley Takase.

9/21/47 Honolulu
Pan Manlapig & Pete Person beat Jacques Manuel & Ted Travis, George Pencheff beat Mike Nazarian, Buck O'Neil drew Ben Pilar, Charley Shiranuhi beat Abel Rodrigues.

9/28/47 Honolulu
Pete Peterson beat George Pencheff, Pan Manlapig beat Jacques Manuel, Jimmy Gonsalves drew Vilai Su'a, Ben Pilar beat Harry Dellis dq, Nick Nichols beat Wimpy Willington.

10/5/47 Honolulu
George Pencheff beat Ali Hassan, Pan Manlapig drew Pete Peterson, Jacques Manuel beat Jimmy Gonsalves, Axel Madsen drew Buck O'Neil, Joe Starkey beat Mike Casey.

10/12/47 Honolulu
George Pencheff beat Pan Manlapig, Ali Hassen beat Jacques Manuel, Ben Sherman beat Vilai Su'a, Kimon Kudo beat Harry Dellis, Abel Rodrigues beat Nick Nichols.

10/19/47 Honolulu
Pete Peterson beat Ali Hassan, George Pencheff beat Ben Sherman, George Manuel beat Bucky O'Neil, Kimon Kudo beat Ben Pilar, Mike Casey beat Buck Lee.

10/26/47 Honolulu
Jules LaRance beat George Pencheff, Ali Hassen drew Jacques Manuel, Jimmy Gonsalves beat Bucky O'Neil, Harry Dellis beat Mike Casey, Abel Rodrigues drew Wimpy Willington.

11/2/47 Honolulu
Sandor Szabo beat Pete Peterson, Jules Larance beat Jacques Manuel, Ali Hassen drew George Pencheff, Kimon Kudo beat Harry Dellis dq, Frank Merrill beat Nick Nichols.

11/9/47 Honolulu
George Pencheff & Pete Peterson beat Ali Hassen & Jules LaRance, Jimmy Gonsalves drew Jacques Manuel, Kimon Kudo beat Bucky O'Neil, Abel Rodrigues beat Buck Lee.

414

11/16/47 Honolulu
Jules LaRance beat Pete Peterson, Maurice LaChapelle beat Jacques Manuel, Ali Hassen beat Kimon Kudo, Buck O'Neil drew Ben Pilar, Mike Casey beat Wimpy Willington.

11/23/47 Honolulu
Maurice LaChappelle beat Ali Hassan, Jacques Manuel drew Pete Peterson, Ben Sherman beat Harry Dellis, Bucky O'Neil beat Mike Casey, Bolo Bataan drew Buck Lee.

11/30/47 Honolulu
Maurice LaChappelle beat Jules LaRance, Ivan Kameroff beat Jacques Manuel, Ali Hassen drew Ben Sherman, Pan Manlapig beat Pete Peterson, Charley Shiranuhi beat Abel Rodrigues.

12/7/47 Honolulu
Ivan Kameroff drew Maurice LaChapelle, Pan Manlapig beat Ali Hassen, Jules LaRance beat Jacques Manuel, Harry Dellis beat Ben Pilar, Mike Casey drew Charley Shiranuhi.

12/14/47 Honolulu
Pan Manlapig beat Jules LaRance, Jimmy Gonsalves beat Jacques Manuel, Ali Hassen drew Ivan Kameroff, Bucky O'Neil beat Harry Dellis, Wimpy Willington beat Buck Lee.

12/21/47 Honolulu
Ivan Kameroff & Maurice LaChappelle beat Ali Hassan & Jules LaRance, Pan Manlapig beat Jacques Manuel, Harry Dellis beat Mike Casey, Stan Miyashiro drew Bull Pugh.

12/28/47 Honolulu
Maurice LaChapelle beat Ali Hassen, Ivan Kameroff beat Jules LaRance, Kimon Kudo beat Harry Dellis, Stan Miyashiro beat Mike Casey, Buck Lee drew Abel Rodrigues.

1948

1/4/48 Honolulu
Ivan Kameroff drew Maurice LaChappelle, Jack Sherry beat Jules LaRance, Tony Felici drew Ali Hassen, Harry Dellis beat Stan Miyashiro, Wally Tsutsumi beat Wimpy Willington dq.

1/11/48 Honolulu
Ted Travis beat Ivan Kameroff, Pan Manlapig beat Ali Hassen, Maurice LaChapelle beat Tony Felici dq, Jimmy Gonsalves beat Jules LaRance, Abel Rodrigues beat Mike Casey.

1/18/48 Honolulu
Pan Manlapig beat Ted Travis, Maurice LaChapelle beat Bob Corby, Buck O'Neil beat Harry Dellis, Ivan Kameroff beat Ali Hassen dq, Bull Pugh beat Mike Casey.

1/25/48 Honolulu
Ed Strangler Lewis beat Butch Levy, Maurice LaChapelle beat Ali Hassen, Bob Corby drew Ivan Kameroff, Al Lolotai beat Bull Pugh, Charley Takase beat Buck Lee.

2/1/48 Honolulu
Ted Travis beat Maurice LaChapelle, Ivan Kameroff & Pan Manlapig beat Bob Corby & Ali Hassen, Buck O'Neil beat Jimmy Gonsalves, Mike Casey beat Wimpy Willington.

2/8/48 Honolulu
Ivan Kameroff drew Ted Travis, Pan Manlapig beat Bob Corby, Al Lolotai beat Kimon Kudo, Harry Dellis beat Abel Rodrigues, Wimpy Willington beat Charley Takase.

2/15/48 Honolulu
Maurice LaChapelle beat Ivan Kameroff, Dude Chick drew Pan Manlapig, Al Lolotai beat Bob Corby dq, Kimon Kudo drew Buck O'Neil, Mike Casey beat Buck Lee.

2/22/48 Honolulu
Ted Travis beat Maurice LaChapelle, Bob Corby beat Dude Chick, Ivan Kameroff drew Ali Pasha, Al Lolotai beat Charley Shiranuhi, Abel Rodrigues beat Mike Casey.

2/29/48 Honolulu
Ted Travis beat Pan Manlapig, Maurice LaChapelle beat Ali Pasha, Ivan Kameroff beat Bob Corby dq, Charley Shiranuhi beat Harry Dellis, Stan Miyashiro beat Bull Pugh.

3/7/48 Honolulu
Ivan Kameroff & Maurice LaChapelle beat Tony Felici & Ted Travis, Bob Corby no contest Ali Pasha, Buck O'Neil beat Axel Madsen, Abel Rodrigues beat Stan Miyashiro.

3/14/48 Honolulu
Ted Travis beat Bob Corby, Maurice LaChapelle beat Tony Felici, Ivan Kameroff drew Ali Pasha, Harry Dellis drew Kimon Kudo, Mike Casey beat Buck Lee dq.

3/17/48 Honolulu
Oki Shikina beat Ali Pasha, Ivan Kameroff beat Kimon Kudo, Charley Shiranuhi beat Harry Dellis, Buck O'Neil beat Stan Miyashiro, Abel Rodrigues drew Charley Takase.

3/21/48 Honolulu
Maurice LaChapelle drew Ted Travis, Bob Corby beat Ali Pasha, Ivan Kameroff beat Charley Shiranuhi, Al Lolotai drew Axel Madsen, Bolo Bataan beat Wimpy Willington dq.

3/24/48 Honolulu
Oki Shikina beat Bob Corby, Kimon Kudo & Charley Shiranuhi beat Harry Dellis & Ali Pasha, Al Galento beat Mike Casey, Stan Miyashiro drew Bull Pugh.

3/28/48 Honolulu
Oki Shikina beat Ivan Kameroff, Maurice LaChapelle beat Bob Corby, Ali Pasha drew Vilai Su'a, Al Galento beat Kimon Kudo, Abel Rodrigues beat Mike Casey.

4/4/48 Honolulu
Oki Shikina beat Ted Travis, Jack Claybourne drew Maurice LaChapelle, Ivan Kameroff beat Ali Pasha, Bob Corby drew Al Galento.

4/11/48 Honolulu
Ted Travis beat Jack Claybourne, Ivan Kameroff beat Red Vagnone, Maurice LaChapelle beat Al Galento, Bob Corby beat Charley Shiranuhi, Abel Rodrigues beat Harry Dellis dq.

4/18/48 Honolulu
Ted Travis beat Oki Shikina, Tony Morelli beat Maurice LaChapelle, Ivan Kameroff beat Bob Corby dq, Mike Casey drew Al Galento.

4/25/48 Honolulu
Ted Travis beat Tony Morelli, Oki Shikina beat Ivan Kameroff, Bob Corby beat Maurice LaChapelle, Vilai Su'a beat Mike Casey, AL Lolotai beat Bull Pugh.

5/2/48 Honolulu
Lee Grable beat Ted Travis won Hawaiian Title, Tony Morelli beat Bob Corby, Harry Dellis beat Abel Rodrigues, Whitey Whittler beat Al Lolotai, Mike Casey drew Bull Pugh.

5/9/48 Honolulu
Oki Shikina beat Tony Morelli dq, Al Lolotai & Leo Wallick beat Bob Corby & Whitey Whittler, Charley Shiranuhi beat Wimpy Willington, Vilai Su'a beat Bull Pugh.

5/16/48 Honolulu
Lee Grable beat Oki Shikina, Leo Wallick beat Tony Morelli, Whitey Whittler beat Bob Corby, Buck O'Neil beat Buck Lee, Harry Dellis drew Abel Rodrigues.

5/23/48 Honolulu
Leo Wallick beat Lee Grable, Pan Manlapig beat Whitey Whittler dq, Bob Corby drew Charley Shiranuhi, Al Lolotai beat Abel Rodrigues, Stan Miyashiro drew Wimpy Willington.

5/30/48 Honolulu
Pan Manlapig & Leo Wallick beat Lee Grable & Whitey Whittler, Bob Corby beat Vilai Su'a, Buck O'Neil beat Wimpy Willington, Harry Dellis beat Buck Lee.

6/6/48 Honolulu
Lee Grable drew Pan Manlapig, Leo Wallick beat Whitey Whittler, Oki Shikina beat Bob Corby, Buck O'Neil beat Harry Dellis, Frank Merrill beat Bolo Bataan.

7/18/48 Honolulu
John Swenski beat Lee Grable, Kimon Kudo & Martin Tanaka beat Jimmy Lott & Tony Ross, Harry Dellis beat Abel Rodrigues, Bolo Bataan beat Fred Tam.

7/25/48 Honolulu
Lee Grable drew John Swenski, Martin Tanaka beat Jimmy Lott, Tony Ross beat Charley Shiranuhi, Harry Dellis beat Axel Madsen, Frank Merrill beat Buck Lee.

8/1/48 Honolulu
Martin Tanaka beat John Swenski, Lee Grable beat Tony Ross, Kimon Kudo drew Jimmy Lott, Vilai Su'a beat Harry Dellis.

8/8/48 Honolulu
Martin Tanaka beat Lee Grable won Hawaiian Title, John Swenski beat Jimmy Lott, Jimmy Gonsalves beat Tony Ross, Charley Shiranuhi beat Buck O'Neil.

8/15/48 Honolulu
Lee Grable & Jimmy Lott beat John Swenski & Martin Tanaka, Kimon Kudo beat Tony Ross dq, Jimmy Gonsalves beat Charley Shiranuhi, Buck O'Neil beat Abel Rodrigues.

8/22/48 Honolulu
Martin Tanaka beat Lee Grable, Bud Curtis beat Jimmy Lott, John Swenski beat Tony Ross, Buck O'Neil beat Harry Dellis.

8/29/48 Honolulu
Martin Tanaka beat John Swenski, Bud Curtis drew Lee Grable, Jimmy Lott beat Tony Ross, Charley Shiranuhi beat Harry Dellis.

9/5/48 Honolulu
Bud Curtis beat Martin Tanaka dq, Lee Grable beat Jimmy Lott, Red Vagnone beat John Swenski, Harry Dellis drew Ben Pilar.

9/12/48 Honolulu
Martin Tanaka beat Lee Grable, Jimmy Lott beat John Swenski, Bud Curtis beat Red Vagnone dq, Wimpy Willington beat Harry Dellis.

9/19/48 Honolulu
Martin Tanaka beat Jimmy Lott, Lee Grable drew Red Vagnone, Bud Curtis beat Charley Shiranuhi, Kimon Kudo beat Abel Rodrigues.

9/26/48 Honolulu
Red Vagnone beat Martin Tanaka, Jimmy Gonsalves beat Lee Grable, Bud Curtis drew Jimmy Lott, Buck O'Neil beat Wimpy Willington.

10/3/48 Honolulu
Oki Shikina beat Red Vagnone, Oki Shikina beat Bud Curtis, Oki Shikina beat Jimmy Lott, Red Vagnone beat Lee Grable, Red Vagnone beat Jimmy Gonsalves, Jimmy Lott beat Kimon Kudo, Vilai Su's beat Charlie Shiranuhi, Jimmy Lott beat Vilai Su's, Ben Pilar beat Bucky O'Neil.

10/10/48 Honolulu
Jack Claybourne & Oki Shikina beat Lee Grable & Jimmy Lott, Red Vagnone beat Bud Curtis, Stan Miyashiro beat Wimpy Wellington, Ben Pilar drew Abel Rodrigues.

10/17/48 Honolulu
Jack Claybourne beat Red Vagnone, Oki Shikina beat Lee Grable, Bud Curtis drew Jimmy Lott, Stan Miyashiro beat Abel Rodrigues.

10/24/48 Honolulu
Martin Tanaka beat Jimmy Lott, Jack Claybourne drew Oki Shikina, Charley Shiranuhi beat Frank Merrill, Bud Curtis drew Brother Frank.

10/31/48 Honolulu
Jack Claybourne beat Martin Tanaka won Hawaiian title, Jimmy Gonsalves beat Buck O'Neil, Brother Frank beat Jimmy Lott, Bud Curtis drew Kimon Kudo, Bolo Bataan drew Wimpy Willington.

11/7/48 Honolulu
Jack Claybourne beat Chief Little Wolf, Brother Frank drew Oki Shikina, Dick Raines beat Bud Curtis, Jimmy Gonsalves beat Jimmy Lott, Stan Miyashiro beat Bolo Bataan.

11/14/48 Honolulu
Chief Little Wolf & Dick Raines beat Kimon Kudo & Oki Shikina, Jack Claybourne beat Brother Frank, Jimmy Gonsalves beat Charley Shiranuhi, Stan Miyashiro drew Buck O'Neil.

11/21/48 Honolulu
Jack Claybourne drew Dick Raines, Chief Little Wolf beat Oki Shikina dq, Brother Frank beat Jimmy Gonsalves, Earl Rasmussen beat Buck O'Neil, Abel Rodrigues beat Wimpy Willington.

11/28/48 Honolulu
Jack Claybourne beat Brother Frank, Chief Little Wolf beat Dick Raines, Jimmy Gonsalves drew Oki Shikina, Earl Rasmussen beat Abel Rodrigues.

12/5/48 Honolulu
Jack Claybourne beat Chief Little Wolf, Stan Miyashiro drew Buck O'Neil, Leo Wallick beat Dick Raines, Seelie Samara beat Brother Frank, Vilai Su'a beat Earl Rasmussen.

12/12/48 Honolulu
Jack Claybourne & Seelie Samara drew Brother Frank & Dick Raines, Leo Wallick beat Chief Little Wolf dq, Vilai Su'a beat Kimon Kudo, Abel Rodrigues beat Charley Takase.

12/19/48 Honolulu
Dick Raines beat Jack Claybourne, Seelie Samara beat Chief Little Wolf, Leo Wallick beat Brother Frank, Oki Shikina beat Vilai Su'a.

12/26/48 Honolulu
Seelie Samara beat Dick Raines, Henry Kulkovich beat Jack Claybourne dq, Basher Donald drew Leo Wallick, Ben Pilar beat Buck O'Neil, Earl Rasmussen beat Bolo Bataan.

1949

1/2/49 Honolulu
Jack Claybourne beat Dick Raines, Seelie Samara beat Basher McDonald, Henry Kulkovich drew Leo Wallick, Ben Pilar beat Earl Rasmussen.

1/9/49 Honolulu
Jack Claybourne beat Seelie Samara, Leo Wallick beat Dick Raines, Basher McDonald beat Henry Kulkovich dq, Ben Pilar beat Stan Miyashiro, Buck O'Neil beat Charley Takase.

1/16/49 Honolulu
Jack Claybourne beat Leo Wallick, Henry Kulkovich beat Basher McDonald, Kenny Ackles drew Seelie Samara, Jimmy Gonsalves drew Ben Pilar.

1/23/49 Honolulu
Henry Kulkovich beat Seelie Samara, Kenny Ackles drew Jack Claybourne, Basher McDonald beat Leo Wallick, Jimmy Gonsalves beat Stan Miyashiro.

1/30/49 Honolulu
Henry Kulkovich beat Jack Claybourne dq, Kenny Ackles beat Basher McDonald, Leo Wallick beat Mike Connors, Bucky O'Neil beat Earl Rasmussen.

2/6/49 Honolulu
Johnny Sepeda beat Henry Kulkovich, Kenny Ackles beat Leo Wallick, Basher McDonald beat Curley Connors, Vilai Su'a beat Stan Miyashiro.

2/13/49 Honolulu
Jack Claybourne beat Kenny Ackles, Johnny Sepeda beat Leo Wallick, Henry Kulkovich beat Basher McDonald, Curley Conners beat Buck O'Neil.

2/20/49 Honolulu
Johnny Sepeda beat Jacques Manuel, Henry Kulkovich drew Leo Wallick, Kenny Ackles beat Basher McDonald, Jimmy Gonsalves beat Curley Connors.

2/27/49 Honolulu
Jack Claybourne beat Johnny Sepeda, Herny Kulkovich beat Leo Wallick, Kenny Ackles beat Jacques Manuel, Al Lolotai beat Basher McDonald.

3/6/49 Honolulu
Jack Claybourne beat Kenny Ackles, Vic Christy beat Henry Kulkovich, Johnny Sepeda beat Bobby Ford.

3/13/49 Honolulu
Vic Christy beat Johnny Sepeda, Kenny Ackles beat Henry Kulkovich, Bobby Ford beat Jacques Manuel, Al Lolotai beat Earl Rasmussen.

3/20/49 Honolulu
Jack Claybourne beat Vic Christy, Lofty Blomfield beat Henry Kulkovich, Lee Grable beat Johnny Sepeda, Kenny Ackles drew Bobby Ford, Jacques Manuel beat Buck O'Neil.

3/27/49 Honolulu
Vic Christy & Ted Travis beat Kenny Ackles & Bobby Ford, Tommy O'Toole beat Lofty Blomfield, Lee Grable drew Pierre LaSalle, Al Lolotai beat Jacques Manuel.

4/3/49 Honolulu
Jack Claybourne beat Tommy O'Toole, Ted Travis beat Lee Grable, Vic Christy drew Antone Leone, Pierre LaSalle beat Bobby Ford, Jimmy Gonsalves beat Jacques Manuel.

4/10/49 Honolulu
Jack Claybourne beat Ted Travis, Antone Leone beat Vic Christy, Kenny Ackles beat Pierre LaSalle, Oki Shikina beat Tommy O'Toole, Jacques Manuel beat Bobby Ford.

4/17/49 Honolulu
Jack Claybourne drew Ben Sherman, Kenny Ackles beat Antone Leone, Pan Manlapig beat Jacques Manuel, Charley Shiranuhi beat Bobby Ford, Ben Pilar beat Bucky O'Neil.

4/24/49 Honolulu
Kenny Ackles beat Ben Sherman, Antone Leone beat Butch Levy, Charley Shiranuhi beat Red Vagnone dq, Oki Shikina beat Jacques Manuel, Jimmy Gonsalves beat Bobby Ford.

5/1/49 Honolulu
Antone Leone beat Kenny Ackles, Jack Claybourne drew Ben Sherman, Red Vagnone beat Oki Shikina, Rocco Toma beat Jimmy Gonsalves, Jacques Manuel drew Vilai Su'a.

5/8/49 Honolulu
Antone Leone beat Ben Sherman, Ray Daoang beat Pierre LaSalle, Kenny Ackles drew Rocco Toma, Al Lolotai beat Jacques Manuel, Stan Miyashiro beat Ben Pilar.

5/15/49 Honolulu
Antone Leone beat Jack Claybourne, Ray Daoang beat Ben Sherman, Rocco Toma beat Red Vagnone, Kenny Ackles drew Charley Shiranuhi, Jacques Manuel beat Stan Miyashiro.

5/22/49 Honolulu
Antone Leone & Rocco Toma beat Jack Claybourne & Ray Daoang, Kenny Ackles drew Red Vagnone, Oki Shikina beat Al Lolotai, Jacques Manuel beat Earl Rassmussen.

5/29/49 Honolulu
Jack Claybourne beat Antone Leone, Ray Daoang beat Red Vagnone, Kenny Ackles drew Rocco Toma, Jimmy Gonsalves beat Jacques Manuel, Vila Su'a beat Abel Rodrigues.

6/5/49 Honolulu
Kenny Ackles drew Antone Leone, Rocco Toma beat Ray Daoang, The Bat beat Charley Shiranuhi, Oki Shikina drew Red Vagnone, Jacques Manuel no contest Vilai Su'a.

6/12/49 Honolulu
Jack Claybourne beat Rocco Toma, Red Vagnone beat Kenny Ackles, The Bat drew Ray Daoang, Jimmy Gonsalves beat Fred Wright, Kimon Kudo beat Jacques Manuel.

6/19/49 Honolulu
Jack Claybourne beat Red Vagnone, Kenny Ackles beat Rocco Toma, The Bat beat Fred Wright, Charley Shiranuhi beat Ray Daoang, Earl Rasmussen drew Abel Rodrigues.

6/26/49 Honolulu
Jack Claybourne beat Kenny Ackles, The Bat beat Red Vagnone, Rocco Toma beat Ray Daoang, Oki Shikina beat Fred Wright, Count Von Busing beat Earl Rasmussen.

7/3/49 Honolulu
Jack Claybourne beat Oki Shikina, The Bat beat Kenny Ackles, Rocco Toma beat Jimmy Gonsalves, Red Vagnone beat Fred Wright.

7/10/49 Honolulu
George Pencheff beat Jack Claybourne dq, The Bat beat Rocco Toma, Tiger Joe Marsh beat Red Vagnone, Kimon Kudo drew Fred Wright.

7/17/49 Honolulu
George Pencheff beat The Bat, Kay Bell drew Tiger Joe Marsh, Oki Shikina beat Rocco Toma, Red Vagnone beat Fred Wright.

7/24/49 Honolulu
Jack Claybourne beat Kay Bell dq, George Pencheff beat Joe Marsh, Pete Managoff beat Red Vagnone, Jimmy Gonsalves beat Fred Wright.

8/7/49 Honolulu
Jack Claybourne beat Kay Bell, George Pencheff drew Pete Managoff, Don Kindred beat Joe Marsh dq, Red Vagnone beat Charley Shiranuhi.

8/13/49 Hilo
Harold Sakata beat Bucky O'Neill, Jack Claybourne beat Red Vagnone, Ben Sherman beat Ben Pilar,

8/14/49 Honolulu
Kay Bell & Pete Managoff beat Jack Claybourne & Don Kindred, George Pencheff beat Oki Shikina, Joe Marsh drew Red Vagnone, Kimon Kudo beat Earl Rasmussen.

8/21/49 Honolulu
George Pencheff beat Kay Bell, Jack Claybourne beat Pete Managoff, Ben Sherman beat Don Kindred, Joe Marsh beat Red Vagnone.

8/28/49 Honolulu
Jack Claybourne drew George Pencheff, Pete Managoff beat Joe Marsh, Harold Sakata beat Earl Rasmussen, Red Vagnone beat Ben Sherman, Charley Shiranuhi beat Don Kindred.

9/4/49 Honolulu
Ray Gunkel beat Jack Claybourne Pete Managoff drew George Pencheff, Harold Sakata beat Charley Takase, Tarzan White beat Red Vagnone, Joe Marsh beat Don Kindred.

9/11/49 Honolulu
Ray Gunkel beat Jack Claybourne, Bobby Managoff beat George Pencheff, Tarzan White beat Ben Sherman, Harold Sakata beat Fred Tam, Jimmy Gonsalves drew Joe Marsh.

9/18/49 Honolulu
Bobby Managoff beat Pete Managoff, Jack Claybourne beat Tarzan White, George Pencheff drew Ben Sherman, Oki Shikina beat Joe Marsh, Harold Sakata beat Wimpy Willington.

9/25/49 Honolulu
Jack Claybourne & Don Kindred beat Ben Sherman & Tarzan White, Ray Gunkel drew Bobby Managoff, George Pencheff beat Pete Managoff, Charley Shiranuhi beat Joe Marsh.

10/2/49 Honolulu
Bobby Managoff beat Pat Fraley, Ray Gunkel beat George Pencheff, Sonny Kurgis beat Don Kindred, Jimmy Gonsalves drew Ben Sherman.

10/9/49 Honolulu
Bobby Managoff beat Jack Claybourne, Ray Gunkel beat Sonny Kurgis, Pat Fraley beat George Pencheff, Oki Shikina beat Don Kindred.

10/16/49 Honolulu
Bobby Managoff beat Lee Grable, Ray Gunkel beat Pat Fraley dq, Sonny Kurgis drew Tommy O'Toole, Ben Sherman beat Charley Shiranuhi.

10/23/49 Honolulu
Pat Fraley drew Bobby Managoff, Tommy O'Toole beat Sonny Kurgis, Ray Gunkel beat Lee Grable, Charley Shiranuhi beat Jimmy Gonsalves.

10/30/49 Honolulu
Earl McCready & Tommy O'Toole beat Ray Gunkel & Bobby Managoff, Sonny Kurgis drew Oki Shikina, Ben Sherman beat Kimon Kudo, Harold Sakata beat Abel Rodriguez.

11/6/49 Honolulu
Earl McCready beat Bobby Managoff, Ray Gunkel drew Oki Shikina, Sonny Kurgis beat Charley Shiranuhi, Tommy O'Toole beat Johnny Sepeda.

11/13/49 Honolulu
Bobby Managoff beat Tommy O'Toole, Dick Raines beat Sonny Kurgis, Ray Gunkel drew Johnny Sepeda, Charles Shiranuhi beat Count Von Busing dq, Earl Rasmussen beat Wally Tsutsumi.

11/20/49 Honolulu
Bobby Managoff beat Dick Raines, Dean Detton beat Ray Gunkel, Chief Little Wolf beat Tommy O'Toole, Johnny Sepeda drew Oki Shikina.

11/27/49 Honolulu
Bobby Managoff beat Chief Little Wolf, Dean Detton beat Oki Shikina, Martin Tanaka beat Johnny Sepeda dq, Ray Gunkel drew Sonny Kurgis.

12/4/49 Honolulu
Dean Detton beat Bobby Managoff won Hawaiian title, Ray Gunkel beat Ben Sherman, Sonny Kurgis drew Johnny Sepeda, Martin Tanaka beat Jimmy Gonsalves.

12/11/49 Honolulu
Dean Detton beat Bobby Managoff, Flash Gordon beat Ray Gunkel, Mickey Gold beat Johnny Sepeda, Sonny Kurgis drew Martin Tanaka.

12/18/49 Honolulu
Hans Schnabel beat Dean Detton, Flash Gordon drew Bobby Managoff, Mickey Gold drew Martin Tanaka, Ken Kenneth beat Sonny Kurgis.

12/25/49 Honolulu
Hans Schnabel beat Mickey Gold, Ken Kenneth no contest Fritz Schnabel, Flash Gordon drew Martin Tanaka, Sonny Kurgis drew John Swenski.

1950

1/1/50 Honolulu
Fritz & Hans Schnabel beat Ken Kenneth & Martin Tanaka, Mickey Gold drew Ben Sherman, Flash Gordon beat Sonny Kurgis, Charley Shiranuhi drew John Swenski.

1/8/50 Honolulu
Hans Schnabel beat Flash Gordon, Fritz Schnabel beat Ken Kenneth, Mickey Gold drew Martin Tanaka, Oki Shikina drew John Swenski.

1/15/50 Honolulu
Hans Schnabel beat Martin Tanaka, Ken Kenneth beat Fritz Schnabel, Mickey Gold drew Flash Gordon, Ben Sherman drew John Swenski.

1/22/50 Honolulu
Primo Carnera beat Hans Schnabel, Ken Kenneth beat Flash Gordon, John Swenski beat Fritz Schnabel dq, Mickey Gold drew Martin Tanaka.

1/29/50 Honolulu
Ken Kenneth & Sandor Szabo beat Fritz & Hans Schnabel, Flash Gordon beat Martin Tanaka, John Swenski beat Mickey Gold.

2/5/50 Honolulu
Sandor Szabo beat Hans Schnabel won Hawaiian Junior Heavyweight title, Flash Gordon beat Fritz Schnabel, Brother Frank drew Ken Kenneth, Martin Tanaka beat John Swenski.

2/12/50 Honolulu
Jack Claybourne beat Hans Schnabel, Flash Gordon drew Ken Kenneth, Martin Tanaka beat Fritz Schnabel, Mickey Gold beat Charley Shiranuhi.

2/19/50 Honolulu Att 5000
Jack Claybourne drew Flash Gordon, Bomber Henry Kulkovich beat Mickey Gold, Ken Kenneth beat Martin Tanaka, Oki Shikina drew John Swenski.

2/26/50 Honolulu
Ken Kenneth beat Jack Claybourne, Flash Gordon beat Bomber Kulkovich dq, Mickey Gold drew John Swenski, Jimmy Gonsalves beat Martin Tanaka.

3/5/50 Honolulu
Jack Claybourne beat Flash Gordon, Bomber Kulkovich beat Ken Kenneth, Oki Shikina beat Mickey Gold, Kimon Kudo drew John Swenski.

3/12/50 Honolulu
Primo Carnera beat Jack Claybourne, Antone Leone beat Ken Kenneth, Flash Gordon beat Mickey Gold, Vilai Su'a beat Kimon Kudo.

3/19/50 Honolulu
Jack Claybourne beat Ken Kenneth, Chico Gracia beat John Swenski, Vilai Su'a beat Kimon Kudo, Antone Leone beat Flash Gordon.

3/20/50 Guam
Primo Carnera beat Bomber Kulkovich.

3/26/50 Honolulu
Sandor Szabo drew Primo Carnera, Jack Claybourne beat Antone Leone, Jesse James beat Chico Garcia, Bomber Kulkovich beat Ken Kenneth.

4/2/50 Honolulu
Bomber Kulkovich & Antone Leone beat Flash Gordon & Sandor Szabo, Jesse James beat Jack Claybourne, Armand Tanny beat Chico Garcia.

4/9/50 Honolulu
Jesse James & Sandor Szabo drew Bomber Kulkovich & Antone Leone, Jack Claybourne beat Flash Gordon, Armand Tanny beat Chico Garcia.

4/16/50 Honolulu
Sandor Szabo beat Jack Claybourne, Jesse James drew Antone Leone, Chico Gracia beat Vilai Su'a, Bomber Kulkovich beat Armand Tanny.

4/23/50 Honolulu
Antone Leone beat Jesse James, Sandor Szabo beat Bomber Kulkovich dq, Rey Urbano beat Chico Garcia, Flash Gordon drew Ken Kenneth.

4/30/50 Honolulu
Bomber Kulkovich & Antone Leone beat Jesse James & Ben Sherman, Rey Urbano beat Joe Benincasa, Earl Rasmussen drew Vilai Su'a.

5/7/50 Honolulu
The Angel (Maurice Tillet) beat Bomber Kulkovich, Jesse James drew Antone Leone, Joe Benincasa beat Armand Tanny, Ben Pilar drew Earl Rasmussen.

5/14/50 Honolulu
Sandor Szabo beat Maurice Tillet, Antone Leone beat Ben Sherman, Jesse James beat Joe Benincasa dq, Oki Shikina drew Rey Urbano.

5/21/50 Honolulu
Bomber Kulkovich & Antone Leone beat Jesse James & Sandor Szabo, Arjan Singh beat Joe Benincasa, Oki Shikina drew Joginder Singh.

5/28/50 Honolulu
Sandor Szabo beat Antone Leone, Arjan Singh beat Bomber Kulkovich, Jesse James beat Tiger Joginder, Rey Urbano beat Joe Benincasa dq.

6/4/50 Honolulu
Arjan Singh beat Sandor Szabo, Jesse James beat Antone Leone, Joe Benincasa no contest Bomber Kulkovich, Ben Sherman beat Rey Urbano.

6/11/50 Honolulu
Bomber Kulkovich beat Jesse James, Arjan Singh beat Oki Shikina & Joe Benincasa, Ben Sherman drew Vilai Su'a.

6/18/50 Honolulu
Arjan Singh beat Sandor Szabo won Hawaiian title, Ray Eckert beat Jesse James, Bomber Kulkovich drew Frank Taylor, Joe Benincasa beat Vilai Su'a.

6/25/50 Honolulu
Ray Eckert drew Sandor Szabo, Jesse James & Frank Taylor beat Joe Benincasa & Bomber Kulkovich, Wally Tsutsumi beat Ben Pilar.

7/2/50 Honolulu
Ray Eckert beat Arjan Singh, Frank Taylor beat Joe Benincasa, Jesse James drew Bomber Kulkovich, Wimpy Willington beat Wally Tsutsumi.

7/9/50 Honolulu
Ray Eckert & Bomber Kulkovich beat Arjan Singh & Frank Taylor, Oki Shikina beat Jesse James, Joe Benincasa drew Jimmy Gonsalves.

7/16/50 Honolulu
Ray Eckert beat Arjan Singh won Hawaiian Title, Terry McGinnis beat Bomber Kulkovich, Frank Taylor beat Jesse James, Oki Shikina beat Joe Benincasa.

7/23/50 Honolulu
Terry McGinnis beat Ray Eckert - Won Hawaiian Title, Frank Taylor beat Bomber Kulkovich, Arjan Singh drew Lou Sjobert, Earl Rasmussen beat Wimpy Willington.

7/30/50 Honolulu
Terry McGinnis beat Juan Humberto, Frank Taylor beat Bomber Kulkovich, Lou Sjoberg drew Bill Sledge, Earl Rasmussen beat Leo Lynne.

8/6/50 Honolulu
Juan Humberto beat Frank Taylor, Terry McGinnis beat Lou Sjoberg, Bill Sledge beat Bomber Kulkovich, Wimpy Willington drew Wally Tsutsumi.

8/13/50 Honolulu
Terry McGinnis beat Bill Sledge dq, Juan Humberto beat Joe Campbell, Lou Sjoberg beat Frank Taylor, Charley Takase beat Wimpy Willington.

8/20/50 Honolulu
Terry McGinnis & Frank Taylor drew Juan Humberto & Bill Sledge, Joe Campbell beat Lou Sjoberg, Stan Skieski beat Charley Takase.

8/27/50 Honolulu
Terry McGinnis & Frank Taylor beat Juan Humberto & Bill Sledge, Oki Shikina beat Lou Sjoberg, Joe Campbell beat Stan Skieski.

9/3/50 Honolulu
Sandor Szabo beat Terry McGinnis - Won Hawaiian Title, Juan Humberto beat Frank Taylor, Charro Azteca beat Lou Sjoberg, Joe Campbell drew Bill Sledge, Jimmy Gonsalves beat Stan Skieski.

9/10/50 Honolulu
Sandor Szabo beat Juan Humberto dq, Charro Azteco beat Bill Sledge, Joe Campbell beat Lou Sjoberg, Earl Rasmussen drew Vilai Su'a.

9/17/50 Honolulu
Sandor Szabo drew Juan Humberto, Charro Azteco beat Johnny Mars dq, Joe Campbell beat Ray Daoang, Bill Sledge beat Lou Sjoberg.

9/24/50 Honolulu
Juan Humberto & Johnny Mars beat Charro Azteco & Joe Campbell, Ray Daoang drew Bill Sledge, Stan Miyashiro beat Abel Rodrigues.

10/15/50 Honolulu
Charro Azteca beat Johnny Mars, Juan Humberto beat Joe Campbell, Bill Sledge beat Ray Daoang dq, Ray Daoang drew Ben Sherman.

10/22/50 Honolulu
Charro Azteca beat Flash Gordon dq, Earl McCready beat Johnny Mars, Bill Sledge beat Ben Sherman dq, Ray Daoang drew Oki Shikina.

1951

3/4/51 Honolulu
Buzz Armstrong drew Sugy Hayamaka, Stan Miyashiro beat Earl Rasmussen, Gordon Hessell beat Glen Detton won 6-man battle royal.

3/11/51 Honolulu
Sugy Hayamaka drew Gordon Hessell, Eric Pederson beat Buzz Armstrong, Glen Detton beat Bucky O'Neil, Stan Skieski beat Wally Tsutsumi.

3/18/51 Honolulu
Gordon Hessell beat Sugy Hayamaka, Buzz Armstrong beat Bucky O'Neil dq, Eric Pederson beat Glen Detton, Earl Rasmussen drew Abel Rodrigues.

3/25/51 Honolulu
Ben Sherman beat Buzz Armstrong, Gordon Hessell drew Eric Pederson, Sugy Hayamaka beat Glen Detton.

4/1/51 Honolulu
Woody Strode beat Buzz Armstrong, Gordon Hessell drew Eric Pederson, Sugy Hayamaka beat Ben Sherman dq, Stan Skieski beat Glen Detton.

4/8/51 Honolulu
Jack Claybourne & Woody Strode beat Bobby Bruns & Gordon Hessell, Sugy Hayamaka drew Eric Pederson, Earl Rassmussen beat Stan Miyashiro.

4/22/51 Honolulu
Masahika Kimura beat Ben Sherman judo match, Toshio Yamaguchi beat Sugy Hayamaka Judo match, Andre Asselin beat Eric Pederson, Woody Strode beat Fred Bozic.

4/29/51 Honolulu
Masahika Kimura beat Eric Pederson, Ted Travis beat Laverne Baxter, Toshio Yamaguchi beat Woody Strode, Andre Asselin beat Sugy Hayamaka.

5/6/51 Honolulu
Masahika Kimura beat Joe Benincasa, Toshio Yamaguchi beat Ted Travis judo match, Andre Asselin drew Woody Strode, Ben Sherman beat Eric Pederson dq.

5/13/51 Honolulu
Andre Asselin drew Masahika Kimura, Ted Travis beat Woody Strode, Toshio Yamaguchi beat Joe Benincasa, Ben Sherman beat Eric Pederson.

5/20/51 Honolulu
Masahika Kimura beat Ben Sherman, Ted Travis beat Toshio Yamaguchi, Andre Asselin drew Oki Shikina, Woody Strode beat Joe Benincasa.

5/27/51 Honolulu
Oki Shikina & Toshio Yamaguchi beat Andre Adoree & Andre Asselin, Masahika Kimura drew Ted Travis, Woody Strode beat Joe Benincasa dq.

6/3/51 Honolulu
Andre Adoree & Andre Asselin beat Buddy Jackson & Woody Strode, Ted Travis beat Joe Benincasa, Stan Skieski drew Wally Tsutsumi.

6/10/51 Honolulu
Ted Travis beat Andre Asselin, Terry McGinnis beat Bob Wagner, Andre Adoree drew Woody Strode, Buddy Jackson beat Fred Bozic dq.

6/17/51 Honolulu
Ted Travis beat Andre Asselin, Terry McGinnis beat Woody Strode, Andre Adoree beat Fred Bozic, Buddy Jackson beat Earl Rassmussen.

6/25/51 Honolulu
Ted Travis beat Andre Asselin won battle royal, Vilai Su'a beat Stan Skieski, Buddy Jackson beat Bucky O'Neil, Terry McGinnis drew Woody Strode.

7/2/51 Honolulu
Andre Asselin & Terry McGinnis drew Pete Peterson & Ted Travis, Oki Shikina beat Woody Strode, Andre Adoree drew Buddy Jackson.

7/9/51 Honolulu
Andre Asselin & Terry McGinnis beat Pete Peterson & Ted Travis, Mike Mazurki beat Andre Adoree, Vilai Su'a beat Buddy Jackson.

7/16/51 Honolulu
Mike Mazurki beat Andre Asselin, Terry McGinnis drew Ted Travis, Joe Marsh beat Buddy Jackson, Andre Adoree beat Vilai Su'a.

7/23/51 Honolulu
Mike Mazurki & Ted Travis beat Andre Asselin & Terry McGinnis, Andre Adoree drew Joe Marsh, Ben Sherman beat Buddy Jackson.

7/30/51 Honolulu
Andre Asselin & Terry McGinnis beat Mike Mazurki & Ted Travis, Earl McCready beat Andre Adoree, Joe Marsh drew Oki Shikina.

8/6/51 Honolulu
Andre Asselin & Terry McGinnis drew Earl McCready & Ted Travis, Dave Levin beat Wally Dusek, Andre Adoree beat Joe Marsh dq.

8/12/51 Honolulu
Terry McGinnis beat Wally Dusek, Ted Travis beat Dave Levin, Harold Sakata beat Andre Adoree.

8/19/51 Honolulu
Terry McGinnis beat Ted Travis won Hawaiian title, Dave Levin & Harold Sakata beat Andre Adoree & Wally Dusek, Andre Asselin drew Joe Marsh.

8/27/51 Honolulu
Terry McGinnis beat Dave Levin, Andre Asselin drew Wally Dusek, Harold Sakata beat Joe Marsh dq, Bucky O'Neil drew Ben Pilar.

9/3/51 Honolulu
Andre Asselin & Terry McGinnis beat Laverne Baxter & Wally Dusek dq, Kay Bell beat Dave Levin, Joe Marsh drew Harold Sakata.

9/10/51 Honolulu
Terry McGinnis beat Laverne Baxter, Kay Bell beat Bobby Bruns, Dr. Len Hall beat Casey Berger, Don Arnold no contest Wally Dusek.

9/17/51 Honolulu
Kay Bell & Wally Dusek beat Bob McCune & Terry McGinnins, Dr. Len Hall beat Casey Berger, Don Arnold no contest Wally Dusek.

9/24/51 Honolulu
Terry McGinnis beat Abe Kashey dq, Kay Bell beat Joe Marsh, Bob McCune beat Wally Dusek, Earl Rasmussen drew Abel Rodriguez.

10/1/51 Honolulu
Terry McGinnis beat Kay Bell, Abe Kashey beat Bob McCune, Wally Dusek beat Joe Marsh, Bob Shibuya beat Buck O'Neil.

10/8/51 Honolulu
Abe Kashey beat Terry McGinnis, Kay Bell drew Earl McCready, Gino Vagnone beat Wally Dusek, Bob McCune beat Joe Marsh.

10/15/51 Honolulu
Abe Kashey & Pete Peterson beat Kay Bell & Terry McGinnis, Earl McCready beat Wally Dusek, Bob McCune beat Gino Vagnone.

10/22/51 Honolulu
Abe Kashey beat Terry McGinnis - won Hawaiian Title, Kay Bell drew Pete Peterson, Earl McCready beat Bob McCune, Bob Shibuya beat Earl Rasmussen.

10/29/51 Honolulu
Bob McCune & Terry McGinnis beat Abe Kashey & Pete Peterson, Kay Bell beat Earl McCready dq, Bob Shibuya drew Vilai Su'a.

11/5/51 Honolulu
Abe Kashey & Earl McCready beat Kay Bell & Bob McCune, Lucky Simunovich beat Pete Peterson, Herman Cheong beat Wally Tsutsumi.

11/12/51 Honolulu
Abe Kashey beat Terry McGinnis, Lucky Simunovich beat Earl McCready, Pete Peterson drew Bob McCune, Yukio Kato beat Vilai Su'a.

11/18/51 Honolulu
Jack Claybourne & Lucky Simunovich beat Abe Kashey & Pete Peterson, Terry McGinnis beat Dick Raines dq, Kay Bell drew Bob McCune.

11/25/51 Honolulu
Abe Kashey & Pete Peterson beat Jack Claybourne & Lucky Simunovich, Dick Raines beat Kay Bell, Bob McCune beat Chief Little Wolf dq.

12/9/51 Honolulu
Lucky Simunovich beat Dick Raines, Abe Kashey beat Chief Little Wolf, Kay Bell beat Jack Hader, Bob McCune drew Pete Peterson.

12/16/51 Honolulu
Abe Kashey beat Lucky Simunovich, Dick Raines beat Bob McCune, Kay Bell beat Chief Little Wolf, Pete Peterson beat Jack Hader.

12/23/51 Honolulu
Lucky Simunovich beat Pete Peterson dq won battle royal, Andre Asselin drew Abe Kashey, Dick Raines beat Bob McCune, Gino Vagnone beat Andre Adoree.

12/31/51 Honolulu
Abe Kashey & Pete Peterson beat Andre Asselin & Bobby Bruns, Dick Raines drew Lucky Simunovich, Gino Vagnone beat Ben Sherman.

1952

1/6/52 Honolulu
Bobby Bruns drew Abe Kashey, Dick Raines beat Onoumi, Pete Peterson beat Fujiayama, Andre Asselin beat Gino Vagnone.

1/13/52 Honolulu
Bobby Bruns & Lucky Simunovich beat Abe Kashey & Pete Peterson, Dick Raines beat Andre Asselin, Armand Tanny drew Gino Vagnone.

1/20/52 Honolulu
Bobby Bruns & Lucky Simunovich beat Abe Kashey & Pete Peterson, Dick Raines beat Seelie Samara, Harold Sakata beat Gino Vagnone, Andre Asselin drew Armand Tanny.

1/27/52 Honolulu
Chicf Little Wolf beat Vilai Su'a, Bobby Bruns beat Andre Asselin, Dick Raines beat Armand Tanny, Pete Peterson beat Bob Shibuya, Lucky Simunovich beat Harold Sakata, Bobby Bruns beat Pete Peterson, Lucky Simunovich beat Chief Little Wolf, Dick Raines beat Lucky Simunovich, Bobby Bruns beat Dick Raines for the right to meet Abe Kashey for Hawaiian title next week.

2/4/52 Honolulu
Abe Kashey beat Bobby Bruns, Dick Raines beat Chief Little Wolf, Red Scorpion drew Lucky Simunovich, Pete Peterson beat Andre Asselin.

2/10/52 Honolulu
Bobby Bruns & Lucky Simunovich beat Pete Peterson & Dick Raines, Red Scorpion beat Andre Asselin, Chief Little Wolf drew Harold Sakata.

2/17/52 Honolulu
Abe Kashey beat Dick Raines dq, Lucky Simunovich beat Red Scorpion, Rikidozan beat Chief Little Wolf, Andre Asselin drew Harold Sakata.

2/24/52 Honolulu
Dick Raines beat Lucky Simunovich, Bobby Bruns drew Abe Kashey, Rikidozan beat Andre Asselin, Red Scorpion beat Pete Peterson, Chief Little Wolf beat Bob Shibuya.

3/2/52 Honolulu
Dick Raines beat Abe Kashey dq, Red Scorpion beat Bobby Bruns, Rikidozan drew Lucky Simunovich, Pete Peterson beat Armand Tanny.

3/9/52 Honolulu
Red Scorpion beat Abe Kashey, Lucky Simunovich beat Dick Raines, Rikidozan beat Pete Peterson, Chief Little Wolf drew Harold Sakata.

3/16/52 Honolulu
Bobby Bruns & Lucky Simunovich drew Bud Curtis & Red Scorpion, Rikidozan beat Dick Raines, Abe Kashey beat Gene Dubuque, Amand Tanny beat Harold Sakata.

3/23/52 Honolulu
Lucky Simunovich beat Red Scorpion, Bobby Bruns beat Abe Kashey, Bud Curtis drew Rikidozan, Harold Sakata drew Armand Tanny.

3/30/52 Honolulu
Lucky Simunovich beat Abe Kashey - won Hawaiian title, Rikidozan beat Bud Curtis, Red Scorpion beat Frank Hurley, Bob Shibuya beat Chief Little Wolf.

4/6/52 Honolulu
Karl Davis & Red Scorpion beat Rikidozan & Oki Shikina, Lucky Simunovich beat Bob McCune, Bobby Bruns drew Bud Curtis, Bob Shibuya beat Armand Tanny.

4/13/52 Honolulu
Bobby Bruns & Lucky Simunovich beat Red Scorpion & Hans Schnabel, Bud Curtis beat Jim Mitchell, Rikidozan beat Karl Davis, Iwalani Tanaka beat Sally Lee - Judo Match.

4/20/52 Honolulu
Fritz & Hans Schnabel beat Bobby Bruns & Lucky Simunovich, Rikidozan beat Ivan Kameroff, Red Scorpion beat Earl McCready, Bud Curtis beat Armand Tanny.

4/27/52 Honolulu
Lucky Simunovich beat Hans Schnabel dq, Rikidozan & Toshi Yamaguchi drew Bud Curtis & Red Scorpion, Johnny Sepeda beat Fritz Schnabel.

5/4/52 Honolulu
Rikidozan beat Lucky Simunovich, Bud Curtis & Red Scorpion beat Fritz & Hans Schnabel, Johnny Sepeda drew Toshio Yamaguchi, Earl Rasmussen beat Wally Tsutsumi.

5/11/52 Honolulu
Red Scorpion beat Rikidozan, Bobby Bruns beat Bud Curtis, Ray Daoang drew Johnny Sepeda, Toshio Yamaguchi beat Armand Tanny, Toshio Yamaguchi beat Armand Tanny - judo match.

5/17/52 Honolulu
Red Scorpion beat Lucky Simunovich won Hawaiian Title, Bud Curtis drew Rikidozan, Johnny Sepeda beat Toshio Yamaguchi, Ray Daoang beat Armand Tanny.

5/25/52 Honolulu
Irish Jackie & Sky Low Low beat Sonny Boy Cassidy & Farmer Pete, Lucky Simunovich beat Bud Curtis, Rikidozan beat Johnny Sepeda, Toshio Yamaguchi beat Ray Daoang.

6/1/52 Honolulu
Sonny Boy Cassidy & Farmer Pete beat Irish Jackie & Sky Low Low, Red Scorpion beat Rikidozan, Bud Curtis drew Johnny Sepeda, Ray Daoang beat Lou Britton.

6/8/52 Honolulu
Bobby Bruns & Lucky Simunovich beat Bud Curtis & Red Scorpion won Hawaiian tag titles, Albert Mills beat Johnny Sepeda, Rikidozan beat Armand Tanny, Ray Daoang drew Rikidozan.

6/15/52 Honolulu
Red Scorpion beat Bobby Bruns, Albert Mills drew Lucky Simunovich, Johnny Sepeda beat Bud Curtis dq, Ray Daoang beat Jesse James could not continue.

6/22/52 Honolulu
Leo Nomellini & Lucky Simunovich beat Bud Curtis & Red Scorpion, Bobby Bruns drew Albert Mills, Johnny Sepeda beat Armand Tanny, Ray Daoang drew Stan Skieski.

6/29/52 Honolulu
Leo Nomellini & Lucky Simunovich drew Al Mills & Red Scorpion, Bobby Bruns beat Johnny Sepeda, Bud Curtis drew Seelie Samara, Armand Tanny beat Ray Daoang dq.

7/6/52 Honolulu
Red Scorpion beat Lucky Simunovich, Bobby Bruns drew Baron Leone, Albert Mills beat Seelie Samara, Bud Curtis drew Johnny Sepeda.

7/13/52 Honolulu
Baron Leone beat Bobby Bruns, Bud Curtis & Al Mills beat Johnny Sepeda & Lucky Simunovich, Red Scorpion drew Seelie Samara, Masahiko Kimura beat Ray Daoang.

7/20/52 Honolulu
Baron Leone drew Red Scorpion, Gene Dubuque beat Bud Curtis dq, Al Mills beat Ray Daoang, Al Mills drew Seelie Samara, Masahiko Kimura drew Johnny Sepeda, Frances Robello drew Larry Tanabe judo match.

7/27/52 Honolulu
Al Mills beat Red Scorpion, Bud Curtis beat Gene Dubuque, Bobby Bruns drew Masahiko Kimura, Seelie Samara beat Johnny Sepeda, Kokichi Endo beat Ray Daoang dq.

8/3/52 Honolulu
Red Scorpion beat Al Mills, Gene Dubuque beat Ray Daoang, Bud Curtis drew Dave Levin.

8/10/52 Honolulu
Bobby Bruns & Dave Levin beat Sammy Menacher & Red Scorpion, Gene Dubuque beat Al Mills dq, Johnny Sepeda beat Ray Daoang, Kokichi Endo beat Larry Tanabe - judo.

8/17/52 Honolulu
Bud Curtis beat Dave Levin, Red Scorpion beat Gene Dubuque, Al Mills drew Joginder Singh, Bob Langevin beat Johnny Sepeda, Kokichi Endo beat Bobby Bruns.

8/24/52 Honolulu
Lou Thesz beat Bud Curtis NWA title defense, Bobby Bruns & Dave Levin beat Bob Langevin & Red Scorpion, Gene Dubuque drew Al Mills, Bob McCune drew Johnny Sepeda.

8/31/52 Honolulu
Lou Thesz beat Red Scorpion (Tom Rice) won Hawaiian title, Bud Curtis drew Al Mills, Dave Levin beat Bob McCune dq, Bob Langevin beat Gene Dubuque, Danny O'Rourke drew Joe Pazandak.

9/7/52 Honolulu
Bud Curtis beat Bob McCune, Bobby Bruns beat Bob Langevin, Dave Levin beat Gene Dubuque, Tom Rice beat Johnny Sepeda, Bobby Bruns beat Bud Curtis, Tom Rice beat Dave Levin, Danny O'Rourke beat Stan Miyashiro, Kokichi Endo drew Auleaga Maivia.

9/14/52 Honolulu
Bobby Bruns beat Tom Rice to win vacant Hawaiian Title, Little Beaver & Tuffy McCrae drew Fuzzy Cupid & Tom Thumb, Bud Curtis no contest Bob Langevin, Dave Levin drew Bob McCune, Gene Dubuque drew Auleaga Maiava.

9/21/52 Honolulu
Fuzzy Cupid & Tom Thumb beat Little Beaver & Tuffy McCrae, Bud Curtis beat Bob Langevin, Tom Rice beat Bob McCune, Dave Levin beat Gene Dubuque, Kokichi Endo beat Jack Britton.

9/28/52 Honolulu
Bud Curtis & Tom Rice beat Bobby Bruns & Dave Levin, Little Beaver beat Fuzzy Cupid, Bob Langevin drew Earl McCready, Gene Dubuque beat Ramon Cernades dq, Auleaga Maiava beat Jack Britton.

10/5/52 Honolulu
Ben & Mike Sharpe beat Bud Curtis & Tom Rice NWA World Tag titles, Bobby Bruns drew Bob Langevin, Dave Levin bet Gene Dubuque, Ramon Cernades beat Bob McCune.

10/12/52 Honolulu
Ben & Mike Sharpe beat Bobby Bruns & Gino Garibaldi, Bob Langevin beat Bud Curtis, Tom Rice beat Ramon Cernades, Dave Levin beat Ben Sherman.

10/19/52 Honolulu
Ben & Mike Sharpe beat Bobby Bruns & Gino Garibaldi, Dave Levin drew Tom Rice, Bob Langevin drew Ramon Cernandes, Auleaga Maiava drew Ben Sherman.

10/26/52 Honolulu
Primo Carnera beat Ben Sharpe, Gino Garibaldi drew Mike Sharpe, Tom Rice beat Hardy Kruskamp, Bob Langevin drew Lucky Simunovich, Dave Levin beat Ramon Cernades.

11/2/52 Honolulu
Primo Carnera & Gino Garibaldi drew Ben & Mike Sharpe, Lucky Simunovich beat Tom Rice dq, Ramon Cernades drew Bob Langevin, Dave Levin beat Hardy Kruskamp.

11/9/52 Honolulu
Gino Garibaldi & Lucky Simunovich beat Bob Langevin & Tom Rice, Mike Sharpe beat Primo Carnera, Ben Sharpe beat Ramon Cernades, Dave Levin beat Hardy Kruskamp.

11/16/52 Honolulu
Gino Garibaldi & Lucky Simunovich beat Ben & Mike Sharpe dq, Bobby Bruns beat Tom Rice, Bob Langevin drew Dave Levin, George Pencheff beat Ramon Cernades.

11/23/52 Honolulu
Ben & Mike Sharpe beat Gino Garibaldi & Lucky Simunovich, Tom Rice beat Dave Levin, Bob Langevin drew George Pencheff.

11/30/52 Honolulu
Mike Sharpe beat Gino Garibaldi, Ben Sharpe drew Lucky Simunovich, Bobby Bruns beat Bob Langevin, George Pencheff beat Tom Rice dq.

12/7/52 Honolulu
Lou Thesz beat Mike Sharpe, Tom Rice beat Ben Sharpe, Gino Garibaldi beat Bob Langevin, George Pencheff drew Lucky Simunovich, Dave Levin beat Stan Miyashiro dq.

12/14/52 Honolulu
Ben & Mike Sharpe beat Bobby Bruns & Lucky Simunovich, Gino Garibaldi drew Tom Rice, George Pencheff beat Dave Levin, Auleaga Maiava drew Stan Miyashiro.

12/21/52 Honolulu
Gorgeous George beat Lucky Simunovich, Gino Garibaldi beat George Pencheff, Dennis Clary beat Tom Rice, Joe Campbell beat Auleaga Maiava.

12/28/52 Honolulu
Bobby Bruns beat Gorgeous George, Tom Rice beat George Pencheff, Dennis Clary drew Gino Garibaldi, Joe Campbell beat Stan Miyashiro.

1953

1/4/53 Honolulu
Mario DeSouza beat Dennis Clary won 8-man battle royal, Bobby Bruns drew Gino Garibaldi, Lee Kolina drew Tom Rice, Hisao Tanaka beat Joe Campbell, Auleaga Maiava drew Earl Rasmussen.

1/11/53 Honolulu
Bobby Bruns & Dennis Clary beat Mario DeSouza & Tom Rice, Gino Garibaldi beat Hisao Tanaka, Joe Campbell drew Jack Terry, Lee Kolima beat Earl Rasmussen.

1/18/53 Honolulu
Bobby Bruns beat Gino Garibaldi, Abe Kashey beat Dennis Clary, Mario DeSouza no contest Tom Rice, Lee Kolima beat Joe Campbell.

433

1/25/53 Honolulu
Verne Gagne beat Jack Terry, Mario DeSouza beat Tom Rice, Abe Kashey beat Gino Garibaldi, Dennis Clary beat Lee Kolima.

2/1/53 Honolulu
Abe Kashey & Tom Rice beat Dennis Clary & Mario DeSouza, Bobby Bruns drew Verne Gagne, Joe Campbell beat Jack Terry, Al Marino drew Earl Rasmussen.

2/8/53 Honolulu
Rikidozan beat Tom Rice, Mario DeSouza drew Abe Kashey, Dennis Clary beat Joe Campbell, Lee Kolima beat Al Marino, Lee Kolima drew Auleaga Maiava.

2/16/53 Honolulu
Bobby Bruns & Rikidozan drew Abe Kashey & Tom Rice, Mr. X (Lou Newman) beat Dennis Clary, Mario DeSouza beat Lee Kolima, Job Campbell drew Auleaga Maiava.

2/22/53 Honolulu
Salie Helassie & Pee Wee James beat Vito Gonzales & Pancho The Bull, Mr. X beat Tom Rice, Mario DeSouza drew Rikidozan, Dennis Clary beat Lou Britton.

3/1/53 Honolulu
Abe Kashey & Tom Rice beat Bobby Bruns & Rikidozan won vacant Hawaiian Tag titles, Mario DeSouza beat Mr. X, Salie Helassie beat Vito Gonzales, Pancho The Bull beat Pee Wee James, Auleaga Maiava beat Lou Britton.

3/8/53 Honolulu
Bobby Bruns drew Abe Kashey, Mr. X beat Mario De Souza, Tom Rice beat Dennis Clary, Jack Hader beat Auleaga Maiava.

3/15/53 Honolulu
Abe Kashey drew Mr. X, Bobby Bruns drew Tom Rice, Bearcat Wright beat Jack Hader, Mario DeSouza beat Dennis Clary.

3/22/53 Honolulu
Bobby Bruns beat Abe Kashey, Bobby Managoff beat Tom Rice, Mr. X beat Bearcat Wright, Mario DeSouza drew Jack Hader.

3/29/53 Honolulu
Bobby Bruns & Bobby Managoff beat Abe Kashey & Tom Rice, Mr. X beat Jack Hader, Mario DeSouza drew Bearcat Wright, Iwalani Tanaka beat Sally Lee Judo.

4/5/53 Honolulu
Bobby Bruns & Bobby Managoff beat Abe Kashey & Tom Rice won Hawaiian tag titles, Mr. X beat Mario DeSouza, Mr. X drew Bearcat Wright, Jack Hader drew Auleaga Maiava.

4/12/53 Honolulu
Mr. X beat Bobby Bruns, Bobby Managoff beat Abe Kashey, Tom Rice drew Bearcat Wright, Al Marino beat Jack Hader dq.

4/19/53 Honolulu
Hombre Montana & Tom Rice beat Bobby Bruns & Bobby Managoff, Pierre LaSalle drew Bearcat Wright, Auleaga Maiava beat Larry Tanabe.

4/26/53 Honolulu
Hombre Montana beat Bearcat Wright, Bobby Managoff beat Pierre LaSalle, Pat McGill drew Tom Rice, Jack Hader beat Auleaga Maiava.

5/3/53 Honolulu
Bobby Bruns drew Hombre Montana, Bobby Managoff beat Tom Rice dq, Mr. X beat Pat McGill, Jack Hader drew Bearcat Wright, Kokichi Tokei beat Wally Tsutsumi.

5/10/53 Honolulu
Bobby Bruns & Bobby Managoff beat Tom Rice & Mr. X, Hombre Montana no contest Hans Schnabel, Jack Hader beat Earl Rasmussen.

5/17/53 Honolulu
Bobby Managoff beat Tom Rice, Hans Schnabel beat Hombre Montana, Bobby Bruns drew Mr. X, Sonny Kurgis beat Jack Hader.

5/24/53 Honolulu
Han Schnabel beat Bobby Managoff, Hombre Montana drew Mr. X, Bobby Bruns beat Jim Mitchell, Sonny Kurgis beat Auleaga Maiava.

5/31/53 Honolulu
Hans Schnabel beat Mr. X, Bobby Managoff beat Lee Grable, Hombre Montanan beat Sonny Kurgis, Jim Mitchell drew Hombre Montana, Al Marino drew Larry Tanaka.

6/7/53 Honolulu
Hans Schnabel beat Bobby Bruns - won Hawaiian title, Lee Grable beat Sonny Kurgis, Hombre Montana & Lou Newman beat Bobby Managoff & Jim Mitchell.

6/14/53 Honolulu
Bobby Bruns & Jim Mitchell beat Lou Newman & Hans Schnabel, Bobby Managoff beat Hombre Montana, Lee Grable drew Sonny Kurgis.

6/21/53 Honolulu
Bobby Managoff & Leo Nomellini beat Hombre Montana & Lou Newman, Hans Schabel beat Sonny Kurgis, Lee Grable drew Jim Mitchell.

6/28/53 Honolulu
Leo Nomellini beat Hans Schnabel dq, Bobby Managoff beat Lou Newman, Jack Witzig beat Lee Grable, Sonny Kurgis drew Jim Mitchell.

7/5/53 Honolulu
Bobby Managoff beat Hans Schnabel, Lee Grable beat Jim Mitchell, Brother Frank & Lou Newman beat Sonny Kurgis & Jack Witzig.

7/12/53 Honolulu
Frank Jares & Hans Schnabel beat Bobby Managoff & Jim Mitchell, Jack Witzig beat Lou Newman, Sonny Kurgis drew Pierre LaSalle.

7/19/53 Honolulu
Bobby Managoff beat Hans Schnable - won Hawaiian title, Jack Witzig beat Pierre LaSalle, Frank Jares beat Sonny Kurgis, Larry Tanabe drew Wally Tsutsumi.

7/26/53 Honolulu
Ray Eckert beat Hans Schnabel, Bobby Managoff beat Frank Jares, Jack Witzig beat Jim Mitchell, Sonny Kurgis beat Pierre LaSalle.

8/2/53 Honolulu
Ray Eckert drew Bobby Managoff, Bobby Managoff beat Joe Marsh, Ray Eckert beat Jack Witzig, Frank Jares beat Lee Grable, Sonny Kurgis beat Jim Mitchell.

8/9/53 Honolulu
Lou Thesz beat Bobby Managoff, Ray Eckert beat Frank Jares, Sonny Kurgis drew Jack Witzig, Joe Marsh beat Auleaga Maiava.

8/16/53 Honolulu
Lou Thesz beat Ray Eckert dq, Bobby Managoff drew Ben Sharpe, Jack Witzig beat Frank Jares, Sonny Kurgis drew Joe Marsh.

8/23/53 Honolulu
Ben Sarpe beat Bobby Managoff - won Hawaiian title, Bobby Bruns beat Ray Eckert, Jack Witzig beat Joe Marsh, Frank Jares beat Sonny Kurgis.

8/30/53 Honolulu
Ben & Mike Sharpe beat Bobby Managoff & Jack Witzig, Pat McGill beat Frank Jares, Mario DeSouza beat Joe Marsh.

9/6/53 Honolulu
Ben Sharpe drew Bobby Bruns, Jack Witzig beat Mike Sharpe dq, Tommy O'Toole beat Mario DeSouza, Pat McGill beat Joe Marsh.

9/13/53 Honolulu
Bobby Bruns & Jack Witzig drew Ben & Mike Sharpe, Tommy OToole beat Pat McGill, Mario DeSouza beat Joe Marsh.

9/20/53 Honolulu
Jack Witzig beat Bud Curtis dq, Bobby Bruns drew Tommy O'Toole, Pat McGill beat Mario DeSouza, Joe Marsh beat Al Marino.

9/27/53 Honolulu
Bud Curtis & Tommy O'Toole beat Bobby Bruns & Jack Witzig, Frank Valois beat Pat McGill, Mario DeSouza beat Joe Marsh.

10/4/53 Honolulu
Pat McGill & Jack Witzig beat Bud Curtis & Tommy O'Toole, Frank Valois beat Bobby Bruns, Hank Metheny beat Mario DeSouza.

10/11/53 Honolulu
Pat McGill & Jack Witzig drew Bud Curtis & Tommy O'Toole, Frank Valois beat Earl McCready, Bobby Bruns beat Hank Metheny.

10/18/53 Honolulu
Gorgeous George beat Pat McGill, Bobby Bruns drew Frank Valois, Jack Witzig beat Tommy O'Toole dq, Bud Curtis beat Hank Metheny.

10/25/53 Honolulu
Jack Witzig beat Gorgeous George dq, Bobby Bruns beat Pat McGill, Bud Curtis & Tommy O'Toole beat Hank Metheny & Frank Valois.

11/1/53 Honolulu
Frank Valois beat Jack Witzig, Vito Gonzales & Sky Low Low beat Pee Wee James & Tuffy McCrae, Bobby Bruns drew Tommy O'Toole, Bud Curtis beat Jack Britton.

11/8/53 Honolulu
Bobby Bruns & Jack Witzig drew Bud Curtis & Tommy O'Toole, Sky Low Low beat Tuffy McCrae, Pee Wee James beat Vito Gonzales, Frank Valois beat Hank Metheny, Frank Valois beat Jack Britton.

11/15/53 Honolulu
Rikidozan beat Tommy O'Toole, Dick Raines beat Jack Witzig, Pee Wee James & Tuffy McCrae beat Vito Gonzales & Sky Low Low, Bud Curtis drew Frank Valois.

11/22/53 Honolulu
Rikidozan beat Dick Raines, Frank Valois beat Tommy O'Toole, Sammy Berg beat Bud Curtis, Bobby Bruns beat Les Grimes.

11/29/53 Honolulu
Sammy Berg beat Rossi Mucciacciaro, Frank Valois beat Bobby Bruns, Rikidozan beat Bud Curtis, Al Lovelock beat Tommy O'Toole, Rikidozan beat Frank Valois, Sammy Berg beat Al Lovelock.

12/6/53 Honolulu
Lou Thesz beat Rikidozan, Frank Valois beat Sammy Berg, Al Lovelock beat Bud Curtis, Dr. John Bonica drew Count Mucciacciaro.

12/13/53 Honolulu
Lou Thesz beat Frank Valois, Rikidozan drew Al Lovelock, Sammy Berg beat Count Rossi Mucciacciaro, Bud Curtis beat Dr. John Bonica.

12/20/53 Honolulu
Sammy Berg & Rikidozan & Pat McGill beat Al Lovelock & Count Mucci & Frank Valois, Bobby Bruns beat Bud Curtis, Al Marino drew Wally Tsutsumi.

12/27/53 Honolulu
Sammy Berg & Bobby Bruns & Pat McGill beat Carlos Freeman & Count Mucci & Frank Valois, Rikidozan drew Al Lovelock.

1954

1/3/54 Honolulu
Al Lovelock beat Pat McGill won battle royal, Luther Lindsay beat Carlos Freeman, Bobby Bruns drew Frank Valois, Sammy Berg drew Count Rossi Mucci, Vilai Su'a beat Al Marino.

1/10/54 Honolulu
Sammy Berg & Pat McGill beat Carlos Freeman & Count Rossi Mucci, Al Lovelock & Frank Valois beat Sammy Berg & Pat McGill, Bobby Bruns & Luther Lindsay beat Carlos Freeman & Count Rossi Mucci, Bobby Bruns & Luther Lindsay beat Al Lovelock & Frank Valois won Hawaiian Tag Titles.

1/17/54 Honolulu
Al Lovelock beat Sammy Berg, Luther Lindsay beat Frank Valois, Bobby Bruns beat Count Rossi Mucci dq, Pat McGill beat Carlos Freeman.

1/24/54 Honolulu
Ed Gardenia & Count Rossi Mucci beat Sammy Berg & Frank Valois, Al Lovelock beat Luther Lindsay, Bobby Bruns beat Pat McGill.

1/31/54 Honolulu
Elmer & Logger Larsen beat Ed Gardenia & Count Rossi Mucci, Al Lovelock beat Bobby Bruns, Luther Lindsay beat Carlos Freeman & Pat McGill.

2/7/54 Honolulu
Ed Gardenia & Count Rossi Mucci beat Bobby Bruns & Luther Lindsay, Rikidozan drew Al Lovelock, Logger Larsen beat Pat McGill, Elmer Larsen beat Carlos Freeman.

2/14/54 Honolulu
Al Lovelock beat Ben Sharpe won Hawaiian Title, Ed Gardenia drew Mike Sharpe, Logger Larsen beat Count Rossi Mucci dq, Pat McGill beat Elmer Larsen.

2/21/54 Honolulu
Larry Moquin beat Ed Gardenia dq, Rey Urbano beat Count Rossi Mucci, Logger Larsen beat Pat McGill, Elmer Larsen beat Earl Rasmussen.

2/28/54 Honolulu
Larry Moquin beat Al Costello dq, Rey Urbano beat Elmer Larsen, Ed Gardenia beat Logger Larsen.

3/7/54 Honolulu
Ed Gardenia & Count Rossi Mucci beat Elmer & Logger Larsen, Al Costello drew Larry Moquin, Rey Urbano beat Al Marino & Earl Rasmussen.

3/14/54 Honolulu
Ben & Mike Sharpe beat Ed Gardenia & Count Rossi Mucci, Bobby Bruns drew Larry Moquin, Al Costello beat Pat McGill, Rey Urbano beat Logger Larsen.

3/21/54 Honolulu
Ed Gardenia & Count Rossi Mucci beat Bobby Bruns & Larry Moquin dq, Al Costello no contest Rey Urbano, Tommy Wright beat Al Camacho.

3/28/54 Honolulu
Ed Gardenia drew Larry Moquin, Al Costello beat Pat McGill, Rey Urbano beat Count Rossi Mucci, Bear Honda drew Wimpy Willington.

4/4/54 Honolulu
Bobby Bruns & Larry Moquin beat Al Costello & Ed Gardenia dq, Karl Von Schober beat Pat McGill, Tinia Su'a beat Al Camacho.

4/11/54 Honolulu
Bobby Bruns & Larry Moquin beat Al Costello & Ed Gardenia, Eric Pederson drew Karl Von Schober, Rey Urbano beat Pat McGill.

4/18/54 Honolulu
Larry Moquin beat Eric Pederson, Karl Von Schober beat Ed Gardenia, Rey Urbano beat Al Costello, Tinia Su'a beat Al Marino.

4/25/54 Honolulu
Karl Von Schober beat Bobby Bruns, Ed Gardenia beat John Paul Henning, Larry Moquin no contest Rey Urbano, Wally Lam Ho beat Wimpy Willington.

5/2/54 Honolulu
Larry Moquin beat Ed Gardenia, Rey Urbano beat Eric Pederson dq, Karl Von Schober beat Don Beitelman, Bobby Bruns drew John Paul Henning.

5/9/54 Honolulu
Bobby Bruns & Larry Moquin beat Ed Gardenia & Eric Pederson, Jungle Boy beat Rey Urbano, John Paul Henning beat Karl Von Schober, Tinia Su'a beat Wimpy Willington.

5/16/54 Honolulu
Ed Gardenia drew Eric Pederson, Jungle Boy beat John Paul Henning, Bobby Bruns beat Rey Urbano, Larry Moquin beat Jungle Boy dq, Karl Von Schober beat Bobby Bruns.

5/23/54 Honolulu
Larry Moquin beat Karl Von Schober won Hawaiian title, Ed Gardenia & Jungle Boy beat Bobby Bruns & Rey Urbano, John Paul Henning beat Eric Pederson.

5/30/54 Honolulu
Karl Von Schober beat Larry Moquin, Larry Moquin beat Jungle Boy dq, Larry Moquin beat Pedro Godoy, Karl Von Schober beat Ed Gardenia, Pedro Godoy beat John Paul Henning, Rey Urbano beat Eric Pederson.

6/6/54 Honolulu
Larry Moquin drew Lou Thesz, Karl Von Schober beat Pedro Godoy, Ed Gardenia & Jungle Boy beat John Paul Hennig & Rey Urbano, Wally Lam Ho beat Al Marino.

6/13/54 Honolulu
Lou Thesz beat Karl Von Schober, Pedro Godoy beat Rey Urbano, Ed Gardenia & Jungle Boy drew John Paul Henning & Larry Moquin, Earl Rasmussen beat Wally Lam Ho.

6/20/54 Honolulu
Lou Thesz beat Larry Moquin, Pedro Godoy drew Karl Von Schober, Bobby Bruns & John Paul Henning beat Ed Gardenia & Jungle Boy, Rey Urbano beat Earl Rasmussen.

6/27/54 Honolulu
Cowboy Bradley & Little Beaver beat Fuzzy Cupid & Tom Thumb, Bobby Bruns beat Ed Gardenia, Jungle Boy beat Larry Moquin, Pedro Godoy drew John Paul Henning.

7/4/54 Honolulu
Karl Von Schober beat Jungle Boy, Fuzzy Cupid beat Little Beaver dq, Tom Thumb beat Cowboy Bradley, Pedro Godoy drew Larry Moquin, John Paul Henning beat Jimmy Szikszay.

7/11/54 Honolulu
Karl Von Schober beat Larry Moquin won Hawaiian title, Danno O'Shocker beat Jim Szikszay, Cowboy Bradley & Little Beaver beat Fuzzy Cupid & Tom Thumb, Pedro Godoy drew John Paul Henning, Jungle Boy beat Rey Urbano.

7/18/54 Honolulu
Rocky Brown & Bobby Bruns & John Paul Henning beat Pedro Godoy & Jungle Boy & Karl Von Schober, Danno O'Shocker beat Larry Moquin, Earl Rasmussen beat Tinia Su'a.

7/25/54 Honolulu
Pedro Godoy & Karl Von Schober beat John Paul Henning & Danno O'Shocker, Rocky Brown beat Jack Hader, Bobby Bruns drew Jungle Boy, Wally Lam Ho beat Wimpy Willington.

8/1/54 Honolulu
Bobby Bruns & John Paul Henning beat Pedro Godoy & Karl Von Schober - Hawaiian Tag Title, Rocky Brown beat Jungle Boy, Danno O'Shocker beat Jack Hader, Tommy Wright beat Wimpy Willington.

8/8/54 Honolulu
Wladek Kowalski beat Rocky Brown, John Paul Henning drew Karl Von Schober, Bobby Bruns & Danno O'Shocker beat Pedro Godoy & Jungle Boy, Jack Hader beat Al Marino.

8/15/54 Honolulu
John Paul Henning drew Wladek Kowalski, Rocky Brown beat Karl Von Schober, Bobby Bruns beat Jungle Boy, Danno O'Shocker beat Pedro Godoy.

8/22/54 Honolulu
Wladek Kowalski bet Karl Von Schober, Rocky Brown beat Mike Sharpe, John Paul Henning beat Pedro Godoy, Danno O'Shocker beat Jack Hader.

8/29/54 Honolulu
John Paul Henning beat Karl Von Schober won Hawaiian Title, Wladek Kowalski drew Mike Sharpe, Bobby Bruns beat Rocky Brown dq, Pedro Godoy beat Danno O'Shocker.

9/5/54 Honolulu
John Paul Henning beat Wladek Kowalski, Bobby Bruns beat Pedro Godoy, Don Arnold drew Danno O'Shocker, Earl Rasmussen beat Wally Lam Ho.

9/12/54 Honolulu
Bobby Bruns & John Paul Henning beat Pedro Godoy & Wladek Kowalski, Don Arnold drew Vic Christy, Jack Pesek beat Danno O'Shocker, Tinia Su'a beat Earl Rasmussen.

9/19/54 Honolulu
Bobby Bruns & Vic Christy & John Paul Henning beat Don Arnold & Bob Corby & Pedro Godoy, John Paul Henning beat Pedro Godoy, Don Arnold drew Bobby Bruns, Vic Christy beat Jack Pesek, Danno O'Shocker beat Bob Corby dq.

9/26/54 Honolulu
Don Arnold beat Pedro Godoy, John Paul Henning drew Jack Pesek, Vic Christy beat Bob Corby, Bobby Bruns beat Danno O'Shocker.

10/3/54 Honolulu
John Paul Henning no contest Hans Schnabel, Don Arnold drew Lou Newman, Vic Christy beat Jack Pesek, Bob Corby beat Earl Rasmussen.

10/10/54 Honolulu
Lou Newman & Hans Schnabel beat Bobby Bruns & John Paul Henning won Hawaiian Tag titles, Don Arnold beat Vic Christy, Bob Corby beat Pedro Godoy, Al Marino beat Wally Lam Ho.

10/17/54 Honolulu
Shoulders Newman beat John Paul Henning, Don Arnold beat Hans Schnabel dq, Bobby Bruns drew Zebra Kid (George Bollas), Don Beitelman beat Pedro Godoy, Vic Christy beat Bob Corby.

10/24/54 Honolulu
John Paul Henning beat Lou Newman, Zebra Kid beat Don Arnold, Hans Schnabel beat Vic Christy, Don Beitelman beat Bob Corby.

10/31/54 Honolulu
Shoulders Newman & Hans Schnabel beat Bobby Bruns & John Paul Henning, Don Beitelman beat Zebra Kid dq, Don Arnold drew Vic Christy, Wally Lam Ho beat Wimpy Willington.

11/7/54 Honolulu
John Paul Henning beat Hans Schnabel dq, Zebra Kid beat Lou Newman, Don Beitelman beat Don Arnold, Roger Mackay beat Bobby Bruns.

11/14/54 Honolulu
Roger Mackay beat John Paul Henning, Dick Raines beat Hans Schnabel, Don Beitelman beat Zebra Kid dq, Don Arnold drew Shoulders Newman.

11/21/54 Honolulu
Roger Mackay beat John Paul Henning won Hawaiian Title, Don Arnold beat Lou Newman, Hans Schnabel beat Zebra Kid dq, Dick Raines beat Don Beitelman, Don Arnold beat Hans Schnabel.

11/28/54 Honolulu
Don Beitelman & Roger Mackay beat Shoulders Newman & Hans Schnable won Hawaiian Tag titles, Dick Raines beat Don Arnold, John Paul Henning beat Ed Gardenia.

12/5/54 Honolulu
Lou Thesz beat Dick Raines, Don Beitelman & Roger Mackay drew Ed Gardenia & Zebra Kid, Don Arnold drew Bobby Bruns.

12/12/54 Honolulu
Lou Thesz beat Ed Gardenia, Lou Thesz drew Zebra Kid, Don Beitelman beat Dick Raines, Roger Mackay beat Don Arnold.

12/19/54 Honolulu
Fuzzy Cupid & Irish Jackie beat Black Panther & Little Beaver, Ed Gardenia drew Roger Mackay, Zebra Kid beat Don Beitelman dq, Bobby Bruns beat Don Arnold.

12/26/54 Honolulu
Don Beitelman & Roger Mackay drew Ed Gardenia & Zebra Kid, Little Beaver beat Fuzzy Cupid, Irish Jackie beat Black Panther, Bobby Bruns beta Al Warshawsky.

1955

1/2/55 Honolulu
Black Panther & Little Beaver beat Fuzzy Cupid & Irish Jackie, Roger Mackay beat Zebra Kid dq, Tosh Togo beat Al Warshawsky, Don Beitelman beat Ed Gardenia.

1/9/55 Honolulu
Tosh Togo beat Don Beitelman won battle royal, Roger MacKay beat Ed Gardenia, Buddy Lenz drew Zebra Kid, Al Marino drew Earl Rasmussen.

1/16/55 Honolulu
Don Beitelman & Roger MacKay beat Ed Gardenia & Zebra Kid dq, Tosh Togo beat Buddy Lenz, Al Marino beat Wally Lam Ho.

1/23/55 Honolulu
Tosh Togo beat Roger MacKay, Lucky Simunovich beat Ed Gardenia, Bobby Bruns drew Zebra Kid, Don Beitelman drew Buddy Lenz.

1/30/55 Honolulu
Tosh Togo beat Bobby Bruns, Lucky Simunovich drew Zebra Kid, Roger Mackay beat Buddy Lenz, Don Beitelman drew Ed Gardenia.

2/6/55 Honolulu
Lucky Simunovich beat Tosh Togo, Don Beitelman beat Zebra Kid, Bobby Bruns drew Roger Mackay, Ed Gardenia beat Buddy Lenz.

2/13/55 Honolulu
Lucky Simunovich beat Roger Mackay won Hawaiian title, Zebra Kid beat Don Beitelman, Tosh Togo beat Ed Gardenia, Buddy Lenz beat Earl Rasmussen.

2/20/55 Honolulu
Bobby Bruns & Lucky Simunovich beat Don Beitelman & Roger Mackay Won Hawaiian tag titles, Zebra Kid beat Tosh Togo, Ed Gardenia beat Buddy Lenz.

2/27/55 Honolulu
Bobby Bruns & Lucky Simunovich drew Ed Gardenia & Zebra Kid, Roger Mackay beat Tosh Togo, Don Beitelman beat Buddy Lenz.

3/6/55 Honolulu
Lucky Simunovich beat Zebra Kid dq, Roberto Pico beat Don Beitelman, Ed Gardenia drew Roger Mackay, Bobby Bruns beat Buddy Lenz.

3/13/55 Honolulu
Gene Stanlee beat Ed Gardenia, Don Beitelman drew Lucky Simunovich, Roberto Pico & Zebra Kid beat Bobby Bruns & Roger MacKay.

3/20/55 Honolulu
Gene Stanlee beat Don Beitelman, Lucky Simunovich beat Roger Mackay, Bobby Bruns drew Zebra Kid, Roberto Pico beat Ed Gardenia.

3/27/55 Honolulu
Doc Gallagher & Roberto Pico & Zebra Kid beat Don Beitelman & Bobby Bruns & Lucky Simunovich, Gene Stanlee beat Roger Mackay.

4/3/55 Honolulu
Lucky Simunovich beat Gene Stanlee dq, Rikidozan beat Don Beitelman dq, Roberto Pico & Zebra Kid beat Bobby Bruns & Doc Gallagher.

4/10/55 Honolulu
Zebra Kid beat Lucky Simunovich - won Hawaiian Title, Azamafuji beat Don Beitelman, Rikidozan beat Roberto Pico, Bobby Bruns drew Doc Gallagher.

4/17/55 Honolulu
Rikidozan & Azamafuji beat Bobby Bruns & Lucky Simunovich to win Hawaiian tag titles, Doc Gallagher drew Roberto Pico, Al Marino beat Wimpy Willington.

4/24/55 Honolulu
Bobby Bruns & Doc Gallagher beat Zebra Kid - Handicap match in which Zebra Kid failed to pin both opponents within 45 minutes., Rikidozan drew Lucky Simunovich, Azamafuji beat Roberto Pico, Oki Shikina beat Al Marino.

5/1/55 Honolulu
Rikidozan & Azamafuji beat Roberto Pico & Zebra Kid dq, Tony Angelo beat Bobby Bruns, Doc Gallagher beat Oki Shikina.

5/8/55 Honolulu
Zebra Kid beat Rikidozan dq, Azamafuji beat Doc Gallagher, Bobby Bruns & Nick Roberts drew Tony Angelo & Roberto Pico, Earl Rasmussen drew Tinia Su'a.

5/15/55 Honolulu
George Bollas drew Nick Roberts, Azamafuji & Oki Shikina beat Tony Angelo & Roberto Pico, Bobby Bruns beat Doc Gallagher, Tinia Su'a beat Buckets Schnabel dq.

5/22/55 Honolulu
George Bollas beat Tony Angelo dq, Azamafuji beat Doc Gallagher, Azamafuji beat Roberto Pico, Bobby Bruns drew Nick Roberts.

5/29/55 Honolulu
Bobby Bruns & Nick Roberts beat George Bollas & Roberto Pico, Azamafuji beat Tony Angelo, Oki Shikina beat Doc Gallagher dq.

6/5/55 Honolulu
Azamafuji beat George Bollas, Bobby Bruns & Oki Shikina beat Doc Gallagher & Roberto Pico dq, Tony Angelo beat Nick Roberts.

6/12/55 Honolulu
George Bollas beat Azamafuji, Nick Roberts beat Roberto Pico won battle royal, Bobby Bruns beat Tony Angelo, Oki Shikina beat Doc Gallagher dq.

9/11/55 Honolulu
Ben & Mike Sharpe beat Johnny Barend & Clyde Steeves, Riccardo Gattoni beat Ramon Cernandes, Johnny Brown beat Tony Vagnone.

9/18/55 Honolulu
Ben Sharpe beat Ricardo Gattoni, Johnny Barend drew Mike Sharpe, Clyde Steeves beat Tony Vagnone dq, Ramon Cernandes beat Johnny Cabral.

9/25/55 Honolulu
Lou Thesz beat Ben Sharpe, Mike Sharpe beat Clyde Steeves, Johnny Barend beat Ramon Cernandes, Ricard Gattoni drew Tony Vagnone.

10/2/55 Honolulu
Ben & Mike Sharpe beat Lou Thesz & Johnny Barend, Tony Vagnone beat Frank Marconi, Clyde Steeves beat Ricardo Gattoni, Johnny Brown drew Ramon Cernandes.

10/9/55 Honolulu
Primo Carnera beat Clyde Steeves, Johnny Barend beat Ben Sharpe, Mike Sharpe beat Frank Marconi, Tony Vagnone beat Ramon Cernandes, Ricardo Gattoni beat Hardy Kruskamp.

10/16/55 Honolulu
Ben & Mike Sharpe beat Johnny Barend & Primo Carnera, Clyde Steeves beat Bob Leipler, Ramon Cernandes beat Hardy Kruskamp, Ricard Gattoni drew Tony Vagnone.

10/23/55 Honolulu
Johnny Barend & Sandor Kovacs drew Ben & Mike Sharpe, Tony Vagnone beat Ricardo Gattoni, Clyde Steeves beat Ramon Cernandes.

10/30/55 Honolulu
George Bollas beat Mike Sharpe, Sandor Kovacs drew Ben Sharpe, Johnny Barend beat Tony Vagnone, Clyde Steeves beat Ricardo Gattoni.

11/6/55 Honolulu
Johnny Barend & Sandor Kovacs beat Ben & Mike Sharpe, George Bollas beat Clyde Steeves, Tony Vagnone beat Al Szasz.

11/13/55 Honolulu
Johnny Barend & Sandor Kovacs beat George Bollas & Tony Vagnone won vacant Hawaiian tag titles, Lord Blears beat Clyde Steeves, Max Steyne beat Al Szasz.

11/20/55 Honolulu
Johnny Barend beat Lord Blears, Al Lolotai beat Tony Vagnone, George Bollas drew Clyde Steeves, Johnny Brown beat Al Marino.

11/27/55 Honolulu
George Bollas beat Johnny Barend, Lord Blears drew Sandor Kovacs, Al Lolotai beat Clyde Steeves, Kokichi Endo beat Tony Vagnone, Johnny Cabral drew Earl Rasmussen.

12/4/55 Honolulu
Lord Blears & Gene Kiniski beat Johnny Barend & Sandor Kovacs, George Bollas drew Kokichi Endo, Al Lolotai beat Earl Rasmussen, Al Marino beat Johnny Cabral.

12/9/55 Honolulu
Lord Blears & Gene Kiniski drew Kokichi Endo & Sando Kovacs, Al Lolotai beat Johnny Barend, George Bollas beat Cyclone Wright, George Bollas beat Johnny Cabral, George Bollas beat Earl Rasmussen, Johnny Brown beat Al Marino.

12/16/55 Honolulu
Al Lolotai beat George Bollas won Hawaiian Title, Kokichi Endo beat Don Beitelman dq, Lord Blears & Gene Kiniski beat Doug Dawkins & Sandor Kovacs.

12/23/55 Honolulu
Doug Dawkins & Al Lolotai & Sandor Kovacs beat Lord Blears & George Bollas & Gene Kiniski, Kokichi Endo beat Don Beitelman, Earl Rasmussen beat Johnny Brown.

12/30/55 Honolulu
Leo Nomellini beat George Bollas, Lord Blears & Gene Kiniski beat Kokichi Endo & Tosh Togo, Sandor Kovacs drew Al Lolotai, Doug Dawkins beat Earl Rasmussen dq.

1956

1/6/56 Honolulu
Al Lolotai beat Tosh Togo to win battle royal, George Bollas drew Kokichi Endo, Leo Nomellini beat Gene Kiniski dq, Sandor Kovacs beat Earl Rasmussen, Lord Blears beat Doug Dawkins.

1/13/56 Honolulu
Sandor Kovacs & Al Lolotai & Leo Nomellini beat Lord Blears & George Bollas & Gene Kiniski dq, Hans Schnabel beat Kokichi Endo, Johnny Brown drew Doug Dawkins.

1/20/56 Honolulu
Lord Blears & Gene Kiniski beat Dick Beyer & Al Lolotai, Hans Schnabel beat Sandor Kovacs, Doug Dawkins beat George Bollas dq.

1/27/56 Honolulu
George Bollas & Hans Schnabel beat Lord Blears & Gene Kiniski, Dick Beyer drew Sandor Kovacs, Kokichi Endo beat Doug Dawkins.

2/3/56 Honolulu
Al Lolotai beat Hans Schnabel dq, Kokichi Endo beat George Bollas, Sandor Kovacs beat Gene Kiniski dq, Dick Beyer beat Doug Dawkins.

2/10/56 Honolulu
Lord Blears & Gene Kiniski beat George Bollas & Hans Schnabel, Sandor Kovacs drew Al Lolotai, Kokichi Endo beat Dick Beyer.

2/19/56 Honolulu
Lord Blears & Gene Kiniski drew Sandor Kovacs & Billy Varga, Al Lolotai beat Kokichi Endo, Dick Beyer beat Hans Schnabel dq.

2/24/56 Honolulu
Hans Schnabel beat Gene Kiniski 30-falls to a finish - each had 6 falls when Kiniski refused to continue after midnight, Billy Varga beat Dick Beyer, Lord Blears no contest Al Lolotai.

3/2/56 Honolulu
Billy Varga beat Al Lolotai, Gene Kiniski beat Sandor Kovacs, Hans Schnabel beat Lord Blears, Dick Beyer no contest Kokichi Endo.

3/9/56 Honolulu
Lord Blears & Gene Kiniski beat Sandor Kovacs & Al Lolotai, Billy Varga beat Hans Schnabel dq, Dick Beyer beat Kokichi Endo.

3/16/56 Honolulu
Billy Varga beat Al Lolotai won Hawaiian title, Tony Morelli beat Dick Beyer, Lord Blears & Gene Kiniski drew Sandor Kovacs & Hans Schnabel.

3/25/56 Honolulu
Dick Beyer & Al Lolotai & Billy Varga beat Lord Blears & Gene Kiniski & Hans Schnabel, Tony Morelli beat Sandor Kovacs, Earl Rasmussen beat Max Steyne.

4/1/56 Honolulu
Gene Kiniski beat Hans Schnabel, Lord Blears & Tony Morelli beat Bob Leipler & Billy Varga, Dick Beyer beat Sandor Kovacs.

4/8/56 Honolulu
Rikidozan & Kokichi Endo beat Lord Blears & Gene Kiniski, Tony Morelli drew Billy Varga, Don Beitelman beat Dick Beyer.

4/15/56 Honolulu
Lord Blears & Gene Kiniski beat Rikidozan & Kokichi Endo, Billy Varga beat Don Beitelman, Tony Morelli beat Dick Beyer.

4/22/56 Honolulu
Lord Blears & Tony Morelli beat Dick Beyer & Billy Varga, Gene Kiniski drew Don Beitelman, Ramon Cernandes drew Ray Urbano, Buddy Gilbert beat Earl Rassmussen.

4/29/56 Honolulu
Great Togo & Tosh Togo beat Lord Blears & Gene Kiniski - won Hawaiian tag titles, Tony Morelli beat Ramon Cernades, Rey Urbano beat Buddy Gilbert.

5/6/56 Honolulu
Tony Morelli beat Billy Varga, Al Lolotai drew Tosh Togo, Great Togo beat Rey Urbano, Ramond Cernandes beat Buddy Gilbert.

5/13/56 Honolulu
Great Togo beat Tony Morelli dq, Tosh Togo drew Billy Varga, Jerry Christy beat Ramon Cernades, Rey Urbano beat Johnny Brown, Buddy Gilbert beat Johnny Walker.

5/20/56 Honolulu
Great Togo no contest Billy Varga, Tony Morelli beat Tosh Togo, Jerry Christy beat Buddy Gilbert, Doug Dawkins beat Rey Urbano, Johnny Brown drew Ramon Cernandes.

5/27/56 Honolulu
Lou Thesz & Billy Varga beat Great Togo & Tosh Togo, Tony Morelli beat Jerry Christy, Ramon Cernandes drew Doug Dawkins, Johnny Brown beat Buddy Gilbert.

6/3/56 Honolulu Att 4000
Lou Thesz drew Leo Nomellini, Great Togo & Tosh Togo beat Jerry Christy & Doug Dawkins, Tony Morelli beat Billy Varga.

6/10/56 Honolulu
Leo Nomellini & Billy Varga beat Great Togo & Tosh Togo, Tony Morelli beat Doug Dawkins, Danny O'Rourke beat Ramon Cernandes, Jerry Christy beat Earl Rassmussen.

6/17/56 Honolulu
Ben & Mike Sharpe beat Great Togo & Tosh Togo, Billy Varga beat Ramon Cernandes, Tony Morelli beat Danny O'Rourke, Jerry Christy beat Zach Malkov.

6/24/56 Honolulu
Billy Varga beat Tony Morelli, Zach Malkov drew Sam Steamboat, Danny O'Rourke beat Great Togo dq, Tosh Togo beat Jerry Christy, Ramon Cernandes drew Doug Dawkins.

7/1/56 Honolulu
Billy Varga beat Great Togo, Tosh Togo beat Danny O'Rourke, Sam Steamboat beat Ramon Cernandes, Zach Malkov beat Doug Dawkins, Jerry Christy drew Johnny Walker.

7/8/56 Honolulu
Pedro Godoy & Zack Malkov & Tosh Togo beat Danny O'Rourke & Sam Steamboat & Billy Varga, Jerry Christy beat Ramon Cernandes, Johnny Brown beat Johnny Walker.

7/15/56 Honolulu
Billy Varga drew Zach Malkov, Tosh Togo beat Jerry Christy, Pedro Godoy beat Danny O'Rourke, Ramon Cernades drew Rey Urbano.

7/22/56 Honolulu
Billy Varga beat Pedro Godoy, Tosh Togo beat Zach Milkov, Doug Dawkins beat Jerry Christy, Danny O'Rourke beat Ramon Cernandes.

7/29/56 Honolulu
Tosh Togo beat Billy Varga - won Hawaiian Title, Pedro Godoy beat Doug Dawkins, Sam Steamboat beat Jerry Christy, Zach Malkov drew Danny O'Rourke, Johnny Brown beat Ramon Cernades.

8/5/56 Honolulu
Sam Steamboat & Billy Varga beat Tony Gardenia & Tosh Togo - won Hawaiian Tag titles, Pedro Godoy beat Rey Urbano, Doug Dawkins beat Danny O'Rourke, Johnny Brown beat Earl Rasmussen dq.

8/12/56 Honolulu
Pedro Godoy drew Billy Varga, Tosh Togo beat Doug Dawkins, Tosh Togo dew Rey Urbano, Sam Steamboat beat Tony Gardenia dq, Danny O'Rourke beat Johnny Walker.

8/19/56 Honolulu
Tosh Togo beat Pedro Godoy, Vic Christy drew Billy Varga, Jack Claybourne beat Tony Gardenia, Ray Duran beat Danny O'Rourke.

9/2/56 Honolulu
Vic Christy & Jack Claybourne beat Aldo Bogni & Pedro Godoy, Tosh Togo beat Lee Grimes, Sam Steamboat beat Doug Dawkins, Chief Vili Ava beat Ray Duran.

9/9/56 Honolulu
Jack Claybourne no contest Tosh Togo, Lord Layton beat Aldo Bogni, Vic Christy beat Ray Duran, Vili Ava beat Earl Rasmussen.

9/16/56 Honolulu
Aldo Bogni & Tom Rice beat Vic Christy & Jack Claybourne, Lord Layton drew Mike Mazurki, Ray Duran beat Rey Urbano.

9/23/56 Honolulu
Tosh Togo beat Mike Mazurki, Lord Layton beat Vic Christy, Jack Claybourne drew Tom Rice, Aldo Bogni beat Rey Urbano.

9/30/56 Honolulu
Jack Claybourne beat Tosh Togo, Lord Layton no contest Tom Rice, Vic Christy beat Aldo Bogni, Ray Duran beat Johnny Walker.

10/7/56 Honolulu
Tom Rice beat Tosh Togo - won Hawaiian Title, Jack Claybourne no contest Red Shoes Duggan, Aldo Bogni & Lord Layton drew Sammy Berg & Vic Christy, Wong Buck Lee beat Ray Duran.

10/14/56 Honolulu
Aldo Bogni & Lord Layton & Tom Rice beat Sammy Berg & Jack Claybourne & Vic Christy, Tosh Togo beat Red Shoes Duggan, Johnny Brown drew Johnny Walker.

10/21/56 Honolulu
Lord Layton & Tom Rice beat Sammy Berg & Vic Christy, Jack Claybourne beat Tosh Togo dq, Aldo Bogni beat Red Shoes Dugan, Wong Buck Lee beat Johnny Walker.

10/28/56 Honolulu
Jack Claybourne & Pat O'Connor beat Lord Layton & Tom Rice, Don Beitelman beat Vic Christy, Sammy Berg drew Aldo Bogni.

11/4/56 Honolulu
Pat O'Connor beat Lord Layton, Tom Rice beat Jack Claybourne, Kokichi Endo beat Aldo Bogni, Don Beitelman drew Sammy Berg.

11/11/56 Honolulu
Pat O'Connor beat Tom Rice, Don Beitelman drew Sammy Berg, Aldo Bogni & Lord Layton beat Jack Claybourne & Kokichi Endo.

11/18/56 Honolulu
Jack Claybourne beat Tom Rice dq, Sammy Berg & Pat O'Connor beat Aldo Bogni & Lord Layton, Kokichi Endo beat Don Beitelman.

11/25/56 Honolulu
Jack Claybourne & Pat O'Connor drew Lord Layton & Tom Rice, Don Beitelman beat Aldo Bogni, Kokichi Endo beat Sammy Berg.

12/2/56 Honolulu
Pat O'Connor beat Gorgeous George, Don Beitelman beat Lord Layton dq, Jack Claybourne drew Kokichi Endo, Sammy Berg beat Aldo Bogni.

12/9/56 Honolulu
Pat O'Connor drew Billy Watson, Don Beitelman drew Tom Rice, Lord Layton beat Sammy Berg, Jack Claybourne beat Joe Mitchell, Kokichi Endo beat Wong Buck Lee.

12/16/56 Honolulu
Tom Rice drew Billy Watson, Lord Layton beat Don Beitelman dq, Jack Claybourne beat Sammy Berg, Kokichi Endo beat Prince Charming, Joe Mitchell drew Johnny Walker.

12/23/56 Honolulu
Lord Layton & Tom Rice & Great Zorro (Jacob Grobbe) beat Don Beitelman & Joe Blanchard & Jack Claybourne, Sammy Berg drew Kokichi Endo, Wong Buck Lee beat Joe Mitchell.

12/30/56 Honolulu
Lou Thesz beat Great Zorro, Joe Blanchard drew Lord Layton, Kokichi Endo beat Sammy Berg, Prince Charming beat Joe Mitchell, Tom Rice beat Don Beitelman.

1957

1/6/57 Honolulu
Lou Thesz beat Tom Rice, Joe Blanchard beat Sammy Berg, Lord Layton & Great Zorro beat Don Beitelman & Kokichi Endo, Wong Buck Lee drew Kanak Victorino.

1/13/57 Honolulu
Lucky Simunovich beat Great Zorro, Charro Azteca drew Al Costello, Joe Blanchard drew Kokichi Endo, Lucky Simunovich & Great Zorro beat Lord Layton & Tom Rice, Johnny Walker beat Kanak Victorino.

1/20/57 Honolulu
Charro Azteca & Lord Layton & Tom Rice beat Al Costello & Kokichi Endo & Lucky Simunovich, Joe Blanchard beat Mark Tendler, Johnny Brown beat Johnny Walker.

1/27/57 Honolulu
Al Costello & Kokichi Endo & Lucky Simunovich beat Charro Azteca & Lord Layton & Tom Rice, Johnny Brown beat Wong Buck Lee, Mark Tendler beat Johnny Walker.

2/3/57 Honolulu
Al Costello beat Lord Layton dq, Kokichi Endo drew Tom Rice, Lucky Simunovich beat Charro Azteca, Joe Blanchard beat Adrian Baillargeon.

2/10/57 Honolulu
Tom Rice beat Al Costello, Lord Layton beat Lucky Simunovich, Joe Blanchard drew Kokichi Endo, Charro Azteca beat Johnny Walker, Charro Azteca drew Johnny Brown.

2/17/57 Honolulu
Lord Layton & Tom Rice beat Joe Blanchard & Kokichi Endo, Rikidozan beat Al Costello, Toyonobori beat Charro Azteca, Wong Buck Lee drew Mark Tendler.

2/24/57 Honolulu
Rikidozan & Kokichi Endo & Toyonobori beat Charro Azteca & Lord Layton & Tom Rice, Joe Blanchard drew Lucky Simunovich, Johnny Brown beat Mark Tendler.

3/3/57 Honolulu
Rikidozan drew Lucky Simunovich, Bobo Brazil beat Sammy Berg, Toyonobori beat Joe Blanchard, Kokichi Endo drew lord Layton, Earl Rasmussen beat Johnny Walker.

3/10/57 Honolulu
Tom Rice beat Lucky Simunovich, Bobo Brazil beat Kokichi Endo, Toyonobori beat Lord Layton dq, Joe Blanchard drew Johnny Brown.

3/17/57 Honolulu
Bobo Brazil beat Lord Layton, Kokichi Endo & Toyonobori beat Jan Gotch & Tom Rice, Joe Blanchard beat Wong Buck Lee, Earl Rasmussen beat Mark Tendler.

3/24/57 Honolulu
Lord Layton & Tom Rice beat Joe Blanchard & Bobo Brazil, Toyonobori beat Jan Gotch, Kokichi Endo beat Earl Rasmussen.

3/31/57 Honolulu
Bobo Brazil & Jack Claybourne beat Lord Layton & Tom Rice, Kokichi Endo & Toyonobori beat Joe Blanchard & Sam Steamboat, Jan Gotch beat Earl Rassmussen.

4/7/57 Honolulu
Kokichi Endo & Toyonobori beat Bobo Brazil & Jack Claybourne, Lord Layton beat Joe Blanchard, Tom Rice beat Jan Gotch, Sam Steamboat beat Wong Buck Lee.

4/14/57 Honolulu
Lord Layton & Tom Rice beat Kokichi Endo & Toyonobori, Hans Schnabel beat Joe Blanchard, Jack Claybourne beat Jan Gotch.

4/21/57 Honolulu
Al Lolotai & Lucky Simunovich beat Lord Layton & Tom Rice, Hans Schnabel drew Toyonobori, Kokichi Endo beat Jack Claybourne, Johnny Brown drew Jan Gotch.

4/28/57 Honolulu
Lord Layton & Tom Rice beat Al Lolotai & Lucky Simunovich - won vacant Hawaiian tag titles, Sammy Berg & Rocky Brown beat Jan Gotch & Hans Schnabel, Jack Claybourne drew Kokichi Endo.

5/5/57 Honolulu
Hans Schnabel beat Kokichi Endo, Al Lolotai beat Lord Layton, Jack Claybourne drew Tom Rice, Sammy Berg beat Rocky Brown dq.

5/12/57 Honolulu
Tom Rice & Lord Layton & Hans Schnabel beat Rikidozan & Toyonobori & Sammy Berg, Al Lolotai beat Great Zorro, Jack Claybourne beat Rocky Brown.

5/19/57 Honolulu
Al Lolotai beat Tom - won Hawaiian title, Lord Layton & Hans Schnabel drew Jack Claybourne & Toyonobori, Sammy Berg beat Rocky Brown.

5/26/57 Honolulu
Lou Thesz beat Bobo Brazil, Toyonobori beat Lord Layton, Hans Schnabel beat Al Lolotai dq, Jack Claybourne no contest Tom Rice.

6/2/57 Honolulu
Lou Thesz beat Toyonobori, Al Lolotai beat Hans Schnabel, Lord Layton & Tom Rice beat Sammy Berg & Jack Claybourne, Wong Buck Lee drew Mark Tendler.

6/9/57 Honolulu Att 5000
Lou Thesz drew Al Lolotai, Jack Claybourne beat Hans Schnabel, Tom Rice beat Sammy Berg, Kokichi Endo beat lord Layton dq.

6/16/57 Honolulu
Kokichi Endo & Toyonobori beat Lord Layton & Tom Rice, Al Lolotai beat Lucky Simunovich, Jack Claybourne beat Sammy Berg.

6/23/57 Honolulu
Brown Panther & Lord Littlebrook beat Fuzzy Cupid & Ivan The Terrible, Al Lolotai beat Lord Layton, Lucky Simunovich beat Jack Claybourne, Tom Rice beat Kokichi Endo, Martino Angelo drew Abe Zvonkin.

6/30/57 Honolulu
Al Lolotai & Lucky Simunovich beat Kokichi Endo & Toyonobori, Fuzzy Cupid beat Lord Littlebrook, Brown Panther beat Ivan The Terrible, Tom Rice beat Martino Angelo, Abe Zvonkin beat Earl Rasmussen.

7/7/57 Honolulu
Lord Littlebrook beat Fuzzy Cupid - won battle royal, Brown Panther drew Ivan The Terrible, Toyonobori beat Abe Zvonkin, Al Lolotai & Lucky Simunovich drew Tom Rice & Abe Zvonkin.

7/14/57 Honolulu
Al Lolotai drew Toyonobori, Fuzzy Cupid & Ivan The Terrible beat Brown Panther & Lord Littlebrook, Lucky Simunovich beat Abe Zvonkin dq, Martino Angelo drew Al Marino.

7/21/57 Honolulu
Al Lolotai beat Toyonobori, Tom Rice drew Lucky Simunovich, Martino Angelo & Doug Dawkins & Lord Littlebrook & Brown Panther beat Al Marino & Abe Zvonkin & Ivan The Terrible & Fuzzy Cupid.

7/28/57 Honolulu
Al Lolotai & Jack Witzig beat Tom Rice & Abe Zvonkin, Lucky Simunovich drew Toyonobori, Fuzzy Cupid & Ivan The Terrible beat Brown Panther & Lord Littlebrook dq.

8/4/57 Honolulu
Gorgeous George beat Lucky Simunovich dq, Bill Savage beat Jim Wright, Al Lolotai & Jack Witzig drew Lou Newman & Tom Rice.

8/11/57 Honolulu
Lucky Simunovich beat Gorgeous George, Shoulders Newman drew Jack Witzig, Tom Rice & Bill Savage beat Al Lolotai & Tinia Su'a, Al Marino beat George Kongozan dq.

8/18/57 Honolulu
Herb Freeman & Al Lolotai beat Lord Blears & Gorgeous George, Bill Savage beat Jack Witzig, Shoulders Newman drew Lucky Simunovich.

8/25/57 Honolulu
Bill Savage beat Al Lolotai COR, Herb Freeman & Lucky Simunovich no contest Shoulders Newman & Tom Rice, Jack Witzig beat Al Marino, Tinia Su'a beat Wong Buck Lee.

9/1/57 Honolulu
Herb Freeman & Lucky Simunovich & Jack WItzig beat Shoulders Newman & Tom Rice & Bill Savage dq, Al Marino drew Tinia Su'a, George Kongozan beat Mark Tendler.

9/8/57 Honolulu
Shoulders Newman & Tom Rice & Bill Savage beat Herb Freeman & Lucky Simunovich & Jack Witzig, George Kongozan beat Al Szasz.

9/15/57 Honolulu
Herb Freeman & Lucky Simunovich beat Tom Rice & Bill Savage dq, Dick Hrstich drew Shoulders Newman, George Kongozan beat Al Marino.

9/22/57 Honolulu
Lord Blears & Tom Rice beat Dick Hrstich & Lucky Simunovich, Herb Freeman no contest Bill Savage, Shoulders Newman beat Tinia Su'a, George Kongozan drew Lou Newman.

9/29/57 Honolulu
Lord Layton & Shoulders Newman & Tom Rice beat Bobo Brazil & Herb Freeman & Lucky Simunovich, Lord Blears drew Bill Savage, Dick Hrstich beat George Kongozan.

10/6/57 Honolulu
Bill Savage beat Dick Hrstich, Shoulders Newman & Tom Rice drew Herb Freeman & Lucky Simunovich, Lord Blears beat Bulldog Drummond.

10/13/57 Honolulu
Herb Freeman & George Pencheff beat Lord Layton & Tom Rice, Dick Hrstich drew Bill Savage, Armand Tanny beat Wong Buck Lee.

10/20/57 Honolulu
Herb Freeman beat Sky Hi Lee dq, George Pencheff & Lucky Simunovich drew lord Blears & Shoulders Newman, Bill Savage beat Dick Hrstich.

10/27/57 Honolulu
Lou Thesz beat Ski Hi Lee, Lord Blears beat George Pencheff, Tom Rice & Lew Newman drew Dick Hrstich & Herbie Freeman, Dr. John Bonica drew George Kongozan.

11/3/57 Honolulu
Lou Thesz drew Sky Hi Lee, Ricky Waldo & Herbie Freeman beat Tom Rice & Bill Savage, Lucky Simunovich beat Lou Newman, Dick Pencheff drew Dick Hrstich.

11/10/57 Honolulu
Sky Hi Lee beat Dick Hrstich, Ricky Waldo beat Sky Hi Lee, Herb Freeman drew Tom Rice, Lord Blears drew Lucky Simunovich, Shoulders Newman drew Tinia Su'a.

11/17/57 Honolulu
Lucky Simunovich & Ricky Waldo beat Lord Blears & Shoulders Newman, Tom Rice beat Herb Freeman, Dick Hrstich beat Al Marino.

11/24/57 Honolulu
Ricky Waldo beat Shoulders Newman, Lord Blears & Tom Rice beat Lucky Simunovich & George Kongozan dq, Dick Hrstich beat Herb Freeman.

12/6/57 Honolulu
Ricky Waldo beat Dick Hrstich, Tom Rice beat George Kongozan, Lucky Simunovich beat Lord Blears, Ricky Waldo beat Tom Rice dq, Lucky Simunovich beat Ricky Waldo, Herb Freeman beat Shoulders Newman dq.

12/11/57 Honolulu
Al Lolotai beat Lucky Simunovich, Lord Blears & Tom Rice beat Herb Freeman & Ricky Waldo, Dick Hrstich beat George Kongozan dq, Tinia Su'a drew Mark Tendler.

12/15/57 Honolulu
Lucky Simunovich & Ricky Waldo beat Lord Blears & Tom Rice, Nelson Royal beat Herb Freeman, Dick Hrstich drew George Kongozan.

12/22/57 Honolulu
Tom Rice beat Lord Blears dq, Lucky Simunovich & Ricky Waldo drew Dick Hrstich & Nelson Royal, Al Marino beat Tinia Su'a.

12/29/57 Honolulu
Lord Blears & Lucky Simunovich beat Tom Rice & Bill Savage, George Bollas beat Dick Hrstich, Nelson Royal drew Ricky Waldo.

1958

1/5/58 Honolulu
Bill Savage beat Dick Hrstich won battle royal, George Bollas beat Ricki Waldo dq, Lord Blears drew Tom Rice, Nelson Royal drew Lucky Simunovich, George Kongozan beat Al Marino.

1/12/58 Honolulu
Kokichi Endo beat Bill Savage, Lord Blears & Lucky Simunovich & Ricky Waldo beat George Bollas & Tom Rice handicap match, Nelson Royal beat George Kongozan.

1/19/58 Honolulu
George Bollas & Bill Savage beat Kokichi Endo & Nelson Royal, Tom Rice beat Lord Blears, Lucky Simunovich drew Ricky Waldo.

1/26/58 Honolulu
Lord Blears & Kokichi Endo & Nelson Royal beat George Bollas & Tom Rice & Bill Savage, Lucky Simunovich beat Ricky Waldo dq, George Kongozan beat Al Marino.

2/2/58 Honolulu
Billy Darnell beat Bill Savage, George Bollas & Tom Rice beat Lord Blears & Kokichi Endo, Nelson Royal drew Ricky Waldo.

2/9/58 Honolulu
Tosh Togo beat Nelson Royal, George Bollas & Tom Rice beat Lord Blears & Kokichi Endo, Nelson Royal drew Ricky Waldo.

2/16/58 Honolulu
George Bollas & Tom Rice beat Bob McCune & Lucky Simunovich dq, Tosh Togo beat Ricky Waldo, Kokichi Endo beat Nelson Royal.

2/23/58 Honolulu
Kokichi Endo & Tosh Togo beat Nelson Royal & Ricki Waldo, Tom Rice beat Lucky Simunovich, Bob McCune beat George Bollas.

3/2/58 Honolulu
George Bollas & Tom Rice & Fred Wirght drew Kokichi Endo & George Kongozan & Tosh Togo, Luigi Macera beat Ricky Waldo dq, Bob McCune beat Nelson Royal.

3/9/58 Honolulu
Tosh Togo beat Tom Rice, Ricky Waldo beat Bob McCune, George Bollas drew Kokichi Endo, Luigi Macera beat Fred Wright dq.

3/16/58 Honolulu
Al Lolotai drew Tosh Togo, Bob McCune beat Kokichi Endo, Luigi Macera beat George Bollas dq, Ricky Waldo drew Fred Wright.

3/23/58 Honolulu
Bob McCune beat Tosh Togo dq, Kokichi Endo & Luigi Macera & Ricki Waldo beat George Bollas & Tom Rice & Fred Wright, Tinia Su'a drew Mark Tendler.

3/30/58 Honolulu
Tosh Togo beat Luigi Macera, Bob McCune beat Ricky Waldo, Kokichi Endo & George Kongozan beat George Bollas & Fred Wright.

4/6/58 Honolulu
Kokichi Endo beat Ricky Waldo, Tosh Togo beat Tom Rice, Jack Bence & George Bollas beat Nick Kozak & Luigi Macera.

4/14/58 Honolulu
George Bollas & Tom Rice beat Nick Kozak & Tosh Togo, Jack Bence drew Luigi Macera, Ricky Waldo beat Fred Wright.

4/20/58 Honolulu
Tosh Togo beat George Bollas, Kokichi Endo beat Jack Bence, Ricky Waldo beat Nick Kozak, Luigi Macera drew Tom Rice.

4/27/58 Honolulu
Sky Hi Lee beat Tosh Togo, Lucky Simunovich beat Luigi Macera, Charro Azteca & Tom Rice beat Kokichi Endo & Ricky Waldo.

5/4/58 Honolulu
Leo Nomellini & Lucky Simunovich beat Sky Hi Lee & Tom Rice, Kokichi Endo drew Ricky Waldo, Doug Dawkins beat Charro Azteca dq.

5/7/58 Honolulu
Al Lolotai beat Sky Hi Lee, Leo Nomellini beat Ricky Waldo, Charro Azteca & Tom Rice beat Doug Dawkins & Lucky Simunovich.

5/11/58 Honolulu
Sky Hi Lee drew Leo Nomellini, Lucky Simunovich beat Charro Azteca, Tom Rice beat Kokichi Endo dq, Ricky Waldo beat George Kongozan.

5/18/58 Honolulu
Kokichi Endo & Jerry Gordet & Lucky Simunovich beat Sky Hi Lee & Tom Rice & Ricky Waldo, Sky Hi Lee beat Lucky Simunovich dq, Jerry Gordet beat Ricky Waldo, Kokichi Endo no contest Tom Rice, Charro Azteca drew George Kongozan.

5/25/58 Honolulu
Kokichi Endo & Jerry Gordet & Lucky Simunovich beat Sky Hi Lee & Tom Rice & Ricky Waldo dq, Charro Azteca & Wong Buck Lee beat George Kongozan & Mark Tendler.

6/2/58 Honolulu
Sky Hi Lee beat Kokichi Endo, Lucky Simunovich beat Ricky Waldo, Charley Kalani beat Mark Tendler, Jerry Gordet drew Tom Rice, Charro Azteca drew George Kongozan.

6/8/58 Honolulu
Stan Kowalski & Sky Hi Lee & Tom Rice beat Kokichi Endo & Jerry Gordet & Lucky Simunovich, Charley Kalani beat Wong Buck Lee, Charro Azteca drew Ricky Waldo.

6/15/58 Honolulu
Kokichi Endo & Toyonobori beat Stan Kowalski & Tom Rice, Charley Kalani beat Charley Azteca, Sky Hi Lee drew Lucky Simunovich, Jerry Gordet beat Ricky Waldo.

6/22/58 Honolulu
Little Red Feather & Tiny Tim beat Beau Brummel & Klondike Jack, Toyonobori beat Tom Rice, Stan Kowalski beat Jerry Gordet, George Kongozan drew Jim Szikszay.

6/29/58 Honolulu
Kokichi Endo & Toyonobori beat Stan Kowalski & Tom Rice, Sky Hi Lee beat Lucky Simunovich, Klondike Jack beat Tiny Tim, Beau Brummel beat Little Red Feather, Jerry Gordet beat Jim Szikszay.

7/6/58 Honolulu
Rikidozan & Kokichi Endo & Toyonbori beat Stan Kowalski & Sky Hi Lee & Tom Rice, Beau Brummel drew Tiny Tim, Little Red Feather beat Klondike Jack dq, Jerry Gordet beat Jim Szikszay.

7/13/58 Honolulu
Rikidozan beat Stan Kowalski COR, Toyonobori beat Sky Hi Lee dq, Jerry Gordet drew Tom Rice, Red Feather & Tiny Tim beat Beau Brummel & Klondike Jack.

7/20/58 Honolulu
Rikidozan drew Sky Hi Lee, Toyonobori beat Lucky Simunovich, Beau Brummel drew Tiny Tim, Red Feather beat Klondike Jack dq, Jerry Gordet & Bob McCune beat Stan Kowalski & Jim Szikszay.

7/27/58 Honolulu
Toyonbori beat Sky Hi Lee, Bob McCune drew Lucky Simunovich, Stan Kowalski beat Jerry Gordet, Little Red Feather & Tin Tim beat Beau Brummell & Klondike Jack, George Kongozan beat Jim Szikszay.

8/3/58 Honolulu
Rikidozan & Toyonobori beat George Bollas & Sky Hi Lee, Tiny Mills beat Bob McCune, Lucky Simunovich beat Stan Kowalski dq, Jerry Gorden drew Clyde Kennedy.

8/10/58 Honolulu
Jerry Gordet & Lucky Simunovich drew Stan Kowalski & Tiny Mills, George Bollas drew Sky Hi Lee, George Kongozan beat Clyde Kennedy.

8/17/58 Honolulu
Lucky Simunovich & Toyonobori beat George Bollas & Stan Kowalski, Tiny Mills beat Sky Hi Lee, Charley Kalani beat Clyde Kennedy.

8/24/58 Honolulu
Johnny Barend & Toyonobori beat Stan Kowalski & Tiny Mills dq, Lucky Simunovich beat Sky Hi Lee dq, George Bollas drew Jerry Gordet, Wong Buck Lee beat Clyde Kennedy.

8/31/58 Honolulu
Toyonobori beat Tiny Mills, Don Leo Jonathan drew Lucky Simunovich, Stan Kowalski beat Johnny Barend, Jerry Gordet beat Sky Hi Lee dq.

9/7/58 Honolulu
George Bollas & Stan Kowalski & Tiny Mills beat Jerry Gordet & Lucky Simunovich & Toyonobori, John Swenski beat George Kongozan, Charley Kalani beat Wong Buck Lee.

9/13/58 Honolulu
Toyonobori beat George Bollas, Lucky Simunovich beat Jack Bence, Stan Kowalski & Tiny Mills beat Jerry Gordet & John Swenski, Charley Kalani drew George Kongozan.

9/21/58 Honolulu
Jerry Gordet & Lucky Simunovich & Toyonobori drew George Bollas & Stan Kowalski & Tiny Mills, Juan Humberto beat John Swenski, Tinia Su'a beat Wong Buck Lee dq.

9/24/58 Honolulu
Al Lolotai beat Toyonobori, Jerry Gordet beat George Bollas, Juan Humberto & Lucky Simunovich no contest Stan Kowalski & Tiny Mills, George Kongozan beat Tinia Su'a.

9/28/58 Honolulu
Stan Kowalski & Tiny Mills beat Lucky Simunovich & John Swenski dq, Jerry Gordet beat George Bollas, Juan Humberto drew George Kongozan.

10/5/58 Honolulu
Hard Boiled Haggerty beat Juan Humberto, Lucky Simunovich beat Stan Kowalski, Jerry Gordet drew Tiny Mills, John Swenski beat George Bollas dq.

10/12/58 Honolulu
Hard Boiled Haggerty beat Lucky Simunovich, Stan Kowalski & Tiny Mills beat Jerry Gordet & Dick Hrstich, Juan Humberto beat John Swenski.

10/19/58 Honolulu
Hard Boiled Haggerty beat Tiny Mills dq, Lord Blears beat Juan Humberto, Stan Kowalski beat Dick Hrstich, Jerry Gordet drew Lucky Simunovich, George Kongozan drew John Swenski.

10/26/58 Honolulu
Hard Boiled Haggerty beat Stan Kowalski, Joe Blanchard beat Tiny Mills, Lord Blears drew Lucky Simunovich, Jerry Gordet beat John Swenski, Juan Humberto beat George Kongozan.

11/2/58 Honolulu
Joe Blanchard & Lord Blears beat Stan Kowalski & Tiny Mills, Hard Boiled Haggerty beat Jerry Gordet, Lucky Simunovich beat Juan Humberto.

11/9/58 Honolulu
Hard Boiled Haggerty drew Sky Hi Lee, Don Leo Jonathan beat Tiny Mills, Johnny Barend beat Stan Kowalski, Joe Blanchard & Lord Blears beat Jerry Gordet & Lucky Simunovich dq.

11/12/58 Honolulu
Al Lolotai beat Hard Boiled Haggerty, Don Leo Jonathan beat Joe Blanchard, Lord Blears drew Sky Hi Lee, Johnny Barend drew Jerry Gordet.

11/16/58 Honolulu
Don Leo Jonathan beat Hard Boiled Haggerty, Sky Hi Lee beat Jerry Gordet, Johnny Barend no contest Lord Blears, Joe Blanchard drew Lucky Simunovich.

11/23/58 Honolulu
Don Leo Jonathan beat Sky Hi Lee dq, Joe Blanchard & Lord Blears beat Johnny Barend & Lucky Simunovich, Elephant Boy beat George McKay, Abe Jacobs beat Jerry Gordet.

11/30/58 Honolulu
Don Leo Jonathan beat Sky Hi Lee, Joe Blanchard & Lord Blears drew Jerry Gordet & Lucky Simunovich, Baron Von Schober beat Abe Jacobs.

12/7/58 Honolulu
Sky Hi Lee & Carl Von Schober beat Joe Blanchard & Lord Blears, Don Leo Jonathan beat Jerry Gordet, Don Leo Jonathan drew Lucky Simunovich, Abe Jacobs drew Charley Kalani.

12/14/58 Honolulu
Dick Hutton beat Don Leo Jonathan NWA defense, Lord Blears drew Carl Von Schober, Sky Hi Lee beat Joe Blanchard dq, Abe Jacobs beat Jerry Gordet.

12/17/58 Honolulu
Dick Hutton beat Al Lolotai, Don Leo Jonathan beat Lucky Simunovich, Joe Blanchard & Lord Blears drew Sky Hi Lee & Carl Von Schober, Abe Jacobs beat Charley Kalani.

12/20/58 Honolulu
Dick Hutton drew Don Leo Jonathan, Joe Blanchard & Lord Blears beat Sky Hi Lee & Carl Von Schober, Lucky Simunovich beat Abe Jacobs.

12/27/58 Honolulu
Don Leo Jonathan & Sky Hi Lee & Carl Von Schober beat Joe Blanchard & Lord Blears & Lucky Simunovich, Neff Maiava beat Jerry Gordet, Abe Jacobs drew Sam Steamboat.

1959

1/7/59 Honolulu
Lord Blears & Al Lolotai beat Don Leo Jonathan & Bob Shibuya dq, Don Leo Jonathan & Bob Shibuya won 11-man battle royal, Sky Hi Lee drew Lucky Simunovich, Neff Maiava beat Baron Von Schober, King Curtis beat Al Marino.

1/14/59 Honolulu
Al Lolotai beat Don Leo Jonathan, Bob Shibuya beat Lord Blears, Sky Hi Lee drew Neff Maiava, Joe Blanchard beat Baron Von Schober dq, Abe Jacobs beat Al Marino.

1/21/59 Honolulu
Joe Blanchard & Lord Blears & Neff Maiava drew Elephant Boy & Sky Hi Lee & Baron Von Schober, Bob Shibuya beat Abe Jacobs, Magnificent Mackay beat Al Marino.

1/28/59 Honolulu
Bob Shibuya beat Joe Blanchard, Neff Maiava beat Sky Hi Lee, King Curtis drew Carl Von Schober, Lord Blears beat Elephant Boy, Magnificent Mackay drew Kanek Victorino.

2/4/59 Honolulu
Bob Shibuya & Carl Von Schober beat Joe Blanchard & Lord Blears, Magnificent Mackay beat King Curtis dq, Elephant Boy drew Neff Maiava, Kanek Victorino beat Wong Buck Lee.

2/11/59 Honolulu
Al Lolotai & Neff Maiava beat Bob Shibuya & Carl Von Schober, Lord Blears drew Lucky Simunovich, Kokichi Endo beat Elephant Boy, Reggie Parks beat Magnificent MacKay.

2/18/59 Honolulu
Bob Shibuya beat Al Lolotai, Lucky Simunovich beat Elephant Boy, Kokichi Endo beat Magnificent Mackay, Joe Blanchard & Neff Maiava drew Reggie Parks & Baron Von Schober.

2/25/59 Honolulu
Al Lolotai & Neff Maiava drew Reggie Parks & Carl Von Schober, Bob Shibuya beat Joe Blanchard, Kokichi Endo beat King Curtis, Wally Tsutsumi beat Wong Buck Lee - judo match.

3/4/59 Honolulu
Al Lolotai beat Bob Shibuya, Neff Maiava beat Clyde Steeves dq, Joe Blanchard & Lord Blears beat Karl Von Schoberg & Reggie Parks, Tsutsumi beat Kanak Victorino.

3/11/59 Honolulu
Al Lolotai beat Primo Carnera defended Hawaiian title, Lord Blears & Neff Maiava & Joe Blanchard beat Bob Shibuya & Clyde Steeves & Karl Von Schoberg, Reggie Parks beat Endo, Tsutsumi beat Charley Kalani.

3/18/59 Honolulu
Karl Von Schoberg & Clyde Steeves & Reggie Parks beat Lord Blears & Neff Maiava & Joe Blanchard, Bob Shibuya drew Al Lolotai, Endo beat King Curtis.

3/22/59 Honolulu
Joe Blanchard & Lord Blears beat Clyde Steeves & Bob Shibuya - Hawaiian tag titles, Neff Maiava drew Karl Von Schoberg, Reggie Parks beat King Curtis, Endo beat Charley Kalani.

3/29/59 Honolulu
Ed Francis beat Reggie Parks - Junior Heavyweight Title, Neff Maiava beat Clyde Steeves, Joe Blanchard drew Karl Von Schoberg, Bob Shibuya drew Lord Blears, Kokichi Endo beat Wally Tsutsumi, Rikidozan was a spectator.

4/1/59
Honolulu
Ed Francis beat Joe Blanchard – retains NWA Junior Heavyweight title, Rikidozan & Neff Maiava beat Clyde Steeves & Reggie Parks, George Drake beat Baron Von Schober, Kokichi Endo beat Hawaii Maiava – Judo match.

4/8/59 Honolulu
Ed Francis beat Lord Blears – retains NWA Junior Heavyweight title, Rikidozan & Kokichi Endo drew Neff Maiava & Al Lolotai, George Drake beat Reggie Parks.

4/15/59 Honolulu
Ed Francis beat George Drake – nontitle match, Lord Blears & Joe Blanchard beat Rikidozan & Kokichi Endo – retain Hawaiian tag titles, Sam Steamboat & Neff Maiava drew Reggie Parks & Baron Von Schober.

4/22/49 Honolulu
George Drake & Lord Blears beat Ed Francis & Jack Bence, Joe Blanchard drew Reggie Parks, Baron Von Schober beat Kokichi Endo.

4/29/59 Honolulu
Ed Francis beat Neff Maiava, Lord Blears beat Reg Parks, George Drake drew Baron Von Schober, Joe Blanchard beat Kokichi Endo – Judo match, Kokichi Endo beat a fan Reuben Corpuz – Judo match.

5/6/59 Honolulu
Al Lolotai & Neff Maiava beat Joe Blanchard & George Drake, Ed Francis drew Lucky Simunovich, Wally Tsutsumi beat Reuben Corpuz – Judo match.

5/13/59 Honolulu
Ed Francis beat Al Lolotai – wins Hawaiian Heavyweight title, Lucky Simunovich beat Dizzy Martin, Neff Maiava beat Joe Blanchard – DQ, George Drake & Lord Blears drew Baron Von Schober & Reg Parks, Wally Tsutsumi beat Hawaii Maiava – Judo match.

5/20/59 Honolulu
Ed Francis beat Al Lolotai – retains Hawaiian Heavyweight title, Neff Maiava beat Baron Von Schober, George Drake drew Sammy Steamboat, Joe Blanchard beat Reg Parks.

5/27/59 Honolulu
Ed Francis beat Neff Maiava – DQ, Al Lolotai beat Joe Blanchard, Sam Steamboat beat Reg Parks, Baron Von Schober drew Lucky Simunovich, Young Maiava drew Naleieha Solomon – Judo Match.

6/3/50 Honolulu
Al Lolotai, Lucky Simunovich, Neff Maiava beat Ed Francis, Reg Parks Baron Von Schober, Irish Jackie & Fuzzy Cupid beat Farmer McGregor & Klondike Jake – midget match, Danny Farazza drew George Drake.

6/10/59 Honolulu
Al Lolotai beat Karl Schoberg, Ed Francis drew Lucky Simunovich, George Drake & Sam Steamboat beat Benny Ferazza & Taro Miyaki (Kongozan), Fuzzy Cupid beat Klondike Jake.

6/17/59 Honolulu
Lucky Simunovich beat Ed Francis, Neff Maiava beat Benny Ferazza, George Drake drew Taro Miyaki, McGregor & Klondike Jake beat Fuzzy Cupid & Irish Jackie.

6/24/59 Honolulu
Lord Blears beat Ed Francis dq, Neff Maiava drew George Drake, Taro Miyaki beat Benny Ferazza, MacGregor & Klondike Jake beat Fuzzy Cupid & Irish Jackie.

7/1/59 Honolulu
Al Lolotai beat Lucky Simunovich, Ed Francis beat George Drake, Neff Maiava & Lord Blears & Klondike Jake & MacGregor beat Fuzzy Cupid & Irish Jackie & Taro Miyaki & Benny Ferazza.

7/8/59 Honolulu
Al Lolotai beat Ed Francis regained Hawaiian title, George Drake beat Dizzy Martin, Killer Kowalski & Tiny Mills beat Lucky Simunovich & Neff Maiava, Karl Von Schoberg drew Taro Miyaki.

7/15/59 Honolulu
Tiny Mills & Stan Kowalski & Karl Von Schoberg beat Geroge Drake & Neff Maiava & Lord Blears, Ed Francis drew Lucky SImunovich, Taro Miyaki beat Al Marino.

7/22/59 Honolulu
Al Lolotai & Neff Maiava beat Tiny Mills & Killer Kowalski, Sonny Pascua beat George Drake, Lord Blears drew Taro Miyaki, Neff Maiava drew Al Marino.

7/29/59 Honolulu
Neff Maiava beat Tiny Mills dq, Sonny Pascua beat Taro Miyaki, Don Manoukian beat Killer Kowalski, Karl Von Schoberg beat Al Marino.

8/5/59 Honolulu
Al Lolotai beat Tiny Mills, Don Manoukian beat Neff Maiava, Killer Kowalski drew Sonny Pascua, Lord Blears beat Taro Miyaki.

8/12/59 Honolulu
Enrique Torres & Lord Blears & Neff Maiava beat Tiny Mills & Killer Kowalski & Karl Von Schoberg, Sandor Kovacs drew Don Manoukian, Sonny Pascua beat Clyde Steeves dq, Fred Atkins drew Lucky Simunovich.

8/18/59 Honolulu
Enrique Torres beat Clyde Steeves, Don Manoukian beat Sandor Kovacs, Fred Atkins beat Neff Maiava, Lord Blears & Sonny Pascua drew Killer Kowalski & Tiny Mills.

8/26/59 Honolulu
Don Manoukian beat Enrique Torres, Al Lolotai beat Fred Atkins, Tiny Mills & Killer Kowalski beat Lord Blears & Neff Maiava, Sonny Pascua beat Karl Von Schoberg.

9/2/59 Honolulu
Al Lolotai beat Don Manoukian, Gene Darvel beat Lucky Simunovich dq, Lord Blears beat Killer Kowalski, Sonny Pascua drew Tiny Mills.

9/9/59 Honolulu
Gene Darvell & Steve "Mr. America" Stanlee & Don Manoukian beat Lord Blears & Sonny Pascua & Lucky Simunovich, Tiny Mills beat Neff Maiava, Steve Stanlee drew Sonny Pascua, Killer Kowalski beat Al Marino.

9/16/59 Honolulu
Toyonobori & Yoshimura beat Tiny Mills & Killer Kowalski, Gene Darvel beat Lucky Simunovich, Lord Blears beat Steve Stanlee dq, Don Manoukian drew Sonny Pascua.

9/23/59 Honolulu
Al Lolotai & Lucky Simunovich & Lord Blears beat Steve Stanlee & Gene Darval & Don Manoukian dq, Toyonobori beat Karl Von Schoberg, Yoshimura beat Red Shoes Duggan.

9/30/59 Honolulu
Yoshimura beat Gene Darval, Toyonobori beat Don Manoukian, Andre Drapp beat Red Shoes Duggan, Sonny Pascua & Lord Blears beat Karl Von Schoberg & Steve Stanlee.

10/7/59 Honolulu
Bill Savage & Don Manoukian beat Toyonobori & Yoshimura, Andre Drapp beat Gene Darval, Steve Stanlee beat Karl Von Schoberg, Sonny Pascua beat Red Shoes Duggan.

10/14/59 Honolulu
Andre Drapp beat Al Lolotai, Bill Savage & Don Manoukian beat Lucky Simunovich & Lord Blears, Toyonobori beat Steve Stanlee, Yoshimura beat Sonny Pascua.

10/21/59 Honolulu
Andre Drapp drew Lord Blears, Steve Stanlee drew Sonny Pascua, Neff Maiava drew Kanek Victorino, Toyonbori & Yoshimura beat Don Manoukian & Bill Savage.

10/28/59 Honolulu
Al Lolotai beat Toyonobori, Bill Savage drew Yoshimura, Buck Lee drew Kanek Victorino, Don Manoukian beat Bill Savage, Andre Drapp beat Lord Blears.

11/4/59 Honolulu
Toyonobori & Yoshimura & Lord Blears beat Steve Stanlee & Karl Von Schoberg & Bill Savage, Andre Drapp drew Lucky Simunovich, Sonny Pascua beat Don Manoukian.

11/11/59 Honolulu
Al Lolotai beat Andre Drapp, Yoshimura beat Sonny Pascua, Lord Blears drew Don Manoukian, Tsutsumi beat Wong Buck Lee, Toyonobori beat Bill Savage dq.

11/18/59 Honolulu
Great Bolo & Don Manoukian & Karl Von Schoberg beat Toyonobori & Yoshimura & Sonny Pascua, Lord Blears drew Lucky Simunovich, Andre Drapp beat Bill Savage.

11/25/59 Honolulu
Bill Savage beat Andre Drapp, Toyonobori & Yoshimura beat Great Bolo & Karl Von Schoberg, Lucky Simunovich beat King Curtis dq, Don Manoukian drew Sonny Pascua.

12/2/59 Honolulu
Pat O'Conner beat Lou Thesz - World Title, Yoshimura drew Bill Savage, Toyonbori beat Don Manoukian, Lucky Simunovich & Lord Blears beat Great Bolo & Karl Von Schoberg.

12/9/59 Honolulu
Pat O'Conner beat Al Lolotai - NWA World Title, Lou Thesz beat Toyonbori, Sonny Pascua beat Great Bolo dq, Lord Blears & Yoshimura beat Bill Savage & Don Manoukian.

12/16/59 Honolulu
Al Lolotai beat Great Togo - Hawaiian title, Yoshimura beat Great Bolo unmasked as Al Lovelock, Don Manoukian & Bill Savage beat Lord Blears & Lucky Simunovich, King Curtis beat Sonny Pascua.

12/23/59 Honolulu
Al Lolotai & Toyonbori & Yoshimura beat Bill Savage & King Curtis & Don Manoukian, Taro Miyaki drew Lord Blears, Lucky Simunovich beat Karl Von Schoberg.

12/30/59 Honolulu
Yoshimura & Toyonbori & Al Lolotai beat King Curtis & Bill Savage & Don Manoukian, Lucky Simunovich beat Taro Miyaki, Lord Blears beat Karl Von Schoberg.

1960

1/6/60 Honolulu
Al Lolotai won battle royal, Al Lolotai & Toyonobori beat King Curtis & Karl Von Schoberg, Taro Miyaki beat Kay Bell, Don Manoukian beat Wong Buck Lee, Bill Savage drew Lucky Simunovich, Lord Blears drew Yoshimura.

1/13/60 Honolulu
Al Lolotai & Lord Blears & Toyonobori & Yoshimura beat King Curtis & Karl Von Schoberg & Bill Savage & Taro Miyaki, Lucky Simunovich beat Don Manoukian.

1/20/60 Honolulu
Hard Boiled Haggerty beat Lucky Simunovich, Dr. Jerry Graham beat Angelo Savoldi, Lord Blears beat Taro Miyaki, Yoshimura & Toyonobori beat Bill Savage & Don Manoukian.

1/27/60 Honolulu
Bill Savage & Hard Boiled Haggerty beat Lord Blears & Jerry Gordet to win Hawaiian tag titles, Toyonobori beat King Curtis, Yoshimura beat Don Manoukian, Lucky Simunovich drew Sonny Pascua.

2/3/60 Honolulu
Hard Boiled Haggerty & Bill Savage beat Toyonobori & Yoshimura, Jerry Gordet beat Karl Von Schoberg, Herb Freeman beat King Curtis dq.

2/10/60 Honolulu
Yoshimura beat Hard Boiled Haggerty dq, Bill Savage drew Herb Freeman, King Curtis beat Sonny Pascua, Jerry Gordet & Lord Blears beat Al Marino & Karl Von Schoberg.

2/17/60 Honolulu
Hard Boiled Haggerty & Bill Savage beat Lord Blears & Jerry Gordet, King Curtis drew Lucky Simunovich, Al Marino beat Kanek Victorino, Al Lolotai beat Yoshimura.

2/24/60 Honolulu
Bill Savage & Hard Boiled Haggerty drew Lucky Simunovich & Yoshimura, King Curtis beat Jerry Gordet, Herb Freeman beat Al Marino, Lord Blears drew Sonny Pascua.

3/2/60 Honolulu
Karl Von Schoberg & Hard Boiled Haggerty beat Yoshimura & Endo, Herb Freeman beat Bill Savage, King Curtis drew Lucky Simunovich, Jerry Gordet beat Sonny Pascua.

3/9/60 Honolulu
Lord Blears & Herb Freeman beat Hard Boiled Haggerty & Bill Savage for Hawaiian tag titles, Lucky Simunovich beat Karl Von Schoberg, Endo drew Jerry Gordet, Sonny Pascua beat Al Marino dq.

3/23/60 Honolulu
Al Lolotai beat King Curtis, Nick Kozak beat Sonny Pascua, Lucky Simunovich & Jerry Gordet beat Lord Blears & Hans Herman.

3/30/60 Honolulu
Lord Blears & Nick Kozak & Herb Freeman beat Hard Boiled Haggerty & Paul Butcher Vachon & King Curtis, Al Martino beat Wong Buck Lee.

4/6/60 Honolulu
Hard Boiled Haggerty beat Al Lolotai, Butcher Vachon beat Herb Freeman dq, Lucky Simunovich drew Jerry Gordet, Lord Blears & Nick Kozak beat Louie Miller & Endo.

4/13/60 Honolulu
Butcher Vachon & Hard Boiled Haggerty beat Lord Blears & Herb Freeman to win tag titles, King Curtis beat Jerry Gordet, Nick Kozak beat Karl Von Schoberg dq, Lucky Simunovich beat Sonny Pascua.

4/22/60 Honolulu
Al Lolotai beat Butcher Vachon, Lord Blears drew Hard Boiled Haggerty, Takamura beat Al Marino, Jerry Gordet & Nick Kozak beat King Curtis handicap match.

4/27/60 Honolulu
Paul Vachon beat Herb Freeman, Freeman had his beard shaved off, Nick Kozak & Jerry Gordet beat King Curtis & Hard Boiled Haggerty, Lucky Simunovich beat Wong Buck Lee, Lord Blears drew Karl Von Schoberg.

5/4/60 Honolulu
Al Lolotai beat Hard Boiled Haggerty to defend state title, Lucky Simunovich beat Toshi Takamura, Lord Blears drew Sonny Pascua, Jerry Gordet & Nick Kozak beat King Curtis & Paul Vachon.

5/11/60 Honolulu
Jerry Gordet & Nick Kozak beat Paul Vachon & Hard Boiled Haggerty to win tag titles, King Curtis beat Lucky Simunovich, Toshi Takamura drew Sonny Pascua, Lord Blears beat Al Marino.

5/18/60 Honolulu
Leo Nomellini beat Hard Boiled Haggerty, Elliott Hardy beat King Curtis, Hans Herman & Bob Orton drew Nick Kozak & Jerry Gordet, Lord Blears drew Paul Vachon.

5/25/60 Honolulu
Leo Nomellini beat King Curtis, Al Lolotai & Elliott Hardy & Leo Nomellini beat King Curtis & Bob Orton Sr & Hans Herman, Nick Kozak beat Paul Vachon, Jerry Gordet beat Toshi Takamura.

6/1/60 Honolulu
Al Lolotai beat Bob Orton, Hans Herman drew Eliott Hardy, Nick Kozak & Jerry Gordet beat Paul Vachon & Don Manoukian, Sonny Pascua drew Toshi Takamura.

6/8/60 Honolulu
Pancho Lopez & Brown Panther beat Sky Low Low & Fuzzy Cupid, Hans Herman beat Nick Kozak, Eliott Hardy beat Tony Terrazze, Don Manoukian drew Jerry Gordet, Ronnie Etchinson drew Butcher Vachon.

6/15/60 Honolulu
Big Daddy Lipscomb beat Hans Herman, Fuzzy Cupid & Sky Low Low beat Brown Panther & Pancho Lopez, Hard Boiled Haggerty beat Ronnie Etchison, Elliott Hardy beat Paul Vachon, Lord Blears drew Tony Terrazze.

6/22/60 Honolulu
Big Daddy Lipscomb & Brown Panther beat Hard Boiled Haggerty & Sky Low Low, Elliott Hardy beat Tony Terrazze, Pancho Lopez beat Fuzzy Cupid, Paul Vachon beat Jerry Gordet.

6/29/60 Honolulu
Pancho Lopez & Brown Panther beat Sky Low Low & Fuzzy Cupid, Lucky Simunovich beat Paul Vachon, Lord Blears drew Nick Kozak, Jerry Gordet beat Tony Terrazze, Hard Boiled Haggerty beat Eliott Hardy.

7/6/60 Honolulu
Al Lolotai & Vili Ava beat Hard Boiled Haggerty & Paul Vachon, Nick Kozak beat Elliot Hardy, Brown Panther beat Fuzzy Cupid, Sky Low Low beat Pancho Lopez, Lord Blears beat Jerry Gordet COR, Kimo Mahi beat Tony Terrazze.

7/13/60 Honolulu
Nick Kozak beat Sonny Meyers, Al Lolotai beat Paul Vachon, Brown Panther beat Sky Low Low dq, Pancho Lopez beat Fuzzy Cupid, Jerry Gordet & Dan Miller drew Paul Vachon & Karl Von Schoberg, Lucky Simunovich beat Tony Terrazze.

7/17/60 Hilo
Pancho Lopez & Brown Panther beat Fuzzy Cupid & Sky Low Low, Lord Blears beat Shoulders Newman dq, Lucky Simunovich beat Jerry Gordet.

7/20/60 Honolulu
Brown Panther & Pancho Lopez beat Sky Low Low & Fuzzy Cupid, Nick Kozak beat Jack Laskin, Lord Blears beat Dan Miller, Jerry Gordet beat Paul Vachon dq.

7/27/60 Honolulu
Al Lolotai beat Nick Kozak, Hans Schnabel beat Lord Blears, Herb Freeman beat Tony Ferazza, Vili Ava beat Paul Vachon.

8/3/60 Honolulu
Hans Schnabel & Shoulders Newman & Karl Von Schoberg beat Nick Kozak & Vili Ava & Jerry Gordet, Leo Garibaldi beat Herb Freeman, Hans Schnabel beat Lucky Simunovich,

8/7/60 Hilo
Hans Schnabel & Shoulders Newman beat Lucky Simunovich & Lord Blears, Vil Ava beat Jerry Gordet, Nick Kozak beat Herb Freeman.

8/10/60 Honolulu
Al Lolotai beat Nick Kozak to defend state title, Lucky Simunovich beat Herb Freeman, Vili Ava beat Karl Von Schoberg, Jerry Gordet drew Hans Schnabel, Nick Kozak beat Shoulders Newman dq.

8/17/60 Honolulu
Hans Schnabel & Shoulders Newman beat Nick Kozak & Jerry Gordet to win tag titles, Vili Ava beat Karl Von Schoberg, Lord Blears drew Lucky Simunovich.

8/24/60 Honolulu
Hans Schnabel & Shoulders Newman drew Al Lolotai & Vili Ave, Lord Blears beat Nick Kozak, Lucky Simunovich drew Karl Von Schoberg.

8/31/60 Honolulu
Sky Low Low & Fuzzy Cupid beat Pancho Lopez & Brown Panther, Al Lolotai beat Shoulders Newman, Hans Schnabel drew Vili Ava, Lord Blears beat Tony Ferrazza.

9/7/60 Honolulu
Hans Schnabel & Shoulders Newman & Sammy Berg beat Al Lolotai & Vili Ava & Neff Maiava, Leo Garibaldi beat Lucky Simunovich, Seymour Koenig beat Lord Blears.

9/14/60 Honolulu
Al Lolotai beat Hans Schnabel dq, Sammy Berg beat Leo Garibaldi, Shoulders Newman beat Lord Blears, Seymour Koenig drew Lucky Simunovich.

9/21/60 Honolulu
Al Lolotai beat Hans Schnabel to defend Title, Shoulders Newman beat Seymour Koenig, Utica Panther & Bill Wright beat Sammy Berg & Karl Von Schoberg.

9/28/60 Honolulu
Utica Panther & Bill Wright beat Shoulders Newman & Hans Schnabel to win tag belts, Vili Ava drew Lucky Simunovich, Sammy Berg beat Seymour Koenig, Al Marino beat Neff Maiava.

10/5/60 Honolulu
Al Lolotai drew Sammy Berg, Utica Panther & Bill Wright beat Shoulders Newman & Al Marino, Seymour Koenig beat Jim Regonski.

10/12/60 Honolulu
Utica Panther & Bill Wright & Vili Ava beat Shoulders Newman & Sammy Berg & Wild Red Berry, Tom Rice beat Seymour Koenig, Wong Buck Lee drew Wimpy Willington.

10/19/60 Honolulu
Tom Rice & Shoulders Newman beat Vili Ava & Al Lolotai, Sammy Berg beat Utica Panther, Bill Wright drew Lucky Simunovich, Seymour Koenig beat Al Marino dq.

10/26/60 Honolulu
Al Lolotai beat Sammy Berg, Lucky Simunovich beat Seymour Koenig, Shoulders Newman & Tom Rice drew Bill Wright & Utica Panther, Neff Maiava beat Wimpy Wellington.

11/2/60 Honolulu
Shoulders Newman & Tommy Rice beat Utica Panther & Bill Wright to win tag titles, Sammy Berg beat Vili Ava, Karl Von Schoberg beat Seymour Koenig.

11/9/60 Honolulu
Ed Carpentier beat Sammy Berg - World Title, Shoulders Newman beat Utica Panther, Leo Garibaldi beat Bill Wright, Tom Rice drew Lucky Simunovich.

11/16/60 Honolulu
Ed Carpentier beat Shoulders Newman, Al Lolotai beat Sammy Berg, Leo Garibaldi beat Tom Rice dq, Bill Wright beat Karl Von Schoberg.

11/23/60 Honolulu
Leo Garibaldi beat Gorgeous George, Tony Galento was ref, Al Lolotai beat Tex McKenzie, King Curtis beat Bill Wright, Shoulders Newman drew Sammy Berg.

11/30/60 Honolulu
Lou Thesz beat Al Lolotai, Vili Ava beat Chuck Leonardo, Leo Garibaldi beat Shoulders Newman dq, Sammy Berg drew Lucky Simunovich.

12/7/60 Honolulu
Lou Thesz beat Sandor Szabo, Sammy Berg beat Lucky Simunovich, Sam Steamboat beat Leo Garibaldi, Wimpy Wellington beat Kanek Victorino.

12/14/60 Honolulu
Ed Carpentier beat Lou Thesz - World Title, Sandor Szabo drew Al Lolotai, Sam Steamboat beat Sammy Berg dq, Leo Garibaldi beat Karl Von Schoberg, Shoulders Newman drew Lucky Simunovich.

12/21/60 Honolulu
Ed Carpentier & Sam Steamboat beat Sammy Berg & Shoulders Newman, Vili Ava beat Sandor Szabo, Leo Garibaldi beat Karl Von Schoberg dq, Lucky Simunovich drew King Curtis.

12/28/60 Honolulu
Sam Steamboat beat Sammy Berg, Mitsu Yoshimura beat Lucky Simunovich, Neff Maiava beat Al Marino dq, Shoulders Newman drew Leo Garibaldi.

1961

1/4/61 Honolulu
Maurice LaPointe beat Sammy Berg, King Curtis drew Vili Ava, Yoshimura beat Shoulders Newman dq, Sam Steamboat drew Leo Garibaldi, Al Lolotai beat Karl Von Schoberg.

1/11/61 Honolulu
Tournament: Leo Garibaldi beat Karl Von Schoberg, Sam Steamboat beat King Curtis, Dick Hutton beat Maurice LaPointe, Yoshimura beat Shoulders Newman, Dick Hutton beat Yoshimura, Sam Steamboat beat Leo Garibaldi, Dick Hutton drew Sam Steamboat, Dick Hutton won coin toss.

1/18/61 Honolulu
Dick Hutton beat Al Lolotai to win Hawaiian Title, Sam Steamboat drew Shoulders Newman, Mitsu Yoshimura beat Leo Garibaldi, Maurice LaPointe drew King Curtis.

1/25/61 Honolulu
Sam Steamboat beat Dick Hutton to win Hawaiian State Title, Michiaki Yoshimura beat Shoulders Newman, Leo Garibaldi drew Maurice LaPointe, Prince Moretana beat Curtis Iaukea.

2/1/61 Honolulu
Sam Steamboat drew Mitsu Yoshimura, Al Lolotai beat Maurice LaPointe, Shoulders Newman beat Leo Garibaldi, Prince Moretana beat Karl Von Schoberg.

2/8/61 Honolulu
King Curtis & Clyde Steeves & Shoulders Newman beat Sam Steamboat & Leo Garibaldi & Mitsu Yoshimura, Maurice LaPointe drew Prince Moretana, Young Maivia beat Kanak Victorino.

2/15/61 Honolulu
Sam Steamboat beat Shoulders Newman, Al Lolotai beat Mitsu Yoshimura, Clyde Steeves beat Maurice LaPointe, King Curtis drew Leo Garibaldi.

2/22/61 Honolulu
Al Lolotai beat Clyde Steeves, Sam Steamboat beat King Curtis, Mitsu Yoshimura beat Leo Garibaldi, Prince Moretana drew Maurice LaPointe.

3/1/61 Honolulu
Sam Steamboat beat Al Lolotai, Clyde Steeves beat Mitsu Yoshimura, King Curtis drew Maurice LaPointe, Nick Schamoff beat Buck Lee, Leo Garibaldi beat Prince Moretana.

3/8/61 Honolulu
Neff Maiava beat Clyde Steeves, Young Maivia drew Nick Schamoff, King Curtis beat Prince Moretana, Lucky Simunovich beat Maurice LaPointe, Leo Garibaldi drew Mitsu Yoshimura.

3/15/61 Honolulu
Sam Steamboat beat Yoshimura, Neff Maiava beat King Curtis, Shoulders Newman beat Leo Garibaldi, Lucky Simunovich drew Clyde Steeves, Maurice LaPointe beat Prince Moretana.

3/22/61 Honolulu
Al Lolotai & Sam Steamboat & Neff Maiava beat King Curtis & Clyde Steeves & Shoulders Newman, Yoshimura beat Leo Garibaldi, Maurice LaPointe drew Lucky Simunovich, Prince Moretana beat Young Maiava.

3/29/61 Honolulu
Sam Steamboat beat Clyde Steeves, Luigi Macera beat Maurice LaPointe, Neff Maiava beat Shoulders Newman, Michiaki Yoshimura beat Prince Moretana, Kanak Victorino drew Wimpy Willington.

4/5/61 Honolulu
Al Lolotai & Neff Maiava beat Karl Von Schoberg & Clyde Steeves, Sam Steamboat drew Neff Maiava, Lucky Simunovich beat Yoshimura.

4/12/61 Honolulu
Sam Steamboat beat Neff Maiava, Clyde Steeves beat Lucky Simunovich, Maurice LaPointe drew Mitsu Yoshimura.

4/19/61 Honolulu
Ed Carpenter beat Clyde Steeves, Al Lolotai drew Sam Steamboat, Luigi Macera drew Neff Maiava, Shoulders Newman, Mitsu Yoshimura, Maurice LaPointe beat Prince Moretana.

4/26/61 Honolulu
Ed Carpentier beat John De Silva, Ed Francis beat Mitsu Yoshimura, Sam Steamboat & Luigi Macera beat Maurice LaPointe & Neff Maiava.

4/30/61 Honolulu
Luigi Macera drew Maurice LaPointe, Little Beaver & Billy The Kid & Cowboy Taylor beat Sky Low Low & Tom Thumb & Klondike Jake.

5/3/61 Honolulu
Ed Francis beat Luigi Macera, Sam Steamboat beat Maurice LaPointe, Red Taylor & Billy The Kid beat Fuzzy Cupid & Tom Thumb, Wally Tsutsumi drew Wong Buck Lee.

5/10/61 Honolulu
Al Lolotai & Neff Maiava beat Ed Francis & Shoulders Newman, Tom Thumb beat Cowboy Taylor, Billy The Kid beat Fuzzy Cupid.

5/17/61 Honolulu
Neff Maiava & Cowboy Taylor & Billy The Kid beat Fuzzy Cupid & Tom Thumb & Shoulders Newman, Ed Francis drew Sam Steamboat.

5/24/61 Honolulu
Argentina Rocco beat Karl Von Schoberg & Shoulders Newman dq handicap match, Al Lolotai & Neff Maiava beat Leo Garibaldi & Luigi Macera, Lucky Simunovich beat Ed Francis dq.

5/31/61 Honolulu
Al Lolotai won battle royal, Luigi Macera beat Karl Von Schoberg dq, Neff Maiava beat Sam Steamboat, Shoulders Newman beat Lucky Simunovich, Al Lolotai dcor Ed Francis.

6/7/61 Honolulu
Neff Maiava & Al Lolotai & Young Maiava beat Shoulders Newman & Ed Francis & Karl Von Schoberg, Lucky Simunovich drew Luigi Macera, Al Marino beat Wong Buck Lee.

6/14/61 Honolulu
Billy Whitewolf beat Shoulders Newman, Neff Maiava beat Luigi Macera to win Hawaiian State Ring Gold Belt, Tiger Ted Travis beat Lucky Simunovich dq, Karl Von Schoberg beat Al Marino.

6/21/61 Honolulu
Luigi Macera beat Neff Maiava dq, Billy Whitewolf beat Ted Travis, Shoulders Newman beat Kenny Ackles, Wally Tsutsumi drew Wimpy Wellington.

6/28/61 Honolulu
Billy Whitewolf & Neff Maiava beat Shoulders Newman & Ted Travis to win Hawaiian tag titles, King Curtis beat Luigi Macera dq.

7/5/61 Honolulu
Billy Whitewolf beat King Curtis, Ted Travis & Shoulders Newman beat Luigi Macera & Kenny Ackles, Neff Maiava beat Karl Von Schoberg - Australian rules.

7/12/61 Honolulu
Ted Travis & Shoulders Newman beat Neff Maiava & Billy Whitewolf, King Curtis beat Ed Francis, Luigi Macera beat Kenny Ackles.

7/19/61 Honolulu
Ted Travis & Shoulders Newman beat Billy Whitewolf & Neff Maiava to win tag titles, Wally Tsutsumi & Kenny Ackles beat King Curtis - Handicap match.

7/26/61 Honolulu
King Curtis beat Billy Whitewolf, Luigi Macera beat Haru Sasaki, Ted Travis beat Kenny Ackles, Neff Maiava beat Shoulders Newman.

7/29/61 Hilo
Billy Whitewolf beat King Curtis, Millie Stafford beat Kathy Starr, Ken Ackles drew Ted Travis.

8/2/91 Honolulu
Neff Maiava & Billy Whitewolf beat King Curtis & Haru Sasaki dq, Shoulders Newman & Ted Travis drew John Brown & Luigi Macera, Kenny Ackles beat Wimpy Wellington, Kathy Starr beat Millie Stafford.

8/9/61 Honolulu
Billy Whitewolf beat King Curtis, Neff Maiava beat Haru Sasaki, John Brown beat Karl Von Schoberg, Luigi Macera drew Shoulders Newman, Ted Travis drew Lucky Simunovich.

8/16/61 Honolulu
King Curtis beat Neff Maiava COR for Hawaii title, Billy Whitewolf drew Luigi Macera, Hogan Wharton beat Ted Travis, Haru Sasaki beat Kenny Ackles.

8/23/61 Honolulu
King Curtis drew Ted Travis defended Hawaiian Title, Billy Whitewolf drew Shoulders Newman, Neff Maiava beat Luigi Macera.

8/30/61 Honolulu
Ted Travis & Shoulders Newman beat King Curtis & Haru Sasaki, Al Lolotai drew Billy Whitewolf, Luigi Macera beat Karl Von Schoberg, Neff Maiava beat Kenny Ackles.

9/6/61 Honolulu
Neff Maiava beat King Curtis, Billy Whitewolf beat Mad Dog Vachon, Al Lolotai beat Luigi Macera Australian Style, John Brown drew Shoulders Newman.

9/13/61 Honolulu
King Curtis & Haru Sasaki beat Lord Blears & Ted Travis, Mad Dog Vachon drew Lord Blears, Billy Whitewolf beat Shoulders Newman dq, Al Lolotai drew Luigi Macera.

9/20/61 Honolulu
King Curtis drew Neff Maiava, Mad Dog Vachon beat Luigi Macera, Billy Whitewolf beat Haru Sasaki, Ted Travis drew Lord Blears.

9/27/61 Honolulu
Lord Blears beat King Curtis, Neff Maiava beat Ted Travis, Mad Dog Vachon beat Kenny Ackles, Al Lolotai beat Karl Von Schoberg.

10/4/61 Honolulu
Lord Blears & Neff Maiava beat Ted Travis & Shoulders Newman, Lucky Simunovich beat King Curtis, Mad Dog Vachon beat Karl Von Schoberg, Luigi Macera beat Kenny Ackles.

10/11/61 Honolulu
Lord Blears & Lucky Simunovich beat King Curtis & Mad Dog Vachon, Ted Travis & Shoulders Newman drew Neff Maiava & Luigi Macera.

10/14/61 Hilo
Kathy Starr beat Judy Glover, Lord Blears beat King Curtis dq, Luigi Macera beat Ted Travis.

10/18/61 Honolulu
Lord Blears won battle royal, Neff Maiava drew Mad Dog Vachon, Lord Blears beat Shoulders Newman, Ed Francis drew Ted Travis, Luigi Macera beat Al Marino, King Curtis drew John Brown.

10/25/61 Honolulu
Lord Blears beat King Curtis for Hawaiian State Title, Shoulders Newman & Ted Travis beat Luigi Macera & Dick Hirsch, Neff Maiava beat Mad Dog Vachon, Vachon head shaved.

11/1/61 Honolulu
Neff Maiava & Lord Blears beat Ted Travis & Shoulders Newman to win Hawaiian tag titles, Mad Dog Vachon beat Luigi Macera, John Brown beat Al Marino, Bobo Shiroma beat King Curtis when Curtis failed to pin him 3 times in 15 minutes.

11/8/61 Honolulu
Neff Maiava & Lord Blears & Ed Francis beat Mad Dog Vachon & Ted Travis & Shoulders Newman, Bolo Shiroma beat King Curtis dq, John Brown drew Luigi Macera, Ed Francis drew Mad Dog Vachon.

11/15/61 Honolulu
Neff Maiava beat King Curtis, Lord Blears drew Mad Dog Vachon, Luigi Macera beat Ted Travis, Fred Blassie beat George Drake WWA World title match.

11/22/61 Honolulu
Lord Blears & Neff Maiava beat Shoulders Newman & Ted Travis to win Hawaiian tag titles, Masked Executioner beat Luigi Macera, Don Manoukian beat King Curtis dq, Mad Dog Vachon drew George Drake.

11/29/61 Honolulu
Masked Executioner beat George Drake, Lord Blears & Neff Maiava beat Don Manoukian & Mad Dog Vachon, Ed Francis drew Ted Travis, Shoulders Newman drew Bolo Shiroma.

12/6/61 Honolulu
Lord Blears & George Drake beat Mad Dog Vachon & Masked Executioner, Ted Travis drew Don Manoukian, Bobo Shiroma drew John Brown.

12/10/61 Hilo
Fred Blassie ddq Lord Blears, Kathy Starr beat Evelyn Stevens, George Drake drew Mad Dog Vachon.

12/13/61 Honolulu
Fred Blassie beat Neff Maiava - WWA World Title, Mad Dog Vachon beat Don Manoukian, Ted Travis & Shoulders Newman beat John Brown & George Drake, Masked Executioner beat Lord Blears to win Hawaiian State Title.

12/20/61 Honolulu
Neff Maiava & Lord Blears beat Mad Dog Vachon & Masked Executioner, George Drake beat Shoulders Newman, Bobo Shiroma beat Ted Travis dq.

12/27/61 Honolulu
George Drake & Armand Tanny & Neff Maiava & Lord Blears beat Ted Travis & Masked Executioner & Mad Dog Vachon & Shoulders Newman, Mad Dog Vachon drew Neff Maiava, George Drake beat Masked Executioner dq, Lord Blears drew Shoulders Newman.

1962

1/3/62 Honolulu
Dick Beyer beat Maurice Vachon, Lord Blears no contest Masked Executioner, Neff Maiava & George Drake beat Shoulders Newman & Ted Travis.

1/10/62 Honolulu
Lord Blears beat Masked Executioner, Neff Maiava drew Mad Dog Vachon, Shoulders Newman beat Ray Stevens, Dick Beyer beat George Drake, Johnny Brown beat Ted Travis dq.

1/17/62 Honolulu
Masked Executioner beat Neff Maiava to defend Hawaiian State Title, Dick Beyer beat Shoulders Newman, Johnny Brown drew Mad Dog Vachon, George Drake beat Ray Stevens Dq.

1/24/62 Honolulu
Fred Blassie beat Dick Beyer WWA World Title, Neff Maiava & Lord Blears beat Mad Dog Vachon & Masked Executioner, John Brown drew Lou Newman, George Drake drew Ted Travis.

1/31/62 Honolulu
Neff Maiava & Lord Blears beat Fred Blassie & Masked Executioner, Dick Beyer beat Ray Stevens, Ted Travis beat Mad Dog Vachon, George Drake drew Johnny Brown.

2/7/62 Honolulu
Masked Executioner beat Mad Dog Vachon Texas Rules match, Dick Beyer & George Drake beat Shoulders Newman & Ted Travis dq, Neff Maiava beat Nature Boy Stevens, Lord Blears beat John Brown.

2/14/62 Honolulu
Dick Beyers ddq Masked Executioner, Lord Blears beat Nature Boy Stevens, Baby Cheryl beat Darling Dagmar, George Drake & Neff Maiava drew Shoulders Newman & Ted Travis.

2/17/62 Hilo
Neff Maiava & Lord Blears beat Mad Dog Vachon & Lou Newman, Baby Cheryl beat Darling Dagmar, Neff Maiava beat Mad Dog Vachon dq, Lord Blears drew Shoulders Newman.

2/18/62 Hilo
Neff Maiava & George Drake beat Lou Newman & Maurice Vachon, Darling Dagmar beat Baby Cheryl, Neff Maiava beat Shoulders Newman, George Drake drew Maurice Vachon.

2/21/62 Honolulu
Neff Maiava & Lord Blears beat Masked Executioner & Ray Stevens to defend Hawaiian title, Shoulders Newman drew Dick Beyer, George Drake beat Mad Dog Vachon, Baby Cheryl beat Darling Dagmar.

2/28/62 Honolulu
Masked Executioner beat Mad Dog Vachon, Ray Stevens & Dick Beyer drew Lord Blears & George Drake, Neff Maiava beat Ted Travis, Wally Tsutsumi beat Kanak Victorino judo match.

3/7/62 Honolulu
Masked Executioner beat Maurice Vachon, Dick Beyer & Nature Boy Stevens drew Lord Blears & George Drake, Neff Maiava beat Ted Travis, Wally Tsutsumi beat Kanak Victorino.

3/14/62 Honolulu
Neff Maiava & Lord Blears & Mad Dog Vachon beat Masked Executioner & Dick Beyer & Shoulders Newman, Ricky Hunter beat Shoulders Newman, Koichi Endo beat Ted Travis, George Drake drew Ray Stevens.

3/21/62 Honolulu
Neff Maiava beat The Elephant Boy, Masked Executioner beat Indio Azteca, Lord Blears & Koichi Endo drew Ted Travis & Shoulders Newman, George Drake beat Mad Dog Vachon dq.

3/28/62 Honolulu
Masked Executioner beat Koichi Endo, Neff Maiava & Lord Blears beat Dick Beyer & Shoulders Newman, Ted Travis drew George Drake, Mad Dog Vachon beat Ricky Hunter.

4/4/62 Honolulu
Neff Maiava beat Masked Executioner to win Hawaiian State Title, Executioner unmasked as Vic Christy, Nick Bockwinkel beat Ted Travis, Lord Blears & George Drake beat Dick Beyer & Ray Stevens, Luigi Macera beat Mad Dog Vachon, Shoulders Newman drew Johnny Brown.

4/11/62 Honolulu
Fred Blassie drew Neff Maiava defended WWA World Title, Nick Bockwinkel beat Duke Hoffman, Lord Blears & Luigi Macera beat Mad Dog Vachon & Eric The Red, Dick Beyer beat Ray Stevens, George Drake drew Shoulders Newman.

4/18/62 Honolulu
Lord Blears & Neff Maiava & Nick Bockwinkel beat Dick Beyer & Maurice Vachon & Ray Stevens, Geroge Drake beat Indio Azteca dq, Luigi Macera beat Ken Lucas, Kanak Victorino no contest Nick Tschamoff.

4/21/62 Hilo
Dick Beyer drew Nick Bockwinkel, Neff Maiava beat Maurice Vachon, Lord Blears beat Shoulders Newman dq.

4/25/62 Honolulu
Neff Maiava beat Dick Beyer to defend Hawaiian State title, Red Shoes Duggan beat Mad Dog Vachon dq, Nick Bockwinkel beat Paul Vachon, Luigi Macera beat Indio Azteca.

5/2/62 Honolulu
King Curtis beat Mad Dog Vachon, Neff Maiava & Lord Blears drew Shoulders Newman & Indio Azteca, Nick Bockwinkel beat Red Shoes Duggan, Luigi Macera beat George Drake.

5/8/62 Hilo Att 2000. All midget card
Lord Littlebrook & Little Beaver beat Fuzzy Cupid & Sky Low Low, Sonny Boy Cassidy beat Brown Bomber, Tiny Tim beat Irish Jackie, Fuzzy Cupid & Sky Low Low won battle royal.

5/9/62 Honolulu
Cowboy Cassidy & Shoulders Newman VS Neff Maiava & Lord Blears, Nick Bockwinkel VS Indio Azteca, King Curtis VS Luigi Macera, George Drake VS Red Shoes Duggan.

5/23/62 Honolulu
King Curtis & Cowboy Cassidy & Shoulders Newman beat Nick Bockwinkel & Lord Blears & Neff Maiava, Dean Higuchi drew George Drake, Luigi Macera beat Pat Mattson.

5/30/62 Honolulu
Nick Bockwinkel beat Cowboy Cassidy, King Curtis beat George Drake, Lord Blears & Neff Maiava beat Luigi Macera & Mr. Fujiwara, Dean Higuchi drew Shoulders Newman, Sweet Georgia Brown beat Etta Charles.

6/4/62 Honolulu
King Curtis & Cowboy Carlson ddq Lord Blears & Nick Bockwinkel, Sweet Georgia Brown beat Etta Charles, King Curtis drew Lord Blears, Cowboy Cassidy drew Nick Bockwinkel.

6/6/62 Honolulu
King Curtis beat Nick Bockwinkel for US Championship, Cowboy Cassidy & Shoulders Newman beat Lord Blears & Pat Mattson, George Drake drew Luigi Macera, Etta Charles beat Sweet Georgia Brown.

6/13/62 Honolulu
Nick Bockwinkel & Luigi Macera & Lord Blears beat King Curtis & Cowboy Cassidy & Tosh Togo, Shoulders Newman beat Mr. Fujiwara, Dean Higuchi beat George Drake dq, Tosh Togo drew Luigi Macera.

6/20/62 Honolulu
King Curtis beat Nick Bockwinkel dq defended US title, Luigi Macera beat Tosh Togo dq, Cowboy Cassidy drew Lord Blears, Neff Maiava beat George Drake.

6/27/62 Honolulu
Neff Maiava & Lord Blears beat Cowboy Cassidy & King Curtis defended Hawaiian tag titles, Tosh Togo beat George Drake, Nick Bockwinkel beat Luigi Macera, Shoulders Newman drew Pat Mattson.

7/4/62 Honolulu
King Curtis beat Mike Sharpe Sr, Nick Bockwinkel & Lord Blears drew Cowboy Cassidy & Tosh Togo, Neff Maiava beat Duke Hoffman, George Drake drew Shoulders Newman.

7/5/62 Hilo. Att 1500
Lord Blears & Neff Maiava beat Cowboy Cassidy & ?, Nick Bockwinkel beat Tosh Togo dq, Lord Blears drew Tosh Togo.

7/7/62 Kealakekua
Tosh Togo beat Shoulders Newman.

7/11/62 Honolulu
Neff Maiava beat Tosh Togo defended Hawaiian title, Lord Blears & Nick Bockwinkel beat Cowboy Cassidy & King Curtis, Buddy Killer Austin beat George Drake, Luigi Macera drew Shoulders Newman.

7/18/62 Honolulu
King Curtis drew Cowboy Cassidy, Nick Bockwinkel & Lord Blears beat Killer Austin & Shoulders Newman, Luigi Macera beat Tosh Togo dq.

7/25/62 Honolulu
Nick Bockwinkel & Neff Maiava & Lord Blears beat Tosh Togo & King Curtis & Killer Austin, George Drake beat Cowboy Cassidy dq, Luigi Macera beat Mr. Fujiwara.

8/1/62 Honolulu
Neff Maiava beat Tosh Togo defended Hawaiian State Title, Buddy Austin & Cowboy Cassidy beat Lord Blears & Pat Mattson, Nick Bockwinkel beat George Drake, Luigi Macera drew Shoulders Newman.

8/2/62 Hilo Att 1700
Lord Blears & Neff Maiava beat King Curtis & Tosh Togo, Nick Bockwinkel beat Buddy Austin, Neff Maiava drew Tosh Togo.

8/8/62 Honolulu
King Curtis drew Nick Bockwinkel defended US title, Neff Maiava & Lord Blears beat Cowboy Cassidy & Killer Austin defended Hawaiian Tag titles, Tosh Togo beat George Drake, Luigi Macera beat Mr. Fujiwara.

8/15/62 Honolulu
Billy Whitewolf beat Killer Austin, Nick Bockwinkel beat Tosh Togo dq, Cowboy Cassidy beat Pat Mattson, Neff Maiava beat Shoulders Newman dq.

8/22/62 Honolulu
Neff Maiava & Lord Blears & Billy Whitewolf beat Shoulders Newman & King Curtis & Tosh Togo, Cowboy Cassidy beat Mr. Fujiwara, Lord Blears drew Tosh Togo, Luigi Macera beat Pat Mattson.

8/29/62 Honolulu
Lord Blears beat Cowboy Cassidy, Billy Whitewolf beat Tosh Togo, Neff Maiava & Rocky Hunter beat King Curtis & Shoulders Newman, Luigi Macera beat Mr. Fujiwara.

8/31/62 Hilo
Cowboy Cassidy ddq King Curtis, Billy Whitewolf & Neff Maiava beat Tosh Togo & Shoulders Newman, Billy Whitewolf drew Tosh Togo.

9/5/62 Honolulu
Billy Whitewolf beat Cowboy Cassidy Indian Death Match, King Curtis & Tosh Togo beat Lord Blears & Rocky Hunter, Luigi Macera drew Neff Maiava.

9/12/62 Honolulu
King Curtis & Tosh Togo beat Lord Blears & Neff Maiava to win Hawaiian tag titles, Billy Whitewolf beat Shoulders Newman.

9/19/62 Honolulu
Tosh Togo & Cowboy Cassidy beat Neff Maiava & Jerry Christy, King Curtis drew Lord Blears, Billy Whitewolf drew Luigi Macera, Lillian (Moolah) Ellison beat Judy Grable.

10/3/62 Honolulu
King Curtis & Tosh Togo beat Billy Whitewolf & Jerry Christy, Lord Blears drew Cowboy Cassidy, Ricky Hunter beat Mr. Fujiwara dq, Little Beaver & Tiny Tim beat Sky Low Low & Fuzzy Cupid.

10/10/62 Honolulu
Billy Whitewolf & Lord Blears & Gil Ane beat King Curtis & Tosh Togo & Cowboy Cassidy dq, Neff Maiava beat Shoulders Newman, Jerry Christy drew Luigi Macera, Tosh Togo beat Ricky Hunter.

10/17/62 Honolulu
Billy Whitewolf beat King Curtis Indian Death match, Luigi Macera beat Tosh Togo, Neff Maiava & Lord Blears beat Cowboy Cassidy & Shoulders Newman, Jerry Christy drew Pat Mattson.

10/24/62 Honolulu
Neff Maiava beat Cowboy Cassidy defended Hawaiian title, Luigi Macera beat King Curtis special rules, Curtis had to pin Macera twice in 20 minutes, Gil Ane & Lord Blears beat Tosh Togo & Shoulders Newman, Billy Whitewolf beat Jerry Christy.

10/31/62 Honolulu
King Curtis beat Ben Sharpe defended US title, Billy Whitewolf & Lord Blears beat Mr. Fujiwara & Cowboy Cassidy, Tosh Togo beat Jerry Christy, Neff Maiava drew Shoulders Newman.

11/7/62 Honolulu
King Curtis & Tosh Togo & Cowboy Cassidy beat Gil Ane & Neff Maiava & Lord Blears; Luigi Macera beat Mr. Fujiwara dq, Lord Blears drew Tosh Togo, Billy Whitewolf beat Kangaroo Kennedy.

11/14/62 Honolulu
King Curtis beat Gorilla Marconi, Gil Ane & Lord Blears beat Tosh Togo & Kangaroo Kennedy, Billy Whitewolf beat Cowboy Cassidy.

11/21/62 Honolulu
Billy Whitewolf beat King Curtis to win US title, Lord Blears & Neff Maiava beat Gorilla Marconi & Tosh Togo to defend Hawaiian tag titles, Luigi Macera drew Cowboy Cassidy.

11/28/62 Honolulu
Tosh Togo & Cowboy Cassidy drew battle royal, Billy Whitewolf & Neff Maiava beat Cowboy Cassidy & Tosh Togo, Shoulders Newman beat Pat Mattson, Luigi Macera drew Lord Blears, King Curtis beat Kangaroo Kennedy.

12/5/62 Honolulu
Neff Maiava beat Masked Executioner, King Curtis & Tosh Togo drew Lord Blears & Billy Whitewolf, Cowboy Cassidy drew Gil Ane.

12/12/62 Honolulu
King Curtis beat Billy Whitewolf to regain US title, Neff Maiava & Lord Blears beat Cowboy Cassidy & Masked Executioner, Boom Boom Michalik beat Luigi Macera, Tosh Togo drew Shoulders Newman, Baby Cheryl beat Dolly Darcel.

12/19/62 Honolulu
Neff Maiava beat Boom Boom Michalik defended his Hawaiian Title, Masked Executioner & Cowboy Cassidy beat King Curtis & Tosh Togo, Billy Whitewolf drew Lord Blears, Luigi Macera beat Pat Mattson.

12/26/62 Honolulu
Tosh Togo beat Cowboy Cassidy, Lord Blears & Gil Ane beat King Curtis & Mr. Fujiwara, Luigi Macera beat Masked Executioner dq, Billy Whitewolf drew Neff Maiava.

1963

1/2/63 Honolulu
King Curtis & Shoulders Newman drew Dean Higuchi & Lord Blears, Masked Executioner drew Great Togo, Billy Whitewolf beat Cowboy Cassidy, Gil Ane beat Harry Fujiwara (Mr. Fuji).

1/9/63 Honolulu
Whipper Watson & Lord Blears beat King Curtis & Tosh Togo, Masked Executioner beat Luigi Macera, Neff Mavia beat Cowboy Cassidy dq.

1/15/63 Hilo Att 2000
Billy Whitewolf & Neff Maiava beat Cowboy Cassidy & Masked Executioner, Lord Blears drew Tosh Togo, Billy Whitewolf drew Cowboy Cassidy.

1/16/63 Honolulu
Billy Whitewolf & Dean Higuchi beat Tosh Togo & King Curtis, Masked Executioner beat Lord Blears, Neff Maiava beat Shoulders Newman dq, Cowboy Cassidy drew Gil Ane.

1/23/63 Honolulu
Masked Executioner beat Billy Whitewolf, King Curtis & Tosh Togo beat Neff Mavia & Sonny Pascua, Cowboy Cassidy drew Lord Blears, Luigi Macera drew Harry Fujiwara.

1/30/63 Honolulu
King Curtis beat Leo Nomellini to defend US title, Billy Whitewolf & Lord Blears beat Harry Fujiwara & Tosh Togo, Masked Executioner beat Dean Higuchi, Cowboy Cassidy drew Sonny Pascua.

2/6/63 Honolulu
King Curtis beat Masked Executioner, Samson Burke beat Cowboy Cassidy, Billy Whitewolf & Lord Blears drew Tosh Togo & Shoulders Newman, Neff Mavia beat Luigi Macera, Gene LeBell beat Pat Mattson.

2/12/63 Hilo Att 2200
Billy Whitewolf & Neff Maiava beat Tosh Togo & Gene LeBell dq, Samson Burke beat Lou Newman, Billy Whitewolf drew Gene LeBell.

2/13/63 Honolulu
Billy Whitewolf beat Gene LeBell Indian Death Match, Samson Burke & Lord Blears beat Cowboy Cassidy & Shoulders Newman, Neff Maiava beat George Drake dq, Tosh Togo drew Dean Higuchi.

2/20/63 Honolulu
Lord Blears & Neff Maiava & Samson Burke beat King Curtis & Tosh Togo & Gene LaBell, Dean Higuchi beat Cowboy Cassidy dq, Gil Ane drew George Drake, Neff Maiava beat Gene LaBell.

2/27/63 Honolulu
Gene LaBell beat Tosh Togo, Gil Ane & Luigi Macera drew King Curtis & Shoulders Newman, Neff Maiava beat George Drake.

3/6/63 Honolulu
Neff Maiava & Lord Blears beat Cowboy Cassidy & Gene LaBell, King Curtis beat Gil Ane, Tosh Togo beat Luigi Macera, George Drake drew Shoulders Newman.

3/8/63 Hilo Att 1500
Dean Higuchi & Gil Ane beat Tosh Togo & King Curtis, Lord Blears beat Gene LeBell, Gil Ane drew Tosh Togo.

3/14/63 Honolulu
Dino Lanza won battle royal, The Brute (Klondike Bill) beat Dean Higuchi, Dino Lanza beat George Drake, Neff Maiava beat King Curtis dq, Cowboy Cassidy beat Pat Mattson, Tosh Togo drew Gene LeBell.

3/20/63 Honolulu
King Curtis beat Gene LaBell Judo jacket match, Lord Blears drew Dean Higuchi, Gil Ane drew Tosh Togo, Dino Lanza beat Cowboy Cassidy.

3/27/63 Honolulu
Don Leo Jonathan beat Dino Lanza, The Brute & Cowboy Cassidy drew Neff Maiava & Luigi Macera, Tosh Togo drew Lord Blears, George Drake beat Gene LaBell dq.

4/3/63 Honolulu
Neff Maiava beat King Curtis, Tosh Togo drew Gene LaBell, The Brute & Cowboy Cassidy drew Lord Blears & George Drake, Don Leo Jonathan beat Shoulders Newman.

4/9/63 Hilo Att 3000
Don Leo Jonathan & Lord Blears beat King Curtis & Tosh Togo, Neff Maiava beat The Brute (Klondike Bill) dq, Lord Blears drew Tosh Togo.

4/10/63 Honolulu
King Curtis beat Don Leo Jonathan to defend US title, Neff Maiava & Lord Blears drew The Brute & Gene LaBell, Abe Jacobs beat George Drake, Tosh Togo drew Dean Higuchi.

4/17/63 Honolulu
Lord Blears beat Gene LaBell dq, Cowboy Cassidy beat Tosh Togo dq, The Brute beat Abe Jacobs, Little Beaver & Tiny Tim beat Billy The Kid & Klondike Jake.

4/24/63 Honolulu
Neff Maiava beat Gene LaBell to win Hawaiian title, Nick Bockwinkel & Lord Blears drew The Brute & Cowboy Cassidy, Tosh Togo beat George Drake, Olga Martinez & Fabulous Moolah beat Ann Casey & Brenda Scott.

4/30/63 Hilo. Att 1600
Nick Bockwinkel & Lord Blears beat The Brute & Cowboy Cassidy, Moolah & Olga Martinez beat Ann Casey & Brenda Scott, Cowboy Cassidy drew Nick Bockwinkel.

5/1/63 Honolulu
Nick Bockwinkel & Lord Blears beat Tosh Togo & The Brute dq, Fabulous Moolah beat Ann Casey defended US title, Luigi Macera drew George Drake, Brenda Scott beat Olga Martinez.

5/8/63 Honolulu
Whipper Watson beat Tosh Togo, Nick Bockwinkel beat The Brute, Dean Higuchi beat George Drake, Neff Maiava & Lord Blears beat Pat Mattson & Shoulders Newman.

5/15/63 Honolulu
King Curtis & Tosh Togo & The Brute beat Nick Bockwinkel & Neff Maiava & Lord Blears, Ricky Hunter beat Shoulders Newman dq, Luigi Macera beat Harry Fujiwara dq, Togh Togo drew Lord Blears.

5/21/63 Hilo Att 1500
Nick Bockwinkel & Neff Maiava & Lord Blears beat King Curtis & The Brute & Tosh Togo, Nick Bockwinkel beat The Brute dq, Neff Maiava drew Tosh Togo.

5/22/63 Honolulu
Neff Maiava beat The Brute, Nick Bockwinkel & Lord Blears beat Tosh Togo & King Curtis, Ricky Hunter beat Harry Fujiwara dq, Dean Higuchi drew Cowboy Cassidy.

5/29/63 Honolulu
King Curtis beat Neff Maiava to defend US title, Nick Bockwinkel & Lord Blears drew The Brute & Cowboy Cassidy, Tosh Togo drew Rocky Hunter, Shoulders Newman beat Dean Higuchi.

6/5/63 Honolulu
King Curtis beat The Brute, Nick Bockwinkel & Luigi Macera beat Cowboy Cassidy & Harry Fujiwara, Lord Blears beat Shoulders Newman dq, Pat Mattson drew Ricky Hunter.

6/10/63 Hilo Att 2400
Masked Executioner & Cowboy Cassidy beat Nick Bockwinkel & Luigi Macera, King Curtis beat The Brute, Cowboy Cassidy drew Luigi Macera.

6/12/63 Honolulu
Nick Bockwinkel won battle royal, Neff Maiava beat Harry Fujiwara, Lord Blears beat Ricky Hunter, King Curtis drew Cowboy Cassidy, The Brute drew Shoulders Newman, Nick Bockwinkel beat The Masked Executioner dq.

6/20/63 Honolulu
Gorilla Monsoon beat King Curtis dq, Nick Bockwinkel beat The Brute, Masked Executioner & Cowboy Cassidy beat Lord Blears & Luigi Macera, Neff Maiava beat Pat Mattson.

7/4/63 Hilo Att 2025
King Curtis beat Gino Marella (Gorilla Monsoon), Nick Bockwinkel & Lord Blears beat Masked Executioner & Cowboy Cassidy dq, Nick Bockwinkel beat Cowboy Cassidy.

7/22/63 Hilo 2605
Nick Bockwinkel & Lucky Simunovich beat Tosh Togo & Shoulder Newman, Masked Executioner beat the Brute, Lucky Simunovich beat Shoulders Newman dq.

8/6/63 Hilo Att 2000
Nick Bockwinkel & Neff Maiava beat Masked Executioner & Cowboy Cassidy, Lucky Simunovich drew Tosh Togo, Cowboy Cassidy beat Neff Maiava.

8/21/63 Honolulu
Neff Maiava beat Don Manoukian, King Curtis beat Masked Executioner dq, Lord Blears & Lucky Simunovich beat Shoulders Newman & Cowboy Cassidy, Nick Bockwinkel beat Tosh Togo.

8/28/63 Honolulu
Masked Executioner beat Cowboy Cassidy, Don Manoukian & Tosh Togo drew Lord Blears & Nick Bockwinkel, Lucky Simunovich beat Mr. Fujiwara, Neff Maiava drew Luigi Macera.

8/30/63 Hilo Att 1500
Nick Bockwinkel & Lord Blears beat Don Manoukian & Harry Fujiwara, Lucky Simunovich beat Masked Executioner dq, Harry Fujiwara beat Lord Blears.

9/4/63 Honolulu
Don Manoukian beat Nick Bockwinkel defended US Title, Neff Maiava & Lucky Simunovich beat Shoulders Newman & Tosh Togo, Pat Mattson beat Cowboy Cassidy dq, Lord Blears drew Mr. Fujiwara.

9/11/63 Honolulu
Lucky Simunovich beat Don Manoukian dq, Killer Austin & Cowboy Cassidy beat Lord Blears & Luigi Macera, Nick Bockwinkel beat Dean Higuchi, Tosh Togo drew Shoulders Newman.

9/18/63 Honolulu
Nick Bockwinkel beat Killer Austin, Lord Blears & Lucky Simunovich beat Don Manoukian & Karl Von Hess dq, Kathy Starr beat Ann Casey defended US title, Sonny Cooper (Don Jardine) beat Tosh Togo.

9/19/63 Hilo Att 1,100
Nick Bockwinkel & Lord Blears beat Cowboy Cassidy & Buddy Austin, Kathy Starr beat Ann Casey, Cowboy Cassidy beat Nick Bockwinkel.

9/25/63 Honolulu
Don Manoukian drew Nick Bockwinkel defended US title, King Curtis beat Sonny Cooper, Al Lolotai & Neff Maiava beat Cowboy Cassidy & Killer Austin, Lord Blears drew Lucky Simunovich.

10/3/63 Honolulu
King Curtis & Tosh Togo drew Lord Blears & Lucky Simunovich, Sonny Cooper beat Mr. Fujiwara, Don Manoukian beat Cowboy Cassidy, Tiny Tim & Irish Jackie beat Sky Low Low & Billy The Kid.

10/8/63 Hilo Att 3,452
Giant Baba beat Don Manoukian dq, Sonny Cooper (Don Jardine) & Neff Maiava beat King Curtis & Tosh Togo, Sonny Cooper drew Tosh Togo.

10/9/63 Honolulu
Giant Baba won battle royal, Don Manoukian beat Tosh Togo, Al Lolotai drew Lucky Simunovich, Cowboy Cassidy & King Curtis drew Lord Blears & Neff Maiava, Sonny Cooper beat Shoulders Newman.

10/16/63 Honolulu
Giant Baba beat King Curtis dq, Don Manoukian beat Sonny Cooper, Lucky Simunovich beat Ricky Hunter, Lord Blears & Neff Maiava beat Tosh Togo & Cowboy Cassidy.

10/22/63 Hilo. Att 2,178
Giant Baba beat King Curtis dq, Lord Blears & Dean Higuchi drew Don Manoukian & Tosh Togo, Tosh Togo beat Dean Higuchi.

10/23/63 Honolulu
King Curtis & Cowboy Cassidy drew Al Lolotai & Neff Mavia, Don Manoukian beat Luigi Macera, Lucky Simunovich beat Shoulders Newman, Lord Blears drew Tosh Togo.

10/30/63 Honolulu
Lord Blears & Lucky Simunovich & Sonny Cooper beat King Curtis & Tosh Togo & Cowboy Cassidy, Sonny Cooper drew Cowboy Cassidy, Al Lolotai drew Don Manoukian, Mr. Fujiwara beat Ricky Hunter.

11/6/63 Honolulu
King Curtis beat Don Manoukian to win US title, Lucky Simunovich & Lord Blears beat Cowboy Cassidy & Mr. Fujiwara, Neff Maiava beat Shoulders Newman, Sonny Cooper beat Dean Higuchi.

11/13/63 Honolulu
Neff Maiava beat Hard Boiled Haggerty, Luther Lindsay beat King Curtis, Sonny Cooper & Lord Blears beat Don Manoukian & Shoulders Newman, Lucky Simunovich drew Cowboy Cassidy.

11/18/63 Hilo Att 2,800
Don Manoukian ddq Fred Blassie, King Curtis beat Luther Lindsay, Cowboy Cassidy drew Lord Blears.

11/20/63 Honolulu
Fred Blassie drew Luther Lindsay, King Curtis beat Lucky Simunovich, Dan Manoukian beat Sonny Cooper, Cowboy Cassidy drew Al Lolotai, Mr. Fujiwara drew Lord Blears.

11/27/63 Honolulu
Neff Maiava beat Don Leo Jonathan defended Hawaiian title, King Curtis & Cowboy Cassidy beat Lord Blears & Sonny Cooper, Don Manoukian beat Mr. Fujiwara, Lucky Simunovich beat Luigi Macera.

12/4/63 Honolulu
King Curtis beat Don Manoukian defended US title, Samson Burke drew Cowboy Cassidy, Lucky Simunovich & Al Lolotai beat Mr. Fujiwara & Shoulders Newman, Lord Blears drew Luigi Macera.

12/11/63 Honolulu
Haystacks Calhoun won battle royal, Billy Whitewolf beat Mr. Fujiwara, Don Manoukian beat King Curtis dq, Cowboy Cassidy beat Lucky Simunovich, Neff Maiava drew Dick The Bruiser.

12/16/63 Hilo. Att 3,000
Haystacks Calhoun & Billy Whitewolf beat King Curtis & Cowboy Cassidy dq, Don Manoukian drew Samson Burke, Billy Whitewolf beat Cowboy Cassidy.

12/18/63 Honolulu
King Curtis & Cowboy Cassidy drew Haystacks Calhoun & Billy Whitewolf, Don Manoukian beat Gil Ane, Samson Burke beat Shoulders Newman, Lord Blears drew Al Lolotai, Lucky Simunovich beat Mr. Fujiwara.

12/25/63 Honolulu
Neff Maiava beat Fred Blassie defended Hawaiian title, King Curtis & Cowboy Cassidy beat Billy Whitewolf & Lucky Simunovich, Don Manoukian drew Lord Blears, Samson Burke beat Gil Ane.

1964

1/1/64 Honolulu
King Curtis beat Fred Blassie to defend US title, Don Manoukian drew Samson Burke, Billy Whitewolf beat Mr. Fujiwara, Lucky Simunovich beat Gil Ane dq, Billy Whitewolf & Lord Blears beat Cowboy Cassidy & Mr. Fujiwara.

1/8/64 Honolulu
Samson Burke beat King Curtis, Hard Boiled Haggerty beat Lucky Simunovich, Billy Whitewolf & Lord Blears beat Gil Ane & Don Manoukian dq, Cowboy Cassidy drew Luigi Macera.

1/16/64 Honolulu
Billy Whitewolf & Neff Maiava & Samson Burke beat Mr. Fujiwara & King Curtis & Cowboy Cassidy, Hard Boiled Haggerty beat Lord Blears, Al Lolotai beat Don Manoukian dq, Neff Maiava beat Mr. Fujiwara.

1/20/64 Hilo. Att 1,200
Billy Whitewolf beat Hard Boiled Haggerty dq, King Curtis beat Neff Maiava, Don Manoukian drew Lord Blears.

1/22/64 Honolulu
Billy Whitewolf beat Don Manoukian Indian Death Match, Samson Burke drew Hard Boiled Haggerty, King Curtis & Mr. Fujiwara beat Lord Blears & Lucky Simunovich, Shoulders Newman drew Al Lolotai.

1/29/64 Honolulu
King Curtis beat Samson Burke to defend US title, Hard Boiled Haggerty beat Gil Ane, Neff Maiava & Lord Blears beat Mike Silva & Cowboy Cassidy, Billy Whitewolf drew Lucky Simunovich.

2/5/64 Honolulu
Hard Boiled Haggerty beat Neff Maiava to win Hawaiian Title, Masked Executioner beat Killer Austin, Billy Whitewolf & Lord Blears beat King Curtis & Cowboy Cassidy.

2/12/64 Honolulu
King Curtis drew Hard Boiled Haggarty defended US title, Billy Whitewolf & Neff Maiava beat Masked Executioner & Shoulders Newman, Cowboy Cassidy drew Lord Blears, Lucky Simunovich beat Luigi Macera.

2/18/64 Hilo Att 2,125
Billy Whitewolf beat Cowboy Cassidy Indian Death Match, Hard Boiled Haggerty beat Lucky Simunovich, Lord Blears beat Masked Executioner.

2/19/64 Honolulu. Att 3,500
Hard Boiled Haggerty beat Neff Maiava defended Hawaiian title, Masked Executioner drew Billy Whitewolf, Cowboy Cassidy & Mr. Fujiwara beat Lucky Simunovich & Lord Blears, Gil Ane drew Al Lolotai.

2/26/64 Honolulu
Hard Boiled Haggerty drew Masked Executioner, Billy Whitewolf & Lord Blears beat Tosh Togo & Mr. Fujiwara, Lucky Simunovich drew Cowboy Cassidy, Shoulders Newman beat Billy Scott.

3/4/64 Honolulu. Att 4,000
Billy Whitewolf beat Hard Boiled Haggerty, Neff Maiava & Lucky Simunovich beat Tosh Togo & Cowboy Cassidy, Lord Blears beat Masked Executioner dq, Luigi Macera drew Gil Ane.

3/11/64 Honolulu
King Curtis beat Kanji Inoki dq defended US title, Billy Whitewolf beat Tosh Togo, Neff Maiava & Lord Blears beat Hard Boiled Haggerty & Masked Executioner dq, Al Lolotai drew Cowboy Cassidy.

3/18/64 Honolulu
Hard Boiled Haggerty beat Billy Whitewolf to defend Hawaiian State Title, Toyonobori beat Cowboy Cassidy, Kanji Inoki & Lord Blears drew King Curtis & Tosh Togo, Masked Executioner beat Lucky Simunovich.

3/23/64 Hilo. Att 1,800
Masked Executioner beat Kanji Inoki, Billy Whitewolf beat King Curtis dq, Lord Blears beat Hard Boiled Haggerty dq.

3/25/64 Honolulu
King Curtis beat Toyonobori, Hard Boiled Haggerty & Masked Executioner beat Kanji Inoki & Lord Blears, Billy Whitewolf drew Samson Burke, Neff Maiava beat Cowboy Cassidy.

4/3/64 Honolulu
Giant Baba beat Hard Boiled Haggerty, Neff Maiava & lord Blears beat King Curtis & Mr. Fujiwara, Masked Executioner drew Cowboy Cassidy, Lucky Simunovich beat Samson Burke dq.

4/8/64 Honolulu
Neff Maiava beat Hard Boiled Haggerty to regain Hawaiian State Title, Lord Blears & Lucky Simunovich beat Masked Executioner & Samson Burke dq, King Curtis drew Billy Whitewolf, Shoulders Newman drew Cowboy Cassidy.

4/15/64 Honolulu
Robert Duranton & Neff Maiava & Lord Blears beat King Curtis & Samson Burke & Masked Executioner, Billy Whitewolf beat Cowboy Cassidy, Lucky Simunovich beat Mr. Fujiwara dq, Neff Maiava drew Masked Executioner.

4/21/64 Hilo. Att 800
King Curtis ddq Hard Boiled Haggerty, Robert Duranton beat Masked Executioner, Lord Blears drew Mr. Fujiwara.

4/22/64 Honolulu
Robert Duranton won battle royal, Neff Maiava beat Mr. Fujiwara, Cowboy Cassidy drew Samson Burke, Masked Executioner & Hard Boiled Haggerty beat Robert Duranton & Lucky Simunovich.

4/29/64 Honolulu
Luther Lindsay beat Masked Executioner, Samson Burke & Cowboy Cassidy drew Lord Blears & Neff Maiava, King Curtis beat Robert Duranton, Hard Boiled Haggerty beat Lucky Simunovich.

5/6/64 Honolulu
Neff Maiava beat Hard Boiled Haggerty to defend Hawaiian title, Cowboy Cassidy & King Curtis beat Robert Duranton & Lord Blears, Luther Lindsay beat Samson Burke, Lucky Simunovich drew Gil Ane.

5/11/64 Hilo. Att 1,400
Robert Duranton beat King Curtis dq, Rita Cortez beat Bambi Ball, Luther Lindsay beat Cowboy Cassidy.

5/13/64 Honolulu
Robert Duranton & Luther Lindsay beat King Curtis & Cowboy Cassidy to win Hawaiian tag titles, Shoulders Newman drew Gil Ane, Mr. Fujiwara drew Lord Blears, Rita Cortez beat Bambi Hall.

5/20/64 Honolulu
King Curtis beat Robert Duranton to defend US title, Gil Ane & Lord Blears beat The Alaskan & Mr. Fujiwara, Luther Lindsay beat Gene LeBell, Lucky Simunovich drew Luigi Macera.

5/27/64 Honolulu
Luther Lindsay beat The Alaskan, King Curtis & Gene LaBell drew Lord Blears & Neff Maiava, Lucky Simunovich drew Robert Duranton, Cowboy Cassidy beat Dean Higuchi.

6/3/64 Honolulu
The Alaskan & Neff Maiava & Robert Duranton beat King Curtis & Cowboy Cassidy & Mr. Fujiwara, Luther Lindsay beat Lucky Simunovich, Gene LaBell drew Lord Blears, Mr. Fujiwara beat Robert Duranton.

6/10/64 Honolulu
King Curtis beat The Alaskan, Lord Blears & Luther Lindsay beat Mr. Fujiwara & Cowboy Cassidy, Gene LaBell beat Robert Duranton, Gil Ane drew Lucky Simunovich.

6/16/64 Hilo. Att 2,000
Luther Lindsay & Robert Duranton beat King Curtis & Cowboy Cassidy, Dean Higuchi beat The Alaskan dq, Cowboy Cassidy beat Robert Duranton.

6/17/64 Honolulu
Billy Whitewolf beat King Curtis, Gene LaBell beat Luther Lindsay, Neff Maiava beat Lucky Simunovich, Robert Duranton & Lord Blears drew Alaskan & Shoulders Newman.

6/24/64 Honolulu
Luther Lindsay beat King Curtis dq, Mr. Fujiwara drew Robert Duranton, Lucky Simunovich beat Gene LaBell, Lord Blears & Neff Maiava beat Alaskan & Cowboy Cassidy dq.

7/13/64 Hilo. Att 2,100
Neff Maiava & Luther Lindsay & Lord Blears beat King Curtis & Gene Kiniski & Gene LeBell, Gene LeBell beat Luther Lindsay dq, Neff Maiava beat King Curtis COR.

7/16/64 Honolulu
Gene Kiniski beat Neff Maiava to win Hawaiian title, King Curtis & Mr. Fujiwara drew Gil Ane & Lord Blears, Luther Lindsay beat Cowboy Cassidy, Luigi Macera drew Gene LaBell.

7/22/64 Honolulu
Neff Maiava & Lord Blears & Luther Lindsay drew Nikita Mulkovich & King Curtis & Gene LaBell, Gene Kiniski beat Gil Ane, Lucky Simunovich drew Shoulders Newman, Neff Maiava beat Gene LaBell.

7/29/64 Honolulu
Luther Lindsay won battle royal, Masked Executioner beat Gil Ane, Mr. Moto beat Ricky Hunter, Neff Maiava drew Gene Kiniski, Cowboy Cassidy drew Lucky Simunovich, Dean Higuchi beat Nikita Mulkovich dq, Luther Lindsay beat Shoulders Newman.

7/29/64 Honolulu
King Curtis beat Luther Lindsay, Tosh Togo drew Jim LaBelle, Gene Kiniski drew Masked Executioner, Neff Maiava & Lord Blears beat Mr. Moto & Nikita Mulkovich.

7/28/64 Honolulu National All Star Promotions
Ray Stevens beat Ed Carpenter US title, Pepper Gomez & Jose Lothario beat Stan Neilson & Karl Von Brock, Charlie Kalani beat Don Duffy, Cowboy Bob Ellis beat Fritz Von Goering, Kinji Shibuya beat Maurice Tapoiate, Dick Steinborn beat Rocky Montero.

8/4/64 Hilo. Att 2,100
Lord Blears & Luther Lindsay beat Gene Kiniski & Nikita Mulkovich, Mr. Moto beat Masked Executioner dq, Luther Lindsay drew Nikita Mulkovich.

8/5/64 Honolulu
Luther Lindsay drew Gene Kiniski, Mr. Moto beat Nikita Mulkovich, King Curtis & Tosh Togo beat George Drake & Lord Blears, Masked Executioner beat Cowboy Cassidy.

8/12/64 Honolulu
Gene Kiniski beat Neff Maiava Hawaiian title defense, King Curtis beat Nikita Mulkovich, Luther Lindsay beat Masked Executioner, Tosh Togo drew Lord Blears, Cowboy Cassidy drew George Drake.

8/19/64 Honolulu
Gene Kiniski & Cowboy Cassidy & Nikita Mulkovich beat Luther Lindsay & Lord Blears & George Drake, George Drake beat Nikita Mulkovich dq, Tosh Togo drew Neff Maiava, King Curtis beat Masked Executioner dq.

8/26/64 Hilo. Att 1,500
Kathy Starr beat Jessica Rogers, Gil Ane beat Nikita Mulkovich, Lucky Simunovich beat Masked Executioner dq.

9/3/64 Honolulu
Johnny Barend beat Lucky Simunovich, King Curtis & Tosh Togo beat Cowboy Cassidy & Nikita Mulkovich, George Drake beat Masked Executioner, Kathy Starr beat Jessica Rodgers US Woman's Title.

9/9/64 Honolulu
Johnny Barend & King Curtis drew Toyonobori & Yoshimura, Nick Bockwinkel beat Tosh Togo, Shag Thomas beat Mr. Fujiwara, Shoulders Newman drew George Drake.

9/15/64 Hilo. Att 1,500
Shag Thomas & Michiaki Yoshimura beat Johnny Barend & Tosh Togo, King Curtis drew Nick Bockwinkel, Michiaki Yoshimura beat Tosh Togo dq.

9/16/64 Honolulu
King Curtis beat Toyonobori US title defense, Nick Bockwinkel & Lord Blears beat Tosh Togo & Johnny Barend, Shag Thomas beat Shoulders Newman, Yoshimura beat George Drake.

9/22/64 Hilo. Att 1,500
Tiny Tim & Jamaica Kid beta Sky Low Low & Vito Gonzales, Johnny Barend beat George Drake, Gil Ane beat Shoulder Newman dq.

9/23/64 Honolulu
King Curtis beat Nick Bockwinkel, Yoshimura drew Johnny Barend, Mighty Ursus beat George Drake but failed to pin Shag Thomas Handicap match, Jamaica Kid & Tiny Tim beat Pancho Gonzales & Sky Low Low.

10/8/64 Honolulu
Johnny Barend beat Neff Maiava for the Hawaiian Title, King Curtis & Tosh Togo beat Nick Bockwinkel & Lucky Simunovich, Shag Thomas beat Mighty Ursus dq, Yoshimura beat George Drake.

10/12/64 Hilo. Att 1,200
King Curtis & Mr. Fuji beat Mighty Ursus & Lord Blears, Shag Thomas beat Johnny Barend dq, Lord Blears beat Mr. Fujiwara.

10/15/64 Honolulu
Shag Thomas won battle royal, Tosh Togo drew Shoulders Newman, Nick Bockwinkel drew Yoshimura, Johnny Barend & Mr. Fujiwara drew Lucky Simunovich & Shag Thomas, Mighty Ursus beat Hooded Terror dq, King Curtis beat Gil Ane.

10/29/64 Honolulu
King Curtis beat Mighty Ursus US title defense, Shag Thomas beat Johnny Barend dq, Masked Executioner beat Lucky Simunovich, Lord Blears drew Mr. Fujiwara.

11/3/64 Honolulu
Johnny Barend beat Masked Executioner Hawaiian title defense, King Curtis & Tosh Togo drew Nick Bockwinkel & Shag Thomas, Mighty Ursus drew Bobby Shane, Lord Blears drew Shoulders Newman.

11/10/64 Hilo. Att 2,000
Don Leo Jonathan & Mighty Ursus beat Johnny Barend & Tosh Togo dq, Nick Bockwinkel beat Masked Executioner dq, Mighty Ursus drew Tosh Togo.

11/14/64 Honolulu
King Curtis beat Don Leo Jonathan US title Defense, Masked Executioner drew Mighty Ursus, Bobby Shane beat Shoulders Newman dq, Nick Bockwinkel & Lord Blears beat Tosh Togo & Mr. Fujiwara, Johnny Barend drew Shag Thomas.

11/20/64 Honolulu
Johnny Barend drew Nick Bockwinkel Hawaiian Title defense, Bobby Shane & Shag Thomas beat King Curtis & Mr. Fujiwara, Enrique Torres beat Mighty Ursus, Tosh Togo drew Lord Blears.

11/28/64 Honolulu
King Curtis beat Shag Thomas, Johnny Barend & Tosh Togo drew Enrique Torres & Neff Maiava, Nick Bockwinkel drew Mighty Ursus dq, Lord Blears beat Bobby Shane.

12/4/64 Honolulu
Johnny Barend drew King Curtis, Neff Maiava & Lord Blears beat Mighty Ursus & Tosh Togo, Enrique Torres beat Mr. Fujiwara, Nick Bockwinkel beat Shoulders Newman, Gil Ane beat Bobby Shane.

12/12/64 Honolulu
Enrique Torres beat King Curtis to win US title, Mighty Ursus drew Gil Ane, Shoulders Newman & The Mongol beat Nick Bockwinkel & Lord Blears, Tosh Togo beat Mr. Fujiwara, Neff Maiava beat Kangaroo Kennedy.

12/14/64 Hilo. Att 2,000
Enrique Torres & Lord Blears beat King Curtis & Mr. Fujiwara, The Mongol beat Nick Bockwinkel COR, Enrique Torres beat Mr. Fujiwara dq.

12/18/64 Honolulu
Enrique Torres beat The Mongol dq defended US title, King Curtis beat Nick Bockwinkel to win Hawaiian title, Mighty Ursus & Tosh Togo drew Lord Blears & Tim Colt.

12/25/64 Honolulu. Att 3,200
King Curtis beat Tosh Togo dq, Nick Bockwinkel & Enrique Torres beat The Mongol & Mighty Ursus, Mr. Fujiwara drew Tim Colt, Neff Maiava beat Gil Ane dq.

12/26/64 Hilo Att 3,100
Nick Bockwinkel beat The Mongol fence match, Enrique Torres beat Mighty Ursus, King Curtis DCOR Tim Colt, Neff Maiava drew Tosh Togo.

1965

1/2/65 Honolulu
King Curtis beat The Mongol, Kurt & Karl Von Stroheim drew Enrique Torres & Tim Colt, Nick Bockwinkel beat Gil Ane, Lord Blears beat Tosh Togo dq.

1/9/65 Honolulu
Enrique Torres drew King Curtis, Kurt & Karl Von Stroheim beat Nick Bockwinkel & Lord Blears, Neff Maiava beat Gil Ane dq, Tim Colt beat Pat Mattson, Shoulders Newman drew Mr. Fujiwara.

1/9/65 Honolulu Different Promotion
Kinji Shibuya beat Mark Lewin defended AWA title, Bearcat Wright beat Mitsu Arakawa, Pat Barret beat Ken Yates, Billy Whitewolf beat Maurice Dupree, Pepper Gomez & Ricky Romero beat Don Manoukian & Killer Buddy Austin.

1/11/65 Hilo. Att 2,900
Nick Bockwinkel won battle royal, Enrique Torres dcor Karl Von Stroheim, Nick Bockwinkel beat Mr. Fujiwara, Lord Blears drew Rey Urbano, Kurt Von Stroheim beat Tim Colt.

1/13/65 Honolulu
Enrique Torres beat King Curtis defended US title, Kurt & Karl Von Stroheim beat Nick Bockwinkel & Lord Blears, Neff Maiava beat Gil Ane dq, Tim Colt beat Pat Mattson, Shoulders Newman drew Mr. Fujiwara.

1/15/65 Honolulu
Kurt & Karl Von Stroheim & King Curtis beat Enrique Torres & Nick Bockwinkel & Tim Colt, Rey Urbano beat Harry Fujiwara dq, Nick Bockwinkel beat Karl Von Stroheim dq, Kurt Von Stroheim drew Tim Colt, Lord Blears beat Pat Mattson.

1/20/65 Honolulu
Kurt Von Stroheim drew Nick Bockwinkel, King Curtis & Mr. Fujiwara beat Enrique Torres & Tim Colt - defended Hawaiian tag titles, Neff Maiava beat The Bandit dq, Lord Blears drew Karl Von Stroheim.

1/26/65 Hilo. Att 2,900
Nick Bockwinkel & Enrique Torres & Tim Colt beat King Curtis & Kurt & Karl Von Stroheim, Kathy Starr beat Barbara Baker, King Curtis beat Enrique Torres COR, Karl Von Stroheim drew Tim Colt.

1/27/65 Honolulu
Kurt & Karl Von Stroheim beat Lord Blears & Enrique Torres, King Curtis beat Nick Bockwinkel dq, Tim Colt beat The Bandit, Kathy Starr beat Barbara Baker Collins.

2/3/65 Honolulu
Enrique Torres beat Kurt Von Stroheim defended US Title, Tim Colt & Nick Bockwinkel beat Mr. Fujiwara & Karl Von Stroheim, Neff Maiava beat King Curtis dq, Lord Blears beat Tim Bandit.

2/10/65 Honolulu
Enrique Torres & King Curtis drew battle royal, Enrique Torres beat The Bandit, Nick Bockwinkel beat Mr. Fujiwara, Karl Von Stroheim drew Shoulders Newman, Tim Colt beat Kurt Von Stroheim dq, King Curtis drew Gil Ane.

2/15/65 Hilo. Att 2,475
King Curtis DCOR Nick Bockwinkel, Enrique Torres beat The Wolfman (Soldat Gorky), Hard Boiled Haggerty beat Lord Blears, Neff Maiava beat Ivan Kameroff.

2/17/65 Honolulu
Hard Boiled Haggerty beat Nick Bockwinkel, Lord Blears & Tim Colt beat The Bandit & Gil Ane, King Curtis drew Russian Wolfman, Enrique Torres beat Ivan Kameroff.

2/24/65 Honolulu
Hard Boiled Haggerty beat Enrique Torres won US title, Nick Bockwinkel beat The Russian Wolfman, Neff Maiava beat Ivan Kameroff, The Bandit & Mr. Fujiwara drew Lord Blears & Tim Colt.

2/25/65 Honolulu
Pepper Gomez & Ricky Romero beat Pat Patterson & Don Manoukian, Kinji Shibuya beat Bearcat Wright, Billy Whitewolf beat Tony Gallarza, Jack Lanza beat Maurice DePare, Mitsu Arakawa beat Pat Barrett.

3/3/65 Honolulu
Hard Boiled Haggerty beat Neff Maiava, Enrique Torres beat Masked Executioner, The Bandit drew Nick Bockwinkel, Shoulders Newman & Mr. Fujiwara beat Tim Colt & Lord Blears.

3/10/65 Honolulu
Enrique Torres & Lord Blears & Luther Lindsay beat Masked Executioner & The Bandit & Hard Boiled Haggerty, Nick Bockwinkel beat Mr. Fujiwara, Neff Maiava beat Gil Ane, Enrique Torres drew The Bandit.

3/12/65 Hilo. Att 1,500
Giant Baba beat The Bandit, Hard Boiled Haggerty beat Neff Maiava COR, Nick Bockwinkel beat The Masked Executioner dq, Enrique Torres beat Shoulders Newman.

3/19/65 Honolulu
King Curtis drew Giant Baba defended Hawaiian title, Hard Boiled Haggerty beat Enrique Torres, Lord Blears & Neff Maiava beat Shoulders Newman & Mr. Fujiwara, Luther Lindsay beat The Bandit, Fred Blassie beat Leo Nomellini, Masked Executioner drew Nick Bockwinkel.

3/22/65 Hilo. Att 1,500
Luther Lindsay won battle royal, Hard Boiled Haggerty beat Nick Bockwinkel, Fred Blassie beat Lord Blears, Enrique Torres beat King Curtis dq, Luther Lindsay beat The Bandit.

3/27/65 Honolulu
Luther Lindsay beat Fred Blassie, King Curtis & Mr. Fujiwara beat Enrique Torres & Gil Ane, Dean Higuchi drew The Bandit.

3/29/65 Hilo. Att 1,465
Hard Boiled Haggerty beat Nick Bockwinkel, King Curtis beat Fred Blassie dq, Luther Lindsay beat Don Duffy, Enrique Torres beat Ripper Collins.

4/2/65 Honolulu
Hard Boiled Haggerty beat Fred Blassie, Enrique Torres drew King Curtis, Luther Lindsay & Nick Bockwinkel beat Ripper Collins & Don Duffy dq, Lord Blears drew The Bandit.

4/9/65 Honolulu
Enrique Torres & Lucky Simunovich & Luther Lindsay beat Ripper Collins & Don Duffy & Hard Boiled Haggerty, King Curtis drew Nick Bockwinkel, Luther Lindsay beat Don Duffy, Lucky Simunovich drew The Bandit, Lord Blears beat Ripper Collins dq.

4/16/65 Honolulu
Hard Boiled Haggerty beat King Curtis defended US title, Luther Lindsay & Nick Bockwinkel beat Ripper Collins & Don Duffy, Lucky Simunovich drew Mr. Fujiwara.

4/17/65 Hilo
Luther Lindsay & Neff Maiava & Lord Blears beat King Curtis & Hard Boiled Haggerty & Ripper Collins COR, Enrique Torres beat The Bandit, Neff Maiava beat King Curtis, Lord Blears drew Ripper Collins.

4/23/65 Honolulu
Luther Lindsay beat King Curtis dq, The Bandit DDQ Shoulders Newman, Hard Boiled Haggerty & Mr. Fujiwara beat Dean Higuchi & Lucky Simunovich, Enrique Torres beat Ripper Collins.

4/30/65 Honolulu
Lou Thesz beat Hard Boiled Haggerty to defend NWA World Title, King Curtis beat The Crusher, Luther Lindsay beat Mr. Fujiwara, Enrique & Alberto Torres beat Ripper Collins & Shoulders Newman, Lord Blears beat The Bandit, Nick Bockwinkel beat Gil Ane.

5/4/65 Hilo. Att 2,200
Lou Thesz beat Hard Boiled Haggerty, Enrique & Alberto Torres beat Mr. Fujiwara & Shoulders Newman, Luther Lindsay beat Ripper Collins, Alberto Torres drew Mr. Fujiwara.

5/7/65 Honolulu
Lou Thesz beat Luther Lindsay, Alberto & Enrique Torres beat Mr. Fujiwara & King Curtis, Hard Boiled Haggerty drew Nick Bockwinkel, Ripper Collins beat Lord Blears.

5/14/65 Honolulu
King Curtis & Ripper Collins beat Luther Lindsay & Dean Higuchi, Nick Bockwinkel drew Lucky Simunovich, Enrique Torres drew Hard Boiled Haggerty defended US title, Lord Blears drew Mr. Fujiwara.

5/18/65 Hilo. Att 2100
Luther Lindsay beat Ripper Collins, Enrique & Alberto Torres beat King Curtis & Hard Boiled Haggerty dq, Lord Blears drew Mr. Fujiwara, King Curtis drew Enrique Torres.

5/21/65 Honolulu
Luther Lindsay beat Ripper Collins dq, Enrique Torres beat Mr. Fujiwara, Hard Boiled Haggerty & Gil Ane beat Lord Blears & Lucky Simunovich, King Curtis beat Alberto Torres.

5/28/65 Honolulu
Enrique Torres & Alberto Torres beat King Curtis & Mr. Fujiwara to win Hawaiian tag titles, Victor The Great (Bear) beat Hard Boiled Haggerty, Fred Blassie beat Dean Higuchi, John Pesek beat Shoulders Newman.

5/31/65 Hilo. Att 2,500
Enrique & Alberto Torres beat King Curtis & Great Muldoon (Haystacks Muldoon), Victor The Bear beat Hard Boiled Haggerty, Fred Blassie drew Luther Lindsay, Jack Pesek drew Lord Blears.

6/4/65 Honolulu
Luther Lindsay won battle royal, Alberto Torres beat The Great Muldoon, Hard Boiled Haggerty beat Jack Pesek, Lord Blears beat Fred Blassie dq, Luther Lindsay drew King Curtis, Enrique Torres beat Dean Higuchi.

6/6/65 Hilo. Att 2,000
Luther Lindsay beat Hard Boiled Haggerty dq, Enrique Torres beat Mr. Fujiwara, Victor The Bear beat King Curtis, Lord Blears beat Shoulders Newman, Alberto Torres drew Jack Pesek.

6/11/65 Honolulu
Enrique & Alberto Torres beat King Curtis & Hard Boiled Haggerty to defend Hawaiian tag titles, Luther Lindsay beat Jack Pesek, Gil Ane drew Shoulders Newman, Lord Blears beat Mr. Fujiwara dq.

6/16/65 Honolulu
King Curtis beat Enrique Torres dq, Hard Boiled Haggerty drew Chief Red Cloud, Luther Lindsay beat Man Mountain Montana, Alberto Torres beat Mr. Fujiwara, Lord Blears drew Jack Pesek.

6/21/65 Hilo. Att 1,800
Hard Boiled Haggerty & Mr. Fujiwara beat Luther Lindsay & Chief Red Cloud (Billy Red Cloud), King Curtis beat Hercules Cortez dq, Enrique Torres beat Lord Blears, Luther Lindsay drew Mr. Fujiwara.

6/23/65 Honolulu
Hard Boiled Haggerty beat Hercules Cortez defended US title, King Curtis beat Chief Red Cloud, Luther Lindsay beat Shoulders Newman, Alberto & Enrique Torres beat Lucky Simunovich & Mr. Fujiwara.

6/30/65 Honolulu
Luther Lindsay beat Hard Boiled Haggerty boxing match, Ripper Collins beat Chief Red Cloud, Alberto & Enrique Torres beat King Curtis & Shoulders Newman, Mr. Fujiwara drew Lord Blears.

7/2/65 Hilo. Att 1,200
Alberto & Enrique Torres beat Ripper Collins & King Curtis, Luther Lindsay beat Hard Boiled Haggerty dq, Lord Blears beat Shoulders Newman, Enrique Torres drew Ripper Collins.

7/7/65 Honolulu
Alberto & Enrique Torres & Dean Higuchi beat Hard Boiled Haggerty & King Curtis & Mr. Fujiwara, Luther Lindsay drew Ripper Collins, Gil Ane drew Lord Blears, King Curtis drew Dean Higuchi.

7/14/65 Honolulu
Ray Stevens & Pat Patterson beat Alberto & Enrique Torres defended World Tag titles, Hard Boiled Haggerty beat Luther Lindsay defended US title, Bearcat Wright drew King Curtis, Ripper Collins drew Dean Higuchi, Jack Lanza beat Great Sinbad.

7/19/65 Hilo
Alberto Torres beat Ripper Collins dq, Moolah beat Dorothy Carter, King Curtis drew Pepper Martin, Enrique Torres beat Mr. Fujiwara.

7/22/65 Honolulu
Moolah beat Kathy Starr, Enrique Torres beat Ripper Collins, Dorothy Carter beat Barbara Collins, King Curtis drew Alberto Torres, Pepper Martin beat Great Sinbad.

7/29/65 Honolulu
Ripper Collins beat Alberto Torres, Moolah & Barbara Collins beat Kathy Starr & Dorothy Carter, Enrique Torres beat Lord Blears, King Curtis drew Pepper Martin.

8/2/65 Hilo
Alberto Torres & Kathy Starr beat Ripper & Barbara Collins dq, King Curtis ddq Pepper Martin, Enrique Torres beat Russian Wolfman.

8/4/65 Honolulu
Enrique & Alberto Torres & Pepper Martin beat Ripper Collins & King Curtis & Mr. Fujiwara, Russian Wolfman beat Dean Higuchi, Bandit drew Lord Blears, Pepper Martin drew Ripper Collins.

8/11/65 Honolulu
Kinji Shibuya drew Hard Boiled Haggerty, Ray Stevens beat Bearcat Wright, King Curtis beat Jack Lanza, Enrique & Alberto Torres beat The Spoiler & Ripper Collins, Pepper Martin beat The Russian Wolfman.

8/16/65 Hilo. Att 1,200
Hard Boiled Haggerty won battle royal, Enrique & Alberto Torres beat King Curtis & Russian Wolfman, Hard Boiled Haggerty beat Pepper Martin, Ripper Collins beat Lord Blears.

8/18/65 Honolulu
Pepper Martin & Kathy Starr beat Ripper & Barbara Collins dq, King Curtis beat Alberto Torres, Enrique Torres drew The Russian Wolfman, Hard Boiled Haggerty beat Dick Steinborn.

8/25/65 Honolulu
King Curtis won battle royal, Pepper Martin drew Ripper Collins, The Bandit drew McRonald Kamaka, Lord Blears beat The Russian Wolfman, Mr. Fujiwara beat Seymour Koenig, Hard Boiled Haggerty beat Ricky Hunter.

8/30/65 Hilo. Att 1,800
Hard Boiled Haggerty beat Pepper Martin, Luther Lindsay & Johnny Kostas beat King Curtis & Ripper Collins, Lord Blears beat Russian Wolfman.

9/1/65 Honolulu
King Curtis beat Pepper Martin defended Hawaiian title, Johnny Kostas beat Ripper Collins, Luther Lindsay & Dean Higuchi beat Hard Boiled Haggerty & The Russian Wolfman, Ricky Hunter beat The Bandit.

9/8/65 Honolulu
Lord Blears beat McRonald Kamaka dq, Hard Boiled Haggerty beat Pepper Martin, Johnny Kostas beat Russian Wolfman, Luther Lindsay drew Ripper Collins, King Curtis beat Ron Reed.

9/15/65 Honolulu
King Curtis beat Hard Boiled Haggerty, Bearcat Wright & Luther Lindsay beat Pat Patterson & Ray Stevens dq, Wilbur Snyder beat Juan Sebastian, Ripper Collins beat Johnny Kostas, Pepper Martin drew Mr. Fujiwara.

9/20/65 Hilo. Att 1,500
Ripper Collins beat Pepper Martin, Luther Lindsay beat Hard Boiled Haggerty boxing, King Curtis drew Johnny Kostas, Lord Blears beat The Bandit.

9/22/65 Honolulu
King Curtis beat Johnny Kostas, Ripper Collins beat Luther Lindsay dq, Shoulders Newman beat McRonald Kamaka, Mr. Fujiwara beat Ricky Hunter, Pepper Martin beat The Bandit.

9/29/65 Honolulu
Killer Kowalski beat Pepper Martin, Bobby Graham drew Ripper Collins, Luther Lindsay beat King Curtis to win Hawaiian Title, Gil Ane drew Mr. Fujiwara, Johnny Kostas beat The Bandit dq.

10/6/65 Honolulu
Killer Kowalski beat Luther Lindsay, Ripper Collins beat Pepper Martin, King Curtis drew Bobby Graham, Johnny Kostas beat Mr. Fujiwara, The Bandit drew Lord Blears.

10/9/65 Hilo. Att 2,300
Killer Kowalski no contest Luther Lindsay, King Curtis beat Bobby Graham, Johnny Kostas beat Pepper Martin, Ripper Collins beat Lord Blears.

10/13/65 Honolulu
Luther Lindsay & Neff Maiava beat Ripper Collins & Beauregard dq, Killer Kowalski beat Bobby Graham, Johnny Kostas beat The Bandit, King Curtis beat Pepper Martin.

10/22/65 Honolulu
Killer Kowalski beat Don Leo Jonathan, King Curtis beat Pepper Gomez US title, Pat Patterson & Ray Stevens drew Luther Lindsay & Bearcat Wright, Neff Maiava beat Ripper Collins, The Alaskan beat Johnny Kostas.

10/27/65 Honolulu
King Curtis & Ripper Collins drew Luther Lindsay & Czaya Nandor, Dean Higuchi beat Mr. Fujiwara dq, Killer Kowalski beat The Alaskan, Jamaica Kid & Pancho Lopez beat Fuzzy Cupid & Sky Low Low.

11/1/65 Hilo
Pancho Lopez & Jamaica Kid beat Fuzzy Cupid & Sky Low Low, Killer Kowalski beat Czaya Nandor, Luther Lindsay beat The Alaskan.

11/3/65 Honolulu
Killer Kowalski beat King Curtis to win US title, Lord Blears & Pancho Lopez beat Ripper Collins & Sky Low Low, Joe Scarpa (Jay Strongbow) beat The Alaskan dq, Jamaica Kid beat Fuzzy Cupid, Luther Lindsay beat Czaya Nandor.

11/10/65 Honolulu
Joe Scarpa & Neff Maiava & Luther Lindsay beat Killer Kowalski & Ripper Collins & The Alaskan, Killer Kowalski drew Joe Scarpa, Czaya Nandor beat The Bandit dq, Gil Ane drew Mr. Fujiwara.

11/17/65 Honolulu
Neff Maiava beat Ripper Collins, Wilbur Snyder beat The Alaskan, Killer Kowalski beat Czaya Nandor, Luther Lindsay beat The Bandit, Joe Scarpa beat Mr. Fujiwara.

11/22/65 Hilo
Bearcat Wright beat Ripper Collins, Killer Kowalski drew Wilbur Snyder, Joe Scarpa beat The Alaskan, Luther Lindsay beat Mr. Fujiwara.

12/1/65 Honolulu
Joe Scarpa beat Killer Kowalski, Luther Lindsay & Lord Blears beat Ripper Collins & Mr. Fujiwara, The Alaskan beat Czaya Nandor, Neff Maiava beat Shoulders Newman dq.

12/6/65 Hilo
Luther Lindsay & Lord Blears beat Ripper Collins & Beauregard, Killer Kowalski dcor Red Bastien, Joe Scarpa beat The Alaskan.

12/8/65 Honolulu
Killer Kowalski beat Red Bastien, Joe Scarpa beat Gil Ane, Luther Lindsay beat The Alaskan, Ripper Collins beat Czaya Nandor, Neff Maiava beat Mr. Fujiwara.

12/15/65 Honolulu
Killer Kowalski beat Joe Scarpa defended US title, Luther Lindsay beat Mr. Fujiwara, Karl Gotch beat Kangaroo Kennedy, Ron Reed drew Beauregard, Gil Ane drew The Alaskan.

12/20/65 Hilo. Att 1,500
Killer Kowalski beat Joe Scarpa, Luther Lindsay DCOR Ron Reed, Karl Gotch beat The Alaskan, Lord Blears drew Mr. Fujiwara.

12/22/65 Honolulu
Bearcat Wright won battle royal, Killer Kowalski beat Pepper Gomez, Karl Gotch drew Joe Scarpa, Neff Maiava & Luther Lindsay beat Pat Patterson & Ray Stevens dq, Ripper Collins beat Kinji Shibuya dq, Ron Reed beat Mr. Fujiwara, Bearcat Wright beat The Alaskan.

12/29/65 Honolulu
Luther Lindsay drew Hard Boiled Haggerty, Dick Steinborn beat Ripper Collins, Nick Kozak beat The Bandit, Ron Reed beat Shoulders Newman, Joe Scarpa drew Beauregard.

1966

1/5/66 Honolulu
Nick Kozak beat Killer Kowalski to win US Championship, Ron (Buddy Colt) Reed beat Luther Lindsay to win Hawaiian Title, Joe Scarpa & Dick Steinborn beat Ripper Collins & Beauregard, Neff Maiava beat The Bandit dq.

1/10/66 Hilo
Johnny Barend no contest Nick Bockwinkel, Nick Kozak beat Ripper Collins, Beauregard beat Ron Reed COR, Joe Scarpa drew Lord Blears.

1/12/66 Honolulu
Ripper Collins drew Nick Kozak, Johnny Barend beat Ron Reed, Neff Maiava beat Joe Scarpa, Nick Bockwinkel & Lord Blears beat The Bandit & Mr. Fujiwara.

1/19/66 Honolulu
Ripper Collins beat Ron Reed, Bearcat Wright beat Johnny Barend dq, Gil Ane beat Mr. Fujiwara, Alberto Torres drew Joe Scarpa.

1/26/66 Honolulu
Neff Maiava & Nick Bockwinkel & Nick Kozak beat Ripper Collins & Johnny Barend & Beauregard, Golden Terror beat Gil Ane, Dean Higuchi drew Mr. Fujiwara, Nick Bockwinkel drew Ripper Collins.

1/31/66 Hilo
Ripper Collins & Johnny Barend beat Nick Kozak & Nick Bockwinkel, Neff Maiava beat Golden Terror dq, Lord Blears beat Beauregard dq.

2/2/66 Honolulu
Johnny Barend beat Nick Kozak to win US Title, Lord Blears & Nick Bockwinkel beat Ripper Collins & Beauregard dq, Neff Maiava drew Golden Terror (Pedro Godoy), Tosh Togo beat Dean Higuchi.

2/9/66 Honolulu
Nick Bockwinkel drew Johnny Barend, Neff Maiava & Gil Ane drew Ripper Collins & Tosh Togo, Dean Higuchi beat Golden Terror dq, Nick Kozak beat Beauregard.

2/14/66 Hilo
Tosh Togo beat Don Manoukian dq, Golden Terror drew Lord Blears, Ripper Collins & Johnny Barend beat Nick Kozak & Nick Bockwinkel COR.

2/16/66 Honolulu
Lou Thesz beat Don Manoukian dq, Golden Terror beat Nick Bockwinkel dq, Neff Maiava & Dean Higuchi drew Ripper Collins & Tosh Togo, Johnny Barend beat Nick Kozak, Ray Stevens & Pat Patterson beat Rene Goulet & Bill Watts.

2/23/66 Honolulu
Johnny Barend & Ripper Collins & Tosh Togo beat Neff Maiava & Nick Kozak & Nick Bockwinkel, Johnny Barend drew Nick Bockwinkel, Dean Higuchi drew Mr. Fujiwara, Golden Terror beat Beauregard.

3/2/66 Honolulu
Lou Thesz drew Luther Lindsay, Johnny Barend & Tosh Togo beat Lord Blears & Nick Kozak, Ripper Collins beat Golden Terror, Neff Maiava beat Shoulders Newman.

3/7/66 Hilo
Nick Kozak & Luther Lindsay beat Johnny Barend & Ripper Collins dq, Neff Maiava beat Golden Terror dq, Lord Blears drew Tosh Togo.

3/9/66 Honolulu
Neff Maiava beat Johnny Barend Samoan Death Match, Nick Kozak & Dean Higuchi beat Ripper Collins & Beauregard, Luther Lindsay beat Golden Terror dq, Shoulders Newman drew Tosh Togo.

3/16/66 Honolulu
Giant Baba drew Johnny Barend, Dale Lewis drew Luther Lindsay, Nick Kozak beat Jack Bence, Neff Maiava beat Ripper Collins dq, Gil Ane beat Golden Terror Dq.

3/23/66 Honolulu
Pat Patterson & Ray Stevens drew Ripper Collins & Johnny Barend, Dale Lewis drew Joe Scarpa, Don Manoukian drew Luther Lindsay, Nick Kozak beat Golden Terror, Bill Watts beat Kinji Shibuya dq, Neff Maiava & Dean Higuchi beat Tosh Togo & Beauregard.

3/30/66 Honolulu
Nick Kozak beat Johnny Barend, Luther Lindsay drew Tosh Togo, Neff Maiava beat Shoulders Newman, Joe Scarpa & Lord Blears drew Ripper Collins & Beauregard.

4/4/66 Hilo
Neff Maiava beat Johnny Barend Samoan Death Match, Ripper Collins & Beauregard beat Joe Scarpa & Lord Blears, Luther Lindsay drew Nick Kozak.

4/6/66 Honolulu
Missing Link Pampero Firpo beat Joe Scarpa, Mr. Fujiwara drew Tosh Togo, Luther Lindsay drew Beauregard, Nick Kozak & Pepper Gomez & Neff Maiava beat Johnny Barend & Ripper Collins & Pampero Firpo.

4/13/66 Honolulu
Johnny Barend beat Pepper Gomez to defend US Title, Joe Carollo & Don Chuy beat Ripper Collins & Beauregard, Pampero Firpo drew Nick Kozak, Tosh Togo drew Dean Higuchi.

4/18/66 Hilo
Don Chuy & Joe Carollo no contest Ripper Collins & Johnny Barend, Nick Kozak dcor Pampero Firpo, Lord Blears beat Beauregard.

4/20/66 Honolulu
Pampero Firpo drew Neff Maiava, Johnny Barend & Ripper Collins beat Nick Kozak & Dick Steinborn to defend Hawaiian Tag titles, Joe Carollo beat Beauregard, Don Chuy drew Tosh Togo.

4/27/66 Honolulu
Pat Patterson & Ray Stevens beat Johnny Barend & Ripper Collins to defend World Tag titles, Bill Watts beat Don Duffy, Don Chuy & Joe Carollo beat Pampero Firpo & Beauregard, Nick Kozak drew Cyclone Negro.

5/4/66 Honolulu
Pampero Firpo won battle royal, Ripper Collins & Johnny Barend beat Don Chuy & Joe Carollo, Sam Steamboat beat Shoulders Newman, Missing Link beat Mr. Fujiwara, Nick Kozak beat Dean Higuchi.

5/9/66 Hilo
Pampero Firpo won battle royal, Johnny Barend beat Joe Carollo, Pampero Firpo beat Beauregard, Sam Steamboat beat Ripper Collins dq, Don Chuy drew Nick Kozak.

5/11/66 Honolulu
Ripper Collins drew Sam Steamboat defended Hawaiian title, Missing Link Pampero Firpo & Neff Maiava beat Beauregard & Dean Higuchi, Nick Kozak beat Mr. Fujiwara, Johnny Barend beat Red Eagle.

5/18/66 Honolulu
Johnny Barend beat Nick Kozak defended US title, Sam Steamboat drew Masked Executioner, Ripper Collins beat Neff Maiava, Pampero Firpo beat Jim Grabmire, Red Eagle drew Mr. Fujiwara.

5/25/66 Honolulu
Pat Patterson & Ray Stevens beat Ripper Collins & Johnny Barend dq, Neff Maiava & Pampero Firpo beat Beauregard & Jim Grabmire, Cyclone Negro drew Pepper Gomez, Masked Executioner drew Red Eagle, Kinji Shibuya beat Nick Kozak.

5/30/66 Hilo
Billy Whitewolf & Red Eagle beat Ripper Collins & Beauregard, Johnny Barend drew Pampero Firpo, Masked Executioner drew Mr. Fuji.

6/1/66 Honolulu
Pampero Firpo & Neff Maiava beat Ripper Collins & Beauregard, Johnny Barend beat Billy Whitewolf COR, Red Eagle beat Kongozan dq, Lord Blears drew Masked Executioner.

6/3/66 Honolulu
Wild Bill Dromo & Ripper Collins & Johnny Barend beat Sam Steamboat & Nick Bockwinkel & Neff Maiava, Billy Whitewolf beat Killer Karl Kox, Nick Bockwinkel beat Beauregard, Kongozan beat Red Eagle.

6/8/66 Honolulu
Billy Whitewolf beat Kongozan COR, Johnny Barend & Ripper Collins beat Pampero Firpo & Neff Maiava, Red Eagle beat Beauregard, Masked Executioner drew Tosh Togo.

6/13/66 Hilo
Neff Maiava & Pampero Firpo beat Johnny Barend & Ripper Collins dq, Billy Whitewolf beat Beauregard, Masked Executioner drew Red Eagle.

6/15/66 Honolulu
Pampero Firpo beat Harry Fujiwara, Red Eagle & Billy Whitewolf & Nick Bockwinkel beat Masked Executioner & Ripper Collins & Johnny Barend, Nick Bockwinkel beat Kongozan, Beauregard drew Tosh Togo.

6/22/66 Honolulu
Pampero Firpo beat Masked Executioner, Billy Whitewolf & Red Eagle beat Johnny Barend & Ripper Collins dq, Kongozan beat Dean Higuchi, Nick Bockwinkel beat Beauregard.

6/29/66 Honolulu
Ripper Collins & Beauregard beat Kongozan & Tosh Togo dq, Johnny Barend beat Pampero Firpo, Pat Patterson & Ray Stevens beat Billy Whitewolf & Red Eagle, Jim Hady drew Masked Executioner, Gorilla Monsoon drew Nick Bockwinkel.

7/2/66 Hilo
Nick Bockwinkel & Billy Whitewolf & Red Eagle & Lord Blears beat Johnny Barend & Ripper Collins & Beauregard & Kongozan, Red Eagle beat Beauregard, Nick Bockwinkel beat Kongozan dq, Ripper Collins drew Tosh Togo.

7/3/66 Kealakekua
Ripper Collins & Beauregard drew Tosh Togo & Red Eagle, Tosh Togo beat Beauregard, Red Eagle drew Ripper Collins.

7/3/66 Naalehu
Nick Bockwinkel & Billy Whitewolf beat Kongozan & Johnny Barend, Billy Whitewolf beat Kongozan, Johnny Barend drew Nick Bockwinkel.

7/4/66 Kapaau
Lord Blears & Billy Whitewolf beat Kongozan & Johnny Barend, Billy Whitewolf beat Kongozan, Johnny Barend drew Nick Bockwinkel.

7/6/66 Honolulu
Ripper Collins beat Billy Whitewolf, Nick Bockwinkel & Sam Steamboat drew Johnny Barend & Beauregard, Red Eagle beat Tosh Togo dq, Kongozan beat Tony Shepard.

7/13/66 Honolulu
Ripper Collins & Johnny Barend & Bill Dromo beat Sam Steamboat & Nick Bockwinkel & Neff Maiava, Kongozan beat Red Eagle, Billy Whitewolf beat Karl Kox, Nick Bockwinkel beat Beauregard.

7/20/66 Honolulu
Ripper Collins beat Kongozan dq, Johnny Barend drew Nick Bockwinkel, Billy Whitewolf & Red Eagle beat Bill Dromo & Karl Kox dq, Sam Steamboat beat Beauregard.

7/25/66 Hilo
Johnny Barend & Ripper Collins - no contest Ray Stevens & Pat Patterson, Billy Whitewolf beat Bill Dromo dq, Nick Bockwinkel beat Tony Shepard, Beauregard drew Lord Blears.

7/27/66 Honolulu
Johnny Barend & Ripper Collins & Gorilla Monsoon beat Ray Stevens & Pat Patterson & Haystack Calhoun, Sam Steamboat drew Bill Dromo, Nick Bockwinkel beat Butch Hoffman, Billy Whitewolf & Red Eagle beat Tosh Togo & Kongozan, Neff Maiava beat Beauregard.

8/1/66 Hilo
Haystacks Calhoun won battle royal, Billy Whitewolf beat Beauregard, Lord Blears drew Ripper Collins, Sam Steamboat beat Mongolian Stomper dq, Bill Dromo drew Nick Bockwinkel.

8/3/66 Honolulu
Haystacks Calhoun won battle royal, Ripper Collins beat Nick Bockwinkel Mongolian Stomper beat Dean Higuchi, Johnny Barend beat Red Eagle, Sam Steamboat beat Duke Savage, Neff Maiava drew Bill Dromo.

8/10/66 Honolulu
Johnny Barend drew Nick Bockwinkel defended US championship, Mongolian Stomper beat Red Eagle, Billy Whitewolf beat Bill Dromo, Sam Steamboat & Kongozan beat Ripper Collins & Beauregard.

8/15/66 Hilo
Billy Whitewolf beat Ripper Collins Indian Death Match, Nick Bockwinkel & Lord Blears beat Johnny Barend & Beauregard, Kongozan dcor Mongolian Stomper.

8/17/66 Honolulu
Johnny Barend & Bill Dromo & Mongolian Stomper & Ripper Collins drew Billy Whitewolf & Neff Maiava & Nick Bockwinkel & Kongozan, Mongolian Stomper drew Sam Steamboat, Billy Whitewolf beat Beauregard, Bill Dromo beat Red Eagle.

8/20/66 Kailua.
Neff Maiava beat Bill Dromo, Beauregard drew Lord Blears, Johnny Barend & Ripper Collins no contest Sam Steamboat & Nick Bockwinkel, Kathy Starr beat Barbara Baker, Billy Whitewolf beat Mongolian Stomper.

8/20/66 Honolulu. Different Promotion Ran Only This Card
Jim Grabmire beat Fidel Grimo, Bruce Kirk drew Gorgeous George Jr, Assassins beat Tito Montez & Ray Gordon, Arman Hussian beat Don Arnold dq.

8/24/66 Honolulu
Neff Maiava beat Ripper Collins to win Hawaii Title, Johnny Barend & Beauregard beat Kongozan & Charlie Kalani, Billy Whitewolf beat Duke Savage, Nick Bockwinkel drew Mongolian Stomper, Sam Steamboat drew Bill Dromo.

8/31/66 Honolulu
Billy Whitewolf beat Johnny Barend Indian Death Match, Ray Stevens & Pat Patterson beat Kinji Shibuya & Cyclone Negro - World Tag Match, Kongozan beat Ripper Collins Judo style match, Beauregard drew Charlie Kalani, Neff Maiava beat Duke Savage, Bill Dromo & Mongolian Stomper beat Sam Steamboat & Nick Bockwinkel.

9/3/66 Hilo
Johnny Barend & Ripper Collins & Beauregard beat Nick Bockwinkel & Billy Whitewolf & Mongolian Stomper, Kongozan beat Bill Dromo, Beauregard drew Lord Blears.

9/7/66 Honolulu
Johnny Barend beat Neff Maiava, Nick Bockwinkel & Mongolian Stomper drew Ripper Collins & Beauregard, Bill Dromo drew Kongozan, Billy Whitewolf beat Shoulders Newman.

9/14/66 Honolulu
Mongolian Stomper drew Johnny Barend, Ripper Collins & Beauregard drew Billy Whitewolf & Kongozan, Bill Dromo beat Dean Higuchi, Nick Bockwinkel drew Shoulders Newman.

9/21/66 Honolulu
Ray Stevens & Pat Patterson & Billy Whitewolf beat Johnny Barend & Ripper Collins & Gorilla Monsoon, Hard Boiled Haggerty drew Mongolian Stomper, Bobo Brazil beat Bill Dromo, Kathy Starr beat Jeannie O'Brien defended US title, Karl Gotch drew Kongozan.

9/26/66 Hilo
Johnny Barend beat Mongolian Stomper Texas Death Match, Kathy Starr beat Jeanine O'Brien, Nick Bockwinkel & Billy Whitewolf beat Ripper Collins & Beauregard.

9/28/66 Honolulu
Johnny Barend beat Kongozan dq, Ripper Collins & Barbara Collins beat Billy Whitewolf & Jeannie O'Brien, Karl Gotch beat Beauregard, Mongolian Stomper drew Bill Dromo.

10/5/66 Honolulu
Johnny Barend beat Nick Bockwinkel defended US title, Missing Link Pampero Firpo beat Bill Dromo, Mongolian Stomper drew Kongozan, Ripper Collins & Beauregard beat Karl Gotch & Billy Whitewolf dq.

10/12/66 Honolulu
Pampero Firpo beat Ripper Collins, Johnny Barend & Mighty Atlas beat Karl Gotch & Mongolian Stomper, Billy Whitewolf beat Bill Dromo, Beauregard drew Kongozan.

10/14/66 Hilo
Billy Whitewolf beat Johnny Barend, Karl Gotch & Lord Blears beat Ripper Collins & Beauregard dq, Neff Maiava beat Mighty Atlas.

10/19/66 Honolulu
Pat Patterson & Ray Stevens beat Victor Rivera & Pepper Gomez, Ripper Collins beat Neff Maiava to win Hawaiian title, Pampero Firpo beat Johnny Barend, Karl Gotch & Billy Whitewolf drew Tarzan Tyler & Beauregard, Kongozan drew Mighty Atlas, Mongolian Stomper beat Dan Miller.

10/26/66 Honolulu
Johnny Barend & Ripper Collins & Mighty Atlas beat Jim Hady & Billy Whitewolf & Kongozan, Jim Hady beat Tony Shepard, Karl Gotch drew Shoulders Newman, Pampero Firpo beat Beauregard.

10/31/66 Hilo
Johnny Barend & Ripper Collins beat Pampero Firpo & Neff Maiava dq, Billy Whitewolf beat Mighty Atlas, Beauregard drew Karl Gotch.

11/2/66 Honolulu
Neff Maiava & Pampero Firpo beat Ripper Collins & Johnny Barend to win Hawaiian tag titles, Kongozan beat Mighty Atlas dq, Jim Hady beat Beauregard, Billy Whitewolf drew Karl Gotch.

11/9/66 Honolulu
Jim Hady beat Ripper Collins, Karl Gotch drew Mike Paidousis, Johnny Barend beat Neff Maiava, Pampero Firpo beat Mighty Atlas, Billy Whitewolf beat Beauregard.

11/16/66 Honolulu
Jim Hady beat Cry Baby Cannon, Beauregard & Johnny Barend beat Billy Whitewolf & Bob Boyer, Pampero Firpo beat Fritz Von Goering, Karl Gotch beat Mighty Atlas, Neff Maiava drew Iron Mike Paidousis.

11/21/66 Hilo
Pampero Firpo & Karl Gotch & Billy Whitewolf drew Johnny Barend & Ripper Collins & Man Mountain Cannon & Mike Paidousis, Billy Whitewolf ddq Johnny Barend, Jim Hady beat Mike Paidousis, Pampero Firpo beat Man Mountain Cannon, Karl Gotch drew Ripper Collins.

11/23/66 Honolulu
Ripper Collins beat Karl Gotch dq, Johnny Barend beat Bob Boyer, Pampero Firpo beat Man Mountain Cannon, Billy Whitewolf beat Mike Paidousis, Jim Hady beat Mighty Atlas.

11/30/66 Honolulu
Johnny Barend beat Pampero Firpo, Bill Watts drew Ripper Collins, Billy Whitewolf & Cry Baby Cannon beat The Mighty Atlas & Beauregard, Karl Gotch beat Sonny Meyers, Tarzan Tyler & Cyclone Negro drew Pepper Gomez & Jim Hady, Johnny Valentine beat Mike Paidousis.

12/7/66 Honolulu
Jim Hady & Billy Whitewolf & Karl Gotch beat Johnny Barend & Ripper Collins & Skull Murphy dq, Mighty Atlas drew Lord Blears, Beauregard beat Tony Shepard, Jim Hady drew Ripper Collins, Pampero Firpo beat Golden Terror dq.

12/14/66 Honolulu
Billy Whitewolf beat Johnny Barend Indian Death Match, Ripper Collins beat Mr. Fujiwara, Karl Gotch & Pampero Firpo beat Mighty Atlas & Beauregard, Jim Hady beat Skull Murphy.

12/19/66 Hilo
Jim Hady & Billy Whitewolf & Ripper Collins beat Johnny Barend & Beauregard & Mr. Fujiwara, Karl Gotch no contest Pampero Firpo, Jim Hady beat Beauregard, Billy Whitewolf drew Mr. Fujiwara.

12/21/66 Honolulu
Ripper Collins drew Billy Whitewolf defended Hawaiian title, Johnny Barend beat Karl Gotch, Pampero Firpo & Neff Maiava beat Mighty Atlas & Beauregard, Jim Hady beat Mr. Fujiwara.

12/28/66 Honolulu
Johnny Barend beat Ripper Collins dq, Pat Patterson & Ray Stevens beat Pampero Firpo & Jim Hady, Billy Whitewolf dcor Cyclone Negro, Karl Gotch drew Tarzan Tyler, Beauregard drew Mr. Fuji, Kongozan & Neff Maiava beat Mighty Atlas & Steve Stanlee.

1967

1/4/67 Honolulu
Jim Hady won battle royal, Ripper Collins beat Kongozan, Jim Hady & Eddie Morrow beat Beauregard & Harry Fujiwara, Neff Maiava drew Steve Stanlee, Pampero Firpo beat Shoulder Newman dq, Hans Mortier beat Mighty Atlas.

1/11/67 Honolulu
Johnny Barend beat Jim Hady dq boxing match, Hans Mortier beat Nick Bockwinkel, Eddie Morrow beat Kongozan dq, Karl Gotch beat Beauregard, Pampero Firpo drew Ripper Collins, Billy Whitewolf beat Steve Stanlee.

1/16/67 Hilo
Ripper Collins beat Johnny Barend, Hans Mortier beat Karl Gotch dq, Pampero Firpo beat Beauregard, Eddie Morrow drew Jim Hady.

1/18/67 Honolulu
Johnny Barend beat Billy Whitewolf, Hans Mortier beat Pampero Firpo, Jim Hady & Eddie Morrow beat Ripper Collins & Steve Stanlee, Karl Gotch drew Kongozan.

1/25/67 Honolulu
Hans Mortier drew Jim Hady, Ray Stevens & Pat Patterson & Ripper Collins beat Johnny Barend & Bill Watts & Cyclone Negro, Missing Link Pampero Firpo & Eddie Morrow beat Kongozan & Steve Stanlee, Karl Gotch beat Tosh Togo, Billy Whitewolf drew Beauregard.

2/1/67 Honolulu
Hans Mortier & Johnny Barend beat Neff Maiava & Pampero Firpo - Hawaiian titles, Jim Hady beat Steve Stanlee, Karl Gotch & Eddie Morrow drew Jim Hady & Steve Stanlee, Ripper Collins lost Beauregard - not getting 2 falls in 30 minutes

2/8/67 Honolulu
Jim Hady beat Johnny Barend, Masked Executioner beat Steve Stanlee, Ripper Collins drew Tosh Togo, Hans Mortier beat Dean Higuchi, Eddie Morrow beat Kongozan.

2/15/67 Honolulu
Ripper Collins beat Eddie Morrow to defend Hawaiian title, King Curtis beat Kongozan, Karl Gotch beat Masked Executioner, Johnny Barend & Hans Mortier beat Steve Stanlee & Jim Hady.

2/20/67 Hilo. Att 1,000
Jim Hady won battle royal, Ripper Collins beat Han Mortier, King Curtis beat Karl Gotch, Johnny Barend beat Jim Hady dq, Lord Blears drew Masked Executioner (Vic Christy).

2/22/67 Honolulu
King Curtis beat Karl Gotch, Ripper Collins beat McRonald Kamaka, Mr. Fujiwara beat Johnny Barend dq, Jim Hady beat Kongozan, Eddie Morrow drew Hans Mortier.

3/1/67 Honolulu
King Curtis beat Johnny Barend to win US title, Ray Stevens & Pat Patterson beat Jim Hady & Eddie Morrow to defend World Tag titles, Masked Executioner & Beauregard drew Kongozan & Tosh Togo, Karl Gotch drew Skull Murphy, Ripper Collins beat Cyclone Negro.

3/8/67 Honolulu
Jim Hady drew Karl Gotch, Hans Mortier beat Masked Executioner, Ripper Collins beat Beauregard, King Curtis beat Eddie Morrow, Johnny Barend beat Kongozan.

3/15/67 Honolulu
Jim Hady beat Ripper Collins to win Hawaiian title, King Curtis beat Masked Executioner, Johnny Barend beat Dean Higuchi, Paul Diamond beat Kongozan, Karl Gotch drew Hans Mortier.

3/20/66 Hilo. Att 1,200
Jim Hady beat Johnny Barend lumberjack match, Paul Diamond beat Ripper Collins dq, Karl Gotch beat Beauregard, King Curtis drew Hans Mortier.

3/22/67 Honolulu
Johnny Barend & Hans Mortier beat Nick Bockwinkel & Paul Diamond to defend tag titles, King Curtis drew Jim Hady, Ripper Collins beat Kongozan, Karl Gotch beat Beauregard.

3/29/67 Honolulu
Ray Stevens & Pat Patterson beat Missing Link Pampero Firpo & Nick Bockwinkel to defend World Tag titles, King Curtis drew Johnny Barend defended US title, Kongozan & Karl Gotch beat Beauregard & Ugly American (Don Duffy), Mongolian Stomper beat Jim Hady, Ripper Collins drew Hans Mortier, Paul Diamond beat Cyclone Negro dq.

4/5/67 Honolulu
Beauregard & Johnny Barend & Hans Mortier beat Paul Diamond & Jim Hady & Nick Bockwinkel, King Curtis & Ripper Collins beat Karl Gotch & Dean Higuchi, Dean Higuchi drew Mr. Fujiwara, Nick Bockwinkel beat Kongozan.

4/12/67 Honolulu
Johnny Barend & Beauregard beat King Curtis & Mr. Fujiwara, Jim Hady beat Don Duffy, Hans Mortier beat Nick Bockwinkel, Paul Diamond drew Dory Funk Jr, Karl Gotch drew Kongozan.

4/17/67 Hilo
King Curtis beat Johnny Barend COR, Jim Hady beat Ripper Collins, Hans Mortier & Beauregard drew Lord Blears & Paul Diamond.

4/19/67 Honolulu
King Curtis beat Dory Funk Jr, Jim Hady beat Tojo Yamamoto, Karl Gotch & Paul Diamond drew Hans Mortier & Beauregard, Johnny Barend beat Ripper Collins.

4/26/67 Honolulu
Beauregard beat Harry Fujiwara, Karl Gotch beat Kongozan, Johnny Barend & Hans Mortier drew Pepper Gomez & Pedro Morales, Mongolian Stomper & Cyclone Negro beat Ray Stevens & Ripper Collins, King Curtis beat Jim Hady.

5/3/67 Honolulu
King Curtis & Ripper Collins beat Johnny Barend & Hans Mortier to win Hawaiian tag titles, Beauregard drew Kongozan, Karl Gotch drew Paul Diamond, Jim Hady beat Tosh Togo.

5/10/67 Honolulu
Jim Hady drew Ripper Collins to defend Hawaiian title, King Curtis beat Paul Diamond, Karl Gotch & Beauregard drew Mr. Fujiwara & Kongozan, Johnny Barend beat Hans Mortier.

5/15/67 Hilo
Jim Hady beat King Curtis Pier 9 brawl, Ripper Collins beat Johnny Barend Texas Death Match, Lord Blears & Beauregard beat Hans Mortier & Kongozan.

5/17/67 Honolulu
Johnny Barend & Jim Hady beat King Curtis & Ripper Collins cage match, Pampero Firpo & Lord Blears beat Hans Mortier & Beauregard, Karl Gotch drew George Drake, Kongozan beat Paul Diamond.

5/24/67 Honolulu
Ripper Collins won battle royal, Ripper Collins drew George Drake, Hans Mortier beat Dean Higuchi, Baby Blimp beat Paul Diamond, Johnny Barend beat Mr. Fujiwara, Jim Hady beat Kongozan.

5/31/67 Honolulu
Jim Hady beat Hans Mortier, King Curtis beat Baby Blimp, Johnny Barend beat Paul Diamond, Billy Whitewolf drew Ripper Collins, Beauregard drew George Drake.

6/7/67 Honolulu
Ripper Collins beat Lord Blears, Jim Hady & Johnny Barend beat Hans Mortier & Baby Blimp, King Curtis beat Kongozan, Billy Whitewolf beat Beauregard.

6/14/67 Honolulu
King Curtis & Ripper Collins beat Johnny Barend & Jim Hady to defend Hawaiian tag titles, Ernie Ladd beat Hans Mortier dq, Nick Kozak beat Skull Murphy, Billy Whitewolf drew Baby Blimp, George Drake drew Mr. Fujiwara.

6/21/67 Honolulu
Johnny Barend beat Hans Mortier, Jim Hady beat Baby Blimp, Billy Whitewolf & Little Beaver & Jamaica Kid beat Ripper Collins & Fuzzy Cupid & Little Brutus, King Curtis beat George Drake, Nick Kozak beat Beauregard.

6/28/67 Honolulu
King Curtis beat Don Leo Jonathan to defend US title, Johnny Barend & Jim Hady beat Mr. Fujiwara & Baby Blimp, Beauregard drew George Drake, Billy Whitewolf & Nick Kozak drew Ripper Collins & Hans Mortier.

7/5/67 Honolulu
Ray Stevens drew Pepper Gomez, Billy Whitewolf & Nick Kozak beat Rip Miller & Art Neilson, Cyclone Negro drew Baby Blimp, Kongozan beat Beauregard judo match, Hans Mortier drew George Drake.

7/12/67 Honolulu
King Curtis & Ripper Collins beat Dick Steinborn & George Drake, Johnny Barend & Jim Hady beat Hans Mortier & Dutch Schultz, Nick Kozak beat Beauregard, Billy Whitewolf beat The Baby Blimp Indian Death Lock Match.

7/19/67 Honolulu
Jim Hady beat Pat Patterson dq defended Hawaiian Title, Johnny Barend dcor Dutch Schultz, King Curtis beat Eric Frolich, Nick Kozak & Billy Whitewolf beat Ripper Collins & Hans Mortier.

7/20/67 Hilo
Johnny Barend beat Pat Patterson, Nick Kozak & Billy Whitewolf beat King Curtis & Ripper Collins, Dutch Schultz drew Jim Hady.

7/26/67 Honolulu
Johnny Barend beat Ripper Collins boxing, King Curtis beat Nick Kozak, Jim Hady drew Dutch Schultz, Billy Whitewolf beat Hans Mortier, Eric Frolich beat Beauregard.

8/3/67 Honolulu
Billy Whitewolf beat King Curtis Indian Death Match, Ray Stevens & Pat Patterson beat Johnny Barend & Jim Hady dq, Ripper Collins drew Pat O'Conner, Nick Kozak & Eric Frolich beat Kurt & Karl Von Stroheim, Pedro Morales beat Hans Mortier, Dutch Shultz beat Beauregard.

8/9/67 Honolulu
King Curtis & Ripper Collins & Dutch Schultz beat Johnny Barend & Jim Hady & Lord Blears, Dutch Shultz drew Nick Kozak, Ripper Collins beat Eric Frolich, Billy Whitewolf beat Mr. Fujiwara, Kathy Starr beat Jessica Rodgers defended US Woman's Title.

8/9/67 Hilo
Johnny Barend & Jim Hady beat Dutch Schultz & King Curtis, Jessica Rogers drew Kathy Starr, Eric Frolich drew Nick Kozak.

8/16/67 Honolulu
Johnny Barend & Jim Hady beat Billy Whitewolf & Nick Kozak, King Curtis beat Kongozan, Ripper Collins beat Beauregard, Dutch Schultz & Jessica Rodgers beat Kathy Starr & Eric Frolich.

8/23/67 Honolulu
Ripper Collins beat Johnny Barend brass knuckles match, Jim Hady beat David Schultz defended Hawaiian title, Nick Kozak & Eric Frolich beat King Curtis & Tank Morgan.

8/30/67 Hilo
Haystacks Calhoun & Jim Hady beat King Curtis & Dutch Schultz, Johnny Barend ddq Ripper Collins, Mr. Fujiwara beat Lord Blears.

8/31/67 Honolulu
Haystacks Calhoun won battle royal, Jim Hady & Johnny Barend beat Masked Enforcers defended Hawaiian tag titles, Ripper Collins beat Kongozan, Tank Morgan drew Dutch Schultz, Ray Stevens & Pat Patterson beat Eric Frolich & Dutch Schultz.

9/6/67 Honolulu
Jim Hady & Johnny Barend & Haystacks Calhoun beat King Curtis & Ripper Collins & Dutch Schultz, Bill Watts beat Mr. Fujiwara, Tank Morgan beat Nick Kozak, Eric Frolich beat Catalina Drake, Haystacks Calhoun beat Johnny Barend dq.

9/13/67 Honolulu
King Curtis beat Bill Watts, Johnny Barend & Jim Hady beat Ripper Collins & Dutch Schultz.

9/20/67 Honolulu
Billy Whitewolf drew Dutch Schultz, Johnny Barend beat Eric Frolich, Jim Hady beat Tank Morgan.

9/27/67 Honolulu
Ray Stevens & Pat Patterson drew Nick Kozak & Billy Whitewolf world tag titles, King Curtis & Dutch Schultz beat Johnny Barend & Jim Hady, Eric Frolich beat Great Malenko, Ripper Collins drew Pepper Gomez, Tank Morgan beat Tiger Andrews.

10//4/67 Honolulu
Nick Kozak & Billy Whitewolf beat Ripper Collins & Tank Morgan, Jim Hady beat Dutch Schultz, Eric Frolich beat Kongozan, Nick Kozak beat Mr. Fujiwara.

10/11/67 Honolulu
David Schultz & Ripper Collins beat Billy Whitewolf & Nick Kozak, Jim Hady beat Tank Morgan, Eric Frolich beat Mr. Fujiwara, Darling Dagmar beat Diamond Lil.

10/18/67 Honolulu
Ray Stevens & Pat Patterson beat King Curtis & Dutch Schultz dq, Nick Bockwinkel & Jim Hady beat The Enforcers, (Clyde Steeves & Bad Boy Shields) Billy Whitewolf beat Fritz Von Goering, Angelo Poffo beat Nick Kozak, Dory Funk Jr. beat Kongozan, Victor the Bear beat Ripper Collins.

10/19/67 Hilo
Angelo Poffo drew Nick Kozak, Victor The Bear beat Dutch Schultz, Jim Hady beat Tank Morgan, Billy Whitewolf drew King Curtis.

10/25/67 Honolulu
Victor The Bear beat Tank Morgan & Dutch Shultz, Jim Hady & Nick Kozak beat The Alaskan and King Curtis by dq, Nick Bockwinkel beat Kongozan, Billy Whitewolf beat Tank Morgan, Angelo Poffo beat Eric Frolich.

11/15/67 Honolulu
Jim Hady beat Dutch Shultz to defend Hawaiian title, Johnny Barend & Nick Bockwinkel beat King Curtis & The Alaskan, Billy Whitewolf beat Killer Kowalski, Kongozan drew Shoulders Newman, Angelo Poffo drew Lord Blears.

11/22/67 Honolulu
Billy Whitewolf & Jim Hady & Johnny Barend beat Kinji Shibuya & Killer Kowalski & Angelo Poffo, The Alaskan beat Frank Allman, King Curtis drew Nick Bockwinkel, Billy Whitewolf drew Dutch Schultz.

11/27/67 Hilo Att 1,825
Johnny Barend & Jim Hady beat Ray Stevens & Pat Patterson, Art Thomas beat King Curtis dq, Killer Kowalski beat Nick Bockwinkel, Billy Whitewolf beat Angelo Poffo dq, Dutch Schultz drew Kinji Shibuya.

11/29/67 Honolulu
Jim Hady & Johnny Barend beat Dutch Schultz & King Curtis to win tag titles, Kinji Shibuya beat Beauregard, Ripper Collins beat The Alaskan, Billy Whitewolf & Nick Bockwinkel beat Ray Stevens & Pat Patterson dq, Sailor Art Thomas & Bearcat Wright drew Angelo Poffo & Killer Kowalski.

12/6/67 Honolulu
Billy Whitewolf beat King Curtis, Jim Hady & Johnny Barend drew Ripper Collins & Dutch Schultz, Angelo Poffo beat Beauregard, Kinji Shibuya beat The Alaskan, Killer Kowalski beat Nick Bockwinkel.

12/13/67 Honolulu
Johnny Barend & Jim Hady beat Killer Kowalski & Angelo Poffo dq, King Curtis & Ripper Collins beat Billy Whitewolf & Nick Bockwinkel, Dutch Schultz beat The Alaskan, Kinji Shibuya beat Frank Allman

12/20/67 Honolulu
Jim Hady won battle royal, Nick Bockwinkel & Victor Rivera drew Ripper Collins & Dutch Schultz, Jim Hady beat Beauregard, Billy Whitewolf drew Kinji Shibuya, Fred Blassie beat Nick Kozak, Johnny Barend beat The Alaskan.

12/25/67 Honolulu. Att 8,000
Johnny Barend beat King Curtis (Paul Boesch ref), Giant Baba beat Dutch Schultz dq, Kinji Shibuya & Ripper Collins beat Victor Rivera & Pepper Gomez, Fred Blassie beat Billy Whitewolf, Cyclone Negro beat Nick Kozak, Jim Hady beat The Alaskan, Angelo Poffo drew Nick Bockwinkel.

12/27/67 Hilo
Angleo Poffo & Ripper Collins & Fred Blassie beat Johnny Barend & Jim Hady & Victor Rivera, Johnny Barend dcor Kinji Shibuya, Lord Blears beat Dutch Schultz dq, Victor Rivera beat Ripper Collins.

1968

1/3/68 Honolulu
Kinji Shibuya beat Jim Hady, Johnny Barend beat Nick Bockwinkel Ripper Collins & Dutch Schultz drew Tony Nero & Lord Blears, Angelo Poffo beat Beauregard.

1/10/68 Honolulu
Pampero Firpo & Neff Maiava & Jim Hady beat Angelo Poffo & Killer Kowalski & Kinji Shibuya, Tosh Togo drew Ripper Collins, Johnny Barend beat Dean (Ho) Higuchi, Dutch Schultz beat Frankie Allman.

1/17/68 Honolulu
Jim Hady beat Johnny Barend, Killer Kowalski & Angelo Poffo drew Pepper Gomez & Pedro Morales, Fred Blassie & Ripper Collins drew Pampero Firpo & Neff Maiava, Kinji Shibuya drew Larry Williams, Bearcat Wright drew Dutch Schultz.

1/22/68 Hilo
Pampero Firpo & Jim Hady & Neff Maiava beat Johnny Barend & Killer Kowalski & Angelo Poffo, Lord Blears beat Ripper Collins dq, Jim Hady beat Angelo Poffo, Killer Kowalski drew Neff Maiava.

1/23/68 Maui
Johnny Barend & Ripper Collins & Killer Kowalski beat Pampero Firpo & Jim Hady & Neff Maiava, Angelo Poffo beat Lord Blears, Neff Maiava drew Ripper Collins, Jim Hady no contest Killer Kowalski.

1/24/68 Honolulu
Ripper Collins & Johnny Barend beat Pampero Firpo & Neff Maiava, Angelo Poffo & Killer Kowalski beat Jack Carson & Dean Higuchi, Kinji Shibuya beat Frankie Allman, Jim Hady beat Dutch Schultz.

1/31/68 Honolulu
Jim Hady beat Kinji Shibuya, Ripper Collins & Johnny Barend beat Tosh Togo & Jack Carson, Pampero Firpo beat Angelo Poffo, Killer Kowalski drew Neff Maiava.

2/7/68 Honolulu
Ripper Collins & Johnny Barend & King Curtis beat Karl Gotch & Ken Hollis & Ricky Hunter, Jim Hady drew Angelo Poffo, Killer Kowalski drew Pampero Firpo, Bill Miller beat Jack Carson.

2/12/68 Hilo
Jim Hady beat Johnny Barend, King Curtis drew Pampero Firpo, Killer Kowalski beat Bill Miller, Ripper Collins beat Ken Hollis, Angelo Poffo beat Jack Carson.

2/13/68 Maui
Jim Hady beat Ripper Collins, Bill Miller beat King Curtis dq, Johnny Barend beat Jack Carson, Killer Kowalski drew Pampero Firpo, Angelo Poffo drew Ken Hollis.

2/14/68 Honolulu
Jim Hady beat Bill Miller, Ripper Collins & Johnny Barend beat Ken Hollis & Jack Carson, Pampero Firpo beat Killer Kowalski dq, King Curtis beat Rick Hunter, Karl Gotch drew Angelo Poffo.

2/21/68 Honolulu
Pampero Firpo & Jim Hady beat Ripper Collins & Johnny Barend to win tag titles, Killer Kowalski drew Pepper Gomez, Bearcat Wright & Art Thomas beat King Curtis & Fred Blassie, Lord Blears drew Mr. Fuji, Angelo Poffo beat Alberto Amessa.

2/28/68 Honolulu
King Curtis beat Jim Hady to win Hawaiian title.

3/6/68 Honolulu
Johnny Barend & Ripper Collins beat Jim Hady & The Missing Link Pampero Firpo in a Pier 9 Brawl, Killer Kowalski beat Rick Hunter, King Curtis beat Ken Hollis, Peter Maivia beat Angelo Poffo.

3/13/68 Honolulu
Pampero Firpo beat Ripper Collins - Hair match, King Curtis drew Killer Kowalski, Johnny Barend beat Ken Hollis, Peter Maivia beat Mr. Fuji, Jim Hady beat Angelo Poffo.

3/20/68 Honolulu
King Curtis drew Pampero Firpo, Johnny Barend beat Bearcat Wright, Ripper Collins & Ray Stevens beat Pepper Gomez & Hahn Lee, Jim Hady beat Fritz Von Goering, Peter Maivia & Neff Maiava beat Killer Kowalski & Angelo Poffo.

3/27/68 Honolulu
Peter Maivia won battle royal, Peter Maivia beat Harley Race, Giant Baba beat King Curtis dq, Jim Hady beat Don Duffy, Ripper Collins drew Neff Maiava.

4/3/68 Honolulu
Peter Maivia & Neff Maiava beat Johnny Barend & King Curtis, Jim Hady beat Tosh Togo, Ripper Collins drew Pampero Firpo, Jerry London beat Ricky Hunter.

4/8/68 Hilo Att 2,256
Joyce Grable & Pat Sherry beat Bette Boucher & Fabulous Moolah, Peter Maivia beat King Curtis, Jim Hady beat Johnny Barend dq, Bette Boucher beat Pat Sherry.

4/10/68 Honolulu
Peter Maivia beat Jerry London, Ripper Collins beat Frankie Allman, King Curtis & Johnny Barend drew Jim Hady & The Missing Link Pampero Firpo, Joyce Grable & Pat Sherry beat Fabulous Moolah & Betty Boucher dq.

4/17/68 Honolulu
Peter Maivia beat Ripper Collins, Johnny Barend & King Curtis drew Neff Maiava & Pampero Firpo, Jim Hady beat Kongozan, Mr. Fuji drew Jerry London.

4/24/68 Honolulu
Jim Hady beat Johnny Barend for US title, Peter Maivia beat King Curtis dq, Ray Stevens drew Bearcat Wright, Neff Maiava & Pampero Firpo drew Ripper Collins & Kinji Shibuya, Pepper Gomez beat Jerry London.

5/1/68 Honolulu
Billy Whitewolf & Jim Hady & Pampero Firpo beat King Curtis & Johnny Barend & Reggie Parks, Peter Maivia & Neff Maiava beat Ripper Collins & Kongozan, Dean Higuchi drew Jerry London.

5/8/68 Honolulu
Pampero Firpo drew Ripper Collins - dcor, Billy Whitewolf & Jim Hady drew King Curtis & Johnny Barend, Peter Maivia beat Kongozan, Neff Maiava beat Jerry London.

5/15/68 Honolulu
Ray Stevens beat Jim Hady US Title, Ripper Collins & King Curtis & Johnny Barend beat Peter Maivia & Neff Maiava & Pampero Firpo elimination match, Bearcat Wright drew Kinji Shibuya, Pedro Morales beat Harry Fujiwara, Billy Whitewolf beat Jerry London.

5/22/68 Honolulu
Jim Hady & Peter Maivia beat King Curtis & Ripper Collins to win Hawaiian tag titles, Pampero Firpo beat Kongozan, Billy Whitewolf beat Tosh Togo, Neff Maiava beat Mr. Fuji.

5/29/68 Honolulu
King Curtis drew Billy Whitewolf, Jim Hady beat Ripper Collins, Peter Maivia & Pampero Firpo beat Tosh Togo & Mr. Fuji, Little Beaver & Joey Russell beat Sky Low Low & Cowboy Bradley.

6/3/68 Hilo Att 1,500
Little Beaver & Joey Russell beat Little Brutus & Sky Low Low, Peter Maivia beat Ripper Collins dq, Billy Whitewolf drew King Curtis.

6/4/68 Maui
Neff Maiava beat Ripper Collins dq, Billy Whitewolf beat King Curtis dq, Little Beaver & Joey Russell beat Little Brutus & Sky Low Low.

6/5/68 Honolulu
Jim Hady beat Killer Karl Kox, King Curtis beat Pampero Firpo, Peter Maivia beat Mr. Fuji, Billy Whitewolf & Little Beaver beat Ripper Collins & Sky Low Low.

6/12/68 Honolulu
Jim Hady beat Ray Stevens to win US Championship, King Curtis drew Peter Maivia, Mr. Fuji beat Neff Maiava, Magnificent Maurice beat Pampero Firpo, Pedro Morales beat Pat Patterson, Ripper Collins beat Hahn Lee, Billy Whitewolf beat Killer Karl Kox.

6/19/68 Honolulu
Billy Whitewolf beat Ripper Collins chain match, Peter Maivia beat Killer Karl Kox, Jim Hady & Dean Higuchi beat Magnificent Maurice & Mr. Fuji, King Curtis beat Samoan Meatoga.

6/24/68 Hilo. Att 1,000
Jim Hady & Billy Whitewolf beat King Curtis & Ripper Collins COR, Peter Maivia beat Magnificent Maurice dq, Lord Blears drew Mr. Fuji.

6/26/68 Honolulu
Billy Whitewolf & Peter Maivia beat Ripper Collins & King Curtis to win Hawaiian tag titles, Jim Hady beat John Bull, Magnificent Maurice beat Ricky Hunter, Mr. Fuji drew Lord Blears.

7/3/68 Honolulu
Jim Hady drew Gene Kiniski NWA title, Magnificent Maurice beat Dino Lanza, Billy Whitewolf beat John Bull, Pepper Gomez & Pedro Morales beat Ripper Collins & Fred Blassie, King Curtis beat John Tolos, Ray Stevens drew Peter Maivia.

7/10/68 Honolulu
Ripper Collins beat King Curtis, Neff Maiava beat Ricky Hunter, Peter Maivia beat John Bull, Jim Hady & Billy Whitewolf beat Magnificent Maurice & Mr. Fuji.

7/17/68 Honolulu
Magnificent Maurice & Johnny Barend beat Billy Whitewolf & Peter Maivia to win Hawaiian tag titles, Ripper Collins drew Jim Hady, King Curtis beat Ricky Hunter, John Bull beat Frankie Allman.

7/24/68 Honolulu
Jim Hady won battle royal, Magnificent Maurice & Johnny Barend beat Ricky Hunter & Neff Maiava, Ripper Collins drew Bearcat Wright, Jim Hady beat Frankie Allman, Billy Whitewolf beat Mr. Fuji.

7/29/68 Hilo. Att 1,500
Jim Hady & Jean Antone beat Magnificent Maurice & Betty Niccoli, King Curtis ddq Ripper Collins, Peter Maivia beat Johnny Barend dq, Lord Blears drew Magnificent Maurice.

7/31/68 Honolulu
Magnificent Maurice & Johnny Barend beat King Curtis & Jim Hady, Billy Whitewolf & Peter Maivia drew Ripper Collins & Fred Blassie, Tosh Togo beat John Bull, Pepper Gomez drew Kinji Shibuya, Jean Antone beat Betty Nicoli.

8/7/68 Honolulu
Jim Hady & Jean Antone & Kathy Starr beat Ripper Collins & Barbara Collins & Betty Nicolli, King Curtis beat Tosh Togo, Peter Maivia beat Magnificent Maurice, Billy Whitewolf drew Johnny Barend.

8/14/68 Honolulu
King Curtis beat Ripper Collins - dq, Peter Maivia & Neff Maiava drew Johnny Barend & Magnificent Maurice, Jim Hady beat Mr. Fuji, Billy Whitewolf beat Ricky Hunter.

8/21/68 Honolulu
Jim Hady & King Curtis beat Johnny Barend & Magnificent Maurice cage match, Ripper Collins & Mr. Fuji beat Dean Higuchi & Ricky Hunter, Klondike Bill beat Moe Smith, Billy Whitewolf beat John Bull.

8/25/68 Kealakekua
Tosh Togo & Dean Higuchi beat Ripper Collins & Klondike Bill, Dean Higuchi beat Ricky Hunter, Tosh Togo beat Klondike Bill dq, King Curtis drew Ripper Collins.

8/26/68 Hilo. Att 2,000
Johnny Barend & Ripper Collins beat King Curtis & Jim Hady cage match, Billy Whitewolf beat Magnificent Maurice Indian Death Match, Klondike Bill beat Dean Higuchi, Lord Blears drew Tosh Togo.

8/28/68 Honolulu
Klondike Bill beat King Curtis for Hawaiian title, Fred Blassie & Ripper Collins beat Pepper Gomez & Pedro Morales, Billy Whitewolf beat Johnny Barend chain match, Peter Maivia & Neff Maiava drew Magnificent Maurice & Mr. Fuji, Jim Hady beat Mr. Saito in a US title match.

9/4/68 Honolulu
Jim Hady beat Ripper Collins - boxing match, King Curtis & Neff Maiava drew Johnny Barend & Magnificent Maurice, Billy Whitewolf beat Baron Scicluna, Klondike Bill beat Dean Higuchi.

9/11/68 Honolulu
King Curtis beat Klondike Bill dq, Johnny Barend & Magnificent Maurice beat Tosh Togo & Kongozan, Jim Hady beat Mr. Fuji, Billy Whitewolf beat Ripper Collins.

9/18/68 Honolulu
Magnificent Maurice won battle royal, Peter Maivia & Pampero Firpo beat Ripper Collins & Klondike Bill, Billy Whitewolf beat Mr. Fuji, Jim Hady beat Jack Pesek, Paddy Barrett drew King Curtis.

9/25/68 Honolulu
Jim Hady & Billy Whitewolf beat Johnny Barend & Magnificent Maurice double chain match, Klondike Bill drew Pampero Firpo, Ripper Collins & Fred Blassie drew Lord Blears & Peter Maivia, Luke Graham beat Hahn Lee, Paddy Barrett drew Mr. Fuji.

10/2/68 Honolulu
Peter Maivia beat Johnny Barend, Jim Hady drew Klondike Bill, Magnificent Maurice drew Tosh Togo, Luke Graham & Ripper Collins beat Paddy Barrett & Billy Whitewolf.

10/9/68 Honolulu
Luke Graham beat Klondike Bill to win Hawaiian title, Johnny Barend & Magnificent Maurice beat Peter Maivia & Lord Blears, Billy Whitewolf beat Tosh Togo, Jim Hady drew Ripper Collins, Paddy Barret beat Kongozan.

10/16/68 Honolulu
Jim Hady & Billy Whitewolf beat Johnny Barend & Magnificent Maurice cage for tag titles, Luke Graham drew Peter Maivia, Paddy Barret beat Ripper Collins dq, Klondike Bill drew Neff Maiava.

10/23/68 Honolulu
Johnny Barend beat Peter Maivia both wore suits, Paddy Barrett beat Jack Pesek, Billy Whitewolf drew Luke Graham, Klondike Bill & Jim Hady & Paddy Barrett beat Ripper Collins & Luke Graham & Magnificent Maurice.

10/30/68 Honolulu
Jim Hady drew Johnny Barend to defend NWA title, Ray Stevens beat Paddy Barett, Magnificent Maurice drew Ripper Collins, Fred Blassie beat Billy Whitewolf, Klondike Bill & Billy Whitewolf & Peter Maivia beat Luke Graham & Fred Blassie & Ripper Collins.

11/6/68 Honolulu
Ripper Collins & Luke Graham beat Jim Hady & Billy Whitewolf to win Hawaiian tag titles, Paddy Barrett beat Johnny Barend dq, Nick Bockwinkel beat Klondike Bill, Mr. Fuji drew Lord Blears.

11/13/68 Honolulu
Giant Baba beat Johnny Barend dq, Mr. X drew Nick Bockwinkel, Jim Hady & Red Bastien beat Tosh Togo & Mr. Fuji, Ripper Collins & Luke Graham beat Lord Blears & Pat Barrett.

11/18/68 Hilo. Att 1,500
Giant Baba beat Ripper Collins dq, Luke Graham drew Red Bastien, Johnny Barend beat Nick Bockwinkel, Mr. X drew Pat Barrett.

11/20/68 Honolulu
Giant Baba & Nick Bockwinkel beat Ripper Collins & Luke Graham, Johnny Barend drew Red Bastien, Pat Barrett beat Kongozan, Jim Hady beat Mr. X.

11/27/68 Honolulu
Gene Kiniski beat Jim Hady NWA World Title, Luke Graham & Ripper Collins drew Man Mountain Mike & Pepper Gomez, Mr. X drew Paddy Barrett, Johnny Barend beat Nick Bockwinkel dq, Giant Baba drew Bill Miller, Joyce Grable & Princess Little Cloud beat Betty Boucher & Barbara Owen.

12/2/68 Hilo. Att 1,000
Princess Little Cloud & Lucille Dupree beat Barbra Owen & Bette Boucher, Johnny Barend ddq Red Bastien, Nick Bockwinkel drew Ripper Collins, Jim Hady beat Mr. X dq.

12/4/68 Honolulu
Donna Christanello won battle royal that included Patti Neilson, Fabulous Moolah, Betty Boucher, Barb Collins, Barbara Owen, Linda Carroll, Princess Little Cloud, Lucille Dupree & Toni Rose, Princess Little Cloud beat Betty Boucher, Ripper Collins beat Paddy Barrett, Johnny Barend drew Neff Maiava, Luke Graham drew Jim Hady, Red Bastein drew Mr. X.

12/11/68 Honolulu
Jim Hady & Red Bastien dcor, Toru Tanaka & Johnny Barend, Ripper & Barbara Collins beat Patty Neilson & Nick Bockwinkel, The Fabulous Moolah beat Donna Christanello, Mr. X drew Neff Maiava, Luke Graham drew Pat Barrett.

12/18/68 Honolulu
Luke Graham & Ripper Collins beat Jim Hady & Red Bastein to defend Hawaiian tag titles, Nick Bockwinkel beat Killer Austin, Prof. Tanaka beat Paddy Barrett, Lord Blears drew Mr. X.

12/25/68 Honolulu
Prof. Tanaka beat Jim Hady to win North American Title, Ripper Collins & Luke Graham beat Al Negra & Pepper Gomez, Ray Stevens drew Tex McKenzie, Nick Bockwinkel beat Man Mountain Cannon – Ring Belt awarded as Johnny Barend no-showed, Red Bastien beat Buddy Austin, Mr. Fuji drew Mr. X.

1969

1/1/69 Honolulu
Ed Francis beat Ripper Collins, Mr. Fuji & Prof Tanaka beat Red Bastein & Paddy Barrett, Tex McKenzie beat Fred Blassie, Nick Bockwinkel beat Mr. X, Luke Graham drew Neff Maiava.

1/8/69 Honolulu
Toru Tanaka & Mr. Fuji beat Neff Maiava & Lord Blears, Ripper Collins beat Pat Barrett, Jim Hady DCOR Luke Graham, Nick Bockwinkel beat Friday Allman, Tex McKenzie beat Mr. X.

1/15/69 Honolulu
Toru Tanaka beat Tex McKenzie dq, Neff Maiava & Nick Bockwinkel & Lord Blears beat Ripper Collins & Luke Graham & Friday Allman, Rocky Montero beat Masa Fuji, Mr. X drew Tosh Togo.

1/22/69 Honolulu
Ripper Collins beat Ed Francis - Cage match, Prof Tanaka beat Ray Stevens, Mr. Saito & Kinji Shibuya beat Tex McKenzie & Nick Bockwinkel, Wahoo McDaniel beat Mr. X, Luther Lindsay beat Tosh Togo, Dr. Bill Miller drew Don Chuy, Luke Graham drew Rocky Montero.

1/27/69 Hilo. Att 1,500
Tex McKenzie beat Professor Tanaka dq, Nick Bockwinkel & Ed Francis no contest Luke Graham & Ripper Collins, Rocky Montero drew Wahoo McDaniel, Lord Blears beat Mr. X.

1/29/69 Honolulu
Prof. Tanaka beat Nick Bockwinkel, Wahoo McDaniel & Tex McKenzie beat Ripper Collins & Friday, Luke Graham beat Kongozan, Rocky Montero beat Mr. X.

2/5/69 Honolulu
Ripper Collins & Luke Graham beat Ed Francis & Wahoo McDaniel, Bobby Shane beat Mr. X, Neff Maiava beat Rocky Montero, Nick Bockwinkel & Tex McKenzie beat Kongozan & Prof. Tanaka.

2/12/69 Honolulu
Nick Bockwinkel won battle royal, Nick Bockwinkel & Tex McKenzie drew Danny Hodge & Rocky Montero, Wahoo McDaniel beat Masa Fujiwara, Prof Tanaka beat Bob Boyer, Ripper Collins drew Bobby Shane.

2/19/69 Honolulu
Gene Kiniski beat Prof Tanaka to win North America Title, King Curtis beat Nick Bockwinkel, Tex McKenzie beat The Mummy, Don Chuy & Ray Stevens & Wahoo McDaniel beat Ripper Collins & Luke Graham & Roger Kirby, Rocky Montero drew Bobby Shane, Billy Whitewolf beat Bob Boyer.

2/26/69 Honolulu
Luke Graham & Ripper Collins drew Wahoo McDaniel & Billy Whitewolf, King Curtis beat Bobby Shane, Toru Tanaka drew Nick Bockwinkel, Tex McKenzie drew Rocky Montero.

3/5/69 Honolulu
Nick Bockwinkel beat King Curtis dq, Ed Francis beat Friday boxing, Ripper Collins & Luke Graham beat Wahoo McDaniel & Tex McKenzie, Toru Tanaka beat Bobby Shane, Rocky Montero drew Lord Blears.

3/12/69 Honolulu
Bobby Shane & Nick Bockwinkel beat Ripper Collins & Luke Graham to win Hawaiian tag titles, Tex McKenzie beat Toru Tanaka Texas Death Match, Wahoo McDaniel beat King Curtis, Rocky Montero & Mr. Fuji beat Tosh Togo & Lord Blears.

3/19/69 Honolulu
Rocky Montero beat Nick Bockwinkel, Ripper Collins beat Bobby Shane, Tex McKenzie beat Mr. Fujiwara, Wahoo McDaniel beat Luke Graham, King Curtis beat Steve Kovacs.

3/26/69 Honolulu
Tex McKenzie drew Gene Kiniski, King Curtis beat Wahoo McDaniel, Nick Bockwinkel & Paul Jones beat Ripper Collins & Luke Graham, Rocky Montero beat Sandor Kovacs, Bobby Shane drew Dave Ruhl.

3/31/69 Hilo. Att 1,500
Pedro Morales won battle royal, Ripper Collins & Buddy Austin beat Bobby Shane & Pedro Morales, King Curtis ddq Tex McKenzie, Lord Blears beat Rocky Montero dq.

4/2/69 Honolulu
Tex McKenzie & Pedro Morales & Nick Bockwinkel drew Ripper Collins & Killer Austin & King Curtis, Pedro Morales beat Dave Ruhl, Bobby Shane drew Rocky Montero, Killer Austin beat Sandor Kovacs.

4/9/69 Honolulu
King Curtis beat Tex McKenzie, Ripper Collins & Killer Austin beat Pedro Morales & Sandor Kovacs, Don Leo Jonathan beat Rocky Montero, Nick Bockwinkel & Bobby Shane beat Mr. Fuji & Dave Ruhl.

4/16/69 Honolulu
Gene Kiniski drew King Curtis defended North American Title, Don Leo Jonathan & Pedro Morales beat Mr. Saito & Kinji Shibuya dq World Tag title, Ripper Collins & Killer Austin beat Bobby Shane & Nick Bockwinkel to win Hawaiian tag titles, Peter Maivia beat Dave Ruhl, Rocky Montero beat Ray Kamaka.

4/21/69 Hilo
Don Leo Jonathan beat Ripper Collins dq, Buddy Austin beat Bobby Shane, Pedro Morales beat Rocky Montero, King Curtis & Mr. Fuji drew Nick Bockwinkel & Lord Blears.

4/23/69 Honolulu
King Curtis beat Don Leo Jonathan, Pedro Morales & Nick Bockwinkel & Lord Blears beat Ripper Collins & Rocky Montero & Buddy Austin, Bobby Shane drew Mr. Fuji, Ray Kamaka drew Buddy Austin.

4/30/69 Honolulu
Ripper Collins & Killer Austin beat Nick Bockwinkel & Bobby Shane, Pedro Morales beat Rocky Montero, King Curtis beat Ray Kamaka, Lord Blears beat Mr. Fuji.

5/7/69 Honolulu
Dory Dixon won battle royal, Ripper Collins beat Ray Kamaka, Bobby Shane drew Friday Allman, Pedro Morales beat Tank Morgan, Dory Dixon beat Mr. Fuji, Billy Robinson drew Nick Bockwinkel.

5/14/69 Honolulu
King Curtis beat Nick Bockwinkel, Buddy Austin beat Bobby Shane, Ray Kamaka drew Bobby Shane, Pedro Morales & Dory Dixon & Billy Robinson beat Rocky Montero & Ripper Collins & Buddy Austin.

5/21/69 Honolulu
Pedro Morales beat King Curtis for Hawaiian title, Nick Bockwinkel beat Chris Markoff, Ripper Collins & Buddy Austin ddq Pepper Gomez & Dory Dixon, Billy Robinson beat Tom Andrews, Bobby Shane drew Kongozan, Rocky Montero drew Ray Kamaka.

5/26/69 Hilo. Att 1,000
Ripper Collins & Buddy Austin beat Nick Bockwinkel & Bobby Shane, King Curtis drew Pedro Morales, Billy Robinson drew Dory Dixon, Lord Blears beat Rocky Montero dq.

6/4/69 Honolulu
Gorilla Monsoon drew Pedro Morales, Billy Robinson beat Killer Austin, Dory Dixon beat Ripper Collins dq, King Curtis & Rocky Montero beat Tex McKenzie & Bobby Shane, Nick Bockwinkel beat Kongozan.

6/11/69 Honolulu
Bobby Shane beat Ripper Collins, Tex McKenzie drew Killer Austin, Karl Gotch beat Kongozan dq, Gorilla Monsoon & Rocky Montero & King Curtis drew Dory Dixon & Pedro Morales & Nick Bockwinkel.

6/18/69 Honolulu
Pedro Morales beat Gene Kiniski to win North America Title, Ripper Collins & Buddy Austin beat Bobby Shane & Tex McKenzie, Ray Stevens beat Pat Patterson, Dory Dixon beat Kongozan, Karl Gotch beat Rocky Montero, King Curtis beat Don Leo Jonathan boxing match.

6/23/69 Hilo
Buddy Austin & Ripper Collins beat Dory Dixon & Pedro Morales, Nick Bockwinkel beat Gorilla Monsoon dq, Rocky Montero & King Curtis drew Lord Blears & Tex McKenzie.

6/25/69 Honolulu
King Curtis beat Tex McKenzie, Gorilla Monsoon & Rocky Montero drew Dory Dixon & Nick Bockwinkel, Pedro Morales beat Killer Austin, Karl Gotch beat Ripper Collins.

7/2/69 Honolulu
Billy Whitewolf beat Killer Austin, Pedro Morales & Ed Francis drew King Curtis & Gorilla Monsoon, Nick Bockwinkel drew Ripper Collins, Dory Dixon beat Rocky Montero, Mr. Fujiwara drew Karl Gotch.

7/9/69 Honolulu
Pat Patterson & Ripper Collins & Killer Austin beat Ray Stevens & Ed Francis & Peter Maivia, Pedro Morales beat Gene Kiniski, Gorilla Monsoon & King Curtis drew Nick Bockwinkel & Dory Dixon, Billy Whitewolf beat Rocky Montero, Little Brutus beat Jamaica Kid, Little Beaver drew Sky Low Low, Karl Gotch drew Killer Austin.

7/14/69 Hilo
Little Beaver & Jamaica Kid beat Sky Low Low & Little Brutus, Gorilla Monsoon dcor Pedro Morales, King Curtis drew Dory Dixon, Nick Bockwinkel drew Rocky Montero.

7/16/69 Honolulu
Ripper Collins & Killer Austin beat Billy Whitewolf & Nick Bockwinkel, Rocky Montero drew Dory Dixon, Pedro Morales & Ed Francis beat King Curtis & Gorilla Monsoon, Little Beaver & Jamaica Kid beat Little Brutus & Sky Low Low.

7/23/69 Honolulu
Pedro Morales & Dory Dixon drew Kurt & Karl Von Steiger, Billy Whitewolf beat Mr. Fujiwara, Rocky Montero drew Karl Gotch, Nick Bockwinkel drew Killer Austin, Dory Dixon won battle royal.

7/26/69 Schofield
Buddy Austin & Ripper Collins beat Dory Dixon & Ricky Hunter, Kurt & Karl Von Steiger beat Lord Blears & Pedro Morales, Nick Bockwinkel drew Rocky Montero, Nick Bockwinkel won battle royal.

7/30/69 Honolulu
Billy Whitewolf & Peter Maivia beat Kurt & Karl Von Steiger, Gorilla Monsoon beat King Curtis cor, Nick Bockwinkel beat Mr. Fujiwara, Pedro Morales & Ed Francis beat Ripper Collins & Killer Austin, Kinji Shibuya drew Dory Dixon, Ray Stevens beat Rocky Montero.

8/6/69 Honolulu
Rocky Montero beat Billy Whitewolf Indian Death match, King Curtis & Kurt & Karl Von Steiger beat Pedro Morales & Pampero Firpo & Dory Dixon, Killer Austin beat Ricky Hunter, Ripper Collins drew Nick Bockwinkel.

8/13/69 Honolulu
Kurt & Karl Von Steiger beat Dory Dixon & Nick Bockwinkel, Pedro Morales & Ed Francis beat Ripper Collins & Killer Austin, Pampero Firpo beat Rocky Montero, Ricky Hunter drew Mr. Fujiwara, King Curtis drew Billy Whitewolf.

8/18/69 Hilo
Kurt & Karl Von Steiger beat Pedro Morales & Dory Dixon dq, Ed Francis beat Buddy Austin, Pampero Firpo beat Ripper Collins dq, King Curtis drew Nick Bockwinkel.

8/20/69 Honolulu
Kurt & Karl Von Steiger beat Billy Whitewolf & Ricky Hunter, Masked Man 1 & 2 & Ripper Collins & Killer Austin beat Dory Dixon & Pedro Morales & Nick Bockwinkel & Pampero Firpo, King Curtis beat Dory Dixon, Pedro Morales beat Rocky Montero.

8/27/69 Honolulu
Kurt & Karl Von Steiger beat Bobby & Jerry Christy, Dory Funk drew King Curtis North American Title, Pedro Morales beat Gorilla Monsoon NWA title, Billy Whitewolf beat Rocky Montero, Killer Austin & Ripper Collins beat Nick Bockwinkel & Dory Dixon.

9/3/69 Honolulu
King Curtis beat Jerry Brisco, Von Steigers beat Billy Whitewolf Handicap match, Pedro Morales beat Killer Austin, Nick Bockwinkel beat Ricky Hunter, Ripper Collins drew Pampero Firpo.

9/10/69 Honolulu
King Curtis beat Billy Robinson, Von Steigers beat Pedro Morales & Ed Francis to win Hawaiian tag titles, Ripper Collins & Killer Austin beat Jerry Brisco & Nick Bockwinkel, Pampero Firpo beat Mr. Fujiwara.

9/15/69 Hilo
Ed Francis & Pedro Morales beat Kurt & Karl Von Steiger, Giant Baba beat Buddy Austin, King Curtis beat Pampero Firpo dq, Nick Bockwinkel drew Ripper Collins.

9/17/69 Honolulu
Von Steigers beat Ray Kamaka & Nick Bockwinkel, Pampero Firpo drew Killer Austin, Mr. Fujiwara beat Ricky Hunter, Pampero Firpo & Giant Baba & Pedro Morales beat King Curtis & Ripper Collins & Killer Austin.

9/24/69 Honolulu
Pampero Firpo beat The Sheik dq, King Curtis beat Pedro Morales to win North American Title, Ripper Collins beat Ricky Hunter, Ed Francis beat Killer Austin, Gene Kiniski drew Giant Baba, Peter Maivia & Neff Maiava drew Kurt & Karl Von Steiger.

10/1/69 Honolulu
King Curtis drew Bob Harris, Ripper Collins drew Nick Bockwinkel, Ed Francis & Pedro Morales beat Von Steigers to win tag titles, Bing Ki Lee beat Mr. Fujiwara, Pampero Firpo beat Tosh Togo.

10/8/69 Honolulu
King Curtis & Ripper Collins beat Bob Harris & Nick Bockwinkel, Pampero Firpo won battle royal, Pampero Firpo beat Mr. Fujiwara, Kurt Von Steiger drew Bing Ki Lee, Ray Kamaka beat Karl Von Steiger dq.

10/15/69 Honolulu
King Curtis beat Ray Stevens, Pedro Morales & Bing Ki Lee beat Stan Nielsen & The Alaskan, Karl Gotch drew Tosh Togo, The Sheik beat Pampero Firpo, Von Steigers beat Ray Kamaka & Bob Harris.

10/17/69 Hilo
Ed Francis & Pedro Morales beat Kurt & Karl Von Steiger, King Curtis DCOR Hahn Lee, George Harris drew Ripper Collins, Pampero Firpo beat Mr. Fuji.

10/22/69 Honolulu
King Curtis & Ripper Collins beat Von Steigers, Friday beat Pampero Firpo, Mr. Fujiwara drew Karl Gotch, Bing Ki Lee & Pedro Morales beat Ray Kamaka & Bob Harris.

10/29/69 Honolulu
Pedro Morales & Bing Ki Lee beat Von Steigers, King Curtis beat Dory Dixon, Bob Harris beat Cowboy Laine, Ripper Collins beat Pampero Firpo.

11/5/69 Honolulu
Pampero Firpo & Rene Goulet beat Ripper Collins & Friday, Bob Harris drew Ray Kamaka, Bing Ki Lee beat Kurt Von Steiger, Pedro Morales beat King Curtis.

11/12/69 Honolulu
Pampero Firpo beat Karl Von Steiger, Don Leo Jonathan beat Kurt Von Steiger, Rene Goulet drew Bob Harris, King Curtis & Ripper Collins beat Pedro Morales & Bing Ki Lee.

11/17/69 Hilo
Cowboy Lang & Wee Willie Wilson beat Little Bruiser & Mighty Atom, Hahn Lee drew Ripper Collins, Pedro Morales beat King Curtis, Pampero Firpo beat Karl Von Steiger.

11/19/69 Honolulu
Pedro Morales & Bing Ki Lee & Rene Goulet beat King Curtis & Ripper Collins & Mr. Fujiwara, Pampero Firpo drew Bob Harris, Don Leo Jonathan beat Karl Von Steiger, Cowboy Lang & Wee Willie Wilson beat Mighty Atom & Little Bruiser.

11/26/69 Honolulu
Pedro Morales beat The Sheik dq, Don Leo Jonathan drew Fred Blassie, Tank Morgan beat Rene Goulet, Bing Ki Lee beat King Curtis, Mighty Atom & Little Bruiser beat Cowboy Lang & Wee Willie Wilson, Pampero Firpo beat Ripper Collins dq, Johnny Barend beat Bobby Shane.

12/3/69 Honolulu
Johnny Barend beat Rene Goulet, Jack Bence drew Pampero Firpo, Kongozan drew Bob Harris, Jack Bence & Ripper Collins & Tank Morgan beat Bing Ki Lee & Pedro Morales & Don Leo Jonathan.

12/10/69 Honolulu
Peter Maivia & Pampero Firpo beat Tank Morgan & Jack Bence, Bing Ki lee beat Mr. Fujiwara, Ripper Collins beat Klondike Bill, Danny Hodges drew Johnny Walker, Bing Ki Lee won battle royal.

12/17/69 Honolulu
Tank Morgan beat Pedro Morales dq, Bing Ki Lee drew Jack Bence, Mr. Fujiwara beat Bob Harris, Johnny Barend & Ripper Collins beat Pampero Firpo & Don Leo Jonathan.

12/25/69 Honolulu
Johnny Barend beat Pedro Morales, Danny Hodge drew Hahn Lee, Ed & Bill Francis beat Ripper Collins & Friday Allman, Giant Baba & Seiji Sakaguchi beat Tank Morgan & Jack Bence, Pampero Firpo beat Johnny Walker, Tex McKenzie beat Mr. Fuji.

1970

1/1/70 Honolulu
Johnny Barend & Ripper Collins beat Giant Baba & Seigi Sakaguchi, Danny Hodge drew Pampero Firpo, Pedro Morales drew Jack Bence, Tank Morgan beat Bing Ki Lee

1/7/70 Honolulu
Pedro Morales & Bill Francis & Bing Ki Lee drew Ripper Collins & Jack Bence & Tank Morgan, Johnny Barend beat Seigi Sakaguchi, Jack Bence drew Don Carson, Pampero Firpo beat Kongozan.

1/14/70 Honolulu
Pampero Firpo beat Ripper Collins, Pedro Morales & Bing Ki Lee beat Jack Bence & Tank Morgan, Little Bruiser & Mighty Atom & Johnny Barend beat Wee Willie Wilson & Cowboy Lang & Don Carson, Cowboy Lang beat Mighty Atom.

1/19/70 Hilo
Pampero Firpo beat Jack Bence, Hahn Lee drew Johnny Barend, Cowboy Lang & Pedro Morales & Wee Willie Wilson beat Ripper Collins & Little Bruiser & Mighty Atom, Mighty Atom beat Cowboy Lang.

1/20/70 Maui
Jack Bence & Little Bruiser & Mighty Atom beat Cowboy Lang & Hahn Lee & Wee Willie Wilson, Pampero Firpo beat Johnny Barend dq, Pedro Morales drew Ripper Collins, Mighty Atom beat Wee Willie Wilson.

1/21/70 Honolulu
Peter Maivia & Ray Stevens drew Pat Patterson & Masked Gladiator, Ripper Collins & Gene Kiniski & Johnny Barend ddq Bing Ki Lee & Pedro Morales & Haystacks Calhoun, Pampero Firpo drew Jack Bence, Don Leo Jonathan drew Tank Morgan, Earl Maynard beat Mr. Fujiwara.

1/28/70 Honolulu
Pedro Morales beat Tank Morgan, Johnny Barend & Ripper Collins beat Ed & Bill Francis, Pampero Firpo beat Mac MacFarland, Bing Ki Lee beat Jack Bence.

2/4/70 Honolulu
Ripper Collins beat Pampero Firpo to win Hawaiian title, Johnny Barend & Frank Allman & Tank Morgan beat Don Leo Jonathan & Sandor Kovacs & Pedro Morales, Pedro Morales beat Jack Bence, Bing Ki Lee beat Mac MacFarland.

2/11/70 Honolulu
Ripper Collins & Johnny Barend beat Rene Goulet & Lou Klein to retain tag titles, Bill Francis beat Frank Allman, Tank Morgan drew Bing Ki Lee, Pedro Morales beat Mac MacFarland, Pampero Firpo drew Tosh Togo.

2/16/70 Hilo
Donna Christanello & Vivian Vachon beat Paula Kaye & Rita Monroe, Friday Allman & Johnny Barend & Ripper Collins beat Bill & Ed Francis & Pedro Morales, Hahn Lee beat Tank Morgan dq, Pedro Morales drew Ripper Collins.

2/17/70 Maui
Bill Francis & Hahn Lee & Pedro Morales beat Johnny Barend & Ripper Collins & Tank Morgan, Donna Christanello & Vivian Vachon drew Paula Kaye and Rita Monroe.

2/18/70 Honolulu
Dory Funk drew Johnny Barend, Don Leo Jonathan & Tex McKenzie beat Bad Boy Shields & Mac MacFarland, Bing Ki Lee beat Mr. Fujiwara, Pampero Firpo beat Frank Allman, Pedro Morales drew Pat Patterson, Donna Christanello & Vivian Vachon beat Rita Monroe & Paula Kay.

2/24/70 Honolulu
Johnny Barend beat Pampero Firpo, Vivian Vachon & Donna Christanello & Pedro Morales beat Paul Kay & Rita Monroe & Ripper Collins, Rene Goulet drew Bad Boy Shields, Bing Ki Lee beat Tank Morgan dq.

3/4/70 Honolulu
Pedro Morales & Bing Ki Lee beat Johnny Barend & Ripper Collins to win tag titles, Tosh Togo beat Tank Morgan, Mac MacFarland drew Rene Goulet, Bad Boy Shields beat Pampero Firpo.

3/11/70 Honolulu
Johnny Barend & Ripper Collins split 14-man battle royal, Giant Baba & Seigi Sakaguchi beat Tank Morgan & Mr. Fujiwara, Pedro Morales beat Mac MacFarland, Bing Ki Lee drew Les Roberts.

3/18/70 Honolulu
Pedro Morales & Bing Ki Lee beat Kinji Shibuya & Mitsu Arakawa retained tag titles, Ripper Collins & Johnny Barend drew Giant Baba & Seigi Sakaguchi, Les Roberts drew Bad Boy Shields.

3/23/70 Hilo
Giant Baba drew Johnny Barend, Hahn Lee & Pedro Morales beat Ripper Collins & Frank Shields, Tank Morgan beat Mac MacFarland, Rene Goulet drew Les Roberts.

3/25/70 Honolulu
Ripper Collins beat Rene Goulet, Pedro Morales beat Johnny Barend stretcher match, Cyclone Negro & Spiros Arion beat Kinji Shibuya & Mitsu Arakawa won International tag titles, Bing Ki Lee beat Bad Boy Shields, Tank Morgan beat Don Carson, Giant Baba beat Les Roberts.

4/1/70 Honolulu
Ed Francis & Bing Ki Lee & Rene Goulet & Donna Christanello beat Johnny Barend & Ripper Collins & Frank Allman & Rita Monroe, Pedro Morales beat Les Roberts, Rene Goulet drew Tosh Togo, Tank Morgan beat Bad Boy Shields.

4/8/70 Honolulu
Ripper Collins drew Bing Ki Lee, Johnny Barend beat Rene Goulet, Pedro Morales beat Bad Boy Shields, Tank Morgan drew Les Roberts, Lord Littlebrook & Mighty Atom beat Cowboy Lang & Wee Willie Wilson.

4/13/70 Hilo
Pedro Morales beat Les Roberts, Ripper Collins beat Rene Goulet, Bing Ki Lee beat Johnny Barend, Cowboy Lang & Wee Willie Wilson beat Lord Littlebrook & The Mighty Atom.

4/14/70 Maui
Ripper Collins drew Rene Goulet, Bing Ki Lee beat Les Roberts dq, Cowboy Lang beat Lord Littlebrook, Johnny Barend & Ripper Collins & Lord Littlebrook & The Mighty Atom beat Cowboy Lang & Bing Ki Lee & Pedro Morales & Wee Willie Wilson.

4/15/70 Honolulu
Johnny Barend beat Bing Ki Lee North American Title, Lord Littlebrook beat Cowboy Lang, Wee Willy Wilson & Pedro Morales beat Ripper Collins & Mighty Atom, Tank Morgan drew Mac MacFarland, Les Roberts drew Rene Goulet.

4/22/70 Honolulu
Ed Francis beat Ripper Collins, Pedro Morales beat Mr. Fujiwara, Johnny Barend & Frank Allman beat Tank Morgan & Rene Goulet, Bing Ki Lee beat Les Roberts dq.

4/29/70 Honolulu
Ray Stevens & Peter Maivia beat The Sheik & Johnny Barend dq World Tag champs, Sam Steamboat beat Ripper Collins dq Hawaiian Title, Kinji Shibuya beat Pedro Morales, Rene Goulet beat Mr. Fujiwara, Tank Morgan beat Les Roberts.

5/6/70 Honolulu
Kinji Shibuya & Ripper Collins & Johnny Barend beat Sam Steamboat & Tank Morgan & Rene Goulet, Kinji Shibuya drew Bing Ki Lee, Pedro Morales beat Les Roberts, Rene Goulet beat Killer Buddy Austin dq.

5/13/70 Honolulu
Pedro Morales & Bing Ki Lee beat Johnny Barend & Ripper Collins Hawaiian Tag titles, Sam Steamboat beat Les Roberts, Kinji Shibuya beat Rene Goulet, Tank Morgan beat Frank Allman.

5/18/70 Hilo
Bing Ki Lee & Pedro Morales & Sam Steamboat beat Ripper Collins & Hard Boiled Haggerty & Kinji Shibuya, Tank Morgan beat Mac McFarland, Rene Goulet beat Friday Allman dq, Ripper Collins drew Bing Ki Lee.

5/19/70 Maui
Friday Altman & Ripper Collins & Hard Boiled Haggerty beat Rene Goulet & Pedro Morales & Bing King Lee, Sam Steamboat beat Kinji Shibuya dq, Tank Morgan beat Mac McFarland, Rene Goulet beat Friday Allman.

5/20/70 Honolulu
Ripper Collins beat Tank Morgan to defend State Title, Hard Boiled Haggerty & Kinji Shibuya beat Jerry Brisco & Sam Steamboat, Pedro Morales beat Mac MacFarland.

5/27/70 Honolulu
Pedro Morales & Bing Ki Lee beat Hard Boiled Haggerty & Kinji Shibuya, Tank Morgan beat Frank Allman boxing match, Ripper Collins beat Mac MacFarland, Sam Steamboat beat Duke Savage.

6/3/70 Honolulu
Sam Steamboat won Texas battle royal, Sam Steamboat drew Billy Robinson, Pedro Morales drew Ripper Collins, Hard Boiled Haggerty beat Tank Morgan, Bing Ki Lee beat Mr. Fujiwara dq.

6/10/70 Honolulu
Sam Steamboat beat Ripper Collins to win Hawaiian title, Billy Robinson beat Bing Ki Lee, Pedro Morales beat The Convict, Tank Morgan beat Mr. Fujiwara, Hard Boiled Haggerty beat Mac MacFarland.

6/17/70 Honolulu
Hard Boiled Haggerty drew Pedro Morales, Sam Steamboat beat Tony Borne, Bing Ki Lee drew Ripper Collins, Billy Robinson beat Tank Morgan, Mr. Fujiwara drew Mac MacFarland.

6/22/70 Hilo. Att 1,100
Johnny Barend & Ripper Collins beat Lord Blears & Sam Steamboat, Pedro Morales drew Billy Robinson, Tank Morgan beat Hard Boiled Haggerty dq, Bing Ki Lee beat Tony Borne, Sam Steamboat won battle royal.

6/24/70 Honolulu
The Sheik no contest Johnny Barend, Ripper Collins beat Sam Steamboat to win Hawaiian title, Billy Robinson beat The Wolfman, Pedro Morales beat Tony Borne, Bing Ki Lee drew Hard Boiled Haggerty, Tank Morgan beat Mac MacFarland.

7/1/70 Honolulu
Johnny Barend & Billy Robinson beat Pedro Morales & Bing Ki Lee to win Hawaiian tag titles, Ripper Collins beat Tosh Togo, Sam Steamboat beat Frank Allman, Tank Morgan beat Tony Borne.

7/8/70 Honolulu
Billy Robinson beat Tosh Togo European Style match, Sam Steamboat & Pedro Morales & Bing Ki Lee beat Ripper Collins & Killer Kox & Johnny Barend, Kinji Shibuya beat Don Karlson, Tank Morgan beat Frank Allman.

7/15/70 Honolulu
Dory Funk Jr beat Ripper Collins, Johnny Barend beat Pedro Morales dq, Kinji Shibuya beat Tank Morgan, Hahn Lee drew Sam Steamboat, Billy Robinson beat Killer Karl Kox, Moolah beat Toni Rose, Vicky Williams beat Fran Gravette.

7/20/70 Hilo
Johnny Barend beat Sam Steamboat dq, Bing Ki Lee drew Billy Robinson, Pedro Morales beat Karl Kox, Ripper Collins beat Lord Blears, Toni Rose & Vickie Williams beat Fabulous Moolah & Fran Gravette.

7/21/70 Maui
Lord Blears beat Karl Kox, Hahn Lee & Sam Steamboat beat Johnny Barend & Ripper Collins dq, Toni Rose & Vickie Williams beat Fabulous Moolah & Fran Gravette.

7/23/70 Honolulu
Johnny Barend & Billy Robinson beat Tank Morgan & Sam Steamboat, Bing Ki Lee drew Ripper Collins, Pedro Morales drew Kinji Shibuya, Vicki Williams & Toni Rose beat Fabulous Moolah & Fran Gravette.

7/29/70 Honolulu
Sam Steamboat beat Ripper Collins to win Hawaiian title, Billy Robinson & Kinji Shibuya beat Tank Morgan & Pedro Morales, Bill Francis beat Johnny Barend dq, Ivan Koloff drew Bing Ki Lee.

8/5/70 Honolulu
Pedro Morales beat Johnny Barend to win North American Title, Ripper Collins & Kinji Shibuya beat Eddie Graham & Sam Steamboat, Billy Robinson drew Ray Stevens European Style match, Cyclone Negro drew Ed Carpentier, Ivan Koloff beat Tank Morgan, Bing Ki Lee beat Mac MacFarland.

8/12/70 Honolulu
Sam Steamboat & Pedro Morales & Ed Carpentier beat Johnny Barend & Ivan Koloff & Billy Robinson, Kinji Shibuya beat Nick Kozak, Bing Ki Lee beat Reggie Parks, Ripper Collins drew Jack Armstrong.

8/18/70 Maui
Johnny Barend & Billy Robinson beat Jack Armstrong & Sam Steamboat, Pedro Morales beat Ivan Koloff, Ed Carpentier drew Kinji Shibuya, Ripper Collins beat Bing Ki Lee.

8/19/70 Honolulu
Sam Steamboat beat Ripper Collins, Kinji Shibuya drew Pedro Morales, Johnny Barend & Billy Robinson beat Ed Carpentier & Jack Armstrong, Bing Ki Lee beat Frank Allman.

8/21/70 Hilo
Bing Ki Lee & Jerry Monti & Pedro Morales & Billy Robinson & Sam Steamboat beat Jack Armstrong & Johnny Barend & Ripper Collins & Destroyer & Kinji Shibuya, Ripper Collins drew Sam Steamboat, Pedro Morales beat Jack Armstrong, Bing Ki Lee beat Kinji Shibuya, The Destroyer beat Jerry Monti.

8/26/70 Honolulu
Dory Funk drew Billy Robinson NWA title match, Johnny Barend beat The Sheik stretcher match, Sam Steamboat beat Les Wolfe, Killer Austin drew Jack Armstrong, Pedro Morales drew Ripper Collins, Bing Ki Lee drew Kinji Shibuya.

9/2/70 Honolulu
Johnny Barend & Billy Robinson beat Pedro Morales & Bing Ki Lee, Kinji Shibuya beat Sam Steamboat, Ripper Collins beat Les Wolfe, Mac MacFarland drew Jack Armstrong.

9/9/70 Honolulu
Pedro Morales drew Billy Robinson, Sam Steamboat drew Johnny Barend, Kinji Shibuya beat Jack Armstrong, Ripper Collins beat Frank Allman, Bing Ki Lee beat Mac MacFarland.

9/16/70 Honolulu
Billy Robinson & Johnny Barend beat Sam Steamboat & Nick Bockwinkel, Kinji Shibuya drew Pedro Morales, Ripper Collins beat Bing Ki Lee, Mac MacFarland beat Jack Armstrong.

9/21/70 Hilo
Pedro Morales & Hahn Lee & Sam Steamboat & Billy Robinson & Jerry Monti beat Jack Armstrong & Kinji Shibuya & Ripper Collins & Johnny Barend & The Destroyer dq, Ripper Collins drew Sam Steamboat, Pedro Morales beat Jack Armstrong, Hahn Lee beat Kinji Shibuya dq, The Destroyer beat Jerry Monti.

9/23/70 Honolulu
Johnny Barend & Ripper Collins beat Hahn Lee & Mac MacFarland, Sam Steamboat beat Kinji Shibuya dq, Pedro Morales beat Abdullah The Butcher dq, The Destroyer beat Jack Armstrong.

9/30/70 Honolulu
Masked Destroyer beat Pedro Morales for North American Title, The Sheik & Ed Francis beat Johnny Barend & Ripper Collins, Bing Ki Lee beat Jack Armstrong, Billy Robinson beat Abdulla The Butcher, Kinji Shibuya beat Jerry Monti.

10/7/70 Honolulu
Sam Steamboat drew Masked Destroyer, Bing Ki Lee & Pedro Morales & Sam Steamboat & Billy Robinson & Frank Allman beat Ripper Collins & Johnny Barend & Destroyer & Kinji Shibuya & Jack Armstrong, Pedro Morales beat Jack Armstrong, Ripper Collins beat Frank Allman, Billy Robinson drew Kinji Shibuya.

10/14/70 Honolulu
Johnny Barend beat Ed & Bill Francis, Destroyer beat Frank Allman, Billy Robinson beat Soldat Gorky, Lord Blears beat Jack Armstrong, Kinji Shibuya & Ripper Collins beat Sam Steamboat & Bing Ki Lee.

10/19/70 Hilo
Bing Ki Lee beat Jack Armstrong, Bill Francis drew Soldat Gorky, Sam Steamboat beat Kinji Shibuya, Bill & Ed Francis & Billy Robinson beat Ripper Collins & The Destroyer & Soldat Gorky.

10/21/70 Honolulu
Ed Francis & Billy Robinson & Sam Steamboat beat Kinji Shibuya & Soldat Gorky & Destroyer, Bing Ki Lee beat Jack Armstrong, Johnny Barend beat Les Wolfe, Ripper Collins beat Frank Allman.

10/28/70 Honolulu
Destroyer beat Sheik dq, Billy Robinson & Ed Francis beat Ripper Collins & Johnny Barend to win Tag titles, Beauregard drew Soldat Gorky, Sam Steamboat drew Dale Lewis, Kinji Shibuya beat Bing Ki Lee, Bill Francis beat Jack Armstrong.

11/4/70 Honolulu
Ripper Collins beat Sam Steamboat, Dale Lewis & Destroyer & Soldat Gorky drew Billy Robinson & Bill Francis & Lord Blears, Johnny Barend beat Bing Ki Lee, Dale Lewis beat Jack Armstrong.

11/11/70 Honolulu
Billy Robinson beat John Quinn, Destroyer beat Johnny Barend dq, Dale Lewis & Ripper Collins drew Nick Bockwinkel & Sam Steamboat, Rocky Johnson beat Soldat Gorky, Bing Ki Lee drew Frankie Laine.

11/18/70 Honolulu
Billy Robinson won battle royal, Dale Lewis beat Bing Ki Lee, Billy Robinson & Sam Steamboat drew John Quinn & Ripper Collins, Nick Bockwinkel drew Rocky Johnson, Destroyer beat Frankie Laine, Johnny Barend beat Soldat Gorky.

11/25/70 Honolulu
Billy Robinson beat Nick Bockwinkel, Dale Lewis beat Rocky Johnson, Bing Ki Lee drew Soldat Gorky, Frankie Laine beat Mac MacFarland.

12/2/70 Honolulu
Billy Robinson & Ed Francis drew Dale Lewis & Ripper Collins, Sam Steamboat beat Soldat Gorky, Johnny Barend beat Mac MacFarland, Frankie Laine beat Destroyer dq.

12/9/70 Honolulu
Johnny Barend beat Ripper Collins to win Hawaiian title, King Curtis & Destroyer beat Sam Steamboat & Frankie Laine, Dale Lewis beat Beauregard, Billy Robinson beat Soldat Gorky.

12/13/70 Maui
Sam Steamboat beat Soldat Gorky, Ripper Collins beat Lord Blears, Billy Robinson beat Dale Lewis dq, Curtis Iaukea beat Frankie Laine, Victor The Wrestling Bear beat the Destroyer.

12/14/70 Hilo
Lord Blears beat Soldat Gorky, Ripper Collins beat Frankie Laine, Dale Lewis drew Sam Steamboat, Curtis Iaukea drew Billy Robinson, Victor The Wrestling Bear beat The Destroyer.

12/16/70 Honolulu
Billy Robinson beat Destroyer to win North American title, Beauregard beat Soldat Gorky, King Curtis beat Bing Ki lee, Dale Lewis beat Rocky Montero, Frankie Laine & Sam Steamboat beat Larry Hennig & Bob Windham (Blackjack Mulligan).

12/23/70 Honolulu
Frankie Laine dcor Ripper Collins, Dale Lewis beat Ed Francis, Sam Steamboat beat Gene LeBell, King Curtis & Mr. Fuji beat Billy Robinson & Beauregard, Rocky Montero beat Mac MacFarland.

1971

1/2/71 Honolulu
Billy Robinson won battle royal, Frankie Laine beat Black Angel dq, King Curtis beat Don Muraco, Billy Robinson beat Gene LeBell, Dale Lewis drew Sam Steamboat.

1/9/71 Honolulu
King Curtis beat Billy Robinson to win North American title, Gene LaBell drew Don Muraco, Frankie Laine ddq Dale Lewis, Sam Steamboat & Beauregard beat Lonnie Mayne & Ripper Collins.

1/16/71 Honolulu
Billy Robinson & Cowboy Laine beat Ripper Collins & Lonnie Mayne, King Curtis beat Beauregard, Sam Steamboat beat Gene LeBell Judo Freestyler, Dale Lewis beat Kongozan, Don Muraco drew Mr. Fuji.

1/23/71 Honolulu
Dory Funk Jr beat Don Leo Jonathan NWA title, King Curtis beat Billy Robinson, Don Muraco & Sam Steamboat beat Lonnie Mayne & Ripper Collins, Beauregard beat Jerry Jarrett, Frankie Laine beat Tojo Yamamoto, Dale Lewis beat Pierre Duranton.

1/30/71 Honolulu
King Curtis & Lonnie Mayne & Ripper Collins beat Sam Steamboat & Frankie Laine & Pierre Duranton, Billy Robinson drew Dale Lewis, Don Muraco beat Tojo Yamamoto, Beauregard drew Mr. Fujiwara.

2/6/71 Honolulu
Frankie Laine beat Ripper Collins to win Hawaiian Title, Lonnie Mayne beat Beauregard, Don Muraco beat Mr. Fujiwara, Dale Lewis beat Pierre Duranton, King Curtis drew Verne Gagne.

2/13/71 Honolulu
King Curtis & Lonnie Mayne & Dale Lewis & Ripper Collins beat Don Muraco & Verne Gagne & Billy Robinson & Frankie Laine, Sam Steamboat beat Bill Dromo, Lonnie Mayne beat Pierre Duranton, Dale Lewis beat Beauregard.

2/17/71 Hilo
Sam Steamboat won battle royal, Ripper Collins & Lonnie Mayne beat Verne Gagne & Sam Steamboat, Frankie Laine beat King Curtis dq, Dale Lewis beat Lord Blears, Don Muraco drew Billy Robinson.

2/24/71 Honolulu
Sam Steamboat beat King Curtis North American title, Lonnie Mayne beat Frankie Laine to win Hawaiian title, Mad Dog & Butcher Vachon beat Billy Robinson & Verne Gagne, Dale Lewis drew Don Muraco, Ripper Collins beat Beauregard.

2/27/71 Honolulu
Lonnie Mayne & Ripper Collins beat Frankie Laine & Billy Robinson, Verne Gagne beat Dale Lewis, King Curtis beat Don Muraco dq, Beauregard drew Mr. Fuji.

3/6/71 Honolulu
Billy Robinson beat King Curtis Pier 9 brawl, Sam Steamboat beat Dale Lewis, Lonnie Mayne & Ripper Collins drew Don Muraco & Verne Gagne, Cowboy Laine beat Beauregard.

3/13/71 Honolulu
Verne Gagne beat Mad Dog Vachon defended AWA title, Lonnie Mayne drew Mil Mascaras, King Curtis beat Bobby Shane, Billy Robinson beat The Pro, Don Muraco & Cowboy Laine beat Ripper Collins & Dale Lewis.

3/24/71 Honolulu
Sam Steamboat beat King Curtis Sicilian Stretcher match loser leaves town, Billy Robinson beat Gene Kiniski, Bearcat Wright beat Dale Lewis, Lonnie Mayne & Ripper Collins beat Ray Stevens & Peter Maivia, Vivian Vachon beat Betty Nicolli, Rocky Montero drew Don Muraco, Cowboy Laine beat The Pro (Doug Gilbert) dq.

3/26/71 Hilo
Vivian Vachon beat Betty Niccoli, Ripper Collins & Lonnie Mayne beat Don Muraco & Lord Blears, Gene Kiniski beat Frankie Laine, Billy Robinson beat Mr. Fuji, Sam Steamboat beat The Professional.

3/27/71 Honolulu
Lonnie Mayne beat Cowboy Laine, Vivian Vachon & Bearcat Wright beat Betty Nicolli & Ripper Collins, The Pro drew Don Muraco, Billy Robinson drew Sam Steamboat, Rocky Montero beat Beauregard.

4/3/71 Honolulu
Don Muraco beat Lonnie Mayne dq, Sam Steamboat drew Ripper Collins, Avenger beat Mr. Fujiwara, Rocky Montero beat Beauregard, Bearcat Wright beat The Pro.

4/10/71 Honolulu
Bearcat Wright won battle royal, Lonnie Mayne beat Beauregard, Avenger drew Bad Boy Shields, Ripper Collins drew Don Muraco, Bearcat Wright drew Rocky Montero.

4/17/71 Honolulu
Neff Maiava beat Lonnie Mayne lights out, Bearcat Wright & Don Muraco & Sam Steamboat beat Rocky Montero & Bad Boy Shields & The Pro, Sam Steamboat beat Bad Boy Shields dq, Mr. Fujiwara beat Beauregard, Avenger beat Don Carson.

4/28/71 Honolulu
Ripper Collins & Lonnie Mayne beat Peter Maivia & Ray Stevens Hawaiian tag titles, Bearcat Wright beat Bad Boy Shields, Steven Little Bear beat Bill White, Don Muraco drew Rocky Montero, Avenger beat The Pro.

5/1/71 Honolulu
Bearcat Wright & Neff Maiava beat Ripper Collins & Lonnie Mayne, Sam Steamboat beat Rocky Montero, The Avenger drew Bill Steele, Don Muraco drew The Professional.

5/5/71 Honolulu
Bearcat Wright & Peter Maivia beat Ripper Collins & Lonnie Mayne, Sam Steamboat beat Rocky Montero, Avenger drew Bill Steele, Don Muraco drew The Pro.

5/8/71 Honolulu
The Avenger no contest Ripper Collins, Lonnie Mayne & Rocky Montero beat Bill Francis & Don Muraco, Bill Steele drew Sam Steamboat, Bearcat Wright beat Mac MacFarland.

5/19/71 Honolulu
Gene Kiniski beat Bearcat Wright North American title, Lonnie Mayne beat Haystacks Calhoun dq, Sam Steamboat & Steven Little Bear beat Pat Patterson & Ripper Collins.

5/22/71 Honolulu
Haystacks Calhoun won battle royal, Don Muraco & Bill Francis beat Rocky Montero & Masked Gladiator, The Avenger beat Nicoli Volkoff, Bearcat Wright beat Joe Turco, Sam Steamboat beat Angelo Mosca.

5/24/71 Hilo
Haystacks Calhoun & Bearcat Wright beat Lonnie Mayne & Angelo Mosca, Sam Steamboat beat The Skull, The Avenger ddq Ripper Collins, Lord Blears drew Rocky Montero.

5/29/71 Honolulu
Haystacks Calhoun & Bearcat Wright beat Lonnie Mayne & Ripper Collins, Billy Robinson beat Angelo Mosca, Gladiator drew Avenger, Sam Steamboat beat The Skull, Don Muraco drew Rocky Montero.

6/5/71 Honolulu
Lonnie Mayne drew Sam Steamboat, Bearcat Wright & Don Muraco beat Gladiator & Rocky Montero, Ripper Collins drew Avenger (Bing Ki Lee), Billy Robinson beat The Skull.

6/16/71 Honolulu
Bearcat Wright beat Gene Kiniski Sicilian Stretcher match, Suni War Cloud & Steve Little Bear beat Lonnie Mayne & Ripper Collins Hawaiian tag titles, Sam Steamboat beat Bing Ki Lee, Tony Borne drew Rocky Montero, Beauregard beat Avenger, Lord Littlebrook & Cowboy Lang beat Little Bruiser & Mighty Atom.

6/19/71 Honolulu
Bearcat Wright & Sam Steamboat & Lord Littlebrook beat Lonnie Mayne & Ripper Collins & Little Bruiser, The Skull drew Tony Borne, Rocky Montero drew Bing Ki Lee, Cowboy Lang beat Mighty Atom, Gladiator beat Beauregard.

6/21/71 Hilo
Cowboy Lang & Lord Littlebrook beat Little Bruiser & Mighty Atom, Ripper Collins drew Sam Steamboat, Gladiator beat The Skull, Hahn Lee beat Lonnie Mayne.

6/30/71 Honolulu
Bearcat Wright beat The Sheik dq, Lonnie Mayne & Ripper Collins beat Steven Little Bear & Suni War Cloud to regain tag titles, Pancho Lopez beat The Skull dq, Rocky Montero drew Bing Ki Lee, Gene Kiniski beat Sam Steamboat North American title.

7/7/71 Honolulu
Sam Steamboat & Neff Maiava beat Rocky Montero & Masked Gladiator, Lonnie Mayne beat Bearcat Wright for Hawaii title, Hahn Lee beat The Skull, Pancho Lopez drew Ripper Collins.

7/14/71 Honolulu
The Sheik & Gene Kiniski drew Bearcat Wright & Pedro Morales, Lonnie Mayne & Ripper Collins beat Pancho Lopez & Peter Maivia, Bill Watts drew Rocky Montero, Sam Steamboat beat Bob Sweetan, Danny Hodge beat Gladiator, The Skull drew Bing Ki Lee.

7/21/71 Honolulu
Sam Steamboat & Bearcat Wright beat Lonnie Mayne & Ripper Collins to win Tag titles, Gladiator & Rocky Montero beat Danny Hodge & Bing Ki Lee, Pancho Lopez beat Bulldog Brown dq, Lord Blears drew The Skull.

7/28/71 Honolulu
Sam Steamboat & Pepe Lopez & Bing Ki Lee beat Lonnie Mayne & Bulldog Brown & Rocky Montero, Bearcat Wright beat Gladiator, Ripper Collins beat Beauregard.

8/4/71 Honolulu. Att 8,000
Lonnie Mayne beat Ripper Collins, The Sheik & Gene Kiniski beat Pedro Morales & Bearcat Wright, Bing Ki Lee drew Jerry Monti, Dino Lanza (Tony Marino) beat Bulldog Brown, Sam Steamboat beat Johnny Kace, Rocky Montero beat Chuck Karbo, Mr. Fujiwara beat Pepe Lopez.

8/11/71 Honolulu
Eddie Morrow won hooded battle royal, Sam Steamboat & Bing Ki Lee drew Rick Renaldo & Mr. Fujiwara, Rocky Montero drew Pepe Lopez, Lonnie Mayne beat Jerry Monti, Dino Lanza beat Chris Markoff.

8/18/71 Honolulu
Man Mountain Mike & Dino Lanza & Bing Ki Lee & Sam Steamboat beat Lonnie Mayne & Rocky Montero & Chris Markoff & Rick Renaldo, Eddie Morrow beat Mr. Fujiwara, Rick Renaldo beat Jerry Monti, Pancho Lopez drew Chris Markoff.

8/23/71 Hilo
Man Mountain Mike beat Lonnie Mayne, Bearcat Wright & Eddie Morrow beat Rick Renaldo & Rocky Montero, Sam Steamboat beat Chris Markoff, Dino Lanza beat Pancho Lopez.

8/25/71 Honolulu
Eddie Morrow beat Gene Kiniski to win North American title, Lonnie Mayne beat Ripper Collins loser leaves town, Man Mountain Mike & Dino Lanza drew Rocky Montero & Rick Renaldo, Sam Steamboat beat Chris Markoff, Bing Ki Lee drew Mr. Fujiwara, The Sheik beat Bearcat Wright African Death match.

9/1/71 Honolulu
Lonnie Mayne beat Dino Lanza, Bearcat Wright & Sam Steamboat beat Rick Renaldo & Mr. Fujiwara, Eddie Morrow beat Pepe Lopez, Bing Ki Lee drew Rocky Montero.

9/8/71 Honolulu
Bearcat Wright beat Lonnie Mayne - won the right to paint Mayne Black, The Sheik beat Steven Little Bear, King Curtis & Mr. Fujiwara beat Bing Ki Lee & Dino Lanza, Sam Steamboat beat Spoiler 2, Rick Renaldo beat Pepe Lopez, Gene Kiniski beat Eddie Morrow to regain North American title.

9/11/71 Honolulu
Bearcat Wright & Sam Steamboat beat Lonnie Mayne & Mr. Fuji, King Curtis beat Dino Lanza, Eddie Morrow beat The Spoiler, Rick Renaldo & Rocky Montero beat Pancho Lopez & Hahn Lee.

9/18/71 Honolulu
King Curtis & Bull Ramos beat Sam Steamboat & Bing Ki Lee, Bearcat Wright beat Lonnie Mayne boxing match, Dino Lanza beat Rick Renaldo, Eddie Morrow beat Rocky Montero.

9/21/71 Hilo
Sam Steamboat won hooded battle royal, King Curtis & Fidel Castillo beat Bearcat Wright & Sam Steamboat, Lonnie Mayne beat Dino Lanza (Tony Marino), Hahn Lee beat Rick Renaldo, Eddie Morrow beat Rocky Montero.

9/29/71 Honolulu
Sam Steamboat beat Gene Kiniski to win North American title, The Sheik drew Peter Maivia, Bearcat Wright & Sandy Parker beat Mr. Fujiwara & Toni Rose, Bing Ki Lee beat Rick Renaldo, Dino Lanza beat Fidel Castillo, Eddie Morrow beat Rocky Montero, King Curtis drew Lonnie Mayne.

10/2/71 Honolulu
Ed Francis beat Lonnie Mayne to win Hawaiian title, King Curtis & Fidel Castillo beat Peter Maivia & Dino Lanza, Sam Steamboat beat Rick Renaldo, Bing Ki Lee drew Mr. Fujiwara.

10/9/71 Honolulu
Lonnie Mayne & Sweet Daddy Siki beat Sam Steamboat & Bearcat Wright to win tag titles, King Curtis beat Eddie Morrow, Jack Pesek beat Mr. Fujiwara, Fidel Castillo drew Bing Ki Lee.

10/16/71 Honolulu
King Curtis beat Lonnie Mayne chain match, Sweet Daddy Siki beat Bing Ki Lee, Sam Steamboat & Bearcat Wright beat Fidel Castillo & Mr. Fujiwara, Eddie Morrow beat Jack Pesek.

10/27/71 Honolulu
Sweet Daddy Siki beat Sam Steamboat US title, Ed Francis beat Lonnie Mayne Hawaiian title, The Sheik & Gene Kiniski beat King Curtis & Peter Maivia, Bearcat Wright beat Mike Loren, Eddie Morrow beat Fidel Castillo & Mr. Fujiwara, Eddie Morrow beat Jack Pesek.

10/30/71 Honolulu
Sweet Daddy Siki & Lonnie Mayne beat King Curtis & Hahn Lee, Sam Steamboat beat Fidel Castillo, Eddie Morrow beat Mr. Fuji, Hahn Lee drew Jack Pesek.

11/6/71 Honolulu
Sam Steamboat drew Sweet Daddy Siki, Lonnie Mayne beat Eddie Morrow, King Curtis beat Jack Pesek, Duncan McTavish beat Mr. Fuji, Fidel Castillo drew Hahn Lee.

11/13/71 Honolulu
Sweet Daddy Siki & Lonnie Mayne & Fidel Castillo beat King Curtis & Sam Steamboat & Duncan McTavish, Jimmy Snuka beat Mr. Fuji, Bing Ki Lee beat Jack Pesek dq, Eddie Morrow drew Fidel Castillo.

11/17/71 Hilo
Sam Steamboat & Jimmy Snuka ddq Sweet Daddy Siki & Lonnie Mayne, Duncan McTavish drew Fidel Castillo, Hahn Lee beat Frank Allman, Jack Pesek drew Joe Scarpello.

11/21/71 Honolulu
Lonnie Mayne & Sweet Daddy Siki beat Jimmy Snuka & Sam Steamboat, Duncan McTavish beat Fidel Castillo, Destroyer drew Bing Ki Lee, Toni Rose & Donna Christanello beat Sandy Parker & Sue Green.

11/24/71 Honolulu
Ed Francis beat Sweet Daddy Siki sleeper VS Claw, Gene Kiniski drew Peter Maivia, Jimmy Snuka drew Destroyer, Duncan MacTavish & Bing Ki Lee beat Fidel Castillo & Mr. Fujiwara, Joe Scarpello beat Jack Pesek, Sue Green & Sandy Parker beat Donna Christanello & Toni Rose.

11/27/71 Honolulu
Sweet Daddy Siki & Lonnie Mayne beat Jimmy Snuka & Sam Steamboat, Toni Rose & Donna Christanello beat Susan Green & Sandy Parker for World tag titles, The Destroyer drew Hahn Lee, Duncan McTavish beat Fidel Castillo.

12/8/71 Honolulu
Johnny Barend beat Sweet Daddy Siki North American title, Ed Francis drew Lonnie Mayne, Jimmy Snuka & Sam Steamboat beat Toru Tanaka & Buck Ramstead, Toru Tanaka beat Bing Ki Lee, Tosh Togo drew Duncan McTavish, Peter Maivia beat Buck Ramstead.

12/11/71 Honolulu
Tex McKenzie & Jimmy Snuka & Sam Steamboat VS Sweet Daddy Siki & Lonnie Mayne & Toru Tanaka, Bob Ramstead VS Johnny Barend, Hahn Lee VS Mighty Brutus, Duncan McTavish VS Toru Tanaka.

12/18/71 Honolulu
Jimmy Snuka won battle royal, Sweet Daddy Siki & Lonnie Mayne beat Duncan McTavish & Don Muraco, Jimmy Snuka beat Mighty Brutus dq, Bob Ramstead drew Tosh Togo, Sam Steamboat drew Toru Tanaka.

12/25/71 Honolulu
Sweet Daddy Siki & Lonnie Mayne VS Johnny Barend & Ed Francis stretcher tag, Giant Baba VS Toru Tanaka, Mad Dog Vachon VS Don Muraco, Jimmy Snuka & Sam Steamboat VS Dingo & Mighty Brutus, King Curtis VS Buck Ramstead, Sandor Kovacs VS Bing Ki Lee.

1972

1/1/72 Honolulu
Sam Steamboat beat Mad Dog Vachon, Sweet Daddy Siki beat Bing Ki Lee, Johnny Barend & Don Muraco beat Jack Bence & Mad Dog Vachon, Lonnie Mayne drew Jimmy Snuka, Pat O'Brien drew Mighty Brutus.

1/12/72 Honolulu
Ed Francis beat Mad Dog Vachon, Sam Steamboat & Jimmy Snuka beat Mike Webster & Jack Bence, Jack Bence drew Pat O'Brien, Sweet Daddy Siki beat Johnny Barend, Lonnie Mayne beat La Pantera Negra, Tosh Togo drew Mighty Brutus.

1/15/72 Honolulu
Johnny Barend beat Lonnie Mayne boxing, Sam Steamboat & Jimmy Snuka drew Sweet Daddy Siki & Mad Dog Vachon, Pat O'Brien beat Mighty Brutus dq, Tosh Togo drew Jack Bence.

1/17/72 Hilo
Johnny Barend & Jimmy Snuka beat Sweet Daddy Siki & Lonnie Mayne, Sam Steamboat beat Mad Dog Vachon, Mighty Brutus beat Pat O'Brien, Jack Bence drew Lord Blears.

1/26/72 Honolulu
Dory Funk Jr beat Sweet Daddy Siki NWA title, Johnny Barend & Jimmy Snuka beat Mad Dog Vachon & Lonnie Mayne, Sam Steamboat beat Jack Bence dq, Ed Francis drew Mighty Brutus (The Skull, Bugsy McGraw), Pat O'Brien beat Soldat Gorky, Dingo The Sundowner drew Tosh Togo.

1/29/72 Honolulu
Ed Francis beat Mad Dog Vachon defended Hawaiian title, Sam Steamboat drew Lonnie Mayne, Sweet Daddy Siki beat Pat O'Brien, Jimmy Snuka & Johnny Barend beat Jack Bence & Mighty Brutus.

2/5/72 Honolulu
Johnny Barend drew Sweet Daddy Siki Pier 9 brawl, Sam Steamboat & Jimmy Snuka beat Lonnie Mayne & Jack Bence, Mighty Brutus beat Chuck Richards, Pat O'Brien drew The Stomper, Bing Ki Lee beat Russian Wolfman.

2/16/72 Honolulu
Johnny Barend & Bobo Brazil drew The Sheik & Sweet Daddy Siki, Lonnie Mayne beat Mad Dog Vachon, Jack Bence beat Chuck Richards, Jimmy Snuka beat The Stomper, Gene Kiniski beat Ed Francis to win Hawaiian title.

2/19/72 Honolulu
Ed & Bill Francis beat Lonnie Mayne & Sweet Daddy Siki dq, Sam Steamboat beat Jack Bence, Johnny Barend beat Chuck Richards, Jimmy Snuka beat Mad Dog Vachon, Mighty Brutus beat Pat O'Brien,

2/26/72 Honolulu
Lonnie Mayne & Billy Graham & Mighty Brutus & Chuck Richards & Jack Bence beat Jimmy Snuka & Sam Steamboat & Jack Carson & Pat O'Brien, Mighty Brutus beat Jack Carson, Sam Steamboat drew Lonnie Mayne, Jimmy Snuka beat Chuck Richards.

3/8/72 Honolulu
Dory Funk Jr beat Johnny Barend NWA title, Gene Kiniski beat Ed Francis, Lonnie Mayne drew Ripper Collins, Sweet Daddy Siki beat King Curtis, Luke Graham beat Jack Carson, Jimmy Snuka & Sam Steamboat beat Mighty Brutus & Jack Bence.

3/15/72 Honolulu
Johnny Barend & Sam Steamboat beat Lonnie Mayne & Sweet Daddy Siki, Jimmy Snuka beat Billy Graham dq, Mighty Brutus beat Jack Carson, Jack Bence drew Pat O'Brien.

3/22/72 Honolulu
Johnny Barend beat Sweet Daddy Siki to win North American title in a loser leaves town match, Gene Kiniski beat Sam Steamboat, Lonnie Mayne drew Ed Francis, Bulldog Brower beat Pat O'Brien, Jimmy Snuka & Manny Soto beat Billy Graham & Sputnik Monroe.

4/12/72 Honolulu
Johnny Barend beat Terry Funk North American Title Defense, The Sheik beat Bobo Brazil, Gene Kiniski & Fred Blassie beat Sam Steamboat & Fred Curry, Tosh Togo beat Lonnie Mayne dq, Jimmy Snuka beat Bulldog Brower, Ed Francis beat Mike Conrad.

5/3/72 Honolulu
Gene Kiniski beat Billy Robinson defended Hawaiian titles, Ed Francis drew Fred Blassie, The Sheik beat Bobo Brazil, King Curtis drew Jimmy Snuka, Sam Steamboat beat Tosh Togo, Bobo Johnson & Cowboy Lang beat Little Bruiser & Little Crusher.

6/14/72 Honolulu
Fred Blassie beat Sam Steamboat lights out match, The Sheik drew Fred Curry, Gene Kiniski beat The Great Kusatsu, Bobo Brazil beat Buck Robley, Jimmy Snuka drew Masked Executioner, Ed Francis & Kinji Matsuta beat Mr. Wrestling & Dan Krow.

7/12/72 Honolulu
Johnny Barend beat Fred Blassie North American title, Fred Curry beat The Sheik, Dory Funk Jr beat Kinji Matsuta, Ed Francis beat Killer Kowalski, Bull Curry beat Sandor Kovacs, Jimmy Snuka & Sam Steamboat beat Mr. X & Masked Executioner.

7/26/72 Honolulu
Johnny Barend beat Fred Blassie North American title match, Fred & Bull Curry beat The Sheik & Abdulla Farouk, Ed Francis drew Bill Miller, Executioner drew Rene Goulet, Jimmy Snuka & Sam Steamboat beat Mr. X & Masked Executioner.

7/31/72 Hilo
Johnny Barend & Fred Curry & Vivian Vachon beat Fred Blassie & Baron Scicluna & Nancy Hart, Sam Steamboat beat Kinji Matsuta, Jimmy Snuka beat Masked Executioner.

8/2/72 Honolulu
Fred Curry beat Gene Kiniski to win Hawaiian title, Haystacks Calhoun & Johnny Barend beat The Sheik & Fred Blassie, Sam Steamboat & Jimmy Snuka beat Executioner & Kenji Matsuta, Ed Francis beat Baron Scicluna, Dawn Lemke beat Vivian Vachon.

8/30/72 Honolulu
Ray Stevens & Nick Bockwinkel beat Wahoo McDaniel & Fred Curry defended AWA tag titles, Lonnie Mayne beat Jimmy Snuka, Johnny Barend drew Dory Funk Jr, Sam Steamboat beat Al Costello, Ed Francis drew Fred Blassie, Tahiti Kid & Farmer Jerome beat Sky Low Low & Little Brutus.

9/20/72 Honolulu
Nick Bockwinkel & Ray Stevens ddq Pedro Morales & Wahoo McDaniel, Ed Francis beat Fred Blassie Cage match, Jimmy Snuka beat Ray Kamaka, Sam Steamboat beat Mr. X, Fred Curry beat John Quinn, Giant Baba ddq The Sheik.

10/11/72 Honolulu
Ray Stevens & Nick Bockwinkel beat Bearcat Wright & Bobo Brazil, Fred Curry beat Fred Blassie, The Sheik beat Tony Rocco, Sam Steamboat beat Fidel Castillo, Ed Francis drew John Quinn.

10/21/72 Honolulu
Billy Robinson beat Ivan Koloff, The Sheik beat Fred Curry, Sam Steamboat beat Ric Ferrara, Ed Francis beat Bill Dromo, Bull Bullinski (Bad Boy Shields) drew Mighty Inoue, Cowboy Lang & Bobo Brazil beat Little Tokyo & Wee Willie Wilson.

11/15/72 Honolulu
Ed Francis & Billy Robinson beat Ray Stevens & Nick Bockwinkel, Dusty Rhodes beat Sam Steamboat to win North American title, Giant Baba beat Bulldog Brown, Lonnie Mayne beat Jack Carson, Tony Borne drew Ray Glenn.

11/29/72 Honolulu
Ed Francis & Billy Robinson beat Nick Bockwinkel & Ray Stevens dq, Destroyer beat Dory Dixon, Tosh Togo drew Jack Carson, Sam Steamboat beat John Foley, Ray Glenn beat Pepo Casto.

12/13/72 Honolulu
Don Muraco won battle royal, Verne Gagne beat King Curtis AWA title, Dusty Rhodes drew Sam Steamboat, Nick Bockwinkel & Ray Stevens beat Don Muraco & Red Bastein, Billy Robinson beat Jack Carson, Ed Francis beat Sueno, Tosh Togo drew Bull Bullinski, Spiros Arion beat Dennis Stamp.

1973

1/17/73 Honolulu
Dory Funk Jr beat Billy Robinson, Dusty Rhodes beat Don Muraco, Ed Francis beat The Sheik to win Hawaiian Title, Ripper Collins beat Rick Drasin, Tony Borne drew Sam Steamboat, Fred Blassie did not beat Lord Blears in 10 minutes.

2/7/73 Honolulu
Dusty Rhodes & Dick Murdoch beat Billy Robinson & Don Muraco, Ripper Collins drew Peter Maivia, Ken Patera beat Tapia, Paul Jones beat Harley Race dq, Ed Francis beat Lord Nelson, Bulldog Brown drew Sam Steamboat, Jimmy Snuka beat Pepo Castro.

3/7/73 Honolulu
The Sheik beat Dory Funk, Billy Robinson & Don Muraco beat Dusty Rhodes & Dick Murdoch, Jimmy Snuka beat Ripper Collins, Ken Patera beat Tony Borne, Sam Steamboat beat The Masked Executioner, Ed Francis beat Haru Sasaki.

4/4/73 Honolulu
Nick Bockwinkel & Ray Stevens beat Billy Robinson & Don Muraco, Dusty Rhodes beat Ken Patera, Ed Francis beat Ripper Collins dq, Sam Steamboat beat Jose Quintero, Jimmy Snuka beat Haru Sasaki, Cowboy Lang & Hillbilly Pete beat Tokyo Kid & Lord Littlebrook.

4/9/73 Hilo. Att 1,200
Cowboy Lang & Farmer Pete beat Billy The Kid & Johnny Reb, Jimmy Snuka ddq Ripper Collins, Sam Steamboat beat Jose Quintero, Tosh Togo beat Bepo Castro.

4/18/73 Honolulu
Wahoo McDaniel beat Billy Graham, Ed Francis drew Sam Steamboat, Tony Borne beat Jimmy Snuka dq, Peter Maivia beat Wild Bill Howard, Sandy Parker beat Bambi Ball, Ray Stevens drew Don Muraco.

5/16/73 Honolulu
Wahoo McDaniel beat Billy Graham Indian Death Match, Dusty Rhodes beat Billy Robinson North American title dq, Ivan Koloff beat Ken Patera, Sam Steamboat & Jimmy Snuka beat Mad Dog Vachon & Lars Anderson, Ed Francis beat Buck Ramstead, Peter Maivia beat The Lumberjack.

6/6/73 Honolulu
Billy Graham & Ivan Koloff beat Ken Patera & Jack Carson, Ed Francis beat Sam Steamboat Hawaiian title, Billy Robinson beat Dusty Rhodes to win NA title, Jimmy Snuka drew Tony Borne, Peter Maivia beat Pepo Castro.

6/20/73 Honolulu
Sam Steamboat beat Ed Francis stretcher match, Ripper Collins beat Jimmy Snuka, Ken Patera beat The Alaskan, Peter Maivia beat Tony Borne, Billy Robinson drew Billy Graham NA title defense, Lord Littlebrook & Haiti Kid beat Tokyo Joe & Frenchie Lamont.

6/25/73 Hilo. Att 1,200
Lord Littlebrook & The Haiti Kid beat Little Tokyo & Frenchy Lamonte, Ken Patera beat The Alaskan, The Alaskan beat Ed Francis, Sam Steamboat beat Tony Borne.

7/25/73 Honolulu
Verne Gagne beat Billy Robinson dq, Nick Bockwinkel & Ray Stevens beat Ken Patera & Billy Robinson, Ripper Collins & Ed Francis beat Peter Maivia & Sam Steamboat to win Hawaiian tag titles, Hard Boiled Haggerty beat Ric Flair, Bill Francis drew Bull Ramos.

8/22/73 Honolulu
Pedro Morales drew Ed Francis, Ken Patera & Billy Robinson beat Ray Stevens & Nick Bockwinkel dq, Sam Steamboat beat Hard Boiled Haggerty, Bill Francis beat Tony Borne dq, Betty Nicolli & Ripper Collins beat Jean Antone & Paul Jones.

8/28/73 Hilo
Sam Steamboat & Jean Antone beat Ed Francis & Betty Niccoli, Neff Maiava beat Tony Borne, Bill Francis beat Hard Boiled Haggerty dq, Tony Borne drew Tosh Togo.

9/12/73 Honolulu
The Crusher beat Billy Graham, Ed Francis beat Sam Steamboat for Hawaii title, Neff Maiava & Tosh Togo beat Tony Borne & Ripper Collins, Nick Bockwinkel beat Ken Patera, Ivan Koloff beat Al Madril, Bill Francis beat Jack Bence.

9/26/73 Honolulu
Red Bastein & Ken Patera beat Ivan Koloff & Billy Graham, Billy Robinson beat Nick Bockwinkel North American title, Sam Steamboat & Peter Maivia beat Ripper Collins & Ed Francis, Tosh Togo beat Johnny Powers, Sandor Kovacs drew Bill Francis.

10/10/73 Honolulu
Ed Francis beat Billy Robinson dq, Peter Maivia & Sam Steamboat beat Ray Stevens & Nick Bockwinkel dq, Ripper Collins beat Al Madril, Tosh Togo drew Rick Drasin, Bill Francis beat Pepo Castro.

11/14/73 Honolulu
Verne Gagne beat Ed Francis AWA title, Nick Bockwinkel & Ray Stevens drew Peter Maivia & Sam Steamboat, Ripper Collins beat Tosh Togo, Ken Patera beat Masked Executioner, Greg Valentine beat Ric Drasin, Bill Francis beat Pepo Castro.

11/28/73 Honolulu
Billy Robinson beat Fred Blassie North American title Defense, Ripper Collins & Greg Valentine beat Sam Steamboat & Peter Maivia to win Hawaiian tag titles, Billy Graham beat Ken Patera dq, Ed Francis drew Al Madril, Bobo Johnson & Haiti Kid beat Little Bruiser & Tokyo Joe.

12/19/73 Honolulu
Ken Patera won battle royal, Giant Baba & Sam Steamboat & Peter Maivia beat Ripper Collins & Greg Valentine & Billy Graham, Barbi Doll beat Sandy Parker, Ken Patera beat Mr. Fujiwara, Bill Francis drew Toru Tanaka, Cowboy Lang beat Lord Littlebrook.

1/9/74 Honolulu
Billy Graham beat Ed Francis to win Hawaiian title, Ray Stevens & Nick Bockwinkel drew Billy Robinson & Red Bastein, Pak Song drew Ripper Collins, Tosh Togo drew Bill Francis, Sam Steamboat beat Peace Brother 1, Peter Maivia beat Peace Brother 2.

2/13/74 Honolulu
Billy Robinson beat Verne Gagne, Chris Taylor beat Butcher Vachon, Billy Graham beat Ed Francis, Ripper Collins beat Guy Larose, Neff Maiava & Sam Steamboat beat Dale Roberts & Jerry Brown, Bill Francis beat The Phantom.

3/27/74 Honolulu
Billy Robinson beat Verne Gagne, Crusher & Ken Patera beat Larry Heinemi & Billy Graham, Ripper Collins drew Ed Francis, Sam Steamboat beat Len Shelly dq, Neff Maiava beat Tony Borne, Harold Sakata beat Peace Brother 1.

6/19/74 Honolulu
Gene Kiniski beat Dory Funk Jr, Sam Steamboat & The Crusher beat Horst Hoffman & Billy Graham, Neff Maiava drew Ivan Koloff, Reggie Parks drew Mad Dog Bob Griffin, The Destroyer beat Pepo Castro, Sue Green beat Paula Kaye.

7/17/74 Honolulu
Verne Gagne beat Gene Kiniski, Ivan Putski & Sam Steamboat beat Peace Brothers, Sam Steamboat beat Peace Brother 1, Neff Maiava beat Pepo Castro, Ed Francis beat Masked Marvel.

1977

6/7/77 Honolulu
Andre The Giant & Don Muraco & Bill Francis beat John Studd & Buddy Rose & Chris Markoff, John Tolos beat Baron Scicluna, Rocky Tomayo beat Mickey Doyle, Buddy Rose drew Bill Francis.

6/22/77 Honolulu
Billy Whitewolf beat Tony Borne, Steve Strong beat Ricky Hunter, Eric Frolich beat John Tolos dq, Giant Baba beat Lonnie Mayne, Bill & Russ Francis beat Gene Kiniski & Apache Gringo.

6/29/77 Honolulu
Eric Frolich drew Sam Steamboat, Ricky Hunter beat Tony Borne, Billy Whitewolf beat Duke Savage (El Gringo), Giant Baba beat Gene Kiniski, John Tolos & Steve Strong beat Bill & Russ Francis.

7/6/77 Honolulu
Sam Steamboat beat Tony Borne, Billy Whitewolf beat Masked Terror, Steve Strong beat Nick Kozak, Duke Savage drew Ricky Hunter, Russ Francis beat John Tolos dq.

7/13/77 Honolulu
Tosh Togo drew Tony Borne, Nick Kozak beat Duke Savage, John Tolos beat Ricky Hunter, Billy Whitewolf & Sam Steamboat beat Steve Lawler & Steve Strong.

7/20/77 Honolulu
Ricky Hunter beat Tony Borne, Nick Kozak & Sam Steamboat beat Steve Strong & Steve Lawler, Hillbilly Pete & Haiti Kid beat Billy The Kid & Little John, Bill Francis drew John Tolos, Nick Bockwinkel beat Billy Whitewolf.

7/27/77 Honolulu
Haiti Kid & Ricky Hunter beat Steve Lawler & Billy The Kid, John Tolos beat Nick Bockwinkel, Hillbilly Pete beat little John, Steve Strong & Jesse Ventura beat Billy Whitewolf & Sam Steamboat to win tag titles.

8/2/77 Honolulu
Jesse Ventura beat Ricky Hunter, Billy Whitewolf beat Gorilla Lawler, Sam Steamboat beat Duke Savage, Steve Strong & Jesse Ventura beat Nick Kozak & Ricky Hunter, Bill Francis beat John Tolos.

8/10/77 Honolulu
Jesse Ventura drew Nick Kozak, Sam Steamboat beat Gorilla Lawler, Ricky Hunter beat Tor Kamata, Jesse Ventura & John Tolos & Steve Strong beat Billy Whitewolf & Nick Kozak & Bill Francis.

8/17/77 Pearl Harbor
Sam Steamboat beat Tor Kamata, Steve Lawler beat Ricky Hunter, John Tolos & Jesse Ventura no contest Billy Whitewolf & Nick Kozak, Bill Francis beat Steve Strong for Hawaii State title.

8/24/77 Honolulu
Ricky Hunter beat Tor Kamata, Gorilla Lawler drew Duke Savage, Bill Francis & Sam Steamboat beat Jesse Ventura & Steve Strong, Wenonah Little Heart & Vicki Williams beat Moolah & Terry Shane, Billy Whitewolf beat Nick Bockwinkel.

8/31/77 Honolulu
Jesse Ventura drew Bill Francis, Nick Kozak beat Steve Strong, John Tolos beat Ricky Hunter, Moolah beat Vicki Williams, Bill Francis & Wenonah Little Heart beat Terry Shane & Steve Lawler.

9/7/77 Honolulu
Nick Kozak drew Duke Savage, Bill Francis beat Steve Lawler, John Tolos beat Ricky Hunter, Jesse Ventura & Steve Strong beat Sam Steamboat & Nick Kozak.

9/14/77 Honolulu
John Tolos beat Tosh Togo, Sam Steamboat beat Duke Savage, Steve Strong & Jesse Ventura beat Bill Francis & Buck Zumhoff.

9/18/77 Honolulu
Buck Zumhoff beat Duke Savage, Tosh Togo drew Steve Lawler, Steve Strong beat Bill Francis, Sam Steamboat & Steve Olsonoski beat John Tolos & Jesse Ventura.

9/21/77 Honolulu
Steve Olsonoski drew Jesse Ventura, John Tolos & Jesse Ventura & Steve Strong beat Bill Francis & Sam Steamboat & Steve Olsonoski, Buck Zumhoff beat Steve Lawler, Tosh Togo beat Duke Savage.

9/28/77 Honolulu
Steve Olsonoski drew Duke Savage, Tosh Togo beat Buck Zumhoff, Sam Steamboat beat John Tolos for North American title, Pampero Firpo beat Steve Lawler, Bill Francis beat Nick Bockwinkel, Greg Gagne & Jim Brunzell beat Jesse Ventura & Steve Strong.

10/2/77 Honolulu
Steve Strong & Jesse Ventura beat Bill Francis & Missing Link to win Hawaiian tag titles, Tor Kamata beat Buck Zumhoff, John Tolos beat Gorilla Lawler, Sam Steamboat beat Steve O.

10/5/77 Honolulu
Sam Steamboat beat Steve Olsonoski, Steve Lawler beat John Tolos, Tor Kamata beat Buck Zumhoff, Bill Francis & Pampero Firpo no contest Steve Strong & Jesse Ventura.

11/2/77 Honolulu
Ed Francis beat Tor Kamata, Pampero Firpo & John Tolos beat Tor Kamata & Killer Christy, Jesse Ventura drew Sam Steamboat, Billy Whitewolf beat Buck Zumhoff, Bill Francis No Contest Steve Strong.

11/23/77 Honolulu
John Tolos beat Steve Strong, Tor Kamata no contest Billy Whitewolf, Sam Steamboat no contest Jesse Ventura, Buck Zumhoff & Cowboy Lang & Hillbilly Pete beat Rocky Tomayo & Little John & Little Tokyo, Pampero Firpo & Bill Francis beat Bobby Heenan & Nick Bockwinkel.

12/14/77 Honolulu
Nick Bockwinkel drew Pampero Firpo, Don Muraco beat Duke Savage, Sam Steamboat beat Tor Kamata, Chris Markoff beat Buck Zumhoff, Bill Francis & John Tolos beat Steve Strong & Jesse Ventura, Billy Whitewolf drew Rocky Tamayo.

12/21/77 Honolulu
Chris Markoff drew John Tolos, Bill Francis beat Steve Strong, Tor Kamata & Rocky Tomayo beat Don Muraco & Billy Whitewolf, Sam Steamboat beat Jesse Ventura.

1978

1/11/78 Honolulu
Tor Kamata beat Billy Whitewolf, Sam Steamboat beat Lindy Calder, Steve Strong beat Pampero Firpo, Rick Martel beat Rocky Tomayo, Jim Brunzell & Greg Gagne beat Blackjack Lanza & Bobby Duncum, John Tolos & Bill Francis beat Bruce Brown & Chris Markoff.

1/25/78 Honolulu
Chris Markoff & Steve Strong beat Bill Francis & John Tolos, Rick Martel beat Tor Kamata, Billy Whitewolf beat Bruce Brown, Sam Steamboat beat Rocky Tomayo.

2/1/78 Honolulu
John Tolos beat Steve Strong for Hawaiian State Title, Tor Kamata & Rocky Tomayo beat Billy Whitewolf & Sam Steamboat, Rick Martel beat Jack Bence, Bill Francis drew Chris Markoff.

2/13/78 Honolulu
Nick Bockwinkel beat John Tolos, Steve Strong & Chris Markoff beat Russ & Bill Francis, Rick Martel beat Tor Kamata dq, Sam Steamboat beat Bruce Brown, Rocky Tomayo beat Tosh Togo COR, Billy Whitewolf beat Duke Savage.

2/15/78 Honolulu
Rick Martel beat Bruce Brown, John Tolos beat Chris Markoff, Bill & Russ Francis beat Tor Kamata & Rocky Tomayo, Billy Whitewolf drew Steve Strong.

2/22/78 Honolulu
Steve Strong & Chris Markoff beat Bill & Ed Francis dq, Billy Whitewolf beat Tor Kamata dq, John Tolos beat Bruce Brown, Sam Steamboat drew Rocky Tomayo, Rick Martel beat Duke Savage.

3/1/78 Honolulu
John Tolos beat Steve Strong, Rick Martel beat Executioner 2 dq, Bill Francis & Billy Whitewolf beat Tor Kamata & Rocky Tomayo, Chris Markoff beat Sam Steamboat.

3/8/78 Honolulu
John Tolos beat Rocky Tomayo, Rick Martel beat Tor Kamata, Executioner 2 drew Bill Francis, Chris Markoff & Steve Strong beat Bill Francis & Billy Whitewolf.

3/15/78 Honolulu
John Tolos & Bill Francis drew Steve Strong & Chris Markoff, Haiti Kid beat Little Tokyo, Billy Whitewolf beat Executioner 2 dq, Lord Little Brook beat Cowboy Lang, Tor Kamata beat Rick Martel.

3/22/78 Honolulu
Sam Steamboat beat Executioner 2, Bill & Ed & Russ Francis beat Nick Bockwinkel & Chris Markoff & Steve Strong, Rick Martel beat Tor Kamata, Rocky Tomayo beat Duke Savage.

3/29/78 Honolulu
Ed Francis beat Rocky Tomayo, Russ Francis drew Tor Kamata, Rick Martel beat Chris Markoff dq, John Anson beat Bill Francis dq, Billy Whitewolf beat Duke Savage.

4/5/78 Honolulu
John Anson beat Russ Francis, Buddy Rose beat Billy Whitewolf, Bill Francis drew Rocky Tomayo, Rocky Tamayo & Chris Markoff & Tor Kamata beat Rick Martel & Bill Francis & Sam Steamboat.

4/12/78 Honolulu
Buddy Rose drew Bill Francis, John Studd beat Duke Savage, Chris Markoff beat Billy Whitewolf, Bill & Russ Francis beat Tor Kamata & Rocky Tomayo dq, Rick Martel beat John Anson.

4/19/78 Honolulu
Rick Martel beat Chris Markoff, Tor Kamata beat George Wells, Billy Whitewolf beat Rocky Tomayo, Bill & Russ Francis beat John Anson & John Studd.

4/26/78 Honolulu
George Wells beat John Anson for Hawaiian title, Rick Martel beat Nick Bockwinkel, Bill & Russ Francis beat Steve Strong & Chris Markoff, Ed Francis beat Bobby Heenan dq, Billy Whitewolf beat Tor Kamata, Buddy Rose drew Russ Francis.

5/1/78 Hilo
Bill Francis drew Chris Markoff, Billy Whitewolf & Rick Martel beat John Studd & Buddy Rose, Ed Francis beat Rocky Tamayo, Russ Francis beat Tor Kamata.

5/3/78 Honolulu
Ed & Bill & Russ Francis no contest John Studd & Tor Kamata & Rocky Tomayo, Rick Martel beat Buddy Rose, Billy Whitewolf beat Chris Markoff.

5/10/78 Pearl Harbor
Russ Francis beat Tor Kamata, Joyce Grable & Rick Martel beat Le Lani Kai & Buddy Rose, John Studd beat Billy Whitewolf.

5/15/78 Hilo
Rick Martel & Joyce Grable beat Chris Markoff & Le Lani Kai, John Studd & Buddy Rose beat Bill & Russ Francis, Tor Kamata beat Billy Whitewolf.

5/17/78 Honolulu
John Tolos beat Chris Markoff dq, Tor Kamata beat Billy Whitewolf loser leaves town, Nick Bockwinkel beat Rick Martel, Joyce Grable & Vicki Williams beat Pepper LaBianco & Leilani Kai, Big John Studd & Buddy Rose beat Russ & Bill Francis, George Wells beat Rocky Tomayo.

5/24/78 Honolulu
John Tolos beat John Studd dq, Joyce Grable beat Pepper LaBianco, Buddy Rose beat George Wells to win Hawaiian title, John Tolos & Russ Francis teamed to have Francis win pole battle royal.

5/29/78 Hilo
Bill Francis won battle royal, John Studd & Buddy Rose beat Bill & Russ Francis, John Tolos & Vicki Williams beat Rocky Tamayo & Pepper LaBianco, Bill Francis drew Chris Markoff.

5/31/78 Pearl Harbor
Mickey Doyle drew Duke Savage, Don Muraco beat Chris Markoff, John Tolos no contest Rocky Tomayo, John Studd & Buddy Rose beat Bill & Russ Francis.

6/7/78 Honolulu
Andre The Giant & Don Muraco & Bill Francis beat John Studd & Buddy Rose & Chris Markoff, John Tolos beat Baron Scicluna, Rocky Tomayo beat Mickey Doyle, Buddy Rose drew Bill Francis.

6/14/78 Honolulu
John Tolos & Steve Strong beat Buddy Rose & John Studd, Russ Francis beat Nick Bockwinkel dq, Don Muraco beat Rocky Tomayo, Chris Markoff beat Mickey Doyle, Bill Francis beat Duke Savage, Little John & Cowboy Lang beat Little Tokyo & Lord Littlebrook.

6/21/78 Honolulu
Mr. Fuji & Tor Kamata beat Mickey Doyle & Bill Francis dq, John Tolos & Cowboy Lang beat Chris Markoff & Little Tokyo, Russ Francis beat John Studd, Don Muraco beat Buddy Rose, Ed Francis beat Chris Markoff.

6/28/78 Honolulu
Don Muraco beat Rocky Tomayo, Chris Markoff beat Mickey Doyle, Andre The Giant & John Tolos beat John Studd & Buddy Rose, Bill Francis drew Buddy Rose.

7/5/78 Honolulu
Malo The Wonder Boy Satoa drew Tama Togo, Randy Morse beat Mickey Doyle, Don Muraco beat John Studd dq, Chris Markoff beat Ed Francis, Steve Strong & John Tolos beat Mr. Fuji & Tor Kamata, Chris Markoff drew Bill Francis.

7/11/78 Honolulu
Sam Steamboat drew John Studd, Randy Morse beat Mickey Doyle, John Tolos no contest Mr. Fuji, Tor Kamata & Mr. Fuji beat Bill Francis & Don Muraco.

7/19/78 Honolulu
Tor Kamata beat Nick Bockwinkel dq, Sam Steamboat drew Bill Francis, Ed Francis beat Chris Markoff, King Curtis drew Pampero Firpo, Don Muraco & John Tolos beat Mr. Fuji & Randy Morse, Steve Strong drew John Studd, Mickey Doyle drew Malo Satoa.

7/20/78 Honolulu
Nick Bockwinkel beat Billy Whitewolf, Tosh Togo beat Duke Savage, Nick Kozak & Sam Steamboat beat Steve Strong & Gorilla Lawler, Rocky Hunter beat Tony Borne, Bill Francis drew John Tolos, Haiti Kid & Hillbilly Pete beat Billy The Kid & Little John.

7/26/78 Honolulu
Steve Strong beat John Studd, Don Muraco beat Sky Hi Morse, John Tolos beat Mr. Fuji, Don Muraco beat Randy Morse, Tor Kamata beat Bill Francis.

8/3/78 Honolulu
Jesse Ventura beat Ricky Hunter, Billy Whitewolf beat Steve Lawler, Sam Steamboat beat Duke Savage, Jesse Ventura & Steve Strong beat Ricky Hunter & Nick Kozak, Bill Francis beat John Tolos.

8/9/78 Honolulu
Tor Kamata beat Don Muraco, Steve Strong beat Randy Morse, John Tolos drew Big John Studd, Karl Von Steiger & Mr. Fuji beat Sam Steamboat & Bill Francis.

8/10/78 Honolulu
Jesse Ventura drew Nick Kozak, Sam Steamboat beat Steve Lawler, Ricky Hunter beat Tor Kamata, John Tolos & Steve Strong & Jesse Ventura beat Billy Whitewolf & Bill Francis & Nick Kozak.

8/16/78 Honolulu
Sam Steamboat beat Randy Morse dq, Bill Francis drew John Studd, Don Muraco beat Tor Kamata, Karl Von Steiger & Mr. Fuji beat John Tolos & Steve Strong.

8/17/78 Pearl Harbor
Sam Steamboat beat Tor Kamata dq, Steve Lawler beat Ricky Hunter, John Tolos & Jesse Ventura no contest Nick Kozak & Billy Whitewolf, Bill Francis beat Steve Strong for Hawaiian title.

8/23/78 Honolulu
Mike Cunningham & John Tolos & Steve Strong beat Mr. Fuji & Prof Tanaka & Karl Von Steiger, Andre The Giant beat Nick Bockwinkel, Mr. Fuji beat Pampero Firpo, Don Muraco drew Tor Kamata, Peter Maivia drew John Studd, Bill Francis beat Randy Morse.

8/24/78 Honolulu
Steve Lawler drew Duke Savage, Ricky Hunter beat Tor Kamata dq, John Tolos beat Nick Kozak, Bill Francis & Sam Steamboat beat Jesse Ventura & Steve Strong dq, Vicki Williams & Wenonah Little Heart beat Moolah & Terri Shane, Billy Whitewolf beat Nick Bockwinkel Indian Death Match.

8/30/78 Honolulu
Don Muraco beat Karl Von Steiger, Pampero Firpo beat Mike Cunningham, John Tolos drew Mr. Fuji, Tor Kamata beat Bill Francis dq, Steve Strong beat Big John Studd.

8/31/78 Pearl Harbor
Bill Francis & Wenonah Little Heart beat Steve Lawler & Terry Shane, Moolah beat Vicki Williams, John Tolos beat Ricky Hunter, Nick Kozak beat Steve Strong dq, Bill Francis drew Jesse Ventura.

9/6/78 Honolulu
Mr. Fuji beat Pampero Firpo dq, Don Muraco beat Duke Savage, Bill Francis drew John Studd, Tor Kamata & Karl Von Steiger drew John Tolos & Steve Strong.

9/7/78 Honolulu
Nick Kozak drew Duke Savage, Bill Francis beat Steve Lawler, John Tolos beat Ricky Hunter, Jesse Ventura & Steve Strong beat Sam Steamboat & Nick Kozak.

9/13/78 Honolulu
Mr. Fuji & Karl Von Steiger beat Pampero Firpo & Bill Francis, Steve Strong beat John Studd, Don Muraco beat Randy Alls, Sam Steamboat drew Tor Kamata.

9/14/78 Honolulu
Steve Lawler beat Barto Castro, John Tolos beat Tosh Togo, Sam Steamboat beat Duke Savage, Jesse Ventura & Steve Strong beat Bill Francis & Buck Zumhoff.

9/16/78 Hilo
Pampero Firpo beat Randy Morse, Mr. Fuji beat John Tolos, Steve Strong drew John Studd, Don Muraco beat Tor Kamata.

9/18/78 Honolulu
Steve Lawler drew Tosh Togo, Steve Strong beat Bill Francis COR, Buck Zumhoff beat Duke Savage, Sam Steamboat & Steve Olsonoski beat John Tolos & Jesse Ventura.

9/20/78 Honolulu
Don Muraco beat Tor Kamata, Jim Brunzell & Greg Gagne beat Mr. Fuji & Karl Von Steiger, Larry Sharpe beat John Tolos, Steve Strong beat Randy Alls, Bobo Johnson beat Little John, Pampero Firpo drew John Studd, Bill Francis drew Sam Steamboat.

9/21/78 Honolulu
Tosh Togo beat Duke Savage, Buck Zumhoff beat Steve Lawler, John Tolos & Steve Strong & Jesse Ventura beat Bill Francis & Sam Steamboat & Steve Olsonoski, Jesse Ventura drew Steve Olsonoski.

9/23/78 Honolulu
Steve Olsonoski drew Duke Savage, Tosh Togo beat Buck Zumhoff, Sam Steamboat beat John Tolos for North American title, Pampero Firpo beat Steve Lawler, Bill Francis beat Nick Bockwinkel dq, Greg Gagne & Jim Brunzell beat Jesse Ventura & Steve Strong.

9/27/78 Honolulu
Larry Sharpe beat Bill Francis, Billy Whitewolf beat Mr. Fuji, Don Muraco drew John Studd, Ed Francis drew Karl Von Steiger, Steve Strong & Bobo Johnson beat Randy Alls & Little John.

10/4/78 Honolulu
Ed & Bill Francis drew Mr. Fuji & Karl Von Steiger, Steve Strong beat Randy Alls, Billy Whitewolf drew John Studd, Don Muraco drew Larry Sharpe.

10/8/78 Kona
Missing Link drew Karl Von Steiger, Steve Strong beat Randy Alls, Larry Sharpe beat Don Muraco, Billy Francis beat Mr. Fuji dq, Don Muraco won battle royal.

10/9/78 Hilo
Randy Alls drew Steve Strong, Don Muraco beat Larry Sharpe dq, Pampero Firpo beat Mr. Fuji dq, Bill Francis beat Karl Von Steiger.

10/11/78 Honolulu
Tama Samoa beat Randy Alls, Larry Sharpe drew Sam Steamboat, Karl Von Steiger beat Steve Strong, Larry Sharpe & Randy Alls & Mr. Fuji & Karl Von Steiger beat Tama Samoa & Don Muraco & Sam Steamboat & Bill Francis.

10/18/78
Ripper Collins beat Bill Francis, Pampero Firpo beat Whipper Watson Jr, Tama Samoa beat Randy Alls, Larry Sharpe beat Steve Strong, Billy & Benny McGuire beat Mr. Fuji & Karl Von Steiger, Nick Bockwinkel beat Don Muraco.

10/28/78 Hilo
Bill Francis drew Steve Strong, Pampero Firpo no contest Larry Sharpe, Don Muraco & Tama Samoa beat Steve Strong & Mr. Fuji, Billy & Benny McGuire beat Ripper Collins & Whipper Watson Jr.

11/1/78 Honolulu
Tama Samoa & Bill Francis beat Whipper Watson Jr & Ripper Collins dq, Larry Sharpe beat Don Muraco dq, Mr. Fuji drew Steve Strong, Karl Von Steiger beat Randy Alls.

11/2/78 Honolulu
Ed Francis beat Tor Kamata, Pampero Firpo & John Tolos beat Tor Kamata & Killer Christy, Bill Francis no contest Steve Strong, Jesse Ventura drew Sam Steamboat, Billy Whitewolf beat Buck Zumhoff.

11/6/78 Hilo
Whipper Watson Jr beat Randy Alls, Bill Francis beat Ripper Collins, Steve Strong drew Larry Sharpe, Don Muraco & Tama Samoa beat Mr. Fuji & Karl Von Steiger.

11/8/78 Honolulu
Don Muraco beat Whipper Watson Jr, Steve Strong drew Karl Von Steiger, Larry Sharpe beat Randy Alls, Bill Francis beat Mr. Fuji dq, Ripper Collins drew Tama Samoa.

11/15/78 Honolulu
Tama Samoa beat Whipper Watson Jr, Don Muraco beat Larry Sharpe, Ripper Collins drew Bill Francis, Mr. Fuji & Karl Von Steiger beat Randy Alls & Steve Strong.

11/20/78 Hilo
Larry Sharpe beat Randy Alls, Steve Strong drew Karl Von Steiger, Bill Francis & Tama Samoa beat Ripper Collins & Whipper Watson Jr, Don Muraco beat Mr. Fuji.

11/22/78 Honolulu
Pampero Firpo & Bill Francis beat Nick Bockwinkel & Bobby Heenan, John Tolos beat Steve Strong, Tor Kamata no contest Billy Whitewolf, Buck Zumhoff & Cowboy Lang & Hillbilly Pete beat Rocky Tomayo & Little John & Little Tokyo, Sam Steamboat drew Jesse Ventura.

11/29/78 Honolulu
Larry Sharpe beat Bill Francis, Karl Von Steiger beat Steve Strong, Ripper Collins beat Tama Samoa COR, Mando Guerrero beat Whipper Watson Jr, Don Muraco beat Mr. Fuji dq.

12/2/78 Kapa'a
Armando Guerrero & Tama Samoa VS Whipper Watson Jr & Ripper Collins, Don Muraco VS Mr. Fuji anything goes.

12/6/78 Honolulu
Whipper Watson Jr beat Ricky Morton, Bill Francis drew Karl Von Steiger, Steve Strong drew Larry Sharpe, Don Muraco beat Ripper Collins, Tama Samoa & Mando Guerrero beat Mr. Fuji & Karl Von Steiger.

12/20/78 Honolulu
Andre The Giant beat Nick Bockwinkel cage match, Don Leo Jonathan beat Tor Kamata, Ripper Collins & Whipper Watson beat Mando Guerrero & Tama Samoa, Don Muraco drew Larry Sharpe, Steve Strong beat Karl Von Steiger.

12/27/78 Honolulu
Tor Kamata beat Don Muraco, Ripper Collins beat Steve Strong, Bill Francis drew Karl Von Steiger, Mando Guerrero & Tama Samoa beat Larry Sharpe & Whipper Watson.

1979

1/3/79 Honolulu
Steve Strong drew Tor Kamata, Bill Francis drew Larry Sharpe, Don Muraco beat Karl Von Steiger, Tama Samoa & Mando Guerrero beat Ripper Collins & Whipper Watson.

1/6/79 Hilo
Tama Samoa beat Karl Von Steiger, Mando Guerrero beat Larry Sharpe, Ripper Collins & Tor Kamata beat Don Muraco & Bill Francis. Victor The Bear beat Whipper Watson.

1/10/79 Honolulu
Mando Guerrero beat Karl Von Steiger, Larry Sharpe drew Tama Samoa, Tor Kamata beat Don Muraco, Ripper Collins & Whipper Watson Jr beat Tosh Togo & Bill Francis.

1/17/79 Honolulu
Tor Kamata beat John Tolos COR, Bill Francis beat Texas Red, Victor The Wrestling Bear beat Ripper Collins, Buck Zumhoff beat George Allen, Don Muraco beat Whipper Watson Jr, Mando Guerrero & Tama Samoa beat Larry Sharpe & Karl Von Steiger.

1/20/79 Hilo
Buck Zumhoff drew Whipper Watson, Don Muraco beat Tor Kamata, Mando Guerrero beat Larry Sharpe, Victor The Bear beat Ripper Collins & Whipper Watson, Tama Samoa & John Tolos beat Ripper Collins & Karl Von Steiger.

2/14/79 Honolulu
Tama Samoa & Mando Guerrero drew Bill Francis & Don Muraco, Jumbo Tsuruta beat Nick Bockwinkel dq, Tor Kamata beat Ripper Collins dq, Curtis Dudit (Coconut Willie) & Cowboy Lang beat Billy The Kid & Bruiser Morgan, Giant Baba beat Karl Von Steiger, Whipper Watson Jr beat Buck Zumhoff.

2/17/79 Hilo
Tama Samoa beat Chris Markoff, Mando Guerrero beat Karl Von Steiger, Tor Kamata & Clayton Rodriguez beat Ripper Collins & Whipper Watson, Don Muraco beat Bill Francis.

2/21/79 Honolulu
Clayton Rodriguez beat Whipper Watson, Don Muraco beat Tor Kamata, Mando Guerrero & Tama Samoa beat Ripper Collins & Karl Von Steiger, Peter Maivia beat Chris Markoff.

2/28/79 Honolulu
Mando Guerrero beat Karl Von Steiger, Buck Zumhoff beat Chris Markoff, Tama Samoa beat Whipper Watson, Don Muraco beat Bill Francis, Tor Kamata beat Ripper Collins, Harley Race beat Peter Maivia.

3/7/79 Honolulu
Ripper Collins beat Brian Blair, Chris Markoff beat Buck Zumhoff, Tama Samoa beat Karl Von Steiger, Don Muraco beat Mando Guerrero, Brian Blair drew Ati Tago.

3/11/79 Honolulu
Tama Samoa beat Don Muraco, Karl Von Steiger beat Brian Blair, Buck Zumhoff beat Whipper Watson Jr, Armando Guerrero & Ati Tago drew Ripper Collins & Chris Markoff.

3/14/79 Honolulu
Don Muraco beat Brian Blair, Karl Von Steiger beat Buck Zumhoff, Armando Guerrero drew Chris Markoff, Tama Samoa & Ati Tago beat Ripper Collins & Whipper Watson Jr.

3/21/79 Honolulu
Kevin Von Erich beat Whipper Watson Jr, Ripper Collins & Whipper Watson beat Mando Guerrero & Clayton Rodriguez, Kevin Von Erich beat Karl Von Steiger.

3/26/79 Honolulu
Buck Zumhoff beat Ed Dean, Kevin Von Erich beat Whipper Watson, Karl Von Steiger beat Mando Guerrero, Tama Samoa & Ati Tago no contest Ripper Collins & Chris Markoff.

4/4/79 Honolulu
Kevin Von Erich beat Jim Dillon, Karl Von Steiger beat Chris Markoff, Tama Samoa beat Jerry Monti, Buck Zumhoff beat Clayton Rodriquez, Ripper Collins beat Tama Samoa, Karl Von Steiger beat Buck Zumhoff, Kevin Von Erich beat Ripper Collins, Karl Von Steiger beat Kevin Von Erich for Hawaiian State Title.

4/8/79 Honolulu
Ati Tago & Tama Samoa beat Chris Markoff & Ripper Collins, Buck Zumhoff beat JJ Dillion, Buck Zumhoff beat Clayton Rodriguez, Karl Von Steiger beat Jerry Monti.

4/11/79 Honolulu
Tor Kamata drew Ric Martel for Pacific International Title, Ati Tago & Tama Samoa beat JJ Dillion & Karl Von Steiger, Ripper Collins & Chris Markoff beat Buck Zumhoff & Jerry Monti, Sheepherders beat Kevin Von Erich & Dick Slater, Tama Samoa & Ati Tago beat Ripper Collins & Chris Markoff, Sheepherders beat Ati Tago & Tama Samoa.

4/18/79 Honolulu
Ric Martel beat Dick Slater, Siva Afi beat Karl Von Steiger for Hawaiian title, Ric Martel beat Jerry Monti, Ati Tago & Tama Samoa beat Sheepherders.

6/20/79 Honolulu
Raul Castro beat Clayton Rodriguez, Siva Afi drew Brute Miller, Bryan St. John beat Luke Williams, The Beast beat Buck Zumhoff, Rick Martel beat Buddy Rose.

6/27/79 Honolulu
Raul Castro beat Buck Zumhoff, The Bounty Hunter beat Randy Alls, The Beast beat Bryan St. John, Kiwis beat Clayton Rodriguez & Rick Martel, Siva Afi beat Buddy Rose.

6/30/79 Honolulu
Raul Castro beat Clayton Rodriguez, Siva Afi drew Brute Miller, Bryan St. John beat Luke Williams dq, The Beast beat Buck Zumhoff, Rick Martel beat Buddy Rose.

7/1/79 Honolulu
Luke Williams drew Clayton Rodriguez, Sheepherders beat Rick Martel & Bryan St. John, Siva Afi drew Raul Castro, Bounty Hunter beat Buck Zumhoff, The Beast beat Randy Alls.

7/3/79 Honolulu
Clayton Rodriguez beat Buck Zumhoff, Bounty Hunter beat Sgt. Eddie Dean, The Beast beat Randy Alls, Rick Martel beat Raul Castro, Sheepherders beat Bryan St. John & Siva Afi.

7/11/79 Honolulu
Siva Afi & Bryan St. John beat Sheepherders, Roddy Piper beat Clayton Rodriguez, Bounty Hunter beat Buck Zumhoff, Raul Castro beat Randy Alls, Rick Martel beat The Beast.

7/18/79 Honolulu
Jay York beat Randy Alls, Roddy Piper beat Malo The Wonder Boy, Raul Castro beat Siva Afi, Tor Kamata & Rick Martel beat The Beast & The Bounty Hunter.

7/25/79 Honolulu
Jay York beat Clayton Rodriguez, Randy Alls beat Roddy Piper dq, Siva Afi beat Raul Castro, Tor Kamata beat Bounty Hunter, Rick Martel beat The Beast.

8/8/79 Honolulu
Clayton Rodriguez beat Randy Alls, Roddy Piper beat Buck Zumhoff, Siva Afi beat Jay York, Malo The Wonder Boy beat Raul Castro, Rick Martel beat The Bounty Hunter unmasked as Mad Dog Martin.

8/15/79 Honolulu
Raul Castro beat Randy Alls, Roddy Piper beat Buck Zumhoff, The Alaskan beat Siva Afi, Coconut Willie beat Little Tokyo, Mad Dog Martin beat Rick Martel.

8/22/79 Honolulu
Raul Castro beat Buck Zumhoff, Roddy Piper beat Clayton Rodriguez, Coconut Willie beat Little Tokyo, Siva Afi beat Mad Dog Martin, Peter Maivia beat Jay York, Nick Bockwinkel beat Rick Martel.

9/2/79 Honolulu
Raul Castro beat Tui, Siva Afi drew Karl Von Steiger, Jay York drew Clayton Rodriguez, Rick Martel & Siva Afi & Clayton Rodriguez beat Roddy Piper & Raul Castro & Jay York.

9/12/79 Honolulu
Pat Barrett beat Jerry Monti, Jay York & Raul Castro beat Clayton Rodriguez & Jerry Monti, Ripper Collins beat Buck Zumhoff, Siva Afi beat Roddy Piper dq.

9/16/79 Honolulu
Siva Afi & Clayton Rodriguez beat Roddy Piper & Raul Castro, Ripper Collins beat Jerry Monti, Buck Zumhoff beat Jay York, Karl Von Steiger drew Pat Barrett.

9/19/79 Honolulu
Jay York & Karl Von Steiger beat Buck Zumhoff & Jerry Monti, Clayton Rodriguez beat Al Costello, Rocky Johnson beat Roddy Piper, Ripper Collins beat Siva Afi, Peter Maivia beat Harley Race COR NWA title.

9/30/79 Honolulu
Malo the Wonder Boy drew Clayton Rodriguez, Pretty Boy Larry Sharpe beat Buck Zumhoff, Ripper Collins beat Matt Borne, Peter Maivia beat Jerry Monti, Karl Von Steiger beat Rocky Johnson.

10/3/79 Honolulu
Rocky Johnson beat Larry Sharpe, Peter Maivia beat Karl Von Steiger, Ripper Collins beat Jerry Monti, Mr. X beat Buck Zumhoff, Matt Borne drew Clayton Rodriguez.

10/24/79 Honolulu
Ripper Collins beat Clayton Rodriguez, Siva Afi beat Buck Zumhoff, Peter Maivia & Billy Whitewolf beat Karl Von Steiger & Matt Borne, Rocky Johnson beat Larry Sharpe, Vickie Williams & Fabulous Moolah beat Judy Martin & Princess Little Cloud.

11/14/79 Honolulu
Don Muraco beat Malo, Ati Tago & Tama Tango beat Mr. X & Larry Sharpe, Rocky Johnson beat Bob Adonis, Ripper Collins beat Siva Afi, Andre The Giant beat Larry Sharpe & Karl Von Steiger.

11/28/79 Honolulu
Karl Von Steiger drew Ati Tago, Siva Afi beat Don Muraco dq, Ripper Collins & Mr. Fuji beat Ati Tago & Toma Tonga, Mr. X beat Peter Maivia.

12/2/79 Honolulu
Rocky Johnson beat Ripper Collins dq, Peter Maivia beat Mr. Fuji COR, Siva Afi beat Mr. X, Tama Tonga drew Karl Von Steiger, Don Muraco beat Ati Tago.

12/5/79 Honolulu
Rocky Johnson beat Karl Von Steiger, Ati Tago & Tama Tonga beat Ripper Collins & Mr. Fuji, Billy Whitewolf beat Karl Von Steiger, Don Muraco beat Siva Afi, Peter Maivia beat Mr. X (Baron Scicluna).

12/19/79 Honolulu
Siva Afi beat Mr. Fuji, Ricky Rickard beat Kung Fu Lee, Ati Tago & Tama Tonga beat Karl Von Steiger & Hans Schroader, Rocky Johnson drew Don Muraco, Billy Whitewolf drew The Sheik, Peter Maivia beat Ripper Collins to win Hawaiian title.

12/30/79 Honolulu
Ricky Rickard beat Al Rosen, Tama Tonga beat Kung Fu Lee dq, Hans Schroeder beat Lindy Caulder, Billy Whitewolf drew Don Muraco, Siva Afi & Peter Maivia beat Karl Von Steiger & Kung Fu Lee.

1980

1/2/80 Honolulu
Ricky Rickard beat Lindy Caulder, Tama Tongo beat Hans Schroader dq, Siva Afi & Billy Whitewolf beat Karl Von Steiger & Kung Fu Lee, Don Muraco beat Peter Maivia.

1/16/80 Honolulu
Tama Tonga beat Kung Fu Lee, Ricky Rickard drew Bruce Hart, Ati Tago beat Don Muraco dq, Billy Whitewolf beat Hans Schroader, Peter Maivia & Neff Maiava beat Ripper Collins & Karl Von Steiger.

1/20/80 Honolulu
Kung Fu Lee drew Ati Tago, Bruce Hart beat Karl Von Steiger dq, Hans Schroader beat Ricky Rickard, Billy Whitewolf beat Ripper Collins dq.

1/23/80 Honolulu
Ricky Rickard drew Kung Fu Lee, Karl Von Steiger beat Bruce Hart, Don Muraco beat Billy Whitewolf, Pat Patterson beat Tommy Rich, Peter Maivia beat Hans Schroeder dq, Ati & Tama Tonga beat Ripper Collins & Mad Dog Vachon.

2/6/80 Honolulu
Tama Tonga ddq Ripper Collins, Peter Maivia no contest Don Muraco, Bruce Hart beat Hans Schroeder, Ricky Rickard beat Karl Von Steiger, Bruce Hart drew Kung Fu Lee.

2/13/80 Honolulu
Ricky Rickard beat Eddie Dean, Dynamite Kid beat Karl Von Steiger, Tama Tonga & Billy Whitewolf beat Bruce & Keith Hart, Don Muraco beat Rocky Johnson dq, Mighty Goliath beat King Ripper Collins, Kung Fu Lee drew Malo, Peter Maivia beat Hans Schroader.

2/20/80 Pearl Harbor
Malo beat Eddie Dean, Billy Whitewolf & Malo beat Bruce & Keith Hart, Dynamite Kid & Tama Tonga beat Hans Schroeder & Karl Von Steiger, Rocky Johnson beat Don Muraco.

2/22/80 Honolulu
Billy Whitewolf beat Karl Von Steiger, Rocky Johnson no contest Hans Schroeder, Peter Maivia beat Don Muraco, Dynamite Kid & Tama Tonga drew Bruce & Keith Hart.

2/27/80 Honolulu
Tama Tonga ddq Bruce Hart, Malo beat Karl Von Steiger, Bruce & Keith Hart beat Tama Tonga & Dynamite Kid, Don Muraco & Hans Schroeder beat Peter Maivia & Rocky Johnson.

3/2/80 Honolulu
Billy Whitewolf beat Don Muraco, Tama Tonga beat Karl Von Steiger, Rocky Johnson ddq Hans Schroeder, Bruce & Keith Hart beat Malo & Tama Tonga.

3/5/80 Honolulu
Karl Von Steiger beat Malo, Rocky Johnson beat Don Muraco, Hans Schroeder beat Peter Maivia, Tama Tonga & Billy Whitewolf drew Bruce Hart & Keith Hart.

3/16/80 Honolulu
Bruce Hart drew Clayton Rodriguez, Rocky Johnson beat Keith Hart, Hercules Cortez Jr beat Hans Schroeder dq.

3/19/80 Honolulu
Clayton Rodriguez drew Malo, Siva Afi ddq Bruce Hart, Hercules Cortez Jr beat Karl Von Steiger, Victor Rivera no contest Billy Whitewolf, Hans Schroeder beat Rocky Johnson, Siva Afi & Tama Tonga beat Bruce & Keith Hart.

4/2/80 Honolulu
Malo The Magnificent no contest Clayton Rodriguez, Tama Tonga beat Butts Girard, Siva Afi beat Jose Romero dq, Billy Whitewolf & Tama Tonga beat Carlos Mata & Butts Girard.

4/16/80 Honolulu
Ultraman Hiro beat Clayton Rodriquez, Tama Tonga beat Carlos Mata, Billy Whitewolf beat Pete Austin dq, Siva Afi no contest Jose Romero.

5/3/80 Honolulu
Clayton Rodriguez beat Wildman Austin, Jose Martinez no contest Ultraman Hiro, Billy Whitewolf beat Wildman Austin, Victor Rivera & Buddy Diamond beat Siva Afi & Tama Tonga.

5/11/80 Honolulu
Clayton Rodriguez DCOR Wildman Austin, Billy Whitewolf no contest Ultraman Hiro, Jose Martinez beat Mighty Duke, Buddy Diamond & Don Fulton beat Siva Afi & Tama Tonga,

5/21/80 Honolulu
Jose Martinez beat Buddy Diamond dq, Siva Afi beat Ultraman Hiro dq, Billy Whitewolf no contest Missing Link, Tama Tonga beat Wildman Pete Austin, Ultraman Hiro & Buddy Diamond beat Jose Martinez & Clayton Rodriguez.

5/28/80 Honolulu
Buddy Diamond drew Billy Whitewolf, Missing Link beat Clayton Rodriguez, Jose Martinez beat Ultraman, Tama Tonga beat Victor Rivera, Wildman Austin beat Peter Maivia.

6/4/80 Honolulu
Siva Afi no contest The Convict, Tama Tonga beat Lumberjack Larson dq, Buddy Diamond beat Clayton Rodriquez, Wildman Austin & Victor Rivera beat Missing Link & Peter Maivia, Jose Martinez beat Ultraman Hiro.

6/8/80 Honolulu
Tama Tonga drew Ultraman Hiro, Missing Link beat Lumberjack Larson dq, Jose Martinez drew Tito Santana, Andre The Giant beat The Convict, Siva Afi & Tama Tonga & Billy Whitewolf no contest Ultraman, Wildman Austin & Buddy Diamond.

6/11/80 Honolulu
Andre The Giant VS Lumberjack Larson, Tito Santana VS Wildman Austin, Handsome Diamond VS Tama Tonga, Jose Martinez VS Siva Afi, Billy Whitewolf VS Ultraman Hiro.

6/22/80 Honolulu
Ultraman Hiro drew Billy Whitewolf, Clayton Rodriguez beat Lumberjack Larson dq, Peter Maivia beat The Convict, Mike Masters beat Buck Zumhoff.

10/15/80 Honolulu
Peter Maivia VS Ernie Ladd, Ivan Putski VS Don Muraco, Tiki Kamaka VS Wildman Austin, Leilani Kai VS Wendy Richter, Ripper Collins & Saslia VS Tama Tonga & Siva Afi, Jerry Graham Jr VS Hiro Sasaki.

11/12/80 Honolulu
Samoans VS Tor & Tiki Kamata, Don Muraco VS Pedro Morales, Chief Maivia VS Tama Tonga, Jerry Graham Jr VS Ripper Collins, Hiro Sasaki VS Cyclops.

1982

2/10/82 Honolulu
Dynamo Milo beat Mike Allen, Siva Afi beat Sebastian Stone dq, Rocky Johnson no contest Victor Rivera, Sal Bellomo no contest Roy Starr, Bob Backlund drew Don Muraco, Mr. Sakalia & Super Fly Tui beat LeRoy Brown & Farmer Boy Ipo.

2/11/82 Hilo
Roy Starr beat Sebastian Stone, Peter Maivia beat Victor Rivera, Siva Afi beat Sal Bellomo, Bob Backlund beat Don Muraco, Siva Afi & Roy Starr beat Sal Bellomo & Sebastian Stone.

1983

6/29/83 Honolulu
Scott Casey beat Lars Anderson, Tully Blanchard beat Steve Collins, Mr. Z drew Mighty Milo, Coconut Willie beat Wee Willie Wilson, Farmer Boy Ipo & Leroy Brown beat Bruiser Stevens & Superfly Tui, Siva Afi beat The Samoan Mako.

8/3/83 Honolulu
Great Samoan drew Johnny Lee, Roy Starr drew Super Samoan Sakalia, Diamond Fannene beat Tiger Lady, Mighty Milo beat Robert Toronto, Tor Kamata beat Iron Duke, Leroy Brown & Farmer Boy Ipo beat Bruiser Stevens & Super Sly Tui, Mr. Z drew Roy Starr, Tully Blanchard beat Lars Anderson dq.

10/12/83 Honolulu
Lars Anderson beat Super Samoan Sakalia, Farmer Boy Ipo beat Superfly Tui.

10/26/83 Honolulu
Lars Anderson beat Mr. Z, Superfly Tui & Super Samoan Sakalia beat Farmer Boy Ipo & Roy Starr dq.

11/2/83 Honolulu
Lars Anderson beat Mr. Z, Farmer Boy Ipo & Roy Starr no contest Super Samoan Sakalia & Superfly Tui.

1984

1/27/84 Honolulu
Jay Youngblood no contest Superfly Tui, Roy Starr no contest Farmer Boy Ipo, Super Samoan Sakalia beat Robert Toronto, Terry Savage & Sam Sampson beat Richie Magnett & Little Kevin, Mighty Milo beat Fua Mamea, Lars Anderson beat Leroy Brown.

1/30/84 Honolulu
Farmer Boy Ipo no contest Roy Starr, Super Samoan Sakalia beat Robert Toronto, Terry Savage & Sam Sampson beat Little Kevin & Richie Magnett, Mighty Milo beat Fua Mamea, Jay Youngblood no contest Super Fly Tui Selinga, Lars Anderson beat Leroy Brown.

2/25/84 Honolulu
Farmer Boy Ipo beat Roy Starr, Lars Anderson beat Mad Dog Vachon dq, Superfly Tui & Super Samoan Sakalia beat Matt Zoe & Leroy Brown, Fua Mamea beat Sam Sampson, Mighty Milo beat Richie Magnett, Terry Savage beat Little Kevin.

3/10/84 Honolulu
Farmer Boy Ipo beat Roy Starr, Lars Anderson beat Robert Toronto.

3/24/84 Honolulu
Superfly Tui & Super Samoan Sakalia beat Matt Zoe & Lars Anderson, Richie Magnett beat Matt Zoe, Samula beat Mighty Milo.

4/7/84 Palama
Sam Sampson beat Fua Mamea, Richie Magnett beat Sam Sampson, Roy Starr beat Leroy Brown, The Mighty Milo beat Richie Magnett, Lars Anderson beat Samoan Sammy dq, Leroy Brown & Farmer Boy Ipo beat Super Samoan Sakalia & Superfly Tui.

4/21/84 Honolulu
Roy Starr beat Lars Anderson, Jimmy Gilbert & Farmer Boy Ipo beat Super Samoan & Roy Starr & Superfly Tui.

5/19/84 Honolulu
Lars Anderson & Leroy Brown & Farmer Boy Ipo beat Royce Starr & Superfly Tui & Samoan Sakalia, Hoagie Young beat Sam Sampson, Farmer Boy Ipo no contest Superfly Tui, Mighty Milo beat Richie Magnett, Fua Mamea beat Robert Toronto.

6/2/84 Palama
Roberto Toronto beat Hoagie Young, Richie Magnett drew Mighty Milo, Roy Starr beat Farmer Boy Ipo, Superfly Tui & Super Samoan Sakali beat Lars Anderson & Leroy Brown.

6/16/84 Palama
The Mighty Milo drew Richie Magnett, Roy Starr beat Robert Toronto, Super Samoan Sakalia beat Sam Sampson, Farmer Boy Ipo beat Hoagie Young, Lars Anderson dcor Superfly Tui.

6/29/84 Honolulu
Mighty Milo beat Fua Mamea, Wild Bull beat Robert Toronto, Peter Maivia Jr beat Richie Magnett, Siva Afi beat Hoagie Young, Super Samoan Sakalia & Superfly Tui beat Farmer Boy Ipo & Leroy Brown, Tatsumi Fujinami beat Rick Oliver, Kevin Von Erich ddq Michael Hayes, Seiji Sakaguchi beat Bad News Allen dq, Lars Anderson beat Roy Starr to win title.

7/21/84 Palama
Prince Kamehameha beat Super Samoan Sakalia dq, Roy Starr & Richie Magnett beat Farmer Boy Ipo & Mighty Milo, JR Hogg beat Fua Mamea, Lars Anderson beat Super Fly Tui dq.

8/16/84 Honolulu
Terry Savage beat Despina Montagas forfeit, Matt Borne beat The Mighty Milo, Peter Maivia Jr beat Hoagie Young, Roy Starr & Richie Magnett beat Sam Sampson & Prince Kamehameha, Farmer Boy Ipo beat JR Hogg, Kevin Von Erich beat Michael Hayes, Lars Anderson & Seiji Sakaguchi beat Superfly Tui & Super Samoan Sakalia to win tag titles.

10/3/84 Honolulu
Mighty Milo drew Richie Magnett, Matt Borne beat Sam Sampson, Hoagie Young beat Prince Kamehameha, Farmer Boy Ipo beat Doug Somers dq, Rocky Johnson beat Masked Superstar dq, Siva Afi beat Bad News Allan dq, Kerry Von Erich beat Missing Link, Superfly Tui & Super Samoan Sakalia beat Lars Anderson & Seiji Sakaguchi to win tag titles, Don Muraco no contest Mark Lewin.

11/14/84 Honolulu
Mighty Milo beat Bulldog Johnson, Prince Kamehameha beat Mr. Florida, Farmer Boy Ipo & Leroy Brown beat Roy Starr & Richie Magnett, Siva Afi beat Hoagie Young, Super Samoan Sakalia & Superfly Tue beat Matt Borne & Doug Somers, Terry Gordy beat Killer Kahn dq, Lars Anderson beat Mark Lewin dq, Don Muraco beat Kevin Sullivan dq.

12/19/84 Honolulu
Richie Magnett beat Roy Starr, Farmer Boy Ipo & Leroy Brown beat Doug Hui & Don Stevens, Samoan Sammy (Samu) beat Prince Kamehameha, Doug Somers beat Matt Borne, Jimmy Snuka beat Tiger Toguchi, Don Muraco dcor Bad News Allen, Siva Afi & Lars Anderson beat Kevin Sullivan & Mark Lewin, Kevin Von Erich beat Chris Adams, Ricky & Rocky Johnson beat Hoagie Young & Roger Starr, Seiji Sakaguchi & Tatsumi Fujijnami dcor Super Samoan Sakalia & Superfly Tui, Andre The Giant won battle royal.

1985

2/13/85 Honolulu
Ric Flair drew Kerry Von Erich, Antonio Inoki beat Hacksaw Higgins, Super Samoan Sakalia & Superfly Tui beat Seiji Sakaguchi & Atisanoe dq, Lars Anderson & Siva Avi beat Mark Lewin & Kevin Sullivan, The Cobra beat Richie Magnett, Tatsumi Fujinami beat Super Strong Machine 1, Samoan Sammy beat Kini Popo, Mr. Florida beat The Louisiana Cowboy, Farmer Boy Ipo & Leroy Brown beat Royce Starr & Gypsy Joe.

3/27/85 Honolulu
Mr. Florida beat AK Hammer, Richie Magnett beat Kini Popo, Mighty Milo beat the Louisiana Kid, Super Samoan Sakalia & Superfly Tui & Doug Hui beat Farmer Boy Ipo & Leroy Brown & Steve Collins, Tonga Kid beat Royce Starr, Samoan 3 beat Mike Miller, Bad News Allan beat Strong Machine 1, Ricky & Rocky Johnson beat Adrian Adonis & Dick Murdoch, Siva Afi beat Mark Lewin, Lars Anderson beat Kevin Sullivan.

4/17/85 Honolulu
Farmer Boy Ipo & Leroy Brown beat Doug Hui & Kinipopo, The Mighty Milo & Richie Magnett beat The Louisiana Kid & AK Hammer, Royce Starr beat Prince Kamehameha, Superfly Tui docr Steve Collins, Angelo Mosca Sr & Lars Anderson beat Kevin Sullivan & Mark Lewin, Ricky Johnson beat Super Samoan Sakalia, Alexis Smirnoff beat Samoan 3 dq, Siva Afi beat Buck Robley.

5/22/85 Honolulu
Kinipopo beat Alapata Purcell, The Mighty Milo & Richie Magnett beat Doug Hui & Prince Kamehameha, Farmer Boy Ipo & Leroy Brown beat Chick Donovan & Doug Somers, Steve Collins beat Superfly Tui lumberjack match, Samoan 3 beat Alexis Smirnoff, Bad News Allen beat Lars Anderson for Polynesian Pacific title, Ricky & Rocky Johnson ddq Len Denton & Tony Anthony, Bruiser Brody & Angelo Mosca & Siva Afi beat Kevin Sullivan & Mark Lewin & Buck Robley barbed wire match.

6/12/85 Honolulu
Lars Anderson beat Bad News Allen dq, Ricky & Rocky Johnson beat Dirty White Boys, Angelo Mosca beat Mark Lewin dq stretcher match, Siva Afi beat Kevin Sullivan blindfold match, Bruiser Brody beat Buck Robley Texas Death Match, Alexis Smirnoff beat Sam Anoia Russian Chain match, Doug Hui & Roy Starr beat The Mighty Milo & Richie Magnett, Superfly Tui beat Steve Collins high platform sumo match, Farmer Boy Ipo & Leroy Brown beat Rugger Rowles & Kini Popo, Mr. Bombay beat Alapata Purcell.

8/3/85 Aiea
Richie Magnett beat Gypsy Joe, Little Kevin beat Pancho Boy, Debbie Combs beat The Fallen Angel dq, Steve Regal drew The Mighty Milo, Manny Fernandez beat Black Bart dq, Jimmy Snuka beat Mike Sharpe, Tatsumi Fujinami & Kengo Kimura beat Gene Lewis & Gary Fulton, Seiji Sakaguchi beat Matt Borne, The Cobra Beat Superfly Tui, Farmer Boy Ipo & Doug Hui & Kini Popo & Leroy Brown beat Royce Starr & Fui Mamea &? & ?, Antonio Inoki dcor Bruiser Brody, Dusty Rhodes & Magnum TA beat Nikita Koloff & Krusher Khruschev, Lars Anderson beat Bad News Allan to win Pacific title, Andre The Giant & Angelo Mosca & Steve Collins beat Kevin Sullivan & King Kong Bundy & Mark Lewin dq, Rocky & Ricky Johnson beat Len Denton & Tony Anthony, Ric Flair ddq Siva Afi.

11/13/85 Honolulu
Little Kevin beat Pancho Boy, Richie Magnett beat Kini Popo, Maya Singh (Bob Roop) beat Doug Hui, Bad News Allen beat Mr. Florida, Roy Starr beat Mighty Milo, Farmer Boy Ipo & Leroy Brown beat Superfly Tui & Buddy Wolfe, Siva Afi beat The Russian Exterminator (Dave Barbee), Russian Eliminator beat Clint Terrell, Lars Anderson beat Kevin Sullivan, Ricky & Rocky Johnson beat Scott & Bill Irwin, Jerry Lawler beat Anoaro Atisanoe.

12/18/85 Honolulu
Mighty Milo beat Clint Terrell, Jerry Lawler beat Mr. Wrestling 2, Farmer Boy Ipo beat Curt Hennig & Royce Starr, Roxanne Rush beat Liz Chase, Aaori Atisanoe & Doug Hui beat The Spoiler & Superfly Tui, Chilly Bo Dilly beat Mean Little Kevin, Samoan 3 beat Nick Bockwinkel dq, Ripper Collins no contest Russian Exterminator, Tatsumi Fujinami & Kengo Kimura beat Kendo Nagasaki & Mr. Pogo, Kerry Von Erich beat Gino Hernandez, Antonio Inoki & Andre The Giant beat Joel & Dave Deaton, The Samoans beat Superstar & Les Thornton, Lars Anderson no contest Bad News Allen, Rocky & Rick Johnson no contest Kevin Sullivan & Bob Roop, Jimmy Snuka won battle royal.

1986

3/26/86 Honolulu
Kini Popo beat Nick Kiniski, Samoan Connection (Farmer Boy Ipo & Leroy Brown) no contest Tim Patterson & Billy Anderson, Moses Moli beat Ben Injimet, Farmer Boy Ipo drew Tim Patterson, Robert Toronto beat Billy Anderson, Mighty Milo beat Joe Solo, Lars Anderson beat Buddy Wolfe, Super Fly Tui beat Jerry Lawler won Polynesian title.

3/28/86 Honolulu
Guy Lambert beat Moses Moli, Jerry Monti beat Mighty Milo, Paul DeMarco beat Don Steeves, Tim Patterson & Billy Anderson beat Robert Toronto & Leroy Brown, Super Fly Tui beat Jerry Lawler, Buddy Wolfe beat Lars Anderson.

4/17/86 Honolulu
Super Fly beat Nick Kiniski, Samoan Connection beat Dave Deaton & Solo won Polynesian tag titles, Paul DeMarco beat Lars Anderson COR.

5/21/86 Honolulu
Richie Magnett beat Kinipopo 1 dq, Mighty Milo drew Moses Moli, Toronto beat Kinipopo 2 dq, Farmer Boy Ipo beat Madd Maxx dq, Junior Maivia drew Milo, Super Fly Tui beat Junior Maivia, Super Fly Tui no contest Smith, Farmer Boy Ipo & Brown no contest Madd Maxx & Smith, Lars Anderson & Richie Magnett no contest Kinipopos, Madd Maxx won battle royal.

7/18/86 Honolulu
Jimmy Snuka beat Billy Anderson, Rocky Johnson beat Tim Patterson dq, Crusher Stevens beat Doug Hui, Chi Chi Rodriguez beat Falasia Brown, Clint Terrell beat Assassin.

7/19/86 Honolulu
Chi Chi Rodriguez beat Falasia Brown, Sam Save beat Black Panther, Crusher Stevens beat Doug Hui, Clint Terrell beat The Falcon, Blondes beat Jimmy Snuka & Rocky Johnson

8/9/86 Honolulu
Kinipopo 1 & 2 drew Keith & Owen Hart, Uncle Elmer beat Hans Schroeder COR, Debbie The Killer Tomato beat Spice Williams, Keiji Muto beat Jerry Grey, Seiji Sakaguchi beat Johnny Mantel, Bad News Allan beat Alexis Smirnoff judo match, Farmer Boy Ipro & Leroy Brown beat Mad Maxx & Super Maxx to win tag titles, Bruiser Brody & Grizzly Smith beat Mark Lewin & The Sheik barbed wire match, Tatsumi Fujinami & Kengo Kimura beat Kendo Nagasaki & Mr. Pogo, Antonio Inoki beat Hacksaw Higgins dq, Lars Anderson beat Superfly Tui cage match to win title.

8/20/86 Honolulu
Superfly Tui beat Lars Anderson to win title.

11/19/86 Honolulu
Junior Maivia drew Richie Magnett, Kini Popo 2 no contest Johnny Solo, Tony Anthony beat The Medic, Sgt. Ike & Superfly Tui beat Kini Popo 1 & 2, Bill Toronto beat Rasputin dq.

1987

6/25/87 Honolulu
Robert Toronto & Hawaiian Dream Warrior beat The Fugala'au & Mighty Milo, The Wave beat Coco Rock, Joe Solo beat Crazy Tau dq, The Warlord beat Samoan Joe, Kini Popo 1 beat Fred Taylor, Billy Anderson & Tim Patterson beat Leroy Brown & Farmer Boy Ipo, Prince Kamalamala & Kini Popo 1 beat Tepatasi & Superfly Tui, Mark Lewin beat Wayne Hart.

12/16/87 Honolulu
Mighty Milo & Teufugalaau beat Jumping Solo & Loleni Solo, Coconut Willie beat Little Kevin, Eva Savage beat Miss Pacific Excitement, Robert Toronto beat Kini Popo I, Farmer Boy Ipo & Leroy Brown beat The Hawaiian Dream Warriors, Hiro Sasaki beat Wildman Austin, Tim Patterson & Billy Anderson beat Superfly Tui & Masina Tepatsi, Rocky Johnson beat Kamalamala, Chris Adams beat Buddy Roberts.

1988

5/17/88 Honolulu
Mighty Milo & Mighty Tao won Tag titles.

11/13/88 Wakayama Hilo
Tommy Rich ddq Dan Spivey, Dick Slater beat Mark Starr, Johny Ace & The Terminator beat Mike Graham & Steve Keirn, Dory & Terry Funk dcor Stan Hansen & Terry Gordy.

11/14/88 Wakayama
Stan Hansen beat Moose Morowski, Dory & Terry Funk beat Johnny Ace & Terminator.

11/15/88 Honolulu
Mike Graham beat Brett Sawyer, Johnny Ace & Terminator beat Brian Knobbs & Jerry Sags, Jerry Blackwell won battle royal, Scotty The Body beat Mark Starr, Stan Hansen & Terry Gordy beat Michael Hayes & Tommy Rich, The Great Kabuki beat Steve Keirn, Terry & Dory Funk ddq Danny Spivey & Dick Slater.

About the Author

Mike Rodgers received the 2019 Jim Melby Pro Wrestling Historian of the Year award at Cauliflower Alley. Mike considered a career in Journalism but knew the only thing he wanted to write about was wrestling. So instead, he became a PE teacher. One of the perks of that job was the ability to cut a promo on naughty students.

Mike published a monthly wrestling bulletin called Ring Around The Northwest for thirty years. RATNW included interviews with the top stars, the up and comers, results from around the area, and insights into the workings of pro wrestling. These interviews have been converted into three books, Excitement In The Air: The Voices of NW Wrestling – Volumes 1-3.

In addition, Mike authored Katie Bar The Door, The History of Portland Wrestling. This book looks back at the start of the Owen promotion till the close. It is a must-have for anyone wanting to know the history of the Owen family and the promotion.

Finally, there is The Encyclopedia of Portland Wrestlers. From The House of Action. Over 500 pages with results from every match at the Portland Sports Arena. If a wrestler had a match there, there is a biography for them! The most complete book on Portland Wrestling ever written.

Mike has refereed, done wrestling television announcing, and even had a battle royal match.
Mike is retired from teaching and lives in Troutdale, Oregon with his wife Becky and dog Daisy. He enjoys reading, fantasy football, swimming, and writing wrestling books!

Mike Rodgers accepting the James C. Melby Historian Award from
George Schire at the Cauliflower Alley Club in 2019.
(Photo by Dr. Mike Lano)

Mike with Harley Race

Mike interviewing Playboy Buddy Rose

Moondog Ed Moretti gigs Mike

Dean Higuchi extols a story to Mike

Mike being head locked by Sapphire

Jim Cornette swings his racket at Mike

Mike with Jim Melby, J. Michael Kenyon, Dean Silverstone

Above: Mike with Stu Hart and Rhonda Singh
Below: Mike doing tv announcing with Frank Culbertson at WB's Portland Wrestling

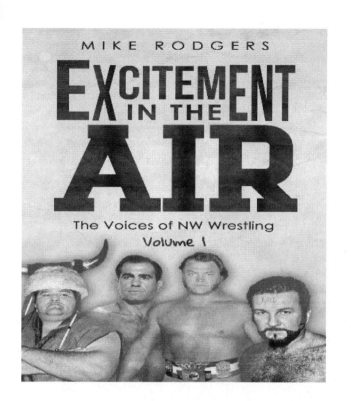

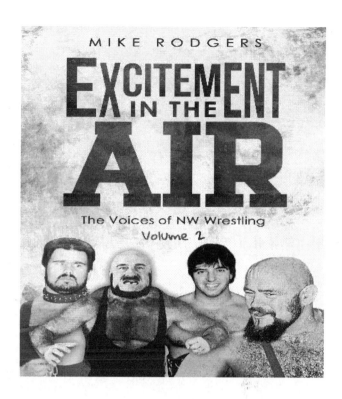

BE SURE TO CHECK OUT THESE GREAT BOOKS BY
MIKE RODGERS
AVAILABLE ON AMAZON

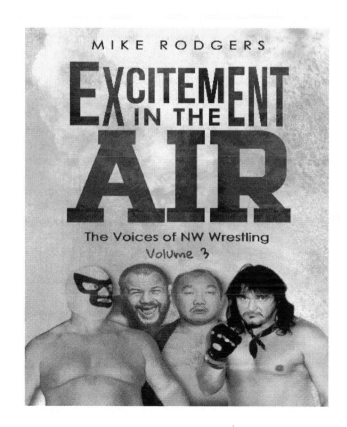

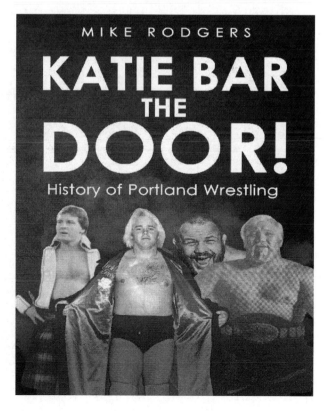

ENCYCLOPEDIA OF
PORTLAND
WRESTLERS

from
The House of Action

MIKE RODGERS

Made in the USA
Las Vegas, NV
28 December 2024